MARTIN LUTHER

HIS LIFE AND WORK

BY

HARTMANN GRISAR, S.J.

PROFESSOR AT THE UNIVERSITY OF INNSBRUCK

Adapted from the Second German Edition

By

FRANK J. EBLE, M.A.

EDITED BY ARTHUR PREUSS

THE NEWMAN PRESS

WESTMINSTER, MARYLAND

1950

NIHIL OBSTAT

Sti. Ludovici, die 29. Julii, 1930,

Joannes Rothensteiner,

Censor Librorum

IMPRIMATUR

Sti. Ludovici, die 30. Julii, 1930,

✠ Joannes J. Glennon,

Archiepiscopus

Manufactured by
Universal Lithographers, Inc.
Baltimore 2, Md.
U. S. A.

PREFACE

The diverse and even profoundly contradictory criticisms to which Luther has been subjected are apt to cause dismay to anyone who undertakes to occupy himself more closely with his biography. This divergence of opinions is a result not only of the divided confessional standpoint, but also of deviating historical evaluations of the facts. Even the Catholic opponents of Luther have never agreed on many points.

In my work on Luther, which appeared in three volumes in the course of 1911 to 1912, I endeavored to the best of my ability to establish a presentment of Luther and his work upon an unimpeachable basis, derived from all genuine sources.[1] For this purpose it was necessary to treat many aspects of the subject quite comprehensively. Others which presented fewer difficulties, could be passed over or summed up briefly. The labor involved in the removal of untenable conceptions prevented me from offering a uniform and well balanced biography in those comprehensive volumes.

For this reason I have always cherished a desire of submitting a more compact description and a proper delineation of the life of Luther in a less voluminous work based on the conclusions that have been established, particularly as supplemented by the researches into Luther's history which have since been instituted with extraordinary activity, especially as a result of the Luther jubilee of 1917. Meanwhile, a large number of special studies, great and small, have been published. Then, too, the Weimar Edition of Luther's works has presented, in its continuation volumes, the writings of Luther in a new form, resulting in considerable improvement over the previously edited texts. The Weimar undertaking has redounded in an eminent degree to the advantage of the Table Talks, which constitute an important source for the biography of Luther. The progress made thus far, was utilized by me, as far as practicable, in the special

[1] *Luther*, 3rd ed., Freiburg i. Br., 1924–1925, Herder. English translation by E. M. Lamond, 6 vols., London 1913–1917.

supplements to the third edition of my above mentioned three-volume work.

In presenting to the public this compendious biography of Martin Luther, which represents the fruit of several years' labor, I may be permitted to call attention to the fact that, in compiling it I have been encouraged by the appreciative reception which has been accorded to my larger work. In their discussion of this work, many Protestants who are not confirmed controversialists, have marked with approval my serious endeavor to observe objectivity and to give a calm, authentic presentation of a delicate subject.[2] Their statements show that an approximation between Catholic and Protestant views of Luther is possible on the basis of unprejudiced historical research. The contentious and irrelevant attacks made upon my work are of no consequence.[3] Similar attacks will not disquiet me even after the appearance of the present biography. On the other hand, I shall gratefully avail myself of any clarification of points offered in a possible new edition of this volume.

It may not be superfluous to mention that the present volume is chiefly concerned with a lucid presentation of the development of Luther, of his mental constitution and the interior impulses which moved him throughout his life. His many frank communications concerning himself as well as his unbridled language about and against others, almost spontaneously lead to a true characterization of him. Luther is so communicative that the afore-mentioned diversity of opinions about him becomes quite inexplicable to the attentive investigator, the more he occupies himself with his writings, letters, and addresses. Owing to Luther's communicativeness, I did not wish to be sparing of the evidences which in part are inserted in the foot-notes of this volume. It was frequently possible to indicate them very briefly by citations of apposite pages in my larger work, "Luther."

Throughout the present work, in the annotations as well as in the

[2] In a volume entitled *Urteile von protestantischer Seite*, the firm of Herder collected and published a large number of these criticisms in 1912. The Swedish-Lutheran Archbishop Söderblom, who delivered a series of lectures on Luther in May, 1923, said of the modern Catholic investigation of Luther in general "that it has extended the horizon of the Reformation and called forth a radical revolution in the conception of Luther." (*Bayerischer Kurier*, Munich, May 9, 1923). His new conception of Luther, however, is certainly not at all acceptable.

[3] Criticisms deserving of consideration were answered by me in part at the end of the third volume of my *Luther*, and also in a more extensive exposition in my article *Bemerkungen zur protestantischen Kritik meines Lutherwerkes* (*Theologische Revue*, 1919, pp. 1 sqq.)

text, I have limited my observations to the great struggle of the sixteenth century without digressing to controversial questions of the present age which suggest themselves almost irresistibly. The question, propounded in this book—and verily it is a sufficiently comprehensive question—rather is: What happened in that period of upheaval and, above all, how is the responsible author of the struggle to be judged in his interior and exterior life? I could impose this restriction upon myself all the more easily, since Luther is regarded by present-day Protestants more and more as a purely historical phenomenon. According to the acknowledgment of Protestant leaders, the present age has in general passed beyond his influence, and the little group which still professes his peculiar doctrines, is diminishing. It may be left to others, be they Protestant or Catholic, to draw appropriate inferences from the texts and facts here presented, which are not the product of theological prepossession, but of an independent study of the facts. In another work, entitled, *Der deutsche Luther im Weltkrieg und in der Gegenwart,* I have frankly discussed certain of these inferences.[4] In the *Lutherstudien,* a selection of more exhaustive contributions on the subject of Luther appearing in single numbers, I have attempted to present in detail the new movements within the Protestant pale, especially as exemplified by the recent jubilee celebrations of the Reformation.[5]

May the present volume be perused by unprejudiced readers.

THE AUTHOR

Innsbruck, December 3, 1925

[4] Augsburg, 1924, published by Haas and Grabherr.
[5] *Lutherstudien,* 6 Hefte, Freiburg, 1921 sqq.

CONTENTS

CHAPTER   PAGE

I   LUTHER'S YOUTH 1
    1. Eisleben and Mansfeld 1
    2. Magdeburg and Eisenach 11
    3. Luther as a Student at Erfurt 19
    4. Luther's Precipitate Entrance into the Monastery . . 37

II   LUTHER'S FIRST YEARS IN THE MONASTERY 44
    1. Novitiate, Profession, First Mass 44
    2. Studies and First Experience as Teacher 48
    3. The Journey to Rome 52
    4. In Wittenberg 55

III   STRIKING OUT ALONG NEW ROADS—THE INTERIOR PROCESS . 58
    1. Luther's First Biblical Lectures—His Mysticism . . 58
    2. Interior State 62
    3. Opposition to Self-Righteousness and Religious Observ-
       ance 65

IV   PROGRESS OF THE NEW DOCTRINE 71
    1. Interpretation of the Epistle to The Romans (1515–
       1516) 71
    2. The Principal Propositions of Luther's Doctrine . . 73
    3. Effects of Luther's First Appearance 74
    4. Historical Background of Luther's Doctrine . . . 79
    5. The Psychological Background 86

V   FROM THE INDULGENCE THESES TO THE DISPUTATION AT
    LEIPSIC (1517–1519) 89
    1. The Controversy on Indulgences 89
    2. The Hearing at Augsburg. Miltitz 100
    3. The Discovery in the Tower 105
    4. The Leipsic Disputation of 1519 and the Papal Primacy . 111

VI   SIGNS OF THE COMING TEMPEST IN STATE AND CHURCH:
    LUTHER'S OPINIONS OF THE AGE 122
    1. Currents of the New Age 122
    2. Abuses in the Life of the Clergy 126

CHAPTER   PAGE

3. Brighter Phases 130
4. Preponderance of Dangerous Elements 135

VII THE YEAR OF THE BAN 141
1. Before the Ban 141
2. Conclusion of the Roman Trial 153
3. The So-Called Two Great Reformation Pamphlets of Luther 157
4. After the Promulgation of the Bull 164
5. The Fire Alarm 173

VIII THE DIET OF WORMS (1521) 180
1. Luther on Trial Before the Empire 180
2. The Sentence of Outlawry 190

IX LUTHER'S SOJOURN AT THE WARTBURG 194
1. Storms Within and Without 194
2. Spirits and Illusions 202
3. "Pecca Fortiter." The Mass 205
4. Confusion at Wittenberg. Other Writings Composed by Luther During His Sojourn at the Wartburg . . . 208
5. The Return. Victory at Wittenberg 212

X THE SPREAD OF LUTHERANISM 221
1. Methods of Propagation 221
2. Auxiliaries from the Monasteries 229
3. The Movement within the Empire 237
4. The Congregational Church 245
5. Divine Service. Multifarious Activities 248
6. The Pen as Luther's Weapon of Continued Attack . . 258
7. Free Christianity and the Freedom of the Will . . 265
8. Companions in Arms at Wittenberg 270

XI THE TEMPESTUOUS YEAR, 1525—LUTHER'S MARRIAGE . 278
1. Luther and the Peasants' War 278
2. Luther's Marriage 289
3. Luther's Principal Work: On the Enslaved Will . . 298
4. The Storms at Erfurt 305
5. The New State Church 311
6. Progressive Destruction of Catholicism 315

XII THE DECISIVE YEARS, 1525-1530 323
1. Charles V, Clement VII, and the Turks 323
2. Luther and the State Church of Saxony 328

CHAPTER PAGE

3. New Doctrinal and Controversial Writings 334
4. Zwingli and the Controversy Regarding the Last Supper 341
5. The Protest of 1529 346
6. Luther and Zwingli in the Castle of Marburg 349
7. Personal Experiences. Temptations 352
8. Catholic Apologetics Against Luther 359
9. Further Spread of the Religious Revolt 371

XIII The Diet of Augsburg (1530) and Luther at Coburg
Castle 374
1. The Diet of Augsburg 374
2. Luther in the Castle of Coburg 380
3. The "Proviso of the Gospel" 387
4. Luther's Writings During His Sojourn at Coburg and the
Following Months 391
5. A Strong Saxon Philippic Against Luther 398

XIV Luther on the Side of the Schmalkaldic League—His
Translation of the Bible 403
1. Luther's Change of Opinion Relative to Armed Resistance 403
2. The Schmalkaldic League After 1531 408
3. The Religious Peace of Nuremberg (1532) and Subsequent Events 410
4. Luther's Translation of the Bible (Completed in 1534) . 420
5. Luther's Literary Activity 433

XV Session of the Schmalkaldic League, 1537. Literary Bat-
tles. Luther's Co-workers 438
1. The Schmalkaldic Articles. Repudiation of the Proposed
General Council by the Schmalkaldians 438
2. Luther's Illness at Schmalkalden. New Polemics . . . 441
3. Further Violent Measures 446
4. Belligerent and Pacific Movements in the Empire . . . 450
5. Literary Defenders of the Catholic Cause After 1530 . 454
6. Luther's Fellow-Combatants 461

XVI Personal and Domestic Affairs 470
1. Engaging Characteristics 470
2. Religious Poetry and Church Hymns 477
3. The Table Talks 479

CHAPTER   PAGE

XVII   PERSONAL AND DOMESTIC AFFAIRS (CONTINUED) . . . 486
      1. Duration and Waning of Temptations 486
      2. Abnormal Psychological Traits 490
      3. From Freedom to Violent Intolerance 498

XVIII   LUTHER ON MORALITY AND MATRIMONY. THE BIGAMY OF
      PHILIP OF HESSE 505
      1. Luther's Ethical Teaching in General 505
      2. Matrimony and Sacerdotal Celibacy 509
      3. The Bigamy of Philip of Hesse 515
      4. "The Bold, Lusty Lie" 526

XIX   THE ECCLESIASTICAL SCHISM ANTERIOR TO LUTHER'S DEATH 528
      1. The Eve of the Religious War. The Council 528
      2. "Consecration" of the Bishop of Naumburg and Dedica-
      tion of the Church at Torgau 532
      3. Attacks upon the Archbishopric of Cologne and the
      Duchy of Brunswick 537

XX   LUTHER'S FINAL STRUGGLES AND DEATH 542
      1. The Militant Spirit of Luther in Word and Picture . . 542
      2. In the Midst of Ruins 549
      3. At Death's Door 563
      4. Luther's Death 567
      5. After Luther's Death 580

      BIBLIOGRAPHY 586

      INDEX 601

CHAPTER I

LUTHER'S YOUTH

I. EISLEBEN AND MANSFELD

In the night of November 10–11, 1483, there was born to the miner John Luther at Eisleben a son who was destined to achieve distinction. The house in which Martin Luther was born was situated on the socalled Lange Strasse, in the southwestern part of the little city, which was encircled by walls and towers. Even at the present day the somewhat deteriorated building is partially preserved, the upper story only having been reconstructed because of a fire in 1689.

The house in which Martin first saw the light of day lay within the limits of St. Peter's parish. On the day succeeding his birth, the infant was brought to the parish church. As it was the feast of St. Martin of Tours, a bishop and monastic founder, the name Martin was given to the child in baptism; and thus the saint who was commemorated on that day became his patron. In accordance with this custom, the name of Martin was presumably likewise selected for Bucer, who will be frequently mentioned as a subsequent helper of Luther. The Sacrament which ushered the son of John Luther into the halls of Catholic Christianity was administered by the pastor, Bartholomew Rennebecher. The sacred rites were performed in the Gothic tower chapel which is still preserved in its pristine condition. Upon entering the chapel, one is vividly carried back to that hour. Profound thoughts are aroused by the impression of the hallowed semi-darkness of the venerable walls and the sight of the precious side-altar, ornamented with ancient statues of saints that look down solemnly upon the worshippers. The local memorials of men frequently mentioned in history, which are so sedulously sought to-day, possess an undoubted historic value. The traces related to Luther's person, were preserved with an uncommon love by his friends and adherents. Tradition, however, has interwoven errors with the truth. There is no historical warrant either for the baptismal font, which is pointed out in the chapel as Luther's, or for the older superimposed part, despite its inscription which proclaims that Martin was baptized here.[1]

As one steps out of the chapel, which is surmounted by a tower, into the church of St. Peter and contemplates its stately exterior, the Gothic forms still recall the period of Luther's youth. The church had been gradually completed by 1513; but the tower, without its present crown and the baptistery upon which its heavy pile is erected, dates from 1474.

The friendly little city of Eisleben participated in the general zeal for building churches which at that time proclaimed the religious devotion and Christian charity of the faithful in many parts of Germany. The large church which was dedicated to St. Andrew and in which Luther delivered his last sermons, was rebuilt in the fifteenth century in conformity with an older plan and adorned with two tall, pointed spires. In the year 1462, the church of St. Nicholas was completed. In that part of the town called the "new city," built by Count Albrecht von Mansfeld in 1511, a church was erected in honor of St. Ann, the patroness of the mining industry, for the benefit of the resident miners. The mining of copper ore, extracted from the near-by hills, constituted even then, as it had for a long time previously thereto, the chief industry of the city. The industry was very much promoted by the counts of Mansfeld, who ruled Eisleben as the capital of their county.

Martin's father at the time of his son's birth resided only temporarily in the beautifully situated and ambitious city. He had settled with his family in this city some time before, in the hope of acquiring a better income. Previously he had lived in Möhra, a village near Eisenach, whence the Luthers originated. There he lived, a descendant of a race of peasants, engaged in husbandry. In his Table-Talks, Martin Luther says: "My great-grandfather, my grandfather, and my father were real peasants." [2] In another passage, after stating: "I am the son of a peasant," he adds, to indicate that he is not ashamed of his descent: "Peasants have become kings and emperors." [3] Indeed, he ever remained conscious of the fact that something of the sturdiness of the Saxon country-folk inhered in him.

[1] *Beschreibende Darstellung der älteren Bau- und Kunstdenkmäler der Provinz Sachsen,* Heft XVIII: *Mansfelder Gebirgskreis,* von H. Grössler und A. Brinkmann (Halle, 1893), p. 145.
[2] *Tischreden,* Weimar ed., V, Nr. 5574.
[3] *Ibid.,* Nr. 6250: *"Ego sum rustici filius,"* etc.

The hardy population of Möhra counted among its number a younger brother of John Luther, who also bore the name of John, which had been given to him in honor of his god-father, regardless of its being a repetition of the same name in the family. The first John was referred to as the elder, or big John; his younger brother as the younger, or little John. In the extant fragmentary court records of Mansfeld, whither he had gone, the name of the younger brother occurs repeatedly. According to these documents little John achieved notoriety on account of certain brutal acts for which he was sentenced. During one of his frequent visits to the tavern, he struck his neighbor's hand with a knife or inflicted bleeding gashes on his head. Once in the course of a brawl he beat his opponent on the head with a tankard until the blood flowed.[4] Perhaps it was this same irascible uncle of whom James, an elder brother of Martin, states in the Table Talks of 1540, that he trapped two Franciscan monks in a hole that was infested by wolves.[5]

It is related of Luther's father that he was a serious-minded, severe, and industrious man. At times, however, he drank to excess, so the Table Talks assure us; and then, contrary to his habitual nature, he was in high spirits and jovial. In this respect he differed, as Luther tells us, from a nephew named Polner, who became vicious and dangerous and compromised the Gospel in his frequent lapses from sobriety.[6] The father, according to Luther's expression, was endowed with "a robust, solid body." As he practised hard manual labor, so too, Margaret his wife, was habituated to unremitting toil. From the scanty notices which history has preserved, she appears to have been an industrious housewife. Besides Martin, Margaret had a number of other children who caused her sufficient cares and worry. Luther recalls that she was wont to carry home on her back the wood that was needed for the household. Margaret Luther, née Ziegler, was a native of Franconia. There was no alien blood in her family, and certain early opponents of Luther were unjustified in claiming to have discovered that Luther's ancestors originated in Slavic Bohemia, in order to connect him with the country of the heretic Hus. Luther is a good Old-Ger-

---

[4] *Zeitschrift des Harzvereins für Geschichte und Altertumskunde*, XXXIX (1906), art. by W. Möllenberg, pp. 169 sqq. In adverting to the acts of violence the name "Hans Luder" is frequently mentioned without distinction of person; so in Nrs. 7 and 8, where the aggressor inflicts bloody blows upon two persons with a knife.

[5] *Tischreden*, Weimar ed., IV, Nr. 4891.

[6] *Ibid.*, Nr. 5050 of the year 1540: "*Reliqui ebrii sunt laeti et suaves, ut pater meus,*" etc.

man name. It is identical with Lothar (Luothar) and signifies: the pure one. This fact is stressed occasionally by Luther in his Table Talks. However, in the first years of his public appearance he spelled his name Ludher or Luder. The form Luder or Lueder likewise appears in the family record. He complained that his enemies spelled the name Lotter (Lotterbube), which signifies a vagrant scamp. In the beginning of his revolt he used, for a time, the more euphonious Greek term Eleutheros or Eleutherius (freeman, liberator). Later on he jocosely derived his Christian name Martin from Mars, the valiant god of war.[7]

The Luthers had left Möhra and removed to Eisleben, because John believed that the mining industry of the latter city would afford him a better subsistence. At Eisleben, according to his son, he became a "metallicus," or poor miner. The poor miner, however, must soon have become conscious of the meagerness of his prospects for advancement, for, in the year succeeding the birth of Martin, towards the middle of 1484, he repaired with his family to Mansfeld, the center of a flourishing mining industry.[8] The traveller of to-day, who follows the road from Eisleben, passes friendly villages of frame dwellings, conspicuous for their protruding upper story, a style of building customary in that country. Continuing his journey, he soon comes upon hills of dross and stones and smoking furnaces, which even to-day form a characteristic picture of the city of Mansfeld, lying between rising hills and green fields and woods. Upon his arrival, he is greeted by the ancient castle of the counts of Mansfeld, majestically enthroned on the hill at his right. To his left and in the immediate vicinity of the small hollow of the valley, lies the moderately sized city itself, situated on a rising plain. A broad street, originally somewhat steep and at Luther's time the only thoroughfare of the city, wends its way upward between the houses. At the right there is an inconspicuous dwelling which is described as the former residence of Luther's parents. Only a small part of the old homestead of the Luthers is preserved. The letters I. L. and the date 1530 are inscribed upon a semi-circular arch above the door. It is reminiscent of James Luther, Martin's elder brother, who, in the

---

[7] Ibid., Nr. 4378; II, Nr. 1829. Briefwechsel I, p. 19 of the year 1514: "F[rater] M[artinus] Luder; cf. pp. 44, 47, 53, 65 of the year 1516.

[8] Tischreden, Weimar ed., V, Nr. 6250: "Darnach ist mein Vater nach Mansfelt gezogen und daselbs ein Bergkheuer worden. Daher bin ich."

year of the death of his father, thus perpetuated his property right. For a long time the parents of Martin lived in poverty and anxiety during their occupancy of this house.

Only gradually did the miner succeeed in improving his condition. In speaking of his early youth, Martin Luther tells us that hard toil was the lot of his parents. At a later date he narrates how he and two other lads once collected sausages. It happened during a procession of poor schoolboys singing in the streets. A burgher approached them, offering to give them sausages, but as he addressed the children, albeit in fun, in a rough tone of voice, they fled, not understanding the well-meant joke. Thus, says Luther, men in their shortsightedness and ignorance often fear God when He wishes to bestow benefits upon them.[9]

He first attended school in Mansfeld. The school was situated somewhat higher up the street than his parental home, to the right of an extended place similar to a plaza. It is partially preserved even to this day. It was one of the elementary schools, known as Latin schools, in which, according to an extensive custom, the students were introduced to the rudiments of Latin immediately after their first lessons in reading and writing. Reading was learned by means of the catechism and the primer; the elements of Latin were acquired by the recitation of the usual Latin prayers, such as the Pater Noster and the Credo. These were arduous and toilsome years for young Martin. The severity of the teachers and the vexatious declensions and conjugations lingered in his memory for many years. According to the customs that obtained in the schools of those days, there was an *"asinus"* (ass) which was wrapped around the lazy or ignorant pupil. There was also among the pupils a *"lupus"* (wolf) appointed to this office by the preceptor; it was his duty to record for punishment the omissions of his schoolmates. Punishment was inflicted summarily at the end of the week. Luther states in his Table Talks that he had once been disciplined with the rod fifteen times on a certain forenoon. If true, this was due either to great lack of diligence, or to stubbornness; or it was a penalty for misconduct of which he had been guilty for a whole week.[10] His later complaints concerning the abuse of the rod in the schools of Mansfeld and in

[9] *Ibid.*, I, Nr. 137: *"cum caneremus ad colligenda farcimina"* etc. Cf. *ibid.*, III, Nr. 2936; V, Nrs. 5804, 5989aa.
[10] *Ibid.*, V, Nr. 5571.

the schools in general, are too specific to exculpate his teachers and many of their colleagues in other places from the charge of excessive severity. The age was strongly biased in favor of the rod. There were laws against such excesses, but we have no guarantee that they were observed.

Undoubtedly the stern discipline of the school contributed to intimidate the character and depress the spirits of young Luther.

He retains one pleasant reminiscence of his school days, when he gratefully mentions in his writings how an elder pupil, Nicholas Semler, often carried him to school in his arms; for the ascent of the street, especially when covered with ice and snow, was assuredly a hardship.

There were not many pleasant memories of his paternal home which accompanied him in life. He did not experience the joyousness of youth.

He avers, it is true, that his parents meant it well with him. His father, ordinarily not communicative, with thoughts engrossed in his labors, and his mother, who was similarly inclined, undoubtedly told him about religion and its consolations; for they were loyal Catholics. Thus, Martin heard from his father the edifying narrative of the happy death of Count Günther of Mansfeld (1475), made beautiful by the great trust he placed in the redemptive merits of the death of Christ.[11] When, in 1530, the dying John Luther, who at the time espoused the religious party of his son, was asked whether he confidently accepted the traditional teachings of salvation, he replied with simplicity and bluntness: "I would in truth be a knave did I not believe in them." He had never been qualified by his educational attainments to pass judgment on the orthodoxy of the new doctrines. For the rest he respected the sacerdotal state during Martin's youth, though he freely indulged in criticisms of it after his own blunt manner. On occasion, too, he expressed his indignation at monasticism, perhaps on account of its obvious faults or because it was the fashion of the age, when monasteries, their possessions or mendicant practices were disliked by many.[12]

Despite the high veneration in which the Church was held in his

[11] M. Ratzeberger, *Chronik*, ed. by Neudecker (Jena, 1850), p. 42, who, however, disregarding other matters, distorts the affair in conformity with the idea of the new Gospel.

[12] *Tischreden*, Weimar ed., III, Nr. 3556a: *"Er hat der Mönche Schalkheit wohl erkannt."* Thus Luther in 1537, undoubtedly because of his father's opposition to his entering the monastic state. In this connection it is also necessary to take into consideration Luther's

parental home, young Luther did not enjoy an excessive amount of loving and solicitous religious care. The school and the Church had to supply the deficit; and they did.

In general, the external discipline to which his parents subjected him was too rigorous. This caused an aversion to the father on the part of the son, which lasted for a long time, so that, as the latter says, the father found it necessary to regain the lost affection of his són. Unfortunately both father and mother, Luther subsequently complains, could not distinguish between the disposition and ' the spirit of their children and drove the son to despondency (*usque ad pusillanimitatem*).[13] His own sad experience is reflected in his admonition to all parents not to indulge in excessive severity, but to "associate the apple with the rod" in the training of their offspring. "My mother," he says, "flogged me until I bled on account of a single nut." [14] It is surprising that Luther never in later life mentions his mother with a friendly and warm feeling, despite the frequency with which he recalls the days of his childhood and boyhood. The consoling picture of a mother's love, which accompanies most men on their journey through life, was apparently denied him. Mother and father, it appears, often acted in anger. The latter, for example, became "thoroughly enraged," as Luther himself says, when his son entered the monastery. Hence, there is no exaggeration in the statement of Albert Freitag that there is discernible in the boy Luther "a substratum of the melancholy which pervaded his parental home"; [15] nor in that of Friedrich von Bezold who says that his "disposition was intimidated and wrapped in gloom" early in life.[16]

The pupils of the Mansfeld school were obliged to attend divine service diligently. They worshipped in the parish church which was dedicated to St. George and lay almost directly opposite the school. This church originated in the thirteenth century. Rebuilt in the year 1497, when Luther was a boy, it still exhibits the same form in which his eyes beheld it. A large statue of St.

---

disposition relative to his former vocation. The same is true of his expression concerning his father in the *Tischreden*, Weimar ed., I, Nr. 881: *"Semper fruit iniquus monasticae vitae."* Cf. *In Genesim*, Weimar ed., XLIV, p. 411, and Ratzeberger, *Chronik*, p. 49.

[13] *Tischreden*, Weimar ed., III, Nr. 3566.

[14] *Ibid.*

[15] *Historische Zeitschrift*, 1918, Heft 2, p. 264.

[16] *Geschichte der deutschen Reformation* (Berlin, 1890), p. 248.

George, the gallant knight, in the act of slaying the dragon, graces the beautiful Gothic portal. The windows are exquisitely decorated. The interior is adorned with richly carved Gothic altars ornamented with figures of the saints. An altar of St. Ann, patroness of miners, was erected in 1502.

The well-regulated divine services were bound to send more cheerful thoughts into the soul of the child and to touch his heart with the supernatural destiny of man.

The singing of the congregation and of the boys' choir was especially treasured in the memory of Luther. They produced a beneficial influence upon him. The boy was endowed with a high voice. Docile and highly talented, he mastered the melody both according to form and spirit. He remained a life-long friend of sacred music. We may picture him in imagination as he and the other youthful choristers, vested in their white gowns, are led by the cantor or the sub-cantor from school to church to participate in the liturgical solemnities. The psalms, responsories, antiphons, the Magnificat and the litanies still lived in him when he had attained to a man's estate. They were venerable melodies, handed down from former ages, in the Latin text of which the singers were carefully exercised by the cantor. Instruction in ecclesiastical chant constituted an important part of the educational methods of the school; it was adapted to their spiritual content as well as to their external rendition. Besides the liturgical hymns there were the religious songs of the people, such as the "fine hymn" at Pentecost, as Luther styles it: *"Nu bitten wir den Heiligen Geist,"* and the Easter hymn, *"Christ ist erstanden,"* etc. "In the days of the papacy," says Luther at a later period of his career, "there were excellent songs." That Luther was the first to introduce congregational singing is a claim not founded on fact, but on prejudice. He himself adequately refutes this prejudice. "Congregational singing flourished before the Reformation." [17]

The boy learned and loved every phase of the regular ecclesiastical life of Catholicism without meeting with any "reformatory" tendencies. The veneration of the Saints, reminiscent of the august communion of all the servants of God here on earth and in the realms of Heaven, the reception of the Sacraments and attendance at the holy Sacrifice of the Mass, the processions in the cemetery and to

[17] Hans Preuss, *Luthers Frömmigkeit* (Leipzig, 1917), p. 52.

the chapel of the departed, as well as those through the decorated streets of the little city, the blessings and ceremonies of the Church no less than the sermons of the clergy—everything made him feel at home in the great spiritual house of God founded by Jesus Christ. There is prejudice in the frequent assertion of non-Catholics that there was "over-emphasis of good works in Roman piety and divine service" which thus "suppressed pious impulses." The congregation and the boy Luther, on the contrary, knew "that men assembled to praise and worship God"; "the heart was truly raised aloft and joyousness replete with life was imparted to it." [18] Luther heard of the Vicar of Christ, Innocent VIII (1484–1492), who governed all Christendom with spiritual power from his see at Rome. He sympathetically sensed the danger with which the advancing forces of Islam threatened the faithful, and which urged the latter to have recourse to prayer, and perhaps his lips recited the prayer for deliverance from the Turkish menace at the sound of the "Turkish bell," a practice introduced about the year 1456. He always treasured the memory of St. George, the patron saint of his church, to whose legendary story it was his delight to give a beautiful spiritual significance. Of the public customs of his boyhood he boasted that all games, such as dice and cards and even dances, had been prohibited, whereas, in his old age, he saw them gain ground.[19] It is known that the most widely read book of those days, which was probably also perused by the boy Martin, who had a passion for reading, was the excellent life of Christ written by the Carthusian, Ludolph of Saxony (died 1377), a work firmly grounded upon Christian doctrine and following in the attractive footsteps of St. Bernard. Rivaling Ludolph's book as a guide to the interior life was Henry Seuse's "Of Eternal Wisdom" and the "Imitation of Christ" by the immortal Thomas à Kempis. All these writings were permeated with genuine religiosity and the most solid piety, undiminished by even a taint of "reformatory" thought. The principal spiritual companion of youth, however, was the catechism, concerning which Luther's pupil, Mathesius, admits that God has "wonderfully retained it in the parish churches, for which we must thank our God and the ancient schools." [20]

---

[18] Otto Scheel, *Luthers Stellung zur hl. Schrift*, I, pp. 17, 19.
[19] *Tischreden*, Weimar ed., IV, Nr. 126.
[20] Mathesius, p. 16.

According to the latter authority, young Luther learned his catechism "diligently and rapidly." [21]

On the other hand, his boyhood days were unfortunately contaminated by the superstitions which prevailed in his parental home and, in general, among his Saxon and German contemporaries. Incredible notions of the devil, expressed in the crassest of anecdotes, haunted the minds of the people. Mysterious and credulous meanings were attached to ordinary phenomena of nature. This evil of superstition was deeply rooted especially among the miners. Their dangerous occupation in the mysterious bowels of the earth awakened dismal phantasies. They feared that preternatural powers spied on them with evil intent; then, too, they expected their assistance in discovering rich ores; or, finally, as Luther's speeches attest, they were familiar with queer deceptions which they imputed to them. The death of a younger brother in the parental home was attributed to witchcraft.[22] Many stories were told about Dame Hulda and her strange apparitions. Luther learned that devils inhabit forests, lakes, and streams, and use water-sprites to deceive men. He was told of a lake in the neighborhood of Mansfeld which was filled with captive devils who caused a storm whenever a stone was cast into the water. In conformity with his traditions, Luther steadfastly maintained that the devil had carnal intercourse with women. Changelings as well as goiters were caused by him. In his childhood, he says, there were many witches in Saxony. One of these lived in the vicinity of his father's house, and his mother had to make every possible effort to protect the family against her. It often happened that the children screamed frantically when subjected to incantations. The same witch, by means of her diabolical craft, brought on the death of a clergyman who had opposed her activity, by means of the ground over which he passed. In his youth Luther had seen many persons whose sickness or death had been caused by witches. "When I was a boy," he says, "I was told of an old woman who had brought misfortune upon a peace-loving husband and wife" against whom the devil had attempted his insidious wiles in vain. The witch induced them to lay sharp knives under their pillows and influenced them to believe that one party intended to murder the other; this

[21] *Ibid.*
[22] Weimar ed., XL, I, p. 315: *"Frater mihi occisus per veneficia."*

being so true, she averred, as the fact that they would discover knives under their respective pillows. As a consequence, the husband cut his wife's throat. Thereupon the evil one appeared to the old woman and, without approaching her, presented her with a pair of shoes on a long pole. Why do you not approach more closely? asked the witch, and the devil replied: Because you are more wicked than I, you have succeeded wherein I failed.[23]

In his early sermons, delivered in 1516 and 1518, Luther mentions the most superstitious things; indeed, strange ideas of this character permeate his entire life. The excrescences of popular credulity, into which he was introduced as a boy, were combated by the Church, but without avail. Books that were held in high esteem even furthered the abuse, as for instance the "Hexenhammer," which was published in 1487 by two Inquisitors. Ofttimes superstitious powers were ignorantly ascribed to ecclesiastical practices, such as the sacramentals and the veneration of the Saints. It is scarcely necessary to emphasize that the rational use of the blessings of the Church and the veneration of the Saints were as little favorable to these errors as the doctrinal teachings of the Church and of Sacred Scripture concerning the devil. The popular imagination created its own worlds. What was invisible was distorted and rendered visible; what was sacred was subjected to profanation. Thus statues of St. Christopher that were erected on the gates of the cities, and on the churches, even in the churches, were made immensely large, because numerous prayer books declared that whoever saw Christopher once a day, was protected against the evil spirits and sudden death. In his youth, these giant statues were round about him. The legend of St. Christopher made a lasting impression upon his mind, but, like that of St. George and other legends, he interpreted it critically and in a spiritual sense. Nevertheless, his criticism of the legends did not dispel his other superstitions.

2. MAGDEBURG AND EISENACH

About Easter, 1497, when Martin was fourteen years of age, his parents sent him to Magdeburg to continue his studies. The eminent talents which he displayed were deserving of a better education than that which Mansfeld offered. In the city on the Elbe there lived a

---

[23] *Tischreden,* Weimar ed., II, Nr. 1429.

citizen of Mansfeld, Paul Mosshauer by name, who was an official at the
archiepiscopal curia. It appears that the poor boy had been recommended to him, for Martin ate his meals with him and, perhaps,
also lodged in his house. The range of his ideas was enlarged in that
ancient city, which even at that time was famed for its magnificent
cathedral and other splendid buildings. Martin had reason to be satisfied with the teaching and the treatment he received at school. He
was instructed by the Brethren of the Common Life,[24] who undoubtedly furnished the major portion of his higher training.[25]

In respect of educational and ecclesiastical matters, the road he
now trod was decidedly a fortunate and very fruitful one; for the
Brethren belonged to a community that was permeated by a profoundly religious spirit, whose efforts of reform within the Church
blossomed forth splendid results at that time. Originating in the
Netherlands through the efforts of Geert Groote, who distinguished
himself by his labors for the Church, the society of the Brethren
spread to Germany. They were representatives of the so-called
"*devotio moderna*," a new conception of monastic piety more in
conformity with the requirements of the age, according to which,
in addition to prayers and begging, an active and timely efficacy
was to be cultivated in behalf of mankind. The Brethren particularly
devoted themselves to the education of the youth who attended the
existing schools, but they also erected schools of their own. Everywhere they laid special emphasis on devotional lectures, by means of
which they desired to foster the religious life of their pupils.[26] Among
their students who became celebrated men were the pious Thomas à
Kempis, the scholarly Gabriel Biel, the astronomer Nicholas Coper-
nicus, and Cardinal Nicholas of Cusa. Thomas à Kempis, having
completed his studies under the guidance of the Brethren, became
a canon regular of the Order of St. Augustine in the monastery of
Agnetenberg near Zwolle, where he died in 1471, in the ninety-
second year of his life. His writings, above all his *Imitation of Christ*,

---

[24] Undoubtedly their popular name (Loll Brothers) was derived from *lulhen*, to sing
softly (in choir).

[25] *Briefwechsel*, II, p. 402, 15 June, 1522. Cf. E. Barnikol, *Luther in Magdeburg* (see note
26), pp. 3 sqq., 54. Probably Luther attended the elementary instructions of the pensioners
of the Brethren.

[26] Cf. Barnikol, "*Die Brüder vom gemeinsamen Leben*," in the *Zeitschrift für Theologie
und Kirche*, Supplementary number, 1917; *ib.*, "*Das Magdeburger Brüderhaus*," in the
Theolog. Arbeiten aus dem rhein.-wiss. Predigerverein, Series of 1922, pp. 8 sqq., and
"*Luther in Magdeburg und das dortige Brüderhaus*," *ib.*, series of 1917, pp. 1 sqq.

faithfully reflect the spirit which he imbibed in his youth from his teachers, the Brethren of the Common Life. The Fraternity lived and labored in complete harmony with the Church. It was absolutely free from that aversion to the existing hierarchy which was formerly ascribed to it by uninformed Protestant writers. Those so-called "reformatory tendencies" which would qualify the Fraternity as a kind of precursor of the Protestant Reformation cannot be attributed to it in any sense. The constitutions, which were composed by Henry of Ahaus, the founder of the German Brethren, are animated throughout by the spirit of ecclesiastical submission; and the documents which we possess descriptive of the activities of the Brethren, confirm their loyalty to the Church.[27]

Luther's sojourn at Magdeburg lasted but a year, and few details of it have been handed down to us. Mathesius, a pupil of Luther, says: "The boy, like many a child of honest and wealthy parents, begged for bread and cried out his *panem propter Deum.*"[28] Luther also confesses that he was "Partekenhengst" during his stay at Magdeburg and subsequently at Eisenach.[29] This was a term of contempt applied to scholars who collected small donations contributed for their sustenance, by singing before the residences of the burghers or in other ways. Mathesius is correct in his assertion that even sons of well-to-do parents were sent out to engage in this humiliating practice of begging so that they might learn humility and sympathy for the poor. In Luther's case it can hardly have been the impoverished condition of his paternal home that compelled him to go begging.

Once, while sick with a fever in Magdeburg, he dragged himself to the kitchen and, without stopping, drank the contents of a vessel of fresh water. Thereupon he was seized with a profound slumber. When he awoke, the fever had left him. This event is narrated by Luther's friend, the physician Ratzeberger, who was impressed by it on ac-

---

[27] Paul Mestwerdt, *Die Anfänge des Erasmus, Humanismus und der devotio moderna* (Vol. II of *Studien zur Kultur und Geschichte der Reformation*, ed. by the Verein für Reformationsgeschichte), Leipzig, 1917. The author, on pp. 83 sqq., establishes proof of the decidedly Catholic attitude of the Brethren. He calls (p. 86) the writings of Thomas à Kempis "a classical memorial of the piety of the adherents of the 'devotio moderna.' "— O. Scheel I, p. 85: "The Brethren never abandoned Catholicism. Their 'modern' devotion was erected entirely on the foundation of Catholic piety. This must, alas, be emphasized to-day; for the Brethren have been made precursors of the Reformation."

[28] *Ibid.*, p. 17.

[29] Weimar ed., XXX, II, p. 576.

count of its peculiar circumstances. He perceived that the robust frame of the boy was endowed with endurance.[30]

Luther tells us how deeply impressed he was by an edifying scene he once witnessed in the streets of Magdeburg. A certain prince William of Anhalt-Zerbst, who had become a Franciscan monk and assumed the name of Lewis, passed him with a begger's sack hanging about him. The body of the prince had been reduced to a shadow from fasting, night watches, and flagellations. A strapping brother of the Order, a companion of his, more competent to carry the sack and its burden, walked alongside of the staggering man, because the latter, imbued with a spirit of penance, wished to bear the burden alone.[31] For thirty years the noble brother Lewis, a disciple of the Saint of Assisi, had borne the habit of his Order with honor until his 48th year, in 1504, when death relieved him of his burden. He performed the functions of a guardian in the houses of his Order in Magdeburg and Halle. He was known for his kindness and charity, no less than for the fearlessness with which he criticized the sins of the mighty, for his delicate art of mediation in their quarrels, and for his solicitude in behalf of the poor and oppressed. The establishment of new houses of his Order, especially in Prussia, was attributed to his successful labors.[32] The rare example of renunciation of the world which he displayed, was highly esteemed, especially because he was the eldest child of his parents. Four sons of these parents embraced the religious state. The historian of the Reformation in the city of Zerbst praises "the earnest and profoundly sincere piety" which characterized the princely family during the time prior to the religious schism.[33] In his Magdeburg days Luther was filled with admiration for the man whose countenance he was often privileged to see. He was yet free from the animus that impelled him in later days to condemn him and his monastic state.

If the lad had been given an opportunity to extend the time of his sojourn at Magdeburg, there is no doubt but that the instructions imparted at that place, and his association with the Brethren of the

[30] Ratzeberger, pp. 41 sq.: *"Er kreuchet auf Händen und Füssen abwärts in die Kuchen,"* etc.

[31] Weimar ed., 38, p. 105: *"Er trug den Sack wie ein Esel, das er sich zur Erde krümmen musste,"* etc.

[32] L. Lemmens, O.F.M., *Aus ungedruckten Franziskanerbriefen des 16. Jahrh. Reformationsgeschichtliche Studien*, Heft 20 (1911), pp. 8 sqq.

[33] H. Becker-Lindau, *Reformationsgeschichte der Stadt Zerbst*, in *Mitteilungen des Vereins für Anhaltische Geschichte*, Vol. XI, (Dessau, 1910), p. 250.

Common Life, would have affected his career most advantageously. About Easter of the subsequent year (1498), however, he had to transfer his residence to Eisenach, where he continued his studies at the Latin school. It is possible that the internal crisis which overtook the house of the Brethren at Magdeburg, contributed to this exchange.[34] Relatives of his parents lived at Eisenach, with whom the student was expected to establish connections. A brother-in-law, Conrad Hutter, sexton of the church of St. Nicholas, extended a cordial welcome to the young student. In grateful remembrance Luther invited him in after years to attend the celebration of his first Mass.

At Eisenach, too, the industrious scholar experienced the directions of a benevolent Providence and was further inducted into the spiritual life. At school and in the families of his acquaintances the religious life of the town furnished him with an adequate spiritual cultivation and a healthful interior development. In order to sustain himself, the young beggar, who was endowed with the gift of song, continued to solicit alms at the doors of the burghers, at least in the beginning of his student days at Eisenach. Shortly afterwards he was supported by a burgher named Henry Schalbe, designated as Heinricianus in the old report, whose son he escorted to school.[35] Later on a still better home opened its doors to him. It was the residence of Kuntz Cotta. The wife of this opulent native of Eisenach, who was descended from an Italian family, was Ursula Schalbe, a charitable lady who is said to have rescued the poor student from the streets, an act which many later Protestant authors describe with touching sentimentality. Mathesius simply says that the pious matron invited him to partake of the hospitality of her table, "because she cherished a strong affection for the boy on account of his singing and fervent praying in church." [36] Luther does not mention her name; only once does he refer to his "hostess" of Eisenach (a reference which might mean the wife of Henry Schalbe), and avers that he learned from her the saying that there is nothing on earth superior to the love of a woman for one so fortunate as to win it.[37] He entered this saying as a marginal note in his translation of the Proverbs chap. 31, where Solomon sings the praises of the virtuous and industrious housewife, the priceless treasure of her husband. At Eisenach the house where Frau Cotta is sup-

[34] Barnikol, Das Magdeburger Brüderhaus (see note 26), p. 40.
[35] Tischreden, Weimar ed., V, Nr. 5362.
[36] Mathesius, p. 17.
[37] Weimar ed., XLIII, p. 692.

posed to have lavished her benevolence upon Luther is still indicated
to the traveller. According to the better topographers of the town, the
residence of the Cottas is unknown.

Besides the Schalbes and the Cottas, who were devoted to the
Catholic faith, Luther became intimate with the vicar of the collegiate
church of St. Mary at Eisenach, John Braun, and his circle of friends.
Braun was versed in music and the humanities. With gratitude and
love Luther later on recalls his friendly and congenial intercourse with
him, in whose company music and song furnished many a happy and
inspiring hour.[38] In a letter to Braun, written during his student
days at Erfurt, Luther recalls his sister Catherine, whose versatility
in singing induced him to refer to her jocosely as "Cantharina"
(the singer).[39] He also desired the presence of Braun at his first
Mass.

It is probable that Luther underwent his greatest spiritual experience in the small Franciscan monastery at the foot of the Wartburg,
which rises above Eisenach. The monastery was known as the Schal-
bian college, because it depended upon the Schalbe family for its endowment and juridical status. The Fathers at the college became his
dear friends, as is revealed by the correspondence concerning his first
Mass. He says that the excellent men of this monastery deserved well
of him.[40] This monastery of discalced monks beneath the Wartburg
nurtured lively local remembrances of St. Elizabeth, the celebrated
landgravine of Thuringia.

As the talented boy ascended the towering castle which commanded
the surrounding country, it is small wonder that he was animated by
lofty sentiments of veneration for the princess, who was the counter-
part on a larger scale to the Magdeburg monk of princely descent.
There his ideas of the service of God and the significance of the things
of this world became enlarged. The example of the sainted princess,
who ministered with her own hands to the sick and indigent in the
hospital she herself had founded at Eisenach, was for him an effective
and beautiful illustration of applied Christianity in the most attractive form of humility, charity, and heroism. The beautiful popular

[38] *Briefwechsel*, I, p. 1, letter to Braun, April 22, 1507. Cf. Degering (see following
note), p. 88.
[39] H. Degering, *Aus Luthers Frühzeit: Briefe aus dem Eisenacher und Erfurter Luther-
kreise, 1497–1510*, in the *Zentralblatt für Bibliothekswesen*, Vol. XXXIII (1916), Heft
3 and 4; Sonderdruck, p. 78.—*Briefwechsel*, XVII, p. 82.
[40] *Briefwechsel*, I, p. 3, to Braun, April 22, 1507.

legend of the miracle of the roses and the narrative of the cruel banishment of Elizabeth and her children moved him more than the living monuments of the days of German knighthood and the contests of troubadours which were enclosed by the walls of the castle. Thence he would cast his eyes upon Eisenach itself, a city of churches and replete with pious traditions of Elizabeth. The city was girdled by a large wall, surmounted by many round, square and hexagonal towers, and a moat filled with water. In the fifteenth century, the city with its vast belt of walls, was no longer the residence of counts. Like the one-time lively Wartburg, it had become a quiet place. The churches, however, were the scenes of an active religious life. This was especially true of the three parish churches, each one of which boasted a school. The Romanesque church of St. Nicholas was located in the north of the town, the church of Our Lady in the south. Another church, dedicated to St. George, had been practically reconstructed in 1515. In addition to the churches, several monasteries opened their chapels to the faithful. There were about seventy priests in the town, of whom some were not actively engaged in the ministrations of religion. All too generous provision had been made for the religious requirements of the population.

The school which Luther attended, the so-called trivium, was situated in the immediate vicinity of the parish church of St. George. John Trebonius—such was the humanist form of his name—was its rector. "He was an imposing and a learned man and a poet," in the words of the physician Ratzeberger. Melanchthon reports that Luther in later life praised his talents. He drilled his pupils thoroughly in the Latin grammar of Donatus and in the syntax book of Alexander. The "asinus" and the "lupus" were not absent. It was customary to study ecclesiastical as well as classical literature. In order to master the church calendar, the students of Eisenach, as in many other places, memorized the so-called "cisio-janus," a composition in Latin hexameters which rendered the sequence of the feasts of the ecclesiastical year by abbreviation of the introductory words. "Cisio" signified circumcisio, the feast of the Circumcision of Christ, the first feast in January. Prosody and the preliminaries of the "art of oratory," and poetry were taught. The cantor played an important part. Besides the cantor, there were a master and probably other preceptors, who functioned under the rector, Trebonius. The latter manifested great respect towards his pupils. When he entered the class-room, he was wont to remove his biretta until the pupils were seated, because, so he said, there might be some among his scholars who were destined to occupy stations of dignity, such as the office of burgomaster, chancellor, doctor or regent. Luther long maintained grateful and friendly connections with the urbane Trebonius.

A prophet lived at that time in the larger Franciscan monastery of Eisenach. The privilege of indulging in public prophecy was denied to him, since the Brethren wisely confined the fantastic and dangerous man to his cell. The name of this prophet was John Hilten. Luther scarcely heard of him during his sojourn at Eisenach, but afterwards, in 1529, he got Hilten to communicate his prophecies to him. He then pretended to discover that his own opposition to the Pope had been foretold by Hilten "at the time of his youth." [41] By means of astrological calculations and a bold application of passages of Daniel and the Apocalypse to the evils of the age, against which he agitated with excessive zeal, Hilten had discovered that Rome was destined to fall about the year 1514. He never mentioned Luther. According to his prognostications, the year 1651 would witness the end of the world. Prophecies which actually came true, such as the advance of the Turks, invested him with a certain reputation. Towards the close of his life, at the end of the fifteenth century, Hilten is said by witnesses to have recanted his various theological errors, especially his erroneous and invidious propositions concerning the monastic life, which he uttered in his exaggerated enthusiasm for the Franciscan rule. He died at peace with his Order and the Church. It is not true that he was immured alive, as asserted by Ernest L. Enders. [42] In his Apologia for the Augsburg Confession, Melanchthon erroneously cites him as a papal witness to "evangelical truth." It was even greater perversion of the truth when Luther stated some years afterwards that Hilten was murdered because he foretold that the execution of John Hus "must be avenged; another shall come, whom the contemporaries will yet see." [43]

After a three years' stay Luther left Eisenach. The memory of the town always remained dear to him. His father ordered him to continue his studies at the university of Erfurt in Thuringian Saxony. Erfurt, with its struggling university, was the property of the arch-

---

[41] *Tischreden*, Weimar ed., III, Nr. 3795, of the year 1538.

[42] *Briefwechsel*, I, p. 198, in note 1 to Friedrich Myconius's letter to Luther concerning Hilten.

[43] *Tischreden*, Weimar ed., III, Nr. 3795, of the year 1538.

bishop of Mayence and subject to the protectorate of the Elector of Saxony. John Luther was determined that Martin should become a proficient jurist, one who could qualify for dignities and offices. In order to achieve this object, Martin had first to complete what is now called the curriculum of the liberal arts as a preparation for a professional course.

In the interim, John Luther had so improved his financial status that he was able to support his son adequately during his academic years. Whereas previously, according to Luther's admission, his parents had been engaged in a bitter struggle for the necessities of life, in later years the industrious father became the lessee of a number of forges and pits. Mines at that time were operated under a leasehold, and often subleased. Moreover, as early as 1491, John had become a member of the "Council of Four" of the section of the city in which he resided. He held the same office again in 1502. The members of the "Council of Four" were associated with the city council in the government of their district. John's repeated elections indicate that he was regarded as an intelligent and a practical man who gradually improved his economic condition. In the spring of 1501, he sent his promising son, now in his eighteenth year, to the university city on the Gera.

3. LUTHER AS A STUDENT AT ERFURT

Young Luther was next concerned with his reception into one of the existing students' inns of the university town. "Burses" or "contubernia" were terms used to designate the homes to which all students of the Alma Mater were obliged to belong, in virtue of a time-honored prescription. Here they usually lived under the supervision of one of the masters of the university. Aided by the master, or by someone else, the students were directed in their scientific pursuits. By the payment of a small tuition fee they had board and lodging in common. At first Luther resided in the "burse" known as Porta Coeli, which he afterwards exchanged for that of St. George in the parish of that name. Thus St. George, the patron saint of his Mansfeld parish, accompanied him also on his road to knowledge. In a verbose letter, the earliest preserved from his pen, Luther announced his residence at the Porta Coeli to his paternal friend Braun at Eisenach. He signs "Martinus viropolitanus" (Martin of Mansfeld), and refers to himself as the "bothersome hair-splitter,"—an allusion, no doubt, to his inclination to criticize.[44]

Erfurt at that time enjoyed an eminent reputation for learning. Since the university of Prague, in consequence of the Hussite controversy and the consequent emigration of the Germans, had lost its exalted position in the academic world, Erfurt was called the New Prague. Its faculty of law in particular became celebrated. No less distinguished were the members of the philosophical faculty and its preparatory courses in the quadrivium of the liberal arts. In respect of the study of philosophy, strictly speaking, Luther came under the influence of two excellent teachers, Jodocus Trutvetter and Bartholomew Arnoldi of Usingen. Prior to his admission to the higher branches of learning, custom constrained him to complete the study of grammar, rhetoric, and poetics. This preparatory discipline was indispensable for those students whose knowledge of these branches of learning was incomplete. Martin, though he was well versed in these branches, availed himself of this course in order to perfect his style, as evidenced by the fluent Latinity of his later writings as well as his early letters. He endeavored to catch the spirit of the classical authors. Among the poets, he first familiarized himself with the writings of an excellent neo-Latin poet, who was highly celebrated in his day, Baptista Mantuanus, whose real name was Giovanni Spagnolo. At one time general of the Carmelite Order, he was a pious and austere man, who was later beatified by Leo XIII. In due course of time Luther read Ovid's Heroics or Love Epistles and the poems of Vergil. The study of scholastic theology, he asserts, prevented him from reading more of these authors. This statement, however, is not to be accepted literally, for he found time to read the comedies of Plautus, and, either at the same time or somewhat later, Horace, Juvenal, and Terence, from whom he was able to quote in his later years. Jerome Emser, his subsequent adversary, explained to him Reuchlin's comedy of "Sergius."

The so-called "minor logic" constituted a part of the subject-matter of the first lectures in the faculty of liberal arts. The Old and the New Logic, interpreted by the aid of Aristotle, was the next

---

[44] Letter of September 5, 1501, with excuse for delay. First appearance of text in H. Degering, *Aus Luthers Frühzeit*, in the *Zentralblatt für Bibliothekswesen*, Vol. XXXIII, (1916), p. 78. Afterwards in Luther's *Briefwechsel*, Vol. XVII, ed. by P. Flemming (Leipzig, 1920), p. 82. The letter is undoubtedly authentic.

step in his studies. With the Stagirite as a guide, the student then learned "natural philosophy, *i. e.*, the physics of Aristotle, and read his treatises on the soul and on spherical astronomy. Although the subjects of the ancient trivium still pertained to the faculty of arts, the subjects of the quadrivium were freely treated. The lectures were delivered in the "burses" or in the auditorium of the so-called Old College. They were accompanied by constant exercises and disputations. These "exercises and disputations" often commenced as early as six in the morning; they stimulated industry, sharpened the wits, and cultivated the faculty of oral expression.

In this respect, too, the faculty of arts of the University of Erfurt revealed itself as a medium of a general academic training, well adapted to the requirements of the age, preparing the student for the higher branches of learning, theology, jurisprudence, or medicine. Aristotle, who was celebrated almost universally as the Philosopher, was the supreme pathfinder to scholarly independence.

The bachelor's degree, the lowest academic honor, was the proximate aim of Luther. He obtained this degree as soon as possible, in the autumn of 1502, by means of a severe test in the presence of five examiners. As "baccalaureus of the liberal arts" he now wore the gown of his office according to the constitutions of the faculty, since he was now a member of the teaching staff. This first academic distinction prepared the way for the master's degree. But, before he could achieve this honor, it was necessary for him to devote himself to protracted study. In the meantime he was obliged to assist beginners in the studies he had completed. This was the rule of the university. A strict law regulated the curriculum of studies and the scientific occupation of the teachers at the universities of that day.

Nevertheless, a certain freedom of life prevailed, and the students found frequent opportunities for pleasantries and merriment.

Young Luther had experienced this at the very threshold of his academic career, when he was obliged, like all newcomers, to take the so-called "deposition" in order to become a full-fledged student in the eyes of his associates. On this occasion the newcomer (*Bean*) was compelled to masquerade with horns and elongated ears, and swine's teeth were attached to the corners of his mouth. Then, by means of a plane, he was fashioned into the proper academic form. The merry procedure was crowned by a baptism with water or wine. Originally a certain spiritual significance had been attached to this ceremony: it was intended to hold up to the freshman the moral aims which he was to pursue through the renunciation of his shortcomings. When Luther was professor at Wittenberg in later years, he alluded to the symbolic meaning of this "deposition."

The life of the beneficiaries of the various "burses" was invested with manifold privileges. Although the constitutions of some, *e. g.*, the Porta Coeli, were strict and decisive in their religious and educational import, they were not always conscientiously observed. In comparison with the beginnings of the "burses," there was possibly a lack of zeal and vigilance in Luther's student days. In some instances, the frequentation of taverns was expressly permitted. The life of the students at Erfurt must have been rather unrestrained. The relatively large number of students (at that time an average of over 300 were enrolled annually) leads us to expect excesses. In 1530 Luther says that the University of Erfurt was "a place of dissolute living and an ale-house," in which subjects the students were interested in preference to everything else.[45] His added remark that "there were neither lecturers nor preachers" at this institution, is evidently to be characterized as a polemical exaggeration directed against a Catholic university. For there were deserving preachers at Erfurt, though they did not preach the new Gospel; and there were also respectable professors, as he himself attests in his reference to Trutvetter and Usingen. Nevertheless, the acrid judgment just cited reveals a modicum of evil experiences made at Erfurt. The city council in a measure harbored immorality by allowing prostitutes to live together upon the payment of a tax, a custom which prevailed also in other cities. Even among the clergy of Erfurt there were open infractions of chastity. It is questionable, however, whether Luther meant Erfurt, when in his Table Talks he said he knew a city where the mistresses of clergymen were honored as Madame Deaconess, Madame Provost, Madame Cantor, etc.[46] "Gossip may have seized upon many a story and embellished it with its own peculiar frivolity," says Otto Scheel.[47] When, at a later period, Luther speaks of his own youth he states that the clergy were not suspected of adultery and immorality, whereas, since then, dissoluteness had constantly increased.[48] At all events, Erfurt,

45 *Tischreden*, Weimar ed., II, Nr. 2719b.
46 Erlangen ed., LX, p. 280 (Chap. 27, Nr. 1301).
47 Scheel, I, p. 136.
48 *Opp. Exeg.*, IX, p. 260.

during the student days of Luther, was a city whose inhabitants observed the moral law and were imbued with a profound religious faith—a city replete with well-attended churches and numerous busy monasteries whose bells never ceased ringing by day and by night.

The splendid church of Our Lady excelled all other churches. Erected on a hill, it overlooked the entire city. The church of St. Severus, which was situated next to it, still presents a magnificent sight. A few decades before Luther used to visit this church, St. John Capistran preached from the lower steps of the mighty terrace which leads up to the hill, and stories were told of numerous conversions and miraculous cures. In the year 1502, while Luther was present, the city and the plaza witnessed the solemn procession of the jubilee which was arranged under the auspices of the papal legate, Raymond Peraudi of Gurk, accompanied by the general reception of the Sacraments and a plenary indulgence. Like the jubilee indulgence granted on a previous occasion, in 1488, that of 1502 was a source of spiritual renovation for citizens and students. For a number of years the voice of an Augustinian monk, John Genser (Jenser) von Paltz, the scholarly promoter of papal indulgences, resounded through the spacious edifice. He was a profoundly pious man, endowed with a powerful gift of speech. His associate, the Augustinian John von Dorsten, rivaled him as a preacher of great popularity and impressive forcefulness. Indeed, the Augustinian monastery excelled all others in learning and practical activity. By means of their confraternities, monasteries, and churches, these monks educated the faithful to a more active religious life. Perhaps young Luther, the son of a miner, may have experienced a sort of predilection for the confraternity of St. Ann, the patroness of miners, which was directed by the Augustinians. We shall see that he supplicated St. Ann, when, during a storm, he made his vow to enter a monastery.

But, until that time, he devoted two years to preparing himself for the master's degree. During this time he studied the logic of Aristotle, certain questions of natural philosophy, mathematics in general, and several minor branches of the old quadrivium; and, finally, moral philosophy, politics, and metaphysics. All these subjects were learned in the light of Aristotle and with the assistance of preceptors who explained the writings of the Stagirite to the student.[49]

---

[49] Cf. Scheel, I, pp. 157 sqq.; 170 sqq., where the branches of study are set forth in detail for the period before and after the baccalaureate.

In its application of the Aristotelian philosophy, and in the study of philosophy in general, the University of Erfurt claimed to pursue a purified course, which at that time was designated as "modern." Trutvetter and Usingen, the principal teachers of Luther, were outspoken representatives of the *via moderna,* as were also their fellow-instructors. At other universities there were advocates of the new as well as adherents of the old method. The old system favored the so-called philosophy of realism, whereas the new system betrayed a nominalistic tendency. The latter originally derived its name from the fact that it held that all universal concepts were mere names (*nomina.*) The better class of Nominalists were strictly Catholic and avoided the dangers ordinarily attached to Nominalism. William of Ockham, the daring and skeptical *"Doctor invincibilis"* (died at Munich in 1347), was the accepted leader of the Nominalist school. But there were men like the learned and influential Gabriel Biel, as well as the Erfurt professors mentioned above, who knew how to avoid the reefs of Ockhamism.

Nominalism was a stage in the decline of Scholasticism. The heyday of Scholasticism was past; logical investigations and useless hair-splitting were in vogue. The barren subtleties of Terminism, so-called, were an evil, though a very large and living stream of learning was still flowing. The Scholastics of the thirteenth century, especially Thomas of Aquin, who followed a moderate realism, had offered a better foundation and, according to content and form, a better school. St. Thomas had brought the Aristotelian philosophy into a better organic union with Catholic truth. But his writings were not properly utilized. We shall see how certain deficiencies of his Erfurt training avenged themselves upon Luther. In many respects he claimed to be a consistent Ockhamite; in some points he went beyond him, in others he abandoned him. It is important to bear in mind, however, that he imbibed no reformatory ideas from his teachers at Erfurt, but learned to combat the Nominalism of Ockham, wherever it deviated from true philosophy to the detriment of dogma.

The same attitude was maintained toward the authority of Aristotle. Although he reigned supreme in natural philosophy, the Catholic school contradicted his theses as far as they were in conflict with the Christian faith. Divine revelation as a source of knowledge was rightly regarded as inviolable against the objections of pagan philosophy.

As yet Luther had not occupied himself with the study of the Sacred Scriptures, with which he was acquainted only through the widely spread excerpts of the *postillæ* or *plenaria*. These books, which contained principally the pericopes of the Sunday gospels and epistles, as well as the very sententious so-called history-bibles, all composed in German, were in the hands of the clergy and laity.

Luther relates in his Table Talks how, while yet a student at Erfurt, he accidentally happened upon a complete Bible, and how the Old Testament story of Anna, the mother of Samuel, made him realize what inspiring narratives were contained in the historical books of the Old Testament.[50] The book with which he became acquainted on that occasion, was a volume of the university library. He was unable to read the whole Bible at the time, but he felt a lively desire to make himself more familiar with the Sacred Scriptures. But the great expense of a complete Bible in those days, when the art of printing was in its infancy, permitted him to buy only a *postilla* for his own use. He was amazed to discover many passages which did not appear in the liturgy of the Church. According to his own testimony, Luther was twenty years of age when he made his first acquaintance with the complete Bible. This late discovery, however, is not surprising. How many persons twenty years of age may there have been, even among the highly educated, who never had a complete Bible in their hands, and how many such individuals might not be found to-day? There was no reason for Protestant writers to adorn the story of this event with romantic embellishments and to assert that Luther then and there became the great discoverer of the Bible, which, in the days that preceded his birth, lay hidden under a bench and fastened to a chain. At most it was fastened to a chain in this sense that it was secured for the sake of safety and general utility. Even at the present day, all manuscripts in the Laurentian Library of Florence are secured by a chain.

Luther also informs us that once, when he and a companion journeyed to Mansfeld, he injured his leg with the sword, which he, as a bachelor, was wont to carry as a badge of his academic

[50] *Tischreden*, Weimar ed., I, Nr. 116; III, Nr. 3767; 5, Nr. 5346. I see no reason to doubt this statement.

status. The accident happened half a mile from Erfurt, and blood flowed so profusely from the wound that he was in danger of death. He lay helpless on the ground, pressing the swelling wound with his hand until his companion had summoned a surgeon from the city, who bandaged the wound. At death's door, he tells us, he implored the aid of the Mother of God. "Then would I have died, placing full confidence in the help of Mary." In his room at Erfurt, the following night, the wound broke open. Feeling faint, he once more invoked the Bl. Virgin Mary. While lying convalescent on his bed, he sought distraction by learning to play the lute, an accomplishment which he ever afterwards cherished.[51]

The playing of the lute proved a great advantage to him. It helped him to dispel a natural tendency to melancholia, and also enabled him to amuse and entertain his fellow-students. Crotus Rubeanus, who in later years became a celebrated free-thinker, was a room-mate of Luther's. In a letter to the latter, dated April 28, 1520, Crotus writes: "You were at one time the musician, you were the learned philosopher in my *contubernium*." [52] This statement reveals not only Luther's musical accomplishment, but also his zeal in the pursuit of his studies. His success in philosophy was especially esteemed by his fellow-students. Mathesius ascribed to him "a great earnestness and special diligence" in his studies. "Though naturally an alert and jovial young fellow," he says, "yet he commenced his studies every morning with prayer and a visit to the church." Mathesius writes this in his sermons on Luther in order to represent the piety of his young companion as exemplary.[53]

Luther at this time had deeply-rooted Christian convictions as well as loyalty to the clergy and the head of the Church. The anti-ecclesiastical ideas of Ockham were completely alien to him. According to his subsequent declarations, he dismissed, by means of prayer and acts of faith, the objections to the teaching of the Church which he occasionally met with in Ockham's works. He heard bitter complaints about the condition of the Church, but they did not produce any impression upon him at the time. An old man from Meiningen, with whose son, who was also a student at Erfurt, Luther was well acquainted, visited him during his illness and spoke to him

---

[51] *Tischreden*, Weimar ed., V, Nr. 6428. Cf. I, Nr. 119.
[52] *Briefwechsel*, II, p. 391.
[53] Mathesius, p. 19. The laudatory expression of Crotus also serves a partisan purpose.

about a great change which was bound to come, since the present state of affairs could not continue. When Luther complained of his indisposition, the man consoled him, saying: "Do not feel aggrieved, you will be a great man some day." Luther mentions this conversation in his Table Talks for the year 1532, and comments upon it as follows: "There I heard a prophet." "I mean," he adds, "that the change of which the old man spoke, has taken place." [54] Such fanciful prophecies as those of the man of Meiningen and of Hilten of Eisenach, captivated him, not in his student days, but in later life.

During 1503 and 1504 his mind was absorbed by his efforts to qualify himself for the attainment of the degree of master of arts. At the beginning of 1505, he took the examination, which was held around the feast of Epiphany. Among the seventeen students who were examined, Luther took second honors. The examination was followed by the solemn presentation of the insignia of the master's office, a brown biretta and a ring. Luther informs us that on such occasions the new masters were publicly honored amid great pomp. At eventide, accompanied by torch-bearers, they rode horseback through the city amid flourish of trumpets, the noisy acclamation of the populace, and the pleasures of Bacchus. They were obliged to give a supper to the faculty, for which, characteristically enough, the minimum and not the maximum number of participants was designated.

In compliance with his father's wishes, Luther, now a master of arts, entered the faculty of law. He commenced to study in preparation for the secular career which his parents had chosen for him. His father was even planning an advantageous marriage for him. Formerly he addressed his son, while yet a bachelor, with the familiar personal pronoun "du" (you); but henceforth he addressed him with the honorary title "Ihr" (you). With a great outlay he purchased a *Corpus Juris* for the young law student.

The faculty of jurisprudence of the University of Erfurt in those days had several professors of renown. Henning Göde in particular was an excellent representative of Canon Law. We do not know what lectures Luther attended during the first few months, that is, the period which preceded his sudden entrance into

---

[54] *Tischreden*, Weimar ed., I, Nr. 223; II, Nr. 1368, 2520. The visitor designated in these passages probably was one and the same person.

the monastery. He appears not to have been satisfied. It is fair to assume that he had no inclination for the study of law. His subsequent strong condemnation of lawyers and their science justify the inference of an early opposition. Then, too, his mind was so much taken up with spiritual matters that he regarded the lectures on law and the private studies which it entailed as too arid, of small profit for heart and head. He did not suffer from a lack of emotional capacity, as the near future soon revealed, but rather possessed a superabundance of emotion, which was destined to become dangerous for him.

Did he, perhaps, permit his philosophy of life to be influenced at that time by the humanistic tendencies, whose history in Germany is so intimately connected with that of the University of Erfurt? Some writers have assumed that a very strong influence was exerted upon the impressionable youth by the neo-humanistic movement which commenced at that time, and which was fostered to excess by certain circles in Erfurt. It has been alleged that the seeds of the future reformer were sown in Luther's soul by the poets and the untrammeled critics who had been alienated from the Church. This view needs rectification. To a certain extent, young Luther became surcharged with the ideas of his age, which sought to imitate the classical form of the ancients without becoming enthusiastic over their pagan philosophy. The school of the trivium, especially under Trebonius at Eisenach, formally directed his mind into that channel. His first Latin essays manifest an affected, humanistically inspired style. Usingen and Trutvetter, his Erfurt teachers of the "liberal arts," although Scholastics and Nominalistic philosophers, were neither unfamiliar with nor hostile to humanism. They cultivated the sound old German humanism which, corresponding with that of the Middle Ages, was favored by the statutes of the University. This was the kind of humanism of which they endeavored to learn the forms and which fructified their ideas. It was devoid of that corrosive and repulsive element which characterized the new humanism about to commence at Erfurt. The movement with which Luther had affiliated himself, was marked by a reverential attitude towards the Church. As yet he did not study Greek, but he read the Latin classics with such enthusiasm that it redounded to his great advantage in acquiring versatility of form in Latin as well as in his German mother-tongue. When he entered the monastery, he took with him the comedies of Plautus and the poems of Vergil and disposed of all his other books to a bookseller. It was only in proportion as his devotion to the Bible increased that his predilection for humanism declined.

The neo-humanistic school did not assume shape at Erfurt until after the doors of the monastery had closed behind Luther.[55] He was not in contact with its spirit, least of all with the anti-ecclesiastical endeavors of the canon Mutianus Rufus (Conrad) of Gotha, the chief of the rising neo-humanism, who, since 1507, gradually formed more intimate connections with the Erfurt humanists, Eobanus Hessus, Crotus Rubeanus, John Lang, Peter and Henry Eberbach, and others. From 1515 to 1520 the neo-humanists prevailed mightily at the University. In collaboration with the talented and frivolous Crotus Rubeanus, they launched, in 1515, a hostile publication against the Scholastics and the monks, which appeared under the title of *Epistolae Obscurorum Virorum.* Luther's contact with Crotus, of which the latter afterwards boasted, was restricted to their association in the burse of St. George. Both were members of that small band of young friends (*consortium*) who celebrated Luther's departure from the University and accompanied him to the gates of the monastery.

Another humanist, George Spalatin, a native of Spalt, afterwards Luther's friend and most effective helper in the religious innovations, was a student of Erfurt from 1498 to 1502, and returned thither for a brief period in 1505 as a private tutor, when through the mediation of Mutianus he obtained a position as teacher at the monastery of Georgental. We have no authority for saying that this man exerted a strong influence upon Luther during the days he spent at Erfurt while yet a layman. But a strange tradition among Catholics in Spalt, which originated there several decades later, attached itself to the name of Spalatin and other natives of Spalt who associated with Luther in Erfurt.[56] It is to the effect that Luther, while a young monk, became enamored of the daughter of a widow whose acquaintance he made in Spalatin's home. This affair, so it was alleged, was the beginning of his renunciation of the monastic life and of the Catholic faith. It is not necessary to refute this fable. The fall of the Augustinian friar is not to be attributed to a desire

[55] Proof offered by Scheel I, pp. 223 sqq.
[56] Grisar, *Luther,* III, pp. 284 sqq.

for matrimony, but to quite other causes. The story of Luther's love affair in Erfurt was probably circulated by George Ferber, a native of Spalt.[57]

In addition to the men mentioned above, Luther in his academic years was associated with Caspar Schalbe, who was happy to procure Luther's intercession with the Elector of Saxony when accused of a crime against morality before that sovereign in later years.[58]

Certain declarations of his contemporaries are not favorable to Luther's student life. We refer to Jerome Emser of Dresden, who came in contact with him at Erfurt, and to Jerome Dungersheim, a professor at the university of Leipsic. Emser, who was secretary of the Duke of Saxony, was engaged in open warfare with Luther in 1520 because of the latter's writings against the Catholic Church. At that time he wrote a letter to him containing personal reproaches which is no longer preserved. Thereupon Luther upbraided him because of his past life. Emser, indeed, was not innocent, according to his own admission. In a counter-reply he says, among other things: "What need was there for you to reproach me publicly with past mistakes, most of which are inventions, because of a letter which tells the truth about you? What do you think is known to me of great derelictions (*flagitia*) on your part?" He did not desire to mention these derelictions because it was not his purpose to repay evil for evil. "That you also fell," he continues, "I believe to be attributable to the same cause which effected my fall, namely, the cessation in our day of that public morality which permits young men to live as they please, unpunished, and to take all sorts of liberties." [59] Luther never replied to these reproaches.

The other witness is Dungersheim of Leipsic. He was a scholarly man and zealous in behalf of the Church. In a printed pamphlet directed against Luther he appeals directly to communications which, as he avers, originated with one of the companions who escorted him to the portals of the monastery and charges him with gross shortcomings in his student years. Besides these reproaches, he mentions, in another polemical writing, "bad habits" which were attributed to Luther and says it must have been due to the latter and the neglect of prayer that Luther now maintained the impossibility for a monk

[57] *Ibid.*, p. 287.
[58] *Ibid.*, I, p. 7.
[59] *Ibid.*, p. 27.

to observe his vow of chastity.[60] It must be remembered, however, that at that time a strong sentiment prevailed against Luther at Leipsic and many an unfavorable rumor was launched against him which had no foundation in fact, as, for instance, his alleged petition to the Holy See for permission to marry on the occasion of his pilgrimage to Rome, in 1510. But Dungersheim reëchoes the report of a companion of Luther. It is possible that both witnesses relied upon the communications of a comrade of Luther. As in the previous instance, so now Luther prefered to ignore the allegations made against him.

Luther afterwards denied that he suffered strong temptations against chastity while he was a monk.[61] In his bizarre manner he repeatedly asserts that the devil reproached him not with moral transgressions, but with his monastic virtues and the celebration of Mass: these were the sins of his youth. On one occasion, however, at the conclusion of his solemn profession of the Last Supper, he concedes that he "spent his youth in a damnable manner and lost it"; but he adds that the greatest sin he committed was the celebration of the Mass.[62] At another period of his later life, he once more alludes to the sins of his youth, namely, the Mass "and this or that youthful act"; that he often enjoyed internal "rest and good days" until he was shaken with fright "of despair and the fear of God's wrath." [63] Spiritually he often vacillated between extremes. All depended, as the last quotation shows, on his ability to form a strong conception of God's mercy. Then he imagined—we speak of his later years—that "it is only a temptation of Satan, the greatest temptation, in fact, when he says: God hates sinners, and you are a sinner." "It is simply false that God hates sinners." "If He hated sinners, He would not have sacrificed His Son for them." "We have the forgiveness of sins," etc. "However, many whom we do not know must thus struggle in the world." [64] These violent and sudden internal transitions are a sample of his temperament in later years.

---

[60] Ibid., pp. 26 sq. The two documents of Dungersheim of Ochsenfurt, quoted in this passage, were combined by him with others in 1531 in a volume which bears the title: Aliqua Opuscula Magistri Hieronymi Dungersheim . . . contra Lutherum edita.

[61] Grisar, Luther (original German ed.), III, p. 1003.

[62] Erlangen ed., XXX, p. 371; Grisar, I, p. 27.

[63] Tischreden, Weimar ed., I, Nr. 141: "quod sacrificavi in missa, quod hoc aut illud feci adolescens."

[64] Ibid.

It is possible that his soul was afflicted with a similar tension, albeit in a milder degree, already in his youth.

While a student at Erfurt, Luther maintained friendly and stimulating relations with his benefactors and friends at Eisenach. Trebonius, his former teacher, inquires sympathetically of Luther's friend, the student Louis Han at Erfurt, concerning the welfare and progress of "my Martin." He sends him a message encouraging him to strive after "wisdom and discipline." The letter is one of a recently published (1916) collection pertaining to the Eisenach circle, with whom Trebonius and Luther's benefactor at that place, John Braun, were associated.[65]

What is still more important, some of the letters of this collection seem to be written by Luther himself. The Latin inscription of the old collector over the Latin letters, which had been copied in many instances without the address or name of the sender, reads very definitely: "Twenty-four letters of Luther and his teachers and friends of Eisenach and Erfurt." [66] The letters were collected shortly after 1507, supposedly at Eisenach, for the purpose of furnishing models of style in epistolary correspondence for the use of schools. Luther is the author of the verbose letter of the 27th or 28th of April, 1507, in which he invites Trebonius to attend his first Mass, and jocosely subscribes himself as "Martinus Lutherus Augustiniaster," an attempted witticism meaning "an inferior Augustinian." [67] Luther is also to be regarded as the author of the letter to Braun, dated September 5, 1501, in which he speaks of the commencement of his studies at Erfurt. It is probable that a third letter, dated February 23, 1503, is likewise the product of his pen.[68] The editor of the collection refers to the spirit and mood of this letter as a proof of Luther's authorship. The unsigned document was addressed to a spiritual "benefactor and dearest friend." Others have rejected this assumption on the ground that the contents do not quite agree with what we know of Luther the student (or rather with what some pretend to know!). An eminent Protestant theologian, however, has taken exception to this criticism by remarking that the supposition that Luther must have been entirely free from the

[65] Cf. note 44, supra; Degering, p. 90, letter of February 5, 1505.
[66] Degering, p. 71.
[67] Briefwechsel, XVII, p. 84; Nr. 16 of Degering's collection.
[68] Cf. text and note in Degering, p. 85.

mistakes of his fellow-students has no "historical support." [69] The recipient of the letter had praised the writer, who declines the compliment in stilted humanistic phraseology and says that he "is surfeited with human weakness, dereliction, and negligence in every respect, interiorly and exteriorly," "that habit rules like a second nature" and "the times are evil, men are worse, their works replete with wickedness. Prevented by gluttony and drunkenness, I have hitherto [since my last letter?] neither written nor read anything good; for, being placed in the midst of men, I have lived with men. But as soon as I had torn myself away, I at once seized my pen, in order to reply to you, most cherished father." [70] In the course of the letter, which does not offer anything very remarkable, the writer requests the loan of a work by Nicholas of Lyra, which he had seen in the library of his correspondent. Reference is probably made to one of the religious tracts of Lyra, who was famous as a Biblical commentator. The style of the letter, both in its humanistic composition and in various peculiarities, corresponds entirely with the two other letters of the collection ascribed to Luther no less than with his oldest previously known letters. The letter, moreover, harmonizes with the above-mentioned accusations against the young student. It must be noted, however, that a certain exaggeration attaching to the form of his admissions is attributable to the style and character of the writer. In a letter written to Staupitz in 1519, and in another written to Melanchthon in 1521, Luther also complains of his gluttony, though the expression is not to be taken in its literal sense.[71] The vigorous words, in which the young student emphasizes the decline of morality, are quite as energetic as those contained in his first lectures, sermons and letters at the commencement of his public career.

Taking all things into consideration, it cannot be denied that young Luther was very probably the author of the letter with which we are concerned. In a publication on Luther which appeared in 1917, at the time of the Luther jubilee, a certain Lutheran churchman

[69] Hermann Jordan in *Theologie der Gegenwart*, 1917, pp. 158 sq.: "I regard Degering's assumption as not absolutely impossible; but it is as much a pure hypothesis lacking historical support as the assumption that Luther as a student must have been entirely free from the intemperance of his comrades."

[70] "*Crapulis et ebrietatibus impeditus hucusque minime quid boni scripserim aut legerim, quia constitutus cum hominibus conversabar cum hominibus.*"

[71] Grisar, *Luther*, II, p. 87.

writes: "Must we not believe that the man who was seized with fear of sin in the monastery, who was personally acquainted with sin, possessed a weak heart of profound depth and obscure corners, at the sight of which he, at times, closed his eyes with trembling, but into which he had descended with wide-open and burning eyes when his evil hour was upon him? Why, else, should he have experienced such biting qualms of conscience and such indescribable fear?" [72]

For the rest Luther already in his youth suffered from a natural inclination towards melancholia. Nature, the severe discipline of his parental home, and the first school which he attended, produced a certain depressed atmosphere in his soul. This never quite left him, although it was frequently interrupted by intermittent periods of great mental uplift and inspiration. Of his inclination to religious melancholia, not to say despair, he wrote in 1528, in a letter to one who suffered from the same malady, that he "was not unacquainted with it since his youth." [73] He regarded melancholia and despondency as the inseparable portion of man. "Melancholia is born in us, the devil fosters the *spiritus tristitiae*." [74] "From the days of my boyhood (*a pueritia mea*)," we read in the Table Talks, "Satan foresaw in me something of that which he must now suffer [in virtue of my Gospel]. Therefore he sought with incredible frenzy to injure and obstruct me, so much so that I often asked myself in amazement: 'Am I the only one of all mortals whom he pursues?'" [75]

There is another indication that a very singular temperament resided in the highly gifted soul of Luther. This must be taken into consideration in judging the catastrophe which drove him precipitately into a monastery.

"Despairing of myself" (*desperans de me ipso*), he tells us, he entered the monastery. [76]

"Internal anxiety," says a Protestant student of Luther, "or despair of himself led him into the monastery," [77] at the same time emphasizing the "godliness" in which Luther learned to exercise him-

---

[72] G. Tolzien, Landessuperintendent, *Martin Luther* (Schwerin, 1917), p. 4. Tolzien seems to be ignorant of the testimonies of Emser and Dungersheim. It is remarkable how consistently they are passed over by all, even scholarly, Protestant biographers of Luther.
[73] *Briefwechsel*, VI, p. 173.
[74] Weimar ed., VIII, p. 574.
[75] *Tischreden*, Weimar ed., II, Nr. 1279; cf. Nr. 2342ab.
[76] Text from Rörers *Handschriften*, published by E. Kroker in the *Archiv für Reformationsgeschichte*, Vol. V, (1908), p. 346.
[77] Scheel, *Martin Luther*, II, 2nd ed., p. 7.

self already as a layman. However, godliness was not the sole driving power which impelled young Luther. In view of his early religious training it is hardly possible to dispute that the most pious impulses often influenced him. Yet, despite his sentiment of despair, he was subject to other factors, namely, in addition to his natural temperament, the well-founded premonition that the life of a layman was accompanied by moral dangers with which he felt himself unable to cope. In his subsequent attacks upon the monastic vow of chastity, he applies a proverb which says: "Monks and clerics are mostly the product of despair." In the case of Luther, "despondency" connotes chiefly a depressing sense of moral incompetence and the experienced inability to preserve chastity.[78]

Another Protestant biographer speaks of the "psychical abnormality" of Luther in his youth, though, of course, his "especially tender and impressionable conscience" is again emphasized.[79] A third author exaggerates when he says that the young man's "nervous system was unsettled from early youth," and attributes this trouble to his excessively severe training.[80] These statements indicate that we are confronted with a complicated phenomonon. At all events, the existence of a somewhat disordered constitution, grounded in his very soul, must be assumed. It was united to the depressing idea of guilt, to which the ambitious youth appears often to have given free rein. Both together, the disordered condition of his nerves and the strong sense of guilt, may possibly explain the fear which, as we shall see, pursued him in a most terrifying manner in the monastery, and which reappeared ever and anon throughout his life. During his monastic years, according to his own statements, he ever sought the aid of a merciful God in his struggles amid great despair, without being able to discover Him in the Catholic faith, and most Protestant biographers hold that he was taken up with this quest even in his student days, until he finally sailed into the haven of rest upon the discovery of the new Gospel. This theory, as we shall show later, is not correct. There is no proof whatever that Luther, prior to the time when he entered the monastery, had a sense of insufficiency of the Catholic faith and consequently struggled to find a merci-

---

[78] Erlangen ed., XXI, p. 359. Cf. *ibid.*, X, p. 400, and XIII, p. 130, where he adduces the "proverb": "Despair makes the monk," applying it to the necessity of gaining a livelihood.

[79] Böhmer, p. 50.

[80] A. Hausrath, *Luthers Leben*, Vol. I, p. 4.

ful God. Let us quote here the words of another Protestant biographer, who, in this instance, judges correctly. Such a construction, he says, "is neither supported by the facts known to us, nor has it any probability." "He [Luther] does not doubt the sufficiency of ways and means. All things as yet co-exist 'naïvely' or succeed one another in the normal Catholic rotation." [81]

The same author rightly rejects the favorite assumption that the generality of mankind at that time was agitated by a knowledge or feeling of the insufficiency of the Catholic way of life and yearned for better things—which yearning was bound to captivate the frank soul of young Luther. "It is an erroneous impression to hold that the human race, prior to the rise of Luther, was moved by a passionate spiritual commotion and an impatient quest after a more profound religious philosophy of life." [82] Many authors endeavored to discover in that age such a highly significant preparation, a great prelude, as it were, to the Reformation. Leading authors have discussed "the lively consciousness of guilt which inspired the people of that age, for the relief of which many thousands made great exertions," but in vain, until Luther appeared as the liberator and prophet. Up to his advent "the mighty desire for certitude in matters of salvation exhausted itself in a gra-

[81] Scheel, I, p. 26. Scheel properly excludes from the juvenile period of Luther a struggle for a merciful God in the sense of most biographers of Luther and as a motive for his entrance into the monastery (pp. 242 sqq.). According to him, Luther's resolution to become a monk was not "the natural result of a long struggle for God's mercy" (p. 243). The hastily composed Latin and German transcript of a sermon delivered by Luther on February 1, 1534, furnished by Rörer, supplies us with the following reading: *"Ego fui XV annis monachus et tamen nunquam potui baptismo me consolari. Ach quando vis semel fromm werden? donec fierem monachus. Non edebam, non vestiebar, friere, papa, antichristus treib mich da hin, qui abstulit baptismum"* (Weimar ed., XXXVII, p. 661). In this entire passage Luther speaks of his monastic period; hence the words *"donec fierem monachus"* are to be attributed to a misconception of the copyist, as Scheel observes in his notes (Weimar ed., XXXVII, p. 519). While it is not permissible to translate these words by: "as long as I was a monk," especially on account of the *fierem*, it is probable nevertheless that Luther intended to say something similar. The German text of the whole passage (Weimar ed., XXXVII, p. 661), which appears in the form of a sermon originally reported by Cruciger, concludes with the following words: "and by such thoughts I have been driven to embrace monasticism." The text is a corruption without foundation in fact. Luther apparently had made his polemical assertion, that he arrived at his new doctrine in consequence of his struggle for a merciful God, so popular that his followers unconsciously extended his struggles and doubts to the time prior to his entrance into the monastery, though he himself does not supply us with one word to that effect.

[82] K. Holl, *Luther*, Tübingen, 1923, p. 13.

dation and excess of ecclesiastical performances without obtaining any repose." [83] This is not the place to present a characterization of the true ecclesiastical state of affairs. We are at a point in the development of Luther, when he had had no opportunity to survey the surrounding world. The student is still traveling his own road, immersed in his studies and occupied with the affairs of his soul.

While he traveled this road, did the thought of embracing the monastic state occasionally arise in his mind? Although he himself is reticent about this matter, we may well believe that this thought did engage his attention. For it is not likely that when his sudden resolve was forced from him, the idea of the monastic life entered his mind all at once. It is to be assumed psychologically that the question of the monastic state had agitated him for some time, even though he had not made a decision.[84] May not the wish to secure the salvation of his soul by becoming a monk have dawned on him while he was in a melancholy frame of mind, overwhelmed with a sense of weakness, vacillation and fear of going completely astray on account of his youthful frivolity? His assertion that he became a monk out of despair, points to such a strong impulse. His early religious education, then the active religious life at Erfurt, the example and activity of the religious Orders at the latter place, e. g., the Carthusians, whose very strict life he had observed; furthermore, his intercourse with pious preceptors, such as Usingen, who eventually became an Augustinian; finally, reminiscences of Magdeburg, such as that of the princely discalced monk and mendicant: all these things might have induced him to contemplate the monastic life.

An event, however, was destined to happen which impelled him to form a precipitous and premature resolution which was fraught with momentous consequences.

4. LUTHER'S PRECIPITATE ENTRANCE INTO THE MONASTERY

On July 2, 1505, as the young man was returning from a visit to his parents at Magdeburg, a violent storm overtook him not far from Erfurt. As he was travelling alone near Stotternheim a bolt of lightning struck in his immediate vicinity and prostrated him

[83] F. von Bezold, *Gesch. d. deutschen Reformation*, Berlin, 1890, pp. 248, 242.
[84] Thus H. Preuss in *Theol. Literaturblatt* (Leipsic, 1916), p. 94.

to the ground. In consequence of his fall, as we know from a newly discovered source,[85] his foot sustained a severe injury (*fracto prope-modum pede*). The realization of the danger of death forced this vow from his lips: "Do thou help, St. Ann; I will become a monk." [86] His power of self-control deserted him almost completely. His friend Jonas later would have it that, at the same time "a terrible manifestation from heaven" appeared to him, which the frightened Luther interpreted as a sign that he should become a monk.[87] The idea of some kind of a vision actually formed itself, and Luther himself probably conceived it. For, immediately after the event he expressed the belief that the thunder-clap was for him a call from Heaven to dedicate himself to God in the religious life. He says that "intimidations from heaven had called him to that state." He advised his father that he had received a heavenly call to the monastery. John Oldecop, a pupil of the young monk, following Luther's representation of the event, said that Luther "entered the monastery in consequence of strange fears and specters."

When his father, in opposition to Martin's monastic vocation, used the word "specter," he merely meant, in the usage of those days, a sudden excitement and imagination. Luther himself, after he had deserted the monastery, said that he "made a forced vow while surrounded by death"; that force made him a monk; that he made his vow amid "consternation"; and he adds: "I became a monk against my will and desire." [88] All the references in this passage pertain to the vow he had made in the course of a raging storm, but not to the voluntary profession made at the close of his novitiate upon twelve months' mature reflection, in virtue of which he became a monk.

After his return to Erfurt, having happily escaped the danger, he decided to keep his vow at once and entered the Augustinian monastery. His friends counseled against such a step. He himself

---

[85] *Tischreden*, Weimar ed., V, Nr. 5373.

[86] *Ibid.*, IV, Nr. 4707.

[87] Report of 1538, published by P. Tschackert in the *Theol. Studien und Kritiken* (1897), 578. The report is not reliable in several points.

[88] Weim. ed., VIII, p. 573: *"neque libens et cupiens fiebam monachus"*. Cf. the words to his father in the foreword to *De votis* on his vow during the thunder-storm: *"spontaneum et voluntarium non erat."* K. Zickendraht ("*Was hat Luther im Juli 1505 bei Stotternheim erlebt?*" in the *Zeitschr. für Kirchengeschichte*, 1922, p. 142) correctly conceived the so-called apparition as the "influence of an electric disturbance on the nervous system" and adduces analogous examples.

desisted for a time and even admits that he regretted his vow. Nevertheless, he finally insisted upon keeping it and determined to carry it out without consulting his parents.

The vow, made under pressure of overwhelming fear, cannot be regarded as valid. It lacked the most necessary preliminary condition, namely, freedom of the mind and deliberation. Any well-informed spiritual adviser could have told him that. In view of reasonable doubt, a release from the vow could have been obtained.[89] Luther, however, was obstinately determined to follow the higher voice which he supposed had called him.

Considering the character of Luther, his qualities and natural propensities, as they gradually developed after he had embraced the religious life, we must conclude that this singular man was not made for the monastery.

The monastic vocation presupposes qualifications entirely at variance with those possessed by Luther's undisciplined nature, dominated by imagination, and especially self-will. No one who is conversant with the religious state and its requirements, will attribute to him a genuine vocation to that state, which is one of renunciation, obedience, and peaceful cohabitation with spiritual brethren. Nevertheless, he announced his immediate entrance to the prior, and severed his connection with the burse. Fourteen days after the storm he celebrated his departure in the company of his invited comrades and other guests. He entertained them for the last time on his flute, mingling plaintive strains with merry tunes. He said: "To-day you still see me, but to-morrow you will see me no more." On the following morning—it was the seventeenth of July, the feast of St. Alexius—he went forth with courageous steps to the portals of the monastery, accompanied by a few sorrowing friends. The prior received him with a joyful embrace. He was glad to be able to welcome this promising young scholar into his community.

Luther was twenty-two years of age when the portals of the monastery closed upon him, and a new future began for him within its sacred precincts.

Prior to his entrance and the commencement of his novitiate, he was obliged by custom to spend a short time of probation in a segregated room. Then he was invested with the habit and commenced his probationary year. The habit of his Order consisted of a white

[89] N. Paulus in *Historisches Jahrbuch*, 1921, pp. 85 sq.

gown with a white scapular, over which a black vestment was worn. The scapular was furnished with a white cowl and a white shoulder-cape. The mantle, worn only on official occasions, was equipped with a black cowl and a black shoulder-cape. The habit which Luther wore about the house, was entirely white and had no cowl.

Internal peace was not to be the lot of the entrant. The very haste with which he entered the monastery must have made its impression upon the young monk; for the step he took signified a great and life-long sacrifice. The fright which he had experienced during the storm still agitated him. Amid flashes of lightning he beheld the tribunal of an angry God who demanded an account of him. Moreover, the emotion of fear, which had lately been awakened in him, tortured him. Melanchthon, supported by subsequent communications from him, says that terror had attacked Luther, "at first, and mostly in the course of that year," i. e., about the time he began his monastic career.[90] The same authority, referring to the frequent attacks of terror (terrores), in Luther's subsequent life, writes: "As he told us, and as many know, he was often convulsed when he meditated on the wrath of God, or reflected upon striking examples of punishment inflicted by His justice. He was subject to such profound fear that he almost gave up the ghost." [91] This testimony is very valuable in explaining the condition of Luther's soul at that time as well as afterwards.

When the lightning struck, he sustained a terrible nervous shock, which must have profoundly affected his future. This fact constrains us to reconsider his previous condition.

As we have seen, Luther was inclined to nervousness. The melancholia which always depressed him, was largely of a nervous kind. The thoughts of despondency which accompanied him, arose principally from an unhealthy psychological substratum. It appears that this constitutional evil was in part the result of hereditary oneration. The excitable temperament of his mother, who, on one occasion, chastised him until he bled on account of a nut, may have been transmitted to the son. From his father he had inherited not only tenacity of purpose, perseverance, an indefatigable zest for work, and energy in the pursuit of his aims, but also a conspicuous

[90] Grisar, *Luther*, I, p. 17.
[91] *Ibid.*

irritability concerning his own ideas and contradictions on the part of others.

It is related of his father that he struck a peasant dead in a quarrel at Möhra, in the period preceding his removal to Eisleben and thence to Mansfeld. He beat his adversary so violently with a harness—although he had not intended to kill him—that the man succumbed to the blow. The earliest mention of this homicide is made not two hundred years after the event, as has been maintained, but during the very life-time of Martin Luther; it is publicly averred in print three times by George Witzel (Wicel), a well-informed contemporary, who had formerly been a Lutheran, but afterwards, from 1533 to 1538, functioned as a Catholic priest at Eisleben. The charge of this polemical writer was never denied by Martin Luther. Nor has one word in contradiction to it been uttered by any of his contemporary friends and literary defenders. It was only at a later date that objections were voiced by Luther's friends. According to the Protestant historian, Johann Karl Seideman (1859), "the contention, which has ever and anon been revived, is decided by the testimony of Wicel." [92]

When, furthermore, his father became "thoroughly enraged," as Luther himself puts it, at his son's unexpected and hasty entrance into the monastery; when the father, somewhat reconciled, attended the first Mass of his son at Erfurt and became infuriated at his son on account of his violated paternal right; and when, finally, Martin Luther, mindful of his treatment at home, indulged in the exaggerated expression that his parents had driven him into the monastery by the bad treatment which they accorded him; [93] then, indeed, the character of John Luther appears sufficiently sanguine to favor the assumption that the son inherited this characteristic from his father. The most recent Protestant biographer of Luther describes the father as possessing a sanguinary temperament.

Under these conditions the terrible shock which Martin sustained when the thunderbolt felled him to the ground, was bound to produce incurable results in one whose very constitution was neurotic.

Medical authorities tell us that, as a rule, neither time nor medical skill can completely master the effects of such a nervous shock in

[92] *Ibid.*, p. 16. F. Falk, *Alte Zeugnisse über Luthers Vater und die Möhraer*, in *Hist.-pol. Blätter*, Vol. CXX (1897), pp. 415-425.

[93] Erlangen, ed., LXI, p. 274 (=*Tischreden*, Weimar); Mathesius, *Aufzeichnungen*, p. 235.

the case of neurotics. Recent experiences of those who sustained shell-shock in the World War confirm this conclusion. The former malady of nervous fear usually attained a degree that was beyond control. And even where there was no predisposition, incurable results often supervened. We are constrained, therefore, to regard Luther, after the thunderbolt had driven him into the monastery, as a monk who was afflicted with an extreme case of "nerves" and deserved commiseration; as one who, even in his subsequent career, often was sorely tried by suffering. We are able to comprehend his complaints about the states of fear with which he was seized both during his monastic life and after he had abandoned it, and which he compares with the genuine death agony.

The Augustinians of Erfurt did not perceive this state of affairs. They were too happy at the reception of a new member whose talents for preaching and teaching were so promising. They attached great importance to the reports of the candidate concerning his call from Heaven. A scholarly member of the Order, John Nathin, professor of theology in the *studium generale* of the Augustinians at Erfurt, said at that time to the nuns at Mühlhausen that Luther had entered the monastery like another Paul, miraculously converted by Christ.[94] In later years he spoke of the antagonist of the Church in a different language, saying, *e. g.*, that "the spirit of apostasy had descended upon Luther," *i. e.*, he had evolved his doctrine under the influence of the devil.[95] There were other brethren of the Order who could not understand his peculiarities. They afterwards said superstitiously to John Cochläus, his celebrated opponent, that young Luther must have had intercourse with the devil. Others, again, regarded him as an epileptic.[96] His epileptic or seemingly epileptic attacks in the choir will receive more detailed attention in the sequel.

It did not take long before strange stories began to be told of Luther's tragic resolve to enter the monastery. Thus Mathesius reports that the sudden death of a dear companion who had been stabbed, had frightened Luther quite as much as the thunderbolt, so that he entered the monastery startled at the wrath of God and the Last Judgment. In his brief reference to this matter, Melanchthon says

[94] Grisar, *Luther,* I, p. 4, quoted from Dungersheim.
[95] *Ibid.,* p. 17.
[96] *Ibid.,* IV, 353.

that Luther at that time lost a dear friend, who perished in an accident. According to Oldecop, that friend was "suffocated" by lightning at his side. Ludwig von Seckendorff asserts in his History of Lutheranism (1692), on the authority of Bavarus' manuscripts (1548 sqq.), that the name of Luther's friend who died a sudden death was Alexius or Alexis. It is probable, however, that the name was formed from that of St. Alexius, on whose feastday Luther entered the monastery. Of the other circumstances mentioned, only one appears to be based on certain evidence, namely, that a friend of Luther died rather suddenly in 1505. The public records of Erfurt are silent concerning any murder, although they note that one of the students who was to be promoted to the master's degree with Luther became seized of a severe sickness during the days of the examinations and soon after passed away. Probably this event had a terrifying effect upon Luther. Yet it is striking that Luther himself never makes mention of this comrade whom death carried off so suddenly.[97] He is conscious only of his own danger during the storm and of his sudden vow. Somewhat later an epidemic in Thuringia and Erfurt claimed for its victims two students of Luther's acquaintance. This fact did not, however, influence his resolve. The pestilence spread even after he had taken up his abode with the Augustinians. The tradition of Luther's resolution to become a monk has been correctly preserved by Crotus Rubeanus, who had befriended Luther in his youth. He writes on October 16, 1519, basing his statement on Luther's own words: "While you returned from your parents, a heavenly stroke of lightning dashed you to the ground before the city of Erfurt like another Paul, and drove you into the monastery of the Augustinians."[98]

[97] Scheel, I, p. 246.
[98] Briefwechsel, II, p. 208.

Chapter II

LUTHER'S FIRST YEARS IN THE MONASTERY

I. NOVITIATE, PROFESSION, FIRST MASS

The completion of a year's novitiate was the first obligation incumbent on the new monk. During this probationary period he was not permitted to study. Prayer, pious reading, labor and penances, service in the choir, and mastering the rules and life of the Order occupied his time. For this purpose the novices were assigned to the direction of an elder monk. Luther was placed under an experienced novice-master whom he praised in later years as a wise and sympathetic religious. The master of novices explained to him the statutes of the Order, which John Staupitz, at that time superior of the entire congregation, had composed in 1504 on the basis of the old constitutions, adapted with wise discretion to the needs of the age. They were detailed and precise, but tolerated many dispensations in the monastic observance. The master of novices also saw to it that the young novice entrusted to his care diligently read the Bible.

The statutes enjoined upon all the duty of "reading the Bible with fervor, to hear it read with devotion, and to learn it with assiduity." To hold that the Sacred Scriptures were not in the hands of the faithful, even of the pious, in the days when Luther was a youth, is a wide-spread error. In the case of Luther himself, who afterwards rendered this statement current, there was not a day "on which the Word of the Scriptures was not perceived abundantly by ear and intellect. It came to be a permanent companion, a monitor and comforter, a judge and a benefactor." [1] From that day a pronounced inclination towards the Bible began to take hold of him.

Besides the Bible, the young novice joyfully saturated his mind with the writings of St. Bernard and St. Bonaventure, those profound and sympathetic teachers of the Middle Ages. His spiritual director understood how to comfort and guide the novice, who at

---

[1] Scheel, M. *Luther*, II, 2 ed., p. 2.

times showed a lack of courage. Long afterwards Luther remembered how the good man spoke to him of the remission of sins and occasionally called his attention to the fact that the article of faith on the *remissio peccatorum* must be set up against all scruples.

Brother Martin willingly adapted himself to the discipline of the well-regulated monastery. He learned to love his new abode, was determined to become a good monk, and resolved to devote his energies to the salvation of souls.

At the commencement of his novitiate, he received sad reports from Mansfeld, where his family resided. The pestilence invaded the little town and carried off two of his brothers. His heart, on the other hand, was gladdened at the news of his father's belated consent to his entrance upon a monastic career. It was difficult for the father to relinquish the hopes he had placed in a secular career for his highly promising son. Perhaps the affliction with which his home had been visited moderated his attitude.

When the probationary year had terminated and the hour for the taking of the solemn vows had arrived, Brother Martin, advancing to the altar of the Augustinian church at Erfurt, unperturbed by misgivings and with joy in his heart, made profession of the vows that bind forever. The vows were couched in the usual form: "I, Brother Martin, make profession and vow obedience before Almighty God and the ever Blessed Virgin Mary, and before you, Brother Winand, local prior, in the name and place of the prior general of the Order of Hermits of the holy Bishop Augustine, and his lawful successors, to live without property and in chastity according to the rule of the same Blessed Augustine to the end of my life." No act of his life, no promise ever made by him, took place after such mature deliberation and with such a complete knowledge of the circumstances and obligations, as this oblation of himself to the divine Majesty in the bosom of the universal Church by means of the triple vow of poverty, chastity, and obedience. The act was witnessed by the community of those who were to be henceforth more closely united to him.

Luther was now a full-fledged member of the German Congregation of the Hermits of St. Augustine, who, as a Congregation of Observantines, were subordinated to John Staupitz, the vicar or representative of the general of the Order who resided in Rome. Besides the monasteries of the congregation of the Observantines, there existed in Germany numerous other Augustinian monasteries which had not introduced the Observance. They constituted the so-called Provincia Saxoniae, and extended over central and upper Germany. According to the general administration of the Order, they were under the jurisdiction of a provincial. Both, Observantines and non-Observantines, were classified under the common canonical character of mendicant friars, with this sole exception that the Observantines had their own peculiar exercises which were conducted in the spirit of the enthusiastic founder and father of their Order, Andrew Proles, the predecessor of Staupitz (died in 1503 at Kulmbach).

Luther was not exempt from the task of begging alms. Despite the fact that he possessed the master's degree, he was obliged to assume this task like other humiliating exercises of the Order. Some years afterwards, however, in view of his academic degree and of the studies he was destined to pursue, he was absolved from the obligation of the *"saccum per naccum,"* as begging with a sack about the neck was humorously termed in the monastery.

As the day of his ordination to the priesthood was approaching, Luther read the thoughtful and edifying treatise on the holy sacrifice of the Mass by Gabriel Biel—but as he assures us after his defection from the ancient Church, he did so with a bleeding heart. His disposition inclined him to view with terror the thought of the sublimity of the sacred function no less than the idea of intimate union with God through the sacrifice of the body and blood of Christ. In the second semester of 1506, the preliminary orders of the subdiaconate and diaconate were conferred upon him. These events were followed by his ordination to the priesthood, probably on April 3, 1507. He received holy orders in the magnificent dome of Erfurt, at the hands of the suffragan bishop, John Bonemilch von Lasphe. His soul now highly stimulated, he prepared himself for the celebration of his first holy Mass. The extant letters in which he extended an invitation to his various acquaintances to be present on the greatest day of his life—for it was celebrated with great solemnity—reveal his profound earnestness and lively realization of his own unworthiness. The style of these letters is invested with a certain pathos, be it in consequence of the humanism he formerly cultivated, or as a result of his natural disposition.

While he said his first Mass at the altar of the Augustinian church, the thought of the proximity and magnitude of almighty God caused him to be seized with such fright that he would fain have interrupted the holy Sacrifice and hastened away from the altar, had not the assistant priest held him back. The reports which have come to us from his own lips, as well as those contained in the copy of his lectures on Genesis, are too definite as to permit the possibility of a doubt concerning the abnormal event.[2] Afterwards he said that he always said Mass with a shudder, aye, "with great horror." [3]

His father, accompanied by no less than twenty riders, arrived for the celebration on horseback, defraying his own expenses. At the festive banquet, Martin desired to persuade his father to give a new and open approval to his entrance into the monastery, since his previous consent had not been whole-hearted. Therefore, Martin praised the "pleasant and quiet" life of the monastery and the "divine nature" of his chosen state of life. But when he mentioned the heavenly call on the occasion of the storm at Stotternheim, his father became angry and exclaimed: "Would to God that it was not a hallucination of the devil!" He was a choleric man and his patience was exhausted. The select company which surrounded him did not restrain him from giving vent to his displeasure. He even remarked, though without justification, whether the son had forgotten that children owe complete obedience to their parents as regards entrance into the cloister, that the fourth commandment was above the notion which induced him to select the monastic state, etc. It must have been an unpleasant scene when the monks, who were seated next to them, tried to defend the monastic life and their promising confrère. Thereat the father expressed himself in these acrid words: "I would prefer to be somewhere else rather than to be here, eating and drinking." To such an extent his irascible temperament led him to forget the requirements of the festive occasion. In course of time, however, the old man became reconciled. When Luther, fourteen years later, was in open conflict with his monastic order as a result of the publication of his treatise against the monastic vow, he justified the conduct of his father in the preface of the dedicatory letter which he addressed to him by citing the latter's statement relative

---

[2] See the citations from the sources in Scheel II, pp. 345 sq. I am unable to regard as sound the objections variously raised against Luther's account in the Table Talks and the statements contained in his commentary on Genesis. Cf. Grisar, *Luther*, I, p. 15; VI, pp. 99 sqq., 195 sqq.

[3] Cf. Grisar, *op cit.*, VI, 197.

to the obedience due to parents.[4] It seems never to have disturbed him previously. But in the aforementioned treatise (1521) he assured his readers that the words which his father uttered on the occasion of his first Mass made a deep impression on him, "as if God Himself had spoken them."

2. STUDIES AND FIRST EXPERIENCE AS TEACHER

After his first Mass, Martin began the study of theology. John Nathin, a celebrated teacher of his Order, was prefect of theological studies in the Erfurt monastery. But Martin was not introduced into positive and speculative theology in an orderly fashion. After about a year and a half spent in the study of Gabriel Biel's treatise on the "Sentences" and other Nominalistic writers, his superiors in the autumn of 1508 transferred him to the Augustinian monastery of Wittenberg, where he was ordered to lecture at once on the Nicomachean Ethics while he continued his theological studies.

At Wittenberg Luther came into closer personal contact with Staupitz, the vicar of his Order, with whom he probably had had converse already at Erfurt. At his instigation, he was promoted to the baccalaureate in Sacred Scripture at the university, on March 9, 1509. Luther had made the reading of the Bible his specialty; it appealed to him more than Scholasticism and methodical scientific works. For this reason, and because of his talents, Staupitz kept an eye on him, in order eventually to make him his successor in the academic chair of Biblical science, which had been entrusted to the Augustinians, but to which he could not do full justice on account of his official journeys. The Biblical baccalaureate was a preliminary step for Luther. It obliged him to explain certain parts of Sacred Scripture to his academic audiences. Later he was appointed to the office of *"sententiarius,"* which entitled him to deliver university lectures on the celebrated Book of Sentences of Peter Lombard. He advanced to this dignity in the autumn of 1509. It terminated his first sojourn at Wittenberg. The Order sent him back to Erfurt, where a *sententiarius* was needed. Due to these labors, his own further training must have been considerably neglected.

Luther's interior life during the days spent at Erfurt and Witten-

---

[4] *Werke,* Weimar ed., VIII, pp. 573 sq.

berg was constantly furrowed by deep anxiety. The terrors from which he suffered at the beginning of his monastic life, would not desert him. He continued to worry about the sternness of the divine Judge, the remission of his sins, and the problem of predestination by an alleged and inscrutable divine decree. In part these terrors were caused by his psychological condition, which, when later symptoms are taken into consideration, seems to have been a kind of precordial fear; in part, they were the product of melancholy thoughts which he harbored and which re-acted upon his physical condition. On one occasion, while attending divine service in the choir of the monks, he fell prostrate to the floor and was racked by convulsions, as the Gospel of the demoniac was being sung, and screamed aloud: "It is not I! It is not I!" (meaning that he was not the man possessed).[5] No mention of epilepsy is made in his subsequent history. The many later references made by him to his mental sufferings during this period, lack precision. They may pertain to his sojourn at Wittenberg or to his first residence at Erfurt, or to both.

He says that his life in the cloister was always sad. When he discussed his sins with Staupitz and raised all kinds of imaginary objections, the latter told him to dismiss the specter of his "puppet sins." His thoughts, which were replete with fantasies, appeared unintelligible to others; few knew how to console him as well as Master Bartholomew (Usingen), whom he styled the "best paraclete and comforter" in the Erfurt monastery.[6] Once Staupitz told him: "Master Martin, I do not understand that." On another occasion Luther was deeply impressed as Staupitz admonished him when he was affrighted at the idea of predestination: "Why torment yourself with such thoughts and broodings? Look at the wounds of Christ and His blood shed for you! There you will see your predestination to Heaven shining forth to your comfort." [7] Yet, in many passages of his later writings and addresses Luther says of his monastic life: "My heart trembles and flutters, when I meditate on how God may be merciful to me. Often have I been frightened at the name of Jesus, and, when I looked upon Him as He hung upon the cross, He was as lightning to me." He was often compelled to say: "I wish there were no God." Never, so he says with exaggeration,

[5] Grisar, *Luther*, I, p. 17.
[6] *Ibid.*, I, p. 10.
[7] *Ibid.*, p. 11.

had he been able to recite a prayer properly. He had lived in great tortures and at times so sensed the terrors of God's judgment "that his hair stood on end." He became startled when death or the future life was discussed in the monastery.[8] According to his representations, it was principally his good friend Staupitz who prevented him from being "drowned," as he puts it, in the fear of predestination. But, are not many polemical admixtures recognizable in these portrayals of his depressed and melancholy state of mind in the monastery, from which he alleged he was forced to flee?

When Luther left Wittenberg, he had neglected to deliver the necessary introductory lecture as *sententiarius*. As a consequence the scrupulous theologians of Erfurt did not want to let him lecture on the Books of Sentences there; they may also have been unfavorably disposed toward him for other reasons. However, in the end he was permitted to lecture.

The notes on Peter Lombard which he penned in those days reveal an active mind, but at the same time an adverse and extremely surprising self-conscious mannerism of formulating judgments. He sneers at the drolleries of contemporary theologians, at "the rotten rules of the logicians," at the masks worn by the "philosophers," at "the rancid philosopher Aristotle." For the latter he showed a decided aversion. At the very beginning of his career he styles him a comedian whom he would unmask. The Middle Ages had appreciated Aristotle quite differently. But Luther showed a contentious and an audacious spirit already at Wittenberg. Mathesius, his eulogist, says of him: "Our Frater Martinus there applied himself to the study of Sacred Scripture, and commenced to dispute in the university against the sophistry which was everywhere in vogue at that time. And since all schools, monasteries, and pulpits appealed to the 'master of sublime thought' (Peter Lombard), besides Thomas of Aquin, Scotus, and Albertus, in support of the foundation of Christianity, our Frater Martinus began to dispute against their principles, at which good people were highly amazed even at that time."

The Erfurt professors were probably conspicuous among the "good people" who opposed Luther. It is not incredible that, as he relates afterwards, the Bible, which served the fiery combatant as a means for his boastfulness, may have been withheld from him for a while. In order to understand his beloved Bible properly, Luther began to

[8] *Ibid.*, III, p. 109.

study Greek under the direction of John Lang, a fellow-member of his Order, who had a humanistic training and shared his opinions, Luther's studious spirit also impelled him to take up certain writings of St. Augustine, the founder of his Order and a doctor of the Church. We have marginal notes made by him in 1509 on certain treatises of Augustine. But owing to his lack of leisure and his pre-conceived notions he was not able to fathom their depth. Augustine's teachings on grace, free will, and justification, on natural good works and acts meritorious for Heaven, really remained a sealed book for him all his life. In vain he appealed to particular passages to support his own peculiar opinions.

The town of Erfurt was hardly aware of Luther's residence at the highly esteemed Augustinian monastery. Luther himself is silent for a long time concerning the storms and struggles which the town experienced. It is only afterwards that he mentions Erfurt, and then with a feeling of resentment. In January, 1510, the ancient city council of Erfurt was violently deposed by a popular democratic party. The Saxon Elector opposed both the insurgent workers and the rights of the Archbishop of Mayence, who ruled the town. The spacious "old college" in which the university lectures were delivered, was destroyed on August 4, in a riot between the students and the municipal lansquenets. It was the "frantic year," as it is called in the annals of the city. During this uprising Luther lectured in perfect peace in the quiet halls of the Augustinian monastery.

In this same year, 1510, a grave controversy broke out in the Observantine Augustinian congregation. It was occasioned by the vicar, John Staupitz, who jeopardized the canonical and disciplinary autonomy of the Observantine monasteries entrusted to his care. He intended to affiliate them with the monasteries of the German Augustinian province, who were non-Observantines. The consolidation of the province, which had hitherto been directed by separate provincials, with the monasteries of his own jurisdiction would have greatly extended his authority. He counted upon the support of the General of the Order and increased vigor in the life of the German monasteries, although no noticeable decline had been manifested by them.

The monks of Erfurt and of six other monasteries of the Observantine congregation judged otherwise. They considered their observance jeopardized by the influence of the communities which had affiliated with them and insisted upon the privileges of their congregation, which was protected in virtue of papal legislation against the arbitrary interference of the General. In the Franciscan Order, Brother Louis of Anhalt, whom Luther met at Magdeburg, had effectually defended the Observantine monasteries of St. Francis in Germany, whose constitutions enjoyed papal sanction, in the interests of the stricter life, against Aegidius Delfini, the General of his Order.[9] In this posture of affairs, Luther assumed the rôle of eloquent spokesman against Staupitz and, in behalf of the insurgent monasteries, was sent to Halle in company with the theologian John Nathin, where Adolph von Anhalt, the provost of Magdeburg cathedral, sojourned. Both appealed for assistance to the provost. In order to assure themselves of success, the monasteries decided to send Luther to the headquarters of the order at Rome and to the papal curia. This was the occasion of Luther's journey to Rome, an event destined to become highly significant in his life.

3. THE JOURNEY TO ROME

After having spent a considerable part of his life in the narrow confines of the monastery and in academic halls, the journey to Rome was bound to bring the active mind of young Luther in contact for the first time with the great ecclesiastical world. He was to receive an abundance of new ideas. He was destined also to become aware of the religious and moral abuses which had been accumulating on all sides, but particularly in the Rome of the Renaissance. In the late autumn of 1510 he commenced his journey on foot, in accordance with a custom of his Order, accompanied by a fellow member. They travelled through Bavaria and over the mountains to Tyrol, thence, from Innsbruck over the Brenner Pass to Lombardy and beyond. Following the usual road of the pilgrims, they crossed Central Italy and proceeded via Viterbo and Lake Bolsena to the Eternal City. Whenever practicable, he called upon the numerous monasteries along the road and enjoyed their hospitality. The hardships of the winter season, just previous to the close of the year, were probably not small. With reinvigorated energy he ascended the heights of Mario, whence he obtained his first sight of Rome. Near a chapel he knelt down and recited the customary prayers of pilgrims, in

[9] Cf. Lemmens, *Franziskanerbriefe*, pp. 20 sqq.

greeting the sacred walls and plains, the home of innumerable saints and martyrs. In Rome he took up his abode with his fellow-monks.

To his great disappointment, his mission in behalf of the Observantine faction proved futile. He was advised that he would have to obtain a letter from the legitimate superior of his order in Germany (*i.e.*, Staupitz) in order to gain admission to the papal curia. He had no such a letter, and the General of the Augustinians as well as his procurator, who were not in favor of his mission, refused to intervene in his behalf. The efforts of the seven monasteries were unwelcome to them. Again, he must have poignantly felt another failure, namely, the refusal of the papal authorities to grant a petition which his passionate fondness for study had inspired. In some cases, religious had been given permission to devote certain years to study at the universities, outside of their monasteries and without appearing in the habit of their order. Luther's request to have this extraordinary privilege extended to the German Augustinians was declined because he had no recommendation of his superiors. The report of his pupil Oldecop on this subject is trustworthy, since during his stay at Rome, some time after this incident, Oldecop made inquiries concerning this matter. Luther compensated himself by studying Hebrew with a German Jew at Rome. He also made it his business to visit all the sacred places in Rome, and to become acquainted with the religious monuments of the city. He hunted up, he says, all the churches and crypts. The traditions of the various places edified him; he did not balk even at the false ones. Only at the so-called Stairs of Pilate, in the vicinity of the Lateran palace, which he climbed on his knees in accordance with custom, the question arose in his mind whether the tremendous indulgences connected with these steps were indeed genuine.[10] This doubt, however, was not the germ of his subsequent doctrine of justification without good works, as has been asserted, but was occasioned by the uncritical *Mirabilia Vrbis Romae*—a guide-book for pilgrims which was in circulation at that time. No trace of so-called reformatory ideas can be detected in Luther either at the time of his pilgrimage to Rome or for some considerable time thereafter.

He was, however, deeply depressed by what he saw of the decline of morality in Rome, including the higher and the lower clergy. Especially what he heard concerning the person and court of the

[10] Grisar, *Luther*, VI, 496.

recently deceased Borgia Pope, Alexander VI, his relatives, certain cardinals, the pomp and worldliness of Julius II (Giuliano della Rovere), the then reigning warrior-like successor of Alexander VI, sank deep into the soul of the receptive northerner. These recollections were violently revived during his subsequent contest with Rome and furnished him with weapons against the Roman Antichrist, whose true character he fancied to have discovered in another manner. He appears, while at Rome, to have come in contact with German and Italian residents who collected reproaches against the morals of the curia in an odious and at times frivolously exaggerated form and apparently took less note of the prevailing good traits in the life of the city and the supreme government of the Church. The same holds good in regard to his entire journey through Italy. An honorable exception were the great hospitals he visited, with their ample equipment and the charity which they dispensed. The exemplary care of the sick and of poor pilgrims exhibited at Florence elicited favorable comments from him later on.

It appears that the splendid edifices and the grand works of this period, inspired by the joyousness of creative art, at Rome as well as along the whole way of his journey, failed to attract his attention. Even in his advanced years he relished no taste for the creations of art. As a pilgrim to Rome, he lacked the proper enlightenment to appreciate these matters.

When Luther, after his apostasy, described himself as having been the most pious monk at Rome, who said Mass so solemnly and slowly that several other priests finished saying Mass at the same time, and when he maintains that, inspired by the great Roman indulgences applicable to the souls of the departed, he in his pious zeal wished that his parents had already departed this life, so that he might gain these indulgences in their behalf—we have a series of grotesque exaggerations, suggested partly by his native humor, partly by exaggerated criticism of Roman conditions. We know that he did not say Mass regularly while in Rome. According to a later declaration of his, he desired to make a general confession extending over his whole life, but found the clergy in Rome insufficiently instructed for this purpose. Whatever he says about conditions or his own monastic virtues must be received with a large grain of salt.

At all events, it is certain that his visit in the center of Catholic Christianity did not shake his devotion to the Church, nor his submission to the papal authority, nor his loyalty to the monastic state, though the subsequent crisis was accelerated thereby.

His stay in the city on the Tiber lasted about four weeks. Luther did not get to see Pope Julius, who, on account of threatening war, had betaken himself to Upper Italy. Luther did not return to Germany by way of Lombardy and across the Tyrolean Alps, but, due to the danger of war, made a detour over Nizza and the Avignon country, up the valley of the Rhone towards Switzerland and thence to Bavaria. Some traces of this journey have been preserved.[11] Nor did the pilgrim return to Erfurt, but, in compliance with the orders of his superiors, went to Wittenberg to teach, a choice which probably conformed with his own desire.

4. IN WITTENBERG

The Augustinians of Wittenberg did not participate in the attack upon Staupitz in connection with the Observantine controversy. The party of the vicar was in control there. What attitude did Luther assume towards him? When he re-entered Germany, his views about this internal question of discipline were different from those which impelled him to visit Italy. He became an opponent of the so-called Observantines and espoused the party of Staupitz. What caused this striking change has never been fully cleared up. Perhaps the opposition which he encountered at Rome influenced him. Possibly his transfer from Erfurt to Wittenberg had something to do with his altered attitude. It is also possible that Staupitz himself influenced him decisively. Cochlaeus, his subsequent opponent, who at that time was in touch with the brethren of the Order and had learned from them some things about Luther, drastically expresses the change in his conduct thus: "He has apostatized to his friend Staupitz." For the rest, his change of attitude need not cause too much surprise in view of the sanguine temperament of the young monk. It is also permitted to inquire whether the consolidation contemplated by Staupitz, did not possess some merit. A uniform government of all the Augustinian monasteries in Germany under an energetic general and active provincials, according to the general rule of the order, was in itself a rather desirable thing.

[11] H. Grisar, *Lutheranalekten*, I ("Zu Luthers Romfahrt; Neues über den Reiseweg") in the *Histor. Jahrbuch der Görresgesellschaft*, Vol. XXXIX (1919–1920), pp. 487 sqq.

The internal conflict was settled in May of the following year at a chapter of the Augustinian congregations held in Cologne. The settlement was effected as a result of the conciliatory policy of Staupitz, who had previously brought about a certain union of the seven convents at Jena, in July, 1511. The proposed consolidation of these congregations with the Saxon province, *i. e.*, with the non-reformed German Augustinians, was to be abandoned—a proposition with which the general now agreed. The Cologne chapter was held without the participation of the "Province of Saxony." This fact alone would indicate a certain retreat on the part of Staupitz, even if it was but a temporary one. In the meantime the opposition within the congregation, once having manifested itself, continued to smoulder. There were friends of the Observance, and, as it appears, some enthusiasts, who exhibited a strict compliance with the statutes. On the other hand there were enemies of the Observance, who complained of unkindnesses and calumnies on the part of their opponents. In the congested atmosphere of the monasteries the conflict grew more and more acute.

At Wittenberg, Luther soon became the passionate spokesman of the opponents of the Observantines, who were by far the more numerous party. He had participated in the chapter at Cologne (1512), as his works testify. On the return journey from Cologne, he visited the valley of Ehrenbreitstein near Koblenz, where a monastery of his Order was situated at Mühltal.[12] Paltz, a celebrated Augustinian and a native of Erfurt, had retired to this monastery some time previously, having become dissatisfied with his position as theological teacher at the "studium generale" of his Order at Erfurt. It is possible that Luther, while at Cologne, had been proposed for the doctorate in theology at Wittenberg. According to his later story he raised strenuous objections to the doctorate when Staupitz subsequently discussed this matter with him in more definite terms at Wittenberg. His objections were based principally on the state of his health. In spite of this, however, the superiors would not alter their decision.

In Wittenberg various tasks diverted him from the preparation for the doctorate. Thus he was obliged to preach in the smaller monastery church. He was also made subprior in the monastery. On

[12] H. Grisar, *"Luther zu Köln und Koblenz,"* in the jubille number of the *Koblenzer Volkszeitung,* February, 1922.

October 4th, he obtained the academic title of licentiate in theology. A few days later, on October 9th, we find him at Leipsic, where he writes out a receipt for fifty guldens, which the Saxon Elector, Frederick, had assigned to him out of the local exchequer to pay the expenses of his pending promotion.[13] Staupitz declared to the Elector that the office of Biblical lecturer, which he himself had occupied at Wittenberg, was henceforth to be entrusted permanently to Luther.[14] According to the terms of their endowment these lectures were assigned to the Augustinian monastery. After passing the required examination, Luther was promoted to the doctorate, on October 19, 1512, in the castle-church at Wittenberg. The ceremony was held under the direction of the university professor Andrew Bodenstein of Karlstadt, with whom Luther in after years lived in strained relations on account of the controversies which arose over the new doctrines.

[13] *Briefwechsel*, I, p. 9.
[14] Scheel, II, pp. 311 and 431.

CHAPTER III

STRIKING OUT ALONG NEW ROADS—THE INTERIOR
PROCESS

1. LUTHER'S FIRST BIBLICAL LECTURES—HIS MYSTICISM

The first lectures of the new professor of Biblical science were delivered in the years 1513 to 1515 and dealt with the Psalms. Those of his pupils who were monks and had to recite the Divine Office in choir, were particularly interested in the Psalms. The interpretation offered them by Luther has been preserved in his works. It is, however, not an explanation made in accordance with our modern ideas, but rather a collection of allegorical and moral sentences based upon the text, as was the custom in those days. Luther justly abandoned this allegorical manner of interpretation in later life. Non-Catholics have endeavored, without justification, to discover in these lectures the germs of his later teaching. His manner of expression is often indefinite and elastic and generally more rhetorical than theologically correct. His teaching on justification, grace, and free will, is, like his other doctrines, still fundamentally Catholic, or at least can be so interpreted if the dogmatic teaching of the Church is properly understood. Still there are a few indications of the coming change. Take, for instance, his emphatic assertion that Christ died for all men and his exaggerated opposition to the doctrine of justification by means of good works.[1] In general these lectures reveal talent, religious zeal, and fertile imagination—qualities which must have charmed his auditors to an unusual degree.

Luther was very amiable and communicative towards his pupils. His entire personality, the very gleam of his eye, exerted a certain fascination over those who associated with him.

The young professor of Sacred Scripture displayed a pronounced inclination towards mysticism. Mysticism had always been cultivated

---

[1] Cf. H. Boehmer in *Allg. Evang.-Luth. Kirchenzeitung*, 1924.

to a certain extent in the religious orders of the Catholic Church. The reading of Bonaventure had pointed Luther, even as a young monk, to the pious union with God at which Mysticism aims. Toward the close of his lectures on the Psalms, he became acquainted with certain works on Mysticism which he imbibed with great avidity. They were the sermons of Tauler and the tract *"Theologia deutsch."* They dominate his thoughts in 1515. Although these works were not designed to do so, they helped to develop his unecclesiastical ideas. His lively experience of the weakness of the human will induced him to hearken readily to the mystical voices which spoke of the complete relinquishment of man to God, even though he did not understand them perfectly. His opposition to good works opened his mind to a fallacious conception of the doctrines of those books of the mystical life. It appeared to him that, by following such leaders, his internal fears could be dispelled by a calm immersion in the Godhead.

John Tauler, an ornament of the Dominican Order (died in 1361), was a famous preacher in the pulpits of Strasburg. His writings and sermons are filled with profound thoughts and have a strong popular appeal. They abound in attractive imagery and are replete with devotion. Tauler stands four-square on the basis of Catholic teaching and the best scholastic theology. Two points in his mystical admonitions found a special echo in Luther's soul, namely, the interior calmness with which God's operations are to be received, and the darkness which fills the souls of pious persons, of whom he speaks consolingly. Luther, however, introduced his own erroneous ideas into the teaching of Tauler. His demand that the soul be calmly absorbed in God, Luther interpreted as complete passivity, yea, self-annihilation. And what Tauler says concerning trials arising from the withdrawal of all religious joy, of all emotions of grace in the dark night of the soul, he referred directly to his own morbid attacks of fear, to which he endeavored to oppose a misconceived quietism, a certain repose generated by despair. In brief, he tried to transform all theology into what he called a theology of the Cross. Misconstruing Tauler's doctrine of perfection he would recognize only the highest motives, namely, reasons of the greatest perfection for himself as well as for others. Fear of divine punishment and hope of divine reward were to be excluded.

These were extravagances which could not aid him, but, on the contrary, involved great danger to his orthodoxy; in fact, constituted a serious aberration. But he trusted his new lights with the utmost self-confidence. Writing of Tauler to his friend Lang at Erfurt, who was also fascinated by the works of that mystic, Luther compares him with contemporary and older theologians and says that while Tauler was unknown to the Schoolmen, he offered more real theology than the combined theological professors of all the universities.[2]

The other mystical writer who interested him, was discovered by Luther in a manuscript. He lived in the fourteenth century and was the author of the *"Theologia deutsch."* His name is unknown to us. He was a priest at Frankfort on the Main. His work, which is a didactic treatise on perfection, is Catholic, although not exempt from obscurities. Luther esteemed it as a book of gold, particularly in view of its praise of the sole domination of God in the soul that suffers for Him. He edited this book, at first incompletely, in 1516, then in its entirety, in 1518. It is remarkable that a book on Mysticism was his first publication. Soon he occupied himself with the mystical writings of the so-called Dionysius the Areopagite, the father of Mysticism, and with those of Gerard Groote, a more modern author.

His style in those days, as also later on, reveals how profoundly he was animated by the devout tone of these mystics. Thus, in writing to George Leiffer, a fellow-monk at Erfurt, who was afflicted by persecutions and interior sufferings, he says (1516): "Do not cast away thy little fragment of the Cross of Christ, but deposit it as a sacrosanct relic in a golden shrine, namely, in a heart filled with gentle charity. For even the hateful things which we experience, are priceless relics. True, they are not, like the wood of the Cross, hallowed by contact with the body of the Lord, yet, in as far as we embrace them out of love for His most loving heart and His divine will, they are kissed and blessed beyond measure." [3] In discussing the idea of self-annihilation under the guidance of God, which was his favorite thought in these days, he shows that he has gone astray. He says that man should not choose among good works, but abandon himself to God's inspiration, as the steed is governed by the reins. In an address delivered in 1516 he declares: "The man of God goeth, whithersoever God directs him as a rider. He never knows whither he is headed; he is passive rather than ac-

---

[2] Grisar, *Luther*, Vol. I, p. 87.
[3] *Briefwechsel*, I, p. 68 (April 15, 1516); Grisar, *Luther*, I, 88.

tive. He journeys ever onward, no matter what the condition of the road, through water, mud, rain, snow, wind, etc. Thus are the men of God who are led by the divine spirit." [4] Such are the doctrines which he opposed to those who became distasteful to him on account or their insistence on good works and what he called their Pharisaical observance of external practices.

On May 1, 1515, a chapter of the Augustinian congregation was held at Gotha under the presidency of Staupitz. Luther preached the sermon at the opening assembly. The theme which he selected treated of the contrasts which must have developed in the monasteries of the congregation, namely, the "little saints" and their calumnies against the monastic brethren who disagreed with them in matters of discipline. With extreme acerbity, and employing the crudest and most repulsive figures of speech, he scourged their criticism of others as inspired by love of scandal and malevolent detraction.[5] Apparently the majority of the brethren of his Order sided with him, for they elected him to the office of rural vicar, i. e., special superior of a number of monasteries as the representative of Staupitz.

At stated times he visited the monasteries thus entrusted to him. There were eleven of them, including Erfurt and Wittenberg. After the middle of April, 1516, he made a visitation of the congregations of the Order at Dresden, Neustadt on the Orla, Erfurt, Gotha, Langensalza, and Nordhausen. The letters written by him during his term of office as rural vicar, which normally lasted three years, contain practical directions and admonitions concerning monastic discipline and are, in part, quite edifying. Some of his visitations, however, were conducted with such astonishing rapidity that no fruitful results could be expected of them. Thus the visitation of the monastery at Gotha occupied but one hour, that at Langensalza two hours. "In these places," he wrote to Lang, "the Lord will work without us and direct the spiritual and temporal affairs in spite of the devil." [6] At Neustadt he deposed the prior, Michael Dressel, without a hearing, because the brethren could not get along with him. "I did this," he informed Lang in confidence, "because I hoped to rule there myself for the half-year." [7]

[4] Grisar, *Luther*, VI.
[5] *Ibid.*, I, pp. 69 sq.
[6] *Ibid.*, I, 65.
[7] *Ibid.*, I, 266.

In a letter to the same friend he writes as follows about the engagements with which he was overwhelmed at that time: "I really ought to have two secretaries or chancellors. I do hardly anything all day but write letters. . . . I am at the same time preacher to the monastery, have to preach in the refectory, and am even expected to preach daily in the parish church. I am regent of the *studium* [*i. e.*, of the younger monks] and vicar, that is to say prior eleven times over; I have to provide for the delivery of the fish from the Leitzkau pond and to manage the litigation of the Herzberg fellows [monks] at Torgau; I am lecturing on Paul, compiling an exposition of the Psalter, and, as I said before, writing letters most of the time. . . . It is seldom that I have time for the recitation of the Divine Office or to celebrate Mass, and then, too, I have my peculiar temptations from the flesh, the world, and the devil." [8]

2. INTERIOR STATE

The last sentence quoted above contains a remarkable declaration about his spiritual condition and his compliance with his monastic duties at that time. He seldom found time to recite the Divine Office and to say Mass. It was his duty so to arrange his affairs as to be able to comply with these obligations. The canonical hours were strictly prescribed. Saying Mass is the central obligation of every priest, especially if he is a member of a religious order. If Luther did not know how to observe due moderation in his labors; if he was derelict in the principal duties of the spiritual life; it was to be feared that he would gradually drift away from the religious state, particularly in view of the fact that he had adopted a false Mysticism which favored the relaxation of the rule. As rural vicar, it is probable that he did not sustain among the brethren the good old spirit which the zealous Proles had introduced into the society. Of the "temptations of the flesh" which he mentions we learn nothing definite. He was not yet in conflict with his vows. His wrestlings with the devil may signify the fears and terrors to which he was subject.

He continued to be on good terms with his friend Staupitz, who was interested in the young monk's manifold activities. Staupitz also

[8] *Ibid.*, I, p. 275. October 26, 1516.

posed as a mystic, and favored the spiritual tendency which Luther
followed. This talented and sociable man was very popular as a useful adviser in the homes of the rich and as an entertainer at table.
Whilst Luther could not accompany him on such errands, he enjoyed his company on monastic visitations. In July, 1515, he accompanied Staupitz to Eisleben, when the latter opened the new
Augustinian monastery at that place. As he walked in his sacerdotal
vestments in the procession through the city of his birth at the side
of his vicar, who carried the Blessed Sacrament, Luther was suddenly
seized with unspeakable fright at the thought of the proximity of
Christ. On mentioning the incident to his superior afterwards, the
latter comforted him by saying: "Your thought is not Christ," and
assuring him that Christ did not desire this fear.[9] At times, in consequence either of a disordered affection of the heart or of overwork, he was so distressed that he could not eat or drink for a long
time. One day he was found seemingly dead in his cell, so completely
was he exhausted as a result of agitation and lack of food. His friend
Ratzeberger, a physician, mentions this incident, without, however,
indicating the exact time of its occurrence. Luther was relieved of
this pitiable condition by recourse to music, which always stimulated him. After he had regained his strength, he was able once more
to prosecute his labors. As a result of his suffering and worry he became very much emaciated.

Did Luther subject himself to extraordinary deeds of penance at
any period of his monastic life, as he frequently affirmed in his subsequent conflict with the papacy and monasticism, when he was impelled by polemical reasons to describe himself as the type of a
holy and mortified monk, one who could not find peace of mind
during his whole monastic career? Holding then that peace of mind
was simply impossible in the Catholic Church, he arbitrarily mis-
represents monasticism, in order to exhibit in a most glaring manner
the alleged inherent impossibility of "papistic" ethics to produce the
assurance of God's mercy. "I tormented my body by fasting, vigils,
and cold. . . . In the observance of these matters I was so precise
and superstitious, that I imposed more burdens upon my body than
it could bear without danger to health." "If ever a monk got to
heaven by monkery, then I should have got there." "I almost died

---

[9] *Tischreden*, Weimar ed., Vol. I, Nr. 137.

a-fasting, for often I took neither a drop of water nor a morsel of food for three days." [10]

Such exaggerated penitential exercises were prohibited by the statutes of the congregation, which were distinguished for great discretion, and insisted upon proper moderation as a matter of strict duty.

The above picture of singular holiness is produced not by early witnesses, but by assertions which Luther made little by little at a later period of life. The established facts contradict the legend. Perhaps his description is based partly on reminiscences of his distracted days in the monastery, or on eccentric efforts to overcome his sombre moods by means of a false piety. His greatest error, and the one which most betrays him, is that he ascribes his fictitious asceticism to all serious-minded members of his monastery, yea, of all monasteries. He would have it that all monks consumed themselves in wailing and grief, wrestling for the peace of God, until he supplied the remedy.[11] It is a rule of the most elementary criticism finally to cut loose from the distorted presentation of the matter which has maintained itself so tenaciously in Protestant biographies of Luther.

It may be admitted that, on the whole, Luther was a dutiful monk for the greatest part of his monastic life. "When I was in the monastery," he stated on one occasion, in 1535, "I was not like the rest of men, the robbers, the unjust, the adulterous; but I observed chastity, obedience, and poverty." [12]

Yet, after his transfer to Wittenberg, and in consequence of the applause which was accorded to him there, the unpleasant traits of his character, especially his positive insistence on always being in the right, began to manifest themselves more and more disagreeably. In his opinion, the Scholastic theologians, even the greatest among them, were sophists. They were a herd of "swine theologians," while he was the enlightened pupil of St. Paul and St. Augustine.[13] The finer achievements of Scholasticism, especially those of its intellectual giant, Thomas of Aquin, were scarcely known to him. Could his confused mysticism perhaps supplement his deficient knowledge

---

[10] See the passages quoted by me in *Luther*, Vol. VI, pp. 191 sqq. A special chapter in that volume (pp. 187 sqq.) discusses "Luther's Later Embellishment of His Early Life" in the various phases of its development.

[11] Cf. Grisar, *Luther*, Vol. II, pp. 157 sqq.

[12] *Op. cit.*, Vol. VI, pp. 233 sqq.

[13] *Op. cit.*, Vol. I, pp. 130 sqq.

of Scholasticism? No, it only made him more self-conscious and arbitrary in the sphere of theology. He gave free vent to his criticism of highly respected ascetical writers. An example of his egotistical excess in this respect is furnished by his glosses for the year 1515, which he indited on the Psalter of Mary, a work of Mark of Weida.[14] In addition to these characteristics, there was his peculiar irritability, which is strikingly exhibited in his correspondence during 1514. The theologians of Erfurt, led by Nathin, had reproved him for taking the doctorate at Erfurt instead of at Wittenberg, since the Erfurt school had claims on him as one of its own pupils. It is possible that some harsh words were exchanged in regard to this matter. The young professor in a letter addressed to the monastery at Erfurt says that he had well nigh resolved to "pour out the entire vial of his wrath and indignation upon Nathin and the whole monastery" on account of their lies and mockery. They had received two shocking letters (*litterae stupidae*) from him, for which he now wants to excuse himself, though his indignation "was only too well founded," especially since he now heard even worse things about Nathin and his complaints against his (Luther's) person. In the meantime, God had willed his separation from the Erfurt monastery, etc.

The ill-feeling between Nathin and his Erfurt colleagues, on the one hand, and Luther and his monastic partisans on the other, arose from the controversy concerning the stricter observance of the rule within the Order.

3. OPPOSITION TO SELF-RIGHTEOUSNESS AND RELIGIOUS OBSERVANCE

Contradictory conceptions of monastic life continued to be harbored in the Augustinian congregation even after the settlement of the contention with regard to Staupitz's plans of union.

Those brethren who treasured the ancient monastic discipline, protected by papal privileges and exemptions, were accused of self-righteous Pharisaism and of disobedience towards the General of the order by Luther and his party. They were the "Little Saints" against whom he had inveighed in his impetuous address at Gotha. In his lectures and sermons he reproached, though often only in allusions, their "observantine" practices, their adherence to the doctrine of good works, and their want of charity. His invectives, however,

---

[14] *Theol. Studien u. Kritiken*, 1917, pp. 81 sqq.

were launched with a bitterness which those concerned assuredly did not merit, even though there might have been reasons for complaint. It may be said that the ancient and the modern wings opposed each other in the Wittenberg monastery. Probably there was friction also in the monastery at Erfurt, where Luther's friend Lang was prior, as well as in other monasteries of the congregation. Luther's monastery, however, was the center of the contention. The young students of the Order brought with them their divergent views out of the cloisters whence they came and they carried the new atmosphere of Wittenberg along with them when they left. Luther's partisans at Wittenberg boasted that they were more closely attached to the General of the Order at Rome than their opponents. The General, they contended, was not in favor of the singularities of the Observantines.

At the commencement of his first series of lectures on the Psalms, Luther delivered a sarcastic address on the obedience due to religious superiors. "How many do we not find," he says, "who believe they are very religious, and yet they are, if I may so express it, only men of an extremely sanguine temperament (*sanguinicissimi*) and true Idumaeans [*i. e.*, pagan-minded]. There are people who so revere and praise their monastic state, their order, their Saints, and their institutions, that they cast a shadow upon all others, not wishing to grant them their proper place. In a very unspiritual manner they are humble followers (*observantes*) of their fathers and boast of them. Oh, the frenzy that prevails in this day! It has almost come to this that every monastery repudiates the customs of all others and is imbued with such pride as to preclude taking over or learning anything at all from another. That is the pride of Jews and heretics, with which we, unfortunate ones, are also encompassed," etc.[15] In the addresses which he delivered in the monastery church he frequently alludes to the obstinate pride of the Jews and heretics, in condemnation of those members of his order or of other orders who adhered to the strict observance. These "Observantines, exempted and privileged characters"—thus he fulminates in another lecture, are devoid of obedience, which is the very soul of good works. It will be seen—he continues—how detrimental to the Church they are; in the interests of the rule, they were determined to insist upon exceptions; "but that is a light that comes from the devil." [16]

[15] Grisar, *Luther*, Vol. VI, pp. 497 sqq. *Sanguinosissimi* must probably be read in lieu of *sanguinicissimi*.

[16] *Op. cit.*, Vol. VI, p. 498.

This was the contest which led the fiery monk to enter upon doubtful ways. His opposition to the so-called doctrine of self-righteousness caused him to form a false conception of righteousness; instead of attacking an. heretical error, he combated the true worth of good works and the perfections of the monastic life.

Voluntary poverty, as practiced by the mendicants, was one of the foundations of his Order. The inmates of monastic houses were to live on alms according to the practice introduced by the great Saint Francis of Assisi and for the benefactions received were to devote themselves gratis to the spiritual needs of their fellowmen. Many abuses, it is true, had attached themselves to the mendicant system: self-interest, avarice, and worldly-mindedness infected the itinerant mendicants. But in his explanation of the Psalms Luther attacks the life of poverty *per se:* "O mendicants! O mendicants! O mendicants!" he pathetically exclaims, "who can excuse you? . . . Look to it yourselves," etc. He places the practice of poverty in an unfavorable light.[17] In his criticism of the "self-righteousness" of his irksome enemies, he confronts them with the righteousness of the spirit that cometh from Christ. These people, whom he believed it his duty to expose, were guilty, in his opinion, of a Pharisaical denial of the true righteousness of Christ. His righteousness, and not our good works, effect our salvation; works generate a fleshly sense and boastfulness. These thought-processes evince how false mysticism, unclear theological notions, a darkening of the monastic spirit, and passionate obstinacy conspired in Luther's mind.

In the years 1515 and 1516, the phalanx of the self-righteous, the *justitiarii*, as he styles them, again constitute the object of his attacks. There is Christ, the hen with its protecting wings, which he must defend against the vultures that pounce upon us in their self-righteousness. These enemies of the sweet righteousness imputed to us by God are "a pestilence in the Church; intractable, nay, rebellious against their superiors, they decry others and clothe themselves with the lamb-skins of their good works."[18]

An Augustinian friend of his, George Spenlein, having become weary of certain persecutions, had had himself transferred from Wittenberg to the monastery at Memmingen. Luther sent him a peculiar letter of condolence on April 8, 1516. According to this missive, it would seem that the self-righteous Spenlein had been for a long time "in opposition to the

---

[17] *Op. cit.,* Vol. VI, p. 500.
[18] *Op. cit.,* Vol. VI, pp. 502 sq.

self-righteousness of God, which had been bestowed most lavishly and gratuitously upon him by Christ"; whereas he (Spenlein) desired to stand before God with his own works and merits, which, of course, is impossible. He (Luther), too, had harbored this notion, and says he still wrestles with this error. "Learn, therefore, my sweet brother," thus he addresses Spenlein in the vocabulary of mysticism, "learn to sing to the Lord Jesus and, distrusting yourself, say to Him: Thou, O Lord Jesus, art my righteousness, but I am Thy sin. Thou hast accepted what was mine and hast given to me what was Thine. Oh, that thou wouldst boldly appear thyself as a sinner, yea, be a sinner in reality; for Christ abides only in sinners." "But, if you are a lily and a rose of Christ, then learn to bear persecution with patience, lest your secret pride convert you into a thorn." [19]

The germ of Luther's reformatory doctrine is plainly contained in this species of Mysticism. Step by step he had arrived at his new dogma in the above described manner. The system which attacked the basic truths of the Catholic Church, was complete in outline. Before giving a fuller exposition of it, we must consider the individual factors which co-operated in its development in Luther's mind.

Confession and penance were a source of torturing offense to the young monk. Can one obtain peace with God by the performance of penitential works? He discussed this question with Staupitz on an occasion when he sought consolation. Staupitz pointed out to him that all penance must begin and end with love; that all treasures are hidden in Christ, in whom we must trust and whom we must love.[20] These words contain nothing new; but the exhortation to combine love with penance entered the inflammable soul of Luther as a voice from heaven. According to his own expression, it "clung to his soul as the sharp arrows of the mighty" (Ps. CXIX, 4); henceforward, he says, he would execrate the hypocrisy by means of which he had formerly sought to express a "fabricated and forced" penitential spirit during the tortures of confession. Now that the merits of Christ covered everything, penance appeared easy and sweet to him. He expresses himself on this point in a grateful letter to Staupitz, written in 1518.[21]

On the occasion referred to, it is probable that Staupitz, as was

---

[19] Enders, *Luthers Briefwechsel*, I, p. 29.
[20] *Tischreden*, Weimar, ed., II, Nr. 2654.
[21] Enders, *Luthers Briefwechsel*, I, p. 196 (May 30, 1518.)

his custom, expressed himself in a vague and sentimental manner, rather than in clear theological terms. His writings are susceptible of improvement in many respects. The influence which he exerted on Luther was not a wholesome one. He was too fond of him to penetrate his character. He perceived in him a rising star of his congregation, a very promising ornament of his Order. Even in the most critical period anterior to Luther's apostasy, he eulogized his courage and said: Christ speaks out of your mouth,—so well it pleased him that Luther, in the matter of righteousness and good works, ascribed everything to Christ, to whom alone glory should be given.[22] Certain of a favorable response on the part of his superior, Luther wrote thus in the above letter to him: "My sweet Saviour and Pardoner, to whom I shall sing as long as I live (Ps. CIII, 33), is sufficient for me. If there be anyone who will not sing with me, what is that to me? Let him howl if it please him." The short-sighted Staupitz sided with Luther even after he had been condemned by the Church.

Nor was Staupitz the man who could thoroughly free Luther from his doubts about predestination, although Luther says he helped him. His general references to the wounds of Christ could not permanently set the troubled monk aright. He should have placed definitely before him the Catholic dogma, based on Sacred Scripture, that God sincerely desires the salvation of all men, and should have made clear to the doubter that voluntary sin is the sole cause of damnation. But he himself seems not to have grasped these truths, for in certain critical passages of his writings he allows them to retreat before a certain mysterious predestination. Luther's fear of predestination constituted the obscure substratum of his evolving new religious system. Recalling Staupitz's exhortations, he says, in 1532: We must stop at the wounds of Christ, and may not ponder over the awful mystery. The only remedy consists in dismissing from our minds the possibility of a verdict of damnation. "When I attend to these ideas, I forget what Christ and God are, and sometimes arrive at the conclusion that God is a scoundrel. . . . The idea of predestination causes us to forget God, and the *Laudate* ceases and the *Blasphemate* begins." [23] The part which these struggles had in the origin of his new doctrine, is to be sought in Luther's violent efforts

[22] Weimar ed., XL, I, p. 131.
[23] *Tischreden*, Weimar ed., II, Nr. 2654.

to attain to a certain repose in the face of his presumptive pre-destination.

It is also remarkable that the last-quoted utterance is followed by one concerning his "great spiritual temptations." In contrast with the struggles of despair which he underwent, he is not deeply impressed by ordinary temptations. "No one," he writes, "can really write or say anything about grace, unless he has been disciplined by spiritual temptations." [24] His opponents, he says elsewhere, not having had such experiences, it behooved them to observe silence. When his doctrine encountered opposition in Rome, he wrote to Staupitz that Roman citations and other matters made no impression on him. "My sufferings, as you know, are incomparably greater, and these force me to regard such temporal flashes as extremely trivial." [25] He meant "doubtlessly, personal, inward sufferings and attacks which were connected with bodily ailments . . . , whereby, as formerly, he was always seized with fear for his personal salvation when he pondered on the hidden depths of the divine will." [26]

In his interpretation of the Epistle of St. Paul to the Romans, given during the years 1515 and 1516, Luther completely unfolded his new doctrine.

[24] Grisar, *Luther*, Vol. I, pp. 204 sqq.
[25] *Op. cit.*, Vol. VI, pp. 100 sqq.; cfr. I, 14 sqq.
[26] Julius Köstlin.

CHAPTER IV

PROGRESS OF THE NEW DOCTRINE

1. INTERPRETATION OF THE EPISTLE TO THE ROMANS
(1515–1516)

In none of his other Epistles does St. Paul penetrate so deeply into the questions of grace, justification, and election, as in his magnificent Epistle addressed to the Christians of Rome. Luther believed that this profound Epistle furnished the thread that would lead him out of his labyrinth. Disregarding the tradition of the Church concerning the meaning of the Epistle, he buried himself in its contents and brooded over its many mysterious expressions. For him the sacred document was to become the subject-matter of academic lectures with entirely new ideas. How often may he not have wandered up and down the venerable corridors of the monastery meditating on the significance of the words of the Apostle. His emaciated form may have become animated, his deep-set eyes may have flashed, as he imagined to discover in the Epistle to the Romans the desired solution of his problems. With ever-increasing confidence he imputed to the Apostle the ideas to which he was urged for the sake of the supposed quieting of his scruples. Simultaneously, an arsenal of new weapons against the self-righteous Pharisees within the Church seemed to open itself to him.

St. Paul sets forth the idea that neither the observation of the law of nature nor that of the Mosaic law can justify man before God, but only the grace of God now revealed through the Gospel of Christ. In this exposition Luther erroneously discovered a denial of the natural powers of man and the sole causality of God in His creature—a doctrine utterly foreign to the Apostle's mind. In the propositions on the grace of Christ, as set forth by Paul, he discovered an ascription of the merits of Christ equally foreign to the mind of the Apostle—a purely external imputation without works on the part of man. St. Paul discourses sublimely on the freedom of the Christian believer from the disciplinary law of Moses and on the freedom of the soul that is directed towards God. From this Luther inferred that the true Christian was free from all law and formulated for himself a contrast between the law and the Gospel which implied fatal consequences. The Apostle, again, paints a striking picture of the rejection of the Jewish nation from anterior secret decrees, which prove his notion of predestination to hell. In a similar way his lively imagination interpreted other doctrines of the Epistle, which he confidently undertook to explain, despite the fact that his deficient training rendered him incompetent for the task.

He began to lecture on Romans in the second semester of 1515. We have his own manuscript of the lectures and a faithful copy of it, which is preserved in the Vatican Library. Fr. Henry Denifle, O. P., has the honor of having first edited extensive extracts from the Roman copy in 1904. Four years later John Ficker published the original, the existence of which was till then unknown. It belongs to the Berlin Library.

These publications were of inestimable advantage for the student of Luther. As contrasted with the numerous defective reproductions of these lectures previously circulated, we have here for the first time an authentic insight into the genesis and original form of Luther's teaching. Since that day, investigators have been occupied with the task of analyzing and discussing these lectures. The principal outlines are clear, but there are differences of opinion with respect to various details. This is all the more natural, since Luther, when he delivered these lectures, was still undergoing a spiritual process of development. He sometimes contradicts his own views and retains various elements of Catholic thought which cannot be reconciled with his changed views. The opening sentences disclose the impulsive vigor with which he advances towards his new position. He commences by stating that St. Paul, in his Epistle to the Romans, was desirous of eradicating "all wisdom and righteousness" of the terrestrial man; that he wished to destroy, "in heart and marrow," all man's works, even the best-intentioned and noblest, and all his virtues. Instead, he wished "to cultivate and glorify sin," that is, to describe the permanent hereditary sin of mankind, in order to set up an alien righteousness, i. e., the grace of Christ imputed to us by faith. In this manner, he says, St. Paul inculcates the doctrine of self-annihilation on the one hand, and, on the other, resignation to the sole causality and omnipotence of God.

2. THE PRINCIPAL PROPOSITIONS OF LUTHER'S DOCTRINE

The ancient Church, above all things, upheld the freedom of the human will to do good. She steadfastly maintained that God wills the salvation of all men without exception and to this end offers them the necessary grace, with which men should freely coöperate. Baptism makes a man a child of God by virtue of sanctifying grace; but the inclination to evil remains through no fault of his own, provided he does not consent to sin. Concupiscence is diminished by the means of grace offered by the Church. If any one has been seduced into committing mortal sin, he may confidently hope to regain the state of grace through the merits of the death of Christ, provided he submits to penance and resolves to amend his life. Mere faith in the application of the merits of Christ is not sufficient. Actual grace assists man to be converted and to persevere in doing good.

In these few propositions we have described a splendid system of doctrine, which accords with the free, rational nature of man as well as with the infinite goodness of God. This is not the place to demonstrate its truth from the sources of divine revelation, Scripture and tradition.

Luther, with the Epistle to the Romans in his hand, proclaimed that man was not free to do good; that all his efforts were sinful, because evil concupiscence dwelled in his soul; that God did everything in him, governing him as the rider governs his steed. He did not differentiate between natural and supernatural good. Christ, he said, has fulfilled the law for me and atoned for every weakness and sin. Through His righteousness the believing and trustful sinner is covered, apart from his own works and his own righteousness. He remains a sinner as before, but is justified by the imputation of the justice of Christ and necessarily brings forth good works through the infinite causality of God, just as trust in God is imparted to the hesitating only through the divine omnipotence.

According to Luther's teaching, not all men are thus favored by God, since His inscrutable decree consigns many to eternal damnation. Resignation to hell is the highest virtue because it connotes complete submission to the will of God. But this very resignation reconciles the despondent soul with the thought of a merciful God. Perfect humility and submission (*perfecta humilitas*) must serve us as a kind of anchor. The doctrine of the absolute certainty of salvation, or rather, the certitude of justification through mere belief in Christ, had not yet been discovered by Luther. Instead, he still upheld the Catholic teaching on merit, similarly as when, in connection with justification, he employed Catholic expressions, albeit obscurely and hesitatingly, to set forth his conception of the renovation of the inward man. The renovation, however, which Luther indicates, is far removed from that which the ancient Church teaches on the basis of Sacred Scripture, namely, that the spirit of God, poured forth into the soul, abides in man. Luther ridicules the outpouring of grace in man in virtue of the so-called habits and the implanted supernatural virtues. He had nothing but scorn for the "sophists" who entertained such "silly notions."

His exposition of the new theology, which we have condensed above, is accompanied by a haughty and repellent treatment of the traditional dogmas and theology. He selects some actual deficiencies of the older theologians, in order to stigmatize the entire past, especially the Scholastic system, with which he was but inadequately acquainted.[1]

3. EFFECTS OF LUTHER'S FIRST APPEARANCE

Protests were immediately voiced. In September, 1516, Luther arranged for a disputation at the University of Wittenberg, to be conducted by Bartholomew Bernhardi, a native of Feldkirch in Vorarlberg, for which he himself supplied the theses. They were chiefly concerned with the utter moral incompetence of man in the state of nature. The solemn disputation, according to his own testimony, was intended to silence the "yelping curs" which might rise up against him. The theses stated that man sins even when doing the best he can; for he is absolutely unable by his own unaided efforts to keep the commandments of God.[2]

[1] On the doctrinal content of Luther's Commentary on the Epistle to the Romans, see Grisar, *Luther*, Vol. I, pp. 184 sqq., 374 sqq.

[2] *Op. cit.*, Vol. I, pp. 310 sq.

In October, 1516, he began his celebrated shorter lectures on the Epistle to the Galatians. In the printed edition with which we are familiar, as well as in the condensed form in which they have been recently published, they constitute a still more vigorous expression of his views. These lectures were followed, in 1517, by his prelections on the Epistle to the Hebrews, which have not yet been printed. The Wittenberg disputation and the lectures delivered by Luther at that time were subsequently represented by him and his friends as "the commencement of the gospel business." [3]

Whilst the reports concerning Luther caused the monks at Erfurt and other cloisters to be startled, and whilst the opposition to him at Wittenberg increased, influential professors at the University gradually espoused his cause. Among these were the following: Andrew Karlstadt, who up to this time had labored energetically in the interests of Scholasticism; Nicholas Amsdorf, who was destined to distinguish himself as an ardent enthusiast, more Lutheran even than Luther himself; and Peter Lupinus, a former professor and originally an antagonist of the new thought. Of special importance for Luther was the support and coöperation of the Augustinian, Wenceslaus Link, prior of the Wittenberg monastery and since 1511 a doctor at the University, a confidant of Luther and one of the supporters of Staupitz. After having accompanied the latter on several visitation tours, he arrived in 1517 at Nuremberg, where he pleaded the cause of Lutheranism in eloquent sermons. At Nuremberg, the humanist Christopher Scheurl became a friend of the Lutherans. At Erfurt Luther had an active supporter in his old friend, John Lang, the prior of that place. To him Luther wrote, in 1517, that he contemned the reproaches of the Augustinians of Erfurt for his alleged presumption, since God's work would be realized in him. "Pray fervently for me," he wrote, "as I pray for you, that our Lord Jesus may assist us and help us bear our temptations, which are known to no one but ourselves." [4]

The law faculty of Wittenberg entertained diverse opinions of Luther. Among the first to defend him was the jurist Jerome Schurf, who subsequently became the patriarch of jurisprudence at Wittenberg. The renowned Martin Pollich, who, with Staupitz, was one of the founders of the University, freely acknowledged Luther's extra-

[3] Op. cit., Vol. I, pp. 303 sqq.
[4] Enders, Luthers Briefwechsel, I, p. 124 (November 11.)

ordinary talents.[5] Most of the other professors, however, were either against him or noncomittal, because they disapproved of his opposition to canon law. Already at that time Luther was not fond of the representatives of jurisprudence, to whose legal demands, on the basis of his peculiar mysticism, he opposed an exaggerated "passive" complaisance.

The reformer's most agitated opponents at Wittenberg quite naturally were those monks and clergymen whom Luther in his lectures and in the pulpit was wont to castigate as self-righteous. We know from what has been said above that the high esteem in which the Observance was held by many Augustinians was severely criticized by Luther. Among the younger student monks were some who brought with them from the cloister sound traditions and a spirit of enthusiasm for the external exercises of piety which Luther and his supporters disliked. They became the kernel of an active party who attacked the new theology. Luther assailed the self-righteous and Pharisaical Observantines all the more hotly. At the time of his lectures on the Epistle to the Romans (1515) he delivered a Christmas sermon, in which he raised his voice against them.

As the ancient prophets, philosophers, and scribes who proclaimed the truth were persecuted, so, Luther assures us, he in turn is being persecuted. Men exclaimed that he erred when he called Christ a hen, who, as it were, gathers us under His wings, in virtue of His merits and righteousness, in order to make us righteous. The opponents of the hen should know that their righteousness is sin. Since man is unable to fulfill the law, it behooves him to exclaim: "O sweet hen!" However, one may not seek virtues and gifts according to one's own opinion. Thus, with a lavish hand, Luther casts about him the products of his mysticism in the course of a sermon.[6]

Meanwhile, his adversaries, who were solicitous about the Church and their Order, did not remain inactive. Luther charged them in a sermon in mid-summer, 1516, with shooting arrows at those who are pure of heart. They, in common with countless other contemporaries, he exclaims, are becoming obdurate in their "carnal righteousness and wisdom." They are the greatest evil in the Church; their shibboleth, that one is obliged to

[5] Grisar, *Luther*, Vol. IV, pp. 258 sq.
[6] Grisar, *Luther*, Vol. III, p. 970 (German ed.)

do what is good, is a pestilence whereby they antagonize the goodness of God. He enumerates no less than seven transgressions of which they were guilty.[7]

Luther's enemies were cowed by his vehement attacks. They could not compete with him as an orator. In Wittenberg especially there was no one to challenge him. It was a tragical advantage in his favor that his talents enabled him to stand head and shoulders above all the brethren of his Order. Opposition merely increased his audacity.

On September 4, 1517, he arranged another sensational disputation by his disciple Franz Günther of Nordhausen on ninety-seven theses composed by him against Scholasticism and Aristotle. One of these theses was that man can "desire and do only evil." Another, that "his will is not free." Another, that "the sole disposition for grace is predestination, eternal election by God." Another that "neither the Jewish ceremonial code, nor the decalogue, nor whatever may be externally taught or commanded, is a good law; the only good law is the love of God," etc. At the end of these paradoxical theses we find the assurance that nothing in their contents contradicted Catholic dogma and the ecclesiastical writers. These ninety-seven propositions of 1517 enjoyed a certain circulation prior to the publication, in the same year, of Luther's famous theses on indulgences, which are not nearly so far-reaching. In consequence of this disputation several distinguished men, like Scheurl of Nuremberg, expressed the belief that a "restoration of the theology of Christ" was under way. Some time previously Luther triumphantly wrote to Lang: "Our theology and St. Augustine are making good progress and thanks be to God they prevail at our university. . . . The lectures on the Sentences [delivered by the Scholastic teachers] are completely ignored, and no one can assure himself of an audience who does not profess this [i. e., our] theology." [8]

The assertion that Augustine was coming into his own in virtue of the new doctrine was as little in accord with the truth as the statement that that doctrine was genuinely Pauline. On the contrary, Luther's errors may be refuted point for point from the writings

[7] Op. cit., Vol. III, p. 971 (original German edition; omitted in the English translation which we always quote in this volume, except where the German edition is expressly mentioned.)

[8] Op. cit., Vol. IV, pp. (May 18, 1517.)

of Augustine, who, in his contest with the Pelagians, forcefully points out the rôle of grace, yet neither denies that man has a part in every good deed, nor, much less, that he has a free will. The great Doctor of the Church acknowledges the devastating results of original sin, but he demands the fulfillment of the entire law with divine aid. In the theology of St. Augustine the grace of divine sonship is not merely an imputation of alien righteousness, but a supernatural state of the soul which has been truly cleansed of sin. He admits that the distribution of grace is an inscrutable mystery, but rejects the theory of absolute predestination to hell as an abomination. He frequently argues in favor of the freedom of the human spirit and the dominion of love. But he does not hold man to be independent of the laws of God or the Church; or that love must be the sole motive of action to the exclusion of fear of God's punishments so natural to man. Above all, Augustine is a defender of ecclesiastical authority and tradition, who inexorably combated arbitrariness, the spirit of innovation and subjectivism in doctrinal matters. In spite of Luther's boastfulness, he and Augustine are poles apart. All that may be said in extenuation of Luther is that Augustine's thought is frequently profound, and that, as a rule, he does not propound his doctrines methodically, but either in the service of controversy or adapted to the changing requirements of souls and the Kingdom of Heaven. As a consequence, his teaching in some respects is more easily misunderstood than that of other ecclesiastical writers. Luther repeatedly read his own ideas into Augustine with a rashness that was but little removed from conscious falsification.

For the rest, to understand Luther, we must bear in mind that the theological tradition since the days of Scholasticism was not yet fully clarified. Some of the theological doctrines which he criticized had not been treated adequately in the schools. The subsequent labors of the theologians at the Council of Trent indicate how much still remained to be done in the matter of clearing up such questions as original sin, grace, and justification.

It is highly amazing, however, to see Luther proposing new theories without interrogating more closely the well-established doctrinal tradition of the Church and questioning the latter's prerogative to teach, which had been instituted by Christ for the defense of dogma. We marvel at the fact that this sacred authority is almost completely set aside by him, as though it were non-existent. Luther acts as if his fight were merely a fight against the schools, against Scholastic sophists, against the Aristotelians, against the new writers and their friends, such as the followers of Gabriel Biel, whom he calls "Gabrielists," or against the defenders of such older authors as the "*sententiarii.*" The mighty authority of the Church, which every Catholic theologian must consult at every step, did not impress him sufficiently during his formative period. This deficiency is attributable, in part, to the schools where he studied and disputed, for the later Scholastics, while indulging in hair-splitting investigation, neglected the important doctrine on the Church, or at least did not pay enough attention to it. Too much preference was given to speculation in contrast with authority and the question of its binding power, and, in general, with the positive study of the treasures of tradition entrusted to the Church and her supreme government.

True Luther was not entirely unfamiliar with the doctrinal authority of the Church. On the contrary, it is very remarkable that in his exposition of the Epistle to the Romans, despite his deviations from the faith, he strongly and in vehement language condemns the activities of heretics who separated themselves from the Church. Evidently he did not at that time entertain any idea of revolt against the hierarchy, though his complete defection from the common doctrine of the past, if insisted upon, was bound to lead to a separation from the hierarchy as his next step.

In his resolution to continue his criticism of good works—a criticism dictated by false mysticism—it is notable that he still retains the idea of the monastic state for a number of years. He devotes some beautiful passages to the excellence of the monastic vows in his lectures on the Epistle to the Romans. Hence, he arrived at his new doctrine not as a result of his eagerness to break the sacred bonds, but by following entirely different and most intricate routes, especially that of a morbid mysticism.

4. HISTORICAL BACKGROUND OF LUTHER'S DOCTRINE

The publication of Luther's commentaries on the Epistle to the Romans (1515–1516) and the study of contemporary sources, has clearly demonstrated, among other things, the falsity of the assumption that Luther's innovation originated in the intention of effecting a thorough and universal reform of the Church.

Ideas of powerful external and internal "reforms" have been ascribed to the "reformer" as the starting-point of his public appearance; in reality, however, such ideas did not influence him at all. What he primarily intended was to get his peculiar doctrines accepted and introduced in his monastery and Order, in the University of Wittenberg, and, finally, in the whole realm of contemporary scholarship.

It is true, as the sources mentioned above indicate, he combined with his efforts to impose his doctrines a loud demand for a reformation of ecclesiastical conditions. He ascribed the chief cause of the prevailing abuses in the religious sphere directly to the neglect of the truths newly discovered by him. Blinded by his imagination and by his reckless habit of fault-finding, he exaggerated beyond all measure, both in his exposition of the Espistle to the Romans and in his other addresses, the shortcomings of his age in faith and morals. In matter of fact the young monk of thirty-two years, living within the narrow confines of a monastery, knew but little of the actual conditions existing out in the world! Thus far his contacts with the world had been but few. Nevertheless, he believed he saw a veritable "deluge" of errors and abuses everywhere, because mankind was completely estranged from the "Word," namely, the requirements of the Bible and "righteousness," as he understood them. "The pope and the ecclesiastical superiors"—thus he expresses himself with blind audacity in these lectures—"have rendered themselves execrable in their endeavors [9]; they are now unmasked as seducers of the Christian populace." These superiors, he hotly avers, fill the whole world with their sodomitical and other vices; the faithful have completely forgotten the significance of good works, faith and humility. Even the better class are idolaters rather than true Christians, because they are self-righteous.[10] After such a wholesale condemnation of Christians, he is able, in turn, to describe minutely, in grotesque outlines and with humorous incisiveness, the errors of the narrower world by which he was surrounded, e. g., the monks in choir impatiently hastening to the end of the services. He criticizes those of high degree with a mystical zeal, because they

[9] *"Corrupti sunt et abominabiles facti sunt in studiis suis."* (Ps. XIII, 1).
[10] Grisar, *Luther*, Vol. I, p. 227.

insisted upon their rights in preference to suffering injustice, as true Christians should do. It was his opinion that Pope Julius II should have relinquished the rights of the Church in his conflict with the republic of Venice. Duke George of Saxony, who was engaged in warfare with the rebels in Frisia, would have done better had he and his people patiently suffered chastisement for their sins at the hands of their enemies for God's sake.[11] "I fear," he says, "that we shall all perish on account of our worldliness." These are utterances of a disturbed mind.

The memory of the abominations which he had witnessed, or which he claims to have heard of in Rome, ever rises up before him and fills him with terror. "Should we not regard as sinful the shocking corruption of the entire curia and the mountain of revolting immorality, pomp, covetousness, vanity, and sacrilege prevalent there?" Germany at that time was in an ugly mood, not only because of the avarice of the Roman collectors, but also on account of the reports of lax morality incident to the Renaissance, since and even before the days of the unworthy Borgia Pope, Alexander VI. Staupitz, too, was embittered against Rome and freely vented his feelings in the presence of Luther, who stated subsequently that Staupitz had incited him against Rome.[12]

Did this disaffection, which cropped out in spots already before Luther, lead to any opposition in dogma or practice, similar to his? Did Lutheranism have any precursors? Did it arise from a soil prepared by others?

Many prominent men had raised their voices in protest against the corruption and mistakes of the ecclesiastical authorities, but despite their criticisms, they generally remained loyal to the teachings of the Church, and simply demanded a reform on the basis of the ancient dogmas. Such, for example, was that powerful preacher Geiler von Kaysersberg. Only a few before Luther dared to go as far as did John of Wesel (+ 1481) and Wessel Gansfort (+ 1489). The former, who was pastor of the cathedral at Mayence, was cited before the Inquisition and sentenced to spend the balance of his days in an Augustinian monastery, after he had recanted his erroneous propositions, which, among other things, attacked indulgences and approached the Hussite heresy concerning the Church

---

[11] Op. cit., Vol. I, p. 228.
[12] Tischreden, Weimar ed., IV, Nr. 4707.

and predestination. While still an orthodox theologian, Wesel had taught at the University of Erfurt, but he did not influence Luther's development. Wessel Gansfort, who is often confused with John of Wesel, was celebrated as a great scholar by his admirers, but obscured the doctrine of the Church by many heretical propositions. Thus he affirmed the fallibility of ecumenical councils. The righteous, he taught, have the power of the keys in a certain sense. He asserted that satisfaction for sins committed was superfluous after their remission and there was no need for indulgences, etc. Still he conforms as little with Luther in the principal points of the latter's teaching, as did John of Wesel. He holds that man has a free will, that only faith animated by charity can effect justification, and that justification is not merely a declaration of right-eousness, but an actual process of making man just. Neither the one nor the other of these scholars agrees with Luther in his reformatory demands; and hence they are incorrectly hailed as precursors of the Lutheran movement.

It has been asserted that long before Luther there existed a so-called Augustinian school of theology which propagated Lutheran ideas on liberty, grace and justification down to the days of the Protestant Reformation. In reality, however, no such school existed, either during or at the close of the Middle Ages. Isolated writers, especially during the early period of Scholasticism, did advance risqué propositions that smacked of Lutheranism, but they were not in any true sense precursors of Luther, particularly since they did not create a tradition. At the same time it is difficult, yea impossible, to ascertain to what extent Luther knew and used these earlier writers or appreciated their teaching. There is no reason to challenge his independent discovery of his heresies, hence we may readily concede their originality.[13]

13 On so-called precursors of Luther in the "School of Augustine" see Grisar, *Luther* (German original, Vol. III, pp. 1011 sqq.; this appendix is omitted in the English trans-lation). Grabmann in the *Katholik*, 1913, Nr. 3, pp. 157 sqq. The connection of Fidatus of Cascia (died 1348) with Luther is rejected by N. Paulus in the Innsbruck *Zeitschrift für kath. Theologie*, 1922, pp. 169 sqq.; cf. the same writer in the *Theol. Revue*, 1922, pp. 18 sq. and *Histor. Jahrb.*, 1922, p. 323. Some Protestant authors also reject the theory, *e. g.*, R. Seeberg in *Die Lehre Luthers* (1917), p. 118, and, relative to Fidatus, in *Theol. Literaturblatt*, 1923, pp. 197 sqq.; also Scheel in the *Zeitschrift für Kirchengesch.* 1922, pp. 258 sq. Cf. W. Köhler in the *Histor. Zeitschrift*, Vol. CXI, Nr. 1, p. 153, and W. Braun in the *Evangel. Kirchenzeitung*, 1913, pp. 181 sqq.

The great Luther monument at Worms, which was unveiled in 1868, embraces quite a number of statues of so-called heralds of the Reformation. The central figure of Luther is encircled by statues of Savonarola, Hus, Wiclif, Reuchlin, and Peter Waldus. Do they belong in this constellation? As precursors of Luther's principal doctrines, certainly not; at most they may pass as opponents of the papacy in virtue of other doctrines or because of some particular controversies.

The most advanced of these opponents of the papacy was Hus, whose unfortunate end at the Council of Constance was the result of heretical doctrines subversive of both Church and State. Though Luther agreed with him in some things, and afterwards glorified him exceedingly, he was not a disciple of Hus. When, in his early monastic years, he chanced upon a volume of Hus, he refused to read it, though he noticed some good therein, because of his aversion for the author's name.[14] Soon after his change of front, however, he exploited in the interest of his own cause the unhistorical legend that Hus, when he faced the stake, said: Now they are roasting a goose [Hus in Bohemian signifies goose], but a swan will come which they will not master. Luther, with a power of illusion which considerably exceeded that of the dreaming and meditative figure of Hus on the Worms monument, applied this alleged prophecy to himself.

Nor was there any greater affinity between Luther's teaching and that of Hus's precursor, John Wiclif, or that of Peter Waldus. Savonarola, the eccentric Dominican of Florence, who lost his life because of his unfortunate political activities and his schismatic attitude towards Pope Alexander VI, to some extent shared the stormy temperament of Luther, but he kept aloof from heresy. It has been aptly said of his peculiar posture on the monument of Worms that it appeared as if he wished to run away because he felt he did not fit in properly with Luther's company. Finally, there is Reuchlin, the scholarly founder of Hebrew philology, who remained a loyal Catholic. After a lengthy conflict concerning his theories of the Talmud, his book, "Augenspiegel," was prohibited by Leo X, chiefly on account of the undue use the young German humanists and incipient Lutherans made of his name. It was only the desire of

14 Grisar, *Luther*, Vol. I, p. 25.

throwing Luther into greater relief which procured for this learned writer an unmerited place on the monument at Worms.

The demand for so-called forerunners of the Reformation originated in a tendency of the nineteenth century, which has now been more or less overcome. Scholars admit the disparity of the ways which led away from Rome and regard it as superfluous to posit any precursors for the great and original Luther.

It must be admitted, however, that in the theological schools of Luther's day there were certain preparations for his doctrine. The evidence for this statement is supplied by a glance at Nominalism, particularly in the form in which it was taught by Ockham. True, at the close of the Middle Ages philosophical and theological Nominalism prevailed in many universities, without any particular injury or separatism. The eminent nominalist Gabriel Biel was quite orthodox in his teaching. But here and there dangerous errors crept in with the Nominalism inspired by the singular mind of William of Ockham. Young Luther absorbed some of these with his reading. "I am a member of Ockham's school" (*factionis Occamicae*), he says and acknowledges this passionate and schismatic partisan of Lewis the Bavarian in his contest with the papacy as his teacher. Not as though he had educated himself by means of Ockham's politico-ecclesiastical writings, or that he had imbibed that author's so-called conciliar theories. But certain philosophical and theological views of Ockham and his disciple, Peter d'Ailly, did not fail to influence him and several other theologians of the Augustinian Order.

Ockham disputed the philosophical demonstrability of the existence of God, of the freedom of the will, and of the spirituality of the soul. He taught that these truths can be known with perfect certitude only through faith. A proposition may be false in philosophy but true in theology. The ultimate cause of the eternal law and of the distinction between good and evil is solely the divine will. *Per se* an unworthy individual might be found worthy of eternal life if God has so willed it. All depends upon the will of God (theory of acceptation); and no supernatural *habitus* is necessary in the just.

It is not difficult to discern a trace of these Ockhamist errors in the teaching of Luther. What is more important is that Luther, going beyond Ockham, took that external imputation which the latter propounded only as a possibility, for a reality and entirely eliminated sanctifying grace. Luther, like Ockham, taught that the same thing need not be true in philosophy as well as in theology. His repression of reason and his disregard of ecclesiastical authority were characteristics of Ockham. Both led him to assign to the emotions or to internal divine inspiration the rank of evidence, which, independently of the teaching of the Church, assured man of the true meaning of Holy Writ. The arbitrariness of God according to Ockham confirmed Luther in his dread of predestination. Finally, it is easy to see how Ockham's disregard of true Scholasticism must have reacted upon Luther's attitude towards the old school.

Gabriel Biel, whose works young Luther likewise studied, kept aloof from the Ockhamist errors, for which reason Luther attacked him and the "Gabrielists." Biel, under the influence of Ockham, unduly extended the limit of man's natural faculties in the realm of virtue, mistakenly appealing to St. Thomas and the other great Scholastics in defense of his theory. Biel minimized the effects of original sin, whereas Luther exaggerates them and combats the "sophists" of Scholasticism, as though they were unanimous in over-rating the powers of fallen man.

We are here confronted with the negative influence of Ockham. In contrast with what he had learned at school, Luther was led to adopt an extreme view, namely, the complete degradation of man's natural powers for good. This extreme antithesis confirmed him in his belief that all things are produced by the omnipotence of God. It was for this reason that he denounced the Scholastic theologians of the Middle Ages as well as those of his own time as "swine theologians," because they overestimated the powers of man and failed to appreciate the rôle of grace.

Rationalism and excessive criticism had gone too far in the Nominalistic schools. Luther was not the only one who was frightened by this tendency. But the true antidote did not consist in the extreme position adopted by Luther, asserting the absolute impotence of reason in matters of salvation.

The negative influence of Ockhamism on Luther also appears in his use of Holy Writ. Despite its appreciation of the Bible, Nominalism did not properly avail itself of the truths of Sacred Scripture in its treatment of theological questions. Guided by a correct sentiment, Luther opposes the study of the Bible to the preponderance of dialectics and the neglect of positive facts. But his preference for the Bible is extreme. According to him, the "Word," i. e., the word of God, is almost the only thing that should be considered. The "Word" should abolish the evils of the world. It was but a step from this attitude to proclaiming the Bible as the only source of faith, to the exclusion of tradition and the Church.

Thus Nominalism, in its Ockhamistic form, appears to be one of the factors which coöperated in the birth of the so-called Reformation, partly in virtue of its positive, partly as a consequence of its negative, influence.[15]

5. THE PSYCHOLOGICAL BACKGROUND

At the end of this rather lengthy discussion of the genesis and contents of the Lutheran dogma it is proper to indicate briefly how the principal doctrines of Luther were conformed to the personal mood of their discoverer. The new theories of grace and justification, which were at first intended to quiet the monk afflicted with a disordered temperament, were forthwith raised to a general norm. Precisely because everything was so absolutely personal with him, the discoverer of these ideas, so diametrically opposed to tradition, plunged into them with a vim that would be incredible were it not evidenced by his writings, especially his lectures on the Epistles to the Romans and to the Galatians, and by his disputations. His temperament furnishes the key to this remarkable phenomenon. He felt called upon to reveal to ignorant and misguided humanity the truth that had dawned on him—called by his office as doctor of theology; called upon also to denounce all abuses of doctrine and life. In reality the doctorate obliged him to teach according to the mind of the Church, who had invested him with this dignity and to whom he had promised obedience. He, on the contrary, proclaimed that he would speak freely because he had the apostolic commission to teach. As a doctor, he said, it was his duty to reproach all, even those who occupied the highest places, if they were guilty of wrong-doing.[16] It does not occur to him that, if he was desirous of effecting a genuine reform, he would have to direct his censures to the proper places and utter them in a becoming manner, not by blustering in the pulpit or before immature students.

In fact, he does not reflect at all, but allows himself to be carried away by his emotions. The fatal thing was that he believed himself to be moved by God.

Lacking the true concept of the Church and of ecclesiastical authority, the pseudo-mystic reformer believes that his ideas are inspired from above and his steps directed by God, whose guidance

---

[15] For a more detailed exposition of the influence of Ockhamism on Luther see Grisar, *Luther* (Engl. tr.), Vol. I, pp. 130 sqq., where the researches of Denifle are utilized. The relations of later Nominalism to the Lutheran heresy still await complete clarification.

[16] *Op. cit.*, Vol. I, p. 228.

he professes to follow blindly. He is convinced that he is not seeking temporal advantages, and we may not gainsay him when he declares that he is and desires to remain a poor monk. At the same time he perceives, not without a basis in fact, an excessively large number of evils in the life of Catholics. Their presence seems to justify, nay, to challenge his intervention. Consequently, he reasons, the efficacious hand of God must rest upon him, particularly since he desires only to exalt Christ.

Later, too, he always firmly believed that he was acting in conformity with "God's acts and councils," though this conviction, in matter of fact, did not persist in periods of "temptation."

Reviewing the commencement of his career as a reformer, Luther says that he went ahead "like a blinkered charger." [17] Basing upon his own example and his mystical theories he formulates the following principle: "No good work happens as the result of one's own wisdom; but everything must happen in a stupor." [18] It was not stupor nor intoxication, however, that inspired the great churchmen of the past to give expression to ideas that moved the world or to perform their benign deeds (such as the renewal of medieval life by St. Francis of Assisi, St. Dominic, and Gregory VII). Their achievements were the product of mature reflection, accompanied by humble self-denial, fervent prayer, and close attachment to the heart of the Church. They wrestled with difficulties without self-confidence. Luther is so full of self-confidence that he regards every contradiction as a confirmation of his position. For, as he repeatedly declared, both at the commencement of his career and afterwards, a good cause is bound to meet with contradiction; in fact opposition proves that it is acceptable to God.

And what about responsibility? "Christ may witness, whether the words I utter are His or mine; without His power and will even the pope cannot speak." Thus he writes to his fatherly friend Staupitz after the great movement had begun.[19] Despite the ravings of our opponents, he continues, I must now appear in public, though I have loved seclusion, and would much rather have preferred to be a spectator of the stimulating intellectual movement of our age, than to exhibit myself to the world. "I seek neither money, nor renown,

[17] Op. cit., Vol. VI, p. 163.
[18] Tischreden, Weimar ed., I, Nr. 406.
[19] Briefwechsel, I, p. 199 (May 30, 1518.)

nor glory. I possess only my poor body, which is bowed down with weakness and every kind of affliction. If I, whilst engaged in the service of God, had to sacrifice it to the cunning or power of my enemies, they would but shorten my life by one or two hours." There was no conquering such self-conceit. The appearance of goodness is a powerful motive. Luther during the entire progress of his tragic monastic development was deceived to a certain degree by the semblance of goodness.[20]

The result of his conflicts, as above described, though potentially dangerous to Christianity, is attributable not so much to an evil will or to any conscious intent to destroy, but rather to his abnormal character, to mystical "will-o'-the wisps," and to the prevalence of unusual abuses. It was not internal "corruption" that showed him the way; we have no proofs for such an assumption; but he was goaded by a combination of less culpable factors. In the background there always threatened the terrors of a just God and eternal predestination. The moral phenomena attending his first public appearance, the defects of his character, and his prejudice against good works, would seem to decide the question of responsibility against him. He incurred a clear and terrible responsibility when he was confronted by the adverse decision of the Church and her threat of excommunication. That he refused to submit to the divinely appointed authority was the great fault which entailed his ruin.

[20] Characteristic parallel traits are observable at the beginning of the last century in the religious Separatists in Bavaria, who also arrived at the Lutheran doctrine of justification by faith alone, etc. Cf. the articles on "Boos" and "Gossner" in the *Kirchenlexikon*.

Chapter V

FROM THE INDULGENCE THESES TO THE DISPUTATION
AT LEIPSIC (1517–1519)

1. THE CONTROVERSY ON INDULGENCES

In consequence of recent researches on the development of Luther, far less significance is to be attached to the celebrated controversy on indulgences which followed the theses of 1517, than tradition has ascribed to it. The ninety-five theses nailed to the door of the Wittenberg castle-church do not mark the commencement of the Protestant Reformation. As we have heard Luther himself intimate, the *initium evangelii* is to be sought in the new theology of Wittenberg and in the public movement which it created. The controversy concerning indulgences simply caused the movement to assume universal proportions. It placed the monk Luther upon the stage of the world and offered him an opportunity of gradually unveiling his revolutionary doctrine before all his contemporaries.

There was no room for indulgences in a system of grace and justification which attacked the meritoriousness of good works and the value of atonement.

Even before these ideas had fully matured (July 27, 1516), Luther delivered a sermon in which he expressed himself correctly on the Catholic doctrine of indulgences. Succeeding ages could have been benefited by his instructions. He correctly emphasized that an indulgence is not a remission of the guilt of sin, but "a remission of the temporal punishment due to sin, which the penitent would have to suffer, be it that it was imposed by the priest, be it that he had to suffer for it in purgatory." "In the gaining of a [plenary] indulgence, therefore," he says in conformity with the belief of the age in which he lived, "one may not then and there feel sure of salvation." "Only those gain a plenary remission of punishment who have become reconciled to God by true contrition and confession." At that time Luther still knew and appreciated the value of indulgences for the dead. The application of these, he explains in the same sermon, is made by way of intercession; hence a complete redemption of souls in each instance is not to be assumed. The foundation of indulgences he correctly states in these words: "They are the merits of Christ and His Saints [*i. e.*, they derive their efficacy from this treasury of merits], and we must, therefore, esteem them with all due reverence." Whatever abuses may have crept in, he holds that it is "most useful that indulgences should be offered and gained." [1]

The abuses indicated by Luther had reached a certain crisis in his day. Since good works are requisite for the gaining of an indulgence, and since it was customary at that time to require a small donation to be made to some pious or useful purpose, to procure delivery of the briefs of indulgence, indulgences were frequently made the means of collecting money. Exaggerated recommendations and avaricious practices combined to degrade them. The so-called *quaestores*, who wandered about plying this trade, were the chief culprits. [2] But many ecclesiastical superiors were also guilty of having increased the evil in the temple of the Lord by distributing indulgences with all too temporal trimmings and worldly bustle.

The extent to which even the papal curia went, may be seen in the case of the indulgences granted by Leo X, the proceeds of which were intended for the construction of St. Peter's basilica at Rome. This indulgence provided Luther, who had already drifted away from the Church, with an occasion for entering the lists against indulgences as such, and not merely the abuse of them.

Bishop Albrecht of Brandenburg, who governed the dioceses of Magdeburg and Halberstadt, a thoroughly worldly-minded ecclesiastic, had succeeded in having himself elected archbishop of Mayence. In order to unite these three bishoprics in one hand, he had to contribute no less than 10,000 ducats to the Roman curia. In addition to this, he was obliged to pay 14,000 ducats for the confirmation of his appointment as archbishop of Mayence and for the pallium. It was agreed that he might preach the indulgence for the construction of St. Peter's basilica throughout his extensive jurisdic-

---

[1] Grisar, *Luther*, Vol. I, pp. 324 sq. On the origin and the early development of indulgences cf. the excellent work of N. Paulus, *Geschichte des Ablasses im Mittelalter*, 3 vols., Paderborn, 1922–1923.

[2] N. Paulus, *op. cit.*, Vol. II, pp. 265 sqq., Vol. III, pp. 450 sqq., 471 sqq.

tion in Germany, retaining one-half of the proceeds to reimburse himself for the 10,000 ducats, which he had borrowed from the Augsburg firm of the Fuggers, whilst the other half was to be devoted to the erection of St. Peter's at Rome. Albrecht kept a sharp eye on the filling of the big indulgence chest which accompanied the preachers and was placed under the supervision of the Fuggers. It was a rather disedifying transaction. Even if it did not involve simony, strictly speaking, it was nevertheless reprehensible, and can be explained only as a result of the evil financial practices of the time, which had taken root also in Rome, and of the activities of the agents of Albrecht and an avaricious party of Florentine churchmen at the curia.[3]

Only gradually did Luther become aware of these agreements. The first motive of his intervention was supplied by his exasperation at the new indulgence enterprise and at the existing abuses in general. He personally witnessed an example of the general decline of the system of indulgences. In the castle-church the Elector of Saxony, Frederick "the Wise," kept a casket of relics, partly genuine and partly spurious, for which he succeeded in obtaining incredibly rich indulgences from Rome. Like the Elector Albrecht of Brandenburg, Frederick was a passionate collector of relics. Both were eager to have each relic enriched with great indulgences, so as to attract pious votaries and realize handsome profits at the annual exhibition. Up to the year 1518, Frederick succeeded in obtaining for his sacred casket in the castle-church of Wittenberg indulgences which amounted, all told, to 127,799 years.

Princely interests played a nefarious rôle in connection with the indulgence traffic of the Roman curia. Occasionally the rulers prohibited the too frequent indulgence-preaching within their territories, because they wished to prevent the flow to Rome of money which they needed for their own countries, or its expenditure for other purposes not agreeable to them. Thus the Elector Frederick prohibited the promulgation of the Mayence indulgence in behalf of St. Peter's within the confines of his principality.

Elector Albrecht selected John Tetzel, a popular orator of the Dominican Order, to preach the indulgence at Mayence. Tetzel was not much of a theologian. His morals were beyond reproach, de-

---

[3] Grisar, *Luther*, Vol. I, pp. 347 sqq.

spite the slanders to which he was subjected in the ensuing controversy. In his sermons, which were attended by large numbers of people, he adhered to the explicit directions of the ecclesiastical authorities of Mayence, although he was unable to abstain from rhetorical exaggerations. The directions of the Mayence authorities adequately emphasized that an indulgence is a remission of punishment, not of sin, and expressly required a contrite confession as a condition. In one respect, however, the directions were defective. They declared that an indulgence applicable to the dead became efficacious upon the performance of the prescribed good work, regardless of whether one was in the state of sanctifying grace or not. Some theologians held this opinion and it was embodied in several other episcopal instructions. The problems arising from the Church's teaching on indulgences had not yet all been clearly solved. The very nature of indulgences had not yet been dogmatically defined. It was a matter of practice, taught by the theologians; but its genuineness was warranted by the ordinary teaching authority of the Church (*magisterium ecclesiae ordinarium*).

Tetzel eagerly availed himself of the above-described, now abandoned, opinion concerning indulgences for the departed. It cannot be proved that he used the famous saw which has been attributed to him: "As soon as money in the casket rings—The soul its flight from Purgatory wings," but in substance his words approximated the proverb. Some critics looked with disfavor on Tetzel because he often, *e. g.*, at Annaberg, availed himself of the occasion of fairs with their secular amusements to proclaim the papal indulgence.[4]

There is an unwarranted report to the effect that when Staupitz had apprised him at Grimma of Tetzel's conduct, Luther exclaimed: "I shall put an abrupt stop to this, please God." When Tetzel, in the course of his preaching tour, had arrived at the confines of the electorate and in the vicinity of Wittenberg, Luther decided that the time for intervention had come. On November 1, the castle-church at Wittenberg celebrated its titular feast. The church was dedicated to All Saints and was specially indulgenced for that day. Many worshipers were sure to attend. On the eve of All Saints, Luther caused a Latin placard containing ninety-five theses on the subject of

---

[4] Cf. N. Paulus, *Johann Tetzel, der Ablassprediger*, Mayence, 1899; Grisar, *Luther*, Vol. I, pp. 341 sq.; Vol. IV, pp. 84 sq.

indulgences to be nailed to the door of the church, which was, at the same time, the university chapel.

The placard contained an invitation to a disputation. At first the Latin placard did not attract much attention except among scholars. But when Luther sent copies of it to the theologians of the neighboring universities of Leipsic, Frankfort on the Oder, and Erfurt, his theses began to attract attention. That they "spread throughout Germany in fourteen days" is "an erroneous representation, based on a later expression of Luther." [5] It is in keeping with the fables which have accumulated around the history of the theses. It is true that many, including well-intentioned but short-sighted Catholics, rejoiced that a courageous protest had been raised against the prevalent abuses in connection with the preaching of indulgences. Under the pressure of these abuses, the true meaning and import of the theses were easily overlooked.

Luther's placard was a challenge to a disputation designed to clarify a set of theses which constituted a fundamental, though guarded, attack on the Catholic doctrine of indulgences. The author had no intention of abandoning them in a learned discussion. His theological position would not permit of this. But he did not allow his novel dogmatic teaching, which stood behind the 95 theses, to appear on the surface. He maintained in his theses that indulgences were invalid before God, but were to be regarded only as a remission of the canonical penances imposed by the Church. He denied the doctrine of the treasury of merits earned by Christ and the saints, which constitutes the presupposition of indulgences. In addition to other erroneous views he expresses false notions about the condition of the departed. In defense of his attitude he seeks to place the absurdities of the indulgence preachers in the forefront as the reason and the subject of his theses. He goes so far as to say: "Let him who contradicts the truth of the papal indulgences be anathema and accursed"; and: "Bishops and priests are obligated to receive the commissioners of the papal indulgences with all due reverence." One sneering thesis asks: "Why does not the pope build the basilica of St. Peter with his own money, rather than with that of the poor, seeing that he is wealthier to-day than the richest Crœsus?" Towards the close he clothes his own sharp objections in the artificial garb of a suggestion to the effect that the objections of the laity against the pope and the

[5] Paul Kalkoff, *Luther und die Entscheidungsjahre der Reformation*, 1917, p. 22.

eleemosynary system ought to be clearly and thoroughly refuted, adding that "if sermons were preached after the mind and intention of the pope, these difficulties would be solved." In this manner the author of the theses thought he could, in a measure, safeguard his position.

Not to omit Mysticism, the last theses enjoin the obligation of striving not for the peace which indulgences seem to bring, but for the cross. Not *pax, pax,* should be the watchword, but *crux, crux.* "Christians must follow their Leader through suffering, death, and the pains of hell" (*per poenas, mortes, infernosque*). This corresponds with the idea, likewise expressed in the theses, that it is better voluntarily to suffer the penalties of sin than to escape them by means of indulgences. He also proclaimed (which was a general truth valid in all ages), that a Christian's entire life, according to the will of Christ, should be one continuous atonement.

The celebrated 95 theses are not a candid or an honest document. Neither are they a scientifically constructed or properly co-ordinated whole. Least of all, are they the programme of a reformation, as they are often represented to be.

The movement gradually assumed great dimensions. On the sixteenth of January, 1518, the eve of the feast of the dedication of the castle-church, Luther delivered in that church a sermon on indulgences which was in conformity with his theses.[6]

In a letter to Staupitz he laments in exaggerated language that "godless, false, and heretical doctrines" were propounded with such confidence in sermons on indulgences, that objectors were forthwith declared worthy of the stake. He, on the contrary, had modestly advanced his deviating opinions, which were "founded on the conviction of all the doctors and the entire Church, that it is better to make atonement than to seek for satisfaction by means of indulgences." Thereby he had invited the frightful wrath of the fanatical representatives of papal authority. [7]

We must not overlook the fact that some months before the publication of Luther's theses, Karlstadt had published 152 theses in conformity with the new doctrine. It seems Luther did not wish to be outstripped by his audacious friend. The controversy concerning in-

---

[6] N. Paulus in the *Zeitschrift für kath. Theologie,* 1924, pp. 630 sqq.
[7] *Briefwechsel,* I, p. 198.

dulgences, moreover, afforded him an opportunity of assuming the leadership of the Wittenberg movement in a popular field.

Soon after the posting of his theses, Luther wrote to the Archbishop of Mayence and to Jerome Schultz (Scultetus), bishop of Brandenburg, to whose jurisdiction Wittenberg was subject, in order to give an account of the events as he saw them. Archbishop Albrecht was also informed by the Dominicans, Tetzel and the brethren of his Order, and, for the sake of his own indulgence, immediately brought the matter before the supreme tribunal of the Church at Rome, by submitting a copy of the 95 theses and those of the disputation of September 4, 1517. Thereupon, on February 3, 1518, an Augustinian, Gabriel della Volta, was commissioned by Leo X, as representative of the General of the Augustinians, to charge Luther's superiors with the task of severely dissuading him from his perverted opinions, "lest a greater conflagration ensue as a result of negligence." It cannot be proved that the Pope originally styled the controversy an empty "quarrel between monks." Strict orders were issued by Della Volta to Staupitz, who, however, was not inclined to adopt thorough-going measures—an attitude which can easily be explained in view of his previous relations with Luther. Luther confidently wrote to him on March 31, 1518: "When God acts, no one can prevent Him; when He rests, no one is able to awaken Him." [8] Della Volta meanwhile summoned him to appear before the imminent chapter of his Order at Heidelberg, to give an account of himself. There a district vicar was to be selected to succeed him, since his three years' term of office had expired.

On the other side Tetzel and the Dominicans were not satisfied with a defense of their preaching. At Frankfort on the Oder, Tetzel published a series of theses on the doctrine of indulgences, which were couched in a moderate form and, generally speaking, correctly reflected the position of the Church. They were composed by Conrad Wimpina, a professor of that city, who afterwards became a literary opponent of Luther. Maintaining his position, Luther replied in a pointed sermon on indulgences and grace. Tetzel defended himself, again in a moderate form, in a printed "representation," in which he stressed Luther's violation of the papal authority. He published a second series of theses, which, in turn, were followed by Luther's

[8] *Briefwechsel*, I, p. 176.

booklet entitled: "Freedom of a Sermon on Indulgences." [9] It was written in a more provocative tone than Luther had thus far used.

The first outsider to enter the lists was Dr. John Eck, who was destined to achieve celebrity in his subsequent controversy with Luther. He was a professor of the university of Ingolstadt, a quick-witted humanist and theologian. He circulated "Obelisci," *i. e.*, annotations to Luther's theses in manuscript. Luther replied with "Asterisci," which were also originally circulated in manuscript form.

As the time for the chapter at Heidelberg approached, April, 1518, Luther undertook to safeguard his position. In the event of his refusal to recant, he had to fear that he would be delivered up to the ecclesiastical authorities—for such was the procedure of medieval jurisprudence—and in the event of obstinacy would be confronted with the severest ecclesiastical penalties. He procured from the Elector Frederick of Saxony an order for his unmolested return to Wittenberg. It was the first demonstration in behalf of Luther on the part of that ruler, whose friendship was destined to increase with the coming years.

The members of the chapter, or at least a majority of them, were favorably inclined towards Luther and the result of their deliberations was a verdict in favor of the defendant. It was a result entirely contrary to the expectations of the Roman authorities of his Order. [10] He was even granted the privilege of arranging a great disputation in the auditorium of the Augustinian monastery, which was conducted by Leonard Beier, a Wittenberg master. University professors and many guests attended. Beier and Luther argued against free will and the ancient theology. One of the Wittenberg professors who were in attendance interrupted the disputants when certain strong declarations were made, exclaiming: "If the peasants could hear this, they would stone you!" The Heidelberg chapter, so far as can be inferred, did not treat the problem of indulgences. Luther, now regarded as a courageous ornament of his Order, remained unmolested. Among the students of theology at the university, several were more or less won over by him. Some of them later on became

---

[9] On the correspondence between Luther and Tetzel see Grisar, *Luther,* Vol. IV, pp. 372 sqq., where the calm and heavy publications of Tetzel are compared with Luther's first impetuous polemical broadsides.

[10] Grisar, *Luther,* Vol. I, p. 334.

his helpers, such as John Brenz and Erhard Schnepf, and particularly Martin Butzer (Bucer), a talented young Dominican endowed with a very lively temperament.

On his homeward journey, Luther, who was delighted with the issue, delivered a sermon in Dresden in the presence of Duke George of Saxony and his court. He discoursed on the grace of Christ, eternal salvation, and the conquest of fear before an angry God. The duke, who was loyal to the Church, took great offense at these remarks. Several others also were indignant. When Luther heard of their objections, he disposed of them in these self-conscious words: These babblers desire everything and can do nothing; they are "a serpent's brood," "masked faces" whom I will ignore.[11]

His arrogance increased because of his having escaped punishment, because of the approval he met with, and because of the expected protection of the Elector Frederick. At the same time his writings and letters of those days reveal how he ever and anon calls up before his mind the abuses actually existing within the Church, especially the lucrative practices of the bishops and the Roman curia, in order to encourage himself and excite his anger. Unfortunately, the abuses furnished him with what he wanted. Oldecop, who was his pupil at that time, thus describes Luther's attacks which he continued at home, on the indulgence traffic and the doctrine of indulgences itself: "In his teaching against them, he exceeded all bounds, indulging in every kind of rage and blasphemy." He describes him on this occasion as "naturally proud and presumptuous." In a statement on indulgences and grace, composed at the behest of members of the Heidelberg chapter, Luther assured them that in his theses on indulgences he had spoken only by way of disputation, to ascertain the truth. In this way he constantly concealed his real opinion. However, in the "Resolutions" which he published in connection with his theses he expressed his attitude unequivocally. These Resolutions or "explanations" were intended to elucidate, defend, and confirm the entire series of theses. No dogmatic definition on indulgences having been issued, he pretended that there was no binding doctrine on the subject proposed by the *magisterium ordinarium* of the Church. He now proclaimed to the world his new doctrine on grace in a more definite outline.[12] He conceived the bold idea of dedicating his

[11] *Ibid.*, p. 335.
[12] *Ibid.*, pp. 335, 378 sq.

"Resolutions" to Pope Leo, and of forwarding them to Rome through Staupitz. He prefaced the work with an humble dedicatory epistle addressed to the head of the Church. Couched in superlative phraseology, it was designed to be an apologia of his conduct and an attack on his opponents. True, he tersely says: "I cannot recant," but towards the end of the epistle he bursts forth with the assurance: "Most Holy Father! I prostrate myself before thy feet, and offer myself to thee with all that I am and possess. Do as thou wilt; give life or death, call or recall, approve or disapprove; I will acknowledge thy voice as the voice of Christ who reigneth and speaketh in thee. If I have merited death, I shall not refuse to die." [13] How is this language to be explained? It constitutes one of the many riddles of his psychology. It need not be taken as hypocrisy, but is, rather, a reflection of the restless and profound struggles which buffeted him about between loyalty to the Church and the new position which he had assumed. It is possible that he wished to dispose the pope favorably and he may also have intended to allay the alarm of his many Catholic readers both at home and abroad. Nevertheless, a considerable lack of spiritual equilibrium is plainly noticeable. When his imagination is deeply roused, the ideas which agitate him at the moment often assume most exaggerated forms, but later are in turn easily displaced by contrary and equally vivid ideas. Concerning the pangs of conscience which afflicted him at the beginning of his revolt, he expressed himself thus on one occasion: "I was not happy or confident concerning that undertaking."—"What my heart suffered in the first and second year, and how I lay prostrate on the ground, nay, almost despaired, they [my opponents] did not know, who themselves afterwards attacked the pope with equal audacity." They were, he said, "ignorant of the cross and of Satan," whereas he "was compelled to go through terrible death-struggles and temptations."

In a remarkable passage of the "Resolutions" he describes these phenomena in detail, though he is not aware that his qualms of conscience are closely related to the neurotic precordial fear which he frequently suffered.

Apropos of indulgences for the departed, he wishes to picture the spiritual agonies of the souls in Purgatory, which were understood very well by such

<hr>

[13] *Ibid.*, p. 335; *Briefwechsel*, I, pp. 200 sq.

as at one time or another had suffered similar pains, but of which the indulgence-preachers had no conception. Then he proceeds in fantastic langauge: That eminent doctor [Tauler] with whom the Scholastic theologians are not familiar, speaks of such "dark nights of the soul"; and he himself is acquainted with one so afflicted (*i. e.*, himself; 2 Cor. XII, 2). The agonies are very brief, but so intense and infernal that no tongue can express, no pen can describe, no uninitiate can believe them. Were they to last but the tenth part of an hour, all of a man's bones would be reduced to ashes. "God, and simultaneously with Him, all creation, appears horribly angry. There is no escape, no comfort, whether within or without, only a hollow accusing voice." The sufferer regards himself as a reprobate, and does not even dare to say with the Psalmist: O Lord, rebuke not me in Thy indignation. He believes that he is saved, but suffers eternal punishment, and feels himself stretched on the cross with Christ, so that all his bones are numbered. There is not a nook of the soul that is not filled with bitter anguish, with terror, dread and sadness, accompanied by the stifling sense that it is to last forever. In order to make a weak comparison: when a bullet traces a line, every point in that line sustains the whole bullet, but it does not compass the whole bullet. Thus the soul feels when that deluge of eternity flows over it and drinks naught else but eternal pain; but this pain does not abide; it passes away. It is an infernal torture, an intolerable terror which excludes all consolation! Those who have experienced it must be believed.[14]

This is the language of a sick man. Here Luther actually depicts those phobias of traumatic neurosis which nervous persons experience as a result of a terrible shock. We must regard them as after-effects of the thunderbolt of Stotternheim. In his own opinion they were that darkness of soul so familiar to mystics. In his case physical fear was intimately associated with tortures of conscience, his internal doubts and that abiding sense of fear, in which he imagined God to be "horribly angry." In their most aggravated form, they were movements of precordial fear. Such psychopathic conditions were not adequately known to the medical science of his day. It was no pressure of circular "psychosis" which affected Luther in his monastic years, as a popular Protestant biographer would have us believe, who holds that monastic practices as such, when strictly and conscientiously performed, ordinarily induce a certain degree of

[14] Grisar, *Luther*, Vol. I, pp. 381 sq.; VI, 102; *Werke*, Weimar ed., I, p. 557; *Opp. Lat. Var.*, II, p. 180.

insanity.[15] Insanity cannot be ascribed in any sense to Luther while he was a monk. If one correctly understands his manifold testimonies, he simply experienced the effects of extreme nervousness from early youth to old age.

The "Resolutions" were followed by a tract on the "Force of Excommunication." It was inspired by anxiety about the condemnatory verdict of the pope. In order to allay his own fears as well as the fears of others, he wished to show that an unjust excommunication does not separate one from the soul of the Church. To justify his conduct he describes in lurid colors the abuses which attended the all too frequent use of the power of excommunication by the bishops.

2. THE HEARING AT AUGSBURG. MILTITZ

The German Dominicans reported to the Roman curia fresh accusations against the impetuous Augustinian. A certain rivalry between these two great and influential bodies may have to some extent prompted this procedure; but it was not the decisive motive. Older Catholic authors, relying too confidently on contemporaneous verdicts, have mistakenly endeavored to trace the origin of the religious schism to the jealousy that existed between the Dominican and the Augustinian orders, inasmuch as the former espoused the cause of Tetzel and his indulgence sermons, whereas the latter rose in defense of Luther and his courageous utterances. Whatever may have been in the background, as far as the attitude of Rome was concerned, the documents which were before the papal curia, namely, the Wittenberg theses, the disputations conducted there, the Heidelberg theses of Luther, and his "*Resolutiones*," decided the issue.

The Pope, acting in conformity with the law, through his fiscal procurator and the auditor of the camera, cited Luther to Rome, where he was to present himself within sixty days. At the same time, the theologian of the sacred palace (*magister sacri palatii*), the Dominican Sylvester Mazzolini, a native of Prierio (therefore called Prierias), was entrusted with the task of preparing an expert opinion. As he had evidently been exactly informed of the case some time before, he completed his task within three days. His printed opinion was a complete apologia for Tetzel and his teaching on indulgences.

[15] Adolph Hausrath; cfr. Grisar, *Luther*, Vol. I, p. 383.

He employed unnecessarily bitter expressions against Luther—following a custom in vogue in those times of controversies against heretics. He placed special emphasis on the power of the pope and his right of definitively deciding all ecclesiastical questions, which he set forth in most forceful terms.[16] When Sylvester's pamphlet with the citation to Rome reached Luther, he realized to his consternation, as he tells us, how serious the situation really was. He made a hasty, all too hasty, decision and published an indignant response (*Responsio*) to Prierias.[17] Relative to the citation, he on the very next day issued a written appeal for help to the Elector, requesting that dignitary to insist that the case be tried in Germany. Frederick "the Wise" was in attendance at the diet of Augsburg at the time.

This diet was also attended by the papal legate, Cardinal Cajetan de Vio, a highly respected Dominican theologian. The Elector told him that he would not let his university professor go to Rome. In the meantime (August 9), the Emperor Maximilian had sent a vigorous letter to the Pope, assuring him that he would execute the decision of the Holy See against Luther with all his energy. Luther's efforts to prevent this course had proved futile. Assured of imperial support, the curia decided to accelerate the procedure against the growing evil. It was also intended to comply with the request of the Elector to have the hearing conducted in Germany in order to secure the help of this powerful prince in the war against the Turks. For this reason Cardinal Cajetan received orders from Rome to summon Luther to appear before him in person to recant his errors. The order was accompanied by another, to the effect that Luther, in the event of his refusal to recant, should be apprehended forthwith and delivered to the Roman authorities. The Elector and the provincial of the Saxon Augustinians received simultaneous orders to assist in apprehending Luther in case such a measure should become necessary. On September 11, the legate received a further document from Rome, empowering him to conduct the case against Luther according to his own discretion.

Luther appeared before Cajetan at Augsburg, on October 12. The first hearing and the subsequent meetings were fruitless. With moderation and dignity Cajetan demanded the retraction of two theses of Luther's: one denying the treasury of merits gained by

[16] *Op. cit.*, Vol. IV, pp. 373 sq.
[17] *Op. cit.*, Vol. IV, 374 sq.

Christ and the Saints, which was the foundation of the doctrine of indulgences; the other, contained in the *"Resolutiones,"* asserting that faith alone renders the Sacraments of the Church efficacious. He disregarded the other theses because, although false, they did not so patently offend against theological truths. As to the treasury of merits, many theologians, among them Cajetan himself, held that it had already been defined by Pope Clement VI. In any event, like the independent efficacy of the Sacraments, it constituted an important doctrine of theology.

Despite all his kindness and determined earnestness, Cardinal Cajetan's efforts proved futile. Luther manifested arrogance and offensive obstinacy. Dismissed with the threat of excommunication, he announced to the Cardinal that he would appeal from his tribunal "to the Pope, who would be more correctly informed." To others he said that this was but a preparation for an appeal to a general council, which was bound to follow in case the Pope, "in the plenitude of his authority, or rather tyranny," would reject his appellation. Luther did not tarry for a reply from the hesitating Cardinal, but secretly fled from the city and hastened back to Wittenberg.

The Cardinal had also made advances to the Elector, in order to influence his attitude regarding the election of a German king in conformity with the intentions of Rome. Frederick subsequently asserted that he had obtained from Cajetan the promise that Luther would be returned to Germany in any event. It is certain that the scholarly and gentle prince of the Church was no match for the cunning diplomacy of the Elector.

The formerly popular legend of Cajetan's haughty treatment of Luther is now admitted to be unhistorical even by Protestant writers. The Cardinal is described as "humble, just, and self-sacrificing" and his conduct towards Luther as dignified; he is admitted to have been "an earnest and, in his judgment concerning the abuses prevalent at the curia, a strict and free-spoken thinker." [18] Luther, on the contrary, accuses him of being "most wofully ignorant" and of having treated him like a lion.[19]

---

[18] Paul Kalkoff, *Luther und die Entscheidungsjahre,* pp. 57, 157; IDEM in *Kirchengesch. Forschungen, E. Brieger dargebracht,* 1912, and in the *Theol. Studien und Kritiken,* 1917, p. 246. Similarly Hermelink in the *Theol. Rundschau,* 1917, p. 141.

[19] *Briefwechsel,* I, p. 282.

The question which now tormented Luther was whether he would be safe at Wittenberg. He thought of going to Paris, where the theological faculty of the University was engaged in a quarrel with Rome. But his friend Spalatin, a preacher at the court of the Elector Frederick, provided protection through that ruler. Luther entered into a lively correspondence with Spalatin, through whom he assured the prince that he would gladly go into exile rather than embarrass him through the fury of his enemies. In the interim, on November 28, he appeared before a notary and two witnesses, and drew up a solemn appeal to a general council. In the lengthy formula he declared his intention to do or say naught against the Roman Church, the teacher and head of all the churches, nor against the authority of the Pope—as long as the latter were well advised (*bene consultus*). The affidavit was signed, as the subscription of the notary attests, "in the chapel of Corpus Christi, situated in the cemetery of the parish church." The little church was a pretty structure erected in honor of "Christ's holy body," such as adorned many a churchyard in those days.

Luther's appeal to an ecumenical council, like his former appeal, was inadmissible and ineffective. According to canon law, an appeal to a council was a penal offense. This provision was justified by the answer to the question: Has any individual who wishes to create a schism within the Church the right to convoke all the bishops of the world to a council, prior to his submission?

On December 18, the Elector addressed a letter to Cardinal Cajetan, in which he disclosed to the latter the line of action he had resolved upon with reference to his protégé, and to which he always adhered. Luther's doctrine, he said, had not as yet been proven heretical; Luther was prepared to appear before a university for a disputation and formal examination; hence, nothing could be done to him at Wittenberg. But Rome proceeded directly, though, out of regard for the Elector and his participation in the great questions of ecclesiastical policy which were then pending, it proceeded with notable slowness. At first an attempt was made to influence Frederick by sending him the Golden Rose blessed by the Pope. It was customary to send it annually to a prince as a mark of distinction. The presentation was to have been made by the Roman notary and titular chamberlain, Karl von Miltitz. The selection of this Saxon nobleman was not a happy one. Miltitz undertook his commission with great pomp, but in the end executed it in a very ineffective manner. He was an incompetent man and a seeker of benefices.

In order to persuade Frederick to deliver up Luther, Miltitz, of his own accord, adopted wrong methods. In the Dominican monastery at Leipsic he overwhelmed Tetzel with unmerited and bitter reproaches, which are said to have hastened his death. Luther consented to make a doubtful promise to the importunate agent, who exceeded his commission, namely, to observe silence if his opponents did the same. There could be no question of a general silence on the Catholic side in view of the ever increasing dangers that threatened the Church; and, on the other hand, Luther was far from expecting his opponents to observe silence, or from being silent himself. Under the influence of Miltitz, Luther at that time published a curious work under the title of *"Unterricht"* (Instructions), etc., which contained both affirmations and negations, in order to conciliate his opponents.

Miltitz sent boastful reports of the success of his efforts to the Roma curia, and they were not entirely devoid of effect. The death of Emperor Maximilian, on January 12, 1519, and the fact that Frederick of Saxony had some prospects of becoming emperor, supplied Leo X with a reason for new delays. Finally the Pope, in a friendly brief (*Paterno affectu*), issued March 29, 1519, summoned Luther to Rome to receive personal instructions and abandon his erroneous doctrines. It cannot be proved that the treatment accorded Luther was severe and ill-considered. When the brief arrived, steps had already been taken by Luther for the Leipsic disputation, which destroyed every hope of arriving at an understanding. At Rome this measure occasioned the termination of the trial which had already been too long drawn out.

Luther's pen was not exclusively devoted to attacks. With impetuous activity he had in the meanwhile composed a series of tracts which, beside those mentioned above, were dedicated in part to a glorification of his cause, and in part written to pastoral requirements. His popular religious writings were intended to invest him with the indispensable reputation of a man who was solicitous solely about the welfare of souls. This activity gained for him a large following among religious-minded people. Among other things he published, in that period of stress, a serviceable explanation of the Our Father, a short instruction on confession, a condensed explanation of the Decalogue, and an interpretation of Psalm CIX (Vulg. CX). Even before this he had entered the field of popular literature with an exposition of the seven penitential Psalms, a sermon on the Ten Commandments, and some other smaller writings.

His history of the Augsburg trial (*Acta Augustana*), on the other hand, as well as his edition of the "Replica" of Sylvester Prierias against his "Responses," were polemical. By publishing a reprint of the "Replica" of the Master of the Sacred Palace, he intended to represent Prierias as a man entirely devoid of importance and worthy of disdain.[20]

3. THE DISCOVERY IN THE TOWER

An essential element was still missing in the new theology, as it appears in Luther's exposition of St. Paul's Epistle to the Romans, in his early disputations, and in the writings which he had thus far published.

He was unable to discover an adequate answer to the distressing question: How can we be personally certain that Christ's merits are imputed to us, and that we are in a state of grace? The Church told him that whoever sought justification by true penance, should be certain of it. Faithful souls in a normal state were not tortured by doubts on this point; but they did not conceive this certitude as really a certitude of faith in the strict and proper sense, as an object of revelation, which would have been erroneous. However, the teaching of the Church and her practice did not satisfy the restless soul of Luther; nor was he content with the results of his own study. His demand of perfect surrender (*humilitas*) to almighty God, coupled with resignation to whatever He might decree, appeared insufficient even to himself to engender that perfect certainty of the state of grace for which he longed. The reason was that his God was the arbitrary God of Ockhamism.

Hence, he conceded, in painful language, the endurance, yea the increase of his fear of a wrathful and avenging Deity. The word *justitia*, he said, had ever persecuted him and often entered into his soul like a flash of lightning.[21] Fear agitated the morbid substratum of his soul. He assures us that he felt most distressed at the time he was about to deliver his second series of lectures on the Psalms. It

[20] Grisar, *Luther*, Vol. IV, p. 375.
[21] *Op. cit.*, Vol. I, pp. 374 sqq.

was synchronous with his appeal to a general council, in the winter semester of 1518 to 1519. Beginning with 1516, one is able to see how, step by step, he gradually advances toward the conclusions which he had laid down in his second exposition of the Psalms, namely, the dogmatic certitude of personal justification. In the works which he published in 1518 he confidently announces this result. The publications which embody this conclusion are the second commentary on the Psalms (*Operationes in Psalmos*), the shorter explanation of the Epistle to the Galatians, and the sermons on "twofold and threefold righteousness." [22] In what manner did he arrive at this conclusion? The answer is supplied by the so-called discovery in the tower.

On various occasions during his later life, Luther spoke freely of this capital discovery. Thus in the preface to his Latin works, edition of 1545,[23] he describes how his discovery in the tower of the monastery was connected with a passage in the Epistle to the Romans (I, 17): "For the justice of God is revealed therein [*i. e.*, in the Gospel], leading men from faith unto faith [*i. e.*, unto the believing], according as it is written: The just shall live by faith." (Cf. Hab. II, 4).

"Until now," Luther says in the preface, "the words, 'the justice of God is revealed in the Gospel,' were an obstacle to me. For I hated the words, 'justice of God,' which I had been taught, in conformity with the usage and custom of all doctors [!], to comprehend philosophically, namely, of the so-called formal or active justice, by which God is just and punishes the sinners and the unjust. Although I was a monk without reproach, I felt myself to be a sinner in the sight of God, suffered the greatest spiritual unrest, and could not consolingly imagine God as reconciled by my atonement. Consequently, I did not love, but rather hated the just God who punished sinners." The ancient law of the Decalogue already threatened sinners with dire punishment, and now, as he understood that passage, God intended to proclaim His anger and avenging justice through the Gospel. "Thus I raved (*furebam*), and my mind conjured up terrors and confusion. Importunately I sounded the text and thirsted to know its purport." While in this frame of mind, the significance of the words, "the just man liveth by faith," suddenly became clear to him. He saw that the

---

[22] *Op. cit.*, Vol. I, pp. 386 sq.

[23] *Opp. Lat. Var.*, Erlangen ed., I, pp. 15 sqq. Cf. Grisar, *Luther*, Vol. I, pp. 388 sqq.

"justice of God" was identical with the justice which the just and holy God bestows by means of faith upon those who are to be justified and did not denote avenging justice, as everybody else imagined. He had discovered, not active but passive justice, as he phrases it.

"I felt completely reborn and believed I was entering paradise through open portals. . . . Henceforth I praised the word justice with as much love as I had formerly pursued it with hatred." He concludes that he was confirmed in his interpretation by reading the works of St. Augustine.

Relative to Luther's assertions concerning the sequence of these events, two things should be noted. The assertions were made long after the event. The most detailed, which we have just cited, was made twenty-seven years later, after an agitated life spent in controversies. It is natural, therefore, that the revelation he claimed he had received is no longer as prominent as in other passages of his writings.[24] The definitely expressed content was the alleged efficacy of faith alone, namely, the absolute certitude of personal justification to be obtained from "*sola fides*," i. e., the confidence engendered by faith. As a result of his later experiences and owing to the progress of his doctrines, this idea appears somewhat obscured in Luther's subsequent account. The time and place were more clearly fixed in his memory.

It is not true that "all the doctors" up to his time understood Rom. I, 17, of the avenging justice of God, and that Luther was the first to perceive the correct meaning of the phrase, namely, the concept of justice by which God makes men just. This assertion is reiterated in Luther's commentary on Genesis and was popularized by Melanchthon in his short biography of the Reformer.[25] The very contrary is true. Denifle has reviewed all the ancient commentators in a careful monograph [26] and shows "that not one Christian commentator from the days of Ambrosiaster up to the time of Luther, interpreted the Pauline passage in the sense of an avenging justice or an angry God, but that all understood it as referring to the justifying God, His justifying grace, and the former exegetes had spoken of justifica-

[24] *Op. cit.*, Vol. VI, pp. 504 sqq.

[25] *Commentar. in Genesim*, see chap. 27. *Opp. Exeg.*, VII, p. 74. Melanchthon, *Vita Lutheri* (*Corp. Ref.*), VI, p. 159.

[26] *Quellenbelege zu Luther und Luthertum: Die abendländischen Schriftausleger bis Luther über Iustitia Dei* (*Rom. I, 17*) *und Iustificatio*, pp. xx and 380 with quotations from 65 exegetes (Mayence, 1905).

tion of faith." [27] Hence, Luther had not made a new discovery, but taught the acquisition of justice in a far different manner. Denifle also showed how tradition contradicts Luther and corroborates the ancient teaching of the Church that justification is obtained only through faith animated by charity (*fides caritate formata*) and not through the Lutheran formula *sola fide*. Luther's assertion about the teaching of the ancient commentators can only have originated in the fact that he had not read, or else had not understood some of them we know he had read. His subsequent utterance is a sign of the self-delusion into which he gradually fell under the influence of self-interest.

It was while he was somberly meditating on Rom. I, 17, that, at the end of 1518, his mind was enlightened in a tower at the southeastern corner of the monastery, next to the garden. In the second story of this tower there was a so-called hypocaust, *i. e.*, a furnace-room, and beneath it the toilet (*cloaca*) of the monks. The hypocaust served Luther as a study. [28] He mentions the tower and the *cloaca* in 1532, in a passage of his Table Talks, where he speaks of the place of his illumination. The conversation was recorded by his pupil and friend, John Schlaginhaufen, who wrote down the short conversation at table for his private collection of Table Talks. [29] Schlaginhaufen, since 1531, resided at Luther's house, the former Augustinian monastery, as an expectant for a position as pastor. In the interval between July and September of the following year, Luther spoke in his presence of the terrors he had suffered at the thought of divine justice. While in the tower, he said, he had pondered the words: The just man lives by faith. His spirit rose and the conclusion flashed upon him: Therefore, it is God's justice which justifies and saves us. "Those words became more gratifying to me. On this *cloaca* the Holy Ghost inspired me with this apt interpretation."

The two references of Schlaginhaufen to the Holy Ghost and the tower are repeated in the same connection by other contemporaneous collectors of Table Talks, who were not present at the conversation, but had Schlaginhaufen's manuscript before them. Thus, Conrad Cordatus reports Luther's words as follows: "The Holy Ghost inspired

[27] Thus Denifle summed up the results of his investigation in *Luther und Luthertum*, 2nd ed., pp. 387 sq.

[28] E. Kroker in the *Archiv für Reformationsgeschichte*, 1920, pp. 300 sqq.

[29] *Tischreden*, Weimar ed., II, p. 177, no. 1681. The word *cloaca* is represented by the letters *cl*.

me with this solution in this tower." [30] He, too, lived in the same house with Luther, was familiar with the place, and adds in the introduction to Luther's words that the "privy" of the monastery was there. George Rörer, also a pupil of Luther and a most reliable collector of his *Table Talks*, quotes Luther as saying: "The spirit of God has inspired me with this interpretation on the *cloaca*." [31] Anton Lauterbach reports that Luther concluded his description of this event thus: "The Holy Spirit revealed the Scriptures to me in this tower." [32] The repeated use of the pronoun "this" permits the inference that it was thought that Luther indicated the tower with his finger. The hypocaust is mentioned only by Lauterbach at the beginning of the Table Talk, thus: "Once when I was reflecting in this tower and hypocaust." The question may be raised why he inserted the word *hypocaust* in Schlaginhaufen's story.

It is of little moment, whether the enlightenment came to Luther in the *cloaca* itself, as seems to have happened, or in the hypocaust, which was his study. [33] In fact, it is of even less moment than might appear from the elaborate discussions of Protestant authors who favor the elimination of the word *cloaca* from the narrative. The matter was quite indifferent to Luther and his aforementioned pupils; only the timid Schlaginhaufen seems to have taken offense at it, since he does not write out the word in full, but only insinuates it with the letters *cl*. That he understood that the *cloaca* was meant when Luther pointed out the place, is not subject to doubt, according to the Protestant author of the new critical edition of the Table Talks, though some still place a different and deviating interpretation on the letters *cl*. [34] Luther, as Kawerau emphasizes, was of the opinion that the Spirit of God has a free hand everywhere, even on the *cloaca*. [35]

Such was Luther's experience in the tower, of which he later says

[30] *Ibid.*, III, p. 228, no. 3232a.

[31] *Ibid.*, II, p. 177, n. 1. Here the word *cloaca* is written out in full.

[32] *Ibid.*, III, p. 228, no. 3232c (Bindseil, *Colloquia*). Likewise Kaspar Khumer (*ib.* no. 3232b): *"Diese Kunst hat mir der Heilige Geist auf dieser cloaca auf dem Torm gegeben."*

[33] Kroker assumes the hypocaust to be the place. (*Jahrbuch* etc.; see note 34.)

[34] Kroker in the *Jahrbuch der Luthergesellschaft*, I (1919), pp. 112 sqq., assumes that Schlaginhaufen had misunderstood Luther. This possibility is not to be entirely excluded. Nevertheless Schlaginhaufen was quite certain, since he preferred to conceal what he had heard, yet expressed it with *cl*.

[35] G. Kawerau, *Luther in katholischer Beleuchtung*, Leipsic, 1911, p. 60.

that for a long time he knew not what he was about, when from the verse, "The just man lives by faith," a light burst upon him which terminated one period of his life. "Thereupon," he says, "I went through." [36]

So much is certain: Luther's experience in the tower may claim to be one of the most important and far-reaching events of his life. In its essential features it does not permit of contradiction. The feeling of joy which Luther tells us he experienced immediately after, is quite comprehensible and does not provoke the least historical objection. Psychologically it is not only possible, but characteristic of the spirit which moved Luther. Of course, the Catholic ascetic will view the sudden emotion of joy in quite a different light than Luther's admirers.

It is evident to any impartial observer that the new theological doctrine of the certitude of salvation or, let us rather say, the certainty of justification, was a deduction completely adapted to Luther's state of mind, as it soothed him in his sad personal struggle. He erected it into an article of faith, to be believed by all. That one must firmly believe that one is in the state of grace became a dogma of the Lutheran faith.

In a similar manner Luther erected the personal experiences of his own way of suffering into a general norm for all. Even at that time he taught—and always adhered to this doctrine—that God leads those whom He wishes to justify, through darkness and fears; that the road of despondency *per se* leads to salvation. On one occasion he wrote that no man has a right to converse about divine things unless he has experienced those things, and among those who have not he classes the papists and the visionaries who deviated from his doctrine.

But Luther was not able to maintain himself in the certainty to attain which cost him so much labor. In the sequel he often admitted, sorrowfully, that this was not possible for him except at the cost of severe trials and ever new struggles. [37] He instructed all that life is nothing but a laborious contest for this ineffable good and that assurance of grace depends on vigorous endeavors and daring defiance, which, however, are not everyman's business.

[36] *Tischreden,* Weimar ed., V, no. 5518.
[37] Grisar, *Luther,* Vol. V, Ch. XXXII, especially no. 6.

4. THE LEIPSIC DISPUTATION OF 1519 AND THE
PAPAL PRIMACY

After Luther's trial at Augsburg, the controversy about indulgences began to wane before other more important questions connected with his revolt. Among these the primacy of the pope gradually began to take precedence.

While the subject of indulgences was still burning, Cardinal Cajetan had availed himself of his stay at Augsburg to compose a series of scholarly treatises on the doctrine of indulgences. [38] He also drew up a scheme for a doctrinal decree of Leo X on this question. This highly important papal decree, which definitely determined the traditional teaching of the Church, appeared on November 9, 1518. [39] Cajetan, who was an excellent commentator of St. Thomas Aquinas, also perceived the importance of the doctrine of the primacy in view of the progress of the Lutheran controversy. He began the composition of a scholarly work, On the Divine Institution of the Roman Pontificate over the Universal Church, which appeared in 1521 and was immediately reprinted at Cologne by Peter Quentell. [40]

John Eck, a theologian of Ingolstadt, shared Cajetan's conviction that the question of papal supremacy would become the real and decisive battleground for the future. The Catholic cause is indebted to his versatile and powerful pen for the comprehensive Latin work, Of the Primacy of Peter, Three Books against Ludder, which originally appeared at Ingolstadt in 1520. [41]

In defending the spiritual supremacy of the successors of St. Peter in Rome, both writers, the Italian and the German, appealed most emphatically with the entire Catholic tradition to Christ's words addressed to the Apostle after the latter had solemnly professed his faith in His divinity: "Thou art Peter, and upon this rock I will build my church, and the gates of hell shall not prevail against it" (Matt. xvi, 18). They likewise quoted the immortal words of the Saviour, when, after His resurrection, He confided His sheep to the pastoral care of Peter on the shores of Lake Tiberias: "Feed my lambs, feed my sheep" (John xxi, 15 sqq.). By means of this concept of the Church, founded

[38] F. Lauchert, Die italienischen Gegner Luthers, 1918, p. 141.
[39] Kalkoff, Luther und die Entscheidungsjahre, pp. 86–88.
[40] Lauchert, op. cit., pp. 142–155.
[41] Wiedemann, Dr. Joh. Eck, 1865, p. 517.

by Christ as the visible spiritual kingdom of the faithful, they further-more demonstrated that, subject to its invisible Head, namely, the Son of God, there must be a visible head to govern this spiritual so-ciety, in order to bind its members in the necessary unity and to pre-serve it from dissolution. They appealed to the history of the Church from the time of its inception for illuminating proofs of the fact that the successors of St. Peter in the see of Rome had always possessed the supreme power in governing the Church, though a progressive development in the use of that power must be acknowledged. They emphasized that all centuries, up to their own, were replete with most glorious achievements on the part of the papacy, though there had been a few unworthy popes. Guided by God, the papacy had conferred upon mankind the golden gifts of Christian civilization and culture, resisted the arrogance of mighty rulers, protected the rights of the lowly, and raised the heart of humanity to celestial things. Finally, they maintained, it was a crime against the will of Christ, against the foundation of the divine temple of the Church, against the duty of gratitude towards the society of the faithful which had been nur-tured by the papacy, to attack the rights of the occupant of the Holy See.

John Eck, the most successful and most celebrated defender of the papacy against Luther in Germany, was born in the town of Eck in Swabia. His real name was John Mayr. In 1510 he became a professor at the University of Ingolstadt and, at the same time, canon of the cathedral of Eichstätt. Thoroughly conversant with humanism, this learned theologian corresponded with a large number of the most prominent men of the age. He was known for his cleverness in scientific discussions, was well-read and endowed with a stupendous memory. These gifts were supplemented by extraordinary physi-cal powers; he was a gigantic man who, when engaged in disputation, was wont to dominate the situation with his stentorian voice.

In May, 1518, Karlstadt had published a series of theses against Eck's "Obelisci" at Wittenberg. Eck not only replied with a set of other theses, but challenged him to a public disputation, to be con-ducted at one of the great university cities, Rome, Paris, or Cologne. Leipsic was finally selected, and Eck endeavored to obtain the con-sent of Duke George, who was reputed to be a great patron of schol-arly pursuits. Prior to the meeting, however, Eck published twelve theses, which were expressly, though somewhat covertly, directed against the person of Luther and his doctrines. The final thesis dealt with the Roman primacy. Luther, in the "Resolutions" which he had appended to his theses on indulgences, had asserted (though without denying the rights of the existing primacy) that he knew of no primacy of Rome over the universal Church, at least not over the Oriental Church, before the time of Gregory the Great, *i. e.*, about the year 600. Eck in his final thesis against Luther says: "We deny that the Roman Church had no precedence over the other churches before the age of Sylvester (died 335), and acknowledge him who occupies the see of St. Peter as the successor of Peter and the universal vicegerent of Christ." Luther indignantly declared that he was the one who had been challenged to the projected disputation. In this he was not entirely wrong. Nevertheless he made up his mind to participate in the Leipsic discussion. In the beginning of February, 1519, he published twelve antitheses against Eck, and soon after, boldly added a thirteenth against the authority of the pope. Although his most intimate friends had hitherto cautioned him not to revolt against Rome, "the thirteenth thesis appears entirely too audacious, nay, absolutely untenable, even to more recent Protestant writers." [42] This thesis declared that his opponents could base their proofs for the primacy only on the "frosty decretals of the last four centuries."

Luther expected to take part in the disputation and to surprise his opponents with historical arguments. Accordingly, he delved into history to discover proofs for the negation, which, as far as he was concerned, was irrefragable even without proofs. In his letters of that period he repeatedly spoke of the hydra of the papacy, against which it was his duty to launch an attack. His previous activities, he said, now appeared to him as mere child's-play by comparison. "The Lord pulls me, and I follow Him not unwillingly." In this pseudo-mystical frame of mind—led by the hand of God, as he imagined—he arrived historically and Scripturally at the discovery that the pope was Antichrist. [43] He finds that the mysterious words in the second chapter of Thessalonians, and those in the first Epistle of St. John (ii, 18) on the advent of Antichrist, are not applicable to a particular person, as tradition would have it, but to the papacy as an institution, whose anti-Christian nature, now that the end of the world was nigh, must be exposed by him, the witness chosen of God.

[42] Köstlin-Kawerau, *Martin Luther*, 5th ed., Berlin, 1903, Vol. I, p. 235.
[43] Cf. Grisar, *Luther*, Vol. III, pp. 142 sqq.

This idea, which was to control his later life, soon struck deep roots in him.

On December 11, 1518, he announced his "presentiment" to Wenceslaus Link. In a letter of March 13, 1519, addressed to his friend and helper at the Electoral court, Spalatin, he speaks more clearly: "In connexion with my disputation, I am reviewing the decretals of the popes, and—I whisper it into your ear—am uncertain whether the pope is himself Antichrist, or an apostle of Antichrist, so awfully is Christ, *i. e.*, the truth, crucified in the decretals." He penned these lines only two months after he had addressed his fawning letter of submission to Pope Leo. Soon the mask drops from his face entirely. Without awaiting the disputation, he publishes his conclusions in a set of Latin "Resolutions" on the aforementioned thirteenth thesis, in which he complains that no one wishes to acknowledge that Antichrist "sitteth in the temple of God at Rome." (2 Thess. ii, 4).

The day of the disputation was approaching, and as yet Luther had not been invited. Duke George of Saxony was still opposed to his taking part in it. Some of the bishops attempted to prevent the disputation, because, no matter what its outcome might be, in their opinion it would only serve to spread the innovations, and because the final decision lay solely with the supreme ecclesiastical tribunal. Their efforts, however, were futile.

Impelled by an intense desire to fight, Luther accompanied his friend Karlstadt to Leipsic, where, at the last moment, he was permitted to participate in the disputation. He afterwards said that he entered the disputation under the aegis of Karlstadt. The oratorical contest began June 27, in the great aula of the Pleissenburg, in the presence of the duke and his court, the professors of the university, and many other scholars who had come from far and near.

Karlstadt had first to dispute with Eck. The disputation between these two men, mainly on free will, lasted up to July 2, inclusively. Karlstadt showed himself inferior to Eck in versatility and knowledge. He was small of stature and his voice was hoarse; he was often timid. The audience became bored because his defective memory compelled him to consult books to prove his assertions. The weather was hot and quite a number of professors fell asleep.

The audience was aroused when, on July 4, Luther appeared at the lecturer's desk with a bouquet in his hand, which he, from time to time, held to his nose, after the manner of one who pretends superiority. His finger was adorned with a shining silver ring. For the rest he wore his monastic habit. Mosellanus (Peter Schade of Bruttig), the humanist, who was present, says that, seeing his medium-sized slender frame, one was almost able to count Luther's bones, a condition resulting from worry, study, and labor. He also reports that Luther spoke in a high, clear voice. Tradition has it that he distinguished himself by an extraordinary adroitness in the use of Scriptural texts. He did not measure up to the clarity and demonstrative force of Eck, who, moreover, by his ready wit and acuteness in detecting contradictions, defects and sudden transitions, showed up many a weak point in Luther's argument. This is proved by the report of the proceedings drawn up by the notaries who were present.

The two disputants were supposed to discuss, in turn, the papacy, indulgences, Purgatory, and other controversial topics. However, the debate on the papacy consumed almost the entire time. Shrewdly appraising the situation, Eck, on July 5, cited the ecumenical Council of Constance, which had condemned Hus as a heretic for denying the primacy. He did this in order to compel Luther to make a definite profession of faith. Luther at first replied that he was certain that among the condemned propositions of Hus there were many which were quite Christian and evangelical, and which the universal Church could not condemn. From this Eck at once drew the conclusion that he (Luther) did not even recognize the ecumenical councils. His opponent became startled and sought to retrace his steps, saying that perhaps those decrees of the Council of Constance were not genuine; for the rest, he contended, the word of God alone is infallible. Then he modified this latter statement by saying that while conciliar resolutions in matters of faith are binding, they may sometimes be erroneous. Eck pinned him to his assertion that the Council of Constance may have erred in the question of the primacy, and inexorably confronted him with all the inferences implied in that assertion. Indignant at Luther's temerity, bluff Duke George, who was loyal to the Church, exclaimed in a voice loud enough to be heard throughout the great hall: "A plague on it!"

On July 14, Purgatory, indulgences, and penance formed the subject of disputation between Eck and Karlstadt, but nothing further was accomplished except that Eck clearly defined the position of the Church, whilst Karlstadt denied the authority of the Church. At the conclusion of the disputation, on July 15 (16), it was agreed to submit the minutes to the universities of Erfurt and Paris, which, however, also proved ineffective.

Luther was uneasy at the result of the controversy. After he had returned home, he wrote to Spalatin that the Leipsic disputation had commenced badly and ended badly, and that Eck and the men of Leipsic were to blame, because they did not seek the truth, but their own glory. He indemnified himself before the public by publishing, towards the end of August, elucidations on the theses which had been discussed at Leipsic. In these he proclaimed, even more decisively than before his adhesion to his own assertions, and distorted the position of his opponents.

Eck, on the other hand, triumphed, especially for the reason that he had succeeded in exposing Luther as a heretic who wished to destroy the authority of the councils and of the Church. He gained the support of other Catholic writers, who espoused his cause and that of the papacy which had been disparaged. Among those who supported him was the priest Jerome Emser, formerly private secretary to Duke George, a learned humanist and theologian, who attacked Luther in a number of polemical writings, which elicited violent replies.

The number of Luther's friends and followers also increased in consequence of the growing intensity of the battle. It was of less importance that the Hussite opponents of the Council of Constance in Bohemia complimented him on his attitude at Leipsic and his subsequent writings. The Utraquists endeavored to form an alliance with him, but their efforts did not result in any intimate, lasting union. As a result of the terrible Hussite campaigns waged on German soil, the Hussite faction had too bad a name in that country to make it prudent for Luther to form an intimate alliance with them at this juncture. The sympathy of the neo-German humanists, which had been aroused by the Leipsic disputation, was of far greater importance and promise for his cause. Crotus Rubeanus, a leader of this group, wrote Luther from Italy, on October 16, 1519, reminding him of their former association and adding that he had extolled him at Rome as the father of his country, who was worthy of a golden statue because he was the first to rise up in behalf of the emancipation of God's people from false opinions; for this purpose he had been called by divine providence like another Paul when a flash of lightning had prostrated him near Erfurt and driven him into a monastery, a cause of "mourning to us, your companions." [44]

At this time he was also befriended by the Erfurt humanist and jurist, Justus Jonas, subsequently his ally, who applied himself avidly to the study of the new theology.

The most influential accession to the cause of Luther, however, was the support of Melanchthon, who accompanied him to Leipsic and whose enthusiasm for the light of Wittenberg was unbounded.

Philip Melanchthon (Schwarzerd), though but twenty-one years of age, had achieved distinction as a philologist; at the recommendation of Reuchlin he had left Tübingen in the summer of 1518 and went to the University of Wittenberg to teach Greek and to carry out his plan of issuing an edition of Aristotle in the original. His acquaintance with Luther and the latter's active influence attracted the highly gifted young layman to theology, particularly in its Lutheran form. Luther promptly detected the value which the scholarly attainments and the amiability of the "weak little man" would have for his cause. With his dominating nature he completely captivated the pliant and susceptible youth. Even later, when Melanchthon had opposed the doctrinal rigor and harsh conduct of Luther, the pensive bookworm was unable to escape the overwhelming influence of his master. In his antipathy toward Scholastics and "sophists," he at once launched upon the sea of Lutheran theology with such impetuosity that he partly outdid Luther in his theses for the theological baccalaureate which was conferred on him September 9, 1519. His later achievements in behalf of Lutheranism, however, consisted particularly in two things: first, that his erudition and formal training enabled him to cast Luther's ideas into a certain systematic and academical form, and, second, that he possessed a certain skill, prudence, and flexibility which were necessary to insure success in the public negotiations with the empire and with the opponents of the new theology, gifts which Luther himself lacked.[45]

In the first years of his acquaintance with Luther, Melanchthon wrote to Spalatin: "You know how carefully we must guard this earthen vessel which contains so great a treasure. . . . The earth holds nothing more divine than him." [46] He styles Luther "our

[44] Köstlin-Kawerau, *Martin Luther*, Vol. I, p. 251.

[45] *Briefwechsel*, II, pp. 204 sqq.

[46] Grisar, *Luther*, Vol. IV, p. 269; Köstlin-Kawerau, *op. cit.*, I, 442.

Elias." [47] Luther appeared to him as one "destined by God" for his work, "driven by the spirit of God." "Leave him to the working of his own spirit and resist not the will of God." [48] Luther requited him with exuberant eulogies. He declared that "almost everything" about this youthful scholar was "superhuman." "He excels me in scholarship by his learning and the integrity of his life." [49] Some of the propositions which the theological "learning" of the philologian was capable of inspiring, are set forth in the *Loci Communes Rerum Theologicarum*, published by Melanchthon in 1521, which will be discussed in the sequel.

In connection with the polemical activity which Luther unfolded in the year of the Leipsic disputation, we must here advert to his pamphlet against Eck concerning the affair of the Franciscans of Jüterbog. The latter had courageously preached against Luther's doctrines. Eck had seconded their efforts by means of printed theses. Luther attacked the friars and Eck, their counselor, in a rude pamphlet in which he styled them "vipers and a brood of vipers," and also for the first time inveighed against confession, which, he alleged, was not a divine institution,[50] but introduced by a pope.

Jerome Dungersheim, professor of theology at Leipsic, who by means of irenic and learned letters endeavored to persuade Luther to abandon his course, received from him a private reply in which he said: "We desire to have the Scriptures as our judge, whereas you desire to judge the Scriptures." He warned him not to abuse his patience, since "countless wolves were tugging" at him already.[51] He also reproved the Roman chamberlain Miltitz, when the latter again appeared with conciliatory suggestions and endeavored to induce him to go with him to Treves to let the Elector, Richard von Greiffenklau, arbitrate the controversy. It was all the easier for him to reject this proposal, since Miltitz had no papal approbation for his plan, and since, moreover, the Elector of Saxony objected to the journey to Treves on account of the dangers that beset it. For the benefit of his high protector, Luther, in a letter written in December to Spalatin, said: "I should wish to fall into their hands, so that

---

[47] Grisar, *op. cit.*, III, p. 322.
[48] Grisar, *op. cit.*, III, 263; cfr. 322.
[49] *"Eruditione et integritate vitae."* *Op. cit.*, III, 321.
[50] Köstlin-Kawerau, *Martin Luther*, Vol. I, pp. 254, 257.
[51] *Op. cit.*, I, p. 258.

they could appease their fury, did I not fear for the Word and the as yet small army of God." [52]

The Elector Frederick was very susceptible to the pious suggestions of Luther, whom, however, for prudential reasons, he did not wish to see. At his instigation, he diligently read the Bible. As the prince was ill since the end of August, Luther composed a comprehensive and consolatory treatise for him. It was written during the stress of his polemical writings, many of which he prepared simultaneously for the press. The work, an irenical and sententious treatise for all sufferers in general, appeared in Latin and in German at the beginning of 1520, and bore the title: "Tessaradekas" (the number fourteen). Its fourteen motives for patience were intended to replace the invocation of the Fourteen Holy Helpers. In this work the productivity of his pen is evidenced in a marvellous manner; notwithstanding the constant agitation in which he was steeped, this work shows that he was endowed with ability to write in a tone of sincere piety.

In addition to his polemical writings Luther composed many religious works of a practical nature. His polemical productions however, outnumbered the others. He denounced the distinguished Dominican theologian Hoogstraten, of Cologne, who had appealed against him to the pope, as "an illogical ass and a bloodthirsty enemy of the truth." In editing his lectures on the Epistle to the Galatians, he sharpened his statements about the new Gospel by the use of pointed denunciations, which stand side by side with reflexions savoring of mysticism. He concluded this commentary with a violent tirade, in the style of the Old Testament prophets, concerning the decadence of the Church in his day. In the interval between his bitter invectives against Emser at Dresden and other similar publications of a smaller scope, appeared the printed beginnings of his larger interpretation of the psalms (*Operationes in Psalmos*) and his Latin postil for Advent. Incidentally he composed tracts on the Our Father, the Passion of Christ, preparation for death, usury, and other topics. Prior to Luther no one had ever availed himself as extensively as he did of the infant art of printing in the interests of a cause. Scarcely anyone in succeeding ages attained to such an incessant activity in the use of the press as Luther.

In addition there were many publications by others, either in

[52] *Briefwechsel*, II, p. 275.

his defense or in opposition to him. Many of his sermons were copied and printed either with or without his knowledge. Thus, two sermons which had been carefully copied appeared simultaneously in print, —one "On the Twofold Righteousness," the other, a companion piece, "On the State of Matrimony," in a form which aroused lively objections on account of the unheard-of frankness with which that subject was treated. It is not possible to ascertain the extent to which the printed text departed from Luther's sermon. In consequence of complaints that were made against it, he issued a revised edition of it, in the introduction to which he says that there is "a great difference between giving expression to something *viva voce* and in dead letters." In a letter to Lang at Erfurt he declined responsibility for the first edition of his homily on matrimony, saying that it was produced without his knowledge and caused him to feel disgraced. In the revised edition he deals arbitrarily with the doctrine and practice of the Church and expresses doubts about the validity of clandestine marriages, which at that time were universally regarded as valid. The sermon in its revised edition was extensively circulated.

In the beginning of October, 1519, Luther reported to Staupitz that he was satisfied with his success. Due to representations made to Staupitz because of his favoring of Luther, he assumed a more reserved attitude towards him. Archbishop Lang of Salzburg sought to attract Staupitz to his episcopal city. In the above quoted letter Luther complains: "You turn your back to me too much. As your favorite child I am keenly hurt at this. I pray you, praise God also in me, the sinner. I detest this very wicked life, I have a great fear of death, I am devoid of faith, though richly endowed with other gifts. However, I desire to serve Christ alone with my talents; He knows it." [53]

Eck was a man of quite different character. Luther and Karlstadt having sent their versions of the Leipsic disputation to the Elector Frederick of Saxony, the latter forwarded them to Eck, who in a lengthy publication frankly and honestly corrected the reports of his opponents, showing "how they economized the truth in diverse ways."

Eck had to suffer much on account of the courageous stand he had taken. Among those who inclined to Luther's side Oecolampadius,

[53] *Ibid.*, p. 184; October 3, 1519.

who subsequently became famous, wrote a sharp satire against him. More bitter still was the contumely heaped on him in an anonymous lampoon which bore the title: "The Planed Eck" (*Eccius dedolatus*), supposed to have been written by Willibald Pirkheimer. As late as 1540, Eck, who had been persecuted throughout his life, wrote that his traducers had depicted him in many forms, among others as a man who had been "planed" and roasted.[54] It was not as though Eck had not in his private life furnished occasions for reproach; but in his defense of the Church he permitted nothing to daunt him. Soon after the disputation at Leipsic he ascended the pulpit of the magnificent Gothic Church of Our Lady in Munich, the residential city of the dukes of Bavaria, and raised his powerful voice against the Wittenberg doctrines—the first to point out to Bavaria the ways of defending the faith to which it subsequently adhered. He gradually completed his work on the primacy of the pope, which had not yet appeared in print at that time. The primacy of the pope and the Roman Church in his opinion occupied the forefront in the controversy—so much so that he desired nothing more ardently than a final decision by the Apostolic See. He rejoiced very much, therefore, when a brief of Leo X summoned him to Rome to report on conditions in Germany. In the midst of winter, on January 18, 1520, he proceeded by way of Salzburg to the Eternal City, bringing with him Luther's German works, translated into Latin. On April 1 he presented to the Pope the manuscript of his own work on the primacy.[55]

[54] Th. Wiedemann, *Johann Eck*, p. 141.
[55] *Ibid.*, p. 150.

Chapter VI

SIGNS OF THE COMING TEMPEST IN STATE AND CHURCH

LUTHER'S OPINIONS OF THE AGE

1. CURRENTS OF THE NEW AGE

Powerful movements which, proclaiming an intellectual revolution and connected more or less intimately with the revival of the study of classical antiquity, pervaded the Western world since the fifteenth century, and presaged a new period in the history of mankind. This agitation was bound to react on young Luther.

The newly invented art of printing had at one stroke created a world-wide community of intellectual accomplishments and literary ideas, such as the Middle Ages had never dreamt of. By the exchange of the most diverse and far-reaching discoveries the nations came into closer proximity with one another. The spirit of secular enterprise awakened as from a long sleep at the astounding discovery of new countries overseas with unsuspected treasures.

As a result of the increased facility of intellectual intercourse and of the development of scientific methods, criticism began to function with an efficiency greater than ever before in all departments of knowledge. Yielding to an ancient urge, the larger commonwealths made themselves increasingly independent of their former tutelage by the Church. They strove after liberty and the removal of that clerical influence whence they had largely derived their durability and internal prosperity in the past. And in proportion as they struggled for autonomy, the opulent cities, the knightly demesnes and principalities, particularly in Germany, tried to throw off the fetters which hitherto had oppressed them, and to increase their power. In brief, we find everywhere a violent break with former restrictions, a determined advance of subjectivism at the expense of solidarity and the traditional order of the Middle Ages, but especially at the expense of the supremacy of the spiritual power of the Church, which thus far alone had preserved mankind from the dangers of individualism.

Influenced by the spirit of the Renaissance and the awakening of historical memories, the spirit of nationalism became more powerful than ever before in the life of peoples. The segregation of national ambitions became ever more pronounced, in spite of the increased solidarity of commerce. The Germans became more keenly conscious of being a unit which had a right to develop along its own lines in opposition to the Latin nations. Luther very skillfully utilized this national spirit in his public conflict. He boldly aroused this spirit in the Germans, "his dear brethren," who had been reduced to servitude by the papacy, with a view to separate them from the universal Church. If the patriotic sentiment of the Germans had been kept within due bounds and had been animated by Christian ideals, it would have been a great good. Aside from other considerations, it might have led to a healthy competition with other civilized nations. In reality, however, it descended down to the individual principalities within the boundaries of Germany. The territorial rulers who concurred with Luther, promoted it to the advantage of their own power. In consequence, the empire increasingly became a cumbersome machine, and the authority of the emperor, the august head of the empire in virtue of his coronation by the pope, waned visibly, especially since the imperial reforms so warmly favored by Maximilian I (d. January 12, 1519) virtually failed and the immense and far-flung empire consolidated under Maximilian's successor, Charles V, almost completely absorbed the attention of that ruler to the detriment of his German subjects. not to speak of the impairment which the authority of this Catholic emperor experienced through Luther's widely-published attacks, made partly in the direct interest of his own ecclesiastical revolt and partly in the service of those petty German territorial rulers who were loyal to him and whose interests conflicted with those of the empire.

In course of time the German rulers obtained a certain ecclesiastical régime within their respective countries, and it came to pass that, at the close of the Middle Ages, besides the ecclesiastical princes, the secular princes were vested with extensive authority in the external administration of religious affairs. They derived this authority in part from the Roman See, which sought to protect and promote the interests of the Church by the aid of loyal Catholic rulers; in part they had acquired it as an inheritance from their forebears and maintained it against the passive or active opposition of the bishops.

This ecclesiastical régime exercised by territorial princes was a colossal danger when the religious struggles began in the sixteenth century.

True, some of the princes, e. g., the well-intentioned Duke George of Saxony and the dukes of Bavaria, employed their ecclesiastical power successfully in defense of the existing ecclesiastical conditions. Many others, however, especially Luther's territorial lord, the Elector of Saxony, constantly incited by him, and landgrave, Philip of Hesse, made of the ecclesiastical privileges they had gained a bulwark for the religious innovation. Thus the ecclesiastical authority of the territorial lords formed a convenient transition to the establishment of a Protestant ecclesiastical régime. Manifestly it was a double-edged sword which was thus wielded by the secular arm in the distribution of benefices, the temporal administration or partial disposition of church property, the control of innumerable ecclesiastical patronages and the superintendence of monasteries and ecclesiastical institutions. It happened that large territories were torn with ease from the faith and jurisdiction of the Church, as it were overnight. Even in principalities that remained Catholic, the reforms initiated by the Church authorities, e. g., in the monasteries, were in many instances obstructed or interrupted by selfish rulers. And the acts of the reigning princes were repeated in the great free cities of the empire, and even in smaller cities, where the secular authorities had come into possession of similar powers.

It is remarkable how this tendency of transferring ecclesiastical functions and rights to secular rulers is noticeable in Luther's Commentary on the Epistle to the Romans, written at the time when he began to drift away from the Church. The young monk there asserts that the clergy are remiss in the performance of their duties concerning the administration of pious foundations. "As a matter of fact," he exclaims, "it were better and assuredly safer, if the temporal affairs of the clergy were placed under the control of the worldly authorities." The laity, he explains, are aware of the inefficiency of the clergy, and "the secular authorities fulfill their obligations better than our ecclesiastical rulers." It is a question whether he perceived the far-reaching import of his words as a kind of prelude to the coming secularization.[1]

In any event, Luther was aware of the opposition existing between the secular powers, and even between the common laity, and the clergy, which smouldered in many places at that time. A certain aversion and hostility toward the entire clergy, commencing with the curia and the episcopate, and extending to the lower secular clergy and the monks, had become widely prevalent and was fomented by the secular authorities. In virtue of the pious donations that had accumulated in the course of centuries, the Church had become too wealthy. Thus, in the diocese of Worms, about three-fourths of all property belonged to ecclesiastical proprietors. Everywhere the Church possessed a plenitude of privileges which provoked envy, as, for illustration, in the judicial forum, in her exemption from taxation, and in the honors bestowed upon her. Jealousy and envy engendered hatred and contentions in many places. True, an immense share of the income of the Church constantly flowed to charitable institutions; other sums were alloted with papal sanction to, or else arbitrarily appropriated by, the secular authorities to cover particular needs. Large sums were remitted to the Roman curia in the form of ordinary or extraordinary taxes. The wealth of the Church was alluring, and the large subsidies from Germany to Rome especially were a constant occasion for complaint. The payments to the papal treasury had, as a matter of fact, become too onerous. The urgent requirements of the administration of the universal Church, especially since the exile of the popes at Avignon, had resulted in constantly increasing imposts levied on the faithful in the various countries for the benefit of Rome. The *annates*, the *servitia* and other taxes, and the revenues derived from indulgences had constantly increased. In Germany complaints were rife that the material resources of the country were too heavily assessed. The so-called *"courtesans,"* i. e., benefice-hunters provided with Roman documents entitling them to certain benefices, by their avaricious practices helped to render the papal curia still more odious.

At the commencement of his controversy Luther assiduously collected every unfavorable detail concerning the financial practices of the curia, so as to paint a collective picture of them for propaganda purposes. In this task he was assisted by a former official of the

[1] Grisar, *Luther*, Vol. I, pp. 283 sq.

Roman curia who had come to Wittenberg. True and exaggerated reports of the pomp displayed at the court of Rome and of the papal expenditures for secular purposes reacted upon the discontented like oil poured into a fire.

A historical expression of this bitter feeling is furnished by the so-called *Gravamina,* official lists of complaints submitted to successive diets by the princes and estates against the excessive burdens and the inequality of rights. In many respects these complaints met with the approval of men who were sincerely attached to the Church, such as Dr. Eck. Similarly the cities had their *Gravamina* against the bishops, the citizens and town councilors against the chapters and the other clergy. The spiritual principalities repeatedly experienced a clash of arms as a result of the quarrels pertaining to jurisdiction or possession.

In this way it appeared—and the more recent researches concerning local conditions confirm the impression—that one reason for the great defection was antagonism to the papal government and to the clergy, originating in material interests. The aversion to Rome was all the more dangerous because it was shared by a large number of the clergy, oppressed by taxes. These were clouds that heralded an approaching storm. Nevertheless, the reform for which many serious-minded churchmen clamored was not excluded, but merely delayed. The existing discontent did not engender a desire for a new religion, and the Catholic dogmas remained sacred. But when Luther proclaimed his new doctrines, which implied the destruction of ecclesiastical unity, the existing discontent accelerated the revolution.

2. ABUSES IN THE LIFE OF THE CLERGY

When Cardinal Nicholas of Cusa (d. 1462), a man who has merited the gratitude of Germany, proclaimed his programme of reforms, he indicated with complete frankness the reasons for the corruption of the ecclesiastical system. They were: the admission of many unworthy candidates to the clerical state, sacerdotal concubinage, the accumulation of benefices, and simony. Towards the end of the fifteenth century complaints had multiplied against immorality among the clergy. "The numerous decrees of bishops and synods do not admit of a doubt but that a large part of the German clergy flagrantly transgressed the law of celibacy." [2] A recommendation made to the dukes of Bavaria in 1447, voicing the opinion of many friends and sponsors of a sound reform, declared that the work of reformation had to begin with the improvement of the morals of the clergy, for here was the root of all evils in the Church. True there were districts where the clergy was irreproachable and praiseworthy, e. g., the Rhineland, Slesvig-Holstein, and the Allgäu. But in Saxony, the home of Luther, and in Franconia and Bavaria, there were reports of many and grave abuses. A work entitled De Ruina Ecclesiae, formerly ascribed to Nicholas of Clémanges, says that at the beginning of the fifteenth century there were bishops who, for a money consideration, permitted their priests to live in concubinage, and Hefele in his Konziliengeschichte adduces a number of synodal decrees which prohibited bishops to accept money or gifts in consideration of their tolerating or ignoring the practice of concubinage. [3]

In addition to living in concubinage, many of the better situated clergy were steeped in luxury and presumptuous arrogance, thus repelling the people, and especially the middle class, which was conscious of its own self-sufficiency.

In connection with the unduly multiplied small religious foundations without clergy, the number of clergymen had increased to such an extent that their very number suggests the idea that many of them had no genuine vocation to the clerical state, and that lack of work constituted a moral danger for many. Thus, at the end of the fifteenth century, two churches in Breslau had 236 "altarists," whose only service consisted in saying Mass at altars erected by pious donations and endowed with petty benefices. Besides saying Mass daily, these "altarists," of whom there was a vast multitude throughout the country, had but one obligation, namely, to recite the Breviary. In 1480 there were 14 "altarists" and 60 vicars, besides 14

[2] Janssen-Pastor, Gesch. des deutschen Volkes, Vol. I, 18th ed., p. 709. On the synods, see Hefele-Hergenröther, Konziliengesch., Vol. VIII. Cf. Janssen-Pastor, op. cit., 680 sq., and H. Grisar, Ein Bild aus dem deutschen Synodalleben im Jahrhundert vor der Glaubensspaltung, in the Histor. Jahrbuch, Vol. I (1880), pp. 603–640.

[3] Nicolaus de Clemangiis, De Ruina Ecclesiae, c. 22, in Herm. von der Hardt, Magnum Oecumenicum Constantiense Concilium (Helmestadt., 1700), I, 3, col. 23 sq. Hefele, op. cit., VII, pp. 385, 416, 422, 594; VIII, p. 97. John de Segovia, Hist. Syn. Basil., II (Vindob. 1873), p. 774: "Quia in quibusdam regionibus nonnulli iurisdictionem ecclesiasticam habentes pecuniarios questus a concubinariis percipere non erubescunt, patiendo eos in tali foeditate sordescere."

canons, stationed at the cathedral of Meissen. In Strasburg the minster boasted 36 canonries, St. Thomas Church 20, old St. Peter's 17, new St. Peter's 15, All Saints 12. The number of canonries was augmented by numerous foundations for vicars and "summissaries," so called because they celebrated high Mass in place of the canons. There were no less than 63 "summissaries" at the minster of Strasburg, not to mention 38 chaplains. John Agricola reports—although only on the strength of an *on dit* ("it is alleged")—that there were 5,000 priests and monks at Cologne; on another occasion he estimates the number of monks and nuns in that city alone at 5,000. It is certain that the "German Rome" on the Rhine at that time had 11 foundations, 19 parish churches, more than 100 chapels, 22 cloisters, 12 hospitals, and 76 religious convents.[4]

The bishop of Chiemsee traces the corruption of the clergy principally to the fact that the spiritual and temporal rulers abused the right of patronage, both by their appointments and their arbitrary interference. This opinion is shared by Geiler of Kaysersberg, who blames the laity, in particular the patrons among the nobility, for the deplorable condition of the parishes and asserts that illiterate, malicious, and depraved individuals were engaged in lieu of the good and honorable.

In contrast with "the higher clergy, who reveled in wealth and luxury," the condition of the lower clergy in no wise corresponded to the dignity of their state. "Beyond the tithes and stole-fees, which were quite precarious, they had no stipends, so that poverty, and at times avarice, constrained them to gain their livelihood in a manner which exposed them to public contempt. 'There can be no doubt that a very large portion of the lower clergy had become unfaithful to the ideal of their state, so much so that one is justified in speaking of a clerical proletariat both in the higher sense, as well as in the ordinary and literal sense.' This clerical proletariat was prepared to join any movement which promised to abet its lower impulses." [5]

The condition created by the all too frequent incorporation of parishes with monasteries was deplorable. Where many parishes were incorporated with one monastery, incompetent pastors were frequently sent, there was no supervision, and the care of souls declined.

---

4 Janssen-Pastor, *l. c.*, pp. 705 sq.

5 *Ibid.*, pp. 703–704. J. E. Jörg, *Deutschland in der Revolutionsperiode 1522–1526* (Freiburg, 1851), p. 191, employs the phrase "clerical proletariat."

One of the chief causes of the decline of the higher clergy and the episcopate was the interference of the secular authorities and worldly-minded noblemen in church affairs.

Not only were spiritual prerogatives frequently usurped by the princes and lesser authorities, but large numbers of cathedral benefices and diocesan sees were arbitrarily conferred on noblemen and princely scions, so that the most influential offices were occupied in many places by individuals who were unworthy and without a proper vocation. "When the storm broke loose at the end of the second decade of the sixteenth century, the following archdioceses and dioceses were administered by sons of princes: Bremen, Freising, Halberstadt, Hildesheim, Magdeburg, Mayence, Merseburg, Metz, Minden, Münster, Naumburg, Osnabrück, Paderborn, Passau, Ratisbon, Spires, Verden, and Verdun." [6] As a rule, the bishops who came from princely houses were dependent upon their relatives and were drawn into secular and courtly activities, even if their education had not radically repressed their ecclesiastical sense, as, for instance, in the case of the powerful archbishop of Mayence, Albrecht of Brandenburg.

An additional evil was the concentration of prominent episcopal sees. "The archbishop of Bremen was also bishop of Verden, the bishop of Osnabrück was also bishop of Paderborn, the archbishop of Mayence was also archbishop of Magdeburg and bishop of Halberstadt. George, palsgrave of the Rhine and duke of Bavaria, was provost of the cathedral of Mayence when but thirteen and successively became vicar capitular of Cologne and Treves, provost of the foundation of St. Donatian at Bruges, incumbent of the parishes of Hochheim and Lorch on the Rhine, and, lastly, in 1513, bishop of Spires. By special privilege of Pope Leo X, conferred under date of June 22, 1513, he, a sincere and pious man, was given possession of all these benefices in addition to the bishopric of Spires." [7] "The higher clergy," laments a contemporary in view of the worldly bishops," are chiefly to blame for the wretched condition of the parishes. They appoint unfit persons to administer parishes, whilst they themselves collect the tithes. Many endeavor to concentrate as many benefices as possible in their own hands, without satisfying the obligations attached to them, and dissipate the ecclesiastical revenues in luxurious expenditures lavished on servants, pages, dogs, and horses.

[6] Janssen-Pastor, *l. c.*, p. 703.
[7] *Ibid.*

One endeavors to outdo the other in ostentation and luxury." [8] The decline and indolence of the episcopate furnishes one of the most important explanations of the rapid defection from the ancient Church after Luther had set the ball a-rolling.

The religious tragedy of the sixteenth century is a perfectly insoluble riddle except on the assumption that there was great corruption within the Church. It is, however, a mistake to think that the abuses were engendered by the nature of the Church, and that, therefore, her doctrines and her hierarchy had necessarily to be abandoned. Her exterior life, it is true, was greatly disfigured; yet there was vitality in her soul and her salutary powers were unbroken. Placed in the midst of mankind and exposed to the frailties of the world in her human element, the Church, as the preceding centuries of her existence show, is subject to periods of decline in her exterior manifestation, without, however, being deprived of the hope of seeing her interior light shine forth anew and her deformity vanish in God's appointed time. She celebrated such a renaissance after the decline of the spiritual life in the eleventh century, in consequence of the warfare which the great pope Gregory VII and his successors waged upon the tyranny of the secular rulers and the numerous infractions of clerical celibacy. She experienced a similar rejuvenation in the sixteenth century, after the anti-ecclesiastical elements had drained off into the new ecclesiastical system, to which they had been attracted by the offer of emancipation from the commandments of the Church.

3. BRIGHTER PHASES

For the rest there are many bright spots in the ecclesiastical conditions of pre-Lutheran Germany. This is true especially of the life of the common people, which went on in conformity with the old spirit, nay, even became more truly religious despite all obstacles. It is true also of the various religious orders, such as the Franciscans and Dominicans, as well as of many portions of the secular clergy. A modern Protestant historian writes: "We hear of grave defects. . . . And again we hear of so many monasteries imbued with seriousness and character, of so many diligent efforts made for the improvement of the parochial clergy, of such eager solicitude for the faithful, of such fruitful fostering of studies within the Church, that we

8 *Ibid.*, p. 700.

hesitate to assume that vice and loathsomeness ruled absolutely. We shall be compelled to establish the fact that gratifying and deplorable things are to be found side by side; that there are some phenomena which are depressing in the highest degree, but many others which are elevating; and that the relationship which they bore to one another was such as no one may venture to describe in numbers." [9]

From the very beginning of his internal defection from the dogmatic teaching of the Church, Luther had no appreciation of these elevating and gratifying conditions. His preconceived delineation of affairs does not constitute an objection to the brighter pages which ought to be adduced.

As an illustration: in his commentary on the Epistle to the Romans, where he expresses the thought that "the temporalities of the clergy ought to be administered by the secular authorities," he outdoes himself in unduly generalized complaints against the clergy. Thus he says: What Paul demanded of the servants of the Church, is "done by no one at the present day. They are priests only in appearance. . . . Where is there one who does the will of the Founder? . . . The laity are beginning to penetrate the mysteries of our iniquity (*mysteria iniquitatis*). . . . Beyond proceeding against such as violate their liberties, possessions, and rights, the ecclesiastical authorites know naught else but pomp, ambition, unchastity, and contentiousness." They are one and all "whitened sepulchres." [10]

Such exaggerated invectives are associated in his earliest literary productions and letters with those fantastic descriptions which we were constrained to adduce on previous pages.

Thus, in 1516, he wrote to Spalatin to dissuade the Elector of Saxony from promoting Staupitz to a bishopric: He who becomes a bishop in these days falls into the most evil company; all the wickedness of Greece, Rome, and Sodom were to be found in the bishops. A pastor of souls was regarded as quite exemplary if he merely pushed his worldly business, and prepared for himself an insatiable hell with his riches. [11]

Everywhere he perceived only dark gloom, because he discovered that the Gospel as he understood it was everywhere forgotten; for, where the "word of truth" does not reign, there can be only "dark iniquity." "The whole world," he exclaims as early as 1515, or in the period immediately succeeding, "the whole world is full of, yea, deluged with, the filth of false doctrine." Hence, it is not astonishing that there is prevalent in Christen-

[9] G. von Below, *Die Ursachen der Reformation*, in the *Histor. Bibliothek*, ed. by the *Histor. Zeitschrift*, München, 1917, pp. 19 sq.

[10] Grisar, *Luther*, Vol. I, p. 284.

[11] *Ibid.*, I, p. 57.

dom "so much dissension, anger, covetousness, pride, disobedience, vice, and intemperance, in consequence of which charity has grown completely cold, faith has become extinguished, and hope has vanished." etc.[12]

In view of these unrestrained and exaggerated effusions on the decline of the Church, which pervade his whole life and are expanded into a condemnation of all previous ages as the kingdom of Antichrist, it is well to observe that they are inspired mainly by his new dogmatic and pseudomystical views. They are anything but historical and balanced judgments, and one can but marvel at the thought that they have influenced the evaluation of the Middle Ages for so long a time among Protestant scholars. To-day, however, well informed Protestant writers are beginning to speak differently of Luther's unjustified and impassioned verdicts.

It is conceded that his discourses were based on "a one-sided and distorted view" of things, and that he painted the history of the Middle Ages, directed by the popes, as "a dark night." [13]

With respect to medieval theology, we read that it is necessary to repudiate resolutely "the caricature we meet with in the writings of the reformers" and "the misunderstandings to which they gave rise." [14]

A historian of the Reformation, writing in 1910, conceded that the history of the close of the Middle Ages was "an almost unknown terrain up to a few years ago;" "the later Middle Ages seemed to be useful only to serve as a foil for the story of the reformers, whose dazzling colors, when superimposed on a gray background, shone forth with greater brilliancy;" only since Janssen has "a more intensive study of the close of the Middle Ages" been made, and it has been discovered that "the Church had not yet lost its influence over souls." "An increasing acquaintance with the Bible toward the end of the Middle Ages must be admitted" and "preaching in the vernacular was not neglected to the extent frequently assumed." [15]

The first volume of Janssen's History, despite the necessary modifications made in later editions, clearly reveals that there was a striking revival in many spheres of ecclesiastical life before Luther.

[12] *Sermo praescriptus praeposito in Litzka*, Weimar ed., I, pp. 10 sqq.; *Opp. Lat. Var.*, I, pp. 29 sqq.

[13] Walter Koehler, 1907; Grisar, *Luther*, Vol. IV, p. 116.

[14] Wm. Maurenbrecher, 1874; *ibid*.

[15] Walter Friedensburg, quoted by Grisar, *Luther*, Vol. IV, p. 117.

Popular religious literature flourished to a certain extent under the fostering care of the new art of printing. It is impossible to assume that such excellent and frequently reprinted works as *Der Schatzbehälter des Heils* (The Treasure Trove of Salvation), *Das Seelenwurzgärtlein* (The Little Aromatic Garden of the Soul), *Der Christenspiegel* (The Mirror for Christians), *Der Seelenführer* (The Spiritual Guide of the Soul), etc., should not have awakened a response in the morals of the people and the general sentiment of the age. Booklets on penance and confession, treatises on matrimony, books on death, pictorial catechisms with instructive illustrations, explanations of the faith and the current prayers, printed tables with the commandments of God and a catalogue of domestic duties, as well as many similar publications were widely disseminated among the people. Excellent books of sermons were found in the hands of the clergy. The classic work of Thomas à Kempis went through no less than fifty-nine editions in several languages before the year 1500. The admirable pedagogical writings of Jacob Wimpfeling, who was styled the "teacher of Germany," were published in thirty different editions within twenty-five years. Among the products of the press the Bible ranked supreme. The first artistic work from the press of Koberger (in Nuremberg) was the splendid German Bible of 1483, which Michael Wohlgemut had oramented with more than a hundred woodcuts. It was entitled "the most excellent work of the entire Sacred Scripture . . . according to correct vernacular German, with beautiful illustrations." [16]

The making of religious woodcuts and copper-plate engravings flourished as perhaps never before. Sculptures and paintings vied with one another in fervor, depth of thought, and beauty of execution. Like all the artistic products of that day, they are permeated by tenderness and sincere piety. This phase of art production is a favorable mirror of the life of the people.

In the town-church of Wittenberg, sculpture has bequeathed to us two splendid models in the richly ornamented baptismal font of 1457, a creation of Herman Vischer, and in the artistically constructed pulpit of the Luther Hall, in which Luther is said to have preached frequently. The principal portal of the church is still adorned with figures sculptured in the lovely style in vogue at the

[16] Janssen-Pastor, *Gesch. des deutschen Volkes*, Vol. I, 20th ed., p. 23.

close of the Middle Ages. In the center the enthroned Madonna with her Child looks down upon and invites the worshipers. Sculptures such as this attractive group of saints reveal as clearly as the popular books just mentioned, how far the people were removed from regarding religion as a source of horror and fear, as Luther will have it. In life as well as in art, they, on the contrary, harmoniously combined a loving trust in Jesus, the Divine Lord, and confidence in the intercession of His servants, the Saints, grouped around Mary, with the gravity of the idea of the eternal Judge, who appears on the outside of the town-church of Wittenberg, a large statue set in the wall. The majestic figure, with a sword protruding from the mouth, in compliance with the Bible, inspires the beholder with a sense of awe. It is not impossible that Luther's morbid fear of God's judgment attached itself to such pictures, for the healthy piety of the Middle Ages was wont to place them beside the monuments of its confidence and childlike hope of salvation, as a counterpoise to the spirit of levity.

Ecclesiastical architecture, finally, constituted a splendid field of artistic endeavor. It was the center of all art. There is scarcely another age in the history of architecture like the century from 1420 to 1520, in which town and country witnessed the erection of so many houses of worship—most of them still in existence—constructed in the devotional and joyful style of the late Gothic. The confraternity of the German builders was the chief bearer of this great movement, and it was one of the most popular institutions of the time. The large sums which the faithful contributed towards the erection of these often marvelous structures, attest the charity and the idealism that actuated the soul of the nation.

In his journey to Rome, which took him through the heart of Germany, Luther had ample opportunities of seeing and admiring the artistic creations of architecture, sculpture, and painting, some of which are still extant, whilst others have perished. But the monk of Wittenberg had no taste for such things. There is not a sentence of his writings or addresses which betrays any appreciation of the mighty impetus of ecclesiastical life represented by the works of art in churches and monasteries. In fact, neither his tongue nor his pen reveals any genuine appreciation of art. He lived a secluded life in his own narrow world, which fact explains the rigor of many of his judgments.

4. PREPONDERANCE OF DANGEROUS ELEMENTS

.Having depicted the favorable aspects of the age, it is necessary once more to revert to its shadows. They must have constituted a source of grave danger to the Church, to judge of certain writings of unbiased and noble-minded contemporaries, such as the indictment of the bishop of Chiemsee, Berthold Pirstinger, published in 1519 under the title, *Onus Ecclesiae*, a phrase borrowed from the Apocalypse. True, in spite of the "burdens" imposed upon the Church he hoped for an internal restoration of the same, based on the unchangeable foundation of the faith. He mournfully addresses Christ as follows: "Grant that the Church may be reformed, which has been redeemed by Thy blood, and is now, through our fault, near destruction!" After a dismal description of existing conditions, he says that the "episcopate is now given up to worldly possessions, sordid cares, tempestuous feuds, worldly sovereignty." He complains that "the prescribed provincial and diocesan synods are not held"; that the shepherds of the Church do not remain at their posts, although they exact heavy tributes; and that the conduct of the clergy and the laity had become demoralized, and so on.[17]

Trithemius, Wimpfeling, Brant, Geiler von Kaysersberg, and Dr. John Eck, joined in the lament of the Bishop of Chiemsee.

"Of the Lamentation of the Church" (*De Planctu Ecclesiae*) was the title of a work which had enjoyed quite a wide circulation before Luther's day. It was reprinted at Ulm in 1474, and again at Lyons in 1517. It was originally composed against the faults of the papacy during the Avignon period, by the Franciscan Alvarez Pelayo, a man of strict morality and whole-heartedly devoted to the Church. The new reprints of this work addressed the contemporaries of Luther in the severe language of Pelayo on the persecution of the Church by those who were instituted as her protectors.[18] In another censorious composition, *De Squaloribus Curiae*, many justifiable complaints were registered side by side with unfounded reproaches. The work entitled *De Ruina Ecclesiae* gained new importance at the end of the fifteenth century.

Luther's mental depression and distorted notions cannot be traced to this kind of literature. Yet it is known from reliable sources that he read other books of a similar tenor, such as the elegant works

---

[17] Grisar, *Luther*, Vol. I, p. 48; Vol. II, pp. 45–47.
[18] *Ibid.*, p. 55.

of the pious Italian poet Mantuanus, who indignantly describes the moral corruption of his country, extending to the highest ecclesiastical dignitaries at Rome. In the writings of the new humanists he found an echo, alloyed with bitter contempt, of what he himself had heard at Rome, fortified by all the complaints of the age against the clergy and the monks. We know that he did not approve their attitude, in so far as it antagonized religion, nor was he himself a humanist; but humanism with its critical activity, as developed everywhere, especially in Germany under the influence of Erasmus, proved to be a great help to him in his revolt against the Church authorities.

The papacy gradually came to regret the favor which it had extended to, and the hopes it had placed in, the nascent humanism in Rome and Italy. Among the German Humanists, Conrad Mutianus of Gotha (d. 1526) was the chief promoter of the anti-ecclesiastical movement. He was a man who had gone so far as to abandon Christianity for a time. From this group originated the "Epistolae Obscurorum Virorum," a clever and biting satyre on monks, scholastics, and friends of the papal curia. Crotus Rubeanus, its principal author, had gathered a circle of younger Humanists about him at an earlier stage of his career, among them Eobanus Hessus, Peter and Henry Eberbach, John Lang, Spalatin for a time, and other talented men desirous of innovation. Erfurt became the headquarters of this group, which was very clamorous in prose and verse.

Justus Jonas also lived at Erfurt. He was a Humanist who later associated himself for life with Luther. While yet a student of law in 1506, he became affiliated with the Humanistic circles of that city. He called Erasmus his "father in Christ" and, in company with Caspar Schalbe, made a pilgrimage to him in the Netherlands. In the same year Jonas, who was a priest and canon of St. Severus, became rector of the University of Erfurt, an event which greatly fortified the position of the neo-Humanists. The Leipsic disputation and the letters of Luther aroused his enthusiasm. When Luther journeyed to the diet of Worms, in 1521, Jonas set out to meet him at Weimar, accompanied him to Worms, and subsequently was called to Wittenberg as provost of the castle-church and professor of canon law. Here, as early as 1521, having obtained his doctorate, Justus Jonas taught theology in concordance with the ideas of Luther. By his intimate attachment to Luther he gained the praise and friendship of such a questionable man as Ulrich von Hutten.

Ulrich von Hutten, humanist and knight, took an active part in the literary feud of Reuchlin against the "Obscurantists." In 1517 he circulated the treatise of Laurentius Valla, an Italian, against the so-called Donation of Constantine, with a view of making a breach in the system of the Roman hierarchy and in a malicious libel ridiculed the conduct of the celebrated theologian Cajetan at the diet of Augsburg. In 1519 he dedicated to his patron, Archbishop Albrecht of Mayence, a work on a cure for syphilis which he had taken with temporary success. He had contracted this disease in consequence of his dissolute life. Wielding a pen skilled in polemics this adventurous Humanist launched his attacks on Rome, thereby becoming the pathfinder of religious schism. Towards his offers of forcible support, Luther prudently assumed a reserved attitude, preferring the protection of his prince to the mailed fist of the revolutionary. Politically, too, Hutten was a revolutionist. Like his friend Franz von Sickingen, he was inspired by the ideal of a powerful and independent knighthood. He fought with Sickingen in the army of the Swabian League when it undertook the expulsion of Duke Ulrich of Württemberg. Afterwards he lived in the Ebernburg, Sickingen's castle in the Palatinate, the so-called "Inn of Justice." Here he devoted himself to the composition of popular and witty writings directed against the clergy and the princes.

The highly revered prince of the Humanists was Erasmus of Rotterdam, at one time an Augustinian canon of Emaus at Gouda, a scholar of prodigious learning and an epoch-making critic, whose ambition it was, not only to introduce a new Humanistic form of speech into ecclesiastical science, but also to reconstruct theology along Humanistic lines, thereby exposing its dogmas to the danger of extinction. While he wished to remain loyal to the Church, his caustic and frequently derisive criticism of things ecclesiastical, Scholasticism, monasticism, and the hierarchy, so influenced the minds of his idolizing followers, both learned and illiterate, as to render the greatest assistance to the work of Luther. His opponents coined the phrase that his writings contained the egg which Luther hatched. At all events, his initial sympathy for Luther was one of the causes that induced almost the entire powerful and wide-spread neo-Humanistic party to join the reform movement of Wittenberg, until finally, about 1524, when it had been clearly demonstrated that the religious struggles were redounding to the disadvantage of the sciences, a reaction set in and Erasmus began to write against Luther.

The great services which Erasmus rendered in behalf of the text of Sacred Scripture and his excellent editions of the writings of the Fathers, remained undisputed and were acknowledged even by his adversaries. In 1516 he issued his first edition of the Greek New Testament, accompanied by a translation into classical Latin, which was followed by his Biblical "Paraphrases." In 1521 he took up his abode near the printing-presses of Basle, whence, in 1529, the disturbances caused by the new religion compelled him to remove to Freiburg in Breisgau. Everywhere in his solitary greatness he was an oracle of the learned. But his character was disfigured by weakness of conviction and pronounced self-conceit. He lacked the power of leadership, such as that trying and dangerous epoch demanded, especially since his unfavorable characteristics were also impressed upon his Humanistic admirers.

Besides Humanism, there were in those critical decades certain other factors which constrain us to speak of a preponderance of imminent dangers.

The minds of men had not yet completely divested themselves of the consequences of the conciliar theories begotten in the unhappy period of the Council of Basle, and of the schisms that preceded it, with its two anti-popes in addition to the one true pope. Here and there the Hussite theories, which had taken deep root in Bohemia, made themselves felt in Germany. A worldly spirit and an unbridled desire for wealth, which the newly inaugurated international commerce and the attractive trade-routes to distant countries aroused in the upper classes of society, were evidenced by the growing evil of usury, against which Luther took a stand in two sermons delivered in 1519 and 1520, though he lacked "an adequate comprehension of the existing conditions." [19] In the lower strata of society, especially among the peasant class, the long-nurtured discontent with oppressive conditions began here and there to issue in unrest and revolt. Lingering politico-social ideas of Hussitism coöperated in this respect with aspirations after a higher standard of living, awakened by the influx of wealth. The unrest was increased by opposition to the introduction into Germany, about 1520, of the Christian-Roman system of jurisprudence, interspersed with Ger-

[19] Thus Köstlin-Kawerau, *Martin Luther*, Vol. I, p. 279.

manic principles. A fanatical preacher of social revolution in favor of the lower classes was the prophet Hans Böhm, a piper of Niklashausen in the Tauber valley. The "Bundschuh"—*i. e.*, the strapped shoe commonly worn by peasants—was the symbol of revolts which broke out in many places, first in 1486, then in 1491 and 1492, but especially in 1513 and 1514, and again in 1517. The social revolution of 1525, with the new Gospel of the "liberty of the Christian man" as its background, was thus gradually prepared.

Only a man of superhuman powers could have banished the threatening dangers of the age in the name of religion and an amelioration of the traditional social order. Who can tell what course events might have taken if at that time saintly men had inspired the people with a reviving spiritual vigor, repeating the example of ancient leaders in reshaping their age? But the teacher of Wittenberg, who took it upon himself to direct the course of events, was no such leader, as the sequel showed.

Many hailed the generous young emperor, Charles V, as the leader who would conduct men out of the religious and social crisis. This young ruler of a world-wide monarchy was animated by the best of intentions. In all sincerity he, as emperor-elect, rendered the customary oath of fealty to the Church on the occasion of his coronation, before he was anointed by the archbishop of Cologne and girded with the "sword of Charles the Great." The oath he took bound him "to preserve and defend in every way the Holy Catholic Faith, as handed down," and "at all times to render due submission, respect, and fealty to the Roman Pontiff, the Holy Father and Lord in Christ, and to the Holy Roman Church." During a life replete with wars and disappointments, Charles honestly endeavored to perform in his beloved Germany the duties which he had assumed; but the religious schism overwhelmed him and finally paralyzed the vigor and determination with which he had begun his career despite constant diversions.

The papacy, too, after Leo X, manifested many hopeful traits of energy and efforts at reform, especially in the brief pontificate of Adrian VI; but there was missing that towering personality on the pontifical throne which might have averted the catastrophe. It was necessary that the idea of a true, distinct from a false, reform of the Church should make its way gradually at Rome and in Germany, until it triumphed at the great Council of Trent in Charles Borromeo and Pope St. Pius V, after the Church had sustained immense losses. But no matter what the popes of Luther's day might have done in the interest of reform, in Luther's eyes their endeavors would have been futile; for he was firmly convinced that they had become rulers of the kingdom of Antichrist.

CHAPTER VII

THE YEAR OF THE BAN

I. BEFORE THE BAN

The friendly invitation which had been extended to Luther to visit Rome, occasioned by the distorted reports of Miltitz, was barren of results. The papal brief addressed to the "beloved son" was suppressed by the Saxon court, and Luther never knew of it. Nor was this a misfortune; for it would only have been the occasion of misinterpretation and derision. Luther was unflinchingly resolved to carry out his programme and the Saxon Elector artfully and perseveringly continued his maneuvers to shield the rebellious monk.

It was to the advantage of both that Miltitz with his unfortunate efforts at reconciliation did not disappear from the scene. He invented the proposal that Luther should present himself to the archbishop-elector of Treves as a non-partisan judge. In the course of these negotiations he pretended that this archbishop· had been legitimately appointed by Cardinal Cajetan to render a judicial verdict in the matter. It was a phantom that did not materialize. Extremely strange and dubious is the statement which Frederick of Saxony attributed to the archbishop of Treves, that Pope Leo X was prepared to make Luther a cardinal if he would retract his errors.

Relative to the policy of Leo X in the great questions of that day, especially in that of the election of a German emperor, there is no doubt that it strongly affected his attitude toward the Saxon Elector and, mediately, toward the latter's protégé. For some time Leo had favored the promotion of Frederick of Saxony, the most esteemed and influential German prince of the time, to the dignity of emperor to succeed the deceased Maximilian I. Subsequently he promoted the cause of the youthful Charles V, even though his election to that dignity would have placed him in dangerous proximity to the capital of Christendom as King of Naples.

The most decisive step taken by Luther after the Leipsic disputation and prior to his condemnation by Rome, was the publication, in

June, 1520, of his work, "On the Papacy at Rome." [1] He now intended to strike the Church a mortal blow by disproving the doctrine of the primacy. The occasion was the written attack made on him by a learned Franciscan of Leipsic, Augustine Alfeld, professor of Biblical science in the monastery of his Order in that city, who had publicly espoused the cause of the divine right of the papacy. The subject had aroused the sympathy of Catholics, who correctly perceived that here was the center of the conflict and the decisive battle-field of the future. The other errors would be defeated if the authority of the papacy was firmly established from Holy Writ and the tradition of fifteen centuries. In his hastily compiled reply to the "highly celebrated Romanist of Leipsic," Luther undertook to refute this "monkish booklet," as he styled it, on a broad basis. In his own book, which he had composed in German for the masses to read, Luther expounded his doctrine that the Church does not require a pope, that a visible head is inconsistent with its nature, and that the attachment of that head to a definite place such as Rome, is inconsistent with its character as a spiritual, invisible kingdom, a congregation of all the faithful who cannot be differentiated individually according to their interior dispositions. The true Church of Christ, who is its only Head, is made manifest only by certain signs, namely, Baptism, the Eucharist, and the preaching of the true Gospel (as purified by Luther). The power of the keys is conferred upon all Christians collectively, including the laity, and does not consist in the absolute sovereignty of any spiritual government, but is solely the assurance to be awakened by Christians of divine forgiveness and mercy for consciences in need of consolation in their brethren. Here the old starting-point of Lutheranism emerges once more: Quiescence of the timorous soul as the supreme end.

In the course of his work Luther indulges in unprecedented invectives against the covetousness of the pope, whom he constantly implicates in the shocking villainies of the Romanists. He passionately invokes the patriotism of the Germans and, in particular, the economic and nationalistic ambitions of the princes and the nobility against the ecclesiastical régime of the Italian curia. At Rome, he says, they speak of the drunken Germans who must be fooled. They regard us as beasts. They say: "The German fools must be separated from their money by all manner of means." "If," he finally exclaims,

---

[1] *Werke*, Weimar ed., Vol. VI, pp. 285 sqq.; Erlangen ed., XXVII, pp. 86 sqq.

"if the German princes and nobility do not bestir themselves very soon, Germany will become a desert or it will have to eat itself." This pamphlet contains many violent invectives but no solid argument. A Protestant critic (Vorreiter) correctly judges that it is filled with "consummate sophistry" and "defies the most elementary logic."

The courageous Alfeld was denounced by Luther as "an uncivil ass which cannot even bray!" But he did not permit himself to be frightened. Subsequently he penned still other solid treatises on the debated questions of the day.

About this time Luther was engaged in the composition of his exhaustive "Sermon on Good Works"—a work which is very important for a deeper understanding of his mental development. [2] He says that it treats of "the greatest question that has arisen," and that the publication of the book appeared to him to be more necessary than any of his sermons or smaller works. [3] For, on account of his doctrine that man is saved by faith alone he was loudly accused of being opposed to good works. He now wishes to restore them to honor, and, at the same time, glorify faith, as he understood it, as the pillar of good works. He dedicated this "Sermon," which had grown into a book in consequence of his rapid industry, to the brother of his territorial lord, Duke John of Saxony, who was very favorably inclined to him and sought edification in religious books. Thus, in a certain sense, this book was a parallel to his consolatory tract "Tessaradekas," which he had shortly before dedicated to the sick Elector Frederick. Luther's precarious position at Wittenberg moved him to correspond with the court which protected him. Throughout this tract he appears to be very solicitous about true virtue. It has been characterized by Protestants, even in recent years, as "the first description and demonstration of evangelical morality by the reformer." [4]

This is an added reason for subjecting it to a closer inspection. Luther's alleged true conception of Christian liberty had its origin in the Epistles of St. Paul, particularly in his commentary on Galatians, published in 1519. The liberty of the believing soul be-

[2] *Werke*, Weimar ed., VI, pp. 202 sqq.; cf. IX, pp. 229 sqq.; Erlangen ed., XVI (2nd ed.), pp. 121 sqq.
[3] See the dedication.
[4] J. Köstlin, M. *Luther*, I, 5th ed., p. 291.

came his favorite theme. Somewhat later, at the time of the proclamation of the ban, he developed it in his well-known treatise, *On the Liberty of a Christian*. For the sake of his attitude toward good works, he pushes his conception of freedom from commandments and obligations somewhat into the background. In this book he teaches: Although the true Christian is subject to no law, faith alone being necessary for him, whilst everything else is voluntary, yet because of this very faith, and impelled by it, he submits to the commandments, which are necessary on account of the weak sinners; indeed, a Christian is constantly occupied with good works. His faith urges him to do good. Where there are no good works, there is no true faith. Faith, however, according to Luther, is never anything else but an uninterrupted trust in God's mercy through the merits of Christ. This joyous confidence he regards as the sole source of morality. The sentences which we have quoted and which, in part, are echoes of the work's mystical aberrations have about them something deceptive and apparently attractive. But his glorification of faith, *i. e.,* trust inspired by faith, is permeated by that forcible struggle for the quieting of his own inner needs and fears which led him to cling to the doctrine of faith as the sole means of salvation.

The fundamental deficiency of his theory of good works cannot escape the critical eye.

In the first place, he says, good works are only such as have been commanded by God. Such a thing as the voluntary assumption of a moral act that is not commanded by God does not exist for him. Consequently, the main artery of the perfect life is severed. There is no foundation for the intense pursuit of virtue or for heroism. The saints of the Bible or of Church history, whose wondrous deeds were not inspired by divine command, were simply fools.

Hence, according to Luther, good works flow spontaneously from confident faith in the blood of Christ. But neither his own life nor that of others confirms this doctrine.

The self-righteous, of whom the world under the rule of the papacy is full, are supposed to know nothing of faith in the blood of Christ. They err, according to Luther, because, without Christ, they invest their own works with value for salvation. Luther's utterly false arraignment of the Catholic doctrine of good works is here again resuscitated in drastic form.

His assertion that the self-righteous papists sinned against faith in the blood of Christ, was bound to meet with speedy and decisive retorts on the part of Catholics. The Humanist Pirkheimer, after renouncing Lutheranism, which he had favored for a while, wrote: "we know that we are justified gratuitously by the grace of God and the atonement which is in Christ Jesus, through which we obtain the remission of sins"; we are not justified by our works alone, but by the death of the Son of God; nevertheless, "we cannot have life without good works, and if they are performed for no other reason, then they should be performed out of gratitude to God and His only begotten Son." Others very appropriately referred Luther to the known bases of good works, namely, the necessity of doing penance and atoning for sins, the need of supplicating God's help in the affairs of temporal existence, and above all else the command of the Bible that we must gain Heaven through the merits of good works performed with grace. Everyone was familiar with the concept that the love of God must sustain and ennoble all good works.

In the formulation of this new doctrine, Luther is governed by the idea, conceived during his mystical period, that those works only can be called good which proceed from the motive of absolutely perfect love. Hence he likes to portray how this love, as an activity in man and an efficient motive urging him to goodness, is joined with the fiduciary faith that springs from his gospel. For the rest, moral spontaneity is suppressed in his system. The contradiction is obvious.

Man, according to Luther, is not free to do good. God alone is the cause of everything. Even reason does not attain to the truly spiritual, and the co-operation of man in working out his salvation is, according to a casual expression of his, only a figment of "that mad harlot," the brain.[5]

Luther pretends to ignore the doctrine of faith (*fides formata caritate*) as taught by the Catholic Church. But in opposition thereto, in his above-quoted sermon, glorifies faith because love abides in faith and results in good works. Thus generally, in his practical writings he abandons his theories of the unfree will and the faith produced by God, invariably demands self-activity, and represents love as an element of faith. This contradiction apparently remains hidden to him because of his quite intelligible effort to appear as a promoter of good works, as the founder of true morality in contrast with the self-righteousness of the papal system.

"The Catholic conception of faith by its emphasis on good works is something so natural, something that so obtrudes itself upon the Christian and

[5] *Werke*, Weimar ed., Vol. XVII, I, p. 58.

natural conscience, that we need not be surprised if Luther, in contradiction with his reformatory principle, frequently testifies to this truth." [6] Luther himself says on one occasion: "The entire nature (of man) seeks good works, when he is not subject to temptation." [7] The new system had been suggested to him by his so-called temptations.

Certain extreme expressions employed by Luther were derived from this same false principle. Thus he says in 1520: "Let us beware of sin, but much more of laws and good works; and let us only observe well the divine promise and faith; then good works will readily follow." Now, good works are prescribed by God in Sacred Scripture. Here we perceive a new contradiction in Luther's teaching. One of the most eminent theologians of modern Protestantism aptly wrote: "If it is asked why God, who connects salvation with justification by faith, prescribes good works and wishes to be honored by them, the arbitrariness of this disposition cannot be concealed. . . . Nor it is evident that good works should serve every man as the *ratio cognitionis* of his own justification." According to Luther, he adds, the value of good works must not be considered at all, and yet his doctrine bases the certain consciousness of justification on a measure of good works. "Confronted with these contradictory judgments of moral action, shall anyone find that repose which justification is supposed to guarantee him?" (Albrecht Ritschl).

But, to continue with the characterization of the much discussed Sermon on Good Works, the author, after having announced his new principles, takes up the Ten Commandaments one by one. He wishes to demonstrate how faith works itself out through good works in the case of each commandment. This part of his treatise is full of sound, inspiring ideas, which are identical with the ancient Catholic teaching. Nor does it lack charm and warmth. Duke John and many other readers might be greatly edified by the popular exhortations contained in this work. Though Luther, for instance, does not acknowledge any commandments, such as that of fasting, he asserts that faith leads the devout Christian to chastise his flesh in order that concupiscence might be broken thereby; likewise he intimates that the religious observance of Sunday rest must serve to allay the passions. On the other hand, he adds, on his own responsibility, that physical labor on Sunday, according to Christian liberty, is not to be regarded as prohibited; all days should be holy days and work days. There follow certain recommendations, e.g., to be patient under the

---

[6] Jos. Mausbach *Die katholische Moral und ihre Gegner*, 1911, p. 27.
[7] *Opp. Exeget.*, XX, p. 188.

tyranny of an unjust ruler, since corporal sufferings or material losses
cannot injure the soul; rather, to suffer injustice improves the soul
and injustice is not so dangerous by far to the spiritual as it is to the
temporal authorities.

Here he again seizes the opportunity to inveigh against the abuses
of the spiritual authorities from which the German nation was supposed to suffer.

"Behold, these are the real Turks." "It is not right that we should support
the servants, the subjects, yea the rogues and harlots of the pope to the loss
and injury of our souls." In these words he favored the view of obedience
as conceived by the Elector of Saxony and his court. Now he appeals to the
princes, the nobility, and all public authorities to defend themselves "with
the secular sword" against the burdens imposed by Rome and its clergy,
"since there is no other help or remedy." The bishops and clergy opposed to
the machinations of Rome were full of fear. Hence, "the best and only
remaining remedy would be for kings, princes, nobles, cities, and communes to put a stop to these abuses." These particular Turks "kings, princes,
and nobility should attack first of all;" they should "treat this same clergy
like a father who had lost his reason" and is imprisoned with all honors.[8]

With all honors, he says, and continues: "Thus we should honor the Roman
authority as our supreme father; and yet, since it has become mad and
irrational, we should not allow it to carry out its purpose." It was, of
course, but a figment of Luther's imagination that the expected measure
would be taken "with all honors." The purposely selected phrase "supreme
father" has no weight, but merely indicates the respect which the cautious
court of Saxony still tried to foster toward the pope.

With still less restraint Luther summoned the people to revolt in a
short reply which he published at that time to the *Epitome* of the
papal court theologian Prierias. As an indication of the contempt
with which he regarded this book he had it reprinted in its entirety,
adding a series of violent attacks,[9] in the course of which he made
a formal appeal to bloodshed. This appeal was couched in such violent
language that the early Protestant editors of his works did not dare
to publish it in its entirety; it betrayed a passion no longer master of
itself.[10]

[8] *Schlusswort des Sermons vom Neuen Testament, Werke,* Weimar ed., VI, pp. 353 sqq.
Erlangen ed., XXVII, pp. 141 sqq.

[9] *Werke,* Weimar ed., VI, p. 328; *Opp. Lat. Var.,* II, pp. 79 sqq.

[10] Cf. H. Grisar, *"Cur non manus nostras in sanguine istorum lavamus?"* in the *Histor.
Jahrbuch* of the Görres Society, XLI, 1921, pp. 248–257 *(Luther-Analekten, V).*

"If the fury of the Romanists goes on thus," he writes, "it seems to me there is no other remedy left to the emperor, the kings, and the princes than to attack this pest of the earth by means of arms, and to decide the matter with the sword instead of words. For what else do these lost people, bereft of reason, do than what Antichrist will do according to the prophecy? They hold us to be more unfeeling than all blockheads. If we punish thieves with the gallows, robbers with the sword, heretics with fire, then why do we not equip ourselves with every weapon and proceed against these teachers of corruption, these cardinals, these popes, and this whole swarm from Roman Sodom which corrupts the Church of God without end? Why do we not wash our hands in their blood? We would thus free ourselves and our own from the most dangerous universal conflagration in existence. How fortunate those Christians, wheresoever they may be, who are not compelled to live under such an Antichrist of Rome, as we unfortunate wretches!"

Naturally Luther did not persist in the bloody designs which he conceived in a moment of sudden excitement. It was an impossibility to follow his crazy call. In a calmer hour he afterwards wrote to Spalatin words which were destined for the Saxon Elector: Not by force and murder should the gospel be contended for, but Antichrist is preferably to be crushed by means of the Word; if, as he fears, a revolt against the clergy should break out, he himself would be quite innocent of the calamity, because he—so he now avers—advised the nobility to have recourse, not to the sword, but to "edicts" against the Romanists.[11]

Luther's vehement appeals to the sword and his call for blood, which followed closely upon the publication of the work of Prierias, were not caused by the tone of the Roman tract, but by the clearness with which that writer expounded the doctrine of the primacy of the Holy See. The calmly written tract was really but the table of contents of a larger work which Prierias intended to publish. It was remarkably free from offensive and inflammatory language. In his blind rage, however, Luther directed his whole opposition against spiritual submission to the pope, whom he denounced as Antichrist. The principal objection, so far as he was concerned, were not the acts of robbery imputed to Rome, but the submission which the pope, in the name of his divine primacy, demanded for his false doctrines, deviating from those of Luther. This point is brought out still more clearly by his characterization of Prierias' composi-

[11] Grisar, *Luther*, II, 54 sq.; January 16, 1521.

tion as a heretical, blasphemous, Satanic, Tartarean poison which spreads over the whole earth. He—Prierias—infinitely outdoes Arius, Manichaeus, Pelagius, and all the other heretics. If Rome teaches the doctrine Prierias attributes to her, then fortunate Greece, fortunate Bohemia, fortunate all who have severed their relations with, and wended their own way out of, this Babylon. "Now Satan has taken even the hitherto impregnable fortress of Sion, Sacred Scripture, the tower of David. Fare thee well, thou unfortunate, lost, and blasphemous Rome, the wrath of God has come upon thee." "We wished to heal Babylon, now let us abandon it, that it may become the abode of dragons, ghosts, specters, witches, and that it be what its name indicates—an eternal confusion, full of the idols of avarice, perjurers, apostates, priapists, robbers, simonists, and countless hordes of other monsters, a new pantheon of impiety!"

Those who censured his frenzy he referred to the inflammatory and vehement language of his opponents. But all these combined did not approach the horrible bitterness and the resounding fury of his own effusions. As the *Epitome* of Prierias was free from reproach in this respect, so, too, the writings of Eck, Emser, Alfeld, and the earlier productions of Tetzel were actually moderate in comparison with Luther's. Rome itself had not proceeded against him with excommunication. The Holy See and the bishops had as yet taken no steps against him, which might have conjured up such frenzy. His outbreaks proceeded from his temperament. The cause lay deeper than is usually supposed; it has been partly revealed in the previous remarks about his psychology. It will be made still more apparent by the events of the momentous year 1520.

In the meantime events led to other outbursts of his vehement polemic. In conformity with their position and custom, the faculties of Cologne and Louvain had rejected a number of propositions extracted from his writings. He published a Latin *Responsio,* in which he proposed to demonstrate the vanity and nullity of such academic verdicts in general. Until they would refute him, he says, he would regard their condemnation as one does the imprecations of a drunken wench. The professors of Louvain and Cologne he characterized as "asses" in a letter to Spalatin.[12]

In other writings he undertakes to discuss practical questions. The

[12] Weimar ed., VI, pp. 174 sqq.; *Opp. Lat. Var.*; IV, pp. 176 sqq.

little book on "How to Confess" [13] asked the question whether it was obligatory to confess all secret sins known only to the sinner himself. The author denounces the practice of auricular confession in general as a means of avarice and tyranny.

In a *Sermon on the Blessed Sacrament* [14] he acknowledges the real presence of Christ in the Eucharist, but questions whether it takes place in virtue of transubstantiation, or whether the bread is present simultaneously with the body of Christ. The manner in which he presents the subject amounts to a denial of the sacrificial character of the Eucharist. One may not assume, he says, that this Sacrament is a work *per se* pleasing to God (*ex opere operato*); he maintains, on the contrary, that the work of salvation is wrought by the faith of Christians who are united about this Sacrament, and by that believing conviction of salvation which is nurtured and inflamed by this holy bread as the sign of Christ's Testament. It would be becoming and goodly, he adds, if this Sacrament were dispensed to Christians in the twofold form of bread and wine, and not merely under one species; for it was instituted by Christ under both and should be so ordained by a council of the Church. In this exposition, he did not consider the weighty reasons which had determined the Church in the course of centuries to administer this Sacrament under one form only—a measure which is advocated by many Protestants to-day for hygienic reasons. The Church has always taught that Christ is present whole and entire in, and consumed under, each form, and that the Sacrament is but "partially" present under the form of bread.

The demand for both forms was destined to prove a powerful means for the introduction of the new religion.

The first opposition to this presumptuous demand was made by the bishop of Meissen, John von Schleinitz. In a decree published on January 24, 1520, he ordered the sequestration of Luther's work *On the Sacrament,* and commanded the clergy to inform the people of the reason why, as recently as the fifth Lateran Council, the Church adhered to the decrees which ordained the administration of the Eucharist under one form only. It is worthy of note that this

---

[13] Weimar ed., VI, pp. 157 sqq.; *Opp. Lat. Var.,* IV, pp. 154 sqq.

[14] Weimar ed., II, pp. 742 sqq.; Erlangen ed., XXVII, p. 28, of the year 1519, with the supplements in Luther's *"Verklärung etlicher Artikel,"* Weimar ed., VI, p. 78; Erlangen ed., p. 70, of the year 1520.

was the first public declaration of a German bishop against Luther. The decree was issued in the name of the bishop with the advice and approbation of the cathedral chapter of Meissen. This procedure angered Luther and he at once published two replies, one in German, the other in Latin. To be able to attack the bishop with less restraint, he asserted that the author of the decree, which had been issued at Stolpe, could not possibly be a bishop; that the stupid note had made its appearance quite appropriately during the Lenten season, and that the author probably lost his reason in the carnival. He insisted that the use of the chalice was "an open question."

Luther, as so often happened to him when engaged in controversy, went even further, with fatal results. He discussed the abrogation of clerical celibacy in a manner enticing to the clergy who had taken sides with him or who were undecided in their attitude. Thus he says: "What if I were to say that it appears proper to me that a council should once more permit priests engaged in the cure of souls to have wives? Behold, the Greek priests have wives, and what good man to-day would not, out of sympathy for our own priests, wish that they would enjoy the same liberty, in view of the dangers and scandals that beset them?"

The court of the Saxon Elector now became deeply concerned over Luther's attacks upon the Saxon episcopate and the aggravation of the controversy within the Church. In order to restrain the assailant in the name of the Elector, Spalatin entered upon a more intensive correspondence with Luther, in the course of which the latter revealed even more clearly the illusions under which he labored. He said he did not comprehend the counsels of peace which Spalatin addressed to him. Why did Christ make him a doctor? He was acting in conformity with the will of God and his vocation. He must permit himself to be directed by God, as the ship is driven by winds and waves. The Word of God could not progress without strife, profound agitation, and danger. Let Spalatin caution his raving opponents to be considerate towards him, lest the filth which they had stirred up emit an even greater stench. If he, Luther, permitted himself to be led by human wisdom, it would be a different matter; but his cause had not been prompted by the judgment of men. God carried him along; let Him see to it what He would accomplish through him; he himself had not chosen the task which he must now perform. It was true that he was more violent than necessity called for; but who can observe moderation when he is angry? He feels that his blood boiling, but he is at least plain and frank, etc.[15] It was not difficult for him to admit his violent emotion; but how was he going to prove that he was guided by God? He made no attempt to prove this; he simply felt the divine guidance as anyone else might.

During all these trials he looked with unrest and anxiety toward Rome, whence the ban could not fail to come.

He judged that it would be advantageous for him to prepare the minds of the people for this event by publishing a German tract entitled *A Sermon on the Ban*. [16] He had previously issued a similar work, *On the Validity of the Ban*. His cardinal theme is this: An unjust excommunication (such as he is looking forward to) does not separate a man from communion with Christ, nor deprive him of the intercession and "all the good works of Christendom." It is rather "a noble and great merit before God, and blessed is he who dies unjustly excommunicated." "Christians should learn," he continues, "to love the ban rather than to hate it, just as we are taught by Christ not to fear, but to love punishment, pain, and death." Although he preaches respect for ecclesiastical authority, he expatiates excitedly on the prevalent abuses of the ban and says one may not be astounded that at times the ecclesiastical judges are bloodily avenged by evil-doers, through God's permission. The secular authorities should not tolerate certain abuses of the ban in their countries and among their people.

The Roman curia had too long deferred determined action for political reasons. Luther's writings, which issued in rapid succession from Wittenberg, some of them in inflammatory German for dissemination among the masses, others in learned Latin for the outside world, had ample time to prepare the way for the coming defection. The lamentable delay of a firm decision was attributable to the negligence of the German episcopate, no less than to the illusions to which the learned circles in Germany and abroad, who had been educated in

---

[15] *Briefwechsel*, II, p. 294: "*Quis rogavit Dominum, ut me doctorem crearet? Si creavit, habeat sibi aut rursum destruat, si poenitet creasse,*" etc.—*Ibid.*, p. 323: "*Esto novum et magnum sit futurum incendium; quis potest Dei consilio resistere*"? *Ibid.*, p. 325: "*Non patiar damnatum errorem in evangelio Dei pronuntiari etiam ab universis angelis,*" etc.—*Ibid.* p. 327: "*Ne praesumeres, rem istam tuo, meo, aut ullius hominum iudicio coeptam.*"—*Ibid.* p. 328: "*Verbum Dei, ut Amos ait, ursus in via et laena in silva. . . . Sic Deus me rapit; qui viderit quid faciat per me,*" etc.—Cf. Grisar, *Luther*, Vol. III, pp. 109 sqq.

[16] Weimar ed., VI, pp. 63, 75 sqq.; Erlangen ed., XXVII, pp. 51 sqq.

a one-sided Humanism, were subject concerning the reform movement. Everything conspired to enable the great controversy to vest itself all too long with the character of an undecided issue.

2. CONCLUSION OF THE ROMAN TRIAL

The written representations which Dr. Eck made at Rome after the Leipsic disputation, and the efforts of the Dominicans at last caused final proceedings against Luther to be initiated at the curia. They began before Eck's arrival in the Eternal City. The report of the disputation and the opinions of the theological faculties of Louvain and Cologne did not fail to make a deep impression on the Pope and his entourage. Crotus Rubeanus testifies that even prior to this, and despite various delays, the Lutheran affair was by no means regarded with levity by the Roman curia. With the aid of these official documents, the difficulties were at last surmounted which ignorance of the German language had placed in the way of a proper appreciation of the numerous productions of Luther's pen.

On January 9, 1520, the first consistory met to initiate definite proceedings. Cardinal Cajetan, a theological expert of the first rank, and Cardinal Pietro Accolti, usually called Anconitanus, a distinguished jurist, were particularly active in the formulation of the charges against Luther and his Elector, against whom proceedings were at that time contemplated as an abettor of heresy. With the active participation of these two Cardinals, the matter was debated from February to the middle of March by a commission of theologians and representatives of monastic orders. A smaller commission, under the presidency of Pope Leo himself, then drafted the Bull, containing 41 theses of Luther which had been selected for condemnation. Eck, upon his arrival at the end of March, rendered substantial assistance by the clarifications which he brought. The erroneous opinion of many who were unacquainted with the question at issue may be gathered from the fact that, as late as May, 1521, some at Rome held that the publication of a solemn Bull against Luther would be more damaging than useful, and that the scandal in Germany would only increase if it appeared that so much importance was attached to the new errors.

Knowledge of the proceedings filtered out and reached Luther at Wittenberg. He became alarmed. Among the peculiar opinions which accompanied the report was this, that special difficulties existed, because the necessary proofs against Luther had to be gathered from Holy Writ.[17]

When, at the end of April, the commission had finished its labors, its conclusions were presented to the Cardinals for their final decision. The matter was decided after four consistorial sessions. Cardinal Cajetan had recommended that the forty-one theses be specified in strict theological form, together with the condemnation that attached to each thesis, such as heretical, false, scandalous, etc. The majority, however, were in favor of condemning the theses as a whole, without definitely qualifying each separately, following the example of the Council of Constance when it condemned the errors of Wiclif and Hus. The commission, moreover, unanimously resolved that the forthcoming Bull should be principally a condemnation of the false teachings of Luther, whereas a solemn excommunication from the Church with its attendant temporal consequences was to be pronounced against Luther personally only after the expiration of a certain period of time to be granted to him for the purpose of reconsidering his position.

At the final consistory, Leo X definitely resolved to promulgate the Bull which commenced with the words: *"Exurge Domine et iudica causam tuam."* It was despatched on June 15, 1520.[18]

Most solemn is the introduction to this memorable document, which, in lieu of an address, was superscribed with the customary formula: *"Leo episcopus, servus servorum Dei, ad perpetuam rei memoriam."* "Arise, O Lord" —thus it begins—"arise and distinguish Thy cause, be mindful of the insult which foolish men have heaped upon Thee without intermission. . . . Arise, O Peter, and, mindful of the pastoral office entrusted to thee by God, be thou solicitous of the Holy Roman Church, the mother of all churches and the teacher of the faith which thou hast consecrated with thy blood at the command of God. . . . Arise thou also, O Paul, we beseech thee, thou who by thy teaching and martyrdom hast become the refulgent light of the Church. . . . Let the whole multitude of the Saints arise, and the universal Church, whose true understanding of Sacred Scriptures is contemned and trampled under foot," etc.

[17] Grisar, *Luther*, Vol. I, p. 48; Vol. II, pp. 45–47.

[18] Text in Raynaldus, *Annales*, a. 1520, n. 51 and a somewhat inferior reprint in the *Bullar. Rom.*, ed. Taurin., t. V, pp. 748 sqq. Another reprint, with odious and alien interpolations, in Luther's *Opp. Lat. Var.*, IV, pp. 264 sqq. The 41 condemned theses are reprinted in Denzinger's *Enchiridion*, 26th ed., 1928, pp. 257 sqq.

There follows the condemnation of the forty-one theses, which are specifically designated, without mentioning Luther's name.

Then the Bull proceeds directly against Luther and prohibits his writings, in which "these (forty-one) theses and many other errors are contained." These writings are to be forthwith sought out everywhere and burnt publicly and solemnly in the presence of the clergy and the people. Luther himself is ordered to recant officially, or to appear personally at Rome within sixty days for the purpose of recanting, being given the assurance of a safe papal escort; otherwise the solemn excommunication was to become automatically effective against him with all the consequences established by law. The term of sixty days was to be computed from the time when the Bull was publicly nailed to the doors of the Lateran, the apostolic chancery, and the cathedral churches of Brandenburg, Meissen, and Merseburg.

Luther is reminded of the former citation, when he had been promised a letter of safe-conduct, a friendly reception, nay, even compensation for the expenses of his journey, and of his defiant attitude for more than a year, regardless of the ecclesiastical censures which he had incurred by his appeal to an ecumenical council in violation of the constitutions of Pius II and Julius II, who had prohibited such an appeal under penalties fixed for heretics. Hence, proceedings could be instituted against him forthwith as one "notoriously suspect of heresy, nay, a true heretic." Still, mindful of the mercy of almighty God, all the insults which he had heaped upon the Pope and the Apostolic See would be forgiven him if he would repent, and the Pope would receive him back lovingly, as the prodigal son in the parable was received by his father.

At the same time, however, Luther is firmly reminded of the consequences attendant upon disobedience as implied in the great excommunication and prescribed by medieval and canon law. In this respect the Bull is strictly in line with ancient tradition. It mentions, furthermore, that it was the "illustrious German nation" which had distinguished itself by its loyal and energetic defense of the faith in the past; that the German emperors, with the approbation of the popes, had promulgated the severest edicts for the expulsion and extirpation of heretics throughout their realm, that they had forfeited the territory and sovereignty of all who protected heretics or refused to expel them. (This was a strong reminder to the Elector Frederick of Saxony.) Although there were no certain prospects of success, the Bull was intended as a reminder of the ancient and severe norms of the Christian family of nations, now confronted with the greatest menace to religion that history had ever recorded. Accordingly, all accomplices of Luther, as well as all who received him, were subject to "the penalties provided by law" for insubordination. Under pain of spiritual penalties, all who were invested with authority, in the spiritual as well as in the secular realm, including the highest Christian princes, were commanded to apprehend the monk of Wittenberg, if he proved obstinate, and his abettors, and to have them sent to Rome, or, at least, to expel them from their domiciles. All localities in which the excommunicates resided, were to be under the interdict, *i. e.*, closed for divine service as long as they abided there, and for three days after their departure.

Upon the termination of the above-mentioned respite of sixty days, a proclamation was to be issued in all churches to the effect that Luther and all who remained disobedient were to be shunned by all as declared and condemned heretics; and the Bull *"Exurge"* was to be read and posted everywhere. All transcriptions of the Bull which were made and subscribed by a notary public as well as all printed copies coming from Rome and bearing the seal of an ecclesiastical prelate, were to be regarded as authentic.[19]

Whether Dr. Eck approved all of these penal paragraphs, borrowed from medieval and curialistic tradition, we have no means of knowing. Relative to the selection and arrangement of the forty-one condemned propositions he later expressed certain wishes. Of the Bull in its entirety he heartily approved and assumed the commission, conferred upon him by the Pope, of promulgating it in Germany and securing its observance wherever possible.

Among the principal doctrines which were declared heretical or otherwise worthy of condemnation in the forty-one propositions, are Luther's errors concerning the utter impotence of man to do good, fiduciary faith, justification and grace, the hierarchy and the Church, the efficacy of the Sacraments, Purgatory, Penance, and indulgences. The denial of the authority of the pope and of general councils—the centre of the position which Luther adopted—was sharply and decisively rejected. Thus, this doctrinal utterance of the Holy See was a magnificent manifesto for the orientation of all Christendom. Once more the Apostolic See, in spite of the disturbances caused in the papal curia by the Renaissance and political intrigues, proved itself a beacon light amidst the errors that beset society at this critical juncture. For the rest, the Pope in the Bull *"Exurge"* does not descend to a refutation of the various condemned errors, but adheres to the ancient custom of the Apostolic See. Luther's doctrines had been tested in the light of Sacred Scripture and tradition and the Pope solemnly

[19] The only extant copy of the three originals of the Bull was found in 1920 in the State Archives of Württemberg at Stuttgart. About nineteen original prints are known, of which an account is given by Schottenloher in the *Zeitschrift für Bücherfreunde*, N. F., Vol. IX, No. 2, p. 201.

appeals to the promise of the Divine Saviour to abide with His Church "all days, even to the consummation of the world," and protect her from error. He appeals, finally, to the power conferred upon the Holy See in Blessed Peter and to his authority as the head of the faithful, which bound him to provide for the peace and concord of the Church.

If modern sensitiveness takes offense at some forceful phrases of the Bull, it should be borne in mind that these are almost all passages from Holy Writ which, in conformity with the usage of the papal court, were invoked against heresy as the greatest of all evils. Thus in the introduction of the Bull, which is so frequently criticized by Protestants, the Supreme Pontiff interweaves a number of Biblical texts, such as: Fools cast opprobrium upon God, foxes sought to devastate the vineyard of the Lord, "the boar out of the wood hath laid it waste, and a singular wild beast hath devoured it."

The condemnation of Luther's two propositions concerning the execution of heretics and the Turkish wars has likewise given offense to modern writers, but without reason.[20]

3. THE SO-CALLED TWO GREAT REFORMATION PAMPHLETS OF LUTHER

The reports of his forthcoming condemnation by the Holy See threw Luther into feverish agitation. Notwithstanding his new ideas,

[20] The condemned 33rd thesis of Luther says: *"Haereticos comburi est contra voluntatem Spiritus."* On the meaning of this condemnation, which has given such grave offense to modern writers, see N. Paulus in the *Histor.-pol. Blätter*, Vol. 140 (1907), pp. 357 sqq. Dr. Paulus says that, although the Bull *"Exurge"* is a so-called ex-cathedra decision, not all the condemned theses are "heretical." Relative to the 33rd thesis, it is sufficient to assume the qualification "scandalous" (*scandalosa*), which means not that the proposition is false, but only that it has some other quality deserving of disapproval. Even if the predicate "false" were to be applied to it, the meaning nevertheless would not be that to burn heretics was a work pleasing to the Holy Ghost, but only that it was not contrary to the will of God, etc. But the censure "scandalous" or "objectionable" suffices. "Such propositions as are objectionable or provocative of scandal at any given time and rightly censured as such, may well cease to be objectionable at another time and under different circumstances, and in that case the censure ceases without further ado as no longer possessing a purpose" (p. 364). This will be conceded by all, even those who, with the older theologians, look upon the medieval penalties for heretics as founded upon the public conditions then prevalent in State and Church. Paulus reminds his readers that Luther himself, in later life, and the Protestant theologians of the 16th century, acknowledged and demanded the death penalty for heretics.—The 34th condemned proposition of Luther is on a par with the 33rd: "To go to war against the Turks is to resist God, who punishes our iniquities through them." "To-day circumstances are quite different" from what they were in the age of the Turkish wars and of the Bull *"Exurge."* (Paulus, p. 367).

the solemn ban constituted a blow which stirred the depths of his soul, and which was calculated to alienate from him for all time many of his adherents among the German people and abroad. In this frame of mind, moved by fear and hatred, he composed two vehement polemical pamphlets which were intended to meet the threatening evil and to weaken, as much as possible, the effects of the sentence about to be passed upon him. For he had no intention of bowing his proud head.

The first, written in German, was entitled, "[*An Address*] *to the Christian Nobility of the German Nation on the Improvement of the Christian Estate.*" The second, composed in Latin, bore the title, "*On the Babylonish Captivity of the Church.*"

In "To the Nobility," [21] he addressed the estates of the Empire, especially the governing high nobility, and with inflammatory words summoned them to intervene against the sins and crimes which the Roman curia was perpetrating against the Germans and all Christendom. With the most circumstantial detail he delineates the real or alleged abuses, the perfectly infernal measures which, so he alleged, were being adopted at Rome for the sake of gaining wealth and power, at the expense of German purses and German honor. But he also unreservedly proclaims doctrines destructive of the Church as such. Thus he proclaims that the distinction between the clerical and the secular state is but a hypocritical invention, since all men are priests in virtue of Baptism; that the hierarchy must be removed, if necessary by force; and that the civil authorities have power over it. The office of the temporal authority, to punish the wicked and to protect the good, he exclaims, should be exercised throughout Christendom without let or hindrance, even though it strike priests, bishops, or popes. It is the boast of Luther's Protestant biographers that he thus "laid the foundation for the right of civil authority within Christendom." [22] It would be more correct to say: he indicated the path that led to an intolerable amalgamation of spiritual and temporal power. The Church is reduced to servility. In case of necessity, according to Luther, the civil authority even has the right to convoke a council; indeed, "as a true member of the whole body, and one able to do so most effectively, it should provide a truly free council, which

---

21 Werke, Weimar ed., VI, 381 sq.; Erlangen ed., XXI, pp. 274 sqq. Cfr. Grisar, *Luther*, Vol. II, pp. 26 sq., 31 sq.

22 Köstlin-Kawerau, *Martin Luther*, I, p. 322.

no one is so competent to achieve as the temporal sword, especially since they are now also fellow-Christians, fellow-priests, and fellow-spirituals." [23]

Twenty-five sections of this polemical tract Luther devotes to the evils of the ecclesiastical estate, and an additional section to the injuries inflicted upon the temporal public life. Hence, the deficiencies of the Church, which he assumes the right to reform, constitute the principal burden of this pamphlet. Essentially, however, it contains scarcely anything of importance which he had not previously set forth or at least touched upon. The facts which it stated had already been acknowledged by individual churchmen and even in public gravamina. The Protestant historian Johann Haller remarks: "This is probably the least original of Luther's writings." [24] On the other hand untrue assertions are propounded with so much exaggeration, that the very language in which they were expressed must have prejudiced against them all who thought dispassionately. At every turn the scare-crow of the papal Antichrist is visible in the background. This Antichrist, according to the prophecy of Daniel (XI, 8, 43), must acquire the treasures of the world and destroy everything. Indeed, "most of the popes were devoid of faith"!

One of the tricks employed by Luther to gain adherents was his declaration to the monasteries that he judged they should "become free, everyone to remain as long as he pleased," whereas now every monastery was a life prison for its poor inmates.

His audacious attack upon sacerdotal celibacy, to which "the poor priests," as he puts it, were bound by canon law, must have been an equally effective means of augmenting his strength among the clergy. He would "freely open his mouth, no matter whether it displease pope, bishop or anyone else," and demand that priests be not compelled to live without a ligitimate wife, as they now are by virtue of an institution introduced by the devil through the pope. By means of this device, he asserted, the pope subjected the clergy to his avaricious power. "O Christ, my Lord, look down, let the day of judgment come and destroy the devil's nest at Rome! There is seated the man of whom Paul has said [2 Thess. II, 3 sq.], he shall be lifted up above Thee, and sitteth in Thy temple, shewing himself as if he were a God."

Thus he justifies his provocative summons to the high addressees of his

---

[23] Ibid.
[24] Die Ursachen der Reformation, Tübingen, 1917, p. 5.

book, whom he exhorts: "If we are to attack the Turks, let us begin at
home, where they are most harmful. If it is just that we hang thieves and
decapitate robbers, why should we allow to go unscathed Roman greed,
the greatest thief and robber who has been or may ever be on earth?"

Luther's "Address to the Nobility" became the most widely read
of his works and has remained so up to the present time. Even where
the rest of his books have long ago fallen into oblivion, this work is
still read as a masterly product of the terrific force which that tribune
of the people wielded by his popular invective. It was a trumpet of
war that resounded throughout Germany, as Luther's friend, John
Lang, expressed himself in a letter. Toward "others who were close
to him, Luther had to defend himself against the charge that he
sounded the call to revolt." [25] Conservative Protestants severely criticize this "demagogical book." "It is now fairly conceded," says one
of them, "that Luther, in this book, exceeded the bounds within
which it was his duty to keep." These critics are horrified at its "revolutionary admixture." The course pursued by Luther, says, e. g.,
F. J. Stahl, "was verily gigantic, even in its negations." [26]

Luther at that time hoped for an intervention of the worldly
power. But it failed to eventuate, and as a consequence, his mind,
now aroused by illusions, suffered a disappointment which he soon
admits. For this reason he begins to pursue his object by other means.[27]
Superficially considered, the reforms proposed in the "Address to the
Nobility" appear very fruitful, but when they are closely examined,
they prove to be largely the fruit of the prepossessions of an inex-
perienced monk. In the course of this work his attacks gradually
grow more violent and his style more acrid. This is to be ascribed

---

[25] Theo. Kolde, *Martin Luther*, Gotha, 1884, Vol. I, p. 256.

[26] Stahl, *Die lutherische Kirche und die Union*, 2nd ed., Berlin, 1860, pp. 17 sq. Stahl
also coined the phrase "revolutionary admixture." H. Vorreiter is even more severe in his
criticism (*Luther's Ringen mit den antichristlichen Prinzipien der Revolution*, Halle,
1860). According to him Luther's "Address to the Nobility" is far more destructive than
constructive. His refusal to sever connections with the revolutionary Frankish knights
was a decisive deviation from the path of sound and successful reform (pp. 300 sqq.; 369
sqq.; 377 sqq.; 392 sq.). Leo, Kliefoth, and other Protestants have expressed themselves in a
similar manner, and they are not alone, but have supporters on the Protestant "left."

[27] Cf. P. Drews, *Entsprach das Staatskirchentum Luthers Ideen?* The views of Karl Holl
(*Luther*, 2nd and 3rd ed., pp. 326 sqq.) on the "Address to the Nobility" are to be
received with caution, as this writer interprets the writings of Luther with a view of
justifying his conduct. Luther was neither always deliberate in his actions nor did he
always "remain true" to himself, as Holl would have us believe.

to the circumstance that, in the course of the work, the author became more and more exasperated at the reports from Rome demanding his surrender.

It is probable that the encouragement of the neo-Humanists and the offers of the revolutionary knights, which reached him about this time, contributed to the presumptuous tone of the book. Above all the frivolous and rebellious Ulrich von Hutten endeavored to make common cause with him. Hutten had written to Melanchthon that Franz von Sickingen, a famous mercenary chieftain and notoriously the greatest swashbuckler of the age, who harbored revolutionary ideas similar to those of Hutten, was prepared to protect Luther in his castles if necessary. The Franconian knight Sylvester of Schaumburg also promised to aid Luther until his case was decided and wrote to him that he would place at his disposal a hundred noblemen for his protection.[28] Luther would not have run true to form if such promises had not inspired him with increased boldness. On July 17, 1520, he wrote to Spalatin: "Schaumburg and Franz von Sickingen have insured me against the fear of men; the wrath of the demons is now about to come." [29] And in a letter to his friend Wenceslaus Link, the Augustinian, he thus expresses his triumphant confidence: "To such an extent is the fury of the Romans disregarded by the Germans." [30] He now counseled the court of the Elector of Saxony to write the Pope that Luther had many friends in Germany who would protect him, despite all bans that might be fulminated against him, in the event that he should be driven from Wittenberg.

It was his intention to leave Wittenberg, he averred, in order not to embarrass the Saxon Elector. Nevertheless he was quite certain that Frederick would declare that the university could not dispense with him, and that the controversy would have to be decided by a council. The representations which the Elector had meanwhile made to Rome did not effect any interruption in the proceedings. When writing to Staupitz, not long after, Luther boasted that not only Hutten and many others had written valiantly in his defense, "but also our prince proceeds wisely, faithfully and, at the same time, steadfastly." [31]

---

[28] Grisar, *Luther*, Vol. II, pp. 4 sqq.
[29] *Ibid.*, p. 5.
[30] Letter of July 20, *ibid*.
[31] Grisar, *Luther*, Vol. II, p. 8.

Prior to the arrival of the Bull of excommunication in Germany Luther, at the advice of the Elector, addressed a letter to Charles V, in which he sought to induce him to extend his protection to him, entirely innocent as he was, against the machinations of his enemies.[32] This letter with the supplement ("Oblation or Protestation") which Luther appended to it, is an example of that political art of concealment of which the correspondence of Luther with Spalatin and the court of Frederick offers so many examples.[33] Luther at once published it together with the "Oblation," in Latin for the benefit of readers in other countries.

In the "Oblation" Luther asserts his submission to the holy Catholic Church, as whose devoted son, he says, he wishes with the help of God to live and to die.

To the Emperor, however, he writes that he was forced to go before the public contrary to his wishes, that the hidden life of the cell was the supreme ideal of his life, and that his only desire was to serve the truth against those who in their frenzy disdained it. "In vain do I plead for forgiveness, in vain do I offer to observe silence, in vain do I propose conditions of peace, in vain do I demand to be better instructed." To obtain such instructions and to be convinced by proofs supplied by competent judges, he now appeals to the emperor, before whom, as the king of kings, he humbly appears as an "insignificant flea."

Charles V tore up this letter with his own hands at the diet of Worms. It deserved no better fate, especially in view of the subsequent events.

Towards the end of August, when Luther had signed his letter to the Emperor, he had already in print a part of a second polemical tract, which ranks worthily beside his "Appeal to the Nobility." It was his Latin work *De Captivitate Babylonica*.[34] In the introduction to this work he declared the papacy to be the empire of Babylon, and repudiated the hierarchy and the entire visible Church. According to this book, the Church has been delivered into Babylonian captivity because her doctrines have been falsified and her Sacraments held in bondage. To her falsehoods he opposes his own teachings, derived

---

[32] August 30, 1520; Grisar, *op. cit.*, Vol. II, p. 20.

[33] Cf. Grisar, *Luther*, Vol. II, pp. 15 sqq.

[34] *Werke*, Weimar ed., Vol. VI, pp. 484 sqq., Erlangen ed., *Opp. Lat. Var.*, V, pp. 13 sqq.; Grisar, *Luther*, Vol. II, p. 27.

from the Word of God. He is, for the present, concerned chiefly with dogma. Because of its Latin garb, this book, intended for scholars and foreigners, is not composed in the style of its predecessor, but is prolix and ponderous, as it is intended to be a scientific attack upon the doctrines of the Church.

In his denial of particular dogmas the author advances beyond his previous position, quite in conformity with the principle laid down by him, that if one meets with contradictions, one should advance all the more boldly! The opponents are to be confused and overwhelmed by new assertions.

Above all, the holy Sacraments are to be rescued from the captivity of the papacy. It is an unfortunate and injurious error to hold that there are seven. There are only three, namely, Baptism, Penance and the Eucharist, and these are efficacious through faith alone. As regards the Eucharist, the doctrine of Transubstantiation must be rejected; the bread remains unchanged, only Christ becomes simultaneously present with it. Christ did not prescribe the reception of the Sacrament. The denial of the chalice to the laity is a mutilation of the Eucharistic banquet. The Mass is no sacrifice; nay, not even a meritorious work. The commandments of the Church are contrary to freedom. The Church may not invite vows. Since the so-called Sacrament of Matrimony is a fraud, the entire marriage law must be abolished. The celibacy of the clergy is a damnable institution. And so forth.

It is not worth while to follow up these assertions in detail. They are the fragments of the foundation which Luther had wrecked by his denial of the authority of the Church.

It is more important to establish the fact that he is approaching a complete disintegration without being aware of the fact. With closed eyes he blows up ecclesiastical and religious subordination and the certain outward tradition of positive truth. "Neither the pope, nor a bishop, nor any one else," he declares in his zeal for destruction, "has the right to impose even a syllable upon any Christian without his consent." He deduces this freedom of the faithful solely from Baptism and its obligations toward God and laments "that few know this splendor of Baptism and this boon of Christian freedom." He holds, moreover, that faith originates only in the interior sense of the individual who reads the Bible under the activity of God. There is no need of Church authority; God's Word suffices to make everyone interiorly certain. He himself claims to be conscious of such certainty. It is his opinion, though he does not express it too freely, that all inquirers will agree with him if they permit themselves to be properly directed from above. This was not the case, however, as may be seen from his subsequent bitter complaints about the hordes of sectarians and fanatics within his own church. It is a trait of the power of self-deception which was characteristic of him and which, at times, almost resembles naïveté. The book concludes with invectives against the "despotism, craftiness, and superstition" of the pope, whose adherents are characterized as filled with "stupid ferocity."

What impression did these pages make upon foreign Catholic readers, who were unable to understand the spirit of this "Teuton"? Ambrose Catharinus, a Dominican, who at that time (1520) had already composed his "Apology against Luther's infamous pest of doctrines," regarded Luther as the "intellectual monster" of Wittenberg. The German Franciscan, Thomas Murner, a satyrically inclined antagonist of Luther, undertook to ridicule his *Babylonish Captivity* in a German translation. In the same year, 1520, another German translation of the same work was published by an adherent of the new religion, under the title, *Von der Babylonischen gefengnusz der Kirchen*.

Luther had given to his Latin work the subtitle *Præludium*, i. e., prelude. This prelude and the concluding words indicated that it was to be regarded as the forerunner of another. The author had meanwhile been apprized of the tenor of the Bull directed against him. With the approach of the storm his soul seemed to be endowed with demoniacal power. He concludes by stating that when the Bull arrived, he would, with the help of Christ, issue a sequel "such as the Roman See has hitherto neither seen nor heard," and that the present work might be regarded as a part of his future retraction, lest tyranny appear to have puffed itself up in vain.

4. AFTER THE PROMULGATION OF THE BULL

At the end of September, the papal condemnation of Luther was promulgated in the places designated in the Bull. Dr. Eck, who had been charged by the Pope with this commission, was accused by Luther's adherents of being moved by personal hostility and vindictiveness. There is no proof of such motives extant, though the selection of another person on the part of Rome would probably have been more advantageous. Yet, how many persons were there in Germany whom the Holy See could have engaged for so delicate an undertaking? As the special confidant of Rome, and as one familiar with German conditions, Eck was authorized and commissioned to designate publicly some of the most important partisans of Luther as having incurred the same papal condemnation. Among the six thus selected were Luther's colleague, Andrew Karlstadt, the celebrated Humanist, Willibald Pirkheimer of Nuremberg, and Lazarus Spengler, the town clerk of that city. On October 3, Eck sent the papal Bull to the University of Wittenberg together with a polemic treatise, composed by himself, on the Council of Constance and on certain doctrines which Luther had advocated in his *Address to the Nobility*.

On September 28, Luther, having obtained definite knowledge of the arrival of the Bull in Germany, wrote a letter to Canon Günther von Bünau of Merseburg, in which he declared his intention to ridicule the *bulla* or *ampulla* as an empty bubble.[35] About the middle of October, he published a small tract, *On the New Eckian Bulls and Lies*, in which, contrary to his better knowledge, he asserted that there was no Bull, intimating that it must be another lie or forgery on the part of Eck.[36] This was a political move, designed to evade the blow for the time being, and to create sentiment in his behalf.

Soon afterwards he completed another highly significant German treatise, of which Miltitz sent a printed copy to Pirkheimer, on November 16, while Luther was working on a somewhat enlarged Latin version. It was his famous treatise *On the Liberty of a Christian*. This treatise also appeared in German.[37] Protestant writers esteem it as the third so-called "great document of the Reformation," coordinate with the *Address to the Nobility* and the treatise *On the Babylonish Captivity*. The little work, we are told, embodies Luther's fundamental ideas and, in its "matured and exquisite presentation," ranks equal to "the noblest productions of German mysticism."[38] Luther sent a Latin version to the Pope, accompanied by a

[35] *Briefwechsel*, II, p. 482.

[36] *Werke*, Weimar ed., Vol. VI, pp. 579 sqq.; Erlangen ed., XXIV[2], pp. 17 sqq.

[37] German version, Weimar ed., Vol. VII, pp. 20 sqq.; Erlangen ed., Vol. XXVII, pp. 175 sqq. Latin version, Weimar ed., VII, pp. 39 sqq., *Opp. Lat. Var.*, IV, pp. 206 sqq.

[38] Köstlin-Kawerau, *Martin Luther*, I, p. 363.

letter which he also prefixed to the original edition. This step was taken at the advise of the fantastic Miltitz, who also caused Luther to date this letter as of September 6, whereas it had actually been composed on October 13. It was intended to create the impression that the document was composed prior to the promulgation of the papal Bull, and hence was not influenced by his condemnation. In this way Luther was able to assume a more peaceable air, with the result that he gained sympathizers and disposed the masses against the ban.

It was peace, he told the Pope, that he had aimed at from the beginning; he had earned the "favor and gratitude" of Rome for his resistance to Eck and other knaves. He had always spoken most respectfully of the person of Pope Leo, whose reputation no one could assail; in his generosity the Pope should restrain his enemies, among whom Eck was the worst on account of his insane ambition. "But, that I should recant my doctrines, that cannot be"; "the Word of God, which teaches all liberty, shall not be made captive."

The author again indulges in his usual descriptions of the corruption of the papal court; the papacy, he says, is no longer in existence; poor Leo sits like a sheep amidst wolves, and like Daniel among the lions; the Roman Church is a "den of assassins worse than all others, and a house of knaves more roguish than all the rest."

This letter, ostensibly intended for the Pope, but in reality for the masses, on whom Luther definitely counted, constitutes the introduction to his work On the Liberty of a Christian, by means of which he purposed to set forth "the sum-total of the Christian life," consisting in faith, i. e., trust in God. Such faith produces a splendid good, the true freedom of a Christian. He says he had acquired this faith himself amid great and manifold interior storms and by means of this book now intends to acquaint all "simple folk" with the value of freedom, that treasure contained in faith. He proposes to address only plain people. In the first and principal part of the work he seeks to demonstrate that a Christian, in virtue of his faith, is "a free lord over all things and subject to no one." In the second part, he asserts that "a Christian is the servant of all things and subject to everybody." The two divisions are intended to be complementary to each other.

There is a dual nature in every Christian, he maintains, one interior or spiritual, the other exterior or corporeal. Freedom is the property of the former, servitude that of the latter. In describing the spiritual freedom which flows from faith, he opposes the alleged servile Catholic doctrine of good works, and in doing so makes use of expressions which reveal his entire new system of justification by faith alone.

"Thus, by this faith all your sins are forgiven you, all the corruption within you is overcome, and you yourself are made righteous, true, devout and at peace; all the commandments are fulfilled and you are set free from all things."

"This is Christian liberty . . . that we stand in need of no works for the attainment of piety and salvation."

"The Christian becomes by faith so exalted above all things that he is made spiritual lord of all; for there is nothing that can hinder his being saved. He may snap his fingers at the devil, and need no longer tremble before the wrath of God." [39]

The second part treats of the Christian as a willing servant who is subject to everybody. In as far as the Christian lives in the society of his fellowmen, he says, he must exercise himself in discipline and assist others as a matter of charity. Such good acts are a direct result of faith. Luther first discourses on the manner in which a Christian must discipline himself against the lusts of the flesh. This is followed by a discussion on the works done for the neighbor. All works are done out of the highest and purest love of God. They cause a "pure, joyful life" to dominate the soul of the Christian. Good works are not, however, performed (as the Roman Church teaches) in order that "man may become pious in the sight of God"; they are not meritorious and do not lead to salvation; we must not look to good works and think that we do well in performing many of them." "Good works never make a devout man, but a devout man performs good and pious works." He performs them even though he lovingly trusts that Christ has fulfilled all the commandments for him, and that for this reason a righteous man is in need of no law and no good works. [40]

Luther believed that he had adequately replied to the objection of those who said: "If faith alone is sufficient to produce piety, why are good works commanded? Would it not be better to be of good hope and do nothing?" Nevertheless, this objection naturally persisted wherever the new religion became dominant, and to the end of his life Luther combated the lax practice which prevailed among his fol-

[39] Grisar, *Luther*, Vol. II, p. 28.

[40] Luther had expressed similar ideas in his commentary on the Epistle to the Romans, and hence this present tract contains nothing new. Moreover, the same distinction between the interior and exterior life is found almost literally in Tauler, whose works were known to Luther,—only that Tauler leaves good works intact, nay, expressly emphasizes their meritoriousness. Cf. Grisar, *Luther*, Vol. I, pp. 229 sq.

lowers as the result of his depreciation of good works, which assumed the pseudomystical semblance of an exaltation. The abolition of the laws of the Church as a despicable means of coercion of necessity avenged itself on the masses, who promptly abused the newly proclaimed freedom of the Christian. Luther in his system forgot the earnest and emphatic exhortations of St. Paul, whose teachings he pretended to revive. Paul taught the necessity of zealously performing good works from a motive of both fear and love and in the hope of heavenly reward and forgiveness of sins. He crowned his exhortations with the words: "Be ye steadfast, immovable, always abounding in the work of the Lord, as knowing that your labor in the Lord is not in vain" (1 Cor. XV, 58). Thus the faithful will be free, according to his teaching; not indeed, here below, but in the life to come, they will enjoy perfect liberty of spirit, there where the victory over death hath been given to us through our Lord Jesus Christ (*ibid.*, 56 sq.).

A well-known Protestant writer, speaking of the liberty which Luther wishes to discover in the hearts of believers, says: "The sublime and beatific image of the liberty of the Christian has descended upon the earth in a different manner than Luther once visioned it in golden clouds." "His ideal," the same author adds, "is not organizatory or regulative," but "incomprehensible and almost unlimited"; we shall always be suspicious of such an ideal when there is question of performing the daily duties of life.[41] Other modern Protestant scholars, such as Köhler, Tröltsch, Wernle, and Bess, have frankly criticized this *opusculum* from the same standpoint.[42] Some of them disagree as to the meaning of Luther's work. His Catholic contem-

---

[41] V. Naumann, *Die Freiheit Luthers*, 1919, pp. 44, 15.

[42] B. Bess, *e. g.*, declares (*Zeitschrift für Kirchengesch.*, XXXVII [1917–1918], p. 526): "We must not omit to say that the fundamentation of morality in the second part signifies a limitation of Luther." R. Otto (*Das Heilige*, 7th ed., 1922, pp. 236 sq.) directs attention to the fact that the good thoughts, how to remain attached to God in trustful confidence, were extensively developed long before Luther in the Catholic mystical writings of the Middle Ages, *e. g.*, by Albertus Magnus (*rectius* by the Benedictine John von Kastel), *De Adhaerendo Deo*." This author even says: "If we did not know that 'The Liberty of a Christian' is the work of Luther, we should probably classify it with Catholic mystic literature." Luther's errors, however, prevent this classification. The celebrated saying, "*Ama et fac quod vis*," is quoted by the Catholic mystics of the Middle Ages in a very different sense than that which Luther ascribes to it. On the teaching of St. Thomas Aquinas concerning indifference to exterior works, see Jos. Mausbach, *Die christliche Moral*, p. 225 (tr. by A. M. Buchanan, *Catholic Moral Teaching and its Antagonists*, New York, 1914, pp. 256 sq.)

poraries (*e. g.*, Hoogstraten and Murner) attacked this imaginary freedom as a dangerous and corruptive phantom. Hoogstraten says that Luther's work on *The Liberty of a Christian* is worse than the other products of his pen, because of its seductive and insinuating style and because it is fundamentally destructive of the doctrine of good works.

The fervent mystical note which Luther frequently strikes in this work recalls his former monastic readings, especially from Tauler, and indeed is captivating. It exercised an almost hypnotic effect on the better class of his adherents. The doctrine of pious Christian liberty, though no one really understood it, became a shibboleth of marvelous power. It was a genial trait in Luther's literary career that he knew how to interlard his impetuous speeches wtih winning sentiments and appeals.

The above-mentioned tendency towards radicalism is also ascribed by Protestant authors to Luther's *Liberty of a Christian*. At the time of the Luther jubilee of 1917, the *Christliche Welt* of Marburg said: "From this freedom to Goethe's ideal of humanity is indeed only a short remove." [43] Of the liberty achieved by Luther generally the Heidelberg theologian v. Schubert says: "Whilst by their struggles men gained liberty in the supreme questions of conscience, they blazed a path for all intellectual liberty." It was by following this road that mankind arrived at enlightenment.[44] It will be profitable to discuss this matter a little more fully.

A remarkable picture presents itself when the three so-called great documents of the Reformation are considered as a whole under this aspect. On the one hand, there is the religious sentiment which is apparently spread over the third and wafts its fragrance back upon the two that have preceded it. On the other hand, there is an individualism which is opposed to revealed religion and every form of ecclesiastical solidarity.

In the *Address to the Nobility,* the autonomy of the individual in judging of religious doctrines, is advocated. "If we all are priests," Luther says, "how then shall we not have the right to discriminate and judge what is right or wrong in faith? . . . We should become courageous and free" in the presence of traditional doctrines. We should "judge freely, according to

[43] 1917, p. 690.
[44] *Grundzüge der Kirchengesch.*, 3rd ed., 1906, p. 234.

our understanding, of the Scriptures," and "force" the popes "to follow what is better, and not their own reason." [45]

Reference should be made to the expression previously quoted from the *Babylonian Captivity*, concerning the divine spirit which enlightens every man and imbues him with absolute certitude. Here we have the enthronement of subjectivism.

The doctrine of private judgment inspired by the "whisperings" of God, as Luther subsequently put it, destroys revealed religion and renders impossible the existence of a religious communion with a common creed. Nor does it pause before the body of Sacred Scripture. Luther himself, in the last-mentioned work, undermines the canon of the Bible by his distinction between those writings which manifest the truly Apostolic spirit, and, *e. g.*, the Epistle of St. James, which contradicts his teaching on good works.

We do not mean to assert that Luther had a clear perception of the road he trod to religious nihilism. He wished to be and to remain a believing Christian, and must be vigorously defended against certain of his Neo-Protestant admirers who, in the interests of infidelity, represent the author of the *Freedom of a Christian* as a conscious champion of an undogmatic Christianity, especially in the period of his youthful vigor and the supposed Lutheran fervor. But we may well ask whether many of the expressions which he used in the first flush of revolt are not diametrically opposed to the binding duty imposed by every form of revelation, as well as to his dogmatic attitude in later years. It may also be questioned whether the demand for freedom for the individual and the right of private judgment may not have assisted in laying the foundation of a mere religious humanitarianism.

It is true, as Harnack says, that Kant, Fichte, and Goethe "are all hidden behind this Luther." [46]

A few words more in explanation of Luther's attitude. Luther desired and was compelled to justify his colossal revolt from the creed of a Church that had existed upwards of a thousand years. How could he, a lone individual, expect to succeed in his opposition to millions of the wisest and most excellent men of the past? He simply asserted that no communion has an established right to claim exclusive possession of the faith, but that every individual who correctly inter-

[45] Grisar, *Luther,* Vol. II, p. 31.

[46] Cf. the passage from Ad. v. Harnack quoted in our *Luther,* Vol., II, p. 32. Chapter XXXIV of the fifth volume of my large work on Luther, first section, treats of Luther on his way "towards a Christianity devoid of dogma," based mainly on Protestant opinions.

prets Sacred Scripture, has precedence. Thoughtful critics perceived
in this proposition the dissolution of all religion, but Luther says:
Follow me, for I am certain, and accept the fragments of faith which
I leave to you. That he believed and willed to be perfectly certain,
must be conceded; for the protracted struggle he waged with himself, in order to attain certainty, could not, in view of his psychological
disposition, be devoid of results. But when he perceived that many,
influenced by his rare qualities, his firm stand, and the force of his
language, admiringly accepted his opinions, the notion that he was
sure of his ground became deeply imbedded in him, even though
he was not always able to cope with the doubts that assailed him, as
his own confessions, made both subsequently to and contempora-
neously with that so-called spring-time of the Reformation, show.
Nevertheless, in the introduction of his "Address to the Nobility,"
he finds himself "compelled to exclaim and to shout." He believes he
is promoting only the glory of Christ.

Hence his concluding words, "God has forced me by them [my adver-
saries] to open my mouth still further." He meets with opposition, but is
only confirmed thereby. "Though my cause is good, yet it must needs be
condemned on earth and be justified only by Christ in heaven." [47]
"I feel that I am not master of myself (compos mei non sum)," he
writes to a friend a few weeks later. "I am carried away and know not by
what spirit." [48]
About this time he unburdens his mind to Staupitz, thus: "Our dearest
Saviour, who has immolated Himself for us, is made an object of ridicule.
I conjure you, should we not fight for Him, despite all dangers, which are
greater than many believe? . . . With confidence I have sounded the bugles
against the Roman idol and true Antichrist. The word of Christ is not the
word of peace, but of the sword. . . . If you do not wish to follow me, then
at least suffer me to go on and be carried away [sine me ire et rapi]." [49]
Staupitz, however, deluded and undecided, had himself uttered the words:
"Martinus has undertaken a difficult task and acts magnanimously, il-
lumined by God." [50]
Touching on the cares of his impetuous activity, which allowed him no
time for reflection at the most decisive moment of his life, Luther writes
in a letter: "Labors of the most varied kind carry my thoughts in all direc-

[47] Grisar, Luther, Vol. II, p. 37.
[48] To Konrad Pellikan, end of February, 1521. Grisar, op. cit., Vol. II, p. 52.
[49] Briefwechsel, III, p. 85; Grisar, op. cit., Vol. II, p. 54.
[50] Köstlin-Kawerau, M. Luther, I, p. 371.

tions. Twice a day I have to speak in public. The revision of my commentary on the Psalms engages my attention. At the same time I am preparing sermons for the press. I am also writing against my enemies, opposing the Bull in Latin and in German, and working at my defense. Besides this I write letters to my friends. I am also obliged to receive visitors at home." [51]

In this last-quoted letter he states that he was opposing the papal Bull of condemnation in Latin and in German. Encouraged by the attitude of the University and the Elector's court, which declined to promulgate the Bull, Luther at once followed up his work *On the New Eckian Bulls and Lies* with his *Adversus Execrabilem Antichristi Bullam*, also published in German, though somewhat altered, under the title *Wider die Bulle des Endchrists*.[52] In the Latin text he reiterates his doubts on the authenticity of the Bull, and pronounces anathema upon the authors of this "infamous blasphemy." He volunteers to die, in the event that this damnable tyranny should actually be consummated in him. In the German version he exclaims with demoniacal fury: "What wonder if princes, nobles and laity should smite the heads of the pope, bishops, priests, and monks, and drive them from the land?"

On November 17, he renewed his appeal to a general council of the Church.[53]

In compliance with an order of his Elector, he forthwith undertook to compose a more learned defense of his condemned forty-one articles. It appeared in Latin and in German, about the middle of January, 1521, under the title, *Grund und Ursach aller Artikel (Assertio Omnium Articulorum)*.[54] "Who knows," he says in the German edition, "whether God has not raised me up and that it behoves mankind to fear Him, lest they contemn God in me? Do we not read that God usually raised but one prophet at a time?" In an attack on free-will contained in this book he expressly teaches that "everything happens necessarily," because ordered and effected by God. The Bible is expressly represented as the sole source of faith.

[51] Grisar, *Luther*, Vol. II, pp. 52 sq.

[52] Latin text in the Weimar ed. of Luther's works, VI. pp. 597 sqq.; Erlangen ed., *Opp. Lat. Var.*, V, pp. 134 sqq.; German text in Weimar ed., VI, pp. 614 sqq.; Erl. ed., XXIV², pp. 38 sqq.

[53] Weimar ed., VII, pp. 75 sqq.; Erl. ed., *Opp. Lat. Var.*, V, pp. 121 sqq.

[54] Latin text in Weimar ed., VII, pp. 94 sqq.; Erl. ed., *Opp. Lat. Var.*, V, pp. 156 sqq.; German in Weimar ed., VII, pp. 308 sqq.; Erl. ed., XXIV², pp. 55 sqq.

5. THE FIRE ALARM

On December 10, 1520, Luther solemnly burnt the book of canon law, as he had previously announced.[55]

In response to a poster which Melanchthon had nailed to the door of the Wittenberg church, a large number of students and teachers assembled before the Elster Gate in the forenoon of that day. A funeral pile was built, upon which were placed the papal law books together with some Scholastic and anti-Lutheran treatises. The principal act was the burning of the book of canon law. The papal Bull was not even mentioned in the invitation. Only after the pile of books, to which a master set fire, had commenced to burn, while the students were chanting jeering songs, Luther stepped forth and cast a printed copy of the Bull of excommunication into the fire, saying: "Because thou hast destroyed (*conturbasti*) the truth of God, may the Lord consume thee in this fire. Amen." The words were almost a literary repetition of the report of the judgment visited upon the person of Achan, as related in the Book of Josue (VII, 25). A less reliable tradition reports Luther as having said: "Because thou hast grieved the holy one of the Lord, eternal fire consume thee!" and the anti-Lutheran party erroneously identified Luther with "the holy one of the Lord," whereas the expression probably referred to Christ, who is called the Holy One of the Lord in the Bible.

The burning of the book of canon law (as this act should be called in preference to the burning of the Bull of excommunication) was a sign of conflagration, symbolical of the ecclesiastical revolt which was commencing in Germany and thence was to spread throughout the world and result in civil revolution. The young men who were present, in their enthusiasm for Luther, did not suspect the far-reaching significance of the act. They sang farcical songs, and long after Luther and his friends had departed, continued their buffoonery about the funeral pyre, which they stirred up ever and anon. In the afternoon students rode about the streets of Wittenberg in a carriage, jeering a ridiculous imitation of the papal Bull. On the next day, however, Luther clearly explained the proceedings to his hearers, saying that really "the pope himself, *i. e.*, the Roman See," should have been consigned to the flames, instead of the book of canon law. The exuberant spirit of the students vented itself anew against the pope in

[55] For details see Grisar, *Lutherstudien*, No. 1 (1921), pp. 5 sqq.

the course of the ensuing carnival. Besides other mischievous pranks, a student vested himself like the pope, paraded in great pomp with a masked Roman curia and, according to a previous agreement, was pursued through the streets by a boisterous mob and finally arrested and brought to judgment. Luther gives an account of this affair with characteristic satisfaction.[56]

In consequence of the intervention of Rome, the number of students at the University had at first decreased slightly. But soon afterwards Spalatin found that Luther's lectures were attended by nearly four hundred hearers, Melanchthon's by from five to six hundred.[57] Despite the Bull of excommunication the fame of Wittenberg increased greatly throughout Germany. Many never obtained a correct knowledge of the Bull, and still less of the reasons for the condemnation. After the termination of the respite which had been granted Luther for the purpose of recantation, the Pope promulgated a new Bull, *"Decet,"* dated January 3, 1521, which announced that the ban had gone into effect and contained exhortations to the faithful. On June 12, Luther's writings and a wooden statue of him were consigned to the flames at Rome. In conformity with ancient custom the scene was enacted in the Campo dei Fiori, where the statue of Giordano Bruno now stands.[58]

The proceedings at Rome found no particular echo in Germany, for which indolence the episcopate was chiefly to blame. Too many of the noble lords who held episcopal sees had other interests at heart than meeting hostile attacks upon the Church, which some of them failed to understand, while others feared to promulgate the papal Bull and take corresponding measures. Yet their dioceses were founded upon that very canon law which Luther had consigned to the flames and which formed the basis of the entire ecclesiastical life of the past and of all western civilization. If the flames of Wittenberg could not enkindle the zeal of the bishops, the latter should at least have learned a lesson from the following work of Luther: *Why the Books of the Pope and his Disciples have been burnt by Dr. Martin Luther.* In this work, which appeared in both German and

---

[56] According to Köstlin-Kawerau, *Luther,* I, p. 375; cfr. Grisar, *Luther,* Vol. II, pp. 51 sq.

[57] Grisar, *Luther,* Vol. II, pp. 50 sqq.

[58] Kalkoff in the *Archiv für Reformationsgeschichte,* XI (1914), pp. 165 sq. Cf. *Zeitschrift für Kirchengeschichte,* XXV (1904), p. 578.

Latin,[59] fundamental attacks upon the Church alternate with re-volting misrepresentations. Never did the lack of ecclesiastical loy-alty in the majority of the episcopate prove more fatally injurious to the German Church than in those decisive days. Not until December 30 was the Roman Decree read from the pulpit at Augsburg. At Freising, its publication was postponed to January 10. Eichstätt like-wise neglected to act till January, and, as in the case of other bishop-rics, minimized the document by means of guarded clauses. Even Meissen and Merseburg delayed its dissemination. Ratisbon prudently waited for developments. Passau offered covert resistance. The Upper Rhenish bishops, such as the bishop of Spires, for a long time took no notice of what had happened. The University of Ingolstadt scarcely manifested any interest. The University of Erfurt was openly hostile. The University of Vienna, in opposition to its theological faculty, de-clined to carry out the provisions of the Bull, and, in justification of its refusal, referred to the dilatory conduct of the archbishops of Salzburg and Mayence. In brief, Dr. Eck met with most unpleasant experiences in connection with his efforts to promulgate the papal Bull.

The learned Erasmus confirmed Frederick of Saxony, who inclined to Lutheranism, in his anti-ecclesiastical attitude. Owing to actual or feigned indisposition, the Elector tarried at Cologne at the time of the coronation of Charles V at Aix-la-Chapelle, October 28, 1520. Erasmus made personal representations to him there, contending that Luther should first be tried by learned and pious judges at a place free from suspicion. In judging of the controversy, Erasmus made a sar-castic remark to Frederick: "Luther has sinned in two respects—he has assailed the crown of the pope and the belly of the monks." [60] In conformity with Erasmus's suggestion, Frederick saw the two papal legates, Aleander and Caraccioli, who had been sent to the new king and to the emperor-elect.

These legates of Leo X were more successful with Charles V, who, though only twenty years of age, was a real monarch. He caused the Bull against Luther to be proclaimed in the Netherlands, his hereditary patrimony. At Louvain and Liège the writings of Luther were publicly burned. The same scene was enacted at Cologne, after

[59] Latin text in Weimar ed., VII, pp. 170 sqq.; Erl. ed., *Opp. Lat. Var.*, V, pp. 257 sqq.; German text in Weimar ed., VII, pp. 161 sqq.; Erl. ed., XXIV [2], pp. 151 sqq.

[60] Kawerau, *Reformation und Gegenreformation*, 3rd ed., 1907, p. 30.

Elector Frederick had left that city in November. Aleander succeeded in having the same thing done at Mayence, though amid difficulties and opposition. The strict traditional demands of the Bull and the altered views of the age frequently collided. Even men devoted to the Church voiced their opposition to the forcible removal of heretics. Eck himself was decidedly in favor of the ancient imperial laws which demanded the execution of heretics. He dealt with this question in his widely circulated *Enchiridion adversus Lutteranos,* which abounded in quotations from the Fathers and theologians.[61]

Jerome Emser, who, like Eck, advocated the enforcement of the penal laws, also attacked Luther in print. The replies which he received from the latter were coarse and ironical, as may be seen from the pamphlets *An den Bock zu Leipzig* and *Auf des Bocks zu Leipzig Antwort* (1521).[62]

When the time for Easter confessions approached, in 1521, Luther, taking into account the critical situation of his readers relative to their confessors, published his *Instructions for Penitents on Prohibited Books.* It was a model of his apparently considerate, yet inciting approach to the practical questions involved in the conflict.[63]

He clearly perceived that for many the Easter confession of that year was to be decisive. Therefore he instructed his readers to entreat their confessor if he should question them, "with humble words," not to bother them about the books of Luther; they should simply say that the popes had often changed their opinions after promulgating a prohibition. If they were denied absolution because of their refusal to promise to leave the prohibited books alone, they should not be disturbed in conscience, "but be joyous and certain of absolution, and also receive the Sacrament [Communion] without any fear." The more courageous penitents, who had "a strong conscience," were told to rebuke their confessor to his face for his narrowmindedness. If communion was refused, they should first "humbly beg for it," and, if that were without avail, "abandon Sacrament, altar, priest and churches," for they all teach that "no commandment may be made or may exist in contravention of God's Word and your conscience."

Luther was inventive in the promotion of his cause. In his eagerness to avail himself of whatever appeared likely of serving his ends,

---

[61] Cap. 26: *De haereticis comburendis.*

[62] Weimar ed., VII, pp. 262 sqq., 271 sqq.; Erl. ed., XXVII, pp. 200 sqq., 205 sqq.

[63] Weimar ed., VII, pp. 290 sq.; Erl. ed., XXIV², pp. 204 sqq.; Grisar, *Luther,* Vol. II, pp. 59 sq.

he, towards the close of 1520, made use of a notorious fable attributed to Bishop Ulrich of Augsburg, by providing a Wittenberg reprint of it with a preface of his own. This publication was intended to be an effective weapon against the celibacy of priests and religious. In this letter the saintly bishop is represented as narrating how some 3000 (according to others, 6000) heads of infants were discovered in a pond belonging to St. Gregory's nunnery at Rome. The manuscript with the letter had been sent to Luther from Holland. It is one of the clumsiest forgeries which issued from the ranks of the opponents of Gregory VII, who strictly enforced the ancient law of clerical celibacy. Emser called Luther to task for publishing this questionable letter, and he replied that he did not place much reliance upon it. Nevertheless, thanks to his patronage, the fable was allowed to continue on its harmful career and was zealously exploited.[64]

What was the attitude of the Augustinians towards Luther in these fateful days? The foundation on which the German Congregation of the Order rested, was deeply undermined by Luther's conduct and the undecided attitude of Staupitz. John Lang, Luther's confidant, who had succeeded Luther in the rural vicariate, advanced his cause by preparing the minds of the brethren for Luther's ideas. Wenceslaus Link effectively aided him. In the chapter which met at Eisleben, August 28, 1520, Staupitz resigned the vicariate when the storm broke over his head.[65] Fourteen friars abandoned the monastic life with Lang. Link succeeded Staupitz in the government of the congregation, now tottering to a fall. The monks who remained loyal were decried by their pro-Lutheran comrades as sanctimonious Pharisees, and their position became very difficult. At a meeting of the brethren at Wittenberg, on Epiphany, 1522, it was announced that begging would be officially prohibited. Moreover—and this was more important—it was resolved that, in view of the liberty granted by the Gospel, any monk might leave the monastery, but he must "pro-

---

[64] Grisar, *Luther*, Vol. IV, pp. 89 sq. What Haussleiter, in the passage cited, establishes as a conjecture (that the Wittenberg edition of this fabulous letter and its preface were the work of Luther) was confirmed by Otto Clemen in the *Theol. Studien und Kritiken*, (XCIII 1920–1921), pp. 286 sqq. Luther appeals to the spurious letter of Bishop Ulrich in his Table Talks, Weimar ed., IV, no. 3983, p. 55; cf. also IV, No. 4358, p. 258, and No. 4731, p. 456. His commentary on Genesis, in the passage quoted by Haussleiter (p. 123), likewise refers to this letter. For the text of the forgery, see *Monumenta Germ. Hist.*, *Leges*, I, pp. 254 sq.

[65] Kolde, *Die deutsche Augustinerkongregation*, p. 327.

ceed without scandal, lest the holy evangel be subject to insult." [66]
Among those who remained faithful at Erfurt were Nathin and
Usingen, Luther's former teacher, and a valiant defender of the
Church, who retired to the Augustinian monastery at Würzburg in
1525. Luther in the meantime continued to live outwardly as a monk
in the monastery at Wittenberg. He did not yet attack the validity
and binding power of the monastic vows.

Staupitz, utterly disappointed, but still favorable to Luther and
his doctrine, retired to the Benedictine monastery of St. Peter at
Salzburg. He repeatedly exhorted his protégé not to go too far. In
1522, he even informed him in a letter that he ought to know that
his (Luther's) activities were being "praised by those who keep
houses of ill-fame." [67] Luther, on his part, bombarded him with letters, in which he importuned him to join his party whole-heartedly
and openly. Owing to the restraint exercised by his environment, and
undoubtedly also to the influence of Cardinal Matthew Lang, archbishop of Salzburg, who appointed him abbot of the above-mentioned
Benedictine monastery, Staupitz finally made a fairly satisfactory,
though ambiguous profession of faith and openly rejected Luther's
abuse of Christian liberty. He died in 1524, and was buried in the
monastery graveyard. A large artistic slab, bearing his coat-of-arms,
covers his remains in the chapel of St. Vitus, and an elegant epitaph,
composed in the style of the age, proclaims his eulogy. The monastery preserves his portrait as a Benedictine abbot in a little known but
fine oil-painting, the work of a contemporary artist. [68]

The image of this man, who for many years favored Luther, reminds the beholder of the words which Luther, in a spirit of uncanny
satisfaction at the turmoil prevailing in Germany, wrote in one of his
last letters to Staupitz: "The confusion rages splendidly (*tumultus
egregie tumultuatur*). [69] It seems to me that it can be quelled only
by the break of doomsday; so eagerly are both parties involved in it.
Marvelous things are ready to happen in the history of the time . . .
I have burned the books of the pope and likewise the Bull. In doing
so, I was at first seized with fear, and prayed; but now I take greater

---

[66] *Ibid.*, pp. 378 sq.; Grisar, *Luther*, Vol. II, p. 337.

[67] Grisar, *op. cit.*, Vol. II, pp. 151 sq.

[68] Another, less reliable portrait of a later period is to be found in the series of abbots
depicted on a wall of the monastery.

[69] January 14, 1521; *Briefwechsel*, III, p. 70.

pleasure in this act than in any other act of my life; they are undoubtedly a greater plague than I imagined!"

In the same letter he writes to his spiritual father thus: "At Augsburg [in the days of the trial] you said to me: 'Remember that you
have begun this cause in the name of our Lord Jesus Christ.' . . . Until now it has really been but a trifling! More serious developments are
at hand, and what you have once said is being verified: If God does
not do it, it is impossible. Manifestly everything is in the hands of
God. No one can deny it."

CHAPTER VIII

THE DIET OF WORMS (1521)

I. LUTHER ON TRIAL BEFORE THE EMPIRE

After Luther had been put under the ban, Pope Leo X addressed an earnest letter to Charles V, in which he demanded that those vested with the proper authority should execute its secular effects.

The diet of Worms had been convoked for January 6, 1521. Elector Frederick of Saxony, ever intent upon delaying the trial of Luther, proposed that Luther be permitted to come to Worms for a hearing before the diet. In a letter to Spalatin the rebellious monk expressed his willingness to make the journey.[1] But the opposition of the party loyal to the Church, especially that of Cardinals Aleander and Caraccioli, the papal nuncios attending the diet, the Elector, and subsequently also the Emperor, temporarily abandoned this plan. When Luther was apprised of this decision, he expressed his displeasure (*cum dolore legi*); for he sedulously strove to create the impression that he had not been accorded an adequate hearing. His fancy was charmed by the prospect of appearing on the world stage at Worms. How much could he not expect in furtherance of his cause from a courageous testimony given there in the presence of the empire! What had he to fear, protected as he was by an imperial safe-conduct and the support of his friends among the knights? Courage and presumption he possessed in a plentiful measure.[2]

Luther's opponents at the diet did not tarry in beginning opera-

---

[1] *Briefwechsel*, III, p. 24. Luther here solemnly advises Spalatin (and through him the Elector) of the dedication of his life to the cause he had espoused.

[2] On the preliminaries and Luther's appearance at the diet of Worms see Kalkoff, *Luther und die Entscheidungsjahre*, 1917, pp. 187 sqq., and the same author's *Der Wormser Reichstag*, 1922. Many of Kalkoff's assertions, however, are questionable. Cf. in addition H. v. Schubert, *Quellen und Forschungen über Luther auf dem Reichstag zu Worms*, 1899. A shorter but more reliable description in Janssen-Pastor, *Geschichte des deutschen Volkes*, Vol. II, 20th ed., pp. 173 sqq. See also Grisar, *Lutherstudien*, No. I: *Luther zu Worms*, etc. pp. 18 sqq.

tions against him. On Ash-Wednesday, February 13, Aleander delivered an oration, which lasted three hours and was received with applause. He recommended that the papal Bull of excommunication be promptly enforced. Among other things he pointed out that the Saxon innovator had rebelled also against imperial statutes, and that his agitation enkindled insurrection and civil war. At the conclusion of the address, Charles V declared his intention to proceed at once, and added that it was neither necessary nor expedient to grant Luther a hearing. This was the correct point of view; for after the definitive judgment of the Holy See, the diet was incompetent to reopen the case, especially before the secular authority. If there was merely a question whether Luther recanted or not, this could be decided in the diet without summoning him. Luther himself stated that it was not necessary for him to leave Wittenberg solely for this purpose.

Notwithstanding the activity of Cardinal Aleander to keep the excommunicated monk away from Worms, some members of the diet were in favor of giving him a hearing. This sentiment was nourished by the approval which Luther's pronouncements against the oppressive papal taxation and the Roman procedure in the bestowal of benefices met with in the assembly. The upshot of this dissatisfaction appears in the "grievances" (*gravamina*) voiced by the diet.

On February 19, the estates requested the Emperor to permit Luther to appear at Worms, not, indeed, for the purpose of disputing with him about religion, but that his recantation might be demanded by experts appointed for this purpose. In the event of his recantation, it was intended to interrogate him "about other points and matters." If, however, he refused to recant, the Emperor was to issue a suitable mandate[3] declaring the concurrence of the empire in the papal ban with its penalties.

In consequence of this request of the estates, the Emperor cited Luther to appear in Worms, March 6, 1521.[4] The citation was handed to him at Wittenberg, on March 26, by Caspar Sturm, the imperial herald, who had orders to escort Luther to the diet. An imperial letter of safe-conduct for the journey to and from the diet was issued,[5] for

[3] *Deutsche Reichstagsakten unter Karl V.*, edited by A. Wrede, Vol. II, Gotha, 1869, pp. 316 sqq. Cf. Janssen-Pastor, *op. cit.*, p. 197.

[4] *Briefwechsel*, III, pp. 101 sq.

[5] *Ibid.*, pp. 103 sq.

which reason the summons stated that he had to fear no violence or injustice.

Before he started on his journey, Luther forwarded the printed commencement of his explanation of the Magnificat to the future Elector, Duke John Frederick, who was very favorably inclined towards him, and to whom he had dedicated this work. He also wrote an exhortation to Wenceslaus Link on the completion of the latter's violent diatribe against the Italian Dominican, Ambrosius Catharinus, who had vigorously attacked him. Then, clad in the habit of his Order, and firmly resolved not to recant, Luther confidently set out, on April 2, on his famous visit to the city of Worms.

His adherents saw to it that a welcome was extended to him everywhere. His journey almost assumed the proportions of a triumphal procession. At Erfurt he preached to a great concourse of people on his newly discovered way of salvation. "What matters it," he exclaimed, "if we commit a fresh sin, so long as we do not despair, but remember that Thou, O God, still livest. Christ, my Lord, has destroyed sin; then at once the sin is gone." [6] When, owing to the overcrowded condition of the church, the galleries cracked and a panic ensued, he forthwith adjured Satan and blamed his spite for the disturbance. A chronicler ascribes the restoration of quiet to Luther's powerful command to the devil and says it was the "first miracle" performed by the man of God. During his sermon at Gotha, the devil cast stones from the gable of the church. According to a letter to Spalatin, written in Frankfort, Luther likewise attributed to the devil a severe illness from which he suffered and which seemed to threaten the continuation of his journey. What was more serious, however, was the news which reached him on the way of an edict which the Emperor had issued concerning his books, that they were to be delivered up to the authorities everywhere. This made Luther realize that the Emperor was resolved on intervention. He said later that this realization caused him to tremble with fear. From Oppenheim he addressed a letter to Spalatin, who had cautioned him; he said he would go to Worms, even if the devils were as numerous in that town as the tiles on the roofs.[7] At that time he also wrote: "We shall enter

---

[6] Grisar, *Luther*, Vol. II, p. 339; Vol. III, p. 180. Cf. the section on Luther's journey to Worms and his appearance at the imperial diet, *ibid.*, I, pp. 379 sqq., and Köstlin-Kawerau, I, p. 407.

[7] *Briefwechsel*, III, p. 120.

Worms in spite of all the gates of hell and all the powers of the air." [8] In a tavern at Frankfort he was in such high spirits that he played the lute in the presence of many guests. His opponent Cochlæus afterwards ridiculed this incident and said that here one had an occasion to see Orpheus perform in cowl and tonsure.

At Worms there was a party, centered around the Emperor's confessor, a Franciscan friar by name of John Glapion, who veered to and fro between the papal nuncio and the declared friends of Luther relative to the latter's trial. Glapion wanted Luther to appear before him at the castle of Ebernburg, instead of the diet in Worms. Luther's friend Bucer was instructed to try to induce him at Oppenheim to acquiesce in this proposal. Luther, however, refused to abandon his journey to Worms, particularly since he had been apprised of the plot which the revolutionary knights had formed against Worms and the diet in the extreme case that violence should be offered to his person.

In the forenoon of April 16, the flourish of the watchman's trumpet on the spire of the cathedral announced to the inhabitants of Worms that Luther was entering the city. He was accompanied by an honorary escort of about one hundred knights. A large multitude soon gathered about him. He rode to the residence of the Knights of St. John, where he took up his abode. After he had alighted, he "gazed about with the eyes of a demon," as Aleander says (who, however, never saw him and declined to attend the sessions).[9] "God will be with me," he said. Clad in a cowl, with a leather girdle, and a scanty tonsure about his brow, he exhibited a wretched figure, emaciated as he was by fatiguing labors and the stress of uninterrupted excitement. But his eyes beamed with a brilliant, deeply glowing, and defiant lustre. A faithful representation of his appearance in 1521 is supplied by Lucas Cranach's etching which forms the frontispiece of the German edition of his works. The lower jaw, the nape of the neck, the mouth and the eyes conspire to give an impression of defiant self-reliance. It is the best portrait of Luther which we have, all the others being considerably "toned down."

On the following day Luther was escorted by the marshal of the

---

[8] Cf. *Briefwechsel*, III, p. 122, annotation 5, where Spalatin's (German) *Annals* (ed. by Cyprian, 1718, p. 38) are quoted and reference is made to Luther's address to Sturm recorded in the Table Talks, No. 2609 (Weimar ed., III, No. 3357b, p. 285).

[9] Grisar. *Luther*, Vol. IV, p. 355.

diet and the imperial herald to an assembly of certain members of the diet who had been summoned to meet the Emperor in the bishop's court. The edifice no longer exists. The Wittenberg jurist Schurf accompanied him as his counsel, and, together with the counselors of the Elector of Saxony, assisted him in the preparation of his address. He entered the hall with a forced smile on his countenance, and critically scanned the audience. He was unable, however, to conceal a feeling of depression. He delivered the few brief words that he was allowed to utter, according to a Spanish report, "with great trepidation and little serenity in countenance or gestures." It was not surprising that the gravity of the moment affected even his habitually defiant disposition. The speaker of the assembly, and official of the Archbishop of Treves, the adroit John von Eck (not to be confused with Dr. Eck of Ingolstadt), addressed two questions to him: first, whether he admitted the authorship of the books that had been placed before him; secondly, whether he was prepared to recant. He acknowledged the authorship of the books, after their titles had been read to him. As to the question of recantation, he begged for time to reflect on account of the importance of the matter for his spiritual welfare. He intended to delay matters, but his expectations were disappointed when, after a brief consultation, the Emperor granted him but one day.

After Luther had left, his appearance was being discussed, and the Emperor said: "This fellow will not make a heretic of me." The most diverse opinions were relayed to Aleander in his retirement. He wrote to Rome that some regarded Luther as deluded, others as possessed, and others again as a man filled with a holy spirit.[10]

In the evening Luther, assisted by his counsel, carefully prepared a statement which he intended to make the following day. He was "in good spirits" during his intercourse with others.

The decisive session was held in the same court, but in a more spacious hall and in the presence of a larger audience. Luther appeared with an escort of friends who showed a bold front. He himself was noticeably less timid than on the previous day, and exhibited a more deliberate reverence toward the high assembly. The official of the archbishop of Treves addressed words of admonition to him and inquired whether he was prepared to recant. Thereupon Luther,

[10] Brieger, *Aleander und Luther*, pp. 143, 147; Kalkoff, *Die Depeschen Aleanders vom Wormser Reichstag*, 2nd ed., 1897, pp. 167, 171.

in a firm tone, began the oration which has since became so famous. He contended that his writings were partly of a religious character, partly directed against the pope and his adherents, and partly replies to individual opponents which had been forced from him. They contained nothing that was censurable. He entered upon a detailed explanation of his writings against the pope, designedly availing himself of this occasion to complain bitterly against the Roman tyranny "in my Germany," as he put it, "to which I owe my services." He was relying on the temper of the princely audience who, as he well knew, were ill-disposed toward the abuses prevalent at the papal court. He also spoke of the judgments of God which overtook the rulers of the Old Testament who resisted the Word of God. He was not interrupted. After he had ended, Eck called his attention to the fact that his doctrines had long ago been condemned by the Church, that their condemnation had been reaffirmed by the recent proclamation of the pope, and that it was unthinkable that all Christendom had been groping about in darkness up to then. The official concluded his remarks with the demand that Luther should state clearly and unambiguously whether or not he was ready to retract. Luther replied: "If I am not convinced by proofs from Scripture or clear theological reasons, I remain convinced by the passages which I have quoted [in my book] from Scripture, and my conscience is held captive by the Word of God. I cannot and will not retract, for it is neither prudent nor right to go against one's conscience. So help me God, Amen!" These last words did not resound through the hall with tragic solemnity, as Protestant biographers are wont to put it. On the contrary, they were scarcely audible, according to the oldest sources, because of the great uproar and indignation which ensued, and also because of the fact that the audience began to crowd out of the stifling hall, which was illuminated by torch-lights. Nor did Luther's declaration conclude with the celebrated exclamation: "Here I stand. I cannot do otherwise. God help me, Amen." Long ago even Protestant scholars have demonstrated that this sentence is unhistorical. The expression, "So help me God, Amen," was a formula with which it had been customary, since the Middle Ages, to conclude solemn speeches. It was simply a Christian paraphrase of the Latin *"dixi,"* I have spoken.[11]

After a further exchange of words with the official, Luther, ac-

---

[11] Grisar, *Luther,* Vol. II, pp. 65 sq., 75 sq.; *Lutherstudien,* Vol. I, pp. 26; 42.

companied by his escort, left the episcopal court. Outside, feeling that he had been victorious, he imitated the lansquenets, when they celebrated a successful surprise-attack, by swinging his arms about in the air and spreading out the fingers of his hands. "I have succeeded," he exclaimed; "I have succeeded!" In the tavern he repeated this demonstration, as he greeted those who awaited him at the bar. During the draughts of merriment, to which they abandoned themselves, no one realized the gravity and responsibility of the situation.

Those who had made preparations for a violent *coup d'état* at Worms were also in the main satisfied. As a result of the ferment among Luther's sympathizers, a placard had been posted at the townhall during the night, announcing that hostilities had been declared upon the "Romanists," *i. e.*, the loyal adherents of the Church, by four hundred unnamed members of the nobility, who, it was alleged, were prepared to launch an attack with a force of 6000 men. The revolutionary watch-word "Bundschuh," thrice repeated, appeared in place of the signatures. The word referred to the so-called auxiliaries supplied by the peasant estate. It was a custom of the peasants to wear strapped shoes. Referring subsequently to the protectors of Luther who were prepared to do battle in his defense, Thomas Münzer told Luther: "You would have been stabbed to death by the knights, if you had hesitated or recanted." He said this to expose the vain-glory with which Luther was accustomed to boast of his courage at Worms, in the presence of the great men of the empire. That there was danger of the safe-conduct being violated, is a fable of subsequent invention, nourished no doubt by Luther's assertions.[12] The Emperor was determined that the promise should be kept and that the return of the obstinate monk to Wittenberg should be unmolested.

Prior to Luther's departure, several days were consumed in an endeavor to bring him round. It was done at the instigation of the estates who feared unrest in the city and in the empire. Their decisive declaration, issued on the twentieth of April, was to the effect that, if Luther did not yield, they would sustain the Emperor in what-

---

[12] Cf. Grisar, *Lutherstudien*, I, p. 88. Annotation 63 of the Table Talks, Weimar ed., No. 5432b.

ever measures he might take against the obstinate heretic.[13] The archbishop of Treves, Richard von Greiffenklau, with the assistance of others vainly endeavored to persuade Luther to modify his stand. Equally fruitless were the efforts of the scholarly and highly respected John Cochlaeus, dean of the chapter-foundation of Our Lady at Frankfort on the Main. He narrates that Luther listened to him with tears in his eyes (which the latter afterwards denied) and appealed to a private revelation which he claimed to have received (*est mihi revelatum*).[14] An offer which Cochlaeus made to dispute with Luther in public before authorized judges, likewise proved futile. Luther's friends within the diet encouraged him. The Elector Frederick alone, true to his usually circumspect and diplomatic habit, held back. Never did he converse personally with his Wittenberg professor, but only through intermediaries. He is reported to have said: "Doctor Martinus is far too bold for me."

Before the termination of the imperial safe-conduct, Frederick excogitated a plan to safeguard his protégé against the dangers likely to result from the imminent declaration of the imperial ban. Luther was initiated in the scheme while yet at Worms. A simulated attack was to be made upon him by the soldiers of the Elector on the home-ward journey, and he was to be taken into custody.

Accompanied by his escort, Luther left the city unobserved in a carriage, on April 26. He had received an order not to preach on his journey, but he disregarded it, contending that the Word of God is untrammeled. Having arrived at Friedberg in the Wetterau, he addressed two solemn letters defending himself, one to Charles V, the other to the princes and estates at Worms.[15] These letters were immediately published in order to create sympathy in his behalf. In the first of them, the original of which is now on exhibition in the "Luther-Halle" at Wittenberg, he solemnly appeals to St. Paul and declares that he can no more deviate from the Gospel of Christ than the Apostle, who was ready to anathematize even an angel if he preached another Gospel. It was not the will of God that His Word should be subject to man; in matters pertaining to salvation no one

[13] Cf. N. Paulus, "*War das Wormser Edikt ungesetzlich?*" in the *Histor. Jahrbuch*, 1918–19, pp. 269 sqq.

[14] Grisar, *Luther*, Vol. IV, p. 258; Vol. VI, pp. 143 sq.; *Reichstagsakten* (see note 3 above), p. 630. Luther's denial, *Opp. Lat Var.*, VII, p. 48. The offer of disputation, *Reichstagsakten*, p. 629; cf. Table Talks, Weimar ed., No. 5432b.

[15] *Briefwechsel*, III, pp. 129, 135; both letters are dated April 28.

may depend upon a mere mortal. In saying this, he was oblivious of his own claim that he alone was able to interpret the Gospel properly and thus show men the way to salvation. He pretended to forget the fact that, when the Church requires men to rely on her doctrine and her interpretation of Holy Writ, this is no demand of fallible men, but of a supernatural institution established by God, invested with divine authority and protected against error—an institution in which the living Christ continues His operations until the end of time.

He who understands the true character of this divine institution will take no stock in the assertion, current among Protestants, that Luther represented liberty of conscience when he took his "heroic" stand at Worms. For freedom of conscience is not violated by the demand to submit to a divinely appointed teaching authority; on the contrary, conscience is thereby directed to the certain possession of higher truth, to contentment and true happiness. The statement that Luther at Worms struggled for complete liberty of research and autonomy of reason as the domain of future civilization, must be read in the light of his own express declaration in his concluding address that he was bound by the Word of Scripture, hence by the compelling power of revelation—understood, of course, in the sense in which he interpreted it. In brief, the diet of Worms does not mark the birth of intellectual liberty, neither for conservative Protestantism, nor for that Neo-Protestantism which is rapidly developing into infidelity, nor yet for the modern world.[16]

The tragic schism, caused by subjectivism in breaking away from the ancient and venerable universal Church, is all that remains of the incident at Worms. But if one were to abstract entirely from the religious aspect of the rupture, the consequences of the so-called declaration of liberty would show that no genuine benefit accrued to Germany, which has been growing weaker and more disunited ever since.

Shortly after Luther's appearance before the diet of Worms, this event was so much exaggerated by his friends, that a great many legends entwined themselves about it. As he set out for home, it was impossible for Luther to foresee the halo with which these days would be surrounded in later years. Among the legends referred to is the alleged text of a prayer which he was said to have recited at

---

[16] For more details see Grisar, *Lutherstudien*, I, ch. v: *"Luther zu Worms, ein Kämpfer für Geistesfreiheit?"* (pp. 28 sqq.)

Worms. A staff which he had stuck into the ground, in testimony of the truth of his doctrine, was said to have grown into a marvelous tree. George von Frundsberg, the leader of the lansquenets, was said to have declared in the presence of Luther, prior to his appearance before the princes and estates, that God would not abandon the little monk if he were in the right. The nuncio Aleander is quoted as saying: "If the Germans repudiate the rule of Rome, we shall take care that they perish in their own blood amid internecine struggles." Aleander was falsely reputed to have been a baptized Jew, or, as Luther said, an infidel who had lost faith in Christianity. The only true element in the charges made against him is that his past history was not blameless, because he had been infected by the Italian Renaissance, and that he often expressed himself imprudently in his letters and addresses. Of course, in the eyes of the Lutherans, the representatives of the "papistical" party at Worms were all venal scoundrels devoid of character, who condemned Luther contrary to their own convictions and acted only for the sake of papal favor and reward. The Archbishop of Treves is said to have made an attempt to poison Luther at a banquet, and Cochlaeus' offer of disputing with Luther was a ruse for endangering his personal safety. Luther himself contributed his share to these legends. He later on boasted of the ineffable courage with which, alone and forsaken at the diet, he jumped into the very jaws of "Behemoth." He alleged that the Emperor had outlawed him even before his (Luther's) arrival, by revoking his safe-conduct in virtue of the edict condemning his books. He also claimed that the Emperor proceeded against him after his departure by means of a surreptitious and invalid proscription without the sanction of the diet.[17]

Apprehensive of the future, Luther left Worms in a carriage, on May 4, accompanied by Amsdorf and a fellow-monk from Möhra; he journeyed in the direction of Gotha, when five mounted horsemen, according to a preconcerted plan, stopped the carriage near Waltershausen, dragged Luther out, placed him on a horse, and, by detours selected for the sake of secrecy, brought him to Wartburg castle, near Eisenach, where they arrived about eleven o'clock at night. Amsdorf, who had been initiated into the affair, was permitted to continue his journey, after he had roundly abused his

[17] On these and other false legends cf. *ibid.* VI: *"Lutherfabeln vom Augsburger Reichstag"* (pp. 36 sqq.)

assailants for the sake of pretense. The monk from Möhra escaped.

The Wartburg was the property of the Elector of Saxony; not wishing to know where Luther was, in order to escape embarrassment, he had permitted his counselors to select the place. For a considerable space of time, Luther disappeared from the scene. His patron could not have resorted to a better expedient to save him.

2. THE SENTENCE OF OUTLAWRY

The imperial councilors, even before the opening of the diet, had taken the point of view that the Emperor, by virtue of his own authority, was empowered to pronounce sentence of outlawry against Luther. The two nuncios demanded that he issue the edict as a sacred duty, since by the terms of his royal oath he was the sworn protector of the Church. The high-chancellor, Gattinara, in opposition to the Saxon Elector, announced that the edict of outlawry should be issued "with the knowledge, but not with the counsel and consent of the princes." [18] On February 19, before Luther arrived in Worms, the diet had left it to the Emperor to proclaim "the proper mandate," *i. e.*, the sentence of outlawry in the event of Luther's refusal to recant. On April 20, as we saw above, the diet expressly renewed its consent to this step. When the Emperor, without necessity, but in a spirit of accommodation, inquired as to the best method of procedure, the estates desired that the mandate be submitted to them, so that "at the request of His Majesty they might indicate their opinion in this matter." But, in matter of fact, the edict was not submitted to the diet, whose members had already begun to scatter. Nor was it necessary to do so. The editor of the recently published *Reichstagsakten* writes: "There can be no doubt that the Emperor was now justified in issuing an edict in his own right, without further consultation of the estates." Moreover, the legitimacy of the imperial edict of outlawry was freely admitted by the estates assembled in 1524 for the diet of Nuremberg, which declared that the edict was issued "with mature deliberation and after the Electors, princes, and other estates had been consulted." [19] Hence, the more recent objection to the legality of the edict of Worms as an imperial measure are unfounded.

[18] Kalkoff, *Luther und die Entscheidungsjahre*, pp. 187 sq.

[19] Cf. Paulus, *l. c.* (note 13 above), for the documentary evidence for all these assertions.

The edict was drawn up under date of May 8, after Luther, whose whereabout was kept secret from everybody, had already spent a number of days at the Wartburg, and after his safe-conduct had expired.

This document was chiefly the work of Aleander, who unfolded therein the whole penal system of the Middle Ages. Since the days when Christianity issued from the catacombs, many changes had taken place in the public relationship between Church and State and modifications had become necesssary even in the interest of practicability, if for no other reasons. But the eyes of Aleander, the Italian, only saw the dangers threatened by the negligence of the bishops and the immense growth of the Lutheran movement. For this reason the nuncios, together with other religious-minded people, prevailed upon the young Emperor, who was zealous in his defense of the Church, to invoke the entire legal machinery of the Middle Ages against heresy and the imminent revolt. Nor were the traditional forceful phrases spared which denounced heresy as the greatest of all evils.[20]

In the introductory part of the edict Charles declared that his imperial office obliged him to protect the Church and that he was in duty bound to heed the Providence which had entrusted him with many countries and with greater authority to promote the welfare of Christianity than was wielded by any of his predecessors. The protection of religion was traditional with his family, through which, on his father's side, he was related to the most Christian emperors and archdukes of Austria and the dukes of Burgundy, and also, on his mother's side, which originated in Spain and Sicily. Hence it was his duty to resist the new heresies, which had originated in hell, after the pope had solemnly condemned them and excommunicated the man who propagated them. In vain had Luther been urged to abandon them at Worms.

The edict goes on to enumerate the errors of the heretic and recalls his very words that, if Hus, who had been burned at the stake, was a heretic, he himself (Luther) was a ten times greater heretic than Hus. In addition, it says, Luther destroys obedience to authority and publishes writings which serve but to foment revolt, schism, and bloody dissensions. He proclaims a brand of Christian liberty destructive of all law, the liberty of irrational beasts. The document styles him a devil in human form and says, if Germany and other countries are not to perish, it is the Emperor's duty to enforce,

[20] Text of the Edict in the *Reichstagsakten*, ed. by Wrede, II, pp. 640 sqq.

without delay or mitigation, "the laudable constitutions of the Christian Roman emperors, which they promulgated for the punishment and extermination of heretics." Therefore, Luther is declared outlawed for the whole extent of the empire, "with the unanimous consent and will," as the document has it, of the Electors, princes, and estates of the diet of Worms. Consequently, no one was allowed henceforth to provide him with shelter, food, drink, etc.; on the contrary, he is to be apprehended wherever he may be found and surrendered to the imperial authorities. Those who disobey the edict incur the penalties of high treason and will themselves be treated as outlaws, liable to the forfeiture of all royal prerogatives, feudal tenures, favors, and liberties which they received from the emperor and the empire. The protectors and adherents of the heretic are to be apprehended, and their property is to be given to those who proceed against them, to be used for their own benefit.

All the literary productions of Luther, even if they incidentally contain some good things, are to be burnt and shunned like poison. The plague of anti-religious books, pamphlets, pictures, etc., composed by others, as well as all libels against the pope, prelates, princes, universities, etc., are to be exterminated. Books which in any manner touch on matters of faith may be printed only after they have been submitted to the censorship of a bishop or of the nearest theological faculty. All other literary productions require the episcopal approbation.

The strict ordinance concerning publications was intended to check an evil which had assumed boundless proportions. The edict was in strict accord with the severe prescriptions of Leo X and the Fifth Lateran Council (1515) regarding preventive censorship.[21] The new invention of the "right noble art of printing," as it is styled in the Emperor's edict, had degenerated in virtue of a deluge of writings and pamphlets which disseminated errors, fostered agitation, and preached ecclesiastical and social revolution. Regardless of consequences, wood-cuts were used to heap mockery upon the hierarchy as well as the rulers who did not sufficiently comply with the desires of the nobility or the oppressed peasantry. Luther, by his polemical tracts against the Church, had, from the beginning of his career, set the example of evading the existing censorship laws. During the diet of Worms quite a number of publications appeared in favor of the new doctrines. Aleander complained that his character was subject to defamation by publications and pictures in the city of the high assembly. At the time when Luther himself was

21 Pastor, *History of the Popes*, tr. by R. Kerr, Vol. VIII, 2nd ed., 1923, pp. 397 sq.

condemned, and even prior to his condemnation, there were circulated at Worms and in other places in the empire, pictorial representations of him with the dove, the symbol of the Holy Ghost, hovering above his head. Other pictures represented him with a halo. A booklet on the Passion of Martinus, patterned after the Gospel narrative of the Passion of Christ, was published, in which he was glorified as a persecuted hero.

When the report of the edict of outlawry reached Luther at the Castle of Wartburg, he wrote to Amsdorf:[22] "A cruel edict has gone forth against me, but God will laugh at them" (Ps. xxxvi, 13). Spalatin he informed [23] that he was aggrieved at this procedure, not for his own sake, but because his opponents thereby heaped disaster upon their heads and the time of their punishment was evidently at hand. He adds in reference to his opponent, Duke George of Saxony, a man distinguished by the traits of a noble character: "Would that this swine of Dresden were found worthy to kill me during a public sermon! If it pleased God, I should suffer for the sake of His Word. The will of the Lord be done."

In these first letters he also rejoices in the unchained power of the masses (*moles vulgi imminentis*), who were, he said, preparing terror for the authors of the edict and all his persecutors; it is evident, he adds, that the people are unwilling and unable to tolerate any longer the yoke of the pope and the papists.

Rendered confident by these phenomena, he continues to indulge his scornful denunciation of the edict: "Swine and asses are able to see how stubbornly they act. . . . What if my death should prove a disaster to you all? God is not to be trifled with." Thus he exclaims a few years later, when, to show his contempt, he incorporates the entire lengthy document in his work *Zwei kaiserliche uneinige Gebote* (Two Discordant Imperial Commandments; 1524), and accompanies them with biting comments.[24] In a frenzy of higher inspiration he advises that "everyone who believes in the existence of God keep away from the commandments (of the imperial proclamation)." "If they kill me, there will be such a slaughter as neither they nor their children will be able to overcome."

---

[22] *Briefwechsel*, III, p. 151; May 12.
[23] *Ibid.*, p. 153; same day.
[24] *Werke*, Weimar ed., XV, pp. 254 sqq.

CHAPTER IX

LUTHER'S SOJOURN AT THE WARTBURG

I. STORMS WITHIN AND WITHOUT

At the Wartburg, Luther vested himself in the costume of a cavalier and allowed his beard and hair to grow. In order to conceal his identity, he assumed the name of Squire George (Ritter Görg). He wrote to Melanchthon at Wittenberg that he would not recognize him if he were to meet him. On the tenth day of his stay, he says in a letter to Spalatin: "I sit idle here the livelong day and eat more than enough." But soon he found an occupation; for in the same letter he says: "I read the Bible in Greek and Hebrew. I shall write a German sermon on the freedom of auricular confession; I shall continue my commentaries on the Psalms and my sermons as soon as the necessary materials arrive from Wittenberg. From there I also expect to obtain the Magnificat which I have begun." [1] He did not carry out all these plans, however. But the period of quiet retirement became for him a time of gigantic labors, chiefly devoted to a direct attack upon the teachings and the power of Antichrist, whose determined opposition to the Gospel he believed to have experienced at Worms. In one of his first letters we hear: "While I quietly sojourn here, I contemplate the face of the Church all day, and hear the voice of the Psalmist raised to God: Why hast Thou made all the children of men in vain? (Ps. lxxxviii, 48). O God, what a horrible monster of divine wrath is this execrable empire of the Roman Antichrist. I curse the hardness of my heart, since I do not completely dissolve in tears because of the murdered sons of my people." [2]

The frame of mind expressed in these rhetorical words to Melanchthon, continued during the ten months of his sojourn at the

---

[1] *Briefwechsel*, III, p. 154; May 14, 1521.
[2] *Ibid.*, p. 148; letter to Melanchthon, May 12.

Wartburg. It was there he was to receive, as it were, his spiritual baptism in preparation for his future work.

His room at the Wartburg was an unpretentious cell, situated not within the castle itself, but in the outbuildings set apart for ordinary guests. He had no elevating outlook upon the green mountains, which some biographers picture him contemplating from his room. Nor was his cell equipped with the oft-admired bay-window, which was added to the corner room only about a century ago. The room, which is much frequented to-day, is reached by ascending a steep, narrow flight of stairs. It is stocked with numerous souvenirs of doubtful authenticity. There "Squire George," secluded from intercourse with others, was attended by servants of the castle. The castle itself made a rather unfavorable impression, its upkeep having been neglected for a long time. The bare walls harmonized with the disposition of the new inmate. A priest conducted divine services for the castellan and a few domestics and rare guests. Luther avoided the society of the "mass-priest." At times he participated in the chase, more for the sake of appearances than for diversion.

So secretly kept was his seclusion, that even for months afterwards but few knew of his whereabouts. Many supposed that he had been abducted by his enemies, others that he had been assassinated. Among those who anxiously desired information about him was Albrecht Dürer, the famous painter, who was on intimate terms with Pirkheimer, Luther's patron at Nuremberg, and favorably disposed towards the reforms which Luther had promised, without as yet realizing the full import of his religious changes.[3]

During the first few days of his sojourn at the Wartburg, Luther was very much concerned over reports of violence at Erfurt. In his opinion, the demonstrations in his behalf were going too far. On the day following his departure from Erfurt, which he visited on his journey to Worms, he heard that the students, assisted by a mob, had risen against the canons of the church of St. Severin, who were loyal to their faith, and had stormed the dwellings of the canons, committing all kinds of excesses. These scenes were reënacted with the permission of the academic senate and the authorities on several days in June. Fundamentally Luther himself had furnished the cause of these demonstrations by the hatred which he had aroused against the Catholics at Erfurt. This same hatred burst

[3] Grisar, *Luther*, Vol. II, pp. 39, 41 sq.

forth anew when the clergy, who had participated in the festive reception in honor of Luther, were threatened with exclusion from choral service and from their benefices because they had also become subject to the edict of outlawry. Luther deplored the whole violent movement in a letter to Wittenberg: "This kind of procedure will bring our Gospel into disrepute and justly bring about its repudiation. . . . Satan attempts to mock our endeavors."[4] His Gospel, however, was exposed to other and still greater annoyances from without. In the meantime he sought relief from his own mental storms by resorting to controversy.

During the first two months of his sojourn at the Wartburg, his lengthy reply to Ambrosius Catharinus was printed.[5] In comparison with his previous writings, this reply was especially striking on account of the visionary application of the real or apparent Biblical passages concerning Antichrist. In the application of these texts to his idea of the papacy, he indulges in a kind of dreamy fanaticism. In his opinion the prophet Daniel (viii, 28) had definitely foretold the different characteristics of Antichrist which were realized in the pope. The enemy of God, according to Luther's (false) translation of Daniel, has different "faces," which are all discoverable in minute detail in anti-Christian Rome. According to Daniel, he held, the spirit out of the mouth of God, not force and human fury, will kill Antichrist and that within a brief space; for the Lord and His day are nigh. This work was intended to be that production of which his tract on the Babylonian Captivity was the prelude. Undoubtedly it is representative of the mental excitement with which Luther was seized at the Wartburg.

During his first week at the castle, he composed his treatise *Von der Beicht* ("On Confession—Whether the Pope has Power to Impose it"). It was dedicated on June 1 to Franz von Sickingen as his "special lord and patron." [6] Confession, as imposed by the papacy, he asserts therein, is an unauthorized and insidious institution, whereas private confession made to anyone, even to a layman, if entirely voluntary, is a "precious and wholesome thing," because of the humiliation it involves and the comfort produced by the consolatory words of one's fellowman. Absolution received in this manner alone

4 *Briefwechsel*, III, p. 158; letter to Melanchthon, about the middle of May.
5 *Werke*, Weimar ed., VII, pp. 705 sqq.; Erl. ed., *Opp. Lat. Var.*, V, pp. 289 sqq.
6 *Werke*, Weimar ed., VIII, pp. 138 sqq.; Erl. ed., XXVII, pp. 318 sqq.

corresponds with the liberty of a Christian. In general, no one may
be compelled to receive the Sacraments, just as no one may be or can
be compelled to accept the faith.

It is not likely that Sickingen went to excess either in. receiving
the Sacrament of Penance or free lay-confession. His two castles
in the Palatinate, Ebernburg and Landstuhl, were asylums for the
friends of the new religious movement and the revolution. Elected
captain of the "Fraternal Union of Knighthood," in. August, 1522,
he declared war against the Archbishop of Treves, Richard von
Greiffenklau, and, after an unsuccessful attack upon his episcopal
city, devastated the district about Treves and portions of the Palatinate. In May of the succeeding year, Sickingen succumbed to the
wounds he had sustained at the siege and capture of his fortress
Landstuhl by the princes who had allied themselves against him.

In his reply to Catharinus, Luther had interpreted one of the
"faces" of the supposed Antichrist (Daniel, ch. ix) as referring to
the papal universities. These high schools of Satan, he alleged, are
the waters of the bottomless pit described in the Apocalypse, whence
locusts with the power of scorpions issue as in a thick smoke. In
1518, a book had been issued against him by the University of
Louvain, which Luther declared to be the most thorough and the most
dangerous of all the works written against him. Its author was the
erudite theologian James Latomus (Masson). In the twelve days
intervening between June 8 and 20, Luther composed a reply to
Latomus, entitled, *Rationis Latomianae Confutatio*,[7] wherein he attempts to refute the Catholic doctrine of sin and grace by citations
from the Bible, no other aids being available to him at the time.
A pronouncement made against his heresies by the theological faculty
of Paris he tried to dispose of by publishing a translation of this
document, accompanied by a preface and an epilogue.[8] He denounces
the faculty, which had been the glory of the Middle Ages, as "the
greatest spiritual harlot under the sun and the back-door to hell." [9]
Again he indulges his mania concerning the Antichrist and the end
of the world. The faculty is the sinful chamber "of the pope, the
true Antichrist." "When the belly of these gentlemen of Paris
rumbles," etc., they exclaim: "It is an article of faith." Their actions

---

[7] Weim. ed., VIII, pp. 43 sqq.; *Opp. Lat. Var.*, V, pp. 395 sqq.
[8] Weimar ed., VIII, pp. 267 sqq.; Erl. ed., XXVII, pp. 379 sqq.
[9] At the end of the publication.

are to him an additional proof that the "pope has not regarded us otherwise than as unworthy to be . . . his privy, etc. . . . So many noble-minded persons have been obliged to harbor the stench, dung, and filth," etc. His crudities are not deserving of full quotation.

It is worth while, however, to mention here the works which Luther composed during his brief sojourn at the Wartburg; particular reference will be made to some of them in the sequel. They are: the *Verhandlungen zu Worms* ("Transactions at Worms"); two treatises against monastic vows; two against the Mass; the interpretation of the Magnificat; a "Warning" against rebellion; a discourse on the "Bull Caena Domini"; an illustrated "Passional of Christ and Antichrist," for which he was responsible at least in part; a Christmas postil, and other explanations of Biblical texts, besides smaller polemical tracts, and, finally, his translation of the New Testament. Surely no small amount of labor. Aided by Spalatin, Melanchthon, and other friends, he entrusted the publication of his works to the Wittenberg press.

What a contrast between the tender and charitable activity of the sainted princess whose memory the Wartburg preserved and Luther's agitated labors, sustained mainly by strong hatred, passion, and a slanderous disposition. St. Elizabeth with her loving heart for the poor, with her loyal devotion to the Church, and her soul aglow with prayer, everywhere confronted the man of the violent pen within the castle-walls. There was the *Kemenate* where she had her quarters, still in a state of beautiful preservation; there was the richly adorned chapel, her favorite retreat; there, rising heavenward above the court, was the tower whence she so often contemplated the splendor of her celestial home in the mirror of nature.

The letters he wrote to his friends cast a lurid light upon Luther's frame of mind in the intervals between his oppressive labors. Anyone who reads them would be greatly disillusioned had he expected that the solitude which came to him as an extraordinary grace from above would have induced Luther to reflect seriously upon himself or to examine quietly his activities which were fraught with so much responsibility. Prayers, indeed, there are, brief and ardent prayers, for himself and against his adversaries; but we miss the principal prayer, the petition for complete submission to the divine will and the expression of willingness to be led anywhere, even to the abandonment of his struggle, if it were God's will.[10] Instead of "Thy will be done" one hears everywhere "*My* will be done"; so that the resignation of the soul to God, which Luther had so strongly emphasized in the days of his so-called mysticism, now seems to be forgotten in a cause so decisive for himself and for thousands of others. God should, nay He must, so Luther thinks, place the seal of His approval upon his revolt from the entire past of the Church.

Luther had to suffer much from temptations. These were always combated by devout Catholics by prayer accompanied by penance, but no mention is made of penitential practices in the case of Luther. He himself acknowledged his deficiency in the matter of prayer.[11]

"Alas, I pray too little instead of sighing over the Church of God. . . . For a whole week I have neither written, prayed nor studied, plagued partly by temptations of the flesh, partly by the other trouble [constipation]. Pray for me, for in this solitude I am sinking into sin."

A previous passage in this same letter says: "I burn with the flames of my untamed flesh; in short, I ought to be glowing in the spirit, and instead I glow in the flesh, in lust, laziness, idleness and drowsiness, and know not whether God has not turned away His face from me, because you have ceased to pray for me."

A little later he writes: "I am healthy in body and am well cared for, but I am also severely tried by sin and temptations. Pray for me, and fare you well!" [12]

Here, at all events, powerful sexual temptations (*ferveo carne, libidine,* etc.) are openly acknowledged. As early as 1519, he had written to his superior Staupitz concerning such visitations (*titillationes*).[13] These assaults at the Wartburg, however are disagreeable to him. His self-revelations are somewhat inflated by his habitually superlative style of writing; and he may have referred the "sins" which he mentions to sensuality, on the one hand, and, on the other, to the frailty of his fiduciary faith in God, which he made the center

[10] Grisar, *Luther,* Vol. VI, pp. 511 sq.; more fully in the original German edition, Vol. III, pp. 995 sqq.

[11] Grisar, *Luther,* Vol. II, pp. 82 sq.; cfr. V, pp. 225 sqq., letter to Melanchthon, July 13, 1521.

[12] *Op. cit.,* II, p. 83; letter to Lang, December 18, 1521.

[13] *Op. cit.,* Vol. V, pp. 319 sqq.

of his Gospel. The devil, so he believed, ever and anon sought to deprive him of this faith.

Luther saw the Wartburg filled with devils. This, in part, was the result of the fear of demons which he had imbibed in his youth; while in part it was a consequence of the inquietude caused by his internal doubts and self-reproaches. The voices of self-reproach he imagined to be voices from the Satanic empire.

"Believe me," he wrote on November 1, "that I am cast before a thousand devils in this idle solitude. It is much easier to struggle with men, even if they be incarnate devils, than with the spirits of iniquity that infest the air. I fall, but the right hand of God sustains me." [14]

According to another utterance of his, he wishes to praise God in the name of his Gospel,—God who has not only given us this combat with the spirits of iniquity, but has also revealed to us [revelavit nobis] that in this matter it is not flesh and blood that take the field against us. . . . It is Satan, who rages against us according to his way and within his limits."

Thus convinced of his great struggle against the evil spirits, he discovers, in his own imagination, that they become visible and audible to him, as will be shown in the following pages.

Meanwhile we must mention the internal struggle which he sustained when he had persuaded himself of the invalidity, nay, absolute reprehensibility of the monastic vows and the vow of celibacy. It was a violent struggle. Hitherto he had adhered to his monastic vow of chastity as a matter of principle, but now his false idea of Christian liberty began to seduce him to break his vow.

Bartholomew Feldkirch (Bernhardi), provost of Kronberg, was the first, or one of the first adherents of Luther among the clergy who married during the time of Luther's sojourn at the Wartburg.[15] Karlstadt, Luther's tumultuous theological colleague at Wittenberg, had published a tract against the vows. Not long afterwards, he, too, took unto himself a wife. When Luther first heard of the movement to permit the inmates of monasteries to marry, he was somewhat taken aback and wrote to Spalatin: "O God, shall the Wittenbergers give wives to the monks! But they shall not force a wife

[14] On November 1, 1521, in a letter to Nicholas Gerbel; *Briefwechsel*, III, p. 240: *"Mille credas me Satanibus obiectum in hac otiosa solitudine. . . . Saepius ego cado, sed sustentat me rursus dextra Excelsi."*

[15] Bernhardi is known to us through his part in the Wittenberg disputation of 1516.

upon *me*." [16] He found very many grounds for criticizing the treatise of Karlstadt, especially its method of demonstration. Melanchthon, too, who opposed the monastic vows, had not hit upon the right solution in Luther's opinion. His own fermenting soul now embraced the question, with no intention of dismissing it until the right solution, or rather the least disquieting disposition of the duty of the vows had been found. On August 3, he revealed the state of his mind in a painful discussion with his friend Melanchthon: "You see with what heat I burn [*quantis urgeor æstibus*], and yet I cannot confirm any satisfactory conclusion except that I greatly desire to support your efforts." [17]

As was to be foreseen, however, he soon discovered what he sought. The solution was destined to bring him what he desired, an influx of male and female members of monastic Orders who had grown tired of their vows. He resolved to liberate these "unfortunates" from the "impure and damnable state of celibacy," as he styles it, and to induct them into the "paradise of matrimony." [18] This solution also afforded the advantage to make him independent of his rival Karlstadt, and furthermore, to enable him to watch over the "firstfruits of the spirit" also in this matter. The point of departure was furnished by his idea of evangelical liberty. "Whoever has taken a vow in a spirit opposed to evangelical freedom"—thus he sets forth his saving idea—"must be set free, and his vow be anathema. Such, however, are all those who have taken the vow in the search for salvation or justification." [19] In this spirit all religious, including himself, had taken their vows. This spirit was inseparable from the vow as long as good works were regarded as efficacious; for the voluntary relinquishment of freedom, offered at the throne of the Most High, is always connected with the certain expectation, guaranteed by the Word of God, that the sacrifice will assist in the attainment of salvation and justification, through the merits of Jesus Christ whom the person who takes the vow promises to follow in humility.

For the sake of advancing his new discovery, Luther first wrote "theses" intended "for the bishops and deacons of the church of Wittenberg." [20] These were followed by his momentous work *Ueber*

[16] On August 6, 1521; *Briefwechsel*, III, p. 215.
[17] *Briefwechsel*, III, p. 213.
[18] Grisar, *Luther*, Vol. II, pp. 83 sqq.
[19] Letter to Melanchthon, *op. cit.* II, 84.
[20] Weimar ed., VIII, pp. 323 sqq.; *Opp. Lat. Var.*, IV, pp. 344 sqq.

die Ordensgelübde, ein Urteil Martin Luthers ("On the Monastic Vows: an Opinion of Martin Luther.") [21] It abounds in misrepresentations of the monastic life and the Catholic teaching concerning perfection, good works, and penance as well as in frivolous indecencies and vulgar calumnies. The author prefaced the book with a dedicatory letter to his father, in order to invest it with an attractive foil of personal experience. His father, he writes, should not be angry at him because, by entering a monastery, he had violated the grave commandment of obedience to parents. He now realized that his vow was worthless, for God had released him from his fetters.

Desertion of the monasteries amid strife and tumult such as, for instance, his friend Lang at Erfurt had proposed, Luther at that time censured. Concerning himself, he announced his intention of adhering to his present mode of life. He wore the habit of his Order for several years after his sojourn at the Wartburg.

2. GHOSTS AND ILLUSIONS

Whilst Luther was engaged in the composition of his last-mentioned book, he announced to Spalatin: "I am suffering from temptation, and out of temper; so don't be offended. There is more than one Satan contending with me. I am alone, and yet at times not alone." [22] He believed that he was visibly pursued by infernal powers because of his praiseworthy discoveries. His intimate friend, the physician Matthew Ratzeberger, quotes Luther as saying that, "Because he was so lonely, he was beset with ghosts and noisy spirits which gave him much concern, and he drove them all away by prayer; but did not wish to talk about it." [23]

Nevertheless Luther in his later Table Talks expressed his firm conviction that he had encountered the visible Satan. Both Ratzeberger and Luther make mention of the devil's assuming the form of a dog.[24] A big black bull-dog resisted him one night as he was about to go to bed, and departed only after Luther had recited a verse of

---

[21] Weimar ed., VIII, pp. 573–669; *Opp. Lat. Var.*, VI, pp. 238–376; Denifle, in *Luther und Luthertum*, has subjected the Latin text to a searching and extensive criticism. Cf. Grisar, *Luther*, II, pp. 83 sqq. On the question of Christian perfection and the alleged dual ideal of life fostered by Catholicism, see *op. cit.*, II, 85, Note 3.

[22] Grisar, *Luther*, Vol. II, p. 85.

[23] *Op. cit.*, Vol. II, p. 82.

[24] *Op. cit.*, Vol. VI, p. 123; Köstlin-Kawerau, *M. Luther*, Vol. I, p. 440.

the Psalms. According to Luther's own story, he seized the dog and threw him out of the window. He states that there was no such dog at the Wartburg. On another occasion he was disturbed at night by a sack of hazel-nuts, locked in a chest, which by the power of the evil one were thrown one after another against the rafters of his room, while his bed was violently jolted. At the same time a rumbling noise was heard on the staircase, as if barrels were being rolled down. And yet, the staircase, as Luther convinced himself, was locked below with bolts and chains.[25] Thus, as Mathesius assures us, "he often heard the rumbling noises of the evil spirit at night in his Patmos [*i. e.*, at the Wartburg]." It was frequently a struggle, he continues, like Christ's, when He was tempted in the desert. When he changed his quarters to accommodate the wife of Hans Berlips, she heard such an ado in the room that she fancied a thousand devils were in it." Luther himself reports that "at Eisenach" (*i. e.*, probably at the Wartburg) he had contemptuously called to the devil on such an occasion: "If you are Christ's master, so be it!" "I have learned by experience," he says elsewhere, "that ghosts go about affrightening people, preventing them from sleeping and so making them ill."

But he experienced not only tribulations, but also consolation and encouragement from the world beyond.

"Ten years ago," he said (1532) to his pupil Schlaginhaufen, "God strengthened me in my struggles and writings through His angels." The period thus indicated probably refers to the months he spent at the Wartburg. Perhaps the vision with which his pupils were acquainted also happened at this time. While he, engaged in the service of the Word—thus the story runneth—was praying in his chamber, the image of Christ bearing the five wounds, appeared to him in shining splendor. However, as he was in doubt, thinking it might be the evil spirit, he said: "Begone, thou infamous devil," whereat the image forthwith disappeared. For some definite reason, Luther disliked to indulge in such narratives, because the fanatics, his enemies, piqued themselves on their enlightenment and revelations, instead of abiding by the Biblical texts as propounded by Luther. He did not look favorably upon communications from the other world. If, nevertheless, he exploited his own experiences in terms such as the follow-

[25] *Op. cit.*, Vol. VI, p. 124. This and the next pages of my larger work also furnish the evidence for the following incidents.

ing, their significance is all the more enhanced. "Ah, bah, spirits!" he exclaims, "I too have seen spirits!"

He had other similar experiences both before and after his sojourn at the Wartburg.

His mind was naturally receptive to such experiences. Even as a monk, when he studied at night in the refectory preparing to become a professor, he heard the devil rustling about in the wood-bin, and again later on in his room at the monastery. "The devil," he says, "often had me by the hair of my head, yet was ever forced to let me go." He claims to have seen "grewsome ghosts and visions" from time to time in the monastery, and "no one was able to comfort" him. More important is the following report. In the course of official business with Gregory Casel, a delegate of the reformed theologians of Strasburg, in 1525, Luther assured him that, while in the monastery, he "frequently had inward experience that the body of Christ is indeed in the Sacrament" (a dogma which the Zwinglians did not believe); that he had seen dreadful visions, also angels (*se angelos vidisse*), so that he had been obliged to stop saying Mass." "What do the Strasburgers mean with their alleged ghost?" he asks. "Are they alone in possession of it? But particularly, have they experienced the terrors of death which I have been through (*mortis horrorem expertus*)?"

Luther's visionary experiences cannot be doubted. They were gross imaginings of preternatural annoyances and corroborations, misinterpretations of internal and external experiences which are well established, particularly for the period he spent at the Wartburg. He named the castle his Patmos, evidently because it was there that he, like the Apostle John when in exile on the isle of Patmos, had preternatural experiences. His extremely active imagination rendered him very susceptible to hallucinations and illusions, especially when accompanied by precordialgia, a physical ailment from which he frequently suffered, or by severe constipation, to which he was also subject at times, and of which he complains at the Wartburg, or when his nerves were overwrought in consequence of excessive literary labors.

The enlightenment which he imagined to have received, naturally revolved about his divine vocation as herald of the new gospel. Thus Luther, for all future time, received his spiritual baptism at his Patmos. The most precious "first-fruits of the spirit" (*primitiæ spiritus,* as he calls them), were allotted to him there.[26] He says, apparently in allusion to a mysterious event relative to his doctrine: "Under threat of the curse of eternal wrath, I have been found worthy in no manner to doubt these things" (*fui dignus, cui sub æternæ iræ maledictione interminaretur, ne ullo modo de iis dubitarem*).[27] How then, in Luther's imagination, was it possible that the devil should not have opposed his election?

Legend has expanded this struggle with the devil. There is no certain warrant for the report of the apparition which in time has come to be the most popular of the Wartburg tales. Luther nowhere says that he hurled the ink-well at the devil, nor do his pupils mention the incident. The famous spot on the wall is unattested, and its historicity is not confirmed by the fact that it has constantly been retouched, whenever the devotion of relic-hunters had gradually scraped it off. Such spots, all originating from an ink-well which Luther hurled at his satanic majesty, were formerly to be found also in other places, *e. g.*, in the rooms which Luther occupied in Wittenberg and at the Koburg.[28]

3. "PECCA FORTITER." THE MASS

The famous expression, "Sin boldly, but believe more boldly still," [29] which Luther embodied in a letter written from the Wartburg to his friend Melanchthon, under date of August 1, 1521, is to

[26] *Op. cit.*, Vol. III, p. 116.

[27] The passage is now to be found in *Tischreden*, Weimar ed., IV, No. 4852, among the Table Talks of the Khumer collection, July, 1543, and is reproduced as a copy from Luther's *Psalter*. Luther wrote in almost identical terms to his friend Jonas, when the latter was ill in 1540 and "in the greatest temptation," introducing his letter as follows: "*Contra tentationem indignitatis nostrae sic respondendum est diabolo*" (Weimar ed., *l. c.*, note). He wished to indicate to his frightened friend, how he quieted himself. The possible relation to a single experience of Luther is made clear by the connection of the longer passage: "*Martinus Lutterus indignus sum, sed dignus fui creari a creatore meo, dignus fui redimi a Filio Dei, dignus fui doceri a Filio Dei et Spiritu sancto, dignus fui, cui ministerium verbi crederetur, dignus fui, qui pro eo tanta paterer, dignus fui, qui in toto malis servarer, dignus fui, cui praeciperetur ista credere, dignus fui, cui sub aeternae*," etc. Aurifaber thus reproduced the conclusion: "[Yet I am worthy] that I ought by no means to doubt it, I who have been severely threatened and enjoined by the wrath of God, His displeasure and execration." (Weim. ed., *l. c.*) Luther's idea that God was leading him into hell, in order to assure him of his salvation, seems to have arisen from an "experience" made by him at a certain juncture of his life.

[28] Grisar, *Luther*, Vol. II, p. 96.

[29] *Briefwechsel*, III, p. 208; Grisar, *op. cit.*, Vol. II, pp. 194 sqq.; M. Pribilla, article "*Pecca fortiter*" in the *Stimmen der Zeit*, 1924, Vol. CVII, pp. 391 sqq.

be ascribed to his strong prepossession in favor of his theory of salvation by "faith alone." This paradoxical aphorism was not, as has frequently been assumed, a command to commit sin, against which Luther always wrote and preached, but a very offensive hyperbolical expression of the certitude, inculcated by him, that faith in a merciful God suffices to obtain pardon for all sins, provided that faith in God is "boldly" asserted.

It seems that Melanchthon, who was spiritually weaker than Luther, was afflicted by the fear of sin. Luther, in his robust way, wished to rid him of this fear and hence reminds him that he is "a preacher of grace" who should not occupy his mind with imaginary sins, but rejoice in Christ, the conqueror of sin; for sins are inevitable in this life. Sin, he says in one of his strongest expressions, will "not tear us away" from the pardoning mercy of the Lamb of God, "even if we should have committed fornication and murder a thousand times in one day." Then he arrives at the notorious expression: "God does not save those who merely fancy themselves sinners. Be a sinner, and sin boldly, but believe more boldly still" (*Esto peccator et pecca fortiter, sed fortius fide*). In the context the phrase "sin boldly" conveys a sinister impression, involving as it does, fundamentally, a strong self-condemnation of the Lutheran theory of fiduciary faith and justification. In lieu of interior contrition, self-humiliation and the penitential spirit, justification is made dependent upon the presumptuous apprehension of the merits of Christ, and sin loses its terrifying character for the believer. Möhler rightly detects in these offensive words "an evident mental derangement." It is to be noted, however, that Luther used similar language also on other occasions, for example, abstracting from other instances at the beginning of his reformatory career, in his letter to Spenlein (1518) and, shortly before his death in his extraordinary letter of 1544 to Spalatin, who had become melancholy. The offensive "*pecca fortiter*" flows naturally from his whole system of doctrine.[30]

After Melanchthon had concluded his lectures on the Epistle to Titus, the Gospel of St. Matthew, and the Epistle to the Romans, he was transferred to the theological faculty of Wittenberg and there not only continued his philological labors, but also undertook a theological work, entitled *Loci Communes,* which was destined to be a pillar for the support of the Lutheran doctrine. The work was com-

[30] Cfr. Grisar, *Luther,* Vol. III, pp. 194 sqq.

pleted in December, 1521, and appeared in sixteen editions before
1525. The Latinity of the book is classical, but its theology clearly
betrays the lay-theologian completely enchanted by the new doctrine. The author pretends that, following in the path of Luther, he
must re-create the system of theology, after the greatest minds of
the centuries had supposedly labored in vain on it. Among other
things he teaches that all things happen of necessity (*necessario eve-
niunt*) in accordance with divine predestination, and that the human
will is not free. He gives a decidedly affirmative answer to the question whether God is also the author of moral evil.[31] Luther was delighted with the precious work, which mirrored forth himself. He
termed it an "unconquered work," which, in his opinion, deserved not
only immortality, but also to be received into the canon of the Bible.[32]
Only gradually did Melanchthon recede from his harsh attitude in
subsequent editions of his work, and did not conceal his disapproval
of Luther's denial of free will. Luther repeatedly invited him from
the Wartburg to take up preaching at Wittenberg. This the learned
layman, however, would never consent to do. He preferred the lecture
room and the serenity of home life. In August, 1520, he had married Catherine Krapp, the daughter of the burgomaster of Wittenberg, and thus formed close social connexions with the inhabitants
of that city, which lasted to the end of his life.

The same spirit which impelled Luther to launch his attack upon
monasticism, also led him to attack the Sacrifice of the Mass. The
monastic state and the Mass he regarded as the most important pillars
of the papacy. In the letter in which he informs Melanchthon of his
passionate struggle with his vows, he also announces: "I shall never
again celebrate a private Mass." Thomas Murner's defense of the sacrificial character of the Mass (1520) did not convince Luther. In 1521,
under the influence of his "spiritual baptism" at the Wartburg,
Luther composed a Latin booklet *On the Abolition of the Private
Mass,* of which he published also a German translation under the title,
On the Misuse of the Mass.[33]

This was the alleged justification of the fight upon the holy sacrifice which at that time commenced at Wittenberg.

---

[31] Grisar, *Luther,* Vol. II, pp. 239, 282 sq.

[32] *Op. cit.,* II, 282.

[33] Weimar ed., VIII, pp. 411 sqq.; German version, pp. 482 sqq.; Erl. ed., *Opp. Lat. Var.,*
VI, pp. 115 sqq. and (German version) XXVIII, pp. 28 sqq.

Luther did not favor any overhasty discontinuation of the traditional liturgical celebrations. He knew that any attempt in this direction would meet with resistance on the part of the Electoral court. Nevertheless, he did whatever he could to realize his designs against the Mass in the university town. In the German treatise just quoted he appealed to his "dear brethren, the Augustinians of Wittenberg," who had already discontinued saying Mass in their church and limited themselves to preaching. He tells them that he rejoices in their work and begs them to take up their position on the rock of firm conviction and at the same time to spare the feelings of the weak. He established his thesis by an appeal to the qualms of conscience which he experienced.

"Daily I feel how very difficult it is to lay aside scruples of long standing, controlled by human laws. Oh, with what great pains and labors, and reliance upon Holy Writ, I have scarcely been able to justify my own conscience, that I, one individual, have dared to oppose the pope and regard him as Antichrist, the bishops as his apostles, and the universities as his brothels! How often has my heart been tantalized, how often has it punished me and reproached me with their only strongest argument: Are you alone wise? Can it be supposed that all others have erred, and erred so long a time? What if you should be mistaken and should lead many into error, who would be eternally damned? Thus I felt until Christ fortified and confirmed me with His only certain Word, so that now my heart is uneasy no longer, but resists this argument of the papists, as a stony shore resists the waves, and ridicules their threats and fury." [34]

This strong faith, which the mysterious "only certain Word of Christ" supposedly conferred upon him, he wished to impart to his brethren and all his readers in the course of his arguments against the Mass.

4. CONFUSION AT WITTENBERG. OTHER WRITINGS COMPOSED BY LUTHER DURING HIS SOJOURN AT THE WARTBURG

Luther's attacks on the Mass were attended with greater success at Wittenberg than he had desired. Gabriel Zwilling (Didymus), a young Augustinian, achieved prominence there as an enthusiast for the purified celebration of the Lord's Supper without the Mass. Some

[34] At the beginning of the German text, *Vom Missbrauch der Messe.*

called him the new prophet and a second Luther. Melanchthon took
his part and missed none of Zwilling's sermons. Karlstadt was no
less enthusiastic; he and a committee constituted of like-minded
zealots petitioned the Elector for "the speedy abolition of the abuse
of Masses in his principality." It was the first application of the principle that ecclesiastical reforms were the affair of territorial rulers.
But the circumspect Elector on October 25 issued an order inhibiting
any acts which might result in dissension and uprisings.

When discontent nevertheless increased, Luther became alarmed
and formed a startling resolution. On December 3, he suddenly left
the Wartburg for a secret visit to Wittenberg, clad in his squire's
costume. He remained there from December 3 to 11, in the company of his friends, for the sake of obtaining information on the state
of affairs, but eight days later he was back at the Wartburg.

He used the information thus acquired, which was partly unsatisfactory, in the composition of a tract, entitled *A Sincere Exhortation
to all Christians to Guard against Rebellion*.[35]

It appears, he says, as if an insurrection is threatening, in which priests,
monks, bishops, and the whole clerical estate might be slain. By hearkening
to his words, however, such a general attack might yet be avoided. Christ
had reserved to Himself the punishment of papism, in order to slay Antichrist by the breath of His mouth. People should wait two years, then it
would be accomplished as a result of the gigantic and irresistible progress
of his Gospel, which was very evidently the work of God. "It is not our
work. . . . 'tis someone else who propels the wheel."

In the sequel, he requests his followers to call themselves Christians, not
Lutherans. "Who is Luther? The doctrine is not mine; nor have I been
crucified for anyone."

But above all: The weak and inadequately instructed must not be taken by
surprise or violence. The authorities only, and not "Herr Omnes" (*i. e.*, the
masses) have the right and the duty to intervene against whatever is contrary
to the Gospel. The devil purposes to injure the evangelical doctrine by foment-
ing rebellion.

The extent of his illusion regarding the speedy collapse of the
kingdom of Antichrist may be inferred from the postil he at that
time composed for the second Sunday of Advent. According to the
astronomers, he says, a great constellation of planets was imminent

[35] *Werke*, Weimar ed., VIII, pp. 676 sqq.; Erl. ed., XXII, pp. 44 sq.; written at the
beginning of 1522.

for the year 1524. The powers of heaven, according to the Sunday
Gospel, would be convulsed. God grant that it be the "Day of Judgment to which the signs certainly point." [36]

During his sojourn at the Wartburg Luther also completed his
remarkable interpretation of the Magnificat, which he dedicated to
the heir to the Saxon throne.[37] It is a remarkable production on account of the note of sincere piety which the author, in the very
midst of a hostile and agitated campaign, sounds in these pages; remarkable, too, because of the author's eulogy of the "Blessed Virgin," "the tender Mother of the Lord." The commentary is largely
pervaded by the traditional devotion with which the Augustinian Order revered Mary, though it fails to do justice to her exalted virtues
or to her position as the advocate of Christendom before the throne
of God. Luther mainly extolled the faith of the Blessed Virgin,
as conceived in accordance with his new doctrine of justification.
He was aware of, and carefully took into consideration, the sentiments
of the prince to whom the work was dedicated, and who had a lively
attachment to many practices of the ancient religion which were still
appreciated by Luther. Later on, when the prince warmly supported
his person and his work, he learned that the successor to the throne
regarded him as a profoundly pious man and a peaceful religious reformer. Besides its religious note, Luther's treatise on the Magnificat is
pacific in so far as the polemical ideas which it contains are veiled and
not clothed in his customary harsh language. Fundamentally, however,
it, too, is a controversial treatise, as is indicated by such superfluous admonitions as that Mary is "no helping goddess," even though Luther
does not as yet condemn the practice of praying for her intercession.[38]
While the book is not, as has been asserted, a monument of the
author's profound piety, nevertheless, one must marvel at the ideas in
which it abounds, the dexterity with which the style is varied, and the
adroitness with which the author adapts himself to his readers. For
the rest, Luther always believed in the virginity of Mary, even *post
partum*, as affirmed in the Apostles' Creed, though afterwards he
denied her power of intercession, as well as that of the saints in general, resorting to many misinterpretations and combated, as extreme
and pagan, the extraordinary veneration which the Catholic Church

36 Köstlin-Kawerau, *Martin Luther*, Vol. I, p. 478.
37 Weimar ed., VII, pp. 544 sq.; Erl. ed., XLV, pp. 212 sq.
38 Grisar, *Luther*, Vol. IV, p. 237.

showed towards Mary. His prayer-book, which appeared in 1522, retained the Ave Maria side by side with the Pater Noster and the Creed. As late as 1527 he even acknowledged the doctrine of the Immaculate Conception of Mary, in conformity with the theological traditions of the Augustinian Order.[39]

At the beginning of 1522, Luther dedicated to the Pope his scornful tract *Vom Abendfressen des allerheiligsten Herrn des Papstes*.[40] This crude production is a reference to the Bull *In Caena Domini*, which was published annually on Maundy Thursday at Rome. This document was a comprehensive condemnation of heresy, and it now listed Luther among the condemned heretics. Luther derides the pope as a drunkard who in his frenzy curses and swears and uses the Latin of a "kitchen scullion." He translates the solemn juridicial document and accompanies it with coarse annotations. In the introduction he declares that "the Rhine is scarcely large enough to drown all the scoundrels"—such as the "retailers of bulls, cardinals, legates," etc., besides archbishops, bishops, abbots, etc. Did such language serve his previously mentioned purpose to quell violence and sedition?

It is a puzzle how Luther, during his short sojourn at the Wartburg, in addition to his other work, was able to translate the New Testament from Greek into a German of undeniable excellence. He practically completed this important task within the incredibly short space of three months. We postpone an appreciation of his New Testament to a later page, where we shall deal with his rendition of the Bible as a whole. As a literary document, it is truly monumental.[41] For the present we will consider only its polemical purpose. Luther intended his Bible to be read by the masses, so that it might win followers to his new gospel. To accomplish this purpose he did not scruple to alter the text in numerous places. The aggressive tendency of the translator is emphasized by the wood-cuts which illustrate the Apocalypse. There the woman of Babylon is repeatedly shown crowned with the papal tiara; Catholic dignitaries, and even the Emperor, are depicted as rendering homage to the bearer of the cup of sin and blasphemy; like Babylon, papal Rome collapses and is consumed by fire; the defenders of the papacy are depicted as dragons with

[39] *Op. cit.*, IV, 238 and 500 sqq.
[40] *Werke*, Weimar ed., VIII, pp. 601 sqq.; Erl. ed., XXIV², pp. 166 sqq. *"Fressen"* is a contemptuous term used only of animals.
[41] Grisar, *Luther*, Vol. V, pp. 494 sqq.

seven heads, and so forth. These illustrations escaped observation until quite recently. They are in complete harmony with the utterly abnormal apocalyptical frame of mind in which Luther was at that time. In this respect, Luther's celebrated German version of the New Testament ranks with the polemical illustrations of the "Passionale of Christ and Antichrist," by which at the beginning of the Wartburg period he enlisted the aid of the graphic arts in the campaign against religion.[42]

5. THE RETURN. VICTORY AT WITTENBERG

Whilst Luther was occupied with the translation of the Bible in the solitude of the Wartburg, events happened at Wittenberg which induced him to move back to the university town, in spite of many and great dangers.

On December 3, students and citizens attacked certain priests who intended to celebrate Mass in the parish church there. The monastery of the Discalced Friars as well as a number of cathedral canons were menaced. Worst of all, the tumultous Karlstadt, who cut such a sorry figure at the disputation of Leipsic, set himself up as the leader of the new movement with the intention of becoming not a dilatory, but a consistent Luther. He announced that matrimony must be obligatory for the clergy and that the reception of the Eucharist without the chalice was not permissible. On Christmas he for the first time commemorated the Lord's Supper without celebrating Mass, by administering bread and wine to all who so desired, without previous confession. On January 19, he, as deacon of All Saints, solemnly took unto himself a wife. The Augustinians who still remained at Wittenberg removed every altar but one from their church and burned the images of the saints as well as the holy oils. Karlstadt asserted that images were prohibited by Holy Scripture (Ex. 20, 4) and denounced them as idols. As a consequence, the sacred images and statues were cast out of the various churches. The monk Zwilling conducted a similar iconoclastic campaign in the towns and villages about Wittenberg. He proscribed ecclesiastical vestments and preached his revolutionary innovations clad in the characteristic attire of the students of that time. Confessions were discontinued; the law of fasting was disre-

[42] Grisar-Heege, Luthers Kampfbilder: I. Das Passionale, II. Der Bilderkampf in der deutschen Bibel, with 14 plates.

garded; there was a movement to abolish all feast-days except Sundays; the religious consolations for the sick, prisoners and those about to be executed fell into desuetude. In lieu of these it was proposed to devote greater attention to the alleviation of temporal needs by the institution of a so-called community chest which was enriched by mass stipends and other ecclesiastical funds. Karlstadt introduced a thoroughly shallow lay Christianity. It was his intention to promote a natural but spiritualistic religiosity in opposition to Luther's massive doctrine of the imputation of the merits of Christ.[43] Like Luther he believed that he was inspired from on high.

A new and dangerous element was injected into this movement when, on December 27, the so-called prophets of Zwickau visited Melanchthon at Wittenberg. They were: Nicholas Storch and Mark Stübner, two cloth-weavers, who claimed to have received a direct call from God to preach. They had been inducted by Thomas Münzer into the prophetic life and into direct converse with God and maintained that man is obliged to learn everything through the Spirit, and to aspire to the most complete self-renunciation and apathy. Not only was the Church to be reformed by one greater than Luther, but the civil order, too, was to be altered, all priests were to be slain, and all godless people extirpated. They attacked especially Luther's doctrine of infant baptism and hence were called Anabaptists. If faith alone makes the Sacrament efficacious, they contended against Luther, then adults only can be baptized, since children are incapable of faith. The inference cannot be denied.

Like many others, Melanchthon, who was deficient in intellectual acumen, allowed himself to be taken in by these "prophets." When Luther heard of this he was greatly worried and tried to inspire Melanchthon with distrust toward these fanatics.[44] His troubles were increased in virtue of the tumultous innovations which were introduced in Wittenberg and environs. Luckily, Karlstadt did not make common cause with the "prophets," but the feeble efforts of the Elector were impotent to arrest the innovations of Karlstadt.

These reforms were favored by a semblance of truth—if one took the Lutheran position. Luther himself had set a precedent in

[43] H. Barge, Karlstadt, Vol. I, p. 404.

[44] Briefwechsel III, p. 273, 13th of January, 1522: "Neque enim Deus unquam aliquem misit, nisi vel per hominem vocatum vel per signa declaratum. . . . Quaeras, num experti sint spirituales angustias et nativitates divinas, mortes infernosque." He says God Himself speaks in the verse: "Contrivit omnia ossa mea" (Is. XXXVIII, 13.)

altering the divine services. The others were simply following his example. The enthusiasts of Zwickau were not only justified in their opposition to his doctrine concerning baptism, but their private revelations and theories of interior experience were essentially not far removed from Luther's contention that the Spirit alone must guide man. Nor did they deviate very much from his view of supernatural revelation, although he himself was naturally unwilling to grant that their strange and arbitrary conduct was the result of visions. Strangely enough, he asked Melanchthon to tell the "prophets" of Zwickau that even raptures capable of transporting men into the third heaven furnished no proof of their claims, but they would have to work miracles and also to show that they had been made partakers of the spiritual travails and the divine re-birth which penetrated death and hell—that terrible regeneration which he believed to have experienced and which he maintained to be the standard by which to judge whether one were really and truly justified.

Writing of affairs at Wittenberg, the Elector Frederick said: "Everything went wrong, everybody became perplexed, and no one knew who was cook or cellarer." [45] It was then that the imperial government finally issued a strict warning (June 20, 1522) to all the bishops and to the above-mentioned Elector to ferret out and punish those who disturbed the religious peace and violated ecclesiastical discipline. The bishops of Meissen and Merseburg indicated their intention to obey and Frederick caused representations to be made to Luther.

What was decisive, however, was that Luther himself now resolved to terminate the disorderly state of affairs by resuming his residence at Wittenberg. Naturally he realized that his territorial lord might be seriously embarrassed by the imperial authorities if he openly permitted the outlaw to return to the university and sheltered him in his territory. However, cognizant of the high esteem in which that prince held him, and relying upon Frederick's favorable attitude towards the new religion, Luther ventured upon a course of action which would otherwise have been foolhardy. Moreover, at the conclusion of his last letter, Frederick had practically put the decision up to Luther by saying that he would leave everything to his dis-

---

[45] Köstlin-Kawerau, M. *Luther*, I, p. 495.

cretion, since he was experienced in such important matters.[46] His return was energetically requested by the authorities of the city of Wittenberg as well as by the University, which had been induced to take this step at the behest of Melanchthon, who was completely bewildered. Thus Luther started on the hazardous journey without notifying the Elector.

He left the Wartburg on the morning of March 1, attired in his squire's costume, and rode towards Borna, south of Leipsic, by way of Jena, where he met the Wittenberg student Kessler, a native of Switzerland, with several companions, in the Inn of the Bear. At Borna he wrote a letter to the Elector, which Protestant historians are wont to represent as a marvelous product of devout heroism.

Since he had received his Gospel not from man but from Heaven—thus he writes in a vein of beguiling confidence—he would now return, in order not to yield to the devil, who had caused the consternation at Wittenberg. He realized that he had powerful opponents, such as Duke George of Saxony (who had issued the most dire threats against Luther in a letter to the Elector, his cousin); yet he was not afraid. Even if the state of affairs at Leipsic, where George resided, were as bad as at Wittenberg, he would, nevertheless, proceed to that place, even if the menaces of vain George became nine times more dire and if every inhabitant were nine times worse than he. He was going to Wittenberg under a far higher protection than that afforded him by his Elector. God was with him, and therefore he did not need the protection of the ruler; indeed, he intended rather to protect Frederick than be protected by him; for the Elector's faith was still weak, whereas his own was strong. He requests the prince, in the event that he be apprehended or murdered, not to resist the authorities of the empire, for that would be contrary to the will of God who had instituted them. The empire, he hopes, would not expect the prince to become his [Luther's] jailer. In conclusion he rises to the height of a spiritualistic style: "If your grace would have the faith, you would vision the majesty of God; but as you have not yet the faith, you have seen nothing."

This is Luther's so-called "heroic letter" from Borna. It is undoubtedly the utterance of an incomparably courageous man; but it is also the product of a mind which cannot be comprehended except

[46] *Briefwechsel*, III, p. 295. The importance of these words is enhanced by the fact that shortly before, at the end of February, 1522, Luther had announced to the Elector his early return to Wittenberg. Erl. ed., LIII, p. 183 (*Briefwechsel*, III, p. 291).

on the assumption that he was impelled by the fixed idea of being divinely inspired. No man can write thus unless he pretends to be an ambassador of God and who does not realize that his entire future is at stake. The situation in which Luther found himself compelled him to impress his territorial lord as forcefully as possible in order to assure the success of his move. And he succeeded in doing this because Frederick was a diplomat, sickly, and a Bible reader who favored the Lutheran innovations. Luther, on the other hand, was simply compelled to resume his abode at Wittenberg and to sever the chain which bound him to the Wartburg, if he did not wish to see his life-work shattered. In no other way was he able to keep control of the reins which, as he believed, had been entrusted to him by God. Thus considered, his resolution as well as the letter lose somewhat of their heroic character and enter into the sphere of tangible and practical calculation. At all events, considering the edict of Worms and its threats, his enterprise was a venture which might just as well have led to the fall of Luther's work, as it actually did to its progress. This remains true, even if two other natural motives are taken into consideration. Luther's long confinement was bound eventually to become a stifling burden to a man of his temperament—a burden to be shaken off at any price, even if the effort involved great danger. The second factor is the order issued by the imperial government to the Elector and the bishops. It was bound to move Luther to form a strong resolution to settle the disturbances at Wittenberg. If he succeeded in this, he would be the man of the hour, and would prove himself useful, if not rehabilitated in the eyes of the empire. In the opinion of many, therefore, he would no longer be accounted a noxious revolutionist, as his opponents represented him to be. This is offered in explanation of the "heroic act" of Borna.

"Squire George" made his entry into Wittenberg on March 6, escorted by a number of knights who had joined him on the way. Kessler, the Swiss student, describes his exterior appearance as "quite corpulent"; his bearing was erect, but as he walked, he bent backward rather than forward; his head was lifted high. Kessler particularly observes his "deep-set black eyes and eyebrows, blinking and twinkling like stars, so that it was not comfortable to behold them." In the following year, this striking expression of Luther's eyes is thus described by the bishop of Kulm and Ermland, John Dantiscus, who had seen and conversed with Luther at Wittenberg: "His eyes are penetrating," he says; "they have a certain sinister sparkle, such as one finds from time to time in persons who are possessed by the devil." His features, he added, reminded one of the character of his books, his conversation was excited and replete with risque allusions and ridicule.[47]

In addition to the letter which Luther had despatched from Borna, the Elector was pleased to receive another communication from him upon his arrival at Wittenberg. In this letter, which had been expressly requested by the Elector, Luther spoke of his return to Wittenberg, and the Elector intended to exhibit it in public, to enable Luther to justify his step himself. The letter was actually read by the Elector's representative at the imperial court and by other important persons.

On the following Sunday Luther, elated at his achievement, confidently ascended the pulpit of the town-church, whence for eight successive days he delivered the most vehement sermons imaginable against the prevalent frenzy. Owing to his powerful action, not to say his hypnotic gifts, he was able to repel all opposition and to restore order. His chief thought was that the weak, i. e., those who had not as yet attained to a full conviction of the value and freedom of the Gospel, should not be perturbed by precipitous innovations. The objects of a general amelioration had better be sought by gentle and circumspect methods. By his prudence and the force of his eloquence, he succeeded in gaining control of the situation and forcing Karlstadt with his associates into the background. The text of these famous sermons was subsequently revised by Aurifaber, who published them. Luther made them the basis of his treatise "On the Reception of the Sacrament under Both Forms," which appeared soon after.[48]

In this work he declares that charity was violated towards those who were not of his party, "who belong to us and must be made to join us." A man is not bound to do what he has a right to do. Then, too, he (Luther) should have been consulted, since the town council had conferred the office of preaching in Wittenberg upon him. The Mass was to be abolished, but not by violence. Marriage of the clergy, the monastic life, fasting, images in

[47] Grisar, *Luther*, Vol. IV, p. 357; cfr. Vol. III, p. 429; Vol. I, pp. 86, 279; Vol. II, pp. 158 sq.

[48] Weimar ed., Vol. X, II, pp. 11 sq.; Erlangen ed., Vol. XXVIII, pp. 285 sqq.

the churches, etc., were matters left free by God. Things would right themselves without ordinances and coercion, provided the Word of God entered the hearts of men.

"While I slept and drank beer with my Philippo [Melanchthon] and with Amsdorf in Wittenberg, the Word did so much to weaken the papacy as no prince or emperor ever did before. I have done nothing; the Word has done and achieved everything."

Everyone who is convinced he is right should make a determined use of his liberty. If he is forbidden to eat meat on fast-days, he should straightway eat it; if the pope tries to compel him to remain in the monastic state, he should discard the cowl. Then, contradicting himself, he states that the use of the chalice by the laity is an ordinance of Christ, as it pertains to the essence of the Eucharist, yet it is free and must not be made compulsory. The chalice is to be given to those who desire it, but it is not to be forced upon the congregation. Consequently, here too we have a twofold form of administering the Sacrament with the inevitable danger of provoking a cleavage among the faithful.

Luther's attitude respecting the use of images was equally indefinite. The images of saints, crucifixes, etc., are not to be abolished on their own account, but only to serve God. Because of the harmful abuse to which they have been put, they do not deserve to be retained. If people once find out that images are worthless, they will disappear.

The old form of confession should be abolished and a voluntary confession of sins substituted for it. He says that he himself had experienced the consolation and strength to be derived from this latter kind of confession, without which the devil would have choked him to death long ago. "I am well acquainted with him [the devil]; and he knows me. If you knew him, you would not thus repudiate confession." Luther, therefore, proposes to retain confession on the strength of his own experience and by virtue of his own authority, whereas the Catholic Church appeals to the authority of Christ. He orders the penitent to confess to anyone whom he may select, whereas the Church directs the penitent to an ordained priest. He directs the penitent to confess for the sake of obtaining consolation, whereas the Church directs him for the sake of obtaining remission of his sins through the Sacrament of Penance. He does not acknowledge the sacramental seal of confession which the Church imposes upon the priest.

But this is not the place to emphasize all the defects and contradictions of the ecclesiastical system advocated by Luther as contrasted with the laws that prevailed in the ancient Church. They will suggest themselves spontaneously to the thoughtful reader.

In one particular Luther openly proclaims the necessity, and at the same time the impracticability of a measure proposed by himself. For the practice of auricular confession he would substitute a kind of ecclesiastical ban as

an indispensable disciplinary measure. After exhortations have proved un-
availing, "adulterers, usurers, robbers, and drunkards" should be excommunicated in the name of the congregation. "However," he says, "I do not
venture to carry this out alone." Owing to the internal defects of his religious system, his well-intentioned endeavors in this respect were never fully
successful, though stricter ecclesiastical discipline would have been precisely
the most necessary requirement after the tumultuous scenes witnessed at
Wittenberg.

On the whole, as even the most eminent among the Protestant biographers
of Luther acknowledges, one is "compelled to question whether the way
which Luther in these sermons prescribed for ecclesiastical reforms, was
actually fit to attain the object he had in view, namely, a Christian regimen
with purified regulations." [49] Indeed, the unlucky star of dissension between his basic demand of a false liberty and the need of unity and order
hovered visibly over the beginnings of his practical attempts at reform.

Karlstadt adapted himself grudgingly to the altered state of affairs,
but pursued his own course. He declared that learned studies were
useless and on one occasion, when a young theologian was being promoted to the doctorate, publicly attacked the title of "Master" as
repugnant to the Word of Christ. He said he preferred to live in the
country as a peasant and to learn from peasants the interpretation of
Holy Writ as it had been imparted to them from on high. He chose to
call himself "Neighbor Andrew" and appeared in the grey garb of a
peasant. Having a propensity for false mysticism, he established relations with the seer and reformer, Thomas Münzer.

The "prophets of Zwickau" had abandoned Wittenberg. In the
course of an interview with Mark Stübner, Luther had challenged
him to prove his mission by a miraculous sign. It was a suggestion
which Stübner could have cast back at Luther. Stübner, however,
boldly declared that he would comply with the demand. Thereupon
Luther asserted that his God would prevent the gods of such false
prophets from performing any miracles. This ended the conference,
and Luther saw nothing more of the "prophets of Zwickau." The
restless and fanatical Münzer, on the other hand, endeavored to re-
approach him and explained to him in a letter how, amid inward
fears, he had become assured that his was a true divine revelation. In
spreading his false ideas, therefore, he applied the same standard which
Luther claimed for himself, namely, the way of interior agony. His

[49] Köstlin-Kawerau, *Martin Luther*, 5th ed., Vol. I, p. 507.

claim, however, did not impress Luther, whose practical sagacity would not permit him to place the least trust in this over-excited Communist.

One who entered the parish church of Wittenberg after Luther's victory, discovered that the same vestments were used for divine service as of yore, and heard the same old Latin hymns. The Host was elevated and exhibited at the Consecration. In the eyes of the people it was the same Mass as before, except that Luther omitted all prayers which represented the sacred function as a sacrifice. The people were intentionally kept in the dark on this point. "We cannot draw the common people away from the Sacrament, and it will probably be thus until the gospel is well understood." [50] The rite of the celebration of the Mass he explained as "a purely external thing", and said that the damnable words referring to the sacrifice could be omitted all the more readily, since the ordinary Christian would not notice the omission and hence there was no danger of scandal. The words in question, especially those of the canon, are pronounced almost inaudibly in the popish Church.[51]

[50] *Von beider Gestalt, das ander Teil.*
[51] Köstlin-Kawerau, *op. cit.,* Vol. I, p. 511.

CHAPTER X

THE SPREAD OF LUTHERANISM

I. METHODS OF PROPAGATION

If one were to investigate the means by which Lutheranism established and propagated itself, he would first of all discover the cunning practice of concealment which was indicated towards the close of the preceding section of this work.

The divine service was essentially altered, but suspicion was avoided as much as possible by retaining the external form, so that the common people, as Luther said, "would never become aware of it." It was to be done "without scandal." [1] In justification of this procedure, he asserted that the new religious practices must be "propagated without injury to charity." Thus it ought to be done, he wrote on a subsequent occasion, "if we are not to unsettle and confuse our churches without accomplishing anything against the papists." Melanchthon shared this view. "The world," he said, "is so much attached to the Mass that it seems well-nigh impossible to wrest people from it." [2] Hence, Luther, as a matter of principle, more frequently adopts a calculated accommodation than his impulsiveness would lead one to expect. When Martin Weier, a young student of good family from Pomerania, who was about to return home, asked him how he should behave in the matter of divine worship in the Catholic surroundings of his home and towards his father, who professed the ancient faith, Luther, according to his own account, told him "to fast, pray, attend Mass, and revere the saints, just as he had been doing before," but try to enlighten his father as much as possible; he would commit no wrong if he "took part in the Mass and other profanations for his father's sake." [3] Yet, when referring to his previous practice of celebrating Mass in the monastery, Luther declared that he had offended

[1] Grisar, *Luther*, Vol. II, pp. 321 sq.
[2] *Ib.*, p. 322.
[3] *Ib.*, p. 323.

God most horribly, more so than if he had been "a highwayman or kept a brothel."

It was, undoubtedly, a serious matter thus to deceive the people, who, owing to the retention of the ancient ceremonies, regarded the service of the reformers as Catholic. Cochlaeus, in a tract, speaks of Luther's "hypocritical deception" of the masses. [4] Luther was pleased to see that, despite the contrary urging of many an impetuous fanatic, his principle maintained the upper hand, namely, that anyone unable to understand the sermon, "be he a layman, whether Italian or Spaniard, seeing our Mass, choir, organs, bells, chantries, etc., would surely say that it was a regular papist church, and that there was no difference, or very little, between it and his own." [5]

The progress of Lutheranism was much aided by the favorable moral impression which the new movement made upon many, even well-intentioned Catholics. The reformers' frank criticism of existing evils attracted many who longed for an amelioration. The bold proposals to pursue other paths, brought forward by Luther with an air of intense zeal, allured the masses and their leaders. People heard of interior Christianity, which was to be opposed to exterior semblance, and of a spiritual liberty which was to overcome self-righteousness. A grand upward flight of virtue appeared to arise from the deceptive teaching that everything was to be done at the inspiration of a perfect love, without regard to the motive of fear or the expectation of reward. Seductive words were heard calling Christ the sole Saviour, who redeemed mankind without any merit on its part, and of the unconditioned rule of grace without human co-operation, which is really nothing but sin. These and other errors, which were dangled before the eyes of men, influenced many whose intentions were good, but who did not investigate more deeply. Only by and bye the true nature of the innovation as a complete religious revolution revealed itself to those who were able to see more clearly, especially after the publication of Luther's "Address to the Nobility" and his work "On the Babylonian Captivity."

Of those who afterwards combated the Reformation successfully

[4] *Ib.*, p. 322.

[5] *Ib.* Attention is called to the many borrowings from the Catholic cult still found among the Protestants of Denmark, Norway, and the duchies formerly united with the Danish crown, as a consequence of the method of concealment introduced in the North by Luther's disciple, Bugenhagen.

with their pens, quite a number at first were prepossessed in favor of Luther and his proceedings, *e. g.*, Cochlaeus, Zasius, Witzel, Billikan, Vitus Amerbach, the aged Wimpfeling, and the humanist Willibald Pirkheimer. Especially among the humanists there were deserving men who at first favored, or at least maintained an indifferent attitude towards, the Wittenberg reform movement, such as John Fabri, who afterwards became bishop of Vienna, and John Faber, the Dominican prior of Augsburg, who later opposed the movement when it unmistakably revealed its true nature. Even Erasmus, much as he had favored Luther's procedure, joined the ranks of his determined opponents in 1524. Other intellectuals were misled in joining Luther by the semblance of reform proclaimed by him; and in the case of some, their allegiance to him was lasting and sincere, and in some instances fanatical. One of these literary men thus taken in was Hartmuth (Hartmann) von Kronberg, a knight who could not go far enough in his enthusiastic support of the Lutheran cause. Prompted by "piety," he petitioned the emperor to treat the pope "as an apostate and a heretic," if he refused to renounce his claims. In his religious enthusiasm Kronberg wished to see all ecclesiastical goods confiscated, and published a pamphlet in which he outlawed every Catholic priest who remained loyal to the ancient Church and stated that it was permissible to treat such "in much the same manner as one treats a ravening wolf, as spiritual thiefs and murderers in word and deed." His Protestant biographer styles Kronberg a man of "unshakable character, though somewhat narrow-minded." [6] Such types were naturally rare, but many showed a steadfast devotion to the cause of Luther, which they regarded as noble.

Of far greater influence upon the masses who joined the Reformation than the attractive force of the good or seemingly good features of the movement was the demand for the abolition of oppressive ecclesiastical burdens. The assertion that the commandments of the Church were not binding opened the door to apostasy. The abolition of confession, of the laws of fasting, of the ruling hierarchy, and the assertion of the dissolubility of matrimony—these and all the other gifts of the new Evangel to the free Christian was sure to captivate many. Above all else, the easy doctrine of justification by faith alone was sure to meet with a friendly reception.

George Witzel (Wicel), who was a Lutheran for a while, wrote

[6] Cfr. Grisar, *Luther*, Vol. II, pp. 325 sqq.

subsequently: "Oh, what a grand doctrine that was, not to be obliged to confess any more, nor to pray, nor to fast, nor to make offerings, nor to give alms. With these you ought surely to have been able to catch two German lands, not one only with such a bait. . . ." [7]

Many clerics who had grown weary of the duties of their state, and desired to marry, flocked to Luther's banner. Convents and monasteries opened their portals and monks and nuns who had selected the monastic life without a vocation or who, enticed by the pleasures of the world, had become disgusted with their vows, left the sacred precincts and doffed their habits. The number of clerics who, prompted by worldly motives, joined the new religion and came to Wittenberg to receive appointments as preachers, was so great that Luther exclaimed: "Who can deliver us from these hordes?" The example of the married Wittenberg leaders proved exceedingly enticing. The ranks of the priests who contracted marriage, as mentioned above, were augmented in 1522 by Dr. Justus Jonas and John Bugenhagen. The former, who had been forced upon the monastery of All Saints as provost and who, in his capacity of professor of theology, proved to be one of the most distinguished assistants of Luther, contracted a solemn marriage with a woman of Wittenberg and defended his conduct in a book specifically directed against Faber's defense of celibacy. Bugenhagen, a Pomeranian, was likewise one of the first adherents of the new religion. He had been a priest and teacher of a convent-school at Treptow, and took up his residence at Wittenberg, where, in 1523, he was forcibly installed as pastor of the local church by Luther and the town council. He had married the previous year.

When Erasmus heard of the growing number of married priests, he penned the sarcastic words: "Many speak of the Lutheran affair as a tragedy; to me it appears rather as a comedy, for the movements always terminate in a wedding." [8]

In the various departments of public life the word "liberty" produced favorable results in behalf of the Lutheran apostasy. In many places where the municipal authorities were engaged in a struggle with the territorial jurisdictions of the episcopate, joining the new religion or the threat of apostasy became a slogan in the battle for civil rights.

---

[7] *Ibid.*, pp. 313 sq.

[8] Letter of March 21, 1528, on the occasion of the marriage of the monk Oecolampadius. Cf. Theod. Wiedemann, *Joh. Eck*, p. 246.

The temptation to obtain high office and to appropriate the property of the Church was too strong to be resisted. The desire to obtain relief from economic pressure through the adoption of the new religion penetrated even to the peasants. In many places the rural populace, like the inhabitants of the cities, were affected by the mighty agitation which was conducted by means of the spoken and the printed word on behalf of the new ideas. Dissatisfied clerics joined in the agitation. It was a veritable mass suggestion. The indescribable power of Luther's pen, his forceful language, which was carried to the lowest classes of the population and excited all the instincts of opposition to the Church, actually induced a sort of popular hypnosis. The hero, such as every profound popular movement necessarily requires, was at hand. The evil conditions existing in State and Church furnished a fateful resonance to his voice. The apocalyptical expressions which he employed, supported by drastic wood-cuts, verses and songs, impressed the imagination and powerfully affected the emotions. The seed he sowed found a soil which was all the more favorable as it had not as yet been overrun by any other literature or public agitation, but offered, as it were, a virginal susceptibility.

In addition to all this there was the resort to force—force on the part of the civil authority for the purpose of introducing the new system of religion and advocated by the theological leaders to be exerted upon all who were exposed to their pressure and violence. The conduct of the civil authorities, especially in the electorate of Saxony, will be discussed more fully in the sequel. These authorities imitated the agitators, Anabaptists and others, in the application of violence.

Luther's personal method of procedure was marked by forcible measures in certain places soon after his return from the Wartburg. In these places, as well as elsewhere, the forbearance and consideration which he had recommended yielded to violent disciplinary penalties, when it appeared to be to the advantage of the new Evangel.

He had, it is true, recommended to Gabriel Zwilling, his first preacher who labored in Altenburg, that he should "liberate the consciences of men solely by means of the Word." He said he had promised his sovereign (prudence had compelled him to do so) that his adherents would observe this rule.[9] But when the loyal Augustinian

9 "You must refrain from innovations . . . I gave my word to the prince, etc." (See Grisar, *Luther*, Vol. II, pp. 314, 316 sqq.

canons of Altenburg, who had for generations exercised the uncontested right of appointing the pastor of the local parish, denied the new preacher permission to take possession of their church, Luther addressed a letter to the city council, whose members favored him, and as a consequence the council claimed the right of nominating Zwilling to the position.

In this letter he maintained that aldermen existed not merely for the sake of temporal government, but were also obliged "by brotherly Christian love" to intervene in behalf of the Gospel. For the rest, everyone had the right to repel ravening wolves, such as the canons and their disturbing provost, who, ensnared by false doctrines, unjustly collected the ecclesiastical tithes, and relied on the councils of the Church, whereas the Scriptures did not empower a council, but "every individual Christian" to "judge doctrine and to recognize and avoid the wolves." The canons were told to "observe silence, or teach the new Gospel, or depart."

Violence was resorted to. With the consent of the Elector, Luther's friend Wenceslaus Link, of the Augustinian Order, was appointed to the position in dispute, in place of Zwilling, who was too indiscreet. This was in the summer of 1522. In February, 1523, Link resigned his position as vicar-general of the Augustinian congregation, chose a wife, and was "married" by Luther himself at Altenburg over the protest of the courageous canons, who, although sorely persecuted, remained in the city with the other faithful clergy and personnel of their Order.

In order to sketch the fate of Altenburg during the next few years —a fate which became typical—it should be mentioned that Link, in 1524, succeeded in having the municipal council forbid the Franciscans, who were very much beloved in that city, to celebrate Mass in public and to preach and hear confessions. At the same time the municipal council, in a written address to the Elector, declared that, according to the Old as well as the New Testament, rulers were not allowed to tolerate "idolatry." The bailiff was given a free hand. In August, 1525, Spalatin, after resigning his office of court-preacher upon the death of the Elector Frederick, took over Link's position in Altenburg and married Catherine Heidenreich on November 19. Luther had preceded him. It was an inevitable consequence of Spalatin's marriage that the canons of Altenburg declared his position and benefices forfeited. Serious conflicts resulted from this action in a city already torn by religious dissensions. Luther demanded from John, the new Elector of Saxony, the suppression of Catholic worship at Altenburg, the "Altenburg idolatry," as he styled it, among other offensive invectives. Soon after Spalatin directed to the court a similar demand couched in no less offensive terms, followed by a second demand in January, 1526. It must be considered, he wrote, "that many a poor man would readily embrace the Gospel, if that miserable idolatry were abolished." At the most, the canons might be permitted "to conduct their ceremonies in the greatest secrecy, behind closed doors, without admitting any other person." On February 9, Luther, referring to Altenburg, memorialized the new Elector, who was very accommodating to him, along the following lines:

As a ruler he was bound in conscience "to attack the idolaters" and to suppress "the false, blasphemous cult" as much as possible. Did he wish to be responsible to God for the criminal abominations by supplying the foundation with tithes and property, as heretofore? Moreover, a secular ruler should not tolerate that contradictory preachers (*i. e.*, such whose teachings were at variance) lead his subjects into dissension and schism, whence rebellion and mutiny may ensue. "One and the same doctrine should be preached in the same locality." "For this reason," he added, "Nuremberg has silenced its monks and closed its monasteries."

By means of the deceptive principle of "one doctrine for the same locality" he rests his intolerance upon a plausible foundation which was satisfactory to the mediocre intelligence of the prince. The subversion of the whole political order in the electorate, as well as elsewhere, was thereby accelerated.

The solution of the Altenburg problem was thus made dependent upon the conscience of the somewhat pietistic ruler. Should the canons, says Luther, attempt "to apply their own conscience," "it shall avail them naught" because they cannot prove their position from Scripture! And if they should complain that "they are forced to embrace a certain doctrine, that is not true; they are only forbidden to give public scandal." They are prevented from practicing a cult which they themselves "must confess is not founded in Scripture."

Such was the pitiful justification of that brutal use of force which became habitual afterwards. But the loyal Catholics at Altenburg offered determined resistance. When the Lutheran visitators came to exercise their office, in 1528, the town council informed them that there were still "many papists in the city," yea, that the whole district "fairly swarmed with monks and nuns." It was an honorable testimony to Catholic loyalty, the like of which was also found in other places.

From the introduction of the new Evangel into Eilenburg, in 1522, we learn what was Luther's leading idea: "It is the duty of the sovereign, as a ruler and brother Christian, to drive away the wolves and to be solicitous for the welfare of his people." [10] On the occasion of a first and second visit to Eilenburg, Luther had discovered that the magistrates of that place had failed to show the proper zeal. Like the authorities of many other places, they were desirous of increasing their own power and influence; but their Catholic conscience checked the majority of them. The prince was to remedy this defect by the exercise of his authority. With the aid of Spalatin, Luther at once proposed two new preachers for Eilenburg, of whom one was to be summoned by the town council under the influence of the court, whilst at the same time the afore-mentioned statement about the wolves was to be shown to the sovereign. Thus the matter was settled in a bureaucratic manner with the co-operation of the prince. Andrew Kauxdorf, a native of Torgau, was finally recognized by the magistrates as preacher, entered Eilenburg in 1522, and was permitted gradually to Lutheranize the people who refused to embrace the new religion.

Where the magistrates were unwilling, the powerful nobility, at Luther's instigation, frequently used violence to bring about a change.

Thus, to cite but one striking illustration, Count Johann Heinrich of Schwarzburg became the founder of Lutheranism in his territories in virtue of a decree authorized by Luther.[11] His father, Count Günther, who was loyal to the Church, had legally confirmed the monks at Schwarzburg in the possession of their parishes; now, Johann Heinrich asked Luther how he might deprive them of their rights and possessions in favor of a preacher of the new Evangel. Luther replied on December 12, 1522, that Count Günther had naturally expected the monks to preach the Gospel, but if witnesses could testify that they did not preach the true Gospel (of Luther), but papistical heresies, the Count would have the right, nay, the duty, to

10 Ibid., p. 319.
11 Ibid., p. 318.

oust them from their parishes. "For it is not unlawful," he says, "indeed, it is absolutely right to drive the wolf from the sheepfold. . . . A preacher is not given property and tithes in order that he should do injury, but that he should labor profitably. If he does not work to the advantage of the people, the endowments are his no longer." This principle was promptly applied at Schwarzburg. The Count seized the properties and revoked the privileges which his father had given to the Church. Monks and parishes were subjected to violence, and the new Evangel was introduced.

Luther's reply concerning temporal possessions, taken in connection with certain other statements made by him, reveals an idea truly revolutionary in its consequences. It indicated that, if the clergy refused to preach the new religion, in Germany and in the Church in general, ecclesiastical possessions were no longer secure. Lutheranism needed but to apply this principle, which, undoubtedly, it was strongly tempted to do. If only those priests, abbots, bishops, and other spiritual rulers were to continue in the possession of their benefices who used them to promote the Lutheran innovation, then the foundations of order were overturned. Wyclif and Hus had proclaimed similar doctrines, and the Christian State had been able to defend its legal structure against them only by taxing its energies to the utmost. It is hardly probable that Luther realized in advance all the consequences of his decision in the Schwarzburg affair, though practically it had been acted upon ever since the beginning of the new movement. Only prudent regard for the electoral court prevented the rigorous carrying out of this decision.

2. AUXILIARIES FROM THE MONASTERIES

Lichtenberg in the Saxon Electorate affords an example of how Lutheranism gained ground by enticing the occupants of important clerical positions to violate the vow of celibacy. The appeal to sensuality served as a stimulant. Whereas the measures discussed before were coercive, we have now to consider a kind of moral compulsion whose power over mortal man was fully realized by those who set the evil passions in motion. In this respect the letter by which Luther prepared the way for the change of religion in Lichtenberg is an extraordinary document. In that city there was a famous monastery of Antonine monks, who followed the rule of St. Augustine. It was governed by Wolfgang Reissenbusch, a doctor of laws and a former student of the University of Wittenberg. He was bound to his Order by solemn vows, and discharged the office of "preceptor" of the monastery and administrator of its property. Luther's friends reminded him that Reissenbusch, notwithstanding his scruples, could probably be prevailed upon to marry—a matter which he had already discussed with him. Luther sent him an open letter, which was published at Wittenberg under the title: "A Christian Letter Addressed to Wolfgang Reissenbusch," etc. In it he tries to impress the recipient, as well as all others who are similarly situated, with every conceivable reason to induce them to violate their vow of chastity by an immediate marriage.

As a man, he says, Reissenbusch was "created for and compelled by God Himself to embrace the married state." The monastic vow is void because it demands the impossible. To keep chastity is "as little within our power as to work miracles." As long as one is neither an angel nor a spirit, we are told, "God in no wise bestows or grants this privilege." He who takes such a vow relies "upon works, and not upon the grace of God;" he "takes his stand upon works and commandments" and denies "Christ and the faith."

Then follows a detailed, and, in some places, disgusting exposition of the alleged inevitable necessity of sexual intercourse. The non-satisfaction of the sexual instinct in matrimony had resulted in immorality among the entire clergy and in all the monasteries. Luther overwhelms his tempted friend in sinister language and with a demoniacal style intended to excite the passions. "It is necessary that you be urged thereto, that you be exhorted, driven, incited, and encouraged. Well now! dear sir, I prithee, why do you wish to delay and meditate, etc.? It must not, it ought not, and it will not be otherwise. Banish the thoughts from your mind and go ahead joyously!" True he would thereby become a "matrimonial mantle covering the disgrace" for others; but Christ, too, had become "the mantle that cloaks the disgrace of us all." [12]

The reference to Christ is repulsive. That holy name ought rather to have reminded him of the admonitions of Christ and His disciples, which were the very antithesis of his own exhortations. It should have recalled to him the words which served as a guiding star throughout all the centuries for those who voluntarily bound themselves by a vow of chastity. It should also have reminded him of the grace of Christ in which he who

---

[12] Weimar ed., Vol. XVIII, pp. 270–279; Erlangen ed., LIII, pp. 286 sqq. (*Briefwechsel*, V, p. 145), letter of March 27, 1525. Finally Luther says (*ibid.*): "It is but a matter of a brief hour of disgrace, to be followed by years of honor."

makes this sacrifice places his sole reliance and whereby that which appears impossible to the world is rendered easy and a source of joy. In lieu of these, we have alluring descriptions of the irresistible force of the sexual instinct.

Reissenbusch yielded to Luther's persuasion, bade farewell to the Order to which he had bound himself by a solemn vow, and married Hanna Herzog, the daughter of a poor tailor's widow at Torgau. With the connivance of the Elector he retained his clerical office as "preceptor" and the endowments entrusted to his Order. For the purpose of inviting others to imitate his example, the incident was exploited in the press by Bugenhagen, the Lutheran pastor of Wittenberg, who addressed to the happy groom an "Epistola Gratulatoria de Coniugio Episcoporum et Diaconorum" which he also caused to be published in German. Such great importance was attached at Wittenberg to the marriage of priests and monks as an auxiliary factor in the extension of the new Evangel.

Already at a previous stage of his career Luther had approached, among others, the Order of Teutonic Knights, urging its members to break their vows by marrying. Unfortunately, discipline had declined among these Knights, so that he had reason to hope that they would respond to his public invitation. Like the priests of this Order, the knights, too, were bound by a voluntary vow of chastity. Their contact with the world exposed them to special danger. The general reform by means of which Adrian VI endeavored to check the decline of their monastic discipline, proved to be but partially adequate in view of the dissensions that prevailed among the rulers of the Teutonic Order, especially since the Grand Master of the Order, Albrecht von Brandenburg, a cousin of the Elector Frederick of Saxony, was himself favorably inclined towards Lutheranism. After receiving a visit from the Grand Master at Wittenberg, on November 29, 1523, Luther wrote his "Exhortation to the Knights of the Teutonic Order to Avoid False Chastity and Embrace Lawful Matrimonial Chastity," which was at once published in German.[13]

In this work, the author depicts matrimony in alluring colors, as the proper thing for their state. He tells the knights who had secret and illicit relations with women, "not to despair in weakness and sin," because such extra-matrimonial relations were "less sinful" than to "take a lawful wife"

[13] Weimar ed., Vol. XII, pp. 232 sqq.; Erl. ed., Vol. XXIX, pp. 16 sqq. Grisar, *Luther*, II, 116 sq., 317 sq.

with the consent of a council of the Church, supposing such a permission were given.[14]

In conclusion he says that Christ had reserved to Himself certain bishops who would resign from their office or transform it into a genuinely episcopal office for the sake of the Gospel. Many a bishop or abbot would marry, he says with a significant hint to weak ecclesiastical dignitaries, if the path were only blazed for them and wooing were no longer regarded as a disgrace and a danger.

These alluring appeals did not fail to attain their object in the case of those members of monastic orders to whom they were addressed. With the same energy Luther set about the task of winning over the episcopate, ridiculing the bishops who refused to heed him. When, in compliance with an imperial mandate, the bishops of Meissen and Merseburg proceeded with their visitations and called to account the clerics who had married, he issued a tract in which he gave full vent to his irritation against the hierarchy (1522). His main intention was to brand the higher clergy as immoral and to strengthen his appeals to the lower clergy to marry and preach the pure Gospel. This tract bore the title: "Against the Falsely Named Clerical State of the Pope and the Bishops." [15] In this work he calls himself an "evangelist by the grace of God," declaring he had the same right to style himself thus as they have to call themselves bishops, since he was certain that Christ regardéd him as such and would testify in his behalf on the day of judgment.

Here, too, he teaches that the sexual impulse can be controlled in the clerical state as little as fire can be deprived of its power to burn; that it is either "all fornication" or "impure, involuntary, miserable, lost chastity." There is "scarcely one among a thousand who lives an upright life." These few are "God's special miracles." Pope and bishops permit innocent men to be sacrificed "to Moloch, the fiery idol." "Monasteries and convents are gates of hell, where the faith (*i. e.*, his faith) is not practiced with honesty and vigor." [16] He does not tire of censuring them because of their corrupt life.

But, he interposes, will not a revolt be the final outcome of his attitude against the episcopate? What about it? "It would be better"—thus runs his terrible reply—"that all the bishops were murdered, that all the monasteries

[14] Grisar, *Luther*, Vol. II, p. 120.
[15] Weimar ed., Vol. X, pp. 105 sqq.; Erl. ed., Vol. XXVIII, pp. 141 sqq.
[16] Grisar, *Luther*, Vol. I.

and convents were uprooted, than that a single soul should perish. Of what use are they but to live voluptuously by the sweat and toil of others?" [17] As an ecclesiast by divine right he boldly issues "Doctor Luther's Bull and Reformation," which begins with the solemn declaration: "All who stake their lives, their property, and their honor, that the bishoprics are destroyed and the episcopal régime is exterminated, are dear chilldren of God and true Christians, who observe God's commandments and combat the devil's régime. . . . All who sustain the rule of the bishops and are subject to them by voluntary obedience, are the devil's very own servants and militate against God's order and law." To this inflammatory appeal to violence, however, he appends the modifying clause that he does not wish to destroy with "club and sword," but, as "Daniel teaches (VIII, 25), the Antichrist shall be broken without hand, so that everyone, with God's Word, will talk, teach and stand firmly against the Antichrist, until he be confounded, abandoned, and despised, and come to grief of his own accord. That is a true Christian agitation for which one should stake his all." [18]

Besides the extirpation of the episcopate, Luther had at heart particularly the emancipation of the nuns. Soon after his Wartburg days, he dedicated two tracts to the "pious children" among the nuns, who were desirous of hearing the voice of the Gospel. One of these, published in April, 1523, bears the title: "Reason and Reply, why Virgins may leave Convents with Divine Sanction." The other is entitled: "Story of How God Aided a Nun." In contrast with the preceding appeal to agitate, the latter reads almost like an idyl. It was intended to inspire other nuns to leave their convents.

The occasion of the former publication [19] was furnished by twelve Cistercian nuns, who fled from their convent at Nimbschen near Grimma, with the assistance of a town-councilor, Leonard Koppe of Torgau. Nine of these fugitive nuns came to Wittenberg. Among them were Catherine von Bora and a sister of Johann von Staupitz. According to Luther, this pamphlet was written expressly to illustrate how all nuns should liberate their consciences and save their souls. To the objection that such clandestine flight, combined with a denial of the monastic vow, gives rise to scandal, he replies: "Away with scandal! Necessity knows no law and gives no scandal. . . .

[17] Köstlin-Kawerau, M. Luther, Vol. I, p. 517.

[18] For contrary utterances, see Grisar, Luther, Vol. III, pp. 44 sqq. Likewise Grisar, Lutherstudien, VI (Kampfbilder, Grisar and Heege, Heft IV), pp. 126 sq., and especially pp. 137 sqq.

[19] Weimar ed., Vol. XI, pp. 394 sqq.; Erl. ed., Vol. XXIX, pp. 33 sqq.

I should consult my soul; let the whole world be scandalized!" It is interesting to note Luther's confession that he had himself, with the aid of Koppe, planned the escape of the twelve nuns, who had been enlightened by his writings. They were mostly daughters of the nobility, who had been committed to the convent according to custom and hence failed to honor the state of life which they had embraced voluntarily. Their lodging with relatives or families in Wittenberg was a source of no small anxiety to Luther, since he feared that opportunities of marrying them off might not present themselves so readily.[20]

After several weeks, three more nuns were abducted from the convent of Nimbschen by their families. Simultaneously sixteen escaped from the convent at Widerstett in Mansfeld, of whom five found lodging with Count Albrecht of Mansfeld, who was very friendly to the Lutheran cause.

The heroine of Luther's "Story of How God Came to the Aid of a Nun" was Florentina of Oberweimar, who had abandoned her convent at Neu-Helfta, near Eisleben.[21] She told Luther of alleged bodily torments inflicted upon her because of her religious views. Luther willingly believed her story and immortalized her in a publication which he addressed to Count Albrecht of Mansfeld as a "sign in confirmation of the Gospel"—which sign one may not overlook with indifference.[22] In compliance with the rule of her Order, Florentina had completed her year of probation and taken the vows. Having imbibed other ideas from the writings of the reformers, she was subjected to penalties by her superioress and kept in strict custody. But behold, O miracle, one happy day in February, 1524, "the person who should have locked her up, left her cell open" and she escaped! "God's word and work," Luther writes in all seriousness, "must be acknowledged with fear; nor may His signs and wonders be cast to the winds." Ordinarily, he adds, such "miraculous signs from God" are not properly heeded!

The birth of a deformed calf at Freiberg (Saxony) towards the close of 1522 was regarded by Luther as a miracle wrought by God in

---

[20] Amsdorf offers his assistance in procuring husbands for them; thus he offers the sister of Staupitz to Spalatin, adding: "But if you wish for a younger one, you shall have your choice of the prettiest." (Grisar, *Luther*, Vol. II, p. 137.)

[21] Weimar ed., Vol. XV, pp. 86 sqq.; Erl. ed., Vol. XXIX, pp. 102 sqq. (year 1524.)

[22] Grisar, *Luther*, Vol. III, pp. 159 sq.

condemnation of the monastic life.[23] He found that this monstrosity really represented a cowled monk in the act of preaching—an evident symbol of the divine wrath against the religious state. He published his discovery in a treatise entitled, "Interpretation etc. of the Monk-Calf of Freiberg." [24] The work was composed in a quasi-mystical style. The age was very superstitious about monstrosities, but Luther's pamphlet was unprecedented. In view of this literary product, one would like to wish, in the name of German literature, that the interpretation had been intended to be facetious. In reality an attempt has been made on the part of Protestants to explain the pamphlet as a huge joke. But a careful perusal of it completely destroys this hypothesis. The work on the monstrosity of Freiberg is itself a monstrosity. A terrible seriousness breathes from these prophetical, hyper-spiritualistic pages. The author quotes Sacred Scripture to show that his interpretation is "adequately founded" on the word of God. He intimates that perhaps the portent signalizes the day of judgment, "since many portents have succeeded one another of late." In exhibiting to his readers a distorted illustration of the deformed calf, he hypercritically undertakes to apply the details of this miraculous phenomenon to monasticism. The supposed cowl represents the worship which the monks render to the calf, *i. e.*, "the false idol in their lying hearts." The cowl over the hind-quarters is torn, this signifies the impurity of the monks; the legs are their "impudent doctors"; the monster is blind because they are blind; its ears are grotesque because of the abuse of the confessional; the tightening of the cowl around the neck signifies their obstinacy; the crippled horns indicate God's intention of breaking the power of monasticism; above all, the attitude of the calf is that of a preacher, which means that the preaching of the monks is despicable in the eyes of God.

Melanchthon prefaces the story of Luther's "Monk-Calf" by another treatise, namely, his own interpretation of the "Pope-Ass of Rome," a semi-legendary freak supposed to have been discovered in the Tiber in 1496.[25] The learned humanist was even more absorbed in the mystical world of such portents, than Luther. The latter

---

[23] Relative to the following, cf. Grisar, *Luther*, Vol. III, pp. 149 sqq., and *Lutherstudien*, V (*Kampfbilder*, n. III), pp. 14 sqq., with two illustrations.

[24] Printed with Melanchthon's dissertation on the "pope-ass" in the Weimar ed. of Luther's writings, Vol. XI, pp. 369 sqq.; in the Erlangen ed., Vol. XXIX, pp. 7 sqq.

[25] Grisar, *Lutherstudien*, n. V (*Kampfbilder*, n. III), pp. 1 sqq., with two illustrations.

subsequently approved of and praised the first part of their joint production, in his "Amen to the Interpretation of the Pope-Ass."

"The sublime divine Wisdom itself," he said, "created this hideous, shocking, and horrible image." . . . "Well may the whole world be affrighted and tremble." "God manifests Himself openly in this abomination; great indeed is the wrath impending over the papacy."

"The multitude of signs," which Luther beheld and interpreted, presaged "something greater than reason can imagine," to quote the words of his *Kirchenpostille*.[26]

Both works, that on the "Monk-Calf" and that on the "Pope-Ass," enjoyed the widest circulation, both jointly and separately, in repeated German editions and in translations into foreign languages. The illustrations were circulated as leaflets in order to gain adherents to the Lutheran cause. The "Pope-Ass" constituted a permanent fixture in Luther's polemical vocabulary. As late as 1545, the picture was selected by him for inclusion in his collection of "Illustrations of the Papacy."

The lively conviction with which Luther treated similar portents, in which "God openly manifests Himself," constitutes in some measure an excuse for his conduct. The manner in which he labored to promote opposition to the Church after his return from the Wartburg, reveals a misguided combative spirit, inspired by design, acrimony, hatred, and other reprehensible motives. At the same time, the great power of his own prejudices must always be taken into consideration. His excited state of mind did not permit him to measure his steps with sufficient clearness. His eschatological notions, as revealed by his writings on the monsters just mentioned, limited his intellectual outlook.[27]

We must always remember that the historical portrait of Luther is not devoid of favorable traits, even at the time of his severest polemical strain after his sojourn at the Wartburg. There is, in the first place, his external manner of life. He is remarkably unconcerned about his dangerous status of one declared an outlaw by the empire and is satisfied with the very modest circumstances in his decaying monastery, which was hardly able to provide him with food and

[26] Grisar, *Luther*, Vol. II, p. 150.
[27] *Ibid.*, Vol. III, pp. 153 sqq.; Vol. V, pp. 241 sqq.; Vol. VI, pp. 141 sqq.

lodging. He is always ready to advise his friends, even though he is overwhelmed with letters. He attracts students to himself by his winsome and unassuming ways. In his sermons he preaches a sound morality, often with forceful emphasis and great ardor, always with marvelous clearness, plastic metaphors, and directness of speech. Abandoning the field of controversy for that of practical religion, he publishes popular works, such as his prayer-book, which, as he says, was intended to "propose a simple Christian form and mirror," to help the faithful to "recognize sins and to pray."[28] This is true of many other printed sermons on Biblical subjects, on the commandments, on faith, on the Our Father and the Hail Mary.[29] Even more important was the continued labor devoted to his translation of the Old Testament, of which portions appeared from time to time.

Did he still remain a monk in his exterior appearance? Dantiscus reports that Luther, when he visited him in 1523, no longer wore the Augustinian habit at home. He wore it when he preached, however, until October, 1524, when it was quite threadbare, and then exchanged it for a civilian coat, the cloth for which was presented to him by the Elector.

3. THE MOVEMENT WITHIN THE EMPIRE

After his return to Wittenberg, Luther, as we have seen, labored almost as zealously in behalf of his new religion, as if no measures had been taken against him at Worms. Notwithstanding the imperial ban, his activities were but little restricted. There had been no effective prohibition of his books, no determined prevention of the sending of preachers and the seizure of parishes, no lack of freedom for his personal movements, at least not within the confines of electoral Saxony. What particularly aided his cause was the fact that the Emperor's attention had been almost completely diverted from Germany immediately after the diet of Worms. The long war with Francis I of France occupied all of his time. Henceforth, the forces prepared to offer resistance to Luther—and of these the rulers of the empire had an adequate number at their command—lacked a rallying point and competent leaders. The so-called "imperial

[28] Köstlin-Kawerau, M. Luther, Vol. I, p. 574.
[29] Kawerau, Luthers Schriften, n. 178, 216, 242, 265, and Kirchenpostille, n. 137, 163.

regimen" at Nuremberg was a cumbersome body and with its constant need of funds not adapted to evolve a uniform and effective policy against a prince of the reputation and political acumen of Frederick of Saxony, the protector of Luther, and against the impetuous methods of the theological tribune of Wittenberg, who had succeeded in arousing the masses. The mandatory formulas of the edict of Worms, with their medieval apparatus, may have seemed promising in the eyes of the young emperor, who was zealous in promoting the interests of the Church, and in those of the papal nuncio, Aleander. In reality, however, they had lost much of their former force in view of the changed conditions of the time.

The head of the imperial regimen at Nuremberg was the Emperor's brother, Ferdinand, a sincere Catholic, who acted as viceroy for the empire and was ably assisted in the affairs that pertained to the support of the ancient religion by the courageous Duke George of Saxony. Among the foreign ambassadors accredited to the government the Saxon councilor, John von Planitz, labored energetically and successfully to promote the pro-Lutheran and dilatory policy of his master, Frederick of Saxony. The severe measures which the government had originally adopted to enforce the edict of Worms, found no response, not even in Nuremberg itself. The opposing elements succeeded in protecting themselves by indicating the danger of a revolt on the part of the agitated masses. Above all they pointed out that the theological questions at issue had not as yet been definitively decided. The complaints of the Catholic members of the government against the oppressive financial measures of Rome likewise constituted an obstacle to decisive action.

During this dangerous state of suspense, Pope Leo X passed away, on December 1, 1521. His successor, the pious and scholarly Adrian VI, who had labored in opposition to the ecclesiastical revolution as a professor at Louvain and as cardinal-archbishop of Tortosa, conceived the noble plan of mastering the hostile movement in Germany by means of a thorough reform within the Church, and by openly acknowledging that the curia and the clergy had a share in the guilt. He sent Chieregati as nuncio to the imperial diet which assembled at Nuremberg in the fall of 1522, and commissioned him to deliver a celebrated address on the necessity of a reform of Rome and the entire hierarchy and clergy, which has become a unique document of his unselfish, profound, honest, and candid character. In the strained relations of the time, however, it failed to produce any results.[30] The efforts which he made during his short pontificate of twenty months towards ameliorating conditions in Rome were destined to fail in a great measure, due to the opposition of worldly-minded priests and prelates. It required time to achieve the necessary reforms. This high-minded pope, the last of German race, saw his fondest hopes shattered and was carried off all too prematurely by death.

Chieregati's demand that the edict of Worms be executed, was turned down by the imperial diet for the reason that it might pro-voke civil war. In lieu thereof, the estates demanded a church council, which was to be convoked within one year on German soil, for the purpose of allaying the current controversies. In the meantime the Gospel was to be preached "in conformity with the right Christian understanding." Luther could content himself with this resolution. Under somewhat more favorable auspices, a new diet was opened at Nuremberg in January, 1524.

The new pope, Clement VII (1523–1534), who, as Cardinal Julius de' Medici, had led an irreproachable life, made every possible effort to suppress the religious innovations by enforcing the decrees of Worms. As a result of the activities of his excellent nuncio, Cardinal Lorenzo Campeggio, the majority of the delegates at the diet acknowledged the legality of the edict of Worms and declared their willingness to enforce it "as far as possible." A minority, consisting mainly of representatives of the cities, in which the reform move-ment was stronger, declared that the execution of the edict of Worms was simply impossible and repeated the misguided demand for a "free ecumenical council," to be held in Germany. This was accompanied by the still more misleading demand, in the form of a resolution adopted by the assembly, for the convocation of a national synod at Spires in the autumn, which was temporarily to restore order. Campeggio at once declared the latter resolution to be the beginning of an "eternal schism." The Pope repudiated it most energetically, and the Emperor in forceful language prohibited the undertaking and demanded the enforcement of the edict.

[30] Pastor, *Geschichte der Päpste,* Vol. IV, Part 2, pp. 89 sqq. In his address, Chieregati read his instructions, which, according to Pastor, are "a document unique in the history of the papacy." "We freely confess," the document states, "that God permits this persecu-tion of His Church because of the sins of men, particularly those of the priests and prel-ates. . . . All these evils have perhaps originated with the Roman curia," etc. (Pastor, p. 93).

Luther now resumed the fight against the edict of Worms. He reprinted it with a furious commentary, bearing the title: "Two Discordant Imperial Commandments concerning Luther." [31] He confronted it with the resolution of the diet of Nuremberg in 1524. In it he incites the Germans by appealing to them to consider how, after all, they were "compelled to be the asses and martyrs of the pope, even if they had to be pulverized in a mortar." In heroic words he tells the princes of his willingness to die: "What, is not Luther's life so highly esteemed before God, that, if he died, not one of you would be certain of your life or rule, and his death would be a misfortune for you all? There is no jesting with God." So certain was he of his spiritual mission.

At the instigation of Campeggio, the Catholic princes now adopted practical measures by forming a defensive alliance against Luther and his passionate threats of a revolution, which, in his opinion, could be stemmed by him alone. The idea of an alliance was in the air. Towards the end of June, 1524, Ferdinand with the Bavarian dukes and most of the bishops of Southern Germany founded at Ratisbon a union for the protection of the Catholic religion, the extermination of heresy, and the solidification of the Empire. It was a necessity forced upon them by the dimensions which the religious revolt had assumed and by the dangers which threatened the State. The destruction of German unity was not begun at this time, as Protestant historians maintain; rather, the subsequent decline of unity was caused by the division that had preceded this union and by the religious schism which was accomplished by political measures. The Emperor welcomed the alliance of Ratisbon. It was welcomed still more cordially by Pope Clement because of the hopes it engendered of restraining the religious defection. For the time being, however, the Pope's efforts to extend the alliance of the princes into Northern Germany proved futile.

Among those who inspired the least hope of energetic resistance to the innovation, was the archbishop and elector of Mayence, Albrecht of Brandenburg. This man, who adhered to a frivolous philosophy of life and was known for his loose morals, maintained distinguished Lutherans such as Wolfgang Capito at his court. Luther, who knew that he could depend on him, dared to write to

---

[31] Weimar ed., Vol. XV, p. 254. Erl. ed., Vol. XXIV, 2nd ed., p. 220.

the Archbishop on December 1, 1521, saying that he must not molest the priests who had married and abolish the practice of indulgences in the city of Halle; he added that he expected a reply within fourteen days, and if it were not forthcoming, he would publish his work "Against the Idol of Halle," which he had completed, but never printed.[32] After three weeks, on December 31, Luther received a reply in which the Archbishop addresses him as "Dear Doctor" and states that he had received his letter graciously, that the indulgence at Halle had been discontinued, that he intended to be "a pious, religious and Christian ruler," and, finally, that he purposed "to be favorable and friendly" towards Luther "for the sake of Christ."[33] Luther now waxed more hopeful. But since he was disappointed in his principal expectation, namely, that the Archbishop would marry and convert his spiritual fief into a secular state, he launched a personal attack upon him, in a letter dated June 2, 1525. He positively demanded that the Archbishop "enter the state of matrimony and transform his bishopric into a secular principality." He also stated that the spiritual order was doomed to destruction beyond recovery, and if God did not perform a miracle, it is "terrible if a man were to die without a wife," since God had created him a male. At that time he was about to marry Catherine Bora. Shortly afterwards this letter to Albrecht was printed for the benefit of other spiritual princes of the Empire.[34] A kind fate preserved Albrecht from adopting the proposal of Luther, who directed new outbursts of ill-will against the Archbishop on several later occasions.

In the letter which Luther wrote to Albrecht of Brandenburg, he referred to the general degradation of the clergy manifested by "various songs, sayings, satires," and by the fact that priests and monks were cartooned on walls, placards, and lastly on playing cards. This systematic defamation was common particularly in electoral Saxony, during the reign of Frederick, the protector of the "Reformation," who knowingly permitted the attacks upon Catholicism to increase in every department of life. The deception and duplicity which he practiced casts a dark shadow upon his character and places his customary surname, "the Wise," in a peculiar light.

[32] Erl. ed., Vol. LIII, p. 95 (*Briefwechsel*, III, p. 251).
[33] *Briefwechsel*, III, p. 265.
[34] Erl. ed., Vol. LIII, p. 308 (*Briefwechsel*, V, p. 186).

Up to his death, on May 5, 1525, Frederick practiced double-dealing in religious matters. He never married, but had two sons and a daughter by a certain Anna Weller. He and Albrecht of Mayence were the two most esteemed and powerful German princes of the time, the one a spiritual primate, the other a prince in the temporal order, but neither of them distinguished by high moral qualities.

A few words must be added concerning the attitude of the Saxon Elector towards Catholicism in Wittenberg.

The support which Frederick gave to the religious innovation produced deterrent phenomena, particularly in the stormy fight which Luther waged against the remnants of the Mass at Wittenberg. Notwithstanding his former declaration of tolerance toward the "weak" and his statement regarding the avoidance of force, Luther's intervention against the celebration of the Mass on the part of the last Catholic priest at the electoral chapel and the monastery church became a tragedy of flagrant intolerance.[35] Already in 1522, the Elector, yielding to the pressure of Luther, abolished the customary solemn exposition of relics. On March 1, 1523, Luther invited the chapter to put an end once and for all to the celebration of the Mass, otherwise the capitularies would have to be disfellowshipped from the communion of the Church. In a second letter he seriously threatened to discontinue his prayers for them, which might cause unpleasant consequences before God! A romantic self-deception regarding his influence in Heaven! When the Elector still hesitated to give his consent and warned against disturbances, Luther appealed to the people in a sermon in which he advised them not to lay violent hands on the canons, and stated that the territorial lord had "no authority except in secular matters." A new, sharp letter of Luther to the cathedral canons provoked the censure of the Elector; but Luther knew he could go farther; he felt assured of the final approval of Frederick, and nothing in that letter was more correct than the warning issued to his enemies, that they were not certain of the protection of the Elector. A new sermon in which Luther fulminated against the holy Sacrifice of the Mass, was delivered on November 27, 1524. The princes and the authorities, he exclaimed, ought finally to force "the blasphemous servants of the Babylonian harlot" to stop the devilish practice of saying Mass. It was scarcely

---

[35] For the following cf. Grisar, *Luther*, Vol. II, pp. 88 sqq., and especially pp. 327 sqq.; Vol. IV, pp. 506 sqq.

possible to restrain the people and the students from committing acts of violence. The town-council and the university threatened with the wrath of God the priests who still held out. Finally, Frederick "the Wise" abandoned them ignominiously to their fate. A vigorous word from him, reinforced by his guard, would have silenced the opponents, at least in the city.

The canons finally bowed to the raging elements. On Christmas, 1524, Mass was suspended for the first time, never to be resumed. Referring to the three remaining Catholic canons, Luther, in his characteristic fashion, said that "three swine and bellies" still remained in the church, "not of All Saints, but of all devils."

An echo of his violent sermons against the Sacrifice of the Mass was the tract, "On the Abomination of the Silent Mass, called the Canon," which he published in the beginning of the year 1525.[36] In it he attributes the merit for the deeds of violence perpetrated at Wittenberg to the "secular lords," who, he says, had been obliged to intervene.

In a letter written at the beginning of May, 1525, to the Elector Frederick, who was very ill at the time, Luther's friend Spalatin, Frederick's counselor and guide in the above-described fight on the Mass, unreservedly set forth the duties of secular rulers to promote a religious reformation.[37] This applied to all territorial rulers.

A few days later, on May 5, Frederick died in his castle at Lochau after receiving the Last Supper under both forms, as an adherent of Luther; he was the first German prince thus to pass away. Luther had been summoned to attend him in his last moments, but arrived too late. In fact, he had never met Frederick personally. On the tenth of May, and again on the eleventh, the day of the funeral, he delivered funeral orations in the castle-church, which abounded in exuberant eulogies of his friendly and prudent protector. In a consolatory letter addressed to John, the brother of the deceased, who succeeded him as ruler, he renewed his former, very intimate relations. John proved an even more determined protector than Frederick, and with his assistance Luther was able to exterminate Catholic worship in the electorate of Saxony.

As the Reformation was imposed in electoral Saxony by pressure

---

[36] Weimar ed., Vol. XVIII, pp. 22 sqq.; Erl. ed., Vol. XXIX, pp. 113 sqq.; Grisar, *Luther*, Vol. IV, pp. 508 sqq.

[37] Köstlin-Kawerau, M. *Luther*, Vol. I, p. 724.

from above, so, too, in other German territories. The free imperial cities especially hastened to take the lead in the introduction of the new ecclesiastical régime by recourse to penal measures enforced by the civil authorities.

The tremendous development of the civil power at that time was very advantageous to the extension of the Protestant revolt. A number of practically independent principalities arose from the loose structure of the empire. Due to the long absence of the Emperor, the territorial rulers found themselves thrown upon their own resources. The increase of power which accrued to their scepters in virtue of the new religious system, accelerated their steps in the direction of absolutism.

As early as 1523, Luther had dedicated his treatise "On Secular Authority and the Extent of the Obedience due to it" to John, the heir-apparent to the throne of the Saxon Electorate.[38] It was a sermon which he had delivered in John's presence at Weimar and which was published at the latter's request, after having been enlarged by the author. Luther later on loved to appeal to this work, in order to show that it was he who had indicated the proper measures to the civil governments for emerging from the oppression of the papacy. "I would fain boast," he says of himself, "that, since the age of the Apostles, the secular sword and authority have never been described so clearly or praised so splendidly, as by me, as even my antagonists must acknowledge."[39] However, what good there is in this work had long ago been expounded by Catholic writers, e. g., the demonstration from Holy Writ that the secular power exercises its authority by the will and ordinance of God. Luther's exhortations to the princes in the third part are beautiful, but by no means new.

On the other hand, the new ideas contained in the second part of the treatise on the restriction of the civil power to temporal affairs, and to the punishment of evil-doers and the protection of good citizens were fallacious and contradicted the theories concerning the assistance to be furnished by temporal rulers for ecclesiastical purposes which he himself subsequently enunciated and openly applied. In the second part of the treatise he has in mind only Catholic princes, his intention being to oppose a strong barrier to their

---

[38] Weimar ed., Vol. XI, pp. 245 sqq.; Erl. ed., Vol. XXII, pp. 59 sqq.

[39] Köstlin-Kawerau, M. Luther, Vol. I, p. 584. Cfr. Grisar, Luther, Vol. II, pp. 294 sqq.; IV, 331.

measures against Lutheranism and for the protection of the Catholic religion. Hence the assertion that secular princes have no voice in matters pertaining to religion. Hence, also, the separation in principle of the kingdom of God from the kingdom of the world, which he proposes. The world, he says, is a house of devils which requires the sword for its government. But the true Christian believer lives in a divine kingdom, which needs no laws and no compulsion, but is governed solely by the Word of God. These are hazy and extravagant ideas which led him to make such declarations as the following: a Christian must put up with any injustice committed against him by his fellowmen, and leave it to the authorities to protect him; for Christ in the Sermon on the Mount taught men to resist evil. In general, the Sermon on the Mount, with its passages referring to the blow on the cheek, etc., affords, to the mind of Luther, not only a guide to perfection; it supplies no mere "evangelical counsels," as the papists teach, but real commandments, which are known to and observed only by those who dwell in the kingdom of Christ, but not by those who inhabit the kingdom of the world and by the civil authorities.[40] Here he meets with a dilemma when he invests the prince with a dual personality which, on the one hand, fundamentally degrades him to the rank of a beadle and a "jailer" of the wicked, whilst, on the other, he must satisfy the most exaggerated religious demands as a Christian believer.

At that time Luther never imagined that he would soon be compelled to regard the civil rulers as the real protectors and guardians of religion in their respective territories, whose chief duty was to ward off the "wolves," i. e., the "papistical" antagonists of the Reformation, and to eradicate the "sacrilegious" Mass.

4. THE CONGREGATIONAL CHURCH

At the beginning of his revolt Luther entertained certain pseudo-mystical ideas of a freely operating system of congregations.[41] He soon found it to be impossible to form an organization of those members of former parishes who had been aroused by the new Evangel—an organization which would be purely spiritual and reject

[40] Grisar, *Luther*, Vol. II, pp. 298 sq. On Luther's distinction between the world and the Church see *ibid.*, Vol. V, pp. 55 sqq.

[41] For the following, see *ibid.*, Vol. II, pp. 102 sqq.

coercive measures, whether secular or ecclesiastical. Thus he was necessarily compelled to change his ideal from that of a congregational church to that of a popular church ruled by a spiritual authority under the protection of the State. Thence, by the intrinsic necessity of his new system, he arrived at the compulsory national Church and his original idea of an invisible Church became gradually obliterated.

Yet he always wished to have a separate church for those who truly believed in his Gospel, as distinct from a church which was open to all, even to those who thought in terms of paganism. Repeatedly he voices his longing for such a genuinely Christian church (*ecclesiola*) with a superintendent, ecclesiastical discipline, and the ban, subject, not to the State, but to himself. He admits, however, that he has not a sufficient number of people to join him in this project.[42] Undoubtedly the execution of this plan would have resulted in two ambitious and mutually antagonistic groups of churches. In general, it is evident how instability and disintegration were the sole fruits of Luther's abandonment of the true concept of the Church. Some modern Protestant writers hold that Luther did not establish any church whatever. The separation of the State from the German Protestant ecclesiastical structure, which has taken place in our time, and the disappearance of the supreme episcopate of the Protestant State ruler, has placed this statement in a new light. There is need of reconstructing the church from the foundation up.

It is interesting to review the intended institution and ultimate fate of the congregational church originally planned by Luther.

It was to be a free covenant of brethren without binding laws. Those who had embraced the Gospel of Luther were to remain, without compulsion, under supreme representatives of a corporate body of their own selection, and to call themselves Christians (not Lutherans). They were to have their own Last Supper and their own dogmas. The free covenant was to be an organization for service only, with "unity of spirit," as Luther himself repeatedly says, and not unity "of place, persons, things or bodies." [43] He does not desire a sectarian body. "To create sects," he says, "is neither useful nor helpful." In his opinion, it was, moreover, unnecessary in order to unite into a Christian covenant prior to the proximate end of the world, the still

[42] See *ibid.*, Vol. V, pp. 133 sqq.
[43] *Ibid.*, Vol. II, pp. 107 sq.

faithful members of the papal empire of Antichrist—the pious who were "terrified in conscience."

How is the representative of the brotherhood to be selected? Luther writes: "Those whose hearts have been moved by God" should band together and choose a "bishop," *i. e.*, "a minister or pastor." Even though the congregation number only six or ten persons, they will attract others, "who have not yet received the Word." "They must not act of their own accord, but must allow themselves to be moved by God." "It is quite certain that Christ acts through them." [44]

The first coherent statement of these ideas is to be found in a Latin treatise of 1523, which Luther addressed to the Utraquists or Calixtines of Prague. He entertained vain hopes of winning over this party, which still obeyed the Catholic hierarchy. His instructions to them were also intended for Germany, and above all for Saxony. This explains why he had the Latin treatise published also in German. [45]

About this time he purposed to establish a model congregation of free Christians constituted from among the masses, in Leisnig, a small town situated in the Saxon electorate. [46] He addressed a treatise to the adherents of the new Evangel in that town, the title of which is characteristic of the impracticability of his ideal. The tract was entitled: "Reasons and Scriptural Motives Demonstrating that a Christian Assembly or Congregation has the Right and the Power to pass on all Dogmas and to Summon, Install, and Depose Teachers." [47] The document states that, according to the Scriptures, the universal priesthood of all Christian believers empowers every member of the congregation to exercise independent judgment in matters of faith. Every member may come forward and correct the erring preacher. St. Paul says: "If anything be revealed to another sitting, let the first hold his peace" (I Cor. XIV, 30, where he speaks of the charismata of the first Christians). A Christian congregation is one in which the pure Gospel is preached. It is presupposed, however, that this is the new Evangel which Luther has brought to light and with which all are in accord who speak the truth, since this doctrine "has been received from heaven." The papists, so Luther writes to the inhabitants of Leisnig, "ought to yield to us and to hear our Word."

Events at Leisnig, as everywhere else, failed to justify his sanguine expectations. There was doctrinal confusion and administrative dissension. When, in 1523, in his solicitude for this town, Luther issued an introduction to their new "fiscal regulations," this beneficent measure came to naught. [48]

[44] *Ibid.*, p. 111.
[45] *Ibid.*, p. 112.
[46] *Ibid.*, Vol. V, pp. 136 sqq.
[47] Weimar ed., Vol. XI, pp. 408 sqq.; Erl. ed., Vol. XXII, pp. 140 sqq.
[48] Weimar ed., Vol. XII, p. 11; Erl. ed., Vol. XXII, p. 105.

The town-council confiscated the properties and endowments of the church, but refused to co-operate in the establishment of a common poor-box. Luther's appeal to the Elector for aid was futile. Nothing more is reported concerning the development of the religious life of the congregation in the town of Leisnig.

The fate of this ideal congregation was a great disappointment to Luther. But, as a Protestant investigator writes, "The primitive Lutheran ideal of a congregation forming itself in entire independence was nowhere realized. . . . Thus at an early date Lutheranism took its place among the political factors, and its development was to a certain extent dependent upon the tendencies and inclinations of the authorities, particularly of the ruling sovereigns of that time." [49]

5. DIVINE SERVICE. MULTIFARIOUS ACTIVITIES

In 1523 Luther issued his treatise "On the Order of Divine Service in the Congregation," published in the interest of Leisnig and other expected churches of true believers. It was a provisional collection of counsels—not precepts, as he himself emphasizes—for the conduct of divine service.[50] The Word and the arousing of "faith" are, in his mind, the principal thing in public worship. He would have each congregation regulate these matters by its own authority after the model of the worship practiced in "the Apostolic age." There were to be daily assemblies, if not of the entire population, then at least of the clergymen and scholars, for the purpose of praying and reading the Bible.

Regarding the Mass, which was to be celebrated on Sunday in connection with the Last Supper, Luther, in 1523, issued a small Latin treatise entitled "Formula of the Mass and Communion for the Church in Wittenberg." [51] According to this formula, the so-called Mass is not yet to be celebrated in German. The sequence of parts corresponds rather closely to the Catholic Latin Mass. Even the alb and the chasuble were to be worn by the celebrant in the Lutheran church of Wittenberg.

The Mass commenced with the Introit, Kyrie, Gloria, and an oration, followed by the Epistle with a chanted Graduale or Alleluja, and the Gospel.

[49] Walter Friedensburg, Cf. Grisar, *Luther*, Vol. II, p. 333.
[50] Weimar ed., Vol. XII, pp. 35 sqq.; Erl. ed., Vol. XXII, p. 159.
[51] Weimar ed., Vol. XII, pp. 205 sqq.; *Opp. Lat. Var.*, VII, pp. 1 sqq.

Relative to the traditional pericopes, Luther complained that they did not sufficiently inculcate the saving faith. The sermon was soon given the place of honor in the middle of the function, namely, after the Credo. In accordance with the "Formula," there was an abrupt transition to the Preface: for, since the sacrificial character of the Mass had been denied, the Offertory and the prayers that followed it were omitted. The ancient Canon was omitted, so that the Preface was immediately succeeded by the celebrant's chanting of the Biblical words of the institution of the Holy Eucharist (1 Cor. XI, 23–25). This chant was supposed to signify the consecration of the bread and wine for the Last Supper. Then followed the Sanctus and the Benedictus, the latter united with the Elevation. "For the sake of those weak in the faith," the Elevation was retained in the church at Wittenberg. The Pater Noster and the Pax Domini were succeeded by the communion of the celebrant, followed by the communion, under both species, of those among the faithful who had announced their intention of receiving, provided that such were present, and that they had stood the test of knowledge and worthiness which was demanded by Luther not long afterwards. The close of the Mass consisted of a selection of Catholic prayers after the Communion, the Benedicamus, and a benediction couched in a Biblical phrase.

The Mass, as thus described, was the first transition to the forms of worship still customary in the Lutheran churches. In course of time it was simplified and toned down even more, and, in view of Luther's constant emphasis on freedom, exhibited many local variations. As early as 1523 he had given it a German setting, which superseded the Latin language, through his work, "The German Mass and Order of Divine Service." [52]

Already at an early stage complaints had been heard that divine service had become barren and ordinary, in consequence of the preponderance of the sermon, which often developed into a tedious polemical tirade against papism. The Catholic forms of worship, per se richer and more varied than Luther's borrowings from the ancient liturgy, were animated by the idea of the Eucharistic sacrifice. In the minds of Catholics the entire function was dominated by the idea of a sacrifice of infinite worth, offered by the Son of God through the consecrated hands of the priest—a sacrifice of which the most ancient ecclesiastical writers, such as Justin, Ignatius of Antioch, Clement of Rome, Tertullian, Cyprian, and Irenaeus, speak with great reverence, professing the faith of which the Protes-

[52] Weimar ed., Vol. XIX, pp. 72 sqq. Erl. ed., Vol. XXII, pp. 226 sqq.

tant theologian, Martin Chemnitz, admits that Christian antiquity "constantly expresses it with such nouns as *sacrificium, immolatio, oblatio, hostia, victima,* and such verbs as *offerre, sacrificare, immolare.*" [53] In the divine service devised by Luther, the heart which had formerly pulsated through the divine cult was missing; the whole thing had become a corpse, which even the popular religious hymns soon introduced, impressive though they were, failed to inspire with life.

Beginning with 1523, Luther devoted himself to the composition of liturgical and other hymns. [54] In this field he was very successful. His compositions are models of popularity and unadorned, natural force. They served to edify the people and became a mighty lever in the spread of Lutheranism. The aggressive mood is strongly marked in some of these hymns, as may be seen from the opening words of: "Behalt uns, Herr, bei deinem Wort, Und steur des Papst's und Türken Mord, Die Jesum, Deinen lieben Sohn, Stürmen wollen von Deinem Thron" (O keep us, Lord, true to Thy Word, stay the murders of the Pope and the Turks, who would assail Thy beloved Son Jesus Christ and cast Him from Thy throne). This song was written for the children, by whom "it was to be sung against the arch-enemies of Christ and His holy Church, the Pope and the Turks." [55] Luther's first poetical and political song was "Ein neues Lied wir heben an," commemorating the execution of two Dutch Lutherans at Brussels.

Luther supplied his followers with an ample collection of beautiful hymns, mostly adapted from the ancient Church, and highly esteemed many of the religious folk-songs of the German people, which embodied precious reminiscences of his youth. He is not, as used to be affirmed, the father of the German religious or ecclesiastical folk-song, since German songs had resounded both within and without the Church long before his day. Owing to his efforts, however, they flourished among his followers and in their churches became part of the divine service in lieu of the liturgical hymns of the ancient Church. [56] The first hymn-book intended for the use of the Lutheran churches was supplied by Johann Walther in

[53] *Examen Concilii Tridentini*, Vol. II, p. 782.
[54] Edited by Lucke in Vol. LIII of the Weimar edition of *Luthers Werke*.
[55] Grisar, *Lutherstudien*, Heft IV (*Luthers Trutzlied*), p. 47.
[56] Grisar, *Luther*, Vol. V, pp. 546 sqq.

1524. It was entitled "Geistliches Gesangbüchlein" (Spiritual Hymnbook), and contained in five parts German hymns with appropriate melodies. Luther wrote the preface and the collection went out under his name. It comprised twenty-four hymns composed by himself and was subsequently augmented by twelve others from his pen. The hymn of defiance: "Ein' feste Burg" (A safe stronghold our God is still), which is regarded as the best of his poetical productions, was composed later, in 1527–28, during a strenuous period of interior and exterior stress. [57]

Johann Walther supplied the melodies, which evidenced skill and good taste. They conformed, in part, to the traditions of Catholicism. It is not certain that Luther is the author of even a single melody, although up to the present time Protestant writers persist in glorifying him as a musical composer. A report concerning his alleged compositions made by a visitor at Wittenberg, who claims to have been a contemporary, is a late fabrication, both in this respect as well as in respect of the charge that Luther was a constant visitor at the tavern. [58]

Among the manifold writings which Luther's industry produced in the years that have been reviewed so far, there is one which is entitled, "A Christian Admonition concerning Exterior Divine Worship,"[59] directed to his followers in Livonia. It illustrates the confusion in divine service which necessarily resulted from the religious changes and the liberty granted by Luther. The Lutheran congregations in Livonia were engaged in serious quarrels. In vain the voice of Wittenberg appealed to them: "Be united in regard to these exterior characteristics." Luther admonishes them against the introduction of a coercive discipline, which, he fears, would only lead to worse dissensions. "Who can resist the devil and his satellites?" "Where the divine Word penetrates, Satan must scatter his seeds out of sheer envy." [60]

Naturally there was great discord and perplexity also in other places, not only in liturgical, but likewise in far more important matters.

---

[57] *Ibid.*, Vol. V, pp. 342 sqq.

[58] Grisar, *Ein unterschobener Bericht über Luther als Tonsetzer und Stammgast*, in the *Ehrengabe an Prinz Johann Georg von Sachsen*, ed. by F. Fessler, Freiburg, 1920, pp. 693 sqq.

[59] *Werke*, Weimar ed., Vol. XVIII, pp. 414 sqq.; Erlangen ed., Vol. LIII, p. 315.

[60] Grisar, *Luther*, Vol. V, pp. 151 sq.

At Strasburg there was a profound schism, as is testified, among other things, by Luther's "Epistle to the Christians of Strasburg against the Spirit of Fanaticism," printed in 1524.[61] Karlstadt, whose relations with Luther were strained because of his arbitrary ways, had been banished from Saxony by virtue of an electoral decree issued at the instigation of Luther, and commenced to agitate in Strasburg against images, mural paintings, vestments worn at Mass, and other "pagan" practices which he discovered there. He also propagated his denial of the real presence of Christ in the Eucharist and succeeded in surrounding himself with an active coterie of adherents. Zwingli exerted his influence upon the movement from Zurich. Capito and Bucer, at that time teachers of theology at Strasburg, were in agreement with Zwingli. Certain preachers at Strasburg wrote to Luther, asking him what should be their attitude towards the existing quarrels. Luther hastened to have his reply printed, since he feared that like schisms in other places would be caused by the "fanatics." In his mind all were fanatics who enthusiastically opposed the alleged externality of ceremonies, or who held independent views and were not devoted to his teaching, especially such men as Karlstadt and the "prophets of Zwickau," who believed that they were inspired from on high. Above all, he attributed a fanatical spirit to those teachers who did not advance along the same line with him relative to the doctrine of the Last Supper.

In his letter to the preachers of Strasburg he instructs the questioners to permit themselves to be guided, not by Karlstadt's inconstant prophetical notions, but solely by Christ, our Redeemer and Sanctifier, who imparts the correct precepts and for whom he (Luther) speaks.

In the matter of the Eucharist, Luther champions the literal interpretation of the words of Christ, "This is my body," and makes this remarkable confession: "Had someone told me five years ago that there was nothing but bread and wine in the Sacrament, he would have done me a great favor. I have suffered strong temptations, and have done violence to myself and writhed with pain, so that I would have been glad to be relieved, because I clearly perceived that I could thereby have administered a great blow to the papacy." He adds that the old Adam in him is even now only too much inclined to deny the real presence of Christ in the Eucharist; but the words, "This is my body," are too plain, and Karlstadt's buffoonery had confirmed him all the more in his adhesion to this simple, literal sense.

[61] Weimar ed., Vol. XV, p. 391; Erl. ed., Vol. LIII, p. 270.

He was soon to become involved in a far greater controversy regarding this question with Karlstadt, and later with Zwingli.

Ulrich Zwingli, influenced by the writings of Luther and his own one-sidedly humanistic training, had devoted himself to "reformatory" ideas while yet a pastor at Einsiedeln. After his election as pastor of the grand minster of Zurich, towards the end of 1518, he intensified his devotion to these ideas. He had eulogized Luther as a beacon light of Christian theology, as the fearless hero of truth, as the man of the future. He was, however, very jealous of his own intellectual independence as against the preacher of Wittenberg. "I have not learned the doctrine of Christ from Luther," he stated in 1523, "but from the Word of God. If Luther preaches Christ, he does just what I do." [62] After 1523, the example of the Wittenberg priests who embraced matrimony exerted its influence also upon the numerous adherents of Zwingli. As early as 1522, Zwingli himself had contracted a so-called "marriage of conscience" with Anna Reinhard, and, in April, 1524, he publicly led her to the altar in the minster church. He later admitted that he was at daggers drawn with his vow of celibacy in the days when he was still a Catholic priest,[63] and proclaimed the theory that the devil had introduced sacerdotal celibacy.

The grave controversy between Luther and Zwingli on the Eucharist, to be discussed in detail in the sequel, was occasioned by Zwingli's letter to Matthew Alber, a preacher of Reutlingen, dated November 16, 1524. In this letter he first developed his interpretation of the verb "is" in the text of the institution of the Eucharist in the sense of "signifies." According to his commentary of March, 1525, he does not even wish to raise the question of the corporal consumption of the Body of Christ. [64]

In the meantime Luther published his principal attack upon Karlstadt's doctrine of the Eucharist as well as upon those who sympa-

[62] Grisar, *Luther*, Vol. III, pp. 379 sq. Farner in *Zwingliana* (1918–19) abandons the old notion of Zwingli's self-sufficiency.—"The humanist parson, to whom the Bible is a book on morals, arrives at a true understanding of the Gospel through the agency of Luther in 1519, and echoes his views." Bossert, in the *Theol. Literaturzeitung*, Vol. XIX, p. 206.

[63] See Walter Köhler, *Zwinglis Geisteswelt*, Gotha, 1920, pp. 22 and 31, quoting Zwingli's own confession in a letter to Henry Utinger, December 3, 1518. (Zwingli's *Werke*, ed. by Egli *et al.*, Vol. VII, pp. 110 sq.).

[64] Cfr. Grisar, *Luther*, Vol. III, p. 409, n. 3.

thized with Karlstadt's ideas, in his large treatise "Against the Heavenly Prophets, on Images and the Sacrament." It is a work overflowing with indigation. [65]

He shows that his former friend and colleague is guilty of harboring "a rebellious and murderous spirit." Karlstadt, he says, "openly declares that I am of no account." "If your spirit," thus he addresses Karlstadt and his friends, "had been the true spirit, he would have demonstrated his office with signs and words; but he is a murderous secret devil," whose diabolic nature follows from the fact that they do not know how to teach the principal subject-matter of theology, namely, how "to obtain a clear conscience and a joyful heart at peace with God. . . . They have never experienced it." [66]

The fanatics, to whom Thomas Münzer and Valentine Ickelsamer belonged, in their repeated literary attacks upon Luther, had marshaled many effective arguments against him. The attitude of the so-called "Baptizers" was not as foolish in every respect as Luther represented it. Recent Protestant writers admire their modern rationalistic ideas. Luther was so sensitive to their many effective arguments against his arbitrary conduct that he expressed himself as follows in his book on the "Heavenly Prophets": "As if we did not know that reason is the devil's handmaid and does nothing but blaspheme and dishonor all that God says or does." When confronted with logical arguments he claims they are "mere devil's roguery." [67]

Accordingly, he appeals to the Bible. This he does very effectively in the principal part of the book, where he demonstrates the Real Presence of Christ in the Eucharist against Karlstadt. He exhibits so much ingenuity and erudition in proof of his literal understanding of the verb "is" that even Catholic theologians may learn therefrom. However, he stops halfway, excludes transubstantiation, and holds that Christ is present simultaneously with the bread. If the antipapistical Luther shines forth in this exhibition, he bids defiance still oftener to the fanatics, as, for instance, in the treatment of the elevation during Mass. Karlstadt denounced the adoration of the species during the elevation. Luther writes: "Although I too had intended to abolish the Elevation, yet I will not do so now, the better to defy and oppose the fanatical spirit." [68] In his "Clag etlicher Brüder" (Com-

[65] Weimar ed., Vol. XVIII, pp. 62 sqq.; Erl. ed., Vol. XXIX, pp. 134 sqq. Cf. Grisar, *Luther*, Vol. III, pp. 387, 390 sq.

[66] Grisar, *Luther*, Vol. III, p. 398.

[67] *Ibid.*, pp. 395 sq.

[68] *Ibid.*, p. 394.

plaint of Several Brethren) Ickelsamer reproached him, not without
justification, with producing many anti-Catholic dogmas merely out
of spite, as he himself confesses, because the papists "had pressed him
so hard," and not because of logical necessity or calm reasoning.

The "Complaint of Several Brethren," originating in Karlstadt's
circle, and composed by Ickelsamer at Rothenburg on the Tauber,
aside from many exaggerations and distortions, cast a glaring light upon
Luther's doctrine and character. [69] This is true in an even greater
degree of Thomas Münzer's "Apology against the Unspiritual, Luxurious Lump of Flesh at Wittenberg," which he composed in 1524. [70]
The head of the Wittenberg school was regarded by the genuine
Anabaptists, who claimed to be spiritual, as one who had gone astray
and had been ensnared by the world and sensuality. Even if they went
too far in their personal attacks, they were successful in proving
that there was no evidence for Luther's divine mission, and that he had
no right to condemn whatever ran counter to his opinion. They refused to credit him when, with characteristic self-assertiveness, he
assured them, in his address to the preachers of Strasburg, that he had
hitherto done right and well in the main. "Whosoever asserts the contrary," he thought, "cannot be a good spirit." [71] They reproached
him for his arbitrary treatment of a most important matter, namely,
the interpretation of the Bible, maintaining that it was not the Bible
which governed him, but the nonsense which they designated as "Bible,
Bubble, Babble." [72] From him they claimed to have learned to exercise
freedom in searching the Scriptures, which they said they used with
discretion. He forbade them to do so, whereas, independently of him,
"the Gospel grants freedom of belief and the right of private judgment." "Now settle yourself comfortably in the papal chair," Ickelsamer tells him, "for after all you want to listen to your own singing." [73]

The eccentric character of Thomas Münzer impelled him to advance
farthest in his fanaticism for the Anabaptist system. Since Easter, 1523,
this one-time Catholic priest ruled in Allstedt near Eisleben as preacher
of the new religion, claiming to be guided by a higher spirit. It was his

[69] Ibid., Vol. III, pp. 170 sq., 302.
[70] Grisar, Luther, Vol. II, pp. 364 sq.; Vol. III, p. 302; Vol. II, pp. 130 sq.
[71] Ibid., Vol. III, p. 397.
[72] Ibid., Vol. II, pp. 365, 370 sq.
[73] Ibid., p. 377.

object to exterminate the impious by the use of force and to establish a communistic kingdom, composed of all the good people on earth and modeled upon the supposed ideal of the Apostolic age. His readiness to apply violent measures was manifested by his destruction, with the aid of an excited mob, of a shrine at Malderbach near Eisleben. The spiritual and social revolution, which it was feared he would start, was proclaimed by him in a sermon published later.

It was during this state of affairs that Luther seized his mighty pen and in the last days of July, 1524, published his "Letter to the Rulers of Saxony on the Spirit of Revolt." [74] It was written against Münzer.

He demanded of the princes that they should "suppress disorder and prevent revolution." At the same time he tried to justify his own new religion in the eyes of the princes. He admits that he is "deficient in the spirit and hears no heavenly voices" like the fanatics, but asserts that his cause comes from God, whereas the devil speaks through Münzer. The fanatics, he says, attacked his conduct; they "take offense at our sickly life"; but all depends on doctrine, even if conduct has its shortcomings. "Let them but preach confidently and cheerfully," they will nevertheless succumb. He places his hopes for the true Gospel in the constancy of the Elector, and in that of his brother and son. He refers them incidentally and alluringly to the prospects of material gain, when, relative to former Catholic churches and monasteries, he writes: "Let the territorial lords dispose of them as they see fit." [75]

In his ponderous reply to Luther's letter to the princes, which he entitled "An Apology" (*Schutzrede*), Münzer complained that Luther "exploded with fury and hatred like a real tyrant." He (Münzer) preached from the Bible only, but not, "please God, his own conceits." Luther having boasted of his courageous appearance before the diet of Worms, and of other feats, he terms him "Doctor Liar" and "Lying Luther." "That you appeared before the Empire at Worms at all was thanks to the German nobles whom you had cajoled and honeyed, for they fully expected that by your preaching you would obtain for them Bohemian gifts of monasteries and foundations, which you now promise to the princes." [76]

The noisy criticism of the fanatics, who kept a sharp watch on

---

[74] Weimar ed., Vol. XV, pp. 210 sqq.; Erl. ed., Vol. LIII, pp. 255 sqq.
[75] Grisar, *Luther*, Vol. II, pp. 365 sqq.
[76] *Ibid.*, Vol. II, pp. 367 sq.

their opponent, rendered Luther somewhat more cautious with regard to blemishes in his own life. Whatever I do, he says, is subjected to investigation; I am a spectacle to the world (*spectaculum mundi;* I Cor. iv, 9). He learned to moderate his appeal to the spirit, to the inner voice, and to personal experience, and to attach greater value to the so-called external word, *i. e.,* the teaching of Scripture as he interpreted it. What gave him an advantage over the fanatics was his practical common sense, which made him feel far superior to them.[77] He did not betray such foibles as they either in his concept of God and in his ideas of suffering and affliction, or in the establishment of ecclesiastical communions, or more particularly in his social ideas, even though his teaching in these matters was quite confused.

However, it must be emphasized that the fanatics took their departure precisely from Luther's so-called reform ideas. They went beyond him, partly by logically developing these ideas—a thing which Luther did not want—and partly as a result of arbitrary distortions and additions. At all events, the fanatics are true children of Luther; their dreams and revolutionary projects are fruits raised in his soil. It was a catastrophal punishment for him that he was compelled to fight practically all his life in order to dissociate the fanatics from his work. His rage increased with his resistance and was intensified by jealousy. They intend to invade my field of labor and fame, he declared in substance; they wish to wrest the leadership from me and to appropriate what I have been unable to achieve amid bitterness and distress. "They exploit our victory," he says, "and enjoy it, take wives and abate papal laws—results which they themselves did not obtain by fighting." [78]

Luther was especially interested in retaining infant baptism which the fanatical Anabaptists strove to abolish. He obstinately insisted on the absurdity that an infant received Baptism together with the faith, even if reason were unable to comprehend this. In 1523, he published his "Little Book on Baptism done into German," [79] in which he retains the old rite according to which the infant is thrice breathed upon and the priest pronounces the exorcism, places salt in the infant's mouth, touches his ear with spittle, and anoints him

---

[77] Cf. Karl Holl, *Luther,* 2nd and 3rd ed., (1923), pp. 450 sqq. on the views of Münzer.
[78] Grisar, *Luther,* Vol. II, pp. 367 sqq.
[79] Weimar ed., Vol. XII, pp. 42 sqq.; Erl. ed., Vol. XXII, pp. 157 sq.

on chest and back with sacred chrism. Thus far did his policy of accommodation go at that time.

A movement against infant Baptism had set in in Switzerland in 1523. It was promoted by the social undercurrent of the adherents of the new religion and provided the Anabaptist sects in Germany with a strong impetus. Conrad Grebel, with the aid of his followers, denied the right of the clergy to levy tithes, demanded the execution of the priests, tried to introduce communism and to establish "congregations of the saints" wherever the laws of God were not observed. The semblance of rigorism and pietism was common to the Swiss and the German Anabaptists. In reality they favored a certain emancipation of the flesh and demanded that nuns be permitted to marry.

6. THE PEN AS LUTHER'S WEAPON OF CONTINUED ATTACK

Matrimony almost constantly engaged the attention of Martin Luther after he had divested it of the dignity of a Sacrament and placed it on a level with ordinary civil contracts. It was imperative to devise new regulations in order to avoid a serious decline of morality. At the same time, in the eyes of the scrupulous, the unaccustomed liberty of Christian believers in this department of life had to be justified.

In 1519, Luther published a sermon "On the Married State," [80] which he had to reëdit in a revised edition, because of loud complaints against unbecoming language. He had permitted himself to go too far in his expressions, though to some extent the transcriber may have been to blame. The new and revised edition bore the title "Of Married Life" and was published in 1522.[81] In these pages, too, he treats of sexual intercourse with a strange freedom of language and in his accustomed fashion.[82] He declares that well-nigh all the obstacles or inhibitions to marriage devised by the popes were to be "repudiated and condemned." He shakes the foundation of the indissolubility of the marriage bond by allowing separation and remarriage in certain cases.

---

[80] Weimar ed., Vol. II, pp. 166 sqq.; IX, pp. 213 sqq.; Erl. ed., Vol. XVI, 2nd ed., pp. 60 sqq.

[81] Weimar ed., Vol. X, p. 11, pp. 275 sqq.; Erl. ed., Vol. XVI, 2nd ed., pp. 510 sqq.

[82] Cf., e. g., the coarse expressions quoted in Grisar, *Luther*, Vol. III, pp. 250 sqq.

This latter work contains a passage which has gained notoriety. Luther says that if the wife refuses to render the *debitum* without reason, the husband may use threatening language to this effect: "If you are unwilling, there is another who is; if the wife is unwilling, then let the maid come." [83] In case the wife persists in her refusal, "the marriage is dissolved," and the husband may "take an Esther to himself and let Vashti go, as King Assuerus did"; he should let his wife "go to the devil" and, with the consent of the authorities, contract a new marriage.

Because of such utterances, particularly the passage, "then let the maid come," Duke George of Saxony addressed indignant complaints to his representative in the diet, Dietrich von Werthern. The Catholic controversialists of the time often advert to it. Offense was taken not only at the elimination of the matrimonial tie, but naturally also at the implied permission of extra-matrimonial intercourse with the maid. The phrase, "if the wife is unwilling, then let the maid come," may possibly have been a proverbial phrase in usage among the uncouth peasant class, signifying intercourse outside of wedlock. Since, however, Luther otherwise always inveighs strongly and decisively against extra-conjugal intercourse, it may be that he did not intend this application of the brutal phrase, but merely gave free rein to his pen when he cited the expression.

Luther's work "Of Married Life," taken in connexion with his other writings and pronouncements, clearly reveals how widely he opened the door to the destruction of the conjugal tie. August Bebel justly observes: "With regard to marriage, he [Luther] develops astonishingly radical views." [84] To this category belongs Luther's work on "The Seventh Chapter of St. Paul to the Corinthians" (I, Chap. vii), published in the year 1523. In some passages this work is characterized by a license of language which approaches indecency.[85]

In general, lack of restraint in speech is a prominent fault of Luther's, arising from his endeavor to employ the language of the common people, wherein he was assisted by his descent from the peasantry. It is not true that he found low pleasure in sexual matters. His uncouth expressions are hardly ever employed for the sake of exciting the sexual passion, even though Modesty must often veil her countenance. He fairly wallows in the mire of base bodily

[83] Grisar, *Luther*, Vol. III, p. 253. On the occurrence of this expression prior to Luther, cf. the investigations of G. Buchwald in *Beiträge zur Sächsischen Kirchengeschichte*, 1915, n. 29, Leipzig, 1916.

[84] Cfr. Grisar, *Luther*, Vol. III, pp. 241 sqq., and *infra*, Ch. XVIII, n. 2.

[85] Weimar ed., Vol. XII, pp. 92 sqq.; Erl. ed., Vol. LI, pp. 1 sqq.

functions, especially in his vigorous denunciation of his opponents. He liked to hurl the most vulgar filth into the faces of his enemies, after he had stirred it up with something akin to glee. He was excelled by no one in this respect either among his contemporaries or in the succeeding so-called age of frank utterance, yes, we may add, not even in the earlier centuries of the Middle Ages, which were not exactly noted for delicacy of speech. In this characteristic quality, he stands forth as a giant, even in his earlier writings, which are now under discussion. Later on, his dexterity increased in an astounding degree. The apologetical references of his defenders to the indelicate language of his age, therefore, are valid only in a very restricted measure. His contemporaries, his nearest friends even, are shocked at the filthy material which is at his disposal in his temperamental outbursts against his adversaries.[86]

King Henry VIII, of England, who was well versed in theology, violently attacked Luther as a heretic in 1521, in his "Defense of the Seven Sacraments," for which the Pope conferred upon him the title of "Defender of the Catholic Faith." Luther's reply to Henry's book (1523) was published in both Latin and German.[87] It abounds in vulgar attacks upon the King. In this work he says he wishes once more "to uncover the infamy of the Roman harlot" and declares "the harlot-countenance" of the king is brazen because of his defense of the "purple harlot of Rome, the drunken mother of impurity."

This fool, he says among other things, this excrement of swine and asses, wishes to defile the crown of my heavenly King of glory with the filth of his body; but the dung must be cast upon him, who is nothing but a lying rascal and buffoon, a monstrosity of a fool.[88]

With disgust the highly educated English chancellor, Thomas More, took cognizance of the filthy language in this and other Latin works of Luther. In a "Reply to Luther's Calumnies," which he published in 1523 under an assumed name, this eminent humanist wrote in a style which fortunately was not habitual with him: "[Luther] has nothing in his mouth but stench, filth and dung. These he scatters about him more abusively and obscenely

---

[86] See my *Luther*, references in the index, Vol. VI, *v*. "Abusive language," "Unseemliness of Luther's language."

[87] Weimar ed., Vol. X, II, pp. 180 sqq., 227 sq. *Opp. Lat. Var.*, XI, pp. 385 sqq., and Erl. ed., Vol. XXVIII, pp. 343 sqq.

[88] Cfr. Grisar, *Luther*, Vol. II, pp. 152 sqq.

than ever did churl. . . . If he continues to cultivate this vituperative manner of speech and to talk of nothing else but cloaca, latrines and excrements, then may others do as they please; we shall turn our backs upon his filth and abandon him to his vile discharges." [89]

In this same work against King Henry VIII, Luther says: "Through me Christ has commenced His revelations concerning the abominations in the holy place." "I am certain that I have my dogmas from heaven," "but the devil tries to deceive me through Henry;" "God blinds the devil, that his mendacity is made manifest through me." The King, he says, proves the truth of the saying that there are no greater fools than kings and princes.

One is compelled to ask, what demagogical effects such frenzied language was likely to produce in an agitated world, when the respect due to civil authority was trampled under foot even in such works of Luther as his treatise "On Secular Authority."

Among the other polemical writings which Luther produced during these years mention should be made of his Latin work, "Against the Armed Man Cochlaeus," whom he ridicules as a combative knight because of his report of their interview at Worms and his defense of the Sacraments.[90] Cochlaeus, himself an effective controversialist, replied in a work that bore a no less poignant title, "Against the Cowled Minotaur of Wittenberg," [91] in which he seriously but unsuccessfully applies to Luther the legend of the abortive calf of Freiberg, claiming that it condemned him.

In opposition to the canonization of Bishop Benno of Meissen, Luther, in 1524, wrote his sermon "Against the New Idol and Olden Devil about to be set up at Meissen." [92] By means of this outrageous sermon he intended to counteract the favorable influence which the Catholic cause was likely to derive from the imminent canonization of the venerable Bishop Benno and his elevation as patron saint of Saxony, a project which was promoted by Duke George.

Eager to increase his followers, Luther at that time also cast his eyes upon the Jews. He imagined that the Jews were inclined to favor him and could be attracted to his cause. What gain and glory if he should convert the people of Israel to the true Gospel! These ideas

---

[89] The Latin text in Grisar, *Luther*, Vol. III, p. 237, note 1. It concludes: *"Capiemus consilium . . . sic bacchantem cum suis merdis et stercoribus cacantem cacatumque relinquere."*

[90] Weimar ed., Vol. XI, pp. 295 sq.; *Opera Lat. Var.*, Vol. VII, pp. 44 sqq.

[91] Köstlin-Kawerau, *M. Luther*, Vol. I, p. 644.

[92] Weimar ed., Vol. XV, pp. 183 sqq.; Erl. ed., Vol. XXIV, 2nd ed., pp. 247 sqq. Cf. Grisar, *Luther*, Vol. V, pp. 123.

inspired his little treatise, "That Christ was Born a Jew." [93] In this work, published in 1523, he relies on the prophecies which foretell the conversion of the Jews at the end of the world. "God grant that the time is near at hand, as we hope." His desire to win over the Jews remained unrealized; his hatred of Judaism afterwards induced him to launch the most unheard-of attacks upon them.

In the midst of his fretful and many-sided labors he yet found leisure to write works on social questions. His small tract against usury, published in 1519, and his "Great Sermon" of 1520 on the same subject, were followed, in 1524, by the publication of a pamphlet, "On Mercantile Trade and Usury." [94] His writings on usury, to which was added another work in 1540, testify to the active interest which he took in the moral aspects of the progress of trade and commerce occasioned by the discoveries and the more intimate intercourse between nations resulting from them. In his work "Von Kaufshandlung," he again prohibits the taking of interest. "Whoever lends in such wise as to receive more in return, is a public and condemned usurer." For the rest, this treatise contains many stimulating ideas and furnishes an insight into the conditions of the time. But the author undeniably goes too far in his demand that the existing commerical societies ought to be abolished. He lacked the necessary breadth of view and practical experience to pass judgment on such a question. The desire to represent the new doctrine as useful for a general reform was not sufficient, and Scriptural passages, especially from the Old Testament, could not be generalized so as to apply to all times and conditions.

Luther's modern admirers have highly praised one of his works, written to improve the condition of the schools. It is entitled "To the Aldermen of all the Cities of Germany, that They Should Establish and Maintain Christian Schools," [95] the emphasis being on the word "Christian." This appeal was occasioned by the observation that his cause was injured by the deterioration of the schools resulting from the religious controversy he had started. It was his inten-

---

[93] Weimar ed., Vol. XI, pp. 314 sqq.; Erl. ed., Vol. XXIX, pp. 45 sqq. Cfr. Grisar, Luther, Vol. V, pp. 411 sq.

[94] Weimar ed., Vol. XV, pp. 293 sqq.; Erl. ed., Vol. XXII, pp. 199 sqq. Cfr. Grisar, Luther, Vol. V, pp. 79 sqq.

[95] Weimar ed., Vol. XV, pp. 27 sqq.; Erl. ed., Vol. XXII, pp. 168 sqq. Cfr. Grisar, Luther, Vol. VI, pp. 3 sqq.; also my article on "Luther" in the Pädagogisches Lexikon, new edition by Roloff.

tion, as he himself expressly confessed, to obtain the necessary spiritual and secular forces for the promotion of his Gospel by re-establishing Christian schools, *i. e.*, schools in which the new religion was inculcated. Besides practicable suggestions regarding education, the pages of this work are burdened with inconceivably crass accusations against the educational policy of the ancient Church, on which he wishes to inflict a mortal wound in the name of education by means of the Scriptures.

It was impossible for Luther, in discussing such questions as the nature of trade and education, to abandon the controversial narrowness which marked his ecclesiastical position.

In his literary activity, his predilection was Holy Writ. He provided the books of the New Testament which he translated into German with prefaces that characterize his standpoint in regard to the Bible and theology. The most significant thing in the latter regard is his preface to the Epistle to the Romans. It is little less than an epitome of his theological teaching, especially as it centers around the idea that St. Paul condemns "the entire ulcerous and reptilian complex of human laws and commandments which drowns the world at present" and teaches the doctrine of justification by faith alone.[96] His general preface to the New Testament is equally noteworthy, as it emphasized that those portions of the Scriptures are the best which show "how faith in Christ gives life, justice, and happiness." Hence his preference for "the Gospel of St. John and his first Epistle, the Epistles of St. Paul, particularly those addressed to the Romans, the Galatians, and the Ephesians, and the first Epistle of St. Peter; these are the books which reveal Christ. . . . They advance far beyond the three Gospels of Matthew, Mark, and Luke. . . . Compared with them, St. James' Epistle is an epistle of straw, since there is nothing evangelical about it."

In this manner his criticism of the Bible proceeds along entirely subjective and arbitrary lines. The value of the sacred writings is measured by the rule of his own doctrine. He treats the venerable canon of Scripture with a liberty which annihilates all certitude. For, while this list has the highest guarantee of sacred tradition and the backing of the Church, Luther makes religious sentiment the criterion by which to decide which books belong to the Bible,

[96] See the conclusion of the preface to Romans, 1522. Cfr. Erl. ed., Vol. LXIII, pp. 7 sqq, for a collection of Luther's prefaces.

which are doubtful, and which are to be excluded. At the same time he practically abandons the concept of inspiration, for he says nothing of a special illuminative activity of God in connection with the writers' composition of the Sacred Book, notwithstanding that he holds the Bible to be the Word of God because its authors were sent by God. As is well known, during the age of orthodox Lutheranism its devotees fell into the other extreme by teaching so-called verbal inspiration, according to which every single word of the Bible has been dictated by God. Catholic theology has always observed a golden mean between these extremes.

Luther always adhered essentially to his opinion of the Epistle of St. James as quoted above.[97] Relative to the other Biblical writings, his most striking assertions will be considered in the sequel. Even at the Leipsic disputation he had maintained that the second book of Machabees did not belong to the canon simply because of the difficulty presented by the passage quoted by Eck concerning Purgatory and prayers for the departed.[98] Later he simply excluded the so-called deutero-canonical books of the Old Testament from the list of sacred writings. In his edition they are grouped together at the end of the Old Testament under the title: "Apocrypha, i. e., books not to be regarded as equal to Holy Writ, but which are useful and good to read." Under this title the Lutheran Bible retains the following arrangement even to the present day: Judith, Wisdom, Tobias, Ecclesiasticus, Baruch, Machabees I and II, parts of Esther and of Daniel. Luther's New Testament is somewhat more conservative. After the Gospels, the Acts of the Apostles, and the Epistles, it contains the Epistles to the Hebrews, those of St. James and St. Jude—three epistles which Luther carped at—and, lastly, the Apocalypse of St. John.

It is a fact that must not be overlooked that the parts of the Bible which Luther retained were taken over from the tradition of the past. By way of exception and as a matter of necessity, he thus conceded the claims of tradition. Though otherwise opposed to it, he took it as his guide and safeguard in this respect without admitting the fact. Thus his attitude towards the Bible is really burdened with "flagrant contradictions," to use an expression of Harnack, especially since he "had broken through the external authority of the written word" by his critical method.[99] And of this, Luther is guilty,

[97] Cfr. Grisar, *Luther*, Vol. V, pp. 521 sqq.
[98] *Ibid*.
[99] Cfr. Grisar, *Luther*, Vol. IV, pp. 403 sq,

the very man who elsewhere represents the Bible as the sole principle of faith!

If, in addition to this, his arbitrary method of interpretation is taken into consideration, the work of destruction wrought by him appears even greater. The only weapon he possessed he wrested from his own hand, as it were, both theoretically and in practice.

His procedure regarding the sacred writings is apt to make thoughtful minds realize how great is the necessity of an infallible Church as divinely appointed guardian and authentic interpreter of the Bible. Deprived of the guidance of the Church, with subjectivism as his lodestar, Luther trod the path that led to an independent religion severed from divine revelation and therefore without foundation.

7. FREE CHRISTIANITY AND THE FREEDOM OF THE WILL

When, in the period from 1520 to about 1525, Luther approached his doctrine of so-called free Christianity without binding dogmas,[100] he nevertheless revealed glimpses of an intention of adhering to the norms of the Christian religion. He speaks with vigor about truths undeniably based upon tradition and guaranteed by the Bible. In brief, he desired to be a true Christian. But the inexorable logic of his subjectivistic system produced a different result. It compelled him with the force of gravity, as it were, to abandon his positive foundation, notwithstanding his refusal to admit it to himself, since he does not follow out his conclusions to the end, but turns back after having gone halfway. It is impossible to form any other opinion of his expectorations, so often influenced by passion and saturated with rhetoric. Not infrequently they contain appeals to liberty which are irreconcilable with true Christianity. Evidently this phenomenon is associated with the impetuosity which animated him at the outset of his career. Under unfavorable circumstances he was not capable of moderating his temperament. In the stress of his labors he did not weigh his words. Inclined to doubt and criticism, his great success on the stage of the world swept him on to further doubt and criticism.

Only when the fanatical sects increased in strength, did a reaction set in, which caused him to favor a more positive attitude.

[100] *Ibid.*, Vol. III, pp. 9 sqq.; V, 432 sqq.

In his attacks upon them, his fear of a free Christianity gained the upper hand, prudence asserted her claims, and there came a time when Luther reversed his views and corrected his utterances. Instead of making internal experience and spiritual relish the sole criterion, he now emphasized (especially after 1525) the so-called external Word of God and the authority of the Bible, in so far as they seemed to him clear and indisputable. He placed the *rule* of faith in the foreground and conceded greater importance to good works. The sight of the general decadence and the dissolving effects of his sermons on Christian freedom in opposition to the law, compelled him more and more to desist from his attacks on the motive of fear of punishment in the fulfillment of the commandments. When, finally, the Peasants' Revolt began to shake the foundations of the social and moral order, his return to positive religion became more pronounced, or, as has been said, he turned from the free Evangel to the legal structure of a Protestantism under state control.

Nevertheless, his early utterances on freedom and intellectual liberty are re-echoed in his later ones. The primitive fallacy of his system could not be eradicated. It took only certain impacts to strike his excitable mentality and cause him once more to espouse the cause of unrestricted liberty.

In the period of his early activity, *i. e.*, before 1525, while Luther was engaged in his struggle with the papacy and, in part, with himself, he expressed himself as follows concerning the rights of subjectivism:

"Neither the pope nor the bishop nor any other man has the right to dictate even so much as a syllable to a Christian believer, except with the latter's consent." Formerly, under the papacy, we had "no right to form an opinion," but now "all councils have been overthrown." No one, he says, may "command what men must believe." "If I am to know what is false doctrine, I have the right to judge." Let others arrive at whatever decision they please, "I also have the right to judge, whether I will accept it or not. . . . You yourself must be able to say, this is right, that is wrong. . . . God must tell you deep down in your heart: this is the Word of God." Autonomy, according to him, is to be maintained at all times,[101] even towards the sermons which every member of the congregation may criticize, reject or accept.[102] In fact, private judgment is to be exercised even in relation to himself (so he says incidentally); for "no one is bound to believe me, let each one look to himself. To warn all I am able, but stop any man I can-

---

[101] *Ibid.*, Vol. IV, pp. 482 sqq.
[102] *Supra*, No. 4 of this chapter.

not." [103] "If we all are priests, how then shall we not have the right to discriminate and judge what is right or wrong in faith?" "A lowly man may have the right opinion; why, then, should it not be followed?" The Bible may be interpreted by everyone, even by a "humble miller's maid, nay, by a child of nine if it has the faith." [104]

He intoned hymns of liberty relative to the commandments, particularly in his work on "The Freedom of a Christian," and thus brought about dire results because of the confusion they created. Once you have comprehended the Word by faith, he expressly says, "all commandments are fulfilled and you shall be free in all things." "No one can be forced." [105]

Is the reception of the Sacraments also a free matter? In 1521 Luther declared: "Every individual ought to be free with regard to the reception of the Sacraments. If anyone does not wish to be baptized, let him please himself about it. If anyone does not wish to receive holy communion, that is his precious right. Also, if anyone does not wish to confess, that is his right before God." [106] He had already disposed of confession as a Sacrament. With respect to Baptism and Communion, however, he subsequently defends the necessity of receiving them. In 1521 he writes in another work: "I approve of faith and Baptism, but no one should be compelled; everyone ought to be exhorted and to exercise liberty in these matters." Perhaps his confused declarations relative to Baptism and Communion are intended to exclude only physical coercion, whilst at the same time he completely spurns confession as such. Yet, according to his whole system (as many modern Protestant theologians admit), Baptism would not be necessary because "salvation is possible without Baptism"; since "the salvation dispensed in the Sacrament is none other than that obtained through the instrumentality of the Word of the sermon" (Erich Haupt). The same is to be affirmed of the Lord's Supper. Consequently, according to Luther, Christ instituted Sacraments the use of which depends upon the good pleasure of men.

Such expressions—which could be multiplied considerably—lead us to the very brink of religious radicalism. In the heat of the combat against the dogmatic teachings of the papacy, during which, it is true, he did not always weigh his words, Luther proclaimed complete anarchy. Modern liberal Protestantism loves this kind of so-called liberty. Harnack styles it a "rich spring-tide" in the history of Luther's development, though, unfortunately, it was not followed by a "full-blown summer. . . . In those years," he says,

[103] Grisar, *Luther*, Vol. III, p. 392.
[104] *Ibid.*, Vol. II, p. 31; Vol. IV, p. 389.
[105] *Ibid.*, Vol. III, p. 11; Vol. IV, pp. 487 sq.
[106] *Ibid.*, Vol. III, pp. 9 sqq.

"Luther was elevated above himself and apparently overcame the limitations of his own individuality." In contrast with the demand of numerous contemporary Protestant theologians, who plead for a return to Luther as he appeared in the spring of life, when, as they allege, he was truly liberal-minded, we may quote this remarkable statement by Frederick Paulsen, the famous Protestant philosopher and historian: "The principle . . . to allow no authority on earth to prescribe the faith is anarchical. And on these lines there can be no church with the right of examining candidates for the ministry and holding visitations of the clergy, as Luther did." This author furthermore says that "Luther as pope," which he really wanted to be, glaringly contradicts that principle. "Whoever stands in need of a pope, had better be advised to stick to the real one at Rome." Fundamentally, Paulsen asserts, "an antinomy lies at the very root of the Protestant Church," namely: "There can be no earthly authority in matters of faith, and: There must be such an authority." [107]

The religion which Luther cultivated in spite of his urge for liberty was the *religion of the enslaved will*. He ascribed so much influence to the omnipotence of God and to what he calls grace, that man's liberty to perform moral and meritorious acts was completely shattered. Now free-will was constantly and rightly regarded as the preliminary condition of divine worship. "God created thee without thy aid," says St. Augustine, "but He does not desire to justify thee without thy co-operation." Luther, however, treats man like a block of wood in matters pertaining to salvation. As he expresses it, man is ridden like a beast by God or by the devil.

Erasmus in 1523 decided to publish an attack on Luther's denial of the doctrine of free-will.[108] As a humanist he was particularly interested in defending the freedom of the will. On the other hand, Luther's obstinate negation of free-will was one of the most vulnerable spots in his doctrinal armor, against which an attack could be most easily launched with the prospect of winning wide-spread applause. It had not been an easy matter to persuade Erasmus to take this resolution. For he had long favored Luther at least to the extent of warmly approving his campaign not only against the existing abuses, but also against certain perfectly justifiable religious

[107] *Ibid.*, Vol. IV, p. 485.
[108] Cfr. Grisar, *Luther*, Vol. II, pp. 223 sqq.

usages and necessary ecclesiastical institutions, which he himself
was also wont to criticize. After Luther's open rupture with the
Church (1520) the cautious Erasmus became more and more guarded
in his utterances relative to the religious innovation.[109] Amid his
epistolary compliments to Luther one may read his assurance, that
he would never separate himself from the divinely instituted spiritual authority of the Church; that he did not wish to bother about
the clash provoked by the religious controversy, but desired to pursue
his studies unperturbed; and that God had sent the strong medicine
which Luther administered in order to purge His Church, since
Christ had been well-nigh forgotten. It required remonstrations on
the part of men in high authority, even in Rome, of the King of
England and of the Emperor, to determine Erasmus to take up his
pen against Luther.

In the spring of 1524 Luther heard that his erstwhile patron was
engaged in composing a book against him. He correctly appraised
the influence which Erasmus would exert upon the numerous humanistic parties which had formerly favored him, but had become
estranged from his cause as a result of his violent activities. The
voice of their highly revered leader was bound to turn the scales
against him. Hence, in April, he wrote a strange letter to Erasmus,
then at Basle. He said that he had nothing to fear from an attack, but,
after flattering his antagonist for his rare qualities and merits, begs
him: "Do not write against me, or increase the number and strength
of my opponents; particularly do not attack me through the press,
and I, for my part, shall also refrain from attacking you." "With patience and respect," he continues, he had observed that Erasmus, alas,
did not possess grace from above to comprehend the new Evangel.[110]

Erasmus's treatise appeared at Basle in 1524; it was written in
excellent Latin and bore the title: *"De Libero Arbitrio Diatribe"*
(Discourse on Free-Will). The author triumphantly refutes the
heresy of the enslaved will, and despite his great and often timid
reserve, his critical rejection of the Biblical supports of Luther's
theory is quite as brilliant as his use of the sacred text in defense
of the Catholic doctrine.

According to Luther, he says, not only goodness, but also moral evil must
be referred to God, which, however, conflicts with God's nature and is ex-

109 *Ibid.*, Vol. II, pp. 249 sq.
110 *Ibid.*, p. 260.

cluded by His holiness. Luther maintains that God punishes sinners who cannot be held accountable for their misdeeds. Hence, so far as this earthly life is concerned, laws and penalties are superfluous, because there can be no responsibility without freedom of choice.

"In defending free-will," thus writes the Protestant theologian A. Taube, "Erasmus fights for responsibility, duty, guilt, and repentance—ideas which are essential to Christian piety." "He vindicates the moral character of the Christian religion. . . ."[111]

It was not to be expected that Erasmus, who was a stranger to Scholasticism, would enter upon a technical discussion of his topic. Nor was it exactly necessary, although many points might have been made more telling, as, for instance, the refutation of Luther's doctrine of absolute predestination. The Catholics were highly elated at the "Diatribe" of Erasmus. Duke George of Saxony thanked him in a letter, but, in his frank and honest way, did not suppress the caustic remark: "Had you come to your present decision three years ago, and withstood Luther's shameful heresies in writing, instead of merely opposing him secretly, as though you were not willing to do him much harm, the flames would not have extended so far."[112] The "Diatribe" also met with the approval of close friends of Luther. Wolfgang Capito had previously declared his opposition to Luther's theory of the enslaved will. Peter Mosellanus (Schade) of Leipsic had spoken so strongly against Luther's theses and his teaching on predestination that warning reports were sent to Wittenberg. George Agricola, the learned naturalist, who at first admired Luther, was repelled by his denial of free-will.[113] Melanchthon, to whom, despite his former approval, this denial became painful in the course of time, thanked his friend Erasmus for the moderation which he had observed. He became more and more convinced that Erasmus was right in certain cardinal theological points, and himself became an opponent of determinism.[114]

8. COMPANIONS IN ARMS AT WITTENBERG

Next to Luther, the most attractive personality at the University of Wittenberg was the young humanist and theologian *Philip Me-*

111 *Ibid.*, p. 263.
112 *Ibid.*, pp. 261 sq.
113 *Ibid.*, p. 242.
114 *Ibid.*, pp. 261 sq.

lanchthon, a small and emaciated man, endowed with a pair of glowing eyes. The reputation for learning which this precocious youth enjoyed, powerfully attracted students. He lectured on Homer and St. Paul's Epistle to Titus, on rhetoric and the Gospel of St. Matthew. Even after his transfer, in 1519, from the chair of Greek to the theological faculty, he continued to occupy himself chiefly with humanism, especially in his literary productions. He never became a doctor of theology. He combined an excellent gift for teaching with a love for youth and great sociability. His lectures he flavored with instructive anecdotes, but never became rhetorical or violent, like Luther. He had difficulty in overcoming his habit of stuttering. In addition to his academic lectures he conducted a *schola privata* for beginners, whom he, an ardent friend of youth, prepared for the higher studies. In 1524 he published for their benefit an "Enchiridion of the Elements for Boys." It was a reader composed of church prayers, passages from the Bible, and secular material, such as moral axioms of the Seven Wise Men and excerpts from Plautus. Despite his many labors, Melanchthon knew how to preserve his delicate health by a life of regularity and extraordinary abstemiousness. He rose early and devoted the first hours of the morning to his extensive correspondence. His letters were composed with great care and a facile and fluent Latinity similar to that which distinguishes his printed works. In the use of the German vernacular, however, he was far less skilled than Luther.

Melanchthon's domestic life presented attractive features. In the fortress-like house which he occupied, and which still stands, he constructed a quiet "sanctuary" reserved for intercourse with his familiars and learned friends as well as for study. It was there he was found by a French scholar who paid him a visit, rocking the baby's cradle by means of a ribbon and reading a book which he held in his right hand. The wife of this lay-theologian was the daughter of a burgomaster, a quiet, sensible woman, like himself very charitable towards the poor.

The nuns who left their convents and came to Wittenberg were not welcome in Melanchthon's home. Aside from the fact that there were some among them who, like Catherine von Bora, flaunted their noble descent too ostentatiously in the presence of Melanchthon's wife, who belonged to the middle class, Melanchthon and his spouse regarded with aversion the worldly conduct of these nuns and their fawning upon Luther. Melanchthon, in a confidential letter to Camerarius, couched in Greek, declared that they had "ensnared" Luther "with every kind of strategy." The conduct of many married clergymen and fugitive monks was likewise distasteful to him.

Melanchthon became very sad when, on a journey to his native town of Bretten in the Lower Palatinate (Baden), he was forced to note the moral decadence which had set in as a consequence of the religious controversy. According to a sufficiently authenticated tradition, he frankly encouraged his mother (either at that time or on the occasion of a visit he paid her in 1529) not to be disturbed by the religious controversies.[115] He well remembered the admonition of his father, the strictly religious George Schwarzerd, an armorer by trade, who, nine days before his demise, had adjured his family never to separate from the Catholic Church. The papal nuncio Campeggio, on the occasion of his first visit, endeavored through the instrumentality of his secretary, Nausea, to induce Melanchthon to return to the mother Church, but the attempt proved futile.

In 1521 Melanchthon championed Luther's cause by publishing a work against Thomas Rhadinus, an Italian antagonist of the Reformation. In this work he went so far as to demand that the authorities of the Empire should use force against the Pope. Soon after he penned an attack upon the Paris Sorbonne. He merited Luther's highest esteem by his "Loci Communes Rerum Theologicarum." "I esteem Philip like myself," Luther wrote in September, 1523, "aside from the fact that he puts me to shame, nay, excels me, in learning and virtue." [116]

Despite his disapproval of the extremes to which his friend Luther went, Melanchthon was fascinated by his personality. He was not sufficiently self-reliant, too much of a specialist and pliant Erasmian to adopt a firm and consistent line of conduct. He aided Luther at all times, by polishing with his skilled pen the latter's impetuously uttered thoughts and bringing them into some kind of scientific form, though he would have preferred to escape from the too turbu-

[115] *Ibid.*, Vol. V, p. 270.
[116] Letter to Billikan, September 17, 1523; *Briefwechsel*, IV, p. 230.

lent struggle to devote himself entirely to his humanistic studies, without, of course, abandoning his "honored master" in his conflict with the Roman Antichrist.

As early as 1525, it could be seen more clearly that Melanchthon was animated by a desire to play the rôle of "Erasmian mediator" in Lutheran theology. He thought the breach between the old and the new theology could be healed and hoped for a conciliatory attitude on the part of the Catholic opposition, all the more fervently in proportion as he, who was more timid and more keenly sensitive than Luther, was affrighted at the consequences of the ecclesiastical revolution. Accordingly he devoted himself to the humanities in order to prepare the way for that vague religious unity which ever hovered before his mind. Because of his extraordinary success in the humanistic field of learning his friends bestowed upon him the honorary title of "*Praeceptor Germaniae*." [117]

Of quite a different stamp were the other men who stood closest to Luther as friends and co-workers.

Justus Jonas, provost of the church of All Saints at Wittenberg, was likewise a disciple of Erasmus, but was far less active in behalf of humanism than in his support of Luther.[118] As doctor of both canon and civil law, he had taught the latter at the University of Wittenberg, but after his promotion to the theological doctorate through Luther's influence, entered the theological faculty and boldly lectured on portions of the Bible, such as St. Paul's Epistle to the Romans. The neo-humanists of Erfurt and the school of Mutianus introduced this unfortunate priest to the pleasures of life. He was of a jovial and lively disposition. Luther derived much consolation and relaxation from his company. By translating his Latin works into German, which he accomplished with great facility, Jonas rendered greater services to Luther than by his scholarship. His lack of theological erudition and profundity were compensated by a firm, nay, fanatical attitude. Few men have treated their opponents more disgracefully and unfairly and with worse personal invectives than Jonas. He entitled the Latin apology of his marriage, published in 1522, thus: "In defense of Clerical Marriage against John Faber, the Patron of Harlotry." Among the defects of his character, ac-

---

[117] Cf. Grisar, *Luther*, Vol. III, pp. 319 sqq., 346 sqq., 360 sqq.
[118] *Ibid.*, Vol. III, pp. 413 sqq.

cording to G. Kawerau, was a "constant, often petty concern in the increase of his income." [119]

A third co-worker of Luther was *John Bugenhagen,* a native of Wollin in Pomerania, hence called "Pomeranus," the intruding city parson of Wittenberg.[120] After he had passed through the humanistic current of his age, he attended private lectures in theology at Luther's side; though a priest, he had until then kept himself rather aloof from theology. With his practical talents and energy, which often degenerated into harshness, he, as parish priest of Wittenberg, commenced quite early to unfold an extensive activity for the advancement of Lutheranism, both in the electorate of Saxony and far beyond its confines. His ability as an organizer made him indispensable to Luther, who eulogized him as "Bishop of the Church of Wittenberg," as the chief support of the "Evangel" besides his Philip, as a great theologian and a man of nerve. Because he supplied a (rather deficient) commentary on the Psalms, Luther said that Bugenhagen was the "first on earth who deserved to be called interpreter of the Psalter." [121] The most opposite of these epithets was that of the "man of nerve"—*multum habet nervorum.* Köstlin rightly characterizes Bugenhagen as "merely a subordinate, though endowed by nature with considerable powers of mind and body." [122] His various "church regulations" were of greater importance than his writings. Energetically and successfully he defended Luther's doctrine of the Last Supper when the Swiss theologians denied the real presence of Christ in the Eucharist in Zwingli's letter to Albert of Reutlingen and his treatise "On the True and False Religion," published in March, 1525.

Nicholas von Amsdorf, who first taught theology at Wittenberg, became pastor and superintendent of the new religion in Magdeburg in 1524, and as such always co-operated with Luther as his confidential adviser.[123] Among all his friends he was most closely akin to him in spirit and most appreciative of his mental sufferings and struggles. He heartily concurred in the most unrestrained assertions and outbursts of Luther, nay, possibly even outdid him. Luther called him "a born theologian." Later champions of orthodox

---

119 *Ibid.,* p. 416.
120 *Ibid.,* pp. 405 sqq.
121 *Ibid.*
122 *Ibid.,* p. 407.
123 *Ibid.,* p. 405.

Lutheranism have glorified Amsdorf as the Eliseus of the Elias, Luther, or even as a second Luther. The thick-set man with his sharp features was a reckless enthusiast and became conspicuous by his extreme views at the very outset of the struggle. In 1523 he proclaimed it as his deliberate judgment that a Christian prince is under obligation to bear arms in defense of the true Gospel. Luther dedicated to him his "Address to the Nobility" and Melanchthon his edition of "The Clouds" of Aristophanes. Amsdorf never married, although he affirmed in one of his writings that marriage was a divine command incumbent upon all priests.

Among Luther's sympathizers in the secular faculties of Wittenberg University the jurist *Jerome Schurf* was the most conspicuous.

Luther also had sympathizers and active co-workers in the Augustinian Order during the initial stages of the new movement. Pre-eminent amongst these was *Wenceslaus Link,* a man experienced in business and fluent of speech. The Saxon congregation under Staupitz comprised certain monasteries in the Low Countries, such as Antwerp, Dordrecht, and Ghent. There Lutheranism took root, especially through the efforts of two priors, Jacob Probst and Henry Moller. The former was a native of Ypres, the latter of Zütphen (Sutphen). Probst evaded the severe censures of the edict, first by issuing a denial of his teachings, and later (in August, 1522) by secretly escaping to Wittenberg. Moller likewise succeeded in reaching Wittenberg before the censures became effective. In contrast with these, two younger Augustinians were burned at the stake in Brussels, the capital of the Low Countries, on July 1, 1523, in consequence of their obstinate adherence to their heretical opinions. Their names were Henry Vos and John van Eschen. Luther extolled them in his hymn on the two so-called martyrs. A third Augustinian, Lambert Thorn, who succeeded Probst in the office of preacher, was likewise condemned to death in Brussels, but escaped with his life for unknown reasons.

Luther derived assistance also from the ranks of the Franciscans. Thus he was aided by the popular orators John Eberlin and Henry von Kettenbach, and by the writers Frederick Myconius and Conrad Pellican. Among the Dominicans who rallied round his banner was the talented young monk, Martin Bucer, whom he had partially won over by the disputation at Heidelberg. The German Dominicans did not furnish him with another man of repute, neither from the

Saxon nor from the Upper German province nor from the Upper German congregation. On the whole, the Dominicans as well as the Franciscans consistently and decisively maintained their Catholic position and opposed the religious innovation. They assigned their most capable writers to enter the lists in defense of the ancient faith. Oecolampadius left the Brigittine monastery at Altomünster and Ambrose Blaurer deserted the Benedictine monastery of Alpirsbach to join the new movement. Both labored with success in the interests of the religious revolt.

Caspar Schwenckfeld, an eccentric and fanatical layman, was a friend of Luther for many years. He intended to bring about a reformation of Christianity on the basis of Lutheranism along novel lines of his own. He was born of a noble family in the duchy of Liegnitz. When Luther took his stand against indulgences, Schwenckfeld was already inclined to join him. In the beginning of the twenties he tried to persuade the prince of Liegnitz to introduce the new religion into his native city and into all Silesia. Though a layman, he preached with unction, and his captivating manners, coupled with an impressive appearance, enabled him to win many adherents, especially among the nobility. [124] In his endeavor to arouse men to a realization of the seriousness of life, he took offense at the omission of good works from Luther's doctrine and censured the loose conduct which he observed about him, in his "Admonition" against "carnal liberty and the errors of the common people," published in 1524. In the following year he pretended to have received by private revelation a new doctrine of the Lord's Supper which abandoned the Real Presence of Christ in the Eucharist. His doctrine on the Eucharist was not approved by Luther, Jonas and Bugenhagen, whom he visited at Wittenberg, notwithstanding the fact that he did not incline to the rationalistic theories of Zwingli. In vain he explained to Luther, on December 1, 1525, his supposedly deeper conception of Christ's abiding survival in the faithful without a Eucharist, Sacraments or a church. In the course of his exposition he ardently advised Luther to abandon his idea of a congregational church with general communion and in lieu thereof establish congregations composed of revived Christians, such as Luther himself had dreamed of at times. Luther did not wish to break with this influential man, but a breach did come later. According to Schwenckfeld's statement, Luther had

[124] *Ibid.,* Vol. V, pp. 78 sqq.

admitted the plausibility of his doctrine of the Eucharist, even though it was as yet undemonstrated, and declared: "Dear Caspar, wait a little while." Probably he merely intended in this fashion to get rid of the importunate Schwenckfeld. The latter, however, was not inclined to wait, but provoked an open controversy, in which, without entirely denying Luther's teaching, he frankly and severely exposed its weaknesses, particularly in their moral implications. His example reveals anew how the arbitrary subjectivism of Luther aroused opposition on the part of his adherents and introduced chaos into the very bosom of the new religion.

For the rest, Schwenckfeld was one of the few men who, having entered into relations with Luther, refused to succumb to the fascination of his personality. The friends whom we have enumerated above, and many others, yielded to that exceedingly powerful charm. There is abundant evidence of the superior force which he exercised in his personal intercourse with others, such as John Kessler, Albert Burrer, Peter Mosellanus, and, at a later date, Mathesius, Spangenberg, Aurifaber, Rhegius, and Cordatus. All agree that there was something charming about his affability, his attractive speech, and constancy in the midst of trouble. [125] One may say that he was by nature endowed with an immense power of suggestion, intensified by his exterior appearance, particularly by his flashing eyes. In addition, the influence of his personality was augmented by the glory of his unexampled success.

[125] *Ibid.*, Vol. IV, pp. 268 sqq.

Chapter XI

THE TEMPESTUOUS YEAR, 1525—LUTHER'S MARRIAGE

For various reasons the year 1525 must be called a tempestuous year. First of all the Peasants' War stamped its character upon it. Germany experienced tumults such as it had never seen before, which shook Luther's work and influenced his mind. Seldom was he so vehemently perturbed as during these momentous months, in the course of which, strange to say, occurred his marriage.

The year 1525 witnessed the formation, on the one hand, of a more compact union of the Catholic princes opposed to the new movement, and, on the other, the preparation of the fatal Protestant alliance of Torgau and the emergence of the war-like figure of Philip of Hessen. It marked the energetic assembly of Mayence, which fanned the fury of Luther, but also the defection of extensive territories, among them Prussia, and the violent introduction of the religious change in the electorate of Saxony, brought about by the new Elector. Luther was compelled to wrestle with the Anabaptists and other fanatics, with powerful enemies in the Catholic camp, and with the triumphal march of Erasmus' polemical pamphlet on free-will, to which, in 1525, he opposed his treatise "On the Enslaved Will," a work begotten literally in storm and stress.

Beyond the German frontier Emperor Charles was engaged in a sanguinary contest with the king of France. Francis was captured at Pavia, but the victory of the imperial arms led to serious conflicts with the Italian States and with Pope Clement VII. At the same time, the power of the Turks assumed menacing proportions along the eastern border of the Empire and in the Mediterranean Sea, with no signs of an energetic defense, which was made impossible by the unsettled state of the Catholic forces and Luther's hostility towards Christian undertakings against the Turks.

I. LUTHER AND THE PEASANTS' WAR

In 1524, the cities of Allstedt and Orlamünde in Thuringia had been violently excited by Thomas Münzer and Karlstadt, respectively.

Urged by the electoral court of Saxony, Luther visited these unsettled districts in August. In vain he negotiated with Karlstadt in
an inn called the Black Bear at Jena. (At the end of the conference,
Luther presented Karlstadt with a golden coin as a token that the latter might write against him.) Thence he proceeded to Orlamünde,
where, as he writes, he was lucky that he was not "expelled with
stones and mud." [1] Karlstadt, as we have seen, was thereupon officially banished from the electorate. Soon afterwards, however, he
continued his agitation in the city of Rothenburg on the Tauber.
Münzer meanwhile went to Mühlhausen, a highly developed indus-
trial center, where evangelical preachers had already succeeded in
creating a great ferment. A riot ensued, but Münzer was compelled
to flee from Saxony and thereupon propagated his revolutionary ideas
in southern Germany and allied himself with the Anabaptists of
Zurich.

It was generally believed among citizens and peasants that a serious
revolt against the princes and the clergy was imminent in 1524.

The revolt actually commenced in southwestern Germany in support of the movement which had been started by Münzer and his
associate, Pfeifer, at Mühlhausen. It spread over a large part of
Thuringia and the Harz mountain district. According to an exaggerated expression of Luther, Münzer, after his return to Mühlhausen, was *rex et imperator* of that city. [2] The sanguinary insurrection
was supported by the discontented peasants, who had been misguided
in spiritual matters, and was preached by this fanatic, "the servant of
God against the godless, armed with the sword of Gedeon."

Peasant revolts against the rulers had not been infrequent towards
the close of the Middle Ages, caused partly by the oppressive conditions under which the peasantry lived, and partly by the spread
of insurrectionary and revolutionary social ideas. Now, however,
these insurrections derived their impetus from the Lutheran ideas
and slogans which had permeated the masses. It would be unhistorical
to throw the entire responsibility for the gigantic movement upon
Luther. Nevertheless, it cannot be gainsaid that the ideas and preachers of the new movement were intimately connected with it. The
doctrine of evangelical liberty played the principal rôle.

In most districts the rebellious peasants not only demanded abso-

[1] Köstlin-Kawerau, M. *Luther*, 1903, Vol. I, p. 681.
[2] De Wette, II, p. 644.

lute liberty to change their religion, or at least the confiscation of church property and the cessation of clerical privileges, but they also increased their justifiable temporal demands in the name of the so-called evangelical liberty by claiming the most unwarrantable liberties, privileges, and tributes. This is illustrated by the Twelve Articles, which became current at the beginning of the Peasants' War. They were composed by Balthasar Hubmaier, a native of Waldshut, an apostate priest who had formerly been stationed at the cathedral of Ratisbon, but latterly had become a preacher of the new religion. The very first article demands for every congregation the right to elect and depose its pastor; the elected pastor is obliged to preach the gospel without any admixture and in plain terms. According to the last article, emancipation from most of the tithes, from the status of serfdom, from the manifold feudal burdens and obligations which is insisted on in the remaining articles, should be demonstrated from Sacred Scripture.

Fundamentally, however, brute force governed the movement. For the first time the masses, incited by the preachers of the new Evangel, became conscious of the power that inheres in union.

How often had not Luther himself summoned his followers to destroy the churches, monasteries, and dioceses of Antichrist.[3] True he desired this to be done by the authorities, but the peasants felt that they were the authorities. Then, too, without mentioning the authorities, he repeatedly pointed out, in his violent and inconsiderate language, that an insurrection of the masses was inevitable. It appeared to the peasants that their hour for acting had now arrived.

The conflagration began in August, 1524, in the southern region of the Black Forest, near Waldshut. It burst into flames at the beginning of 1525, in the territory of the prince-abbot of Kempten. In consequence of the advantages which the peasants of that place had gained for themselves, almost the entire peasantry of southwestern Germany, to the Lake of Constance and the Upper Rhine, rose in open rebellion. The resistance of the Swabian League in Württemberg was paralyzed by the invasion of the exiled Duke Ulrich. The peasants stormed and burned castles and monasteries and plundered churches. Priests and noblemen were subjected to horrible maltreatment. From Swabia the horror soon spread to the Odenwald and to Franconia. In the latter region alone 200 monasteries and castles were

---

[3] For examples see the above and later sections.

sacked and wholly or partly destroyed. The atrocities committed at Weinsberg constituted a horrible climax.

In South Germany, however, the irregular peasant bands at the beginning of May succumbed to the strategy of the leader of the Swabian League, Count George Truchsess von Waldburg. They were subjected to severe punishment. Duke Antony of Lorraine put down the peasants in Alsace, Landgrave Philip of Hesse crushed the insurrection in his territory with bloody arms.

Meanwhile, however, Thomas Münzer, operating from Mühlhausen, had incited the peasants of that district and also plunged some cities (Erfurt, Nordhausen, and Eisenach) into the maelstrom of the revolution. His movement was outspokenly communistic and religiously fanatical. It was more conspicuous for cruelty than the other revolutionary movements in Germany. Münzer soon met with his fate. Philip of Hesse, the Elector John, and Dukes George and Henry of Saxony, engaged his forces in a decisive battle near Frankenhausen on May 15, 1525, and defeated them. Three hundred captives, including Münzer, were executed. According to Cochlaeus and Landgrave Philip he died repentant and received the Viaticum in conformity with the Catholic rite.

The great rebellion had been put down and Germany freed from the danger of destruction. The condition of the peasantry became more oppressive than before, while the power of the princes grew.

What attitude did Luther maintain towards the various phases of the Peasants' War?

Prior to the commencement of hostilities, he published his "Exhortation to Peace." He had been requested by certain representatives of the South German peasantry to express himself on the Twelve Articles in the light of Holy Writ. [4] This he does by acknowledging the justice of some of the demands and insisting on reconciliation and peace. However, he employs such violent terms against the "oppression and extortion" of the authorities and the princes, "on whose neck the sword lies," and whose "presumption will break their necks," that the desire for revolution could be only strengthened among the masses.

In his "Exhortations" he is chiefly concerned with the "admonition" that the Gospel be sustained. But he charges the peasants with meddling in his

[4] Weimar ed., Vol. XVIII, pp. 291 sqq.; Erlangen ed., Vol. XXIV, 2nd ed., pp. 269 sqq.

project; you desire to assist the Gospel, he says, yet suppress it by your violent measures. For the rest, if the lords and princes "prohibit the preaching of the Gospel and oppress the people so intolerably, they undoubtedly deserve that God depose them from their thrones." In imagination he already sees the hands outstretched which are to execute the divine judgment. "Since, therefore, it is certain," he tells the princes, "that you govern tyrannically and madly, forbid the Gospel and harass and oppress the poor, you have no consolation nor hope except to be destroyed.

The tide of rebellion had already begun to rise in the district of Mansfeld and in Thuringia when, at the end of April and the beginning of May, Luther left Eisleben and traveled about in the affected districts, unsuccessfully endeavoring to stem the course of the rebellion by his sermons. His journey impressed him with the seriousness of the situation and the danger to his Gospel, nay, even to his life.

"At the risk of body and life," he writes, "I passed through them. In the case of the Thuringian peasants, I personally ascertained that the more one warns and teaches them, the more stubborn, proud, and' furious they wax." [5]

He described his journey to Dr. John Rühel, a counselor of Count Albert of Mansfeld, in terms of great excitement, which dominated him for weeks after the journey. He wrote that "the peasants, no matter how numerous, are after all but robbers and murderers"; "that the devil had particularly aimed at him and by all means wanted him to be dead." He said that after his return home he intended "to prepare himself for death," but would not approve of the deeds of these murderers. He is determined to defy them and all his enemies to the utmost.

Towards the close of his letter, he mentions a particular act, which he is prepared to perform in defiance of the devil: "If I can arrange it, I will, to defy him, marry my Kate before I die, in case I hear that they continue. I hope they shall not deprive me of my courage and joy." [6] This is the first reference to a more intimate relationship existing between him and Catherine of Bora, and to their contemplated marriage.

Luther returned to Wittenberg on May 6. Shortly after his arrival he published a small pamphlet "Against the Murderous and Rapacious Hordes of the Peasants," which is a severe declaration of war against the rebels. It is a demand permeated with the most ardent passion, that the princes crush with inexorable might the rebels in their own

[5] Köstlin-Kawerau, *op. cit.*, Vol. I, p. 709.
[6] Erlangen ed., Vol. LIII, p. 294 (*Briefwechsel*, V, p. 164).

blood. They [the rebellious peasants] "rob and rave and act like infuriated dogs. . . . Therefore, whosoever is able, should dash them
to pieces, strangle them, and stab them, secretly or openly, just as
one is compelled to kill a mad dog." Just now, he says, a prince can
merit Heaven more effectively by shedding blood than by prayer.
He will not forbid the princes to strike at the rebels even "without
a previous offer of justice and fairness," although an evangelical government should make use of this means. He advocates mercy only for
those who have been carried along by the revolutionary movement
involuntarily and under compulsion. Forthwith, however, he drowns
the plea of mercy by shouting: "Strangle them, whoso is able," etc.

The existence of a strange tension in his mind is revealed in his
trembling reference to the proximate end of the world. "Perhaps,"
he says, "God intends to throw the world into a mass of confusion as
a preliminary to the day of Judgment."

Shortly after his anxiety for the "mass of confusion" was relieved
by the victory of the princes, Luther composed a new pamphlet on
the death of Münzer. It was written after the middle of May, and
entitled, "A Horrible Story and Judgment of God on Thomas Münzer." It is a refutation of the latter's prophetical claims and, in addition, an apologia of Luther's own Gospel, directed to his enemies in
the Anabaptist movement. In view of reports of shocking cruelties
perpetrated by the victors, he openly admonishes the princes "to be
merciful towards the prisoners and those who surrendered." This
exhortation, however, was not sufficiently strong. Rühel, counselor to
the Count of Mansfeld, and many others, took offense at the excessive
punishment which Luther wished to inflict upon the guilty parties.
"Many of those who are friendly to you," thus Rühel warns him on
May 26, "deem it strange that you permit the tyrants to strangle
their opponents without mercy. . . . It is necessary that you apolo-
gize for this." Others reproachfully accused Luther of making himself a vassal of princes, because he approved and furthered their
bloody measures. Some apostatized from him, forgetting what, as
Luther complained, God had done for the world through him. The
author of the dreadful pamphlet "Against the Murderous Peasants"
insisted with characteristic obstinacy upon his rights. The devil, he
contended, had possessed Münzer and his hordes. "When the peasants
are seized by such a spirit, it is high time that they be strangulated
like mad dogs," he writes to Rühel in defense of his attitude.

Meantime, however, he was not so indifferent as he pretended to be towards the hostility that had arisen against him. A little while later he published his "Circular Letter on the Severe Booklet against the Peasants," wherein he proposes to render an account of himself to all "wiseacres who would teach him how he should write."

"What I teach and write remains true, even though the whole world should fall to pieces over it." "I will not listen to any talk of mercy, but will give heed to what the Word of God demands."

With his wonted propensity to claim the victory, he repeats his former exhortation: "Let him who is able, in whatsoever manner he can, cut and thrust, strangle and strike at random, as if he were in the midst of mad dogs." "The ass wants to be beaten, and the mob wants to be ruled by force." With the aid of the mob, "the devil intended thoroughly to devastate Germany, since he was unable to prevent in any other way the spread of the evangel." His Gospel was the guiding star of his conduct.

For the rest, Luther says he wrote only for the benefit of the authorities who wished to conduct themselves either as Christians or as honest folks. He hopes to be able to tell the truth "to the ferocious, raging, senseless tyrants" later on.[7]

Apparently he was able to salve his conscience because of his participation in the atrocities connected with the repulse of the Peasants' revolt.

In later years he once said: "I, Martin Luther, have slain all the peasants at the time of their rebellion; for, I commanded them to be killed; their blood is upon me. But I cast it upon our Lord God; He commanded me to speak as I did."

Even in these horrible circumstances he relies upon his usual claim that he is an instrument of God.

In addition to censuring his ferocity, the Catholics frankly reproved him for complicity in the disastrous war, which they attributed to his religious revolution and to his preachers, who had incited the people to rebellion. Cochlaeus and Emser pointed this out in published writings. Erasmus, that acute observer of his age, also told him that he was to blame. Ulric Zasius, a jurist, who at one time had favored him, harbored the same conviction.[8] The author of a polemical work printed at Mayence accused Luther thus: "In your public writings, you declared that they were to assail the pope and the cardinals with every weapon available, and wash their hands in their blood. . . . You called those 'dear children of God and true Chris-

---

[7] Grisar, *Luther*, Vol. II, pp. 208 sqq.
[8] *Ibid.*, pp. 211 sq.

tians,' who make every effort for the destruction of the bishoprics and the extermination of episcopal rule. . . . You called the monasteries dens of murderers, and incited the people to pull them down." [9] Other fair-minded contemporaries held up before his eyes the difference between the rather favorable opinion of the demands of the peasants which he had entertained at the beginning of their uprising, and the violent language in which he assailed them when he believed that his gospel and position were jeopardized by the raging hurricane. They maintained that the characterization of him as the newly risen vassal of the princes was not without foundation.

At the present time even Protestant writers who are unacquainted with the results of historical research, generally lament the unfortunate, nay, disastrous attitude which Luther maintained towards the origin and course of the great social revolution. One of the most esteemed historians of this phase of the Reformation, Fr. von Bezold, recalls Luther's dangerous proclamation of Christian liberty and his criticism of the Catholic clergy. "How else but in a material sense was the plain man to interpret Luther's proclamation of Christian freedom and his extravagant strictures on the parsons and nobles?" He reminds his readers of Luther's mutinous assault upon the decree of the diet of Nuremberg (1524) and of the impassioned invectives he wrote against the "drunken and mad princes." "Luther could not have spoken thus," he writes, "unless he was resolved to set himself up as the leader of a revolution." He wonders "how he could expect the German nation at that time to hearken to such inflammatory language from the mouth of its 'evangelist' and 'Elias' and, nevertheless, to refuse to permit themselves to be swept beyond the bounds of legality and order." However, like other historians who are favorable to Luther, Von Bezold sees an excuse in the latter's "ignorance of the ways of the world and the grandiose onesidedness," which supposedly "attaches to an individual who is filled and actuated exclusively by religious interests." [10]

Genuine religious interests combined with political necessity resulted, at the close of the German revolution, July 19, 1525, in the formation of the League of Dessau, which was patterned after the League of Ratisbon. Joachim of Brandenburg, Henry and Eric of Brunswick, George of Saxony, and Albrecht of Mayence and Magdeburg joined the new League. A report of the Duke of Saxony, who

[9] *Ibid.*, p. 190; cfr. Janssen-Pastor, Vol. II, 18th ed., p. 491.
[10] *Ibid.*, pp. 189 sq. from Bezold, *Geschichte der deutschen Reformation*, Berlin, 1890, p. 447.

was the moving spirit of the League, designated as its object the "extirpation of the root of the rebellion, namely, the damned Lutheran sect," on the ground that the revolt inspired by the Lutheran evangel "could hardly be quelled except by rooting out the Lutherans." [11] At a convention held at Leipsic on Christmas day, 1525, the above-mentioned princes resolved to induce the Emperor to furnish assistance in conformity with the decrees of Worms.

The spiritual estates who assembled at Mayence on November 14 of the same year also adopted a measure with a view to call the Emperor to Germany and to induce him to intervene. Twelve bishoprics of the province of Mayence were represented at this meeting by priests, while the bishops held aloof. When the resolutions taken at Mayence became known to Luther, he attacked them in a pamphlet of terrific vehemence, composed at the behest of the new Elector of Saxony, but it was suppressed because of the intervention of Duke George. [12]

Now that the Catholics had taken a decisive position against the new movement, certain princes who were sympathetic towards Luther also formed an alliance. They had not accepted the invitation extended to them after the suppression of the peasants' uprising to ally themselves with the other victorious princes for the sake of insuring tranquillity for the future. Philip II, the young and proficient landgrave of Hesse, acted as one of the leaders of the new government. He formed an alliance at Gotha with the Elector John of Saxony for the defense and advancement of the new movement and later concluded the treaty of Torgau (May 2, 1526). The threats of the Emperor were of no avail, but merely induced the dukes of Brunswick-Lüneburg and Philip of Brunswick-Grubenhagen, Henry of Mecklenburg, Wolfgang of Anhalt, and Albrecht of Mansfeld to join the Protestant alliance. So little had the Peasants' War taught men that salvation was not to be found in the disruption of the fatherland. Instead of uniting their forces, they were bent upon division.

Above all others Luther himself gave an unhappy example of internal dissension in his attitude towards the peasants. In his writings he treats them as a class with contempt and hatred. The peasantry

[11] *Ibid.*, p. 214.
[12] *Ibid.*, p. 215. The document is printed in the Weimar ed. of Luther's writings, pp. 260 sqq.

repaid him for his attitude during the Peasants' War by open animosity or indifference towards himself and his "gospel." Luther's popularity with the lower classes declined perceptibly. When ill humor was upon him, he could scarcely refrain from heaping insults upon the peasants. [13]

In his estimation they are "swine"; they are "all going to the devil"; they are "not worthy of the many benefits and fruits which the earth yields."

They have not given adequate support to the princes. "You powerless, coarse peasants and asses, would that you were blasted by lightning! You have the best of it, you have the marrow and yet are so ungrateful as to refuse to give anything to the princes?" [14]

He went so far as to declare that it were best if serfdom and slavery were revived.[15]

According to a transcript of a sermon which he delivered in 1526, he declared that the authorities are called by God "to drive, strike, suffocate, hang, decapitate, break on the wheel the mob, so that they [i. e., the rulers] may be feared." As "swine and untamed beasts are driven and forced," so the rulers must insist upon obedience to their laws.[16]

Luther zealously endeavored to gain the support of the high and mighty beyond the circle of the princes and lords who were already attached to his cause. In his desperate boldness he appealed by letter to King Henry VIII of England, who at that time was still loyal to the Catholic Church, requesting that he join him in the interests of his gospel, after he had aspersed him with the basest calumnies. The king sent a very humiliating reply, which was published together with Luther's letter. [17]

In a paroxysm of overwrought expectancy he even applied to Duke George of Saxony, the most active of his opponents, "exhorting" him "to accept the Word of God." On December 22, 1525, he requested the Duke in the humblest terms not to believe the flatterers and hypocrites who surrounded him and to desist from his ungracious resolve of persecuting Luther's teaching, which was certainly "the work of God." It was not "the same thing to fight against Münzer and against Luther." If it came to a test, this could be demonstrated by

---

[13] Grisar, *Luther*, Vol. II, pp. 216 sqq.; IV, pp. 210 sqq.; VI, pp. 70 sqq.

[14] *Ibid.*, VI, 73

[15] *Ibid.*, Vol. II, p. 217.

[16] *Ibid.*, p. 216.

[17] *Briefwechsel*, V, pp. 231 sqq. On the reply (1526), *ibid.*, p. 412.

the effects of his prayer against the Duke. "I regard my prayer and that of my followers as more powerful than the devil himself, and if that were not true, things would long ago have gone differently with Luther; even though people do not yet observe and notice the great miracle which God has wrought in me." [18]

A few days later Luther received a reply from Duke George, which showed him that his plea had failed to make an impression. [19]

In the very beginning of his reply, the Duke returns Luther's compliment concerning the flatterers and hypocrites by inviting him to look for them "in those places where you are called a prophet, a Daniel, an apostle of the Germans, an evangelist." The prophets of old had "all been honest, truthful and pious men," whereas L. was an apostate, surrounded by apostates. He (the Duke) would ever remain loyal to the Church, the rock of truth. There is no new Gospel. Luther pretends to have "pulled it forth from under the bench," but "it were better if it had remained there; for if you bring forth another such gospel we shall not retain a peasant [in Christendom]." "Your fruits cause us to entertain a great horror and aversion for your doctrine and gospels." "When have more sacrileges been committed by con-secrated persons than as a result of your gospel? When was there greater spoliation of religious houses?" The severest censures are accumulated in the Duke's reply. Thus he reproaches Luther for having "slanderously and scandalously" inveighed against the Roman emperor, "to whom we have sworn allegiance"; for having revived all the errors of Hus and Wiclif and despised the councils of the Church; and for having "produced by his doc-trines blasphemy of the Holy Eucharist, the most precious gift of God." Regarding the comparison between Luther and Münzer, he says, he is well aware that Luther is not Münzer, but "that God punished Münzer and his wickedness through us, should be a warning" to Luther. "We shall gladly allow ourselves to be used for this purpose as an unworthy instrument of God's will."

This unmistakable threat is supported by references to Luther's activities in Wittenberg. The Duke points out that Luther had established there an asylum, a citadel for apostates, including such as belonged to his territory. All monks and nuns "who despoil our churches and cloisters," he says, "find a refuge with you." The wretchedness and misery of the fugitive nuns is evident. "Were there ever more fugitive monks and nuns than are now at Wittenberg? When were wives taken away from their husbands and given to others, as is now the case under your gospel? When has adultery been more frequent than since you have written: when a wife cannot become a

---

[18] Erl. ed., Vol. LIII, pp. 338 (*Briefwechsel*, V, p. 281).

[19] *Briefwechsel*, V, pp. 285 sqq. (December 28).

mother by her husband, she shall go to another and bear offspring, which the husband is obliged to support?" [20] Lastly, Duke George mentions Luther's marriage, which had but recently taken place. The devil, he declares, has seduced him through the sting of the flesh. He should have recourse to prayer, in order to free himself from the spell of Eve, who deceived him. If you were able to get along without a wife for a time in order to please man, why are you unable to do so for God's sake? . . . Prostrate yourself at the feet of Christ, "then, by the grace of God, the monk shall be relieved of the nun." The writer recalls the judgment of God, "to whom you both have made a vow" to refrain from unchastity. On his part, he promises to pardon all the injuries inflicted upon him and volunteers to intercede for Luther "with our most gracious Lord, the Emperor," if he will return to his duty and to the Church.

2. LUTHER'S MARRIAGE

The tempestuous year, 1525, as we have seen, was a profoundly stormy one also in Luther's interior life. We have sketched the convulsions into which he was thrown by the peasants' revolt. In addition to this, he was overwhelmed with labor in virtue of his leadership of a new religion. Besides, there were the increasing worries about the durability of the work he had undertaken, and the increase in the so-called temptations which he habitually attributed to the devil.

During that period, Melanchthon, too, was oppressed by worry and lack of sleep; nay, "brought to the brink of the grave." But none of Luther's friends suffered as he did in consequence of the state of fear through which he passed. His correspondence of 1525, especially with Spalatin, reflects these painful struggles. "How does Satan rage," he groans; "how he rages everywhere against the Word." [21] Again he laments: "Satan is enraged against Christ, because he has discovered Him to be the stronger." "The rage of Satan," he says, "is not the least significant sign that the end of the world is approaching." "Of these there are greater signs than many believe." [22] It is astounding that the condition of physical exhaustion which he had experienced shortly before, was not more frequently repeated. Mention was made of the fact that he had once been found lying

[20] Cf. Erl. ed., Vol. XVI, 2nd ed., pp. 513 sq.
[21] Grisar, *Luther*, Vol. II, pp. 167 sq.
[22] *Ibid.*, p. 168.

stretched out on the floor unconscious. He had been overcome by "melancholy and sadness," coupled with incapacity to digest his food.

In 1523 he suffered from a peculiar indisposition. Fever and insomnia were among the symptoms. Johann Eberlin (Apriolus), a renegade Franciscan, and John Magenbuch, a student of medicine at Wittenberg at that time, attended the patient. When his condition had improved, Eberlin sent a detailed account of the sickness, coupled with a request for advice, to his friend Wolfgang Rychard at Ulm, a physician who was personally acquainted with Luther. The account is no longer extant, but the Latin reply addressed to Magenbuch was published by the Protestant historian, Theodore Kolde. It first mentions the necessity of curing Luther's insomnia, calling him the new Elias of whom Eberlin had written, "among other things," that "it is not to be marveled at that a man who, like master Elias, is overwhelmed with so much intellectual labor, should experience dryness of the brain and lose sleep as a consequence." A poultice composed of women's milk and violet oil was to be applied to the patient's head. Then the letter continues: "If the pains of the French sickness disturb his sleep, they may be alleviated by means of a poultice made of the marrow of a stag, mixed with earth-worms, and boiled with some saffron and quicksilver(*vinum sublimatum*). This, if applied on retiring, will induce sleep." [23] These odd remedies are in conformity with the state of medical science at that period. But attention has been attracted by the passage referring to the French sickness. The *malum Franciae* is notoriously syphilis. That Luther was a victim of this disease is not confirmed by any other source, whereas it is known, on the other hand, that this disease spread over Europe from France and Spain as a kind of pestilence at that time. It was also well known from experience that sexual intercourse was not the only means by which venereal diseases could be contracted.

Oppressed by interior afflictions, Luther in March, 1525, wrote a letter to his intimate friend Amsdorf at Madgeburg, beseeching him to come in haste to Wittenberg, in order to aid him "with consolation and friendly services," since he was "very melancholy and much tempted." The captain of the garrison, Hans von Metzsch, also desired his help because of the troubled state of his mind. [24] No other

---

[23] *Ibid.*, p. 163: ". . . *et si cum hoc dolores mali Francie somno impedimento fuerint, mitigandi sunt cum emplastro, quod fit ex medulla cervi,*" etc.

[24] *Ibid.*, p. 169.

details have come down to us. In the case of Metzsch, who was a bachelor, it is highly probable that there was question of interior conditions, such as afflicted him four years later, when Luther urged him to marry forthwith, and hence, it has been assumed by Protestants that Luther's temptations were of the same kind. [25] It was, indeed, related to the serious question of his marriage, which had not as yet been solved at that time.

Although he vigorously recommended marriage to others, even to priests and religious, Luther long resisted the idea of taking a wife unto himself. He feared that such a step would injure his personal reputation and that of his gospel. He foresaw that his opponents would avail themselves of his marriage to launch a more vigorous and successful attack upon him. "We are the spectacle of the world" (*speculum mundi sumus*), was the phrase he used in 1521.[26] Later he said: "The devil keeps a sharp eye on me, in order to render my teaching of bad repute or to attach some shameful stain to it." [27] He knew, moreover—and this helped to decide the issue—that the Elector Frederick, solicitous about conserving the old conditions as much as possible, did not favor the marriage of priests and monks. It is possible also that he was restrained by those moral considerations and qualms of conscience which still survived in him, and at times asserted themselves with tempestuous vigor, since his monastic days, when he had lived in conformity with his sacred vows.

Among others, Spalatin and Amsdorf actively promoted Luther's marriage. On November 24, 1524, he still wrote that he had no inclination to matrimony, but it appears that only a few months afterwards he was ruled by other sentiments. [28] It is quite characteristic of him that these sentiments triumphed at the very height of the Peasants' War, in the days when he was subjected to the greatest mental stress, when he feared that he was destined to die and his work to perish. His titanic nature required a reaction against the devil. Marriage was to furnish this reaction in spite of all the powers of hell and the papacy. His announcement to the counselor of Mansfeld, Rühel, under date of May 4, 1525, referring to "his Katy" and the defiance of the devil, says enough. There are on record other vigorous and defiant declarations relative to his marriage, such as the

[25] *Ibid.*, p. 169. Cfr. Köstlin-Kawerau, M. *Luther*, Vol. I, pp. 796 and 729, note 2.
[26] 1 Cor. IV, 9; cf. *Briefwechsel*, V, p. 218.
[27] *Ibid.*, p. 134.
[28] *Ibid.*, p. 139.

announcement that he was in duty bound to proclaim by his example the value of the married state in the eyes of the world. These declarations were intended to conceal from himself and others the fact that, in the last analysis, the force of nature, which he did not restrain by prayer, impelled him to break the solemn vow he had made.

According to Melanchthon's testimony, Luther entered into too frequent and close relations with the fugitive nuns who had come to Wittenberg. It should be remembered that some of them found lodging with different families in the city, while others found a temporary refuge in Luther's monastery.

In his oral intercourse with people, Luther exercised an even greater freedom of speech than in his writings. He indulged in unbecoming jokes. On Easter, 1525, he jokingly wrote to Spalatin that he himself was a "famous lover" and had set him an example; for he had had three wives on his hands at one time, of whom he had lost two and was scarcely able to keep hold of the third; that it was really astonishing that he had not become a woman long ago, since he had written so often about marriage, and had so much to do with women (*misceor feminis*). [29] The three wives appear to be the three women whom common report had designated as likely to wed Luther.

In the pious style of this letter he described his actual marriage as entirely dependent on the will and direction of God. "Take care lest I do not precede you in marriage, for God is wont to bring to pass what we least expect." In a similar vein he wrote to an inquisitive lady, Argula von Staufen, who inquired about his intentions concerning marriage as early as November, 1524. He told her that he was "in the hands of God, as a creature whose heart He could fashion as He would"; his feelings were yet foreign to matrimony; "but I shall neither set bounds to God's operation in my regard, nor listen to my own heart." [30] Mystical thoughts even in this slippery field. His enemies speak without mysticism. He knows it: "Alas, poor monk, how he must feel the weight of his cowl, how pleased he would be to have a wife"—thus Luther, while he still sojourned at the Wartburg, heard in spirit his Catholic opponents speak against him and his whole undertaking. [31]

These scruples were finally overcome by his peculiar mentality,

[29] *Briefwechsel*, V, p. 157, April 16, 1525. Cfr. Grisar, *Luther*, Vol. II, p. 140.
[30] *Ibid.*, p. 173.
[31] *Ibid.*, p. 87.

"through the operation of God." In a letter dated June 2, 1525, he frankly and freely requested Dr. Rühel to tell the Cardinal of Mayence: "Should my marriage fortify His Grace, I am quite willing to trot on ahead of him by way of example, since it is my intention anyway, before I depart this life, to be in the state of matrimony, which I regard as demanded by God, even if it be nothing more than an espousal or Joseph's marriage." If the Elector desired to know more about the reason why he had deferred his marriage (thus he writes somewhat obscurely to Rühel), tell him "that I have always feared that I was not fit for it." [32] Is it necessary to connect the Joseph's marriage with this unfitness? "Scandal for scandal, necessity breaks even iron and gives no scandal,"—thus he had exclaimed in his published invitation to the nuns to break their solemn vow of chastity. [33] "The desire to be pure"—thus runs another phrase taken from the very heart of his dogmatic system—"may not be brought about by good works, but the birth of Christ must be renewed within us by means of faith. . . . Sin is incapable of injuring me; the force of sin has been spent. We adhere to Him who has vanquished sin." "In sum, despite good works, everything depends upon doctrine and faith." [34] The Catholic view of the matter is that the marriage which he contemplated was not only a shameful sacrilege, but, in addition, invalid because of the sacred vow of chastity made by Luther and its solemn acceptance on the part of the Church.

The flames of the Peasants' Uprising were still ablaze in the background of his mind. The news of the bloody punishment inflicted by the victorious princes harrowed the souls of thousands, but it did not deter Luther from enacting the scene of his marriage before the eyes of the world. On the contrary, the horrors of the age, as we saw, helped to mature his resolution to wed.

His choice fell upon one of the ex-nuns who had left the convent, a circumstance which, in the eyes of Catholics, invested the step he took with the character of a grave scandal. Catherine von Bora herself

[32] Erl. ed., Vol. LIII, p. 308 (Briefwechsel, V, p. 186). On the last passage Enders remarks: "At this late date it is hardly possible to establish whether Albrecht ever entertained the idea of following the example of his relative, the grand master." As late as 1525, after Luther's marriage, he sent a present of 20 gold gulden to Catherine Bora. Köstlin-Kawerau, I, p. 738.—The decisive victory over the peasants at Königshofen was gained on the same day on which Luther promised to "trot on ahead."

[33] Grisar, Luther, Vol. II, p. 143.

[34] Ibid., p. 148.

had been very active in the prosecution of her choice.[35] She spurned other alliances which were open to her. Her mind was set upon higher aims. Either Luther or Amsdorf, she said, would be her husband. She understood how to influence Luther with female artfulness. With her chubby face she was not exactly a striking beauty, but she was endowed with great prudence, energy, and a facile tongue. Luther afterwards said that he had always observed signs of pride about her and pretended that he had not married her for love.[36] She gave promise of becoming an industrious and devoted housewife. In general she satisfied this expectation without any particular display of intellect. The rumors which had arisen to the effect that Luther had had sexual relations with her prior to their marriage are unproved and can be satisfactorily accounted for by the habitual freedom with which he mingled in society and also, partly, by the haste with which he married.

The wedding took place at his home, in the evening of June 13, as the result of a sudden resolve on Luther's part and without the previous knowledge of most of his friends. Bugenhagen, Jonas, Lucas Cranach and his wife, and the jurist Doctor Apel were the only witnesses. Bugenhagen seems to have officiated in his capacity of minister. A public wedding followed on June 27, in which a number of invited guests participated, comformably with the custom that prevailed in those parts.

In one of the first epistolary comments on his marriage, Luther again voices the sentiment with which he had overcome his principal scruple: "I have become so low and despicable by this marriage," he says jokingly, "that I hope the angels will laugh and all the devils weep." Thereby, he says, he had "condemned and challenged the judgment of those who in their ignorance resist things divine."[37] This remark was aimed at his lawyer friend, Jerome Schurf, who had said: "If this monk takes a wife, all the world and the devil himself will laugh, and Luther will undo the whole of his previous work."[38] Schurf afterwards relented somewhat. The jurists generally, how-

[35] Cf. Kroker, *Lutherstudien*, Weimar, 1917, pp. 140 sqq. According to this Protestant writer, Catherine's interview with Amsdorf as mediator, contained in a Vienna manuscript, is quite credible.

[36] Grisar, *Luther*, Vol. II, p. 185.

[37] *Ibid.*, p. 175.

[38] *Ibid.*, p. 176.

ever, supported by canon law, raised objections to the marriage. [39]

Luther, on the contrary, repeatedly indulged in such assurances as: "God willed it"; "the Lord plunged me suddenly into matrimony, while I still clung to quite other views." [40] Jonas, one of the witnesses present on June 13, forces himself to use similar language, although his sentiments were divided. "I do not know," he says, "what strong emotion stirred my soul; now that it has taken place and is the will of God, I wish [them] every happiness." [41] The chief reason for the unprecedented haste was the growth of slanderous rumors. Bugenhagen testifies to this fact with unconcealed discomfiture, when he states that evil tales constrained Luther to marry so unexpectedly. Luther himself announces his marriage to his friend Spalatin in these significant words: "I have shut the mouths of those who slandered me and Catherine von Bora." [42]

For the rest, he is not deficient in adducing reasons for his marriage, but on the contrary, quite resourceful. Beside the law of nature, he mentions the will of God as revealed to him, and the malice of his slanderers. In addition there is the motive that, prior to his imagined assassination, which he believed to foresee in this period of storm and stress, he was bound to "defy the devil" because the latter was causing the world to apostatize from him. [43] Moreover, he was under obligation to annoy and irritate his papistical opponents, "to make them still madder and more foolish" before the end of the world. He likewise felt bound to show obedience to his father, who at one time wanted him to marry. Finally, and as a seventh reason, he was obliged to "have pity" on poor, abandoned Catherine.

A peculiar impression is created by the pleasantries in which he indulges and to which he gives utterance in proportion as the voices of the critics grow louder, even in the ranks of his followers. Thus he writes to his friend Leonard Koppe that he is now "entwined in the meshes of his mistress' tresses." Elsewhere he speaks of the thoughts which come to a man when he sees "two tresses of plaited hair" next to himself upon awakening. [44] Writing to his friend Link, he attempts an indelicate pun on the name of Bora, which sounds like

[39] Erl. ed., Vol. LV, p. 157 (*Briefwechsel*, XI, p. 90).
[40] Grisar, *Luther*, Vol. II, p. 175.
[41] *Ibid.*, p. 174.
[42] *Ibid.*, p. 175.
[43] *Ibid.*, pp. 181 sq.
[44] Köstlin-Kawerau, I, pp. 738 sq.; cfr. Grisar, *Luther*, Vol. II, p. 183.

bier, thus: "I lie on the bier [*Bore* = modern German, *Bahre*], *i. e.*, I am dead to the world. My '*Catena*' [*Kette* or chain] rattles her greetings to you and to your Catena (*catena* meaning chain, hence Katie)." [45] A mannish demeanor, which he perforce observes in his wife, frequently causes him to indulge in a jocose interchange of "Kate" with "Kette" (chain). In the invitation to the public marriage celebration he styles her his "Herr Caterin." Afterwards he frequently calls her his "Herr" (Lord), "Herr Moses," or "Most Holy Doctoress." [46]

His indelicate jests concerning his marriage and the reasons by which he sought to justify it, were of no avail to him in face of the numerous, unpleasant criticisms to which he was subjected. At Wittenberg, those who thought unfavorably of the marriage did their utmost to relay to him every damaging report. The Frankfurt patrician Hamman von Holzhausen wrote as follows to his son Justinian, a student at the University of Wittenberg: "I have read your letter telling me that Martinus Lutherus has entered the conjugal state; I fear he will be evil spoken of and that it may cause him a great secession." [47]

Yet, despite his jocularity, Luther was "sad and uneasy," as Melanchthon says. The latter was filled with bitter indignation. Cautious as he was, he did not express himself openly, but in a Greek letter to his friend Joachim Camerarius he unreservedly revealed his sentiments, or rather the chagrin which struggled within him against his devoted, almost servile demeanor toward the person of Luther. Without reserve he points to the occasion of the misfortune. [48]

In this letter of June 16, 1525, Melanchthon complains, in the first place, that Luther "had not consulted any of his friends beforehand." "Perhaps you will be surprised," he continues, "that at this unhappy time, when upright and right-thinking men everywhere are being oppressed, he is not suffering, but, to all appearance, leads a more easy life ($\mu\tilde{\alpha}\lambda\lambda\text{ov } \tau\text{ov}\phi\tilde{\alpha}v$) and endangers his reputation, notwithstanding the fact that the German nation stands in need of all his wisdom and strength. It appears to me that this is how it happened: The man is approachable in the highest degree, and

---

[45] *Ibid.*, p. 184.

[46] *Ibid.*, Vol. V, p. 309.

[47] *Ibid.*, Vol. II, p. 184.

[48] The whole Greek text of the letter in Grisar, *Luther*, Vol. II, pp. 176 sq., note 3. Cfr. the quotation from Jerome Dungersheim, *ibid.*, p. 145. Melanchthon was more agreeable to Luther and the latter's nearest friends in referring to the marriage.

the nuns who waylaid him with all their snares, have attracted him to themselves. Perhaps his frequent association with them, although he is noble and high-minded, has rendered him effeminate or has inflamed him. In this way it appears that he has come to grief in consequence of the untimely change in his mode of life. It is clear, however, that there is no truth in the gossip that he had previously had illicit intercourse with her [Bora]. Now the thing is done, it is useless to find fault with it, for I believe that nature impels man to matrimony. Even though his life is low, yet it is holy and more pleasing to God than the unmarried state. And since I see that Luther is to some extent sad and troubled about this change in his way of life, I seek very earnestly to encourage him by representing to him that he has done nothing which, in my opinion, can be made a subject of reproach to him."

Concerning Luther's "having come to grief," the writer finds consolation, first, in the fact that advancement and honor are dangerous to all men, even to those who fear God, as Luther does, and, secondly, in the hope that Luther's new state of life may teach him greater dignity, so that he may lay aside the buffoonery (or mania for making ribald jests, $\beta\omega\mu\omega\lambda\omega\chi\acute{\iota}\alpha$), for which we have so often found fault with him. Camerarius, therefore, should not allow himself to be disconcerted, even though he may feel painfully aggrieved. "Through frequent mistakes of the saints of old God has shown us that He wishes us to prove His Word, and not to rely upon the reputation of any man, but only His Word. He would be a very godless man indeed, who, on account of the mistake of the doctor, should judge slightingly of his doctrine."

These forced reflections rather reveal the timid, learned humanist than the open-minded man, let alone the theologian. Melanchthon's displeasure, moreover, may have been increased by the domestic strain that existed between his middle-class wife and Catherine von Bora, who was of noble descent. When Camerarius later on edited the collected letters of Melanchthon, he had the original of the above letter before him, but did not dare to print it as it was, but suppressed some passages and falsified others. The genuine text was not made known until 1876, when it was published by A. Druffel according to the original holograph in the Chigi Library at Rome. The falsified text, however, was incorporated in the *Corpus Reformatorum* (1834), a work which has been frequently used up to the present time.

The newly married couple made their home in the former Augustinian monastery at Wittenberg. Elector John relinquished the one-time abode of the monks, which Luther had turned over to him, to be used by him and his relatives as a residence. Catherine converted the monastic cells into rooms for the students who became her boarders and thereby helped to increase her modest income. With little consideration the entire furnishings of the monastery, including the plates, yea, even pious memorials such as the drinking glass of St. Elizabeth, were turned to profane uses.[49] As master of the house, Luther gradually forgot the sadness and malaise concerning the change in his mode of life, which Melanchthon referred to.

The restless activity with which he continued his literary labors also helped to divert his mind completely at times from his qualms of conscience.

3. LUTHER'S PRINCIPAL WORK: ON THE ENSLAVED WILL

Mention has already been made of Luther's impassioned work, "Against the Heavenly Prophets," which appeared in the beginning of 1525. In a pamphlet boiling with indignation he attacked, about the same time, the two Bulls of Clement VII on the ecclesiastical Jubilee of 1525. Now comes Antichrist again, he writes, with his putrid, reeking, mendacious indulgence-wares, which have long ago been derided by mankind. Germany in the end will fare worse than Jerusalem.[50] He had two "Sermons" printed in order to take the field against the framing of new ecclesiastical ordinances: marriage, the laying aside of the religious habit, the eating of flesh meat and similar matters must not be subject to the tyranny of the pope.[51] An illustrated satire, published by him in the beginning of 1526, was entitled: "The Papacy Described and Depicted in its Members." In this work the secular and regular clergy appear in their habits and are ridiculed in verse. In the introduction Luther says that there is by far not enough of such derision; that kings and princes had flirted with the papal harlot and still indulged in this practice. It is necessary, according to the Apocalypse of St. John (XVII, 1 sqq.), to fill her cup until she lies crushed like dirt in the street, and until there is nothing more despicable than this Jezabel.[52] This he en-

---

[49] Grisar, *Luther,* Vol. III, pp. 313 sqq.

[50] Weimar ed., Vol. XVIII, pp. 255 sqq.; Erl. ed., Vol. XXIX, p. 297.

[51] Köstlin-Kawerau, II, p. 141; Weimar ed., Vol. XV, pp. 571 sqq.; 609 sqq.; Erl. ed., Vol. XVII, 2nd ed., pp. 223 sqq.

[52] Weimar ed., Vol. XIX, pp. 7 sqq.; Erl. ed., Vol. XXIX, pp. 359 sqq.; cfr. Grisar-Heege, *Luthers Kampfbilder* 3 (*Lutherstudien,* n. 5), pp. 24–37, with illustrations.

deavored to do to the best of his ability in many passages of the second part of the *Kirchenpostille*, which he had printed at the end of 1525.

Besides the works mentioned and those which Luther wrote during 1525, especially against the peasants, he now published his exhaustive treatise "On the Enslaved Will" (*De Servo Arbitrio*).[53] According to his own statement, it excels all his other works in importance and is devoted to the principal doctrine and cornerstone of his system.

This Latin work was intended to convey to all countries his defense against Erasmus's attack in the matter of free-will and grace and to demonstrate man's absolute inability to do good. For a long time he had hesitated to engage in an encounter with the great humanist. The pleas of his wife, as he himself confessed at a later period, finally determined him to tackle the task. True, theology was a rather indifferent matter to Catherine, indeed, it was beyond her ken; but she could not tolerate the reproach that Luther was unable to reply.[54] With bitter chagrin she had heard of the triumphs of his adversaries, and that the many humanistic admirers of Erasmus would apostatize from the new "gospel." When Luther began to write his reply, in the second half of 1525, he felt, as he himself expressed it, as if a knife had been placed at his throat by Erasmus.[55] As far as he himself was concerned, he was now resolved to strangle the doctrine of free-will and all its representatives, and to demonstrate that man can do no good without the co-operation of God. He produced a work full of contradictions, marked by passion and irritability, a work which endeavors to worst the adversary with extremes. He not only divests man, by numerous misinterpreted Biblical passages, of his capacity for discerning and choosing what is good, including even the purely naturally good, if God does not substitute his omnipotent efficacy for the human intellect and will; but in Luther's eager desire for combat everything is absolutely subordinated to a blind fate, subject to the sole activity of God. If God foreknows all things, which is beyond controversy, then all things must happen by necessity, and He must be the inevitable cause

---

[53] Weimar ed., Vol. XVIII, pp. 600 sqq.; *Opp. Lat. Var.*, VII, pp. 113 sqq. For detailed information on this work, cfr. Grisar, *Luther*, Vol. II, pp. 223 sqq.

[54] Grisar, *op. cit.*, Vol. II, p. 264.

[55] Köstlin-Kawerau, *M. Luther*, Vol. I, p. 659.

of all. God brings everything to pass even where there is no question of the influence of grace for the salvation of man (*citra gratiam*).

"Whatever God has made," he says, "He moves, impels, and urges forward (*movet, agit, rapit*) with the force of His omnipotence, which none can escape or alter; all must yield compliance and obedience according to the power conferred on them by God. God in particular moves the will "by means of His omnipotence, in consequence of which man necessarily entertains this or that desire, as God gives it to him, and as He forcibly impels it with His movement (*rapit*). . . . Whether good or bad, every volition is driven by force to wish and to act." [56] Luther in other passages conceded the existence of free-will "in inferior matters," but not in respect of the good, which is a contradiction. He himself shows that he "in reality does not wish to be exactly understood in the sense of this restriction." [57]

With the same intensity he assumes the domination of the devil in the realm of morals, but he was not sufficiently concerned with the compatibility of the sovereign authority of God on the one hand and the activity of the devil on the other. "If we believe"—these words of his can be read only with anguish of heart—"if we believe that Satan is the prince of this world, who constantly attacks the Kingdom of Christ with all his might and never releases the human beings he has enslaved without being forced to do so by the power of the Spirit of God, then it is clear that there can be no free-will." [58] Either God or Satan rules mankind. This is his favorite idea, which destroys free-will, the noblest gift of our nature. "The case is simply thus," he resolutely writes; "if God is within us, the devil is not there and we can only desire what is good. But if God is absent, the devil is present, and then we can desire only what is evil."

"The human will," he continues with a figure of speech which has become famous, "stands like a saddle-horse between the two. If God mounts into the saddle, man wills and goes forward as God wills. . . . But if the devil is the horseman, then man wills and acts as the devil wills. He has no power to run to one or the other of the two riders and offer himself to him, but the riders fight to obtain possession of the animal." [59]

With a horrible temerity Luther declares this viewpoint to be the essence and kernel of religion. It is his opinion that, without it, the dogma of the Redemption falls, since with free-will Christ would lose His unique and eminent significance, human works would

[56] Grisar, *Luther*, Vol. II, p. 265.
[57] *Ibid.*
[58] *Ibid.*, p. 273.
[59] *Ibid.*, p. 274.

prevail, and self-righteousness, Pharisaism, and hypocrisy would occupy the place of self-effacing humility.

Thus he leads his readers back to the pseudomystical errors whence his entire system of theology sprang.

Protestant investigators, who generally display annoyance at these propositions, incidentally and briefly touch upon the question whether this "form of piety is not to be judged pathologically." [60] The pseudomystical traces and many of the details concerning the mental constitution of the youthful Luther, which have been heretofore adduced, furnish an affirmative reply to this question. Thus the Protestant theologian Kattenbusch describes Luther's frame of mind when he composed the latter work, as "not normal" nor "religiously healthy." [61] And Otto Scheel speaks of the "fundamental idea" of the "De Servo Arbitrio" as the product of a morbid frame of mind.[62]

As a matter of fact, the morbid state of Luther's soul repeatedly breaks forth in this book. He realizes that the predestination of the damned is an inference from his denial of free-will. He states that he often took grave offense at it and "arrived at the verge of despair," so much so that he "wished he had never been born." But a marvelous change had come over his ideas. He recognized "how salutary and how near to grace this despondency was"; for whoever shares the conviction that all things are dependent upon the will of God, choses nothing for himself in despairing of himself, but only expects God to act. He is next to salvation, although he be dead and strangled in consequence of his consciousness of guilt, and spiritually immersed in hell. Such a one is succored by the belief that the merits of Christ cover his sins, the *sola fides, i. e.*, the conviction that man is justified by faith alone. "This," he says, "is familiar to everyone who has read our works." [63]

This doctrine of determinism, like his whole system, grew out of personal motives and was patterned after his own abnormal mental states.

In his acrobatic exposition he even goes so far as to idolize the consolation which he derives from his denial of free-will: "Without this doctrine I believe I would be constantly tortured by uncertainty and compelled to

[60] Julius Köstlin; cfr. Grisar, *Luther*, Vol. II, p. 274.
[61] *Ibid.*, p. 284.
[62] *Ibid.*, p. 284.
[63] *Ibid.*, p. 279.

expunge all my work. My conscience would never enjoy certain ease. . . . If free-will were offered to me, I would not accept it at all. I would not want anything to be placed within my power, so as to give a practical proof of my salvation, because I would nevertheless fear that I could not withstand the spiritual dangers and the attacks of so many devils." [64]

He arbitrarily conceals from himself predestination to hell with its horrors, but firmly insists upon the monstrosity of the absolute predestination to eternal punishment of human beings who could not act otherwise than they did. He suggests that we simply should not think of it! He has recourse to a mysterious *hidden God,* who, in His unlimited majesty, may have other norms that our human sense of justice can devise. The essence of God is truly inscrutable. The statement in the Apocalypse that God wills the salvation of all men, applies to the *Deus revelatus* in the Gospel of Christ; but there also exists a hidden God, a *Deus absconditus,* whose decrees may be quite different.

Relative to these doctrines, the Protestant theologian Kattenbusch, whom we have already quoted, says: "Luther expressly advances it as a theory that God has two contradictory wills, the secret will of which no one knows anything, and another which He causes to be proclaimed; . . . in other words, that He is free to lie." [65] No less frank are the words of another Protestant theologian, A. Taube: From Luther's statements we must "conclude that God, as He is preached [in Sacred Scripture], is not in every instance the same God as He who actually works, and that in some cases in His revelation He says what is quite untrue." [66] It cannot be denied that Luther, led astray by Ockham's theory of an arbitrary God, introduced a new concept of God, which, however, is forthwith disproved by the inference just described.

Now, while he upholds, by means of his *Deus absconditus,* the absolute predestination to hell of every man as a possibility, and while he represents it as an actuality in the case of such as are already damned, he does not wish this subject to be made a topic of reflexion and discussion. It is a point which he emphasized innumerable times in his books and letters. As a means of preventing despair he recommends, in an almost importunate manner, that no

[64] *Ibid.,* pp. 268 sq.

[65] Kattenbusch, *"Deus absconditus bei Luther,"* in the *Kaftanfestschrift,* pp. 170 sqq. Grisar, *Luther,* Vol. II, p. 169, note 1.—Isaias (45, 15) praises the *Deus absconditus,* but as God of mercy who wills to save all men. Thus in verse 19, according to Luther's own translation: "I have not said in vain to the seed of Jacob: Seek me." Cf. verses 22 and 24. —R. Otto (*Das Heilige,* 7th ed., Breslau, 1922) says (p. 118): Luther flees from the *Deus absconditus* "like a badger into the fissures of a rock," and (p. 120), owing to his personal states of fear he reduces the whole of Christianity to fiduciary faith. According to Scheel, Luther with his *iustitia passiva,* introduces a "completely new theory of God." (Article, "Iustitia Passiva" in the Briegerfestschrift. Cf. Grisar in the *Zeitschrift für katholische Theologie,* Vol. XLII, 1918, p. 599.

[66] Grisar, *Luther,* Vol. II, p. 269. Cfr. *ibid.,* p. 263.

thought be given to predestination; God, the Incomprehensible, must be adored in silent submission. In his practical work, on the other hand, he frequently writes as though man's salvation lay solely within his own power, by co-operating with divine grace. Thus involuntarily he returns to the Catholic doctrine.

There is no fundamental distinction in the dismal doctrine of predestination as taught by Luther, Calvin, and Zwingli, except that the latter two, particularly Calvin, are more systematic in their exposition of it. Köstlin, the biographer of Luther, is constrained to concede this when he says: "In the resoluteness with which Luther accepts the most rigorous consequences of the doctrine of predestination he is essentially one with Zwingli and Calvin, the other leaders of the Reformation." [67]

Luther appeals to the authority of St. Augustine, that famous Doctor of the Church, in confirmation of his doctrine. But he wofully distorts Augustine's utterances and merely asserts without proof: "He is on my side." [68]

Luther never abandoned his position relative to determinism and predestination, though he modified his expressions. He characterized his book "De Servo Arbitrio," while still in its formative stage, as a "thunderbolt" against the Erasmic and popish heresy of free-will,[69] and always regarded it as a work which his opponents "shall not be able to refute in all eternity." [70] "I do not recognize any of my writings as genuine," he writes as late as 1537 to Capito, "except those on the Enslaved Will and the Catechism." He says he would not shed any tears if the others should be lost.[71]

It is incomprehensible that some Protestant theologians extol the deeply religious spirit which is supposed to prevail in the "De Servo Arbitrio." [72] They admire its profound humility in the presence of God's omnipotence and the self-annihilation that pulsates throughout the book. But they do not reflect that the motto of the unfortunate treatise is not true humility, but the suicide of human nature. In his preface to the new critical edition, the Weimar editor styles the "De Servo Arbitrio" "the most splendid Latin and perhaps

---

[67] Köstlin-Kawerau, M. *Luther*, Vol. I, p. 664.
[68] *Ibid.*
[69] Grisar, *Luther*, Vol. II, p. 284.
[70] *Ibid.*, p. 291.
[71] *Ibid.*, p. 292.
[72] *Ibid.*, pp. 292 sq.; cfr. Vol. VI, pp. 452 sq.

the most splendid polemical work of Luther," [73] but adds: "It must not be concealed that the whole conception has a strongly pantheistic and mechanistic appearance." [74]

Luther's attitude towards the Commandments of God also aroused strong opposition. If man is not free to observe the Commandments, why should there be any at all, and why should punishment be threatened for those who despise them? In consequence of this and other writings of Luther, many placed themselves beyond the Commandments. "Let us do as we please." [75] Luther strongly opposes this tendency. But his defense of the Commandments consists in this: God gives His commandments with the wise intention of teaching us how little we can do of our own accord. The law and its threats should arouse within us a sense of our incompetence, enkindle a desire for redemption by grace, and thus lead us to salvation through self-annihilation.

The assertion of God's relation to sin was equally unintelligible to many readers of Luther's treatise.

If man lacks free-will, who is it that causes sin? Luther feels that it will not do to hold God directly responsible for sin. He does not assert that there is an immediate impulse to evil originating with God. But, quite consistently with his system, he speaks of the treachery of Judas thus: "His [Judas'] will was the work of God; God by His almighty power moved his will as He does all that is in this world." [76] He holds that Adam, at least in spirit, was abandoned by God in Paradise and placed in a situation in which he could not but fall.

"He is God," says Luther, "and therefore there is no reason or cause of His willing," because no creature is above Him, and He Himself is "the rule of all things." Whatever He does in His arbitrariness is good, "not because He must or ought to will thus." "His [man's] will must have reason

<hr />

[73] *Ibid.*, p. 284. Shortly after its appearance, the work was translated into German by Jonas under the title, *"Dass der freie Wille nichts sei."* Recently a new edition of this translation was published by Gogarten, with an introduction which strongly assails the appreciation of Luther as a hero of civilization. Albert Ritschl styled the treatise *"De Servo Arbitrio"* "an unfortunate piece of bungling" (Joh. v. Walter, *Das Wesen der Religion nach Erasmus und Luther*, 1906, p. 124). In 1559, Melanchthon, referring to the fantastic ideas of Luther contained in this work, speaks of them as *"stoica et manichaea deliria."* Cfr. Grisar, *Luther*, Vol. VI, p. 153.

[74] *Ibid.*, p. 284.

[75] *Ibid.*, p. 288.

[76] *Ibid.*, p. 282.

and cause, not so, however, the will of the Creator." [77] These are Ockhamistic subtleties and aberrations.

Relative to the Fall of Adam the essential point is that his sin, as the Protestant Kattenbusch puts it, "is caused by God," whereas "fundamentally nothing is gained" by the other reflections of Luther.[78] And that is the sin of our first parents, through which, according to Luther, the whole human race was plunged into original sin, a misfortune which—again following Luther—radically tainted the entire race.

Since Luther held such views of God and sin already at an earlier period of his career, it is no wonder that a controversy arose at Erfurt among the preachers of the new religion, which could not be terminated by the treatise "On the Enslaved Will." In reference to this controversy Luther's friend Lang, the leader of the Reformation at Erfurt, wrote to him for information. "I perceive," Luther replied, "how indolent you are whilst Satan is on the offensive everywhere." "Why do you quarrel among yourselves about the evil which God does . . . we do evil because God ceases to work in us," etc.[79] This advice did not restore peace at Erfurt, since the preachers there were a quarrelsome lot. Luther refused to send them an official letter of instruction as he had been requested to do by Lang, but declared: "Let them practice faith and love; everything else is well known."

Erfurt, the city which had harbored the whilom peaceful cells of Luther and his fellow-monks, was on the verge of a profound agitation.

4. THE STORMS AT ERFURT

The city of Erfurt, which was subject to the archbishop of Mayence, affords a typical illustration of the storms which accompanied the progress of the religious revolution in 1525. It will repay us, therefore, to review the events which occurred there in the course of this year, and Luther's attitude towards them.

After the first "anticlerical upheaval" (*Pfaffensturm*), Luther, who had just returned from the Wartburg, issued a printed "Epistle to the Church of Erfurt," warning the members against disturbances

[77] *Ibid.*, pp. 282 sq.
[78] *Ibid.*, p. 283.
[79] April 12, 1522 (*Briefwechsel*, III, p. 331.)

and setting forth his own attitude: "As yet I have not raised a finger against them [the papists]; Christ has slain them with the might of His tongue." [80] At Erfurt, he delivered a sermon which was calculated to arouse strong animosity against "the fat and lazy priests and monks," as he characterized them, "who only feed their big bellies." "We must crush the seed of this Satanic head." He boldly maintained that the secular rule of the archbishop of Mayence had no right to exist, and "in virtue of the orthodox faith you are spiritual and should judge all things." "Faith does everything, and good works, too, result from it." [81]

The religious upheaval at Erfurt, however, failed to produce these good fruits, but engendered bad moral conditions, so that even Eobanus Hessus, a friend of the Reformation, known as "King of poets," wrote in 1524: "Immorality, corruption of youth, contempt of learning, and dissensions, such are the fruits of your Evangel." "Oh, unhappy Erfurt!"—he cries in a letter of this same year, in which he stigmatizes "the outrageous behavior of these godless men of God," namely, the apostate priests and new preachers. He sees the battle-field of the passions tinged with "blood." [82]

The scholarly Augustinian, Bartholomew Usingen, who had once been Luther's professor at the University of Erfurt, also predicted a bloody revolution for the same year (1524), which was to break out at Erfurt and reach the most remote districts. In his gloomy forebodings he prophesied that the religious storm would bring about the decline of the empire and the loss of Germany's ancient greatness. "Why," he remonstrates with one of the revolutionary preachers of Erfurt, "why have you ordered out the pickax, the mattock, and the spade in your sermons, if the Word of God is sufficient for the Church? Why have you called out to the mob that the peasant must abandon the soil in order to come to the aid of the gospel?" [83] Oblivious of the debt of gratitude which he owed him, Luther, who was familiar with the energy with which Usingen championed the cause of the Church, denounced the venerable man as a fool. In a tone of frivolity he jeered at the teachers of the university to which he was indebted for his education, and who still remained Catholic, decrying them as the "sophists of the biretta and the pointed hats."

[80] July 10, 1522; Erl. ed., Vol. LIII, p. 139 (*Briefwechsel*, III, p. 431).
[81] Grisar, *Luther*, Vol. II, p. 347.
[82] *Ibid.*, pp. 349 sq.
[83] *Ibid.*, pp. 336 sqq., where proof is adduced for the following statements.

The Reformation received every imaginable assistance from the majority of the town-councilors at Erfurt. Thus encouraged, Johann Lang, a renegade Augustinian monk, proposed the slogan, "The gospel must be sustained by the aid of the sword." [84] The Catholic canons of St. Mary's and St. Severin's were repeatedly compelled to protest against acts of violence. By confiscating their possessions the town-council intended to force them and the remaining clergy to yield. On April 27, 1525, when the revolutionary spirit already stalked through wide stretches of Germany, and the war-cries of the peasants resounded, the treasuries of the two afore-mentioned churches were subjected to a close search by the magistrate. Splendid works of art, which had been given by the forefathers, and faithfully preserved by the Church, were squandered and destroyed.

When the day of the peasants' revolt dawned in the vicinity of Erfurt, they impetuously demanded the new liberties. Their object was equality with the citizenry, who were hostile to the magistrates. They made their peremptory demands in the name of the new gospel. "God has enlightened us to march upon Erfurt with arms," one of their leaders exclaimed. [85] The representatives of fourteen villages in the district of Erfurt, having met in a tavern, swore "with upraised hands" "to fortify the Word of God, and to form an alliance for life, with the object of abolishing the ancient tribute of which they had freed themselves." On April 25 or 26, they appeared with scythes, hoes, and carbines beneath the walls of the city. The magistrate at once conceived the clever idea of diverting the malcontents upon the clerical estate and the Electorate of Mayence. Having completed their negotiations with Hermann von Hoff, president of the Erfurt town-council and an opponent of the clergy, they opened the gates of the city to the threatening mob, on condition that it would spare the property of the citizens. The palace of the archbishop and the custom house, however, were turned over to them. The salt-kilns and almost all residences of the clergy were eventually stormed and plundered by the mob, who with unspeakable barbarity disposed of the sacred vessels, images, and relics belonging to the churches, assisted by many of the lower citizenry. "Lutheran preachers like Eberlin von Günzburg, Aegidius

[84] *Ibid.*, p. 350.
[85] *Ibid.*, pp. 357 sqq., there further proofs are adduced, particularly from the excellent work of Eitner, *Erfurt und die Bauernaufstände im 16. Jahrhundert*, Halle, 1903.

Mecheer, and Johann Lang, mingled with the citizens and peasants before the palace at Mayence and harangued them." Every convent occupied by nuns was confiscated, and the inmates were expelled without mercy in order to furnish quarters for the peasants. The Augustinian monastery, where Luther had sojourned as a monk, was desecrated by the invaders.

Sentence of death was pronounced upon the ancient cult by the adoption of a resolution which decreed that pastors were to be installed and deposed only by the congregations and that "the pure Word of God" alone was to be preached in the pulpit, "clearly and without any addition of human commandments, ordinances, and doctrines." Johann Lang, "the apostate, fugitive, and married monk," as a contemporary Catholic writer calls him, was appointed preacher at the cathedral. Most of the clergy left the city.

With the consent of the magistrate the archiepiscopal rule was declared terminated.

The magistrate was soon deposed and replaced by two committees, one constituted of the lower citizenry, the other of the peasants, who jointly assumed the government of the city. The former members of the magistracy were threatened with decapitation. The preachers, however, succeeded in restoring their authority.

As a norm for the future guidance of the community, which was deeply divided, twenty-eight very accommodating articles were proposed by the town-council and received the "new seal" of the municipality and the peasantry. The preaching of the pure Word of God and the free election of pastors again headed the list. For the rest, the citizens and peasants hedged the town-council about with many limitations. On account of certain debatable points, it was agreed to leave the regulation of the town to Luther, who, however, wisely refused. His intervention could only have made matters worse. He was not qualified for such pacific labors and had no talent for public organization. Moreover, at that time, when the defeat and punishment of the peasants had already begun, he was agitated by that unhappy frenzy against the mob which crops out in his writings. On this account, the twenty-eight articles were placed before him only for his written opinion.

The town-council knew how little the demands which had been extorted from it and which were so favorable to the peasants, could be expected to meet with the approval of Luther. In matter of fact he pronounced the articles absolutely "inept" and wrote [86] that they clearly revealed that they were being proposed by "men who are too prosperous," whose demands were being made at the expense of the magistracy and to the detriment of the public welfare. He claimed that "they wanted to subvert the existing order of things with unheard-of presumption and malice"; that these articles reduced the council to the level of servants of the community; that they caused the "city of Erfurt to be lost" to the princes; and that it had even been resolved to withhold from the Saxon Elector, the legal protector of Erfurt, the tax to be paid by his subjects for protection. The "mob" should not be allowed to govern all things, to bind the magistrate hand and foot and set it up as an "idol" and let it see how "the horses drive the coachman." It is worthy of note that, whilst he was in this restraining mood, Luther found it quite inadmissible that congregations should appoint their own pastors and demanded that the town-council should at least exercise a certain "supervision" in this matter.

However, he was pleased with that article which provided that persons who plied an indecent trade should no longer be tolerated, and that the "house of common women" should be closed—a measure which he advocated also for other cities.[87] For the rest, we may remark that, during the archiepiscopal régime, a house of correction for the punishment of loose women had existed at Erfurt, but had been razed to the ground when the peasants entered the town.

Luther is silent about the abolition of the sovereignty of the archbishop of Mayence. In a sharp letter issued May 26 through his viceregent, Archbishop Albrecht had refused to relinquish his rights over the city and demanded the expulsion of the Lutheran sects and an expiatory tribute. But the Elector John of Saxony promised the town-council that he would support them on the religious issue and act as their "liege lord, territorial and protecting prince," since he, too, was devoted to the Word of God. Relative to the secular government of Mayence, John, no less than the other protector, Duke George of Saxony, insisted upon an amicable understanding. This demand became effective only after the Elector of Mayence threatened to appeal for armed intervention to the dreaded Swabian League. The remnant of the peasants withdrew from the

---

[86] On September 19; Erl. ed., Vol. LVI, p. XII (*Briefwechsel*, V, p. 243).
[87] Grisar, *Luther*, Vol. II, p. 359.

occupied city, Albrecht's sovereignty was reëstablished, and the expelled clerics were reinstated. They had yielded only to superior force. The Catholic element at Erfurt was still numerous, wealthy, and influential. The city council was compelled to promise the Archbishop to reconstruct the demolished buildings and to make restitution, as far as possible, for the spoliation which he and the churches had sustained. In addition, the town-council was obliged to pay him 2,500 gulden and to indemnify the two collegiate churches, namely, the cathedral and the church of St. Sever, to the extent of 1,200 silver marks. These two stately churches have remained in the possession of Catholics up to the present time.

On the other hand, however, Lutheranism obtained complete liberty to propagate itself. At the time of the restoration of the two churches, Cardinal Albrecht, who was formally reinstated in 1530, declared with a striking and far-reaching indulgence, "as regards the other churches, and matters of faith and ritual, we hereby and on this occasion neither give nor take, sanction nor forbid anything to any party." [88]

The Augustinian monastery at Erfurt, that submerged seat of Catholic piety, did not survive the revolution of 1525. On July 31 of that year, Adam Horn, the last prior, received permission from John von Spangenberg, the vicar-general of the dispersed Congregation, to abandon the monastery, since he was no longer safe in it. Usingen joined the brethren of his Order at Würzburg. The last trace of Nathin is found in 1523. Of an aged monk, who remained loyal to the Church and was compelled to live outside the cloister, Flacius Illyricus relates that he used to recall the religious zeal which Luther had displayed in the monastery and his dutiful observance of the rule. [89]

A courageous and eloquent Franciscan, Dr. Conrad Kling, rallied the Catholics of Erfurt about himself. When he preached in the capacious hospital, the audience was so numerous as to overflow into the churchyard outside.

The Catholic members of the town-council, encouraged by Kling, to the annoyance of Luther championed the cause of Catholicity with such success that the Lutheran preachers saw their mission in the city rendered precarious. They complained to Luther that their

[88] *Ibid.*, p. 361.
[89] *Ibid.*, p. 361, note 2.

revenues were restricted and they were reduced to "hunger, misery, and destitution." The people demanded to know who had sent them. Suffering from public contempt, they thought of abandoning the town, when, in 1533, Luther encouraged them to remain and sustained them by means of a letter which he had composed jointly with Melanchthon and Jonas.[90] Their mission, he said, was not to be contested, since they had been "openly and unreservedly" called by the town-council; they should "be patient for a year or a short time." Referring to the end of the world, he said that the treatment to which they were subjected was but an "unsightly, horrible aspect of the end of the world, and of the last fury and wrath of Satan, equally terrible to behold." He promised to appeal to the Elector of Saxony, "who does not favor the religious services of the papists," against the reprobate monk Kling.

The acts of the soldiery against the peasants, and Luther's state of mind against the mob, inspired him at that time to compose a work which he curiously entitled: "Whether Soldiers can be in the State of Grace." [91] He says previous ages did not raise this question, and pretends it was the first time that it was found necessary to solve a case of conscience for the soldiers. He tries to show that it is "divine" to subdue the mob and unjust enemies with violence. The plea sounds like a justification of his pronouncements against the murderous peasants, especially when he asserts that it is God, not man, who destroys unjust, hostile force. "It is God who hangs, quarters, decapitates, slaughters, and makes war." [92] Subjects—the mob—may in no instance constitute themselves judges of authority. It is foolish to yield too much to the mob, lest it become frenzied; the mob is rather to bear and suffer the utmost, as a Christian duty, even if the authorities do not observe the oaths they have taken. No one may rise against tyrants; but if the masses, nevertheless, expel or slaughter them, it is to be regarded as a divine fate; the sword of Damocles hangs suspended over their heads all the time.

5. THE NEW STATE CHURCH

Luther was absolutely right in assuring the Erfurt preachers that the Elector John of Saxony was pro-Lutheran. In fact, he put the case too mildly when he said that John did not favor the religious

---

[90] Erl. ed., Vol. LV, p. 25 (Briefwechsel, IX, p. 341).

[91] Weimar ed., Vol. XIX, pp. 628 sqq.; Erl. ed., Vol. XXII, pp. 244 sqq.; this pamphlet was written towards the close of 1526.

[92] Erl. ed., Vol. XXII, p. 250.

services of the papists. The Elector had been completely won over to the new religious system by Luther, who knew how to approach and influence Frederick's successor, who was inadequately instructed in matters of religion.

John of Saxony became the patron of Lutheranism and the founder of the State Church.

The state-controlled Church was greatly promoted by the status of the congregations which had adopted the new religion, but were too weak to stand on their own feet. Sprung from the contests which the members waged against one another, and organized in the main as a result of the violent procedure of the magistrate, these congregations promised little durability, because of the want of internal cohesion. Hence, as was indicated before, Luther considered the territorial lords as the natural pillars of his Church. The secular rulers alone were in a position to defend the preachers of the new evangel, to remove undesirable persons from office, and to overcome the external consequences of the existing dissension among the citizens.

Thus, with Luther's co-operation, the system of territorial churches was born as the result of a certain necessity. It was nurtured and strengthened by the prospects of secularization, held out to the territorial rulers, of the rich ecclesiastical possessions, and also by the prospect of an increase of authority. The prevailing tendency of the age, which consisted in the self-exaltation of the powers of the princes and their endeavor to make themselves independent of the Empire and the authority of the Emperor, aided them very effectively. Since their victory over the peasants, the politicians felt that an approximation to absolutism was the only salvation in these chaotic conditions. For parishes and schools were threatened with extinction, and the rural population was sinking back into barbarism. Hence, it appeared to be the principal social and spiritual task of the government to take complete charge of church affairs, not only for individual communities, but for the country as a whole. After the social revolution had been crushed, the influential classes benevolently and submissively co-operated with the princes to forestall future revolutions.

As long as Spalatin occupied the position of court-preacher at the court of the new Elector of Saxony, he was a helpful assistant to Luther in the latter's attempt to establish a compulsory national church. Both men regarded it as their primary duty to fan the flames of the anti-Catholic prejudice of their ruler.

Spalatin wrote to the Elector on October 1, 1525: "Dr. Martinus also says that your Electoral Grace is on no account to permit anyone to continue the un-Christian ceremonies any longer, or to start them again." [93]

In a letter to Spalatin, dated November 11, which was intended for the Elector, Luther expounded the thesis that by stamping out the Catholic worship rulers would not be forcing the faith on anyone, but merely prohibiting such open abominations as the Mass. Moreover, he demanded that the right to emigrate should be extended to obstinate papists. [94]

The Elector was unable to resist this powerful appeal.

On February 9, 1526, he received a letter directly from Luther, which was intended to encourage him to attack the idolaters. Should he protect them, "every abomination would burden his conscience before God." In the second place, he should reflect that "mutiny and factionism" would sweep over the cities and the rural districts in consequence of the existence of diverse kinds of worship. Again he declares: "Only one kind of doctrine may be preached in any one place." John replied in a friendly tone, assuring Luther that he would "know how to conduct himself in a Christian and correct manner."

Soon the Elector intervened in the appointments to ecclesiastical positions and in the government of the new religious society. The principle of territorial sovereignty in ecclesiastical affairs was established rather by practice than by open declarations. With astounding dexterity Luther often acted as if he regarded the territorial lord as a kind of patriarchal ruler, similar to the rulers of Israel in the Old Testament. He gradually advanced to this position after 1520, when, in his sermon "On Good Works," in which he addressed the secular authority for the first time, he demanded that "kings, princes, and the nobility" should commence to reform ecclesiastical conditions according to his ideas. [95] As long as possible, he had upheld his impractical ideal of a congregational religion, especially since the Elector Frederick was not in favor of a more compact organization of the new religious system. But now, under John, his policy, openly favored by the court, was completely changed.

[93] Grisar, *Luther*, Vol. II, p. 331.
[94] *Ibid.*
[95] K. Holl, *Luther*, 2nd ed., 1923, p. 327.

He considered three points in particular.[96] First the disposition to be made of the property belonging to the Catholic Church. Who was to get this property when confiscated? With a highly characteristic conception of jurisprudence, he answers this question thus: As a matter of course, it accrues to the territorial lord, though it should be preserved as much as possible for ecclesiastical uses. And it will be necessary that the ministers of the new religion be adequately supported therefrom. None other than the prince can look to this, since the nobility, as experience has demonstrated, endeavor to enrich themselves by the confiscation of church property under all kinds of pretexts; and also because the newly established congregations show themselves unwilling or incapable of supplying the ordinary necessities of the preachers.

The second point he stresses is this: Consistent with the utmost liberty possible, doctrine and ritual ought to be made uniform throughout the land; which is impossible without the help of government. As a result Luther now (1525) begins to direct his efforts towards a visitation, to be ordered by the princes.

The third point is the continuation of the Mass in many places. "The unity of our Church," says Luther, "suffers in consequence thereof." [97] The prince alone, he says, can suppress the Mass—an object which Luther pursued with passionate zeal.

On the thirty-first of October he conferred with the Elector relative to the disposition of the church property and the support of his ministers. As John does not show himself averse, Luther takes up the second point, the internal condition of the congregations. This he does at first by innuendo, then by definitely indicating his wishes.[98] On November 30, 1525, he proposed a visitation to be held under the auspices of the Elector. He suggests "that Your Electoral Grace order the visitation of all parishes in the entire principality," so that evangelical preachers may be appointed and properly supported for the congregations that desire them.

The desired visitation was realized by the electoral instruction of 1527, which definitely completed the régime of territorial churches. True, it was not all done according to Luther's notions. He grievously complained of the undue restraints which the State imposed upon the authority of the Church. Thus the contradictoriness of his attitude avenged itself upon him.

Nothing is so little to the point as to say of Luther's attitude and view of things as Holl does: "Everything has been clearly and

96 Cfr. for the following Holl, *op. cit.*, pp. 361 sqq.
97 *Ibid.*, p. 363, n. 1.
98 *Ibid.*, p. 364.

harmoniously worked out." [99] In reality, Luther does not conceive of the Church as a true society and is as little able to appreciate a Christian State "as a Christian cobbler shop," to quote another Protestant author, since he divides the kingdom of the world from the kingdom of God by a deep chasm.[100] Because he repudiated both the ancient Church and the traditional conception of the State, he had no foundation for his church except the good pleasure of the princes.

6. PROGRESSIVE DESTRUCTION OF CATHOLICISM

1525 was a year of tempests in the history of the propagation of Lutheranism, which brought great conquests. The extent to which the religious revolution spread among the higher and lower strata of society was unexpectedly great.

The want of rapidity in the progress of the new movement in the Electorate of Saxony, attributable to the dissatisfaction of the rural population with the leadership of Luther, was supplied by the activity of the territorial government, which was counseled and directed by Lutheran politicians who were zealous for the interests of the crown, particularly by the electoral chancellor, Gregory Brück. It was also supplied by the married preachers, who congregated in this Electorate, and not in the least by the municipal magistrates who, in virtue of their new rôle, had suddenly been projected into important cultural and civil positions.

In the adjacent Duchy of Saxony, on the other hand, the watchfulness and energy of Duke George, the territorial ruler, prevented the new religion from spreading to any large extent.

The gates of Hesse were opened to the new religion by the young Landgrave, Philip II, who has been undeservedly surnamed "the Magnanimous." As a result of the frivolous and immoral life of his mother (commonly called Madame Venus), this ruler lacked a strict religious and moral training. He was lively and talented, but devoid of religious sentiments or wants. A regent when but twenty years old, Philip II met Melanchthon and became interested in Lutheranism. On July 18, 1524, he issued a mandate in which he granted free scope to the propagation of Luther's teachings within his

99 *Ibid.*, p. 350.
100 *Ibid.*, p. 347.

jurisdiction. He embraced the new religion himself and obstinately defended this step against the well-intentioned and forceful remonstrations of his father-in-law, Duke George. In March, 1525, on the occasion of a meeting with the Elector John of Saxony and the latter's son, Philip assured them that he intended to dedicate his country and his people, nay, his very life to the new gospel. He spurned the invitation of Duke George of Saxony to join the League of Dessau for the pacification of Germany after the Peasants' War, and for the suppression of the ferment of unrest, namely, the Lutheran religion.

In opposition to that League, Landgrave Philip conceived the idea of a military league of evangelicals, which was formed at Torgau and Gotha between him and the Elector of Saxony. None of the German princes were more determined than the young ruler of Hesse to gain recognition for this League and to extend it far and wide. In the background of his mind, however, were other soaring ambitions. It was his intention to resist the power of the Hapsburgs and to frustrate the contemplated elevation of the Archduke Ferdinand to the imperial throne. "With Philip's espousal of the evangelical cause," says Theodore Kolde, "a political element [rectius, a new political element] entered into nascent Protestantism." [101] It redounded to its extreme advantage, but also brought with it many disadvantages. For his bold policy soon induced Philip to form a close alliance with the South German and Swiss Zwinglians, with whose aid he expected to oppose the Emperor. His policy, however, was an explosive that created internal dissension.

Philip's dictatorial conduct manifested itself when, on July 12, 1526, accompanied by 200 cavaliers, he entered Spires to attend the diet, where, despite the objections of the presiding officer, Archduke Ferdinand, he permitted the preaching of "evangelical" sermons from the open gallery of his headquarters, which was accessible to the public. His reply to the Archduke's remonstrances was that he would tolerate no interference, even were he to forfeit his life. The insignia which his retinue bore on their sleeves to indicate the new religion they professed, were composed of the initials V.D.M.I.A. (Verbum Dei manet in aeternum). The Elector of Saxony had adopted the same insignia for his followers. Both the Landgrave and the Elector gave expression to their military alliance by vesting their retinue with uniforms of the same color.

[101] Realenzyklopädie für prot. Theologie und Kirche, Vol. XV, 3rd ed., p. 299.

In the beginning of April, 1525, Luther wrote exultingly to George Polentz, Bishop of Samland: "Behold the miracle! With a rapid stride and with full sails the Gospel hastens to Prussia!" [102] In the same year the Grand Master of the Teutonic Order, Albrecht of Brandenburg-Ansbach, illegally proclaimed himself first Duke of Prussia, one of the territories of that Order, thus becoming the founder of the Lutheran State Church in the ecclesiastical district entrusted to his Order.

Albrecht, one of the fifteen children of the Margrave Frederick, had received a defective training, since his father, owing to his limited income and his numerous progeny, aimed at having his son make a living by obtaining a situation with ecclesiastical or secular courts, rather than by means of a thorough education. He procured two canonical benefices at the archiepiscopal court of the Elector of Cologne. Thereafter he plied the soldier's trade and for some time, having been taken ill, stayed at the residence of the Hungarian court. The Knights of the Teutonic Order elected him Grand Master in 1511, at the recommendation of Duke George of Saxony. He took the customary vow of perpetual chastity, as prescribed by the statutes of the Order, and promised, under oath before the altar, to preserve and defend, as a possession of the Holy See, the territory of the Order that belonged to the Church. Allured by material ambitions, however, he formed a secret alliance with Luther, beginning with June, 1521, through his confidential adviser, Oeden. This alliance purposed to effect an arbitrary reorganization of the Order. It was in contravention of the papal directions, to which Albrecht was in duty bound to adhere, and which were designed to effect the amelioration of the condition of the unmarried knights and the clergy of the Order—a condition which was very much in need of reform. Afterwards he paid a personal visit to Luther at Wittenberg. Incompetent to pass judgment on the latter's teachings, he was, nevertheless, familiar with the decision of the Church.

The ardent demands which Luther made upon Albrecht, such as the secularization of the Prussian territory of the Teutonic Order, and that he himself should marry, infatuated his mind. They were invitations which Luther, in his desire to gain a mighty position in the east, confirmed and generalized in his "Admonition to the Teutonic Order to avoid false chastity," published in 1523.

[102] *Briefwechsel*, V, p. 159.

The Grand Master permitted evangelical preachers, such as Briess-mann, Speratus, and, later on, Poliander, to enjoy untrammeled liberty of action in Königsberg, his residential city. Thence they extended their activity into the country. The apostasy of two bishops who belonged to the Prussian territory of the order, Georg von Polentz, bishop of Samland, and Eberhard von Queiss, bishop of Pomesania, opened the gates wide to the Reformation. The Grand Master permitted both apostates to continue in office, while he himself almost continuously sojourned abroad and succeeded in concealing his intentions of secularization and marriage. When the report of his intended marriage was noised about, his brother John warned him in touching words and pleaded with him not to disgrace his name and family by breaking his vow. However, he merely received an evasive reply.

In spring, 1525, Albrecht of Brandenburg believed that the time had arrived for carrying out his plan.

On April 9, he concluded a dishonorable and humiliating peace with King Sigismund of Poland, who had warred upon the territory of the Order. In return, Albrecht accepted as a fief from Poland the entire territory of the ecclesiastical State of Prussia. At the same time he declared himself secular "Duke of Prussia." Six days after this event went forth a ducal mandate ordering a change of religion for all the inhabitants of the territory. It imposed a penalty upon the clergy who were disobedient or rebellious to the new evangel. On July 1, 1526, the castle of Königsberg witnessed Albrecht's solemn marriage to Dorothy, a young daughter of the Danish King. His example was imitated by the two bishops who had become Lutherans. They were the first apostate bishops of the age of the Reformation. In a new ordinance for the government of the territory, the first territorial diet, convened at Königsberg on December 6, 1525, had formulated laws to correspond to the new and altered religious conditions. The banner of ducal Prussia, which Albrecht was forced to accept from King Sigismund, waved over the assembly hall. In place of the former black cross of the Order on a white background, appeared the black eagle, which has remained the Prussian coat-of-arms up to the present day. The protests of the Knights of the Teutonic Order outside of Prussia, the declaration of the ban and the executory mandates of the Empire were alike futile against the accomplished violation. The solemn protest of the Pope, whose right to the territory of the Order had been grossly outraged, was equally futile. Naturally, the opposition of those inhabitants of the territory who remained loyal to the ancient religion and were determined not to adapt themselves to the religious innovation which had come upon them like a raging storm, was likewise ineffectual.

"Thus at an early date," says a Protestant historian of the Reformation, "Lutheranism took its place among the political factors, and its development was to a certain extent dependent upon the tendencies and inclinations of the [civil] authorities and ruling sovereigns of that day." [103]

The forcible intervention of the secular governments furnishes the key to the solution of the mystery why the Reformation made such rapid progress.

As early as 1523, a fanatical furrier named Melchior Hoffmann, a native of Swabian Hall, made his appearance in Livonia as a lay preacher of Luther's doctrines. An attack was made upon the residences of the cathedral canons and upon churches and cloisters at Dorpat, in January, 1525. Owing to dissensions that had arisen between the preachers of the new religion, Hoffmann obtained a favorable testimonial for his person from Luther at Wittenberg. In conjunction with Bugenhagen, Luther wrote his admonition "To the Christians in Livonia." In this letter, which was forthwith published, he exhorts his followers not to cause any trouble on account of differences due to external customs.[104] Following Luther's trail, Hoffmann became absorbed in eschatological chimeras. Thus he prophesied that the year 1533 would witness the end of the world. He became one of the leaders of the Anabaptists. Indeed, it was due chiefly to the influence which he exercised in his ceaseless journeys, that the Anabaptist sect was transplanted from Upper to Lower Germany. After a stormy career at Reval, Stockholm, Holstein (disputation at Flensburg, 1529), in East Frisia, and elsewhere, Hoffmann finally made his appearance in Strasburg, which had been thoroughly upset by the reformers. Owing to the "Gospel of the Covenant" which he preached enthusiastically, he and his followers ("Melchiorites") became accomplices in the atrocities which were perpetrated by the Anabaptists at Münster. Nowhere is the spiritual affinity between the Anabaptist system and Lutheranism so clearly manifested as in the internal ex-

[103] W. Friedensburg, quoted by Grisar, *Luther,* Vol. II, p. 333.
[104] Erl. ed., Vol. LIII, pp. 315 sqq. (*Briefwechsel,* V. p. 198).

periences and inspirations which moved this "apostolic herald," as he described himself, despite the fact that Luther combated him after 1527 and wished to see him return to his former craft of furrier. For this reason Hoffmann in his writings stigmatized Luther as a "Judas" who persecuted the faithful. This remarkable prophet of the Anabaptist movement died as a prisoner of the Zwinglians about 1543 at Strasburg, after extensive wanderings, in which he believed himself accompanied by heavenly voices.

The Anabaptists of Upper Germany possessed a type of over-excited preacher and leader in the weaver Augustine Bader. He was a friend of Denk, Hetzer, and Hut, Anabaptist leaders of Southern Germany, and not only passed himself off for a prophet, but also for a future "king," which rank he intended to obtain with the aid of the Turks. Secretly his adherents had supplied him with the insignia of royalty, made of gold-plated silver, such as a crown, scepter, poniard and chains, together with a sumptuous costume. Destiny, however, overtook him in a nightly assembly at Blaubeuren; he was apprehended as an insurrectionist, tortured with glowing tongs, and burnt in the market-place of Stuttgart on March 30, 1530. [105]

The adherents of the new religion, who proceeded against Melchior Hoffmann, at Strasburg, obtained control of that city in 1529. In that year, the magistrate, being under the dominant influence of Zwinglian-minded preachers, completely abolished the Mass. Even as far back as 1524, the authorities of the city had authorized the destruction of images in churches. The defection from the Church was especially promoted by Matthew Zell, an apostate priest, who had married the daughter of a Strasburg artisan in 1523; also by Caspar Hedio, until 1523 preacher at the court of Albrecht of Mayence; but above all by Martin Bucer, a native of Schlettstadt, at one time a Dominican and afterwards pastor at Landstuhl. In 1523, Bucer entered upon an epistolary correspondence with Zwingli and soon after embraced many of the latter's rationalistic teachings, especially the denial of the Real Presence of Christ in the Holy Eucharist. Owing to the violent procedure of himself and his friends, Strasburg, after 1524, experienced the progressive destruction of sacred images, as demanded by Zwingli. The most severe measures of repression were adopted against the Catholics. The Zwinglian gospel, however, produced so little fruit that Bucer was forced to write after some years: "Among us in Strasburg there is scarcely any church, no recognition of the Word of God, no frequentation of the Sacraments." [106]

As matters fared in the free imperial city of Strasburg, so they developed in other imperial cities and in cities subject to episcopal rule. Insurrection, iconoclasm, and sacrilegious violation of churches accompanied the introduction of the new gospel in Basle by Oecolampadius, in 1529, in St. Gall by Vadian in 1529, and in Constance by Blaurer—to mention only those cities which were Protestantized according to the Zwinglian idea.

The year 1525 also marked a decisive change in the free imperial city of Nuremberg. Here one could observe how another motive fatally co-operated in the religious upheaval, namely, the activity of renegade priests and religious. A number of Augustinians at that place, who were friendly to Luther, commenced by deserting their cloister. Shortly afterwards, apostate members of the secular and regular clergy began to preach the reformed religion. At first the magistrate of the town prohibited only the discussion of controversial questions from the pulpit. Two provosts and the prior of the Augustinians abolished the Mass. John Walther, an Augustinian preacher at the church of St. Sebaldus, the abbot of St. Aegidius, and the provost Pressler embraced the state of matrimony. One of the prime movers was Andrew Osiander, a renegade priest and preacher who later became famous as a Protestant controversialist. He, too, married. At the diet of Nuremberg, in 1524, the Catholic prelates were mocked by the excited mob. The condition of the many loyal or doubting Catholics became even worse after the impetuous Wenceslaus Link, a companion of Luther's in the monastery of Wittenberg, came to Nuremberg from Altenburg in the company of his wife and, in August, 1525, commenced to function there as custodian and preacher in the New Hospital. In this latter year the town-council formally decreed the adoption of the Lutheran religion. Lazarus Spengler, clerk of the town-council, was mainly instrumental in bringing about this decision.

During the period of the religious upheaval, Spengler and other members of the town-council, like Jerome Ebner and Caspar Nützel, succeeded in preserving from destruction at least the images, altars, and other objects of religious art for which the imperial city

---

[106] Janssen-Pastor, *Gesch. d. deutschen Volkes*, Vol. III, 20th ed., p. 106.

was famous. The ornaments of the churches also survived, to a great extent, the subsequent iconoclastic assaults of Zwinglianism; and even at this late day they evidence the profoundly religious life and artistic fervor of Nuremberg's Catholic period.

By the adoption of tyrannical decrees the magistrates shackled the old religion. The exercise of pastoral functions was denied to the religious orders, the clergy were classified as civilians, and those who complied willingly were assured the life-long enjoyment of their benefices. The monastery of St. Aegidius, with a community numbering twenty-five persons, surrendered to the town-council in 1525. The Augustinian convent, of which no less than twenty-five members, allured by liberty and matrimony, had embraced Lutheranism, likewise surrendered. The Carmelite and Carthusian monasteries eventually also surrendered, although many of their inmates remained loyal to the ancient religion, among them being the courageous prior of the Carmelite monastery, Andrew Stoss, a son of Vitus Stoss, the celebrated sculptor. He determinedly resisted the town-council for a long time. Thus, in the course of one single year, 1525, Nuremberg experienced a complete transformation. The Dominicans remained loyal till 1543, when five of the last remaining members surrendered their monastery to the city authorities.

The most notable resistance was offered by the Order of Friars Minor, whose members suffered every kind of persecution and the most bitter poverty until the last survivor passed away, in 1562. The Poor Clares, pious daughters of the Saint of Assisi, remained loyal under the rule of their highly cultured abbess, Charitas Pirkheimer, a sister of the famous humanist, until their gallant community became extinct. Deprived of their preacher and confessor, these nuns, eighty in all, most of whom were of patrician descent, were forced to listen to the sermons of Osiander and other Protestant dominies behind the lattice-work of their cloister. The Gothic choir of their church, preserved to this day, solemnly towers aloft amidst the modern buildings that surround it, a monument to the heroic fortitude of these nuns. The unpretentious old cloister, once the residence of the venerable, prudent, and matronly Charitas Pirkheimer, was demolished only a few years ago.

Chapter XII

THE DECISIVE YEARS, 1525–1530

I. CHARLES V, CLEMENT VII, AND THE TURKS

The first war between Charles V and Francis I of France ended in the defeat of the French at Pavia, on February 24, 1525, and the capture of their king. The imperial army, composed of Spaniards, Italians, and the dreaded German lansquenets, won a decisive victory. The treaty of peace concluded at Madrid between Charles and Francis on January 14, 1526, was entirely too severe for France. The release of the King was purchased at an exorbitant price.

Pope Clement VII, an astute politician, was of the opinion that the treaty and the oath of King Francis were not binding because they had been obtained by force. It has been frequently asserted that he formally released the King from his oath; but the statement is uncertain. [1] Nevertheless the Pope, fearing the ascendancy of the Emperor in Italy, and apprehensive of his own position in Rome, unfortunately shaped his policies to favor Francis. This proved fatal to the status of the Church in Germany. The action of the Emperor and the Empire against the religious upheaval was paralyzed by the demands made upon the latter in the war-like complications which had arisen, especially in Italy. The so-called Holy League of Cognac, which had been formed in opposition to the Emperor between certain Italian States and France, strengthened by the accession of the Pope, led to a profound schism between the supreme spiritual and the first temporal authority in Christendom.

In the new conflict between the Franco-Italian and the imperial forces, which lasted from 1526 to the "Ladies' Peace" of Cambrai (1529), Rome was stormed and fearfully sacked in 1527 by the mutinous soldiers under Bourbon, the imperial field-marshal, and George von Frundsberg, the commander of the "Landsknechte." The capital of Christendom, degraded by the morals of the Renaissance, suffered

[1] Pastor, *Geschichte der Päpste*, Vol. IV, Part II, p. 208.

a most abject decline. Clement VII, made a prisoner in the Castle of Sant' Angelo, was compelled to sign a humiliating capitulation and lived in exile at Orvieto and Viterbo until he was able to return to Rome, on October 6, 1528. The Emperor was exceedingly alarmed at the capture and humiliation of Rome, which were contrary to his intentions, and was told by Francesco Quiñones, the intrepid General of the Franciscan Order, that if he did not hasten to fulfill his obligations toward the Pope, it would be impossible to call him emperor henceforth; men would prefer to regard him as Luther's captain, since the Lutheran mercenaries had committed the most disgraceful atrocities in his name and under his banner. [2]

Luther, on his part, was jubilant at the course of events. When apprised of the misfortune that befell the Eternal City, he wrote to his confidant, pastor Hausmann of Zwickau: "Rome and the Pope have been miserably devastated. Thus Christ governs, since the Emperor, who, being in the service of the Pope, persecutes Luther, is compelled to destroy the Pope on behalf of Luther. Thus Christ must do everything for the sake of His own and against the enemy." [3] In another letter, however, he says: "I would not like to see Rome burned; for it would be too prodigious a sign." [4] Melanchthon, the humanist, was disturbed rather at the destruction of the ancient classical sites. [5]

In consequence of the conciliatory attitude of Charles V and the overtures made by the Pope to the Emperor, a reconciliation was effected between them. Charles V was crowned emperor at Bologna by Clement VII on February 24, 1530. It was bruited about, however, that he did not intend to allow the Papal States to attain to complete sovereignty and independence. [6] His long separation from Germany was a source of grievous injury to Catholicism as against the reform movement. After the Emperor's energetic stand at Worms his failure to intervene in Germany was regretted. The loyal adherents of the Church loudly clamored for his return. But they were disappointed from year to year. In 1530, when the diet assembled at Augsburg, the Emperor returned temporarily to the field of German activity, which was very much desired by himself, as the country was

[2] *Ibid.*, p. 311.
[3] On July 13, 1527; *Briefwechsel*, VI, p. 69.
[4] On November 11, 1527 to Jonas; *Briefwechsel*, VI, p. 117.
[5] Cf. *Corp. Ref.*, Vol. I, n. 445; XI, p. 130.
[6] Pastor, *l. c.*, pp. 382 sq.

in a sorry religious plight. The complaint was heard that neither the Emperor nor the Pope was properly informed about the condition of the Church in Germany.

Besides the absence of the Emperor and the disturbances in Italy, the events on the eastern boundary of the Empire proved of great advantage to Lutheranism. These events completely engaged the attention and the strength of the imperial regent, Ferdinand of Austria. The approaching danger of a Turkish invasion diverted the thoughts of the princes who remained loyal to the Empire, from the religious question.

During his captivity, the French king had appealed to Sultan Soliman for aid. Since his victory over the Knights of St. John on the Island of Rhodes, Soliman was consumed with a strong desire to resume the ancient campaign of the Crescent against the West. He invaded Hungary with an immense army and defeated King Louis, a brother-in-law of Charles V, at Mohacz on the Danube. The King succumbed in a morass on his flight (1526). His crown, together with that of Bohemia, passed over to Ferdinand of Austria. The danger to Germany remained, yea, became even more aggravated, since Ferdinand's rival in Hungary, John Zapolya of Transylvania, favored the Turks. In order to protect Zapolya, Soliman renewed his attack and besieged Vienna (1529), but was repulsed.

Luther for a long time maintained his unfavorable attitude towards united action against the Turks, but finally perceived its necessity.

The cause of his well-nigh inexplicable attitude of aloofness was the prominent participation of the papacy in the Turkish war. By virtue of its primacy, its ancient activities at the head of the Christian family of nations, and its traditional efforts to check the expansion of infidelity, the papacy was the natural leader in this movement. Luther's pseudomystical state of mind originally inclined him to regard the Turks as a scourge of God which neither could nor ought to be resisted, and to expect that that portion of Christendom which suffered from this scourge would accept his gospel. [7] One of his theses, which was formulated in opposition to the Turkish wars, was condemned among other errors in the Bull *"Exurge"* of Leo X in 1520.[8] Luther naturally sustained this theses with all the more energy.

[7] Cfr. his letter to Spalatin, December 21, 1518 (*Briefwechsel*, I, p. 333).
[8] Cfr. Grisar, *Luther*, Vol. III, p. 78.

He accused the Pope of selfish and imperialistic designs because of his demand for a crusade against the Turks. [9] In an impassioned treatise, "Two Discordant Imperial Commandments" (1524), he wrote: "We refuse to obey and to march against the Turks or to contribute to this cause, since the Turks are ten times cleverer and more devout than our princes." Because the Catholic princes had rejected his demands at the diet of Nuremberg, he delivered himself thus in opposition to their resolution in favor of the crusade: "How can such fools [the princes], who tempt and blaspheme God so greatly, expect to be successful against the Turks?" The Emperor— "a perishable bag of worms"—shamelessly constitutes himself, together with the Pope, the supreme defender of the Christian religion," whereas "the divine power of the faith has no need of a protector." [10] He delights in repeating his assurance that "the government of the Pope is ten times worse than that of the Turk. . . . If ever the Turks were to be exterminated, it would be necessary to begin with the Pope." [11]

Thus he availed himself of the extreme need of Christendom to agitate against Rome and to promote the interests of his own cause.

When, finally, in 1529, Vienna was threatened and cries of alarm rang through Europe, he changed his tone. In his little book "On the War against the Turks" he now demanded protection against the Turks and asked that they be proceeded against as robbers and destroyers; but there was to be no crusade such as had been undertaken against the infidels in the foolish days of old.[12]

The edict of Worms had been renewed at Augsburg, where it was further resolved that arrangements be made for a "free general council" to be assembled at some accessible place in Germany. The diet of Spires, in 1526, was forced to wage an even greater battle with the partisans of the new religion who had increased their forces in the interim. Its efforts were but partially successful. The diet, it is true, received a declaration from the Emperor attesting his firm resolve to act. He left no doubt that he meant to uphold the edict of Worms and its demands upon the cities and princes. Nevertheless Electoral Saxony and Hesse boldly led the other friends of Luther-

9 *Ibid.*, p. 79.
10 *Ibid.*, p. 77.
11 *Ibid.*, pp. 79 sq.
12 *Ibid.*, p. 81.

anism in their resistance. If the edict of Worms were upheld, the partisans of the reform movement now threatened to refuse their assistance in the war against the Turks and the necessary contributions for the support of the imperial government. This placed Ferdinand of Austria and the Catholic party in a quandary. Finally the regulation of affairs was once more deferred until the convocation of a general council, which was definitely expected. The recess stated in rather doubtful language that, pursuant to the edict of Worms, the estates had "unanimously agreed, in matters pertaining thereto, so to live with their subjects, to govern, and to conduct themselves, as each expects and trusts to be held accountable for to God and his imperial majesty."

Was this a legal recognition of the new system of territorial churches?

It has been so affirmed, but without any warrant. What is true is that the elastic statement was thus interpreted at an early date.

The declaration, however, "does not imply what was inferred from it; the right of reformation could be deduced neither from its wording, nor from its origin, nor from its spirit." [13] "One can scarcely say that this formula granted a formal right to the evangelicals to secede from the ecclesiastical communion and to institute a reformation on their own responsibility." [14] The wish of the Emperor, referred to in the formula, was quite clear. Then, too, the diet of Spires only intended to promulgate a temporary norm of peace until the assembly of a general council. True, the edict of Worms was not formally renewed, but the German estates could hold themselves "accountable to the imperial majesty" only for conduct in conformity with that edict. Luther himself during the first three years never interpreted the proposition in question as a legal foundation justifying the formation of national churches. It must be admitted, however, that the expression was ambiguous, and can be explained only as a sorry expedient in the situation created by the opposition. It is more excusable in the light of the diet's concomitant appeal to a general council; for this appeal the diet presupposed, "not the dissolution, but rather the acknowledgment of ecclesiastical jurisdiction." [15]

The misuse to which the recess of the diet of Spires was subjected, promoted the development of territorial churches of the new religion

[13] A. Kluckhohn in the *Histor. Zeitschrift*, Vol. LVI, p. 217.

[14] W. Friedensburg, *Der Reichstag zu Speier 1526*, p. 482. Cfr. Janssen-Pastor, Vol. III, pp. 53 sq.; also Köstlin-Kawerau, II, p. 27.

[15] Janssen-Pastor, *l. c.*

which were in process of formation. A fine opportunity was furnished by the delay in the execution of the edict of Worms. Philip of Hesse had a synod held at Homberg in 1526, under the presidency of a Frenchman, the apostate Franciscan, Francis Lambert of Avignon. This body drafted a radically new ecclesiastical regimen, based upon a purely synodical constitution. Mainly on account of Luther's opposition, however, this regimen was never enforced. On the contrary, the landgrave himself assumed the government of the Church and ruled it as supreme territorial bishop. The monasteries were suppressed, sacred images in the churches and shrines abolished, and the ritual ruthlessly altered.

Philip's personal interest in religion was so feeble that, after his change of religion, he partook of the Eucharist but once in fifteen years and lived persistently in adultery and public vice. According to his own confession he did not observe conjugal fidelity towards his wife Christina for even three weeks. As early as 1526 he harbored the idea of taking a second wife during the lifetime of his first spouse—a design which he executed on March 4, 1540, with the sanction of the Wittenberg reformers, as will be set forth in the sequel.

2. LUTHER AND THE STATE CHURCH OF SAXONY

In the Saxon Electorate, which was his home, Luther urged the introduction of visitations by commissioners to be nominated by the secular ruler. This he did with increased zeal, the longer matters were delayed by the prince, who proceeded in an arbitrary and autocratic manner. The decadence of morals and discipline forced him to take this stand.

He deplored "the ingratitude of the people for the holy Word of God." "They live like swine," he says. "There is no longer any fear of God nor discipline, because the jurisdiction of the Pope has ceased and everyone now does as he pleases. . . . If the elders do not want to, let them go to the devil for all I care. But where youth is neglected and raised without discipline, the authorities are to blame, and the land will be filled with dissolute savages." Thus Luther to the Elector John of Saxony, on November 22, 1526.[16]

In respect to parishes and schools he adds: "Since religious compulsion is

[16] Erl. ed., Vol. LIII, pp. 386 sqq. (*Briefwechsel*, V, p. 406).

at an end and all cloisters and foundations fall into the hands of the prince as the supreme ruler, there arises the duty and inconvenience of regulating such matters, to which no one else attends and in which no one can or should be interested." He contends that God has "summoned the prince to attend to these matters in such an event."

He demands, therefore, that the prince should entrust the visitation, which had already begun in a tentative way, to four persons, two of whom were to manage the property and stipends, while the other two—they should go about the matter with "discretion"—were to be entrusted with the regulation of doctrine and personnel.

The Elector's instruction, which followed in 1527, prescribes the course of the visitation and presupposes a direct right of the State in spiritual matters, [17] formally setting up the territorial government of the Church which was already in existence. In doing so, however, the Elector to some extent exceeded the wishes of Luther, who, accordingly, wrote a preface to the "electoral instruction" which in some respects amounted to a restriction. Luther tries to preserve a certain autonomy for the Church and to prevent the danger of a ruinous dependence. In the preface which he added to the published edict of the prince, he tries to justify the extensive measures which the territorial lord was about to exercise in the sphere of religion by the distressed condition of the Church and the fraternal duty of a Christian ruler, whom he characterizes as an "emergency bishop." But his suggestions were disregarded and proved futile. They are an ineffectual monument of his vacillation and embarrassment in a question of fundamentals, namely, the authentic concept of the Church. The voice of the court and its jurists, and the facts created by the government were mightier than the vague and impotent aspirations of Luther.

The ideas of the territorial government were, however, influenced by an humble invitation extended to the Elector John by a friend of Luther. In this invitation the Elector was styled a prince "of sacred Christian lineage and descent" and exhorted to ameliorate the conditions of the Church by becoming an example to other rulers and following in "the heroic footsteps" of the pious Jewish king, Josaphat. The religious functions of the kings of ancient Israel were held up to him as worthy of emulation—an exhortation "afterwards fre-

17 Weimar ed., Vol. XXVI, pp. 195 sqq.; Erl. ed., Vol. XIII, pp. 1 sqq.

quently repeated by the evangelicals." [18] There is no mention of the prince's functions being restricted by the distressed condition of the Church, nor of fraternal duty; but the ruler, in virtue of his plenary powers as prince, is competent to exercise authority over the churches.

In the name of the territorial ruler, Melanchthon supplemented these general instructions by a set of additional "articles" for the guidance of the visitators. They concerned the method of teaching and set up a church discipline effective throughout the country. These supplementary articles met with Luther's approval and, after having been examined and supplemented several times, by order of the Elector, were formally promulgated.

Many individuals, both Lutherans and Catholics, were astonished at the reactionary nature of these articles, which cautioned against a declaration of the forgiveness of sins by faith alone, without previous penance. The law which penalized sin was emphasized much more forcefully than Luther had been wont to do. As a result, Luther had to hear the objection: "We are crawling backwards again." Nevertheless, he stuck to his approbation of the articles of visitation and remarked that they determined everything in the simplest possible manner for the benefit of the mob; the objections of the dissenters, he predicted, would soon cease.[19]

In 1528, he himself composed a set of "Instructions for the Visitators," which was introduced into the territory of Duke Henry of Saxony in 1538, and into the bishopric of Naumburg in 1545. Having become quite disillusioned in consequence of his experiences, Luther began to yield considerably in the matter of law and penance. When his pupil, John Agricola, raised strong objections to the proposed modifications, Luther opposed him.

On account of doctrinal differences, Agricola, at Eisleben, vehemently opposed Melanchthon, with whom he was at personal enmity. In general, he combated penance and, in part, the rules of a devout life. A satire on the Wittenberg theologians classified him as an Epicurean, "a discriminating voluptuary who knows how to choose among pleasures." His opposition to Luther at a subsequent period caused the latter serious trouble in the so-called antinomian controversy. At the same time, however, it gave him an occasion to recede to an even greater extent from his original attitude toward law,

---

[18] Köstlin-Kawerau, M. *Luther*, Vol. II, p. 25.
[19] *Ibid.*, p. 31.

and penance. "The first official act of the evangelical State Church (the announcement of the visitation) thus became an occasion of strife, yea, of charges of heresy within the most intimate circles of the reformatory theologians of Wittenberg." [20]

The protocols of the visitators show the existing conditions among the people, their preachers and new pastors, in the years 1527 to 1529, and later. It is not worth while to enter upon the melancholy details. Luther's summary complaint in a letter to Spalatin will suffice: "Everywhere the congregations present a deplorable picture, since the peasants neither learn, nor pray, nor do anything else but abuse their freedom; they neither confess, nor go to communion, as if they had completely cast off religion." [21] He adds: "Just as they spurned the papal system, so now they condemn ours." It is only fair to remark that no such conditions existed under the papacy. The new gospel of liberty and the Peasants' War which sprung from it had brought a return to barbarism. The vain excuse has recently been put forth that the protocols of the Lutheran visitators exhibit a state of decadence which "originated in the religious life of the Catholic past." [22] Though, as we have seen, the Catholic ages had their shortcomings, it was nevertheless to be expected that a thoroughgoing religious movement, such as the Reformation claimed to be, should have produced a reform precisely at its inception. Indeed it should have manifested decided signs of the spiritual spring which Luther had persistently announced, especially when, in his extravagant manner, he spoke of the breath of God which would renew all things without violence.

An endeavor was made to increase the effectiveness of the visitations by creating the permanent office of superintendent. It was another seal affixed to the State Church. The office was established by the Elector in his instructions governing visitations for 1527, and entrusted to the pastors of the principal cities. It was their duty to supervise the belief, teachings, and official functions of the clergy within their respective jurisdictions and to report those who obstinately persisted in error to the officials appointed by the prince, and through these to the territorial lord. Where else was there authority that could inflict punishment?

[20] *Ibid.*
[21] Middle of January (?), 1529; *Briefwechsel*, VII, p. 45.
[22] Köstlin-Kawerau, *M. Luther*, Vol. II, p. 40.

In order to fortify the new religious system still more, the German Mass was introduced for Sundays, to be uniform throughout Electoral Saxony. It was an arrangement suggested by the territorial lord. Luther had elaborated a set of hymns with the assistance of John Walther, of the castle of Torgau, which was submitted to the Elector towards the end of 1525. This Mass was prescribed for all the pastors in the articles of visitation and was to be introduced with the least possible disturbance. The article pertinent to this point cautiously says: "It is not necessary to preach extensively to the laity about it." The deceptive resemblance to the Latin Mass was retained.

In all these ordinances there was not one word relative to that assembly of "genuine and freely confessing Christians" which Luther had regarded as desirable. The ideal was interred in consequence of the sad results of the visitation. In lieu thereof, the new church was overrun by unspiritual members, whom Luther calls "pagans," and developed more and more into a compulsory organization. The Anabaptists and other fanatics who rebelled against its doctrines, were severely penalized. Luther even went so far as to demand the penalty of decapitation for such heretics as were found guilty, not of insurrection against the State, but of a fundamental deviation from his doctrine.[23]

Walter Köhler, a leading Protestant historian of the Reformation, writes of the tendency resulting from the regulations governing the visitations due to Luther's intervention: "Capital punishment for heresy was legitimized by the Lutheran authorities. . . . Freedom of conscience and of religion was out of the question with Luther." According to this writer, there is no doubt that the trial of heretics by the Protestant churches was introduced by Luther. When the preaching of the Word proved ineffectual, he appealed to the secular authorities, with whom he was closely allied.[24]

The Protestant scholar, P. Wappler, who has made a special study of the Protestant proceedings against heretics, and also of the Anabaptist movement, shows by a number of concrete cases how, shortly after the inception of the visitations, Luther decided in favor of the execution of heretics, especially on account of the teachings of the Anabaptists. "The many executions," says Wappler, "of Anabaptists who are known not to have been revolutionaries and who were put to death on the strength of the declarations of the Wittenberg theologians, refute only too plainly all

[23] Grisar, *Luther,* Vol. VI, index s. v. "Intolerance" and "Heretics."
[24] For the resp. passages see Grisar, *Luther,* Vol. VI, p. 266.

attempts to deny the clear fact that Luther himself approved of the death penalty against such as were merely heretics." [25]

The formula which Luther applied to representatives of the new heresies was that they were to be remanded to "Master Hans," *i. e.*, handed over to the executioner. At Rheinhardsbrunn, for example, six heretics were simultaneously remanded to Master Hans towards the close of 1529 and the beginning of 1530, and were decapitated on January 18, 1530. Of the inquisition of laymen which was provided for in the electoral regulations of 1527, Wappler justly observes: "The principles of evangelical freedom of belief and liberty of conscience, which Luther had championed two years earlier, were most shamefully repudiated by this lay inquisition;" and yet Luther said never a word in protest.

An impartial and critical Catholic historian, Dr. Nicholas Paulus, has filled a whole volume with convincing evidence of the intolerance of the leaders of the religious schism, particularly Luther and Melanchthon, which went even so far as to recommend capital punishment. [26]

Whilst obstinate denial of the faith was to be avenged thus severely, —a measure which, of course, it was impossible to carry out universally—an attempt was made to penalize also gross violations of the moral law within the religious communities. The lack of the Catholic ban was perceptible. The object of the regulations governing visitations was to discipline notorious sinners by a refusal of the Lord's supper. Luther's first aim was to have obstinate sinners declared pagans in the eyes of the congregation, after a futile warning in the presence of witnesses. Later he decided in favor of greater severity by adopting a kind of excommunication. Various efforts on the part of others to install elders for the supervision of morals were condemned to failure.[27] The only measure that was finally retained was the office of beadle, who, according to a phrase of Luther's uttered in 1529, had to hale those to church who despised the catechism, so that they might learn the Ten Commandments, etc. Whoever scorned to learn the catechism, he said, should be exiled by the civil authorities.[28]

[25] *Ibid.*, p. 267.
[26] *Protestantismus und Toleranz im 16. Jahrhundert*, 1911.
[27] Köstlin-Kawerau, *M. Luther*, Vol. II, p. 47.
[28] Grisar, *Luther*, Vol. V, pp. 484 sq.

3. NEW DOCTRINAL AND CONTROVERSIAL WRITINGS

Luther's efforts to regulate doctrine and religious discipline are associated with the publication of his two catechisms, which have attained great significance. They originated in three series of catechetical sermons preached in 1528. At that time it was a prescribed custom at Wittenberg to preach week-day sermons on the catechism four times a year, for two consecutive weeks.

"The Little Catechism, for children and simple folk," first appeared in the form of tables, designed to be affixed to various parts of the home according to Catholic custom. Its arrangement, particularly the sequence of Commandments, profession of faith, and "Our Father," also followed the old tradition. A section on Baptism and another on the Eucharist were appended. Its arrangement in the form of questions and answers is a model of simplicity and clearness. Though heterodox doctrines are emphasized in the Little Catechism, polemical attacks upon the ancient Church are avoided. In the preface, however, the bishops are blamed for the ignorance of Christian doctrine existing among the common people, especially in the villages.[29]

The Large Catechism was intended to instruct pastors and to enable them to explain the smaller one in their sermons. It is not composed in the form of questions and answers, and is rather prolix. Nevertheless, certain characteristic doctrines, which were apt to give rise to dispute, are omitted, as in the case of the smaller book. Thus the readers are not informed of their right to pass judgment on the Bible and on matters of faith, two things formerly so strongly emphasized by Luther. Its pages are silent on the doctrine of original sin as the destroyer of every inclination to good, on the enslaved will, and on predestination.

The two catechisms were very widely adopted and often reprinted. Numerous Electoral regulations provided for their propagation and use. In 1580 they were incorporated in the "Book of Concord" and thereby raised to the rank of symbolical writings of the Lutheran Church.

It cannot be denied that the desire not to be outdone by Luther proved very beneficial to the development of Catholic catechetics. The religious instruction of the people, it is true, had not been neg-

[29] *Ibid.*

lected. To them Luther holds up his own example. Even in his manner of presentation he completely followed the old method.[30] But the copiousness and systematic method of Catholic religious instruction necessitated a certain gradation. It became necessary that it should be transferred from the home, to which it had been previously entrusted, to the school and the church. Then, too, the existing and quite estimable number of elementary text-books had to be multiplied. The splendid work of Peter Canisius perfected the great amount of good literature which was already in existence.

Luther believed himself justified in stating that, prior to his time, there had been "no doctor on earth who had known the whole of the catechism, that is, the Our Father, the Ten Commandments and the Creed, much less understood them and taught them as now, God be praised, they are taught and learned even by little children. In support of this I appeal to all their books, those of the theologians as well as those of the lawyers. If even one article of the catechism can be learnt aright from them, I shall allow myself to be broken on the wheel or bled to death." [31] He is better advised when he recommends people to occupy themselves with the study of the catechism. He makes his recommendations in a manner characteristic of himself. In the preface to the Large Catechism he tells his preachers that whoever does not heed and abide by the catechism, is to be classified with the "shameful gluttons and belly-servers, who are better fitted to look after the pigs and the hounds than to be pastors having the cure of souls." [32] Daily, every morning and evening, he himself, though a doctor and preacher, recited "the Ten Commandments, the Creed, the Our Father, etc., like a child." The preface exhorts all pastors "to practice well and always to occupy themselves with" the catechism, and contains many practical ideas, in proposing which Luther pleads with those "lazy bellies or presumptuous saints, that, for God's sake, they let themselves be persuaded." His words have borne fruit, and in many Protestant districts his catechisms have established and sustained positive Christian beliefs.

Other minor writings support the Little Catechism. Thus, in 1526, he wrote a little treatise on the ceremonies of Baptism, which supplied the majority of Lutheran churches with the trinitarian formula and the exorcism. In 1529, he composed a "Small Book on the Marriage Ceremony for Simple Pastors," which exercised a similar influence on the marriage rite. According to the latter work, the nuptial ceremony

---

[30] *Ibid.*, pp. 489 sqq.
[31] *Ibid.*, p. 485.
[32] *Ibid.*

is a blessing joined with prayer, freely solicited by the bridal couple, but not necessary for the validity of marriage.

At the head of his treatise "Von Ehesachen," [33] which he commenced in 1529 and published in 1530, as well as in other writings, Luther enunciates the doctrine, which he makes the basis and starting-point of his instructions, that Matrimony is not a Sacrament, but "a purely temporal matter, such as raiment and food, house and court-yard, subject to secular authority." The matrimonial problems with which he had been overwhelmed, had crushed him. After the Catholic laws on matrimony had been discarded, great confusion inevitably ensued, and this disorder was augmented by the Peasants' War and the moral decadence which followed. "I have a lot of trouble with it," he writes to Spalatin; "I resist strongly, cry out and exclaim that such matters should be left to the secular authorities." [34] In the treatise mentioned, as elsewhere in his writings, he does not propose to give any regulations pertaining to Matrimony, since temporal matters do not pertain to the clergy and the Church has no right "to govern or to enforce the law," but her province is "to inform and console the consciences." Hence, he speaks only as one offering advice.

It is not necessary to demonstrate that his usual distinction between the Church and the world, between the spiritual kingdom of Christ and the external realm of the civil authority, between the forum of law and the forum of conscience, was bound to involve him in vacillations and contradictions, especially in the realm of Matrimony. An arbitrary subjectivism all too frequently replaces objective law in his teaching. Because this teaching—if it be possible to speak of uniform teaching —sprang from the soil of his passionate attacks on the religious vows and sacerdotal celibacy, it had a sensuous and dangerous aspect. [35]

Nevertheless, he extols Matrimony as a dignified, yea, sublime institution of divine provenience and delineates the natural side of conjugal life in glowing phrases. He even boastfully claims that it was he who "sang the praises" of the matrimonial state "in sermons, writings, and examples," whereas the papists did not recognize harlotry as a sin. [36] It is surprising to note how many Protestant writers repeat this self-

---

[33] Weimar ed., Vol. XXX, III, pp. 205 sqq.; Erl. ed., Vol. XXIII, pp. 93 sqq.

[34] Similarly in a letter to Spalatin, January 7, 1527 (*Briefwechsel*, VI, p. 6), in consequence of the experience "that mankind could not be governed by the gospel."

[35] Cf. S. Baranowski, *Luthers Lehre von der Ehe*, Münster i. W., 1913, especially the summaries at pp. 4 sqq. and 207 sqq.

[36] *Tischreden*, Weim. ed., Vol. IV, n. 5116.

praise and at the same time overlook the tangible shortcomings inherent in Luther's theory of matrimony as well as the fatal consequences of that theory when put into practice.

In his book "Von Ehesachen" Luther refrains from dealing with the confused mass of questions which had arisen from the new concept of Matrimony. For the jurists, even Schurf at Wittenberg, strictly defended many of the traditional canonical regulations and interpretations against his liberal notions. On the matrimonial impediments, particularly those derived from consanguinity, as well as on divorce, Luther expresses himself only in a cursory manner. He concedes the right of divorce on the grounds of adultery and malevolent desertion.

One of the principal objects of this work is to combat clandestine marriages contracted without parental consent. Matrimony, so he teaches, is a public state of life and hence must be contracted publicly, in the presence of witnesses and in the sight of the congregation. Clandestine marriages contracted against the wishes of father and mother or their representatives, are null and void. However, the rights of parents should not be exaggerated. If parents wantonly prevent their children from marrying, he says, the civil authority or, in the event of the latter's refusal, the pastor, with the assistance of worthy friends, should permit and confirm the marriage. Luther was confronted with severe conflicts with the secular authorities because of his opposition to the constantly increasing secret marriages, or secret betrothals, as he termed them. Because of his vexatious experiences with matrimonial problems, his disgust increased to such an extent that he subsequently wrote to Count Albrecht of Mansfeld: "I have cast it [the matter of regulating marriages] from me and have written to several persons that, in the name of all the devils, they should do as they see fit." [37]

Among other works written by Luther, mention should be made of his "Reply to the Libel of the King of England," written in 1527,[38] —a crude rejoinder to the published reply of Henry VIII in which the latter declined to co-operate with Luther, who had previously endeavored to interest the King in his cause. In his rejoinder Luther says that he "upholds his doctrine in defiance not only of princes and kings, but of all the devils." No less violent is his tract "On Secret and

[37] October 5, 1536; Erl. ed., Vol. LV, p. 147 (*Briefwechsel*, XI, p. 90).
[38] Weimar ed., XVIII, pp. 26 sqq.; Erl. ed., Vol. XXX, pp. 1 sqq.

Purloined Letters," [39] written in 1529 against Duke George of Saxony, in connection with the affair of the alleged secret league of the Catholic princes for the destruction of Lutheranism, discovered by Otto von Pack. Luther had written a letter on this subject to his friend Link, which had come into the possession of the Duke and was made public by him, to the chagrin of the writer. In this letter, as well as in the tract written to defend it, Luther asserts the existence of the League, which had already at that time been shown to be a myth, and maintained that George and his counselors were possessed by the devil, and consequently he (Luther) was constrained to believe that they harbored most wicked designs. [40]

In 1527, Luther dedicated two treatises to the two "martyrs" of his theological system, as he calls them. One of these is entitled, "Consolation to the Christians of Halle on the Death of their Preacher, George [Winkler]"; the other is a tract on "Leonard Kaiser, who was Burnt in Bavaria for the Gospel." [41] Winkler had been attacked and murdered in 1527 by unascertained culprits. Without proof, Luther accuses the canons of Mayence of being accessories to the crime. The second "martyr," Leonard Kaiser (Käser), was a Bavarian ex-priest who had studied at Wittenberg and was executed at Schärding after being tried for heresy by Ernest of Bavaria, administrator of the bishop of Passau.

In his printed message "To the Christians of Bremen" [42] Luther glorified several other "martyrs": two Augustinians of Brussels; the Augustinian Henry of Zütphen (Henry Müller, died 1524); Caspar Tauber, who was burnt at the stake in Vienna in 1524; a Lutheran colporteur named George, who was executed in the same year at Ofen, and an unknown individual of Prague. He pathetically exclaims that "their blood would drown the papacy and its god, the devil." [43]

If several of his later utterances were taken seriously, many more bloody victims of his party would have to be included among the "martyrs" of the new faith. The number mentioned has been increased by historical authorities; for the medieval laws against heretics con-

---

[39] Weimar ed., Vol. XXX, II, pp. 25 sqq.; Erl. ed., Vol. XXXI, pp. 1 sqq.

[40] Grisar, *Luther*, Vol. III, pp. 325 sq., V, p. 343.

[41] Weimar ed., Vol. XXIII, pp. 401 sqq.; Erl. ed., Vol. XXII, pp. 294 sqq. and Weim. ed., Vol. XXIII, p. 452; *Briefwechsel*, VI, pp. 156 sqq.

[42] Erl. ed., Vol. XXVI, 2nd ed., pp. 40 sqq. (*Briefwechsel*, V, p. 112.).

[43] Letter to Hausmann, November 17, 1524; Erl. ed., Vol. XXVI, 2nd ed., p. 403 (*Briefwechsel*, V, p. 112).

tinued in operation. According to Riezler it is possible to demonstrate that in Bavaria, which was accused of being especially cruel, relatively few obstinate heretics were executed. In Württemberg, it appears, capital punishment was more frequently inflicted upon apostate Catholics. But it must be recalled that many of those who were executed there and elsewhere were guilty of participation in the revolts connected with the Peasants' War as well as of other crimes which constituted one of the grounds, if not the chief ground, for their execution. Others were put to death because of their Anabaptist doctrines and machinations, which were dangerous to the State; and for this reason Lutheranism cannot claim them as confessors. A case in point is the frequently cited one of Balthasar Hubmaier, who, having come into prominence as an apostle of the revolutionary Anabaptist movement, was burnt at the stake in 1527. In every religious conflict there have been deluded individuals who wrought up their errors to the point of dangerous madness and did not hesitate to risk their very lives. The history of the severe laws formulated against heresy since the early Middle Ages furnishes ample proof of this statement.

Among the polemical tracts which Luther issued against Catholic worship, is his "Advice to a Dear Friend on Both Forms of the Sacrament in Reply to the Mandate of the Bishop of Meissen," published in 1528. [44] The exclusion of the laity from the chalice, decreed for practical reasons by the Church, constituted one of the chief grounds of attack against her. When, in 1528, the bishop of Meissen renewed his regulations proscribing the use of the chalice for the laity, the Lutherans availed themselves of these regulations in order to attack the Church, and this afforded Luther an occasion to recapitulate his former alleged proofs in support of the reception of the Sacrament under both forms by the laity. The papal Church, thus he declared in opposition to the bishop, sets the Word of God at naught in this respect, thereby proving that she is the Church of the devil and the bride of Satan.

The following two years saw a series of excellent Catholic replies relative to the lay-chalice. The authors easily demonstrated that the reception of the Eucharist under the form of bread alone does not constitute a mutilation of the Sacrament, as Luther, appealing to the alleged "clear, forceful words of Christ," contended. They demonstrated that the blood of Christ as well as His divinity were insepa-

[44] Weimar ed., Vol. XXVI, pp. 560 sqq.; Erl. ed., Vol. XXX, pp. 373 sqq.

rably united with His body. The Church in introducing the custom of giving the host alone to the laity, because of the danger that the consecrated wine be spilled or profaned, was within her rights, as she was the administrator of the Sacraments for the glory of God. The demand for the chalice was not prompted by zeal for divine worship, but rather founded upon a spirit of opposition and provocation, since the adherents of the new religion did not exhibit any great activity in the reception of the Eucharist, and since, moreover, most of them did not desire to receive the Eucharist under either form. Among those who defended the traditional practice we find, for example, the Dominican Michael Vehe of Halle, who, in a treatise, "On the Law of the Reception of the Holy Sacrament," composed in 1531, which was a model of objectivity and calmness, demonstrated the right of Cardinal Albrecht to prohibit the faithful at Halle to receive their Easter communion under both species. [45]

By means of popular polemical pictures Luther endeavored to arouse the passions of the people against the papal Church. In a pamphlet, "A Vision of Friar Claus in Switzerland," [46] published in 1528, he circulated an alleged vision of the papacy had by Blessed Nicholas von der Flüe, which, he pretended, exhibited to the world Rome's "tyrannical, murderous, bloody dominion over body and soul." He sees in this utterly unhistorical representation a dismal head, crowned with a tiara, whence six pointed swords are projected. In Luther's mystical interpretation, the triply serrated beard signifies the three classes of men who adhere to the pope, "the sanctimonious, such as monks, priests, and nuns; the scholars, such as jurists, theologians, magistri; the mighty of the earth, such as kings, princes, and lords." The pamphlet is a mental aberration, corresponding to its author's frame of mind.

Very bitter, even if droll, are the supplements which he appends to his "New Intelligence of Leipsic" and "The Fable of the Lion and the Ass." [47] Two authors of Leipsic, John Hasenberg and Joachim von Heyden, had attacked Luther's marriage to Catherine of Bora. The above-mentioned document was intended to be Luther's reply,

[45] N. Paulus, *Die Dominikaner im Kampf gegen Luther*, pp. 219 sq.

[46] Weimar ed., Vol. XXVI, pp. 130 sqq.; Erl. ed., Vol. LXIII, pp. 260 sqq. Cf. Grisar-Heege, *Luthers Kampfbilder*, Vol. III (*Lutherstudien*, n. 5), pp. 44-56, with illustrations, especially p. 53.

[47] Weimar ed., Vol. XXVI, pp. 539 sqq.; Vol. LIII, pp. 549 sqq.; Erl. ed., Vol. LXIV, pp. 324 sqq. Cf. Grisar-Heege, *l. c.*, pp. 37-44, with illustrations, especially p. 43.

or, at any rate, a sort of reply. The former work is ornamented with a square, in which the word ASINI is written with checkered letters in such wise that, commencing with the center, the word "ass" can be read forty times. The fate which, as he tells us, the writings of the two Leipsic authors were to experience at his hands in his private chamber cannot be described in decent language. The second of these tracts depicts how the ass is made king of beasts; it is aimed at the pope, whom the Leipsic professors honored, but whom Luther frequently describes as "pope-ass." An artistic illustration, furnished by Cranach, which accompanies the work, presents two young asses, *asini Lipsienses*, holding a large crown above the head of a braying, lean old ass, which is followed by two young prancing asses, carrying halberds on their shoulders. The text ironically ascribes to the pope-ass "the ability to administer both the temporal and the spiritual government" and asserts that there is "nothing about the entire ass which is not worthy of royal and papal honors."

Quite serious was Luther's literary warfare against the Anabaptists. His "Address to Two Pastors on Rebaptizing," published in 1528, was particularly characteristic.[48] Contrary to the principal objection of the rebaptizers, namely, that infants could not possibly have the faith which Luther required as a condition for the efficacy of the Sacrament, he obstinately asserts that children can and do have the faith and denounces as a vain conceit the statement that they are as yet devoid of reason. The constant practice of the Church supplies him with a bulwark in support of Infant Baptism. The Church could not have been permitted by God to remain in error for so long a time. He speaks on this topic as if he did not accuse the preceding centuries of the Christian era of the most glaring errors in other essential doctrines. When he was in an agitated frame of mind, he took no account of such contradictions.

The writings which were evoked by Luther's controversy with Zwingli occupy a special place among his literary productions.

4. ZWINGLI AND THE CONTROVERSY REGARDING THE LAST SUPPER

In the celebrated controversy on the Eucharist which arose between Luther and the quick-witted Swiss reformer Zwingli, two

[48] Weimar ed., Vol. XXVI, pp. 144 sqq.; Erl. ed., Vol. XXVI, 2nd ed., pp. 281 sqq.

characteristic traits of Luther are made manifest. In the first place, a more credulous tendency is discoverable in him, even to the extent of accepting the miraculous and incomprehensible features of the doctrine of the Eucharist, as contrasted with the subtlety to which Zwingli and his partisans, Oecolampadius and Bucer, inclined. Secondly, there is discernible that uncouth controversial method which seeks to put down an opponent by every available means of rhetoric, even if it be never so insulting, combined with most questionable arguments. In the thought of mankind, the Last Supper is usually enveloped by a divine peace. The Sacrament unites unto itself the souls of men by the strongest bond of union ever bestowed upon mankind. But now the holy table became the arena of a horrible quarrel which was to last for a number of years and led to a desecration of the pearl of Christian worship by the contending factions of the reformed religion.

The controversy was not confined to the two protagonists, Luther and Zwingli, and their more intimate friends, but extended throughout southern Germany, Switzerland, and the neighboring countries.

Zwingli, in virtue of his rationalistic conception of history, as set forth in a letter written in 1524 to Alberus, in his "Commentary on True and False Religion," in which he discussed the words by which Christ instituted the Holy Eucharist, had professed the following proposition: "The Lord understands by bread and eating nothing but the gospel and the faith. . . . He absolutely does not speak of any sacramental food." The consecrated species, according to his idea, are only a symbol of Christ, of His testament and His grace; there is no Real Presence, which reason could not comprehend and which appears contradictory, since the Body of Christ can be only in one place, namely, in Heaven, at the right hand of His Father, and not wherever the Lord's Supper is celebrated.

The literary controversy with Zwingli was taken up on the Lutheran side by Bugenhagen, whereupon Oecolampadius espoused the cause of Zwingli by his denial of the Real Presence. Luther had on a former occasion defended his teaching on the Eucharist against Karlstadt and the "fanatics" and now repeatedly expressed himself against Zwingli, whose bold attacks on the Eucharist filled him with indignation. He persistently classified Zwingli among the "fanatics," though Zwingli had openly declared himself opposed to the views of Karlstadt. Hence, when Zwingli, in his "*Amica Exegesis*" (1527), renewed and intensified his opposition to the doctrine of the Eucharist as formulated by the Wittenberg divines, Luther drew his sword against his rival of Zurich by means of a violent polemical tract entitled, "That the Words: 'This is my Body' are Still Firmly Established." [49] Zwingli replied in a tract which bore the scarcely less vigorous title, "That These Words . . . Shall Retain Their Same Ancient Significance Forever."

Luther at last determined to put an end to the controversy by means of a final tract, which he entitled, "Profession of the Lord's Supper" (1528). [50]

This tract is not merely a summary and expansion of the reasons which he had hitherto advanced against the "abominable heresy" of the "three leaders of the Sacramentarians," Karlstadt, Zwingli, and Oecolampadius, as well as the Silesian Schwenckfeld; but it is at the same time a solemn profession of faith, to which he is resolved to adhere with increased firmness, now that its articles have been imperiled by the Sacramentarians. He analyzes these articles, commencing with that "on the divine Majesty, on the Father, the Son and the Holy Ghost." The earnestness with which he discusses this article is touching. In this part of his work he is also desirous of marking his attitude towards the Catholic Church. He condemns her doctrine of free-will and sin, represents the Mass as an abomination exceeding all other abominations, rejects the invocation of the saints, and, relative to the Zwinglian iconoclasts, asserts that, according to Holy Writ, sacred images are "very useful;" finally, he contends that the Church consists in the communion or assembly of all Christians without a hierarchy.

This so-called "Great Profession" made no impression upon the opponents of Luther. Zwingli and Oecolampadius jointly published a sharp reply. Luther, however, reverted only incidentally to the great question of the Eucharist, until the memorable debate between him and Zwingli at Marburg.

It cannot be denied that his presentation of the case against his Swiss rival possesses certain merits in spite of obvious defects and the injection of personalities. The necessity of adhering to the simple, literal meaning of the words of institution is demonstrated by splendid arguments and with convincing clarity. The obligation of be-

[49] Weimar ed., Vol. XXIII, pp. 64 sqq.; Erl. ed., Vol. XXX, pp. 14 sqq.—On the history of the controversy cf. W. Köhler, *Zwingli und Luther; ihr Streit über das Abendmahl nach seinen politischen und religiösen Beziehungen*, Vol. I, Leipsic, 1924.

[50] Weimar ed., Vol. XXVI, pp. 261 sqq.; Erl. ed., Vol. XXX, pp. 151 sqq.

lieving religious truths that transcend human reason is emphasized in inspiring words. If, he says, Christ after His Resurrection passed through closed doors, then His glorified body in the Eucharist is not bound by the ordinary laws of nature, and it is simply a question of submitting one's intellect to the plain words of the Almighty. He triumphantly appeals to the unequivocal belief of the Church in the real presence, which she has held since the primitive period of her existence. In these pages he is animated by the faith which he had received in the days of his childhood and nurtured during his long monastic career—a faith that resounds in the sonorous verses of the *Lauda Sion* of St. Thomas Aquinas: *"Quod non capis, quod non vides, animosa firmat fides praeter rerum ordinem."* He pretends to have gained a most intimate conviction of the real presence of Christ by personal experience, nay, even to have been instructed in this truth by angels.

A comparison between the two antagonists reveals the fact that both are guilty of monstrous theological errors. Luther stands on Biblical ground with only one foot as it were; his head is enveloped by theological and philosophical clouds which completely obscure the truth. As regards his demonstration from the Bible, he hesitates to make a logical application of the literal interpretation. He rejects the Catholic doctrine of transubstantiation and contends that the body of Christ is simultaneously present with the bread. His arbitrariness is manifested in his denial of the sacrificial character of the Eucharist as maintained in the Bible.

In the theological and philosophical discussions of the past, this sacred mystery, in as far as it was accessible to human reason, was expressed in clear formulas. These Luther, because of his contempt for Scholasticism, rejected as the product of "sophists." As a result, he founders in his attempt to escape the objections of Zwingli, as when, e. g., he asserts that the body of Christ is at the throne of God, but also participates in the divine omnipresence, so that it is found everywhere throughout the universe (ubiquity), and, hence, also in the Eucharist.[51] The important thing is, he says, that Christ, in virtue of a special promise, desired His presence to be tangible to us somewhere, and this precisely in the Eucharist. In Luther's opinion this "special promise" of Christ as regards the Eucharist resides in His intention

----

[51] Erl. ed., Vol. XXX, p. 67.

to strengthen our faith through the Sacrament and thus to mediate our salvation. Nevertheless, he maintains that infidels actually receive Christ when they receive the Eucharist.

Zwingli objected that, according to Luther's doctrine, the Sacrament does not constitute a thing *sui generis,* since there are other and even more effective means of confirming faith in the divine promises, and therefore a superfluous miracle is postulated. Luther can only meet this objection by asserting that in the Eucharist the remission of sins, which is effected in a general way by the preaching of the Gospel, is personally imputed to each individual. His main object is to uphold his contention that the Sacraments do not sanctify *ex opere operato,* as taught by the Catholic Church.

Zwingli is equally arbitrary. It would be a most disagreeable task to follow up this controversy in detail. Frequently one does not even know to what extent both parties are sincere in their assertions, so much are their assertions involved in contradiction. Thus Luther does not approve of the expression that Christ suffered for us only in His human nature, for the reason that this might cast doubt upon the doctrine of the two natures in Christ. Julius Köstlin, the Protestant biographer of Luther, says that, as regards the controversy about the Eucharist, one is "justified in asking whether Luther really understood what he maintained; especially whether he had a definite and clear idea of what we call the distinction between real and merely dynamic presence." [52]

The style in which this, the sublimest doctrine of the Christian religion, is treated by the two leaders of the new theological systems is anything but edifying. Ridicule, animosity, and misrepresentation alternate with one another. Each is determined to remain master of the situation and to capture the reader. How differently the same theme is treated by the defenders of the Catholic doctrine of the Eucharist, as, for instance, the scholarly Bishop Fisher of Rochester in his Latin treatise, "On the Truth of the Real Presence" (Cologne, 1527).

Luther says that either his antagonists, above all Zwingli, or he himself and his followers are servants of the devil; no other alternative exists. Satan, he asserts, has crept into the Bible, which he (Luther) had once more drawn from under the bench, and now produces rubbish and winks his eyes, insinuating that Baptism, original sin, and Christ are of no conse-

[52] Köstlin-Kawerau, M. *Luther,* Vol. II, pp. 100 sq.

quence. Zwingli's objections are dictated by a "desperate black devil" and his interpretations of Luther's words are "impudent lies."

The leaders of the "Sacramentarians," he declares, are not persuaded of the truth of their cause; in fact they cannot be, but must sincerely regret (as he undertakes to demonstrate) that they began the quarrel. But the devil is determined to be victorious.

"Whoever is willing to be warned, let him beware of Zwingli and avoid his books as he would the poison of the infernal Satan; for that fellow is thoroughly perverse and has lost Christ completely."

In discussing Zwingli's objection to Christ's being seated at the right hand of God, he mockingly speaks of the cope which Christ must wear in Heaven, and asks whether all creatures are not there simultaneously with Him, "such as lice and fleas, that infest the monk's cowl." His opponent replies with undignified acerbity that he is not in need of the phantasmagorical heaven of Luther, nor does he want his cowl or dog's hood; Luther should take them home and deck himself out in them.

Such were the depths of triviality to which these controversialists descended. Nevertheless Zwingli assures his readers that he did not intend to berate Luther with such "unrestrained language" as the latter employed to insult him, but that he abstained from the use of such invectives as "fanatic," "devil," "scoundrel," "heretic," "contumacious fellow," "blockhead," etc. Indeed, his tone is more moderate in the beginning of his argument and somehow betrays the cultured humanist. Eventually, however, he repays Luther in his own coin and uses an uncouth, Swiss-German dialect.

In the interests of decency, especially of religious decency, it was well that Luther made no further reply after his "Great Profession," but left the matter where it was by saying that "it was not the proper thing for him to concern himself any longer with the doltish replies and idiotic performances of his opponents." [53]

5. THE PROTEST OF 1529

At the diet of Spires, which convened in April, 1529, under the presidency of Archduke Ferdinand, the Catholic estates of the Empire and their theological advisers appeared to be more united and determined than before. They were prepared to put an end to the abuse to which the recess of the diet of 1526 had been put by the innovators during the last three years. For the flexible phraseology

[53] *Ibid.*, p. 102. Most of the passages cited above appear in Köstlin-Kawerau, *op. cit.*

of the resolution, which had been forced from that assembly, was unscrupulously exploited by the reformers to advance their cause.

Hence, the Catholic majority of the estates at the new diet in Spires succeeded in having the following modification adopted and published by authority of the Emperor:

Those who adhered to the edict of Worms "shall and are required to abide by the same until a future council"; in the case of the other estates, all further "innovations" should be prevented, at least until the assembly of the council, where it is impossible to abolish the new doctrine without disturbance. In those parts where the new doctrine is upheld, preaching against the Sacrament of the altar and placing obstacles to attendance at Mass were specifically prohibited. Severe penalties were prescribed against the Anabaptists and others who incited the people to rebellion. It was finally declared, in order to safeguard religious peace, that no estate was to "protect the subjects and relatives of one 'faith' against the authorities of the other"; that the public peace declared by the diet of Worms was to continue; and, if any one estate be "violently overrun" by another, it was the duty of the "Kammergericht" (supreme court of judicature) to intervene.

There was nothing in these decrees which the reformers could reasonably have represented as unfair, had they sincerely wished to live in peaceful concord and in a temporary arrangement until the assembly of the council which they themselves had desired. But they harbored no such desire; on the contrary, they were eager to advance farther and resolved to make a solemn protest against the legitimate recess of the imperial diet.

This protest was made on the nineteenth of April, 1529, and from it the entire party which made it derived the name of "Protestants." However, not all the princely estates which were favorably inclined either to religious reform or to Lutheranism, concurred in this hazardous protest. The Elector John of Saxony and the Landgrave Philip of Hesse took the lead. They were joined by Margrave George of Brandenburg-Ansbach, Duke Ernest of Brunswick-Lüneburg, and Prince Wolfgang of Anhalt. Their following was considerably increased when thirteen cities of Upper Germany, who were almost exclusively in favor of Zwinglianism, joined their ranks. These cities were Strasburg, Ulm, Constance, Lindau, Memmingen, Kempten, Nördlingen, Heilbronn, Reutlingen, Isny, St. Gall, Weissenburg, and

Windesheim. Nuremberg also went over to their side. On April 22, Electoral Saxony, Hesse, and the cities of Strasburg, Nuremberg, and Ulm secretly formed a defensive alliance.

Whilst the Eucharistic controversy completely separated the majority of the above-mentioned cities of Upper Germany from the Lutheran faith, they nevertheless, in their inglorious procedure against the authority and peace of the Empire, overlooked the religious differences which prevailed in their own ranks and united against the self-defense to which the Catholic Church was bound to resort.

The Protestants, moreover, frustrated the proposed movement against the Turks. When the imperial diet convened, it was impressed in the name of the absent Emperor with the necessity of energetically repelling the danger of a Turkish invasion, which was declared to be the most important subject before the assembly. The report had reached Spires that the Turkish fleet was cruising along the coast of Sicily, threatening the Occident. "It is an undeniable fact," says Wilhelm Walther, a Protestant authority, "that the [Protestant estates] would not promise to render aid against the Turks, unless the Catholic estates of the Empire arrived at some other conclusion concerning the religious question than that under discussion, which [they declared] it was impossible for them to accept." [54]

Luther was naturally very much in favor of the idea that the parties who espoused the new religion should issue a protest against the resolution of the imperial diet. Two things, however, worried him, and Melanchthon even more: namely, the formation of an armed alliance of his followers in opposition to the Emperor; and the approximation to Zwinglianism, which, though so far merely exterior, might result in an intrinsic religious coalescence. Melanchthon implored them not to break with Charles V, with Ferdinand, and the "whole empire"; for thus far the Protestants had maintained the semblance of not actually wishing to secede from the Empire, nor even from the Church, but of desiring only a reform of the same. For Luther, Zwinglianism, which he detested, constituted the chief source of anxiety. In his worry concerning the new alliance, he wrote to the Elector of Saxony on May 22 that the impetuous temperament of the Landgrave [Philip of Hesse] would create havoc in the Empire, that trust was to be placed in God, not in man, but worst of all was the fact that, by uniting with the Zwinglians, the

[54] Grisar, *Luther*, Vol. II, p. 383.

Lutherans would incur the sins of those who antagonized the Sacrament and were deliberate enemies of God.[55] The Elector bowed to his representations and desisted from further attempts to bring about an alliance.

With increased energy Landgrave Philip, on the other hand, pursued his and Zwingli's project of forming a close union of all the adherents of the new religion in Germany and Switzerland, against the Hapsburg power and against the Catholic Church. Before this could be accomplished, however, it was necessary to effect some kind of reconciliation between Luther and Philip. The latter was resolved to go to impossible lengths, and it was decided that a personal conference should take place between Luther and Zwingli.

6. LUTHER AND ZWINGLI IN THE CASTLE OF MARBURG

On April 22, 1529, the Landgrave of Hesse proposed to his friend Zwingli that he and Luther, as well as the principal representatives of the two parties in the controversy concerning the Eucharist, hold a theological disputation. It was not zeal for religion which induced him to suggest this conference, but the desire of realizing his political ambitions, which, in comformity with Zwingli, were directed against the Emperor and the house of Hapsburg. The exiled Duke Ulric of Württemberg had won over the Landgrave to this hopeless idea of a conference. The intrepid Zwingli favored it at once, without, however, holding out any hope of union on his part. When the matter was broached to Luther, he at first expressed himself against it. Melanchthon also had his scruples. The Elector John at that time was not disposed to have anything to do with the Sacramentarians, as he feared the designs of the Swiss. Eventually, however, the urgent invitations of the Landgrave were crowned with success. On September 29, Zwingli and Oecolampadius, representing the Swiss, came to Marburg, as guests of Philip of Hesse. Bucer, Hedio, and Jacob Sturm represented Strasburg; Jonas, Cruciger, Myconius, and Menius; besides Luther and Melanchthon, represented Wittenberg.

At the first meeting, which was held on October 1, Luther and Melanchthon engaged Oecolampadius and Zwingli, respectively, in private conferences. But, apart from the burning question of the Sacrament, the latter only succeeded in removing some suspicions of

[55] Köstlin-Kawerau, M. *Luther*, Vol. II, p. 120.

the Wittenberg theologians against the doctrines of the Zurich reformer.

The second day witnessed a solemn public disputation between Luther, on the one hand, and Zwingli and Oecolampadius on the other. Luther had written on the table the words of institution in large letters: "This is my Body." In response to the sophistical arguments of his opponents, he always repeated, after expounding the contrary thesis, that he would not yield one tittle of these clear words. Without yielding his position, Zwingli cordially demanded that they come to a fraternal agreement.

After the conference had continued for three days, and a number of futile meetings had been held, it was decided, upon motion of the Landgrave, that at least a fraternal union, as desired by Zwingli, should be established. But Luther refused to accept the hand that was extended to him; for to him the existing theological differences about the Eucharist appeared prohibitive. When Zwingli pleaded for Christian charity, Luther was prepared to grant the request, provided it meant love of peace. He stuck to his oft-repeated declaration: "You have a spirit which differs from ours," perceiving and fearing the frank rationalism of Zwingli, and believing it was this spirit which induced Zwingli to regard the existing point of controversy as not so important as to become an obstacle to the union of both parties, and that eventually it would induce him to abandon all religion.

The Fifteen Articles of Marburg, personally composed by Luther, were to constitute a bulwark against the danger of infidelity, which he secretly feared.[56] Contrary to his expectations, however, they were accepted by the Swiss and Strasburg theologians. They expressed Luther's position relative to the Trinity, Christology, faith and justification, Baptism and private confession. A further article, superscribed, "On the Sacrament of the Body and Blood of Christ," agrees with Zwingli in its negative aspect, namely, in its opposition to Catholicism; for it repudiates the reception of the Eucharist under one species and also the sacrifice of the Mass. This is followed by the vague declaration that "the Sacrament is a Sacrament of the true body and blood of Jesus Christ, and the spiritual reception of this same body and blood is necessary for every Christian." It states, furthermore, that "we all believe

56 "Marburger Gespräch und Marburger Artikel," Weimar ed., Vol. XXX, III, pp. 110 sqq.; Erl. ed., Vol. LXV, pp. 88 sqq.

and maintain the custom of receiving the Sacrament, as it has been given and ordained by the Word of God, the Almighty, that the delicate consciences be thereby moved unto faith and love by the Holy Ghost." Thereupon the existing dissension relative to the doctrine of the Eucharist is expressly admitted and the necessity of charity (to a certain degree) is taught: "Although we have not at this time settled the question whether the true body and blood of Christ are corporeally in the bread and wine, nevertheless, Christian charity, to the extent that every one's conscience can tolerate, should be mutually manifested by both factions, who should diligently supplicate Almighty God to confirm us in the right understanding through His Spirit."

Thus the opponents separated, having settled nothing. In the practical field of the religious life the schism opened by the new theology grew proportionately wider. Fortunately for Germany, one good result came of this conference, namely, that the plan of an alliance against the Emperor and the Empire, as fostered by Zwingli and the Landgrave of Hesse, failed to materialize.

Although intimate union with the Swiss reformers was frustrated, the Zwinglian doctrines continued to make progress in a portion of Germany. In many parishes of the Swabian and Alemannic districts, there arose a powerful Zwinglian faction. The Swiss doctrine and idea of the Church, combined with the denudation of altars, the destruction of sacred images, and certain political projects, extended down the Rhine from Basle over Strasburg into the Netherlands.

In virtue of the attitude of Luther and his Elector, an alliance of the Upper German Zwinglians with the Wittenberg reformers became impossible. Nuremberg on the whole followed Luther, whereas Ulm expressly joined the so-called "Burgrecht" of Zurich. The result was dissension everywhere.

Luther looked in vain for another bridge to span the chasm. He caused the so-called Articles of Schwabach to be proposed to the towns of Upper Germany.[57] These articles had been drawn up by the theologians of Wittenberg in July or August, and were more or less opposed to the Zwinglians. On the sixteenth of October they were rejected by Strasburg and Ulm at a congress held in Schwabach

---

[57] Weimar ed., Vol. XXX, III, pp. 86 sqq.; Erl. ed., Vol. XXIV, 2nd ed., pp. 334 sqq. Cfr. H. v. Schubert in the *Zeitschrift für Kirchengeschichte*, XXIX (1918), pp. 342 sqq.

and likewise at a convention held at Schmalkalden on November 29. Landgrave Philip, whom Luther regarded with suspicion, oscillated between the two great factions of the new religion, whilst Zwingli hoped, through the mediation of the Landgrave, "to isolate Wittenberg and thus finally to make it agreeable to his plans." [58]

7. PERSONAL EXPERIENCES. TEMPTATIONS

On his return to Wittenberg from the Marburg Conference, Luther, as he states in a letter to Link, was seized with grave spiritual afflictions and temptations at Torgau.[59] It is possible that the excitement experienced at Marburg and the sermons he preached on his homeward journey may have contributed to this state of soul. While he boasted of his victory over Zwingli, he fully and painfully realized the latter's obstinacy and the dangers that threatened his own doctrine. In addition, terrible accounts of Turkish aggressions tormented him. His heart, which once before, at Wittenberg, had caused him trouble, again became affected. He wrote to Link that he was scarcely able to reach Wittenberg, since Satan's angel had tormented him so that he despaired of being able to return to his own.

At Wittenberg his suffering continued. Whilst blaming the Turks to a great extent for his condition, he complained to his friend Amsdorf that they (the Turks) had been sent by God to chastise the blasphemous enemies of the gospel and to punish the people for their intolerable ingratitude towards him. He said he sensed their fury in the struggles of his soul, but with the aid of Christ hoped to overcome their god, the devil.[60] Only gradually a period of relative quiet assuaged him.

Previously, in July, 1527, Luther had survived an attack which had brought him to the verge of death. At that time his mental sufferings and self-reproaches were preceded and accompanied by fainting spells. Bugenhagen, who attended him and also heard his confession, wrote at the time that Luther's internal sufferings were comparable to the spiritual darkness "which is often mentioned in the descriptions of the infernal torments of the soul that occur in the Psalms"; they were more severe and dangerous than the mortal weak-

[58] G. Kawerau, *Reformation und Gegenreformation*, 3rd ed., p. 104.
[59] Letter of October 28, 1529, from Wittenberg; *Briefwechsel*, VII, pp. 179 sq.
[60] On October 19; *ibid.*, p. 173.

ness of the body. He adds that Luther had "been through a number of such attacks," although they were not all so severe. Luther himself at the time said to his confidant Jonas, that those who observed his exterior conduct were of the opinion that "he lay on a bed of roses, though God knew how it stood with him." [61]

In the language of Luther and his friends, those painful conditions are termed spiritual temptations (*tentationes spirituales*). We learn more about their nature by his frank epistolary communications during this period of severe internal struggles, through which he passed at the close of the year 1529, after a temporary surcease in July. These communications contain a vivid delineation of his despondent mood and his theological fears—they are the most melancholy chords of his entire life.

Undoubtedly his bitter experiences in connection with the visitation of Electoral Saxony, the irritating discussions between himself and Zwingli, the negotiations caused by the alleged papal conspiracy discovered by Pack, the dangerously arbitrary conduct of Philip of Hesse, the latter's violation of the public peace and his hostilities against Bamberg, Würzburg, and Mayence, were contributory causes. Above all, the pathological condition of his nerves and his irregular heart-action must be taken into consideration. When he was attacked by spells of weakness and fear, his physical infirmities would combine with the spiritual unrest caused by his reformatory efforts. His fears centered around such questions as: Why have you disturbed the peace of the Church? Are you sure that your cause is just? How will you account for the ruin of so many souls? The bright memories of his monastic days and of the happy hours he had spent within the Catholic Church simply would not subside. His fears, therefore, did not originate solely in his physical ailments; at least they were frequently present without any concomitant sense of illness, as he protested at times when they were most violent, that "as far as my physical condition is concerned, I find myself tolerably well"; or, "I feel well in body."

"For more than the whole of last week," he writes to Melanchthon on August 2, 1527, "I was tossed about in death and hell, so that I still tremble all over my body and am exhausted. Billows and tempests of despair and blasphemy assailed me, and I had lost Christ almost completely."

[61] Cfr. Grisar, *Luther*, Vol. V, pp. 333 sqq.

He complains to his friends that he is suffering from the buffetings of the prince of this world, the devil, who would be avenged on him; that reason cannot comprehend how difficult it is to know that Christ is our justice; and that "he seeks or thirsts after naught else than a merciful God." Consequently, he had not yet found Him with an abiding certitude, notwithstanding the fact that when he apostatized, he based his entire doctrine and fight against the Church and the pope upon this supposed discovery.

"I am well in body; but as to how it stands with me in spirit I am not certain. . . . I seek only for a gracious Christ. . . . Satan wants to prevent me from writing [in behalf of the gospel], and to drag me down with him to hell. May Christ tread him under foot. Amen!"

"My Katie is strong in faith," he wrote at that time; but of himself he is constrained to say: "I am scarcely able to breathe because of tempests and despondency." He laments that pope and Emperor, princes and bishops, nay, the whole world assail him, including "Erasmus and the Sacramentarians." His very brethren torment him. In the words of St. Paul, he cries aloud: "Combats without, fears within" (2 Cor. VII, 5). By citing his favorite Biblical passages, he endeavored to fortify himself in his own doctrine; but he felt that the "prince of demons," who had risen against him, was "armed to the teeth with Biblical quotations, so that his own knowledge of Sacred Scripture vanished before him."

With foolhardy temerity he nevertheless forces the habitual notions of his own upon his conscience, lest he perish. "Christ, indeed, has become weak" (in him); nevertheless, he would "believe with firmness (*fortiter credo*) that his work was pleasing to the Lord."

What oppressed him most is the thought that Satan alone is active in the attacks upon his conscience; that he (Satan) assumes the form of Christ and decks himself out as an angel of light. Is it not probable that all his spasmodic imaginings of Satan concealed from him the just reproaches with which he accused himself? To him the voice of his conscience is the voice of Satan.

But this is not the place to penetrate more deeply into Luther's dismal mental struggles during those months. It was the most tempestuous period through which he had to pass. It approached its close at the beginning of 1528, but there were painful after-effects. "Blessed be my Christ," he says amid a sight of relief, "blessed in the midst of despair, death, and blasphemy. . . . It is my glory to have lived in the world in conformity with the will of Christ, forgetting the very wicked life of the past." The story of his sufferings reveals the extent to which an impetuous will is capable of torturing the soul. Scarcely another man ever commanded such titanic forces as did Luther in his interior and exterior struggles.

An echo of his internal experiences is his famous hymn, "Ein' feste Burg" (A safe stronghold our God is still), which he composed in those days and which is still widely sung by his admirers, but properly understood only by a few. In its ponderous verses, expressive of the ardor of the battle which he at that time waged against the pope and the devil, against the "ancient evil one," he clung to the Christ of his Gospel: "But for us fights the proper Man, whom God Himself hath bidden. . . . And were this world all devils o'er . . . they cannot overpower us." [62]

Towards the end of January, 1528, he declared to a confidant quite in his own fashion, relative to the Sacramentarians who annoyed him, that he was determined, in order to get rid of his fears still more effectively, "still further to provoke Satan, who was raging against him with the utmost fury." [63]

In the middle of the same year he told another friend that it is always necessary, when temptations assail one, to exert oneself to the utmost against the devil, who is plainly to be discerned; and that "it is imperative to achieve salvation by blindly assuming as certain that all thoughts to the contrary are mere devil's treason." [64]

From time to time, nevertheless, his writings and addresses reëcho his lamentation of a "struggling conscience." He hears how the devil speaks through man: "It will not be easy for you to die." Yet, as time went on, his mental gymnastics increasingly overcame the reproaches of reason and conscience, aided by the distractions of his polemical life, the delirium of his successes, and the intoxicating eulogy of his friends.[65]

His courage found a more worthy cause to display itself when, in mid-summer, a lingering disease, described as the plague (*Pest*), broke out in Wittenberg and the rest of Germany. The university was temporarily removed to Jena; many fled, but Luther and Bugenhagen, the local pastor, remained to administer spiritual consolation to the sick and the dying. The contagion also entered the former

[62] See Grisar, *Luther*, Vol. V, pp. 549 sq., for the full text, and also Grisar, *Luthers Trutzlied "Ein' feste Burg"* (*Lutherstudien*, 1922, n. 4), pp. 14 sqq.

[63] Grisar, *Luther*, Vol. V, p. 338. Letter to John Hess in Breslau, January 27, 1528 (*Briefwechsel*, VI, p. 199.)

[64] *Ibid.*, pp. 338 sq.

[65] *Ibid.*, cfr. pp. 356 sqq.

monastery which was now his home. But he was not concerned about his own life. "Christ is here," he wrote to Spalatin, "so that we may not be alone; and He will be victorious." [66] At that time he composed the little treatise, "Whether one May Flee from Death," [67] intended to inspire courage. Pastors and preachers, such is his exhortation, ought to remain at their post, especially in such dire trouble, when the flock is more than ever in need of spiritual help.

Luther exhibited the same courage during the epidemic of the so-called "English sweat," a fever which broke out in Wittenberg and other cities in 1529. Again, in 1538 and 1539, he braved new outbreaks of the plague at Wittenberg, regarding perseverance as a duty imposed upon him by his office, which was watched by many with distrust. "God usually protects the ministers of His Word," he writes in 1538, "if one does not run in and out of the inns and lie in bed." [68]

Although many demands were made upon him, he willingly succored the suffering and the poor, aiding them as generously as his circumstances permitted. Thus he was able to say in a sermon to the people of Wittenberg that "he himself was poor, but the joy with which he utilized what had been given to him to satisfy his needs exceeded that with which the wealthy among them enjoyed their accumulated riches." At the same time he censured the avarice which he detected at Wittenberg. It was a theme to which he often reverted. He was not accustomed to seek comfort in the pleasures of the table. He loved simplicity in his domestic life no less than in his manners, conversation, and intercourse with men. In this respect he wished to be an example to those who were associated with him in his work. When not afflicted with melancholy, his familiarity and cordiality were a source of refreshment to his friends. He gladly displayed his characteristic humor, occasionally even in dark hours, in order to distract his mind. He speaks of this as a motive of his jovial talks.[69]

It is not true that the scene of his conviviality was a tavern where he was wont to consort of an evening with his friends and pupils. The account in question is a fabrication. As a matter of fact Luther spent his evenings with his family, in the one-time monastery where,

---

[66] On August 19, 1527 (*Briefwechsel*, VI, p. 76.)
[67] Grisar, *Luther*, Vol. IV, p. 272.
[68] *Ibid.*, pp. 272 sq.
[69] Grisar, *Luther*, Vol. V, pp. 306 sqq.

with Catherine von Bora, he was usually surrounded by those who were associated with him in his work, pupils or newcomers.[70]

Nor is it true that he drank to excess.[71] The so-called fanatics, the Anabaptists, who were often strict in outward appearance, as well as misinformed Catholic opponents, propagated unconfirmed rumors to this effect. Some controversial writers discovered a pretext for these accusations in certain misunderstood utterances of his. But these critics overlooked the fact that their charges were based upon jocose speeches or innocent quips by a man who was not always cautious in his utterances. It is nowhere credibly reported that Luther was drunk, even though there is evidence to show that he imbibed rather freely, according to the prevailing German custom. He was not exactly a model of abstemiousness, but he severely censured the excesses of princes and courtiers. In theory he was undoubtedly too compliant when he permitted a "good drink" (which in those days meant a considerable quantity) in cases of depression of spirit due to evil reports, worries, and heavy thoughts in general, oppression owing to troubles and labor, temptations of the "devil" resulting from sorrow and despondency. In his opinion, sleeplessness and spiritual exhaustion alone were sufficient to justify a "good drink." [72]

Mathesius, his pupil and eulogist, who was in many respects his mouthpiece, is even more indulgent. He says in one of his "wedding sermons" that one must have "a certain amount of patience" with those who sometimes, for a quite valid reason, "get a little tipsy" or "kick over the traces." [73]

If Luther had been addicted to the use of wine and beer in an excessive manner, he would not have been able to develop his marvelous energy. A drunkard does not write books and pamphlets filled with serious and thought-provoking ideas with the ease and facility with which Luther composed his writings. Even the violent and indecorous controversial tracts of the later period of his life are not saturated with alcohol, as a Protestant writer in America has recently endeavored to demonstrate; but they evince the spirit of an infernal hatred which is to be adjudged pathological. The so-called "drunken doc-

[70] H. Grisar, "Ein unterschobener Bericht," etc., in Ehrengabe für Herzog Johann Georg von Sachsen, 1920, pp. 693–703.

[71] Grisar, Luther, Vol. III, pp. 294–318.

[72] Ibid., p. 312.

[73] Ibid., p. 310.

tor" (*doctor plenus*) must be obliterated from history. In passing it should be remarked that this description of himself, which was said to have been found in one of his letters, is based upon an incorrect reading.[74]

The existence of natural children of Luther, with which ignorant polemicists of a former age frequently concerned themselves, is also unhistorical. Erasmus says in one of his letters that Catherine von Bora was confined a fortnight after her marriage with Luther. Subsequently he retracted this false rumor.[75] An alleged illegitimate child, called Andrew, born at a later date, proved to be Luther's nephew, Andrew Kaufmann. The maid servant in Luther's home, Rosina Truchsess, turned out to be an immoral woman, but there was not the least excuse for the gossip that Luther had sexual intercourse with her prior to his dismissing her in a fit of anger. The *adulter infans* (adulterine child) discovered in the controversial writings of Aurifaber (1569) is merely a printer's error for *alter infans* (the other child), as correctly printed in the edition of 1568.[76]

History records that five children were born of Luther's union with Catherine von Bora: Hans, born June 7, 1526; Magdalen, born in 1529; Martin, born in 1531; Paul, born in 1533; and Margaret, born in 1534.

In mid-summer, 1525, Luther secretly sheltered among his guests in the Black Monastery, his former friend and Wittenberg associate, Andrew Karlstadt, who had become his bitter enemy. This was a pleasant trait of his character. After the unfortunate issue of the Peasants' War, in which Karlstadt was accused of having participated in virtue of his sermons in Rothenburg ob der Tauber, he lacked the necessities of life and now solicited Luther's aid at any price, prepared to suffer any kind of humiliation. He was willing to keep silence with regard to his own special doctrines and to work for a living, provided he was permitted to return to the Electorate of Saxony. Luther was prepared to intercede for him with his sovereign. Karlstadt came to visit him and secretly spent several weeks in the former monastery. For a time not even Catherine was aware of

---

[74] H. Grisar in *Histor. Jahrbuch*, XXXIX (1919–20), pp. 496–500; cfr. *Luther*, Vol. III, pp. 316 sq.

[75] Grisar, *Luther*, Vol. II, pp. 187 sq.

[76] *Op. cit.*, Vol. III, pp. 280 sq.

his presence. Only Luther's servant Wolf Sieberger had been initiated into the secret and daily brought food to Karlstadt. After Luther had obtained from him a forced declaration concerning his teaching on the Last Supper, he interceded with the Elector John, who gave Karlstadt permission to remain in his Electorate.[77]

After residing at various places, Karlstadt betook himself to Kemberg, where he labored as a peasant and kept a small shop. Luther published several new tracts against this backslider; whereupon he evaded arrest in October, 1529, by fleeing from the Electorate of Saxony to Holstein, where he joined the Anabaptist Melchior Hoffmann, with whom he went to East Frisia. This vacillating man is next found in Strasburg, then in Zurich with Zwingli, and finally in Basle, where he joined the Zwinglians as a teacher in the theological faculty, though still persevering in his peculiar opinions, and completely at outs with Luther.

8. CATHOLIC APOLOGETICS AGAINST LUTHER

The attack on the ancient Church summoned to her defense a great host of writers, among whom were many illustrious minds. The number of theologians, preachers, secular and regular clerics, and laymen who wielded the pen in defense of the Church is surprisingly great. Naturally not all their writings are valuable. The products of the trained theologians transcend the works of mere preachers or occasional writers. Many of these productions bear the stamp of haste, the ephemeral polemics of the day, and the heat of battle; but not a few possess permanent scientific and historical interest.

Unfortunately, it is a fact that this literature has not been sufficiently noted, or at least not properly esteemed in its ensemble,[78] though, on the other hand, it labored too much under the influence of contention and lacked unity and organization in its development. Even to-day, it is often hardly possible to discover the most telling achievements. The odiousness, moreover, with which the Protestant partisans criticized these writings, lay as a heavy weight upon them. In consequence of the disparagement with which these Catholic authors were treated by the victoriously advancing reform move-

[77] *Ibid.*, Vol. III, p. 388. Barge, Karlstadt, Vol. II, pp. 369 sqq., treats extensively of this incident and the sequel.

[78] In G. Wolfs *Quellenkunde der deutschen Reformationsgeschichte* (II, ii, 1922, pp. 206 sqq.) the seventh section: "Die katholischen Gegner," is unduly abbreviated.

ment, it became customary to detect in them impotence of language as contrasted with the fiery eloquence of a Luther, or intellectual poverty in comparison with the bright flashes of his wit. It is true that the recklessness of Luther's language, by which he enthused the masses, was lacking in the replies of those who defended the Catholic Church. They do not possess the tempestuous force of the Wittenberg reformer. In that tempest Luther alone was endowed with an epochal linguistic talent far outdistancing in this respect even his own followers.

In recent times a more appreciative estimate of the Catholic apologists of the Reformation period has gained ground. The general progress of objective historical research has contributed to this, as well as numerous special studies, such as those of the scholarly Dr. Nicholas Paulus. It has been aided particularly by the labors embodied in the monumental *Corpus Catholicorum*, a collection of reprints intended to unite all those old publications in a critical edition.

A more diligent study of these writings has revealed various excellences possessed by many of the apologists of the old theology and the rights of the Church. Versatility and brilliancy preponderate in a surprising degree in the works of Jerome Emser, secretary to Duke George of Saxony. Extensive reading and circumspection dominate the writings of the cathedral canon, John Cochlaeus. Sincerity, directness, and acumen characterize John Eck, the professor of theology. Dignity, nay, even a certain solemnity, are the marks of John Faber, bishop of Vienna. Ingenious, though occasionally unrefined, humor is discoverable in the writings of Thomas Murner, the popular Franciscan. Theological and religious austerity characterize the works of the Dominican Jacob von Hochstraten. Erasmus, who originally inclined towards Luther, in his subsequent controversial writings shows great intellectual power and abounds in satire. These seven men form a constellation of polemical writers around whom many other able and distinguished defenders of the Church grouped themselves.

It was no easy resolve, but rather a certain risk for these men to rise in opposition to the powerful Luther, or to resist the religious revolt in general. These writers could expect no appreciation at the hands of their opponents, but only derision and contempt.

This was particularly the case when Luther took notice of them. He loaded them with opprobrium and often horribly distorted their teachings.

"I despise the opposition," he says, "and regard them as downright fools." His adherents imitated his tactics.[79] In the event that an opponent of his achieved prominence, he was liable to be depicted as a beast in the cartoons and pamphlets of the opposition. Thus Emser was represented as a goat, Cochlaeus as an ass and a snail, Murner as a cat, Lemp as a dog. Luther and his supporters accused the apologists of the Church that deep down in their hearts they were convinced of the untruth of their own writings and the justice of his cause; that they wrote as they did because they were friends of the papacy or expected a liberal reward. If these accusations failed to dissuade a courageous writer from his undertaking, he encountered difficulties in procuring a publisher for his writings, as is evidenced, for example, by the case of Cochlaeus, who made indefatigable efforts to maintain at least two efficient Catholic printing presses. The reformed or religiously indifferent publishers literally flooded the market. What they were after was profit. Their production brought a good return in money, whereas Catholic books and pamphlets were not acceptable to the colporteurs who traveled through the country selling popular literature. Royalties as a rule were paid by neither party. The Catholic apologists were confronted with the additional disadvantage of insufficient material support on the part of the bishops, who were mostly remiss in this respect, and by the absence of any stimulus for the work that was so urgently needed.

If, despite these hindrances, a noteworthy and timely literature was provided in defense of the Church, this fact was due to disinterested zeal for the cause. Timely above all else were the recommendations made by Catholic writers for a reform of the internal conditions of the Church. Correctly sensing the need of the age, many popular writers, whilst combating the new evangelical liberties, endeavored at the same time to bring about a genuine reform of the morals of clergy and laity. In reply to the criticisms of their opponents, they unhesitatingly acknowledged the prevalence of abuses in the Church. In many instances, effective notice of these evils was taken only as a result of public criticism. Thus many Catholics admitted that Lutheranism furnished the occasion for perfecting catechetical instruction. For this reason the apologists of the time also exposed without fear or favor the moral decadence which everywhere accompanied the religious revolt. In forceful language they demonstrated the fatal social consequences of the new gospel, especially on the occasion of the Peasants' War.

The defenders of the Church were benefited by the labors of the

[79] Grisar, *Luther,* Vol. III, p. 172.

theologians, which were often truly profound. They illustrated topics which had hitherto been but inadequately treated, such as the Church and her authority, the papacy as the center of unity, etc. The greatest services in this regard were rendered by Cajetan de Vio. Other Italians, such as Catharinus, as well as Germans, Frenchmen, and Englishmen, followed his example. The foundations were laid for the development of the theology of the Council of Trent and of the flourishing post-Tridentine period *in re* justification and grace. The apologists also discussed Biblical questions more freely than before. This change of tactics was necessitated by the Lutheran principle that the Bible was the sole source of faith, and by the popularity of Luther's German translation of the Bible. As a consequence, several new translations were made, such as those of Emser, Dietenberger and Dr. Eck. Luther himself declared: "I have driven them to the Bible." [80]

In general, the tone and style of these Catholic controversial writings is moderate and convincing, free from the excesses of the opposition. Not as though the indignation of the Catholic apologists did not occasionally flare forth in their writings, as when, *e.g.*, they saw how ecclesiastical institutions and doctrines, with which they had been acquainted since their youth, were subjected to monstrous distortion. In their replies, however, they did not employ the rude style of Luther, not even when, for instance, they, as cloistered religious, defended their state of life against his vile book "On Monastic Vows," or when, as priests, they undertook to defend the most sacred thing in their religion, the holy sacrifice of the Mass, against scandalous defamation.

Many are strikingly calm and conciliatory in their writings. This is true, especially at the beginning of the controversy, of certain Franciscans who had been well educated in the humanities. John Findling, whose Hellenized name was Apobolymaeus, in 1521 published a "Warning" to Luther, in which he addresses him as "dearest friend" and refuses to characterize him as a heretic, although the papal condemnation had already been issued. He challenges Luther's divine mission because of his unheard-of and hostile revolt—of course without any prospect of influencing the reformer.[81] Such works were inspired by the laudable intention of not wishing to aggravate matters, and also by a certain narrowness of view. The basic sentiment under-

[80] Grisar, *Luther*, Vol. VI, pp. 432 sqq.
[81] *Ibid.*, Vol. III, pp. 171 sq.

lying Humanism, which was very pronounced among the learned and which particularly animated Erasmus, proved to be harmful.

Other apologists move more freely, for instance, the accomplished, energetic Franciscan Caspar Schatzgeyer, a model of moderation combined with correctness and vigor. He was the most prominent defender of monastic life in southern Germany. At the time of his death, which occurred in Munich, in 1527, he had composed more than twenty works, most of which are excellent.

One of the grievances against Luther which pervades the works of the Catholic apologists is his obstinate mendacity. They style him a father of falsehood and a gross calumniator, sustaining this severe indictment by many facts. Nearly all of them hold that the ex-monk of Wittenberg is completely under the dominance of the devil, the father of lies. Some of the most daring among them, in speaking of the demoniacal traits in Luther's character, insinuate that his is a case of diabolical possession. It was their persistent belief that his obstinacy and uncanny dexterity in inventing constantly new attacks could not be explained except on the assumption that he was in league with Satan. John Dietenberger, a learned Dominican, author of a catechism and other works, calls Luther "the devil's hired messenger" and says that "here everything reeks of devils; nothing that the devilish man writes can stand without the devil, who endevils all his products." [82] The erudite and moderate Willibald Pirkheimer of Nuremberg writes in a letter, in 1529: "Luther seems to have gone quite mad, or to be agitated by some wicked demon." Elsewhere this author cites more than a dozen passages from varied contemporary writings, which speak of a diabolic activity on the part of Luther.[83] Luther himself gave occasion to the formation of such charges, among other actions by such unintelligible performances as his alleged disputation with the devil concerning the Mass. The general propensity of the time to discover a special intervention of Satan in extraordinary phenomena undoubtedly contributed to the formation of the afore-mentioned accusations. Cochlaeus traces them to certain idiosyncrasies of Luther shown when he was a young friar.

Elsewhere—first of all, so far as we know, in the writings of the former Dominican, Peter Sylvius (who was, by the way a very ordinary writer)—this contention of Satanic intervention is expanded into

[82] *Ibid.,* Vol. IV, p. 355.
[83] *Ibid.,* p. 353.

the fiction, founded on fabulous narratives, that the devil himself had begot Luther. This senseless babble was propagated by other writers.[84] In general, distortions caused by the readily accepted false legends about Luther, crept into the writings of lesser, nay, at times, even of major authors. One of the most common of them concerns his alleged drunkenness. This story plays its part both at home and abroad. Thus, in Italy, the Dominican theologian Catharinus expatiates at length on the inebriety of the religious reformer of the North. Other authors, in view of the uncertain rumors which were spread by the Anabaptists and other fanatics, write more objectively. The learned Cardinal Cajetan, for instance, prefers to clarify the questions at issue, without attacking the person or character of his opponent, with whom he had become sufficiently acquainted at Augsburg.

Only a few of those who discuss Luther's character intimate that he was abnormal in thought and sentiment. His nervous malady and its influence upon his mental life were naturally hidden to the controversialists. Men at that time were not interested in such observations. The keenly penetrating mind of Erasmus, who was kept informed by humanistic acquaintances of Luther, was ahead of his contemporaries in this respect. In his controversial works, "Hyperaspistes" (1526) and "Purgatio" (1534), and also in his letters, he calls attention to this aspect of Luther's nature,[85] though in his unrefined language he at times goes too far. He states that Luther is mentally deranged in various ways, imputes mental and emotional aberrations to him (*insanus, lymphaticus, non sobrius, febricitans, temulentus, sine mente, delirus*, etc.). On one occasion he appraises him as follows: "In writing thus, Luther, abandoned by the spirit, he is not himself active, but there is active within him another spirit with his diatribes." [86] Pirkheimer would not offer an opinion as to whether Luther was "demented or actuated by an evil demon." As early as 1524 John Clichtovaeus describes the mental state of the ex-monk as "drunkenness or demoniacal possession." In 1522, the gentle Schatzgeyer is impelled to use almost similar terms. The phenomenon was inexplicable to him

---

[84] *Ibid.*, pp. 356, 358.

[85] *Ibid.*, p. 353.

[86] *Ibid.*: "*Quis non videt, haec sine mente scribi, nec agere Lutherum, quum haec scribit, sed agi spiritu quodam maledicentiae?*"

and therefore the admixture of falsehoods and exaggerations in the delineation of Luther's character is excusable.

The Catholics but rarely employed cartoons in combating Luther. Their efforts in this direction are lacking in those captivating and mordant elements which Luther did not shrink from applying in his polemical cartoons. These are very vulgar in many respects, and it is evident that the Catholic controversialists preferred to avoid such indecencies on moral grounds. But they also lacked experienced artists of the kind the reformers had in the person of Luther's friend, Lucas Cranach, and others who espoused their cause. Thus, while the well-known effigy of *Lutherus septiceps* (the seven-headed Luther) by John Cochlaeus is based upon a sound idea, *viz.*, to illustrate in graphic fashion the contradictions of Luther and his vacillating attitudes, the artistic representation is very defective and illustrates the impossibility of tolerably representing a human being with seven heads.

In a rapid review of the most prominent protagonists and defenders of the Catholic cause up to about 1520, the names of Eck, Cochlaeus, and Faber must occupy a prominent place.

Dr. John Eck was such a prolific writer that he wrote thirteen short treatises on the religious questions of the day in 1518 and 1519. He combated not only the doctrines of Luther, but subsequently also those of Zwingli. On sundry journeys to Rome he acted as adviser to the popes. As professor of theology at Ingolstadt he founded there a veritable centre for the preservation of the faith. His incessant and prolific literary activity was interrupted only by his pastoral labors. He also achieved distinction as a powerful preacher. After his victory in the disputation at Leipsic, he celebrated a great triumph in 1526 at Baden (Switzerland) when he triumphantly defended the Catholic teaching on the Eucharist in a disputation with the Zwinglians. With a genuine mastery of the subject, he expounded the doctrine of papal primacy in the first of his major works, which appeared in 1520. In a second treatise, published in 1522, Dr. Eck set forth the Catholic practice of penance and confession. He discussed other leading points of the religious controversy in his writings on Purgatory (1523), on the Sacrifice of the Mass (1526), and on the monastic vows (1527). In 1530–1531 he began the publication of his exposition of the Gospels, originally in three parts, a work which achieved great practical results.

The most widely spread of his writings was his excellent and practical "Enchiridion against the Lutherans," a handy synopsis of all the questions at issue, with a concise refutation of errors, accompanied by citations from the Bible, the Church councils, and the Fathers. It was an armory (*armamentarium,* as he himself calls it) against the heretics. No one combined such indefatigable activity with such practical insight and such a forceful style as this Bavarian scholar, whom Luther feared and endeavored to ridicule by applying to him epithets like Dr. Geck (German for coxcomb) and Dr. Saueck (German for sow's comber).[87]

John Cochlaeus, small of stature, but very active—styled the "puppet" in Luther's circle—was a native of Wendelstein near Schwabach (whence the name Cochlaeus). As a humanist he had composed some serviceable text-books.[88] While still a dean at the cathedral of Our Lady at Frankfort on the Main, he was undecided what attitude to take toward Luther, but after 1520 openly opposed him. In 1526 he went to Mayence as a canon of Archbishop Albrecht. Upon the demise of Jerome Emser, in 1528, he obtained the influential position of secretary to Duke George at the court of Dresden, which he held until the latter's death, in 1539. The writings of this industrious and self-sacrificing man number 202 distinct titles. They are noted for their extensive learning and ready wit and, after the death of Eck, advanced him to first place among the defenders of the ancient faith. They are less conspicuous for theological depth. Luther made but one reply to Cochlaeus, whose criticism proved very annoying to him, and then chose to observe silence. The work to which Luther replied was the first published by Cochlaeus. It bore the title, "De Gratia Sacramentorum," and appeared in 1522.[89] Other products of his pen appeared in rapid succession, among them one in which the author, inspired by patriotic motives, deplores the condition of Germany caused by the religious controversy. His "Seven-headed Luther" bore the sub-title: "Luther everywhere in contradiction with himself," and was published in Latin and German; it decisively influenced many of those who still floundered in doubt.[90]

John Faber, a native of Leutkirch in the Allgäu, was frequently

[87] Cfr. Grisar, *Luther,* Vol. VI, Index *s. v.* "Eck."

[88] *Ibid., s. v.* "Cochlaeus."

[89] Luther's Reply was entitled: *Adversus Armatum Virum Cochlaeum.*

[90] Grisar, *Luther,* Vol. IV, pp. 380 sqq.

mistaken for the Dominican writer John Faber of Heilbronn and for John Faber of Augsburg. He was a secular priest and originally assumed an attitude towards the religious innovation which resembled that of Erasmus. Subsequently, however, he initiated a great movement against Lutheranism by his work "Against Certain New Doctrines of Martin Luther" (1522) and his "Hammer against the Lutheran Heresy," which appeared in 1524. He, too, occupied himself, and that most effectively, with the contradictions in Luther's writings, to which he devoted his "Antilogies" of 1530. In the interim he composed other works on the burning questions of the day. As vicar-general of the bishop of Constance, Faber participated with his friend Eck in the religious conference against Zwinglianism which was held in Baden in 1526. In 1527, Archduke Ferdinand sent him on important politico-ecclesiastical missions to Spain and England. In 1528 this prince recalled him to Vienna, where he was to raise the religious consciousness of the university and to oppose the spread of Lutheranism in Austria. In 1530, at the urgent request of Clement VII, he took over the vacant episcopal see of Vienna.[91]

The Dominican John Faber, incidentally mentioned above, was surnamed "Augustanus" (a native of Augsburg), because Augsburg was his native city and for many years the scene of his activities. He was an erudite scholar whose mentality closely resembled that of Erasmus. Towards the close of the year 1520 he wrote a pamphlet ("Ratschlag") in which he judged Luther far too favorably. After the appearance of the latter's book on the "Babylonian Captivity," he decidedly changed his views, severed his connection with the Humanist party, and combated the new theology in his sermons at Augsburg so courageously that he was driven out of the city in 1525. He died abroad in 1530, a victim of his incessant labors.[92]

Faber of Augsburg had been vicar-general of the Dominican Congregation of Upper Germany, which had seceded from the more numerous body of "Observantines" of the same Order, who were subject to the jurisdiction of separate provincials. This Congregation of the Dominicans flourished side by side with the Saxon and Upper German provinces of the same Order. All three of these great

---

[91] Concerning Bishop John Faber, see Grisar, *Luther*, Vol. VI, Index, *s. v.*

[92] Cfr. N. Paulus, *Die deutschen Dominikaner im Kampfe gegen Luther*, p. 292. This substantial and careful monograph also provides more particular information relative to the following defenders of the faith.

bodies produced many learned and enthusiastic defenders of the Catholic religion. The Order of St. Dominic, who had made the defense of the faith a special object of his foundation, shared with the Franciscans the leadership in the contest against Luther.

In the Saxon province of the Dominicans, two men achieved distinction by raising their voices against the Lutheran innovation. They were: John Mensing, a versatile theologian and author, preacher at Magdeburg and Dessau, afterwards preacher and professor at Frankfort on the Oder, and finally auxiliary bishop of Halberstadt; and Peter Rauch, likewise an able protagonist of Catholicism in the pulpit and by means of his pen, who died as auxiliary bishop of Bamberg.

The Upper German province of the Dominican Order, on its part, was proud of Jacob Hochstraten of Brabant, professor, prior, and inquisitor at Cologne. His first work against Luther, entitled, "Conversations with St. Augustine," which appeared in 1521–22, demonstrated that, in virtue of his Scholastic training, he had a more correct and penetrating insight into the errors of Luther than many other contemporary Catholic scholars. His "Conversations" at the same time reveal a comprehensive knowledge of the writings of St. Augustine, the Doctor of the Church, whose utterances he contrasts with the teachings of Luther. The "Conversations" were followed by treatises on the veneration of the saints, Purgatory, Christian liberty, and, finally, on justification and good works. They were composed in a style which at times lacked due moderation. When Hochstraten died, in 1527, the hatred of his enemies pursued him. They charged that he had died amid tortures of conscience, having realized that he had defended error—a calumny which was meted out to a large number of Catholic apologists.

Conrad Köllin, a member of the same province, was a professor at Cologne, celebrated for his knowledge of the writings of St. Thomas of Aquin. Among other theses, he defended the doctrinal infallibility of the pope, the indirect authority of the latter over temporal matters, and the right of resistence to tyrannical rulers. In 1527 he published a ponderous and rather mordant refutation of Luther's doctrine of matrimony. Luther had denounced the Dominicans of the University of Cologne as asses, dogs, and swine.

Ambrose Pelargus of Hesse, John Fabri of Heilbronn, Bartholomew Kleindienst of Annaberg, John Dietenberger, a native of Frankfort on the Main, and Michael Vehe of Biberach were members of the same Dominican province. Dietenberger was the author of an excellent catechism. He also translated the Bible and composed about fifteen controversial works, which are noted for their learning and acumen. They place their author in the first rank of the Dominican champions of the faith. He labored chiefly in Frankfort on the Main, in Treves, and in Koblenz. His works, composed exclusively in German, are written in a plain and fluent style, whereas many other controversialists of the time, less practiced in the use of their mother-tongue, wrote ponderously in Latin.

Michael John Vehe labored in the service of Archbishop Albrecht of Brandenburg. After the diet of Augsburg, he was appointed by the archbishop a member of the "Neues Stift" of Halle, of which he subsequently became provost. In 1531 he published an excellent treatise on the "Reception of the Blessed Sacrament under One Species." It was composed in good German.

Next to the Dominicans, the Franciscans were represented by a gallant host of apologists of the Church. At the close of the Middle Ages, an energetic spirit of religious reform, sprung from the bosom of this Order, had made its influence felt throughout Germany. Life within the monasteries of the Poor Man of Assisi, as described by John Eberlin, a Franciscan who had apostatized to Lutheranism, was very edifying, characterized by penance, prayer, and zeal for souls.[93] Eberlin makes only one, and that a curious, complaint, namely, that "the devil artfully uses their piety in order to corrupt humanity with a false religion." The example of good monastic discipline alone was a defense against the religious innovation—a brilliant refutation of the Lutheran attack upon Catholic morality. This practical defense was seconded by the writings and sermons of excellent and learned religious.

The Franciscan Augustine Alfeld, for example, entered the lists at Leipsic, in the beginning of the religious controversy, with his work "Super Apostolica Sede." Owing to his clear insight, he at once made the question of the primacy of the Roman see the central point of controversy. His industrious and popular pen produced fifteen Latin and German works, the style of the latter being superior to that of the former, "remarkable alike for vigor and fervor." [94] Caspar

93 Grisar, *Luther*, Vol. II, pp. 128 sq.
94 Thus L. Lemmens, O. S. Fr., in his monograph *Pater Aug. v. Alfeld* (1899), p. 99.

Schatzgeyer, provincial of the Upper German province of the Franciscan Observantines, was another capable writer whose works enjoyed even greater popularity. Thomas Murner, John Findling and Conrad Kling were members of the same Order, as were also Nicholas Ferber of Herborn, who labored with success in Hesse and Cologne; John Wild (Ferus), a preacher and writer at Mayence, and many other apologists and controversialists.

Of the Augustinian Order we shall only mention Bartholomew Usingen (Arnoldi), Luther's one-time teacher, and Konrad Träger. The learned Nicholas Ellenbog of Ottobeuren was a member of the Benedictine Order, and Paul Bachmann belonged to that of the Cistercians.

Certain converts who excelled in writing, among them Vitus Amerbach, Theobald Billican, and later George Witzel, constituted a special and very remarkable phalanx of apologists.

A great number of secular priests, besides those already mentioned, deserve recognition for their apologetic labors in the academic spheres and in the pulpit. Let us but mention Jerome Dungersheim of Leipsic, Ottmar Luscinius (Nachtigall) of Augsburg, and Konrad Wimpina, the soul of the newly-founded university of Frankfort on the Oder. An idea of the great number of German authors who wrote prior to the commencement of the Council of Trent, may be formed when it is recalled that the learned historian F. Falk published the names of 105 such writers in the Katholik, in 1891, and Nicholas Paulus, writing in 1892 and 1893, supplemented this list by the addition of 161 names of writers, without making any claim to completeness.[95] Who knows how many wavering souls were brought back to the Church, or confirmed in the faith, through the efforts of these apologists! That German Catholicism laid down its arms and surrendered to Luther is an assertion which, at the present time, can be attributed only to ignorance.

Non-German countries also furnished quite a number of defenders of the faith, some of whom were very brilliant. Thus, in the Netherlands, Jacob Latomus (Masson) of the University of Louvain was very active in opposing Luther as early as 1518, and again in 1525, when his work "De Primatu" appeared. Luther regarded him as superior to all his other opponents, including Erasmus, who, he

---

[95] *Katholik*, 1891, Vol. 71, pp. 450 sqq. (Falk); 1892, Vol. 72, pp. 545 sqq.; 1893, Vol. 73, pp. 213 sqq. (Paulus).

said, in comparison with Latomus, could only croak. In France, Jodo-cus Clichtovaeus, of the Paris Sorbonne, achieved celebrity by his "Antilutherus" (1524) and his "Propugnaculum Ecclesiae adversus Lutheranos (1526)," etc. In England the apologetical writings of King Henry VIII and his famous chancellor, Sir Thomas More, as well as those of John Fisher Bishop of Rochester, published in 1523, 1525, etc., were preëminent. More and Fisher sealed their opposition to the subsequent schism of Henry VIII with their blood and to-day are honored by the Church as martyrs to the faith. The "Italian Opponents of Luther," according to Frederick Lauchert, who published a monograph on this subject in 1912, comprised no less than sixty-six scholars, beginning with Sylvester Prierias, Ambrosius Catharinus, Thomas Cajetán, and Thomas Radinus, who rose in opposition to Luther during the period preceding the Tridentine Council.

9. FURTHER SPREAD OF THE RELIGIOUS REVOLT

Unmindful of refutations, the new doctrine extended its conquests under the influence of a false evangelical liberty and through the forceful intervention of the secular authorities.

In the city of Braunschweig (Brunswick), Bugenhagen, in the spring of 1528, endeavored to strengthen the Lutheran religion, which had been introduced there by the magistrate. The magistrate of Hamburg forthwith summoned him to the latter city to accomplish the same object in the summer of 1529; after a period of intensive organization, he returned to Wittenberg, where Luther, notwithstanding his multifarious labors, had discharged the pastoral duties in place of Bugenhagen. At the solicitation of the town-council of Goslar, Amsdorf, while passing through Magdeburg, where he held a position as preacher, went to Goslar in the same capacity. Luther's messengers had been originally banished from Lübeck, until the magistrate of that town recalled them. In January, 1530, Luther exhorted them to proceed with courage as well as caution.

In Hesse and electoral Saxony, no less than in Nuremberg, Ulm, and Strasburg, Protestantism spread rapidly under the protection of the defensive League formed by the princes and rulers after the protestation of Spires. Ferdinand, the representative of the Emperor, was authorized by a law of the Empire to avenge by force of arms the manifest civil insubordination revealed in the progress of the new theology and the League. But nothing was done. Luther was content to issue a warning against the League, which had allied itself, in part, with Zwinglian elements; he also characterized the rebellion as a misfortune.[96]

In Pomerania, Lutheranism gradually gained ground under the patronage of Duke Barnim XI, who had studied at Wittenberg and remained in communication with Luther.

Paul Speratus, who, having been condemned to the stake at Iglau because he had preached the new religion in Austria, was pardoned and became preacher at the court of Duke Albrecht of Prussia at Königsberg, and later (1530) so-called bishop of Pomesania, where he indefatigably preached the new gospel and combatted the Anabaptists and Schwenckfeldians.

In the electorate of Brandenburg, Joachim I, the elector, vigorously excluded Lutheranism from his jurisdiction. His wife, Elizabeth, who had been captivated by the new theology, secretly escaped from Berlin to Torgau, and thence to the vicinity of Luther, who called her his "Madam Godmother." After the death of the vacillating Margrave Casimir, in 1527, the Frankish-Brandenburgian territory was openly Protestantized by his successor, George, who, residing in Franconia, became one of the most active and influential Protestant princes.

Several times Luther communicated directly with the adherents of the new theology in Livonia, which was subject to the Teutonic Order. Thus, in 1523 and again 1524, he addressed letters to the Christians of Riga. In 1525 he wrote an epistle "to the Livonians." In 1525, the inhabitants of Danzig requested him to send them a preacher. The movement was impetuous, but was suppressed for the time being by the King of Poland.

In July, 1527, Gustavus Wasa forcibly introduced the new religion into the kingdom of Sweden; in doing so, he was "essentially influenced by political motives." [97]

In Denmark, Christian II, who at that time also governed Sweden, had favored Lutheranism for political reasons, because he feared the influence of the Catholic clergy. Having been banished to Germany, he entered upon intimate relations with Luther. The latter, owing to

[96] Cf. Erl. ed., Vol. LIV, pp. 72 and 79 (*Briefwechsel*, VII, pp. 101 and 110), on May 22 and at the end of May, 1529. But see *infra* ch. XIV, no. 1; furthermore, Köstlin-Kawerau, *M. Luther*, Vol. II, p. 184, and Grisar, *Luther*, Vol. III, pp. 44 sq., on Luther's vacillating attitude relative to armed resistance.

[97] Thus Köstlin-Kawerau, *M. Luther*, Vol. I, p. 625.

his ignorance of human nature and because he hoped for a change in religion, supported him; however, Christian was not concerned with religion, but solely with the recovery of his crown. His successor in Denmark, King Frederick, was sincerely attached to the theological innovation, which, however, triumphed only during the reign of the despotic Christian III.

On the basis of certain premature reports concerning Italy, which he had received from Gabriel Zwilling of Torgau, Luther wrote to him on March 7, 1528: "I am delighted to hear that the Venetians have accepted the Word of God." [98] In this instance, as in the case of Christian II of Denmark, he deceived himself. For though the writings of Luther had penetrated Venice, and Italy in general, there was but a slight movement in favor of his cause. In Italy as well as in Spain, the sharp-sighted Inquisition took precautions to prevent the propagation of the new anti-ecclesiastical ideas.

[98] *Briefwechsel*, VI, p. 222.

CHAPTER XIII

THE DIET OF AUGSBURG (1530) AND LUTHER AT COBURG CASTLE

1. THE DIET OF AUGSBURG

Emperor Charles V was finally able to set out on his journey to Germany, for which the German Catholics had ardently longed. The treaty of Barcelona with the pope, and the treaty of Cambrai with Francis, king of France, had opened the way for him.

On January 21, 1530, shortly before his coronation as emperor, Charles published at Bologna the convocation of the imperial diet at Augsburg, in which he himself intended to take an active part. It was his wish that the diet should remove—peaceably, if possible—the grounds for the religious controversy which filled him with anxiety. It was the intention of this zealous Catholic ruler, sincerely to adopt the ways of kindness and to effect an arrangement by peaceful methods. For this reason the convocation adopted a conciliatory tone and assured the Protestants that they would be given a hearing.

The Emperor's brother, Ferdinand, journeyed to the Brenner in Tyrol, to meet Charles as the latter was coming from Italy. At Gries, on the northern declivity of the mountain, there is a monumental inscription marking the spot where the brothers embraced each other. Charles was depressed by Ferdinand's report of the existing conditions. Nevertheless, on June 15, the high-minded Emperor hopefully entered the city of Augsburg.

This ancient free city on the Lech, a flourishing center of art and commerce, still retained its venerable towered walls with moats and gates. Inside were the homes of the wealthy and comfortably situated patricians, and lofty, antique buildings, conspicuous among them the palace of the bishop and the splendid town-hall, where the sessions of the diet were to be held. Both have since been either replaced by other structures or completely remodeled. The banking house of the Fuggers, which had been established ten years before, still exists, a vivid reminder of the great commercial firm which once dominated international trade. The Fuggers remained loyal to the Catholic Church when the new religion established itself in the city.

Bishop Stadion of Augsburg, assisted by the Emperor and the Catholic estates who arrived for the diet, presided over the Corpus Christi procession which wended its way through the streets of the city, and was celebrated with a splendor never before witnessed. The Protestants ostentatiously kept aloof. As a consequence, the Emperor prohibited the preaching of Protestant sermons.

When the sessions of the diet were opened, on June 20, Luther's partisans succeeded in inducing the estates to deliberate on the religious question before devising ways and means of combating the Turkish menace, which Charles wished to be considered first of all. It was their plan to submit an extensive statement justifying their attitude on the religious question. Above all, it was their intention to procure protection for themselves and publicly to advance their efforts at propaganda. The so-called Augsburg Confession constituted a means to this end. The lengthy document had been written by the prudent and pliant Melanchthon, who at that time was very timorous, and had the approval of Luther, who during the sessions of the diet lived in the castle of Coburg, which was situated not far from Augsburg. The Confession was so drawn up as to speak not in the name of Luther or the theologians, but in that of the rulers who had adopted the new creed and by whom it was submitted. Originally, therefore, it was a confession of faith by the princes. Afterwards it became a symbolical document, *i. e.*, the official statement of the Lutheran creed. By means of this instrument, the princes intended to indicate through Melanchthon, their spokesman, the kind of religion they had thus far suffered to be preached within their territories. Melanchthon, whilst engaged in the composition of this document, had also intended it to serve as a refutation of a work of Dr. Eck, who had caused an exhaustive theological indictment of the new religious system, consisting of 404 articles, to be submitted to the Emperor before his arrival in Augsburg.

In order to procure a favorable decision on the part of the diet, the author of the "Confession" tried to show that in reality there were no great differences between the two camps. He proposes certain essentially Lutheran doctrines, but veils them in clever formulas devised to show that they coincide with what the Catholic Church had always held. The question which, according to him, is of prime importance, is about abuses which in the general opinion of men ought to be abolished. In fact, the first official edition of the "Confession," printed in 1530, contained the deceptive declaration (which was subsequently altered) that the impugned doctrines meant no deviation from the Scriptures or the teaching of the Roman Catholic Church, in as far as that teaching could be ascertained from Catholic authors.

The Emperor reluctantly consented to have the "Confession" publicly read in the presence of the estates. It was so read on June 25, not, however, during a regular session of the diet in the town-hall, but in a smaller Gothic hall of the episcopal palace. The twenty-eight articles were read in a stentorian voice by Baier, the Saxon chancellor, who designedly read the German version of the text so distinctly that it was audible through the open windows by those who lingered in the courtyard without.

On closer inspection, the Catholic theologians were compelled to marvel at the ingenuity with which a road to a pseudo-union with the ancient Church had been kept open. They noted the absence of any declaration relative to the pope, whom the Lutherans had come to regard as Antichrist. The declaration was silent about the universal priesthood of all the faithful in place of the clergy, the incapacity of the human will to do good, and absolute predestination, the very pillars of the doctrinal system of Lutheranism. The antitheses between the two religions on the subject of indulgences and Purgatory were likewise hushed up, and the differences in the veneration of the saints had also vanished.[1]

Hence, honest candor, the preliminary condition of reunion, was missing.

Luther himself censured the omission of some of his doctrines. However, he did not wish to disavow the action of Melanchthon, his indispensable, industrious, and respected mediator. He averred that "he could not step as softly and quietly as he" (Melanchthon) [2] and regarded himself as incompetent to deliberate in such an assembly.

By order of the Emperor, Catholic theologians at once undertook

---

[1] *Corpus Ref.*, XXVI, p. 290. Luther also maintains: *"Audita nostrorum confessione primum communis vox et sententia omnium fuit, nos nihil docere contra ullum fidei articulum neque contra scripturam. . . . ."* Letter to Joh. Brismann, November 7, 1530; *Briefwechsel*, VIII, p. 311.

[2] Letter of May 15, 1530, to the Elector John of Saxony; Erl. ed., Vol. LIV, p. 145 (*Briefwechsel*, VII, p. 335). In a letter to Jonas, July 21 (*Briefwechsel*, VIII, p. 133), Luther also says that the Confession conceals important doctrines.

to compose a refutation of the "Confession," in order to expose its errors as well as its vagueness and its omissions. In addition to Eck, Faber, and Cochlaeus, were some of the other Catholic apologists whom we have heretofore mentioned: Usingen, Dietenberger, Wimpina, etc. The opposition was officially asked whether they had any other articles they wished to defend besides those contained in the "Confession" which they had submitted. They replied evasively. The tone of the hastily composed Catholic "Confutatio" appeared too offensive to the Emperor and his advisers. It was revised and, after it had been cast into the form of an answer given by the Emperor, was read aloud on August 3 in the same hall in which the Protestants had been permitted to submit their "Confession."

The Emperor now ordered the Protestants to return to the pale of the Christian communion, which they had deserted, lest he be compelled to proceed against them in his capacity of "guardian and protector of the Church," which was his bounden duty as emperor. At that time Charles was actually inclined to resort to military force, but after October 30, in virtue of the representations of the Catholic estates, he became somewhat reconciled to the idea of a general council, not, however, until the time for waging a successful war had passed.[3] The papal legate, Campeggio, was in favor of the strictest possible execution of the edict of Worms.

In a state of painful anxiety, Melanchthon approached Campeggio with proposals suggested by the delusive hope of coming to a mutually satisfactory agreement. While he shuddered at the thought of an open break, he did not wish to yield in principle, although many of the Catholic leaders hoped for his conversion on account of his conciliatory addresses. In the subsequent negotiations he became more and more a pitiable figure.[4] His depressed condition of mind is the only thing that helps him over the charge of conscious deception. Many friends of the Lutheran cause were opposed to him and to any kind of approach between the two parties. Landgrave Philip of Hesse, to signify his protest, left Augsburg precipitately.

The negotiations which the Emperor had authorized between seven representatives of each faction proved fruitless. In vain did the

[3] Cf. E. W. Mayer, *Forschungen zur Politik Karls V. während des Augsburger Reichstags* (*Archiv für Reformationsgeschichte*, 1916, pp. 40 sqq.).

[4] Grisar, *Melanchtons rätselhafte Nachgiebigkeit auf dem Augsburger Reichstag* (*Histor. Jahrbuch*, XLI [1921], pp. 257–267; *Luther-Analekten* VI). Cf. Grisar, *Luther*, Vol. II, pp. 383 sqq.

Catholic spokesmen, subject to papal approval, offer to have the lay-chalice introduced in the Protestant districts, or to tolerate the marriage of priests until the assembly of a general council. Every effort to restore peace failed in consequence of the inflexible attitude of Luther, who issued frequent letters from the castle of Coburg. Melanchthon indicated his willingness to have the jurisdiction of the bishops restored, but it was an insidious and ineffectual offer, because of the underlying presupposition that the bishops would have to give free scope to the new "gospel." [5] A smaller commission thereupon undertook to effect an understanding. Its Catholic members were: Eck, Cochlaeus and Wimpina, but their efforts were futile.

In the meantime Melanchthon's tireless pen produced an "Apologia Confessionis Augustanae," which was directed against the Catholic "Confutatio." His party, however, did not succeed in having this "Apologia" publicly read. Upon his homeward return, the author privately published a Latin edition of it. The "Apologia," like the "Confession," was soon regarded by Protestants as a symbol of their faith.

Meantime the number of estates who declared their adherence to the Augsburg "Confession" constantly increased. The original signers were: Elector John of Saxony, Margrave George of Ansbach, Duke Ernest of Braunschweig-Lüneburg, Landgrave Philip of Hesse, and Prince Wolfgang of Anhalt. In addition to these names, the Latin copy of the "Augsburg Confession" contained those of John Frederick, heir to the throne of Electoral Saxony, and Duke Francis of Braunschweig-Lüneburg. Nuremberg and Reutlingen were the only cities to subscribe. Four cities which professed Zwinglianism, namely, Strasburg, Constance, Memmingen, and Lindau, submitted a separate profession of faith, composed by Bucer and Capito; it was called "Confessio Tetrapolitana." Other cities of Upper Germany, though favoring the Reformation, kept aloof. In the course of the deliberations at the diet of Augsburg a better understanding was effected between the Lutherans and the Upper Germans with respect

---

[5] Wilhelm Walther, *Für Luther*, p. 434: "Melanchthon was only too ready to acquiesce in equivocal formulas and to make concessions which in truth could not be harmonized with the 'reservation that nothing may be conceded which contradicts the Gospel'; a reservation which was constantly repeated." The Protestant historian A. Berger (*Luther in kulturgeschichtlicher Darstellung* (1889), Vol. II, I; pp. 226 sq.) notes the weak attitude of Melanchthon and says that, "objectively considered," it was "a betrayal of the Protestant conscience."

to the Augsburg Confession, although Article X of the Confession was supposed to be directed against Zwingli. Bucer was a smooth politician and knew how to surmount the difficulties arising from that document. After several of the cities represented in the diet had accepted the Confession, Strasburg also declared its adherence at a conference which was held towards the end of December, 1530, at Schmalkalden. Thus everything conspired towards the creation of the fateful League named after that city.

The Protestant leaders at the diet of Augsburg used the new evangel as the basis of a political alliance designed to divide Germany. Before his departure, the Landgrave of Hesse threateningly declared that if he had to die for the faith, certain leaders of the opposition would die with him.

After some delay, due partly to the Turkish menace and partly to his own scruples, Emperor Charles issued a decree prohibiting all theological innovations. The Protestants were ordered to accept the articles upon which no agreement had been reached, by the fifteenth of April of the next year, at the very latest. They vociferously objected to this and at the same time refused to consent to the required intervention against the German Zwinglians and the danger to the Empire caused by them and by Zwingli at Zurich. Nevertheless, the Emperor, in his *Reichstagsabschied* of November 19, renewed the edict of Worms with its severe measures, but at the same time referred the litigants to the coming ecumenical council, which was expected within a year.[6]

Both the renewal of the edict of Worms as well as the Emperor's reference to the expected convocation of a general council proved ineffectual. The edict could not be enforced because of the united front of the opposition, and the council was postponed by Pope Clement VII because of the fear that schisms would develop among the faithful, because of the expectation of small benefit to those who had separated from the Church, and, still more, because of the political difficulties in the way of holding a council.

Thus the diet of Augsburg, which had been hailed with such great expectations by the Catholics, due principally to the obstinate attitude of the Protestants, in a certain measure furthered the unfortunate schism. On December 12, Luther gloatingly reminded his elector that the schemes of men "always turn out differently than expected, so that one must say: I surely did not intend that. Pope and Emperor did not

[6] Cf. Janssen-Pastor, III, pp. 251 sqq.; Grisar, *Luther*, Vol. II, p. 384.

succeed at Augsburg as they expected; nor shall they succeed henceforth." He imagines that his party is sustained by God and will "remain with God." [7]

Nothing illustrates Luther's way of thinking and proceeding more graphically than a close scrutiny of his behavior during his sojourn in the lonely castle of Coburg at the time of the diet of Augsburg.

2. LUTHER IN THE CASTLE OF COBURG

The ancient castle of Coburg rises above the city of the same name on the south side of the Thuringian Forest, in the midst of attractive rows of hills. A road, rising gently at first, but soon growing steeper, leads up to the castle, which once upon a time was rightly styled "Frankish Crown." Even to-day the visitor beholds in it the best type of the massive, crown-like castle of the Middle Ages, simply yet magnificently constructed.

During the diet of Augsburg, Luther resided in the topmost portion of the edifice, reserved for princes. His suite is still extant. As he walked upon the detached so-called High Bastion on the side of the courtyard, he had an unobstructed and charming view of the splendid landscape in the direction of the city where the fate of his theological system appeared to be at issue. As an outlaw, Luther could not enter Augsburg; therefore the Elector of Saxony, who owned this castle, had assigned it to him for a residence, whence he could easily correspond with his representatives at the diet.

This lonely and almost unoccupied castle became a "Sinai" and a "hermitage" to him. In his first correspondence "from the kingdom of the jackdaws" he humorously describes the antics of the birds about his lofty room, comparing them with the garrulous and agitated assembly at Augsburg. Good humor, he says, was necessary to "repulse the heavy thoughts which rushed in upon him, so far as they permitted themselves to be banished." [8]

The thoughts which occupied his mind during well-nigh the entire time of his sojourn at the castle of Coburg, and which often tortured him, not only concerned the diet; he was afflicted by deep anxiety

---

[7] Erl. ed., Vol. LIV, p. 201 (*Briefwechsel*, Vol. VIII, p. 331).

[8] Köstlin-Kawerau, *M. Luther*, Vol. II, p. 196.

regarding the Turkish menace to Germany, no less than by interior "temptations" against his teaching.

Luther arrived at Coburg on April 15, 1530, and remained in the castle up to October 5. Aside from the inevitable visitors, his only company consisted of a young pupil, Master Vitus Dietrich, and a nephew, Cyriac Kaufmann, a student at Wittenberg.

The first task which he undertook to discharge was the composition of a violent pamphlet by which he intended to intimidate the clerical members of the diet. It appeared under the title: "A Warning to the Clergy assembled at the Diet of Augsburg." [9] With passionate exaggeration he reproaches them on account of their immoral lives, the abuses in the government of the Church, and eulogizes the Reformation. He threatens them with revolution if they obstruct his gospel. In terrifying words he calls out to the assembly: "Alive, I am your plague; dying, I am your death; for God has instigated me against you. I must be unto you, as Osee says (XIII, 7 sq.), a bear and a lion in the way of Assur. Ye shall have no peace before my name, until you amend your ways or perish."

Then he worked on his translation of the Bible, especially Jeremias and Ezechiel. Whilst engaged in the study of Jeremias, his soul was overcome by a profoundly mystical mood. He was captivated by the prophecy concerning Gog and Magog, whose names pertained to the most remote and barbarous period of paganism, and were connected with the destruction within the kingdom of God. Luther interpreted the prophecy as signifying the devastating incursion of the Turks. He published this interpretation in a special work immediately after the publication of his "Warning to the Clergy." [10] From the Psalter, with which he also occupied himself, he next selected for publication, under the title, "The Beautiful Confitemini," his interpretation of Psalm 117 (Vulgate), which he held in great esteem.[11] It is the Psalm which the Breviary prescribes for recitation on Sunday, beginning with "Confitemini Domino quoniam bonus. . . . Dicat nunc Israel," etc. Luther was wont to apply this Psalm to his dangers and his confidence in

[9] Weimar ed., Vol. XXX, II, pp. 268 sqq.; Erl. ed., Vol. XXIV, 2nd ed., p. 356.

[10] Weimar ed., Vol. XXX, II, pp. 223 sqq.; Erl. ed., XLI, pp. 220 sq. In this little tract, Luther, under the influence of a strong illusion, claims that the Turks had special designs against him and his little band of followers, but Christ, according to the prophecy, will destroy both pope and Turk, "with His splendid advent, which we daily expect."

[11] Weimar ed., Vol. XXXI, I, pp. 65 sqq.; Erl. ed., Vol. XLI, pp. 1 sqq.

salvation, the latter especially because of the passage: "I shall not die, but live: and shall declare the works of the Lord." In order to relieve himself in his physical and mental sufferings he inscribed these words with musical notations on the wall of his room at Coburg castle, where they were seen by the physician Ratzeberger twenty years afterwards.

Later, his anxiety concerning the Augsburg diet once more set his pen in motion. He published an "Open Letter" to Archbishop Albrecht of Mayence, who, as yet, was not sufficiently pliable to suit Luther, but took a conciliatory attitude.[12] In terms far milder than those of his "Warning," he demands that, since it was impossible for them to unite, the rival religious parties be unmolested in their respective professions of faith.

In consequence of physical and mental ailments, his literary labors became more and more difficult. His afflictions were partly a result of nervous over-excitement, and partly an effect of the hasty and impassioned labors which he performed. He had not been well even before he left Wittenberg. Beginning with the end of January, 1529, his melancholia was aggravated at times by violent spells of dizziness and a ringing noise in the head. On January 1, 1530, he said in a sermon at Wittenberg that he would not ascend the pulpit any more because of his disgust at the indifference of the people towards the Word of God. According to a remark of the editor of the sermon in the Weimar Edition, this declaration admits that "the only possible explanation of this step is a pathological one." [13] In May he found it impossible to work for weeks at a time on account of buzzing sensations which he described as "thunder in the head," and a tendency to swoon.[14]

He assigned the cause of his afflictions to the devil, who enlivened Luther's imagination with peculiar images during his sojourn at Coburg. The ex-monk firmly believed in the Satanic apparitions and effects which were reported to him at that time. Thus he declared that he had seen a large host of mysterious spirits, who, coming from Cologne, caused themselves to be carried across the river at Spires and marched towards Augsburg to attend the diet. "They were evil spirits,

12 Weimar ed., Vol. XXX, ii, p. 397; Erl. ed., Vol. LIV, pp. 159 sqq. (*Briefwechsel*, VIII, pp. 84 sqq.).

13 Grisar, *Luther*, Vol. VI, p. 168.

14 *Ibid.*, pp. 99 sqq.

devils in disguise." Melanchthon regarded them as omens of a "terrible revolution," and his son-in-law, George Sabinus, described the apparitions in poetical form. Luther afterwards defied the wrath of these spirits by exclaiming: "Let them have their way—those spectremonks of Spires!" [15] Luther avidly accepted the report of Bugenhagen, who wrote from Lübeck at the time that the devil had testified for the new gospel through the medium of a maiden who was possessed by him. "The cunning demon," he wrote, "designs prodigies." [16]

Concerning himself, he complains in a letter to Melanchthon (May 12, 1530) that when he was alone (Dietrich and Kaufmann being absent) the devil sent "his messenger" to him and so overpowered him with gloomy thoughts that he was driven out of his room and forced to seek other companions. "I can hardly await the day," he adds in a characteristic phrase, "when we shall see the great power of this spirit and, as it were, his almost divine majesty." [17]

At Coburg he saw the devil in a phantastic visual illusion. About nine o'clock, on the evening of a rainy day in June, as he stood at his window and looked out over the little forest near by, as Vitus Dietrich bears witness, he saw "a fiery, flaming serpent, which, after twisting and writhing about, dropped from the roof of the nearest tower down into the wood. He at once called me and wanted to show me the ghost (spectrum), as I stood by his shoulder. But suddenly he saw it disappear. Shortly after, we both saw the apparition again. It had, however, altered its shape, and now looked more like a great flaming star lying in the field, so that we were able to distinguish it plainly, even though the weather was rainy." [18] In his fright, Luther regarded the apparition as the devil. It may have been one of the inmates of the castle passing by with a torch or a brightly shining lantern which cast a reflexion on the roof, the woods and field. Whoever visits the place will at once perceive that this is a plausible explanation. Luther, however, was so sure he had seen the devil that he mentioned it in the following year to those who were present to aid him in the revision of his German translation of the Psalms. He said: "I saw my devil flying over the wood at Coburg," adding that Psalm 18 (Vulg. 17), verse

[15] Cfr. Grisar, *Luther*, Vol. II, p. 387; Vol. VI, p. 209.

[16] *Ibid.*, Vol. III, pp. 410 sq.

[17] *Briefwechsel*, VII, p. 332: *"Habuit Satan legationem suam apud me."* He is eager to see his *plane divina majestas.*

[18] Grisar, *Luther*, Vol. VI, p. 130.

15, which they were just then discussing, speaks of a *materia ignita.* [19]

His morbid fancy was followed by an unusually violent buzzing in the head and an increased tendency to faintness in the succeeding night—symptoms which indicated that his nervousness had reached a crisis. To young Dietrich this was but a new proof that all the ailments of his master were caused by the devil who had just appeared to them. It is not surprising that a blotch of ink on the wall of the room which Luther occupied in this castle was later attributed to Old Nick, just as the legendary one in the Wartburg.[20] Outside of this case, we know of no other manifestation of the evil spirit to Luther.

Luther himself tells us many details of the spiritual "temptations" to which he was subject at this time. He compares his soul, assailed by temptations, to a land dried up by heat and wind and thirsting for water.[21] He says that he is far stronger in his public controversies than in these personal struggles.[22] To Melanchthon he writes that he would rather endure this torture of the body than "that hangman of the spirit who . . . will never stop until he has gobbled me up." [23] After his return to Wittenberg, he recalled these spiritual struggles with horror. He was but forty-seven when he wrote to Amsdorf: "I now am really beginning to feel the weight of my years, and my powers are going. The angel of Satan [2 Cor. XII, 7] has indeed dealt hardly with me." [24] On another occasion he said to Dietrich at the Coburg, if he were to die (he had already selected a place for his grave), and his body were cut open, his heart would be found all shrivelled up "in consequence of my distress and sadness of spirit." [25]

These well-attested spiritual agonies of the ex-monk, which were naturally accompanied by qualms of conscience, stand in striking contrast to the narratives of most Protestant biographers, who laud the spiritual repose, the interior joy, and unflinching faith of Luther in the days which he spent in the castle of Coburg. It is true that when storms assailed him he constantly sought comfort in the idea that his restlessness was attributable to the devil and that he finally overcame his scruples with increased defiance.

[19] *Ibid.*
[20] *Ibid.*, Vol. II, p. 96.
[21] *Ibid.*, Vol. II, p. 390, and Vol. V, p. 346.
[22] *Ibid.*, Vol. II, p. 390.
[23] *Ibid.*, Vol. V, p. 347.
[24] *Ibid.*
[25] *Ibid.*, Vol. V, p. 348.

At that time he advised one of his pupils, Jerome Weller, how to conduct himself when assailed by "temptations." The latter was tormented by great fear as to the forgiveness of his sins and the spiritual condition of his soul.[26] Luther assures him that he also had such temptations, which were caused by the devil, who insidiously persecutes us on account of our belief and trust in Christ. Hence, when tempted "to despair and blaspheme," one should disregard the temptation as much as possible. Avoid being alone, he advises him; jest with my wife, imbibe somewhat more freely. Such temptations are useful. By means of them he himself had become "a great doctor." Moreover, Weller should not fear on account of minor moral infractions. When thus afflicted, "some kind of sin should be committed," in order to manifest one's hatred and contempt for the devil. If the devil tempt me, he should "know that I acknowledge no sin and hold myself guiltless. The Ten Commandments, with which the devil afflicts and tortures us so much," ought to be removed from our sight and our mind. Satan is simply to be referred to our Saviour, the Son of God.[27]

In this strange letter Luther also recalls his monastic days. It is possible that, in the lonely life which he led in the castle of Coburg, his monastic past may have impressed itself upon him more forcibly in contrast with his present career; just as, during his seclusion at the Wartburg, he was similarly impressed with the significance of his monastic vows. In his letter to young Weller, he refers to the fearful and terrible thoughts (*horrificae et terrificae cogitationes*) with which he was tortured while a monk.

He persuaded himself more and more that the feeling of depression which he had experienced in the monastery was entirely a result of his observance of the Catholic doctrine of virtue and merit. He now held that a doctrine which makes piety dependent upon meritorious works, instead of on faith alone, was unable to give peace, but could only engender misery and fear in the soul. It was only after he had discovered his new Gospel that the way of interior peace opened to him.

This is Luther's legendary version of his monastic life, an interpretation of his youthful experience made in after years. It is a weapon which after his sojourn at the castle of Coburg he began to use with predilection in his fight upon the ancient Church.[28]

[26] In July (?), 1530; *Briefwechsel*, VIII, pp. 159 sqq. Cf. the letter to the same, dated August 15, 1530; *ibid.*, p. 188.

[27] "*Nonnunquam largius bibendum, ludendum, nugandum, atque adeo peccatum aliquod faciendum in odium et contemptum diaboli. Utinam possem aliquid insigne peccati designare modo ad eludendum diabolum, ut intelligeret, me nullum peccatum agnoscere ac me nullius peccati mihi esse conscium.*"

[28] For additional details see Grisar, *Luther*, Vol. VI, pp. 187 sqq.

Formerly he had hardly made this charge; but now he claims to have been a pious monk, "one of the best," according to the Catholic ideal—a monk who languished unto death in the performance of the works of papism, with its fasting, vigils, freezing, etc.; and if ever anyone entered Heaven by such "monkish" practices, he, too, had been determined thus to get there.[29] Hence, even if he was driven to despair in consequence of it, he was well acquainted by personal experience with the "over-sweetened infernal poison cake" and the untenableness of the Catholic doctrine of good works, which is sure to make all men as unhappy as he had been in the monastery.

In making these charges he fails to take into consideration that the unhappy state in which he found himself after his apostasy was not a result of the doctrine and practice of the Catholic Church, but rather a product of his own over-wrought and sickly condition; that a contributory cause was his willfulness, as opposed to the discreet spirit of the rule and the direction of his religious superiors; and that thousands have attained to the greatest interior happiness by the conscientious observance of the Evangelical Counsels and the performance of good works.

The false notion referred to crops out in the writings which he issued from the castle of Coburg. Thus he says: "If a conscience is intent upon its works and builds on them, it is erected upon loose sand; it is ever slipping and sliding away; it must ever be seeking for works, for one and then for another, and ever more and more, until at last even the dead are clad in monks' cowls, the better to reach Heaven." However, by means of his new doctrine, he had prevented this calamity.[30] The legend of the emancipated holy monk Martin is utilized after his return to Wittenberg in the sermons which he commenced to preach in 1530 on chapters VI to VIII of St. John's Gospel, where he says that he had "mortified and tortured" himself like others, nay, even more than they, and accomplished thereby only this, that while "one of the best" of monks, he was in despair and so far removed from the faith that he "would have been ashamed to assert that Christ was the Redeemer." The papacy did not want a Redeemer, but wished to achieve redemption by means of its works.

Improbable though it was, this legend of Luther's monastic experience became increasingly prominent up to the close of his life, when it grew still more pronounced, and imposed itself upon countless thousands. It is still widely believed to-day.

Besides the tribulations which filled the soul of Luther during his abode in the castle of Coburg, the death of his aged father depressed him greatly. Hans Luther departed this life on May 29, "strong in

[29] Köstlin-Kawerau, M. Luther, Vol. II, p. 305.
[30] Grisar, Luther, Vol. VI, p. 230.

his faith in Christ," as Martin learned.[31] The news of his father's illness having been communicated to him, he addressed a consolatory letter to him from Wittenberg in the middle of February. Gladly, he writes, would he have visited him, had the journey not been fraught with such grave peril to himself; "peasants and princes" were opposed to him, and he did not dare "to tempt God by exposing himself to danger." [32] Yet it was only a matter of a short journey within the territory of the Elector. The words quoted testify to the isolation in which this once popular man now found himself. After the Peasants' War his popularity had waned. Many of the lower classes regarded him as their oppressor, while the upper classes were largely at war with him because they had enriched themselves by robbing the Church.[33] But more of this anon.

3. THE "PROVISO OF THE GOSPEL"

Luther learned with satisfaction that the Augsburg Confession had been read in the presence of the estates of the Empire. But he did not share Melanchthon's expectation that it would lead to some sort of reunion. His opinion was that rejection was the only thing to be expected from the "obduracy" of his enemies. He would "not allow himself to be discouraged, no matter what the course of events" at Augsburg might be, he declared to Melanchthon.[34]

In addition to the latter, Jonas, Agricola, Spalatin, Brenz, and others were active in promoting Luther's cause. It was to them and to Melanchthon that he wrote: "If we fall, Christ, the Ruler of the world, falls with us." [35] The Emperor, though well-intentioned, is unable to prevail against so many devils. Should he, however, "take a stand against the plain Scriptures or the Word of God," his decision cannot bind us.[36] There can be no question of restoring the property of the Church. It would be an advantage for his partisans to demand a council, since the demand could not be satisfied.

At the beginning of the negotiations proposed by Melanchthon, which at first concerned external matters only, Luther declared him-

---

[31] Köstlin-Kawerau, M. Luther, Vol. II, p. 209.
[32] February 15, 1530; Erl. ed., Vol. LIV, p. 130 (Briefwechsel, VII, p. 230).
[33] On Luther's declining popularity, cf. Grisar, Luther, Vol. VI, pp. 75 sqq.
[34] On June 29; Briefwechsel, VIII, p. 43.
[35] On June 30; ibid., p. 51.
[36] Cf. Köstlin-Kawerau, M. Luther, Vol. II, pp. 216 sq., 225.

self in favor of declining all concessions contrary to the Gospel, and demanded courage and perseverance on the part of his representatives. He would prefer—thus he wrote on July 15—that they should depart for home. "Ever and anon homeward, always homeward,", is his watch-word.[37] His letters to the Elector John of Saxony also demonstrate his negative attitude.

Under date of August 26, he writes a curious letter to Melanchthon. He encourages his pusillanimous friend, whom he always treated with great indulgence, in his ambiguous proposals: "I am certain that you will be unable to commit aught, except at the utmost a personal offense against me, so that we shall be charged with perfidy and vacillation. But what will the consequence be? Matters may easily be remedied by the steadfastness and the truth of our cause. True, I do not wish that it should so happen; but speak in such wise that, if it should happen, despondency do not ensue. For, once we shall have attained peace and escaped violence, we shall easily make amends for our tricks (lies) and failings, because God's mercy rules over us. 'Do manfully, and let your heart take courage, all ye who wait for the Lord' (Psalm XXVI, 14)." Later editions have omitted the word "lies" (*mendacia*) which appeared in brackets between "tricks" and "failings." The textual tradition, however, renders it probable that the deleted word appeared in the original, which is lost. But even if it had not appeared there, Luther's mind is sufficiently expressed by the words "tricks" and "failings" (*doli et lapsus*).[38]

His strictures grow more severe in course of the following month, especially when, on September 20, he receives reports from the Nuremberg representatives at the Augsburg diet, bitterly complaining of Melanchthon's obsequiousness. "I am actually bursting with anger and indignation," he wrote to Jonas on this occasion. "I beseech you to cut the matter short and come back home." "They have our Confession and the gospel . . . If war is to come, then let it come. We have done and prayed enough. The Lord has given them over to us as a holocaust 'to reward them according to their works' [2 Tim. IV, 14]; us, His people, He will save from the fiery furnace of Babylon. . . . What I have written for you is meant for all."[39]

[37] Letter to Jonas, etc.; *Briefwechsel*, VIII, p. 113.

[38] On August 28; *Briefwechsel*, VIII, p. 235. For more details on this letter, see my article on the same in the *Stimmen aus Maria-Laach*, 1913, No. 3, pp. 286 sqq.

[39] Grisar, *Luther*, Vol. II, p. 391.

Writing to his friend Link, he expresses the hope that no definite concessions will be made to the opposition; Christ will transform all offers "into a lance by which to play a deceptive game with the opponents who intend to play us false; Christ is preparing their destruction in the Red Sea." [40]

In a more considerate tone he pleads with Melanchthon, who is burdened with so many cares, to furnish him with more accurate information; for he fears that he will be made a victim of violence and deception.

In order to console Spengler, his informant from Nuremberg, who had indulged in laments, he wrote to him: "Though Christ may appear to be somewhat weak, this does not mean that He is pushed out of His seat. . . . In the proviso concerning the Gospel, there are embodied snares (*insidiae*) other than those which our adversaries can employ against us." [41] Hence, in the last analysis, the proviso concerning the Gospel and its secret snares (*insidiae*) was expected to save everything. This means: No agreement may be regarded as valid or binding if it runs counter to the new gospel, even though such concessions are made.

In the meantime events at Augsburg followed the course we have already described.

The greatest sensation was produced by Melanchthon's concession to recognize the jurisdiction of the bishops under certain conditions.

In treating of this proposal, Luther, on September 23, writes to his confidant, Nicholas Hausmann, to the effect that the main condition for the recognition of episcopal jurisdiction was this, that the bishops "were to attend to the teaching of the Gospel"; and he adds in all seriousness that nothing had been done in this direction and hence his enemies had conjured up their own destruction. [42] He speaks as if the concession was not a mere pretense.

Still more characteristic is Luther's excuse after the close of the diet, addressed to Landgrave Philip of Hesse in response to the latter's complaint. Here he frankly admits the true nature of the proposed recognition of episcopal jurisdiction: It was not at all to be feared that this proposal would be accepted; moreover, it never could have been accepted; but, he avers, it served "to raise our repute still

---

[40] Köstlin-Kawerau, *M. Luther*, Vol. II, p. 237.
[41] Grisar, *Luther*, Vol. II, p. 385.
[42] *Briefwechsel*, VIII, p. 269; Grisar, *Luther*, Vol. II, pp. 387 sq.

further" (*i. e.*, to capture public opinion). The offer would have been a mistake only if it had been adopted. Philip, therefore, ought to be satisfied; in his next work, he (Luther) proposes to discuss at length the unfairness of his opponents.[43] In this work, entitled "Warning," he actually boasts of the conciliatory attitude of his partisans at Augsburg. Nevertheless, all peace overtures were lost upon those obstinate men. "Our offers, our prayers, our cries for peace" were all wasted.[44]

The real nature of the "proviso of the Gospel" is revealed only if due consideration is given to all these texts.

Towards the end of his sojourn at the castle of Coburg, Luther was visited by Martin Bucer and John Frederick, the son and future successor of the Elector of Saxony. Both found him in comparatively good health. His exterior appearance had changed, due to a long beard which he wore until his return to Wittenberg. Bucer's object was to effect an approach between his party, which sympathized with Zwingli, and Luther, relative to the controversy on the Eucharist. He by his artful diplomacy succeeded in impressing Luther favorably by means of a vague formula on the Real Presence. After the termination of the diet, Luther probably hoped to resist the Emperor with a more numerous and more compact following. Prince John Frederick, eager to show his respects to Luther, presented him with a precious signet-ring bearing the latter's "escutcheon,"—a heart overlayed with a cross in the midst of a rose. Luther at once found a mystical interpretation for this symbol, by referring it to his doctrine and position.

With a certain resignation he discussed with these and other callers the unfavorable decision of the diet. In reality, and as a matter of course, he did not expect and could not have expected any other.

In his letters he now entrusted everything to Providence. His letters and writings at this period contain pious and beautiful sentiments and abound in phrases calculated to console himself and his friends.

Some historians love to extol the excellence of the prayers which he composed during his solitude. Among others they refer to a collection of exhortations which he compiled at that time. It is, in reality, a treasury of elevating thoughts, taken from Holy Writ to arouse confidence in God.[45] It is apparent at once, however, that all the texts

---

[43] *Briefwechsel*, VIII, p. 295; Grisar, *Luther*, Vol. II, p. 388.

[44] *Ibid.*, pp. 388-389.

[45] Weimar ed., Vol. XXX, ii, pp. 700 sqq.; Erl. ed., Vol. XXIII, pp. 154 sq. Cf. Haussleiter in the *Neue Kirchliche Zeitschrift*, 1917, pp. 149 sqq.

have been selected to serve as a defense and confirmation of the personal standpoint which Luther assumed in his contentions. The same is true of most of his prayers. They are designed to corroborate his presumptive right. Every true prayer ought to contain, above all else, a petition to know and bow before the will of God, even as related to the whole conception of life. In the prayers which Luther composed such willingness is hardly detectable. He will not concede the possibility that another course besides the one which he has entered upon may be the right one.

This observation is applicable also to the frequently cited prayer which Vitus Dietrich is supposed to have heard from Luther's lips, and which culminates in the words addressed to God: "Thou hast power to extirpate the persecutors of Thy children; if Thou dost not do it, the danger is Thine. What we have done, we had to do." [46] Such is not the spirit of resignation as expressed in the *fiat voluntas tua*, the basis and crown of all prayer; but it is a command addressed to God to do the bidding of the supplicant. Dietrich, who was an enthusiastic disciple, also tells us that Luther, while sojourning in the castle of Coburg, devoted at least three hours daily to prayer. It is not unlikely that many an hour may have been spent by him in sighing for relief, especially when he was unfit for work and in periods of protracted sickness and spiritual affliction. Moreover, his work of translation undoubtedly offered him many opportunities of meditating on the Psalms and other Biblical texts. Hence, it is probable that his customary prayer may have often been protracted. But it is difficult to believe that Luther devoted himself regularly to prayers for more than three hours daily. The strenuous literary work which he performed demanded a most diligent use of time.

4. LUTHER'S WRITINGS DURING HIS SOJOURN AT COBURG AND THE FOLLOWING MONTHS

Some of the works produced by Luther's tireless pen during this period have already been mentioned.

Among the others, which are to be classed with them, his treatise on Purgatory should be noted.[47] It was written by Luther to supply

---

[46] Cfr. Grisar, *Luther*, original German ed., Vol. III, p. 998.

[47] *"Widerruf vom Fegfeuer,"* Weimar ed., Vol. XXX, ii, pp. 367 sqq.; Erl. ed., Vol. XXXI, pp. 184 sqq.

the absence of any reference to this subject in the Augsburg Confession, and to disclose all the disgraceful lies and atrocities of this papistical doctrine which, he asserted, had been introduced allegedly for the sake of filthy lucre.

Simultaneously with this work he published a tract in German and Latin, entitled, "Some Articles which Martin Luther will uphold against the entire School of Satan." [48] It comprises forty theses, which had been occasioned by the negotiations at Augsburg. Of these, no less than ten are an attempt to demonstrate the astounding proposition that the marriage of priests is to be regarded as a Christian institution even according to the papists, and that those who inveigh against it, therefore, deserve to be branded as "public assassins, robbers, traitors, liars and miscreants."

The book "On the Keys," to which Luther devoted himself immediately after, and which he rewrote twice, was his most important work on the power of the Church. [49] He teaches here that sins are not remitted by the Church in virtue of an (imaginary) power of the keys, but by the word of grace entrusted to the congregation, of which each individual avails himself in faith. If sins are to be retained instead of forgiven, the congregation must co-operate; it must be the "co-judge"; and hence, for the sake of discipline, sinners must be properly denounced. It was an exaggerated and impracticable demand, as he himself experienced in his several attempts to introduce the ban. [50]

The "Epistle of M. Luther on Translation and on the Intercession of the Saints" [51] in its first and longer section is a defense of the principles followed by him in translating the Bible. Among other things, he undertakes to formulate an extensive justification of his arbitrary insertion of the word "alone" in Rom. III, 28: "For we account a man to be justified by faith ALONE, without the works of the law." The Catholics severely criticized him for inserting the word "alone" in the interests of his doctrine. It was intended to strengthen the Lutheran position, though it must be admitted that the legitimate meaning of the text, as preserved by tradition, is not exactly incompatible

---

[48] Weimar ed., Vol. XXX, ii, pp. 420 sqq.; Erl. ed., Vol. XXXI, pp. 121 sqq.

[49] Weimar ed., Vol. XXX, ii, pp. 435 sqq. Erl. ed., Vol. XXXI, pp. 126 sqq.

[50] Köstlin-Kawerau, M. Luther, II, p. 223: "Luther adheres to this, although he knew how difficult it was to establish ecclesiastical discipline according to this principle in the new evangelical churches."

[51] Weimar ed., Vol. XXX, ii, pp. 632 sqq.; Erl. ed., Vol. LXV, pp. 102 sqq.

with the word "alone." Luther insists most vigorously upon his interpolation. "I will not have either the pope-ass or a mule for judge." "I would not answer such asses, nor reply to their vain, monotonous babbling about the word *sola,* otherwise than to say: Luther will have it so and says, he is a doctor superior to all other doctors in all popedom. Thus shall it be." With an appearance of humor and a high sense of superiority he repeats that, if there be any "papist who would make himself obnoxious on account of the word *sola,*" he "should be told straightway that Dr. Martin Luther will have it so. . . . *Sic volo, sic iubeo, sit pro ratione voluntas.*" He would also "rail and boast for once against the blockheads, as St. Paul did against his crazy saints" (2 Cor. XI, 21 sqq.), etc.[52] Only an abnormal person with a deep-seated grudge could write in this manner. Apart from this, the treatise here under review contains many good suggestions, in particular concerning the task which he proposed to himself of faithfully reproducing, in conformity with the genius of the German language, the ideas of the sacred writer rather than their material words.

The second part, which attacks the Catholic doctrine of the invocation and veneration of saints as a "shameless lie of the pope-ass," constitutes but a loose appendix to this queer "Epistle." Luther incidentally admits that "it has been immeasurably painful" to him to have "torn" himself away from the saints. He is well aware that the veneration of the saints is an ancient heirloom "of all Christendom."

Another literary product of his sojourn at Coburg Castle bears the title, "Admonition relative to the Sacrament of the Body and Blood of Christ." Besides piously exhorting the evangelicals, it attacks the doctrine of the Holy Sacrifice of the Mass as upheld by the Catholics at Augsburg.[53]

By means of his work, "That Children Should be Urged to Attend School," [54] Luther designed to remove a drawback which vexed him very much in connection with the appointment of pastors.

As early as 1524 he had discussed this matter in his "Appeal to the Aldermen of all Cities." In consequence of the religious contentions and the social revolution, the schools had deteriorated very much. He now laments

[52] For further details see Grisar, *Luther,* Vol. V, pp. 515 sqq.

[53] Weimar ed., Vol. XXX, ii, pp. 595 sqq.; Erl. ed., Vol. XXIII, pp. 162 sqq.

[54] Weimar ed., Vol. XXX, ii, pp. 517 sqq.; Erl. ed., Vol. XVII, 2 ed., p. 377 sqq. Cf. my article on "Luther" in the *Pädagogisches Lexikon* of Roloff.

and fears that eventually there will be no fit candidates available for the pastoral office, as a consequence of which there will be but one pastor to every ten villages. The decline of the schools would likewise prove dangerous to the secular offices. The proposals which he develops for the education of youth are good; but here again he treats the Catholic schools of the past with flagrant injustice. According to Frederick Paulsen, author of a "Geschichte des Gelehrten Unterrichts," he regards the "entire basis of artistic education," as given before his time, as "the work of the devil." [55] Education, he claims, ought to be founded exclusively on the Gospel.

The civil authorities are systematically invited in this work to exert pressure upon parents who are remiss in the discharge of their educational duties. This function, moreover, should be exercised by the civil authorities in the interests of procuring suitable candidates for the public offices, "when they see a lad who displays ability." Luther does not advocate universal compulsory education on the part of the State. "It is unfair," Gustav Kawerau truly says, "to represent Luther as the harbinger of universal compulsory education." [56] Neither is there any justification for the assumption that enthusiasm for the humanities and the advance of science and education in themselves constituted the starting-point of this treatise. "The religious viewpoints alone are the decisive ones," remarks Julius Böhmer, a Protestant author. Another Protestant, F. M. Schiele, says Luther was concerned with devising a remedy for the "collapse of an educational system which had flourished throughout Germany"—a collapse "brought about by the preaching of Wittenberg." The damage could be remedied only with great difficulty and very slowly in the course of subsequent years.

Schiele holds that the statement that "Luther's reformation gave a general stimulus to the schools and to education generally," must "melt away into nothing." [57]

Whilst various other writings of Luther may be passed over, there is one more work of his which is deserving of mention, as it reveals a more pleasing aspect of the man. It is his German edition of the fables of Æsop, intended for the use of school children. This work was intended, on the one hand, to furnish a diversion from serious thoughts; on the other, Luther sincerely desired by his edition of Æsop to provide the young with "the finest possible precept, admonition, and instruction" adapted to their "external life in the world." The adaptation was couched in classical language and the indecent

[55] Grisar, *Luther*, Vol. VI, p. 21.
[56] *Ibid.*, p. 8.
[57] *Ibid.*, pp. 20, 26 sq.

admixtures of former editions were omitted. Luther intended to make it a "jovial and lovable, and withal a respectable and decent Æsop." The projected edition was never completed. Only parts of it are available.[58] They are valuable on account of the suitable German proverbs which the editor has inserted. In general, his works abound in proverbs, of which he made a collection in 1535 or 1536.[59]

Two controversial works of Luther remain to be mentioned as belonging in a certain sense to his Coburg productions. Both were directed against the diet of Augsburg and were issued soon after Luther's return to Wittenberg, whilst he was still in an agitated frame of mind and filled with the thoughts of his sojourn at the castle of Coburg. They are entitled: "Warning of Doctor Martin Luther to his Dear Germans," and "Gloss on the Pretended Imperial Edict."

The "Warning" [60] is directed above all else against the use of force on the part of the Empire and the Emperor, which he believed to be impending. Casting the most vulgar and insulting aspersions upon the Catholic members of the diet, he advises his "dear Germans" not to come to the aid of the papists in the event of war or insurrection. Necessity demands, he says, that resistance be offered to every violent attack.[61] The suggestive force of this impassioned work was calculated to inflame the minds of the masses, who had embraced the new theology, with a determination to offer stern resistance. This book was read aloud to the mob in public squares and markets and from it the people learned that if Dr. Martin Luther would be executed, a large number of bishops, priests, and monks would go with him. Luther here spoke to the masses as "the Prophet of the Germans," claiming that it was necessary for him to adopt this title against the papists and asses.

In the "Gloss" [62] he proclaims with the Psalmist (XC, 13): "In the name and calling of God I shall walk upon the lion and the asp and trample under foot the young lion and dragon, and this shall be commenced during my life and accomplished after my death." His

---

58 *Werke*, Weimar ed., Vol. L, pp. 440 sqq.; Erl. ed., Vol. LXIV, pp. 349 sqq.

59 Weimar ed., Vol. LI, pp. 645 sqq.

60 Weimar ed., Vol. XXX, iii, pp. 276 sqq.; Erl. ed., Vol. XXV, 2 ed., pp. 1 sqq.

61 On the "Warning" cf. Grisar, *Luther*, Vol. II, pp. 388 sq., 391 sq.; Vol. III, pp. sq., 442 sq.; Vol. IV, p. 316.

62 Weimar ed., Vol. XXX, iii, pp. 331 sqq.; Erl. ed., Vol. XXV, 2nd ed., pp. 49 sqq.

self-consciousness rises to a dizzy height against the "insipid cattle
and filthy swine" who would conceal the pretended imperial edict,
which is denounced as an invalid, unjust, and surreptitious decree.
All were warned to leave untouched his principal dogma of justification by faith alone. "Thus I, Doctor Martin Luther, most unworthy
evangelist of our Lord Jesus Christ, declare that the Roman emperor,
the Turkish emperor, the Tartar emperor, the pope, all cardinals,
bishops, priests, princes, lords, the whole world and all the devils shall
leave this article stand; and in addition, they shall have the flames of
hell about their heads and no reward. This be my, Dr. Luther's, inspiration from the Holy Ghost." The Catholic leaders saw in this
declaration an inspiration from an entirely different source. The
quixotic exclamations in which Luther indulged at that time almost
approach the border-line of insanity. It is less difficult to understand
why Luther should invoke the nationalistic sentiments of his "dear
Germans," for he wished to incite them against their alien oppres-
sors, especially against "the principal rogue, Pope Clement, and his
servant, the legate Campegius." In both of the works here under
consideration he repeats the most revolting lies about the Augsburg
diet; as, for instance, when he asserts that it was evident at Augsburg, and many admitted it, that he was in the right and that the
Catholic Church was steeped in errors, but tyrannical obstinacy had
triumphed.

Luther was most furious against Duke George of Saxony, the
protagonist of the Catholic cause, in the months following the diet.
On Easter, 1531, appeared his diatribe "Against the Assassin of Dresden," which is a monument of hatred against a noble prince who
remained loyal to the Emperor.[63] In his published reply to Luther's
"Warning to his Dear Germans," George had defended the diet, the
empire, and Catholicism, and represented Luther as a rebel. This forceful reply was published anonymously and is lost, except for a few
lines which have been preserved by Cochlaeus. Another reply directed against Luther's "Gloss" was published by Francis Arnoldi
under the title: "Reply to the Booklet Launched by Martin Luther
against the Imperial Recess." [64] Its author was a pastor in Cöllen
near Meissen, who was well acquainted with Duke George. Arnoldi's

[63] Weimar ed., Vol. XXX, iii, pp. 446 sqq.; Erl. ed., Vol. XXV, 2 ed., pp. 108 sqq.
[64] Erl. ed., Vol. XXV, 2 ed., pp. 88 sqq.

"Reply" most probably embodied some ideas suggested by the Duke.

Luther, in his libel "Against the Assassin of Dresden," endeavored to defend himself particularly against the charge of sedition, which Duke George and others made against him. The word "assassin" in the title signifies "calumniator." But Luther is not satisfied with defending himself; he once more attacks the "blood-hounds" of the opposition and announces that he will continue his attacks in perpetuity. He says he had humiliated himself sufficiently, nay, too often, and it would now be his boast that he would bubble over with invectives and imprecations against the papists. At the close he admits that he is unable to pray without cursing. He could not utter the petition: "Hallowed be Thy Name," without adding the words: "Accursed, damned, disgraced shall be the name of the papists and of all who blaspheme Thy Name." "Verily," he says, "I pray thus every day." And he believes that God hears his prayers; for even now He has miraculously caused "this terrible diet to come to naught." "In spite of all, however, I maintain a kindly, friendly, peaceable, and Christian heart towards everybody; even my greatest enemies know this."

In reply Arnoldi published an answer "To the Libel," etc., which was again inspired by Duke George, who had been so grievously insulted by Luther. [65] Like the first work which bore Arnoldi's name, this one, too, is composed in a very blunt style. It was the Duke's desire that free vent be given to his sentiments of indignation and that satisfaction be rendered to the maltreated Catholics by way of a severe attack upon their opponent. On account of the religious revolt, the Duke had suffered much in his duchy, despite sincere efforts to abolish the prevailing abuses. The monasteries and the clergy were profoundly shaken by the religious revolt, and his people were being corrupted. Luther had only himself to blame if the Duke and Arnoldi, animated by love of the Church, the Emperor and the Empire, and convinced that they were standing before an abyss, to a certain extent imitated his offensive language by using such epithets as blood-hounds, whoremongers, etc. The historian cannot shirk the unpleasant duty of quoting some passages from these violent replies. There is first of all the quotation which Cochlaeus has preserved from the pamphlet entirely composed by Duke George. [66]

[65] *Ibid.*, pp. 129 sqq.
[66] Cochlaeus, *De actis*, etc. (1565), folio 211b; Erl. ed., Vol. XXV, 2 ed., p. 89.

5. A STRONG SAXON PHILIPPIC AGAINST LUTHER

"You have entitled your work against the diet, 'Warning to my dear Germans.' It would have been more correct if you had entitled it, Seduction and Incitement to Rebellion and Insurrection. For you are plainly bent upon inciting the people to revolt against the Emperor and all in authority. You proceed with artful snares, with lies and outcries, with a veritable specter of assertions. The devil is called upon to assist you on every page. May those pass judgment on this pamphlet who call you a living saint and say you are possessed of the spirit of God." Thus far Cochlaeus' quotation from Duke George.

The following quotations are excerpted from the other works mentioned above:

Your "Glosses" contain as many lies as words. You are an infamous apostate and pervert the truth when you say that the married state is prohibited in the Catholic Church. You lie when you maintain that capital punishment is contemplated for those who do not use consecrated salt. You lie when you assert that Duke George of Saxony and the Elector of Brandenburg promised to supply the Emperor with 5000 horses against the Lutherans. You lie when you aver that the Emperor is resolved to make war upon you Lutherans for the purpose of suppressing the gospel. You lie like a conscious, faithless, and perjured scoundrel, when you state that the Catholic princes have formed a league at Dessau for the purpose of attacking you. Thus you heap lie upon lie. Our princes formed a league for the sake of preserving the peace, only to further the welfare of their people, and to the disadvantage of nobody, as events have shown. You inveigh against all papists, including the Emperor, traducing them as traitors, miscreants, sacrilegious blood-hounds. At the same time you falsely pretend not to have spoken against the Emperor or any other ruler; it is as if one said that he intended to produce white, but in reality produced black.

The noble-minded Emperor's sole intention, formed after due deliberation, is to make order prevail in the Church. He will not allow priests to consort with dissolute women. You, evil-minded apostate, interpret this intention in a way which the devil in hell could not surpass in malice.

Everyone knows that your proper sphere is vituperation. Your scolding against me I regard as the vaporings of an old shrew. Your thunderous blows do not intimidate me, but I dare tell you the truth. If you bark at me, I will make you spit fire like a hell-hound. A perjured renegade ought to be answered so that the whole world may know his name. For it is an old saying that a wolf-roast demands canine sauces.

Hear me, Doctor Luther. I wish to propose for your consideration two words which you apply to the princes who are opposed to you, namely, *sacrileger* and *fool*. You, dishonorable and carnal wretch, fly at your opponents as if they were sacrilegious despoilers of churches. But who was it that sacrilegiously robbed the property of Christ, which emperors, kings, princes, noblemen, citizens, and peasants, inspired by ardent Christian charity and cherishing His sacred Passion, donated of old to the monasteries, parish-churches, and altars? Verily, tell me truly, Squire Martin, Doctor Luther, who despoiled the poor village parsons of their wretched income? Tell me, Doctor Swinetrough (*Säutrog*) Luther, who despoiled God of so many thousands of souls during the last twelve years and sent them to Lucifer in hell? Alas, that arch-murderer of souls, Luther! Who robbed Christ of His spouses, the consecrated virgins, many of whom had served God for years in the religious life, and forced them into a miserable, wretched, and erroneous life, so that they now run about in great want and in disgrace? Fie on you, Martin Luther, you perjured, sacrilegious whore-master of runaway monks and nuns, apostate priests and all apostates! Who robbed and despoiled the Roman Emperor, that beloved, innocent flower of Christianity, Charles V, and the kings, princes, and lords, of honor and obedience on the part of their subjects, by spreading false, seditious, and damnable writings and doctrines? It was you, you execrable wretch! Who is responsible for the many thieves and rogues that now infest almost every nook and corner of the land? It is you, Doctor Luther!

Do you not know from Holy Writ what reward is in store for robbers? Luther, your end and reward are known only to God.

The fruits and splendors of the new gospel are to be measured by other standards. Who among you is able to check the growing drunkenness and marital infidelity, the insubordination towards parents and masters? How many violations of property, what crimes of highwaymen and prowling thieves! This is the liberty which you have given to them: these are the noble fruits of your teaching! You owe your success to the false liberty which you have proclaimed.

You can well afford to preach as you do, for you enjoy the support of your government. If you had not been favored by the Elector, much bloodshed, revolt, and dissension, and the resurgence of all the old-time heresies would have been avoided. Your place is the expected church council. There you would meet men who are competent to dispute with you. But you prefer to hurl your invectives from a safe place.

You say you are obliged to speak out because you are a doctor. Now, I well know the oath which the doctors of Sacred Scripture are obliged to take. It binds them to teach in conformity with the Church. You have violated this oath. I fear you will be promoted in a school of which the devil is rector; for, like you, he is all bluster and tumult.

You boast of your proficiency in German. If the German style of your speeches is so subtle, then I know doctors in the country who are quite superior to you in the vehemence of their German rhetoric, especially when they are under the influence of strong drink. Ofttimes they beat with their fists. If you were among them, you would not be taken for a doctor, but for a swine-herd. You try by the raving fire of your words to start a conflagration; but when the fire meets a solid rock, it merely covers it with black soot, but cannot damage it.

You boast in your addresses that St. John Hus predicted your coming. Hus is holy in the same manner in which he is holy who calls him a saint or canonizes him, or has him prophesy about himself. Both he and you are archheretics. It would have been better had you disputed with the learned Master Erasmus of Rotterdam after he told you the truth in his "Hyperaspistes." He has so attuned his chords that you could not reply. When you cease barking, you become silent, but you keep on sneaking about treacherously like a mad dog.

Whilst the Peasants' War was on, you delivered powerful speeches. How many have lost their property and their lives, their bodies and their souls, as a result of your false, seductive writings and your Satanic doctrines and sermons! All the rebellious peasants who have been slain in that war will rise up against you on Judgment Day and exclaim: "Woe to you!" You are an arch-assassin of souls and bodies. You are guilty of their death, even as Pilate is guilty of Christ's. It is you who are a desperate, perjured blood-hound, not they whom you call by this name to-day.

The whole world knows that your conscience upbraids you day and night, and that you can nevermore be glad and enjoy peace of mind, even though exteriorly you display a joyful disposition towards your Catherine von Bora.

In ten years you have been unable to settle in your own mind what you will or ought to believe. You do not know to-day what you will believe a year from now—your own writings prove it. You cannot come to an agreement even with your own followers as to whether you intend to abide by your present doctrines or invent others. As a consequence, the poor have become to obfuscated that they scarcely know what to believe, and almost every village has seen the rise of a new and distinct sect. What prudent man, therefore, would adhere to you and desert the Catholic Church to join your ranks? You have written that everybody ought to preach the Gospel as he understands it. Now Karlstadt, Zwingli, Bucer, Capito, Oecolampadius, the Anabaptists, Hubmaier, Hut, Müntzer, and many others have followed your advice and preached according to their own judgment, thus extending the misery which you have set afoot. You ought to restore order instead of continuously heaping maledictions upon the papists.

Hear me, you arch-blasphemer; you admit before all the world that, when in your daily prayer you say: "Hallowed be Thy Name!" you are perforce compelled to exclaim: "Accursed, damned, reviled be the name of the paptists and all blasphemers." Who blasphemes more outrageously than you? You boast that you are a Christian doctor and preacher. Do you not know that Holy Scripture teaches you not to curse your enemies, but to love them for God's sake? You should pray for them, as Christ did when He hung upon the cross. You curse the papacy when you utter the words: "Thy kingdom come!", but do not forget that no one on earth is so much opposed to the kingdom of Christ as you are. You would dethrone Him if it were possible. Your followers have already cast His images out of the churches and demolished them.

Your writings display the temerity and folly of a poor apostate who has gone astray. If you want to see an arrogant fellow, behold, here is the most arrogant of all. If you wish to see a destroyer of other people's property, behold, here is one from whom even the property of beggars is not safe. If you want to see an unchaste man, behold, here is one who violates the chastity of a nun. If you want to see an agitator and a rebel, behold, here is one guilty of a hundred thousand murders and homicides, one who despises all spiritual and secular authority and stands convicted as a falsifier of Holy Writ.

In you we find the source of every malice, evil, sin, and infamy; an unadulterated rogue.

Had not St. Paul written of Antichrist as he did, I should believe that you were he; but undoubtedly you are his precursor. They are right who maintain that Luther is certainly possessed by the devil. I believe that the whole legion of devils which Christ drove out of the possessed and permitted to enter into a herd of swine, is in you. As the devils made the swine so mad that they drowned themselves in the sea: so the legion of devils has made your monkish cranium so mad and giddy that you are unable to enjoy any peace by day or night, until the Christians of all parties and places are become confused and perplexed and finally plunged into the abyss of hell.

May you and your erring followers by the grace of God be brought back to the way of truth! Would that you had a sincere desire to return! May God grant you repentance for your sins here below, and eternal happiness to us all!

These are freely rendered extracts from the terrible excoriation delivered against Luther from Dresden, especially by the sturdy pastor, Arnoldi, in the course of the recriminations that followed the diet of Augsburg. The language exceeds the bounds of propriety—which is pardonable because of the heat of controversy—and illustrates the fact that those who had become indignant at Luther freely imitated the rhetorical tricks of their antagonist. At all events this denunciation is a historical monument of an age when fierce contrasts reached their climax. Although not by any means exempt from passion, it reveals, by its very ardor, as no description could, the abhorrence with which Catholic spokesmen viewed Luther, as he appeared to them in his actions and writings, and the schism produced by him in peaceful Germany.

CHAPTER XIV

LUTHER ON THE SIDE OF THE SCHMALKALDIC LEAGUE —HIS TRANSLATION OF THE BIBLE

1. LUTHER'S CHANGE OF OPINION RELATIVE TO ARMED RESISTANCE

After the diet of Augsburg, a striking change took place in Luther's attitude toward the question of armed resistance to the Emperor. The stringent measures of the "Reichskammergericht" announced in the "Abschied" of the diet against the secularization of Catholic church property and the rigorous steps which were generally adopted against the new religion, produced a definite attitude on the part of Protestants. The jurists of Electoral Saxony expressed themselves to Chancellor Brück increasingly in favor of preparedness and forceful resistance to the imperial mandates. Philip of Hesse, who had formed ambitious projects against the Emperor, was prepared to open hostilities at the first favorable opportunity and counted on the support of all those who shared his ideas.

Luther personally would have preferred a policy of watchful waiting without the use of violence. He held that the execution of the resolutions adopted at Augsburg should be demonstrated as impossible by permitting the innovations to progress in a peaceful way. He would have been pleased if things had been left as they were and time thus gained for the further propagation of the new gospel. However, circumstances forced him to change his attitude—a change which led to self-contradiction and open sanction of that armed resistance which he had previously condemned.

His former teaching had been that it was not permissible to meet violence with violence, especially against the Emperor; that, according to the gospel, unjust persecution was to be suffered with Christian resignation and in the expectation of final assistance from above. Despite his blustering, various reasons determined him to issue such declarations repeatedly. In the first place, he was influenced by the after-effects of the mystical idealism which he had developed in the monastery, and according to which the kingdom of God knew only a yielding disposition, humility, and submission; every true Christian must allow himself to be "oppressed and disgraced," but the defense of rights was the business of the secular authorities. In addition, he had firmly persuaded himself that God would and must prosper his cause. Luther was convinced that he was right and, consequently, enjoyed the protection of Heaven, while, on the other hand he "knew" that "the Emperor is not and cannot be sure of his cause." [1] Secondly, he was influenced by the consideration that, if military force were to be invoked in support of his gospel, the prospects of success on the part of the princes who favored him were unfavorable and that the frightful misfortune of war had better be averted for humanitarian reasons. "May God preserve us from such a horror!" [2] He exclaims, since, as he puts it, a breach and disturbance of the public peace would be "a stain on our doctrine." [3] His religious innovations would more readily recommend themselves to the princes if they made their way as peaceably as possible, without any disturbance and conflict.

Hence his assertion, repeated particularly during the first years after his apostasy, that the Word alone must accomplish all things, and his appeal to "the breath of Christ," which, according to the Bible, is to destroy Antichrist. Even as late as 1530, Elector John of Saxony was in complete accord with Luther's idea that armed resistance to the Emperor was unlawful. [4]

Nevertheless, it is well known that, from the beginning, Luther allowed himself again and again to clamor for war. It was a demand born of his agitated temperament and his ardent zeal for his gospel. Thus, in 1522, he declared that "every power must yield to the Gospel." [5] "Not only the spiritual, but also the secular power, must yield to the Gospel whether cheerfully or otherwise." "Not a hair's breadth will I yield to the opponents"; and: "If war will ensue, let there be war" (1530). "If Germany will perish, if it will go to rack and ruin, how can I help it? I cannot save it." In 1523 he had already conceded to the Elector Frederick the right to bear arms in defense of the new doctrine, provided he did this "at the call of a singular spirit and faith," not as a Christian prince engaged in his own affairs, but as a stranger who comes to the rescue. In an opinion which he rendered for the successor of Frederick, in 1529, he said: "There must be

[1] Grisar, *Luther*, Vol. III, pp. 47 sq.
[2] *Ibid.*, p. 49.
[3] *Ibid.*, p. 45.
[4] Köstlin-Kawerau, M. *Luther*, Vol. II, p. 249.
[5] Grisar, *Luther*, Vol. III, p. 76.

no resistance unless actual violence is done or dire necessity compels." [6]

These utterances laid the foundation for the change of mind which came over him in 1531.

He was still wavering when, just prior to the assembly of the diet of Augsburg, he explained to his Elector in a rather lengthy memorandum that military resistance "can in no wise be reconciled with Scripture." "In the confusion and tumult which would ensue," he says, "everyone would want to be emperor, and what horrible bloodshed and misery would that not cause!" "A Christian ought to be ready to suffer violence and injustice, more particularly from his own ruler." It were preferable to sacrifice life and limb, *i.e.*, endure martyrdom.[7] It seems that he was at that time very much frightened at the thought of the "disgrace" which would attach to his doctrine if it stirred up a religious war. This memorandum was formulated after Luther had conferred with his three advisers, Jonas, Bugenhagen, and Melanchthon. It was, however, kept secret, perhaps in order to avoid any friction with the electoral jurists, who were rather inclined to war. An abstract was sent only to Spengler at Nuremberg, which city was likewise disposed to disapprove of resistance.

This memorandum caused the adherents of the new religion great embarrassment later on, after Luther had changed his mind and the Protestant Estates, appealing to his authority had entered the Schmalkaldic War. Cochlaeus obtained its text, and published it with glosses directed against its vacillating author. The courageous abbot, Paul Bachmann of Altenzelle, appended a reply to Luther, in which he says that Luther had ever raved against the Emperor and the Pope, as though they were worse than the Turks; but in this memorandum, "being apprehensive of resistance, the old serpent turns round and faces its tail, simulating a false humility, patience, and reverence for the authorities, and says: A Christian must be ready to endure violence from his ruler." [8] Driven into a corner, Luther's advisers, who had approved the memorandum, shortly after his demise tried to impugn its authenticity. Melanchthon did so incidentally, Bugenhagen of set purpose, for which he was justly reproved in public by Ratzeberger, a well-informed friend of Luther.[9]

---

[6] The cited passages *ibid.*, pp. 45–50.

[7] Erl. ed., Vol. LIV, pp. 138 sq. (*Briefwechsel*, VII, p. 239); Grisar, *Luther*, Vol. III, p. 52.

[8] Grisar, *op. cit.*, Vol. III, p. 63.

[9] *Ibid.*, p. 74.

The rapidity with which Luther changed his mind after formulating the above-mentioned memorandum was chiefly owing to the decision of the diet of Augsburg which was so unfavorable to him. His inclination to offer resistance manifests itself at once in his "Warning" to his dear Germans, which he composed shortly after the close of the diet and which has been discussed above, as well as in the tract which he penned against "the assassin of Dresden."

At the end of October, 1530, he was obliged to repair to Torgau with Melanchthon and Jonas for a conference concerning the question of resistance. There he met the legal advisers of his territorial lord and, perhaps, those of other princes. He was unable to resist their influence. At first he refused to declare himself, claiming that the question did not concern him, since it was his sole duty as a theologian to teach Christ. The laws of the Empire ought to be obeyed; what these were, he neither knew nor cared to know. But the jurists insisted that he express an opinion on a lengthy document which they had drawn up in justification of war. After enumerating alleged juridical and theological reasons, this document asserted that the "proceedings and acts" of the Emperor "were in contravention of law"; that, so far as the decision of this matter is concerned, he was "but a private individual." Luther did not contradict them, but placed the responsibility upon the jurists, leaving them to proceed as they pleased. Conjointly with Melanchthon and Jonas he declared that, up to now, he and the theologians, precisely as theologians, had taught that it was "not right to offer outright resistance to the authorities," but they did not know that, as the jurists pointed out, the authorities themselves conferred the right of armed resistance in cases such as that under consideration. Hence, they could "not quote the Bible against such resistance, when necessary for defense, even if it were against the Emperor in person." Taking these things into consideration, all three declared that the warlike preparations were justified.[10]

In writing about this affair to Link, Luther said: "In no wise have we counseled the use of force. But if the Emperor by virtue of his laws concedes the right of resistance in such a case, then let him bear the consequences." In that event, he says, the princes, *qua* princes, and in this capacity only, may offer resistance. "To

[10] *Ibid.*

a Christian, nothing [of that sort] is lawful, for he is dead to the world." [11]

These vexatious and threadbare explanations did not, however, satisfy Link and his followers at Nuremberg, who continued to side with Spengler in his stand against resistance. Neither would the people of the margravate of Brandenburg listen to this over-refined casuistry, but persisted in their refusal to offer resistance. Luther relied all the more on his pretext, that this question should be decided by the politicians and jurists; that he, as a theologian, was obliged to refrain from offering advice; and said he abstained from offering counsel for reasons of a more lofty piety; and that he would have the entire matter rest not on "the power of man," but on that of God; for, then only "it would turn out well, even if it be a downright error and sin." [12] Despite these extenuating phrases, the jurists, as was to be expected, made use of his declaration given at Torgau as a simple and complete acquiescence in their endeavor to bring about the formation of the military League of Schmalkalden. Spengler, who had a copy of Luther's opinion of March, 1530, in which he strictly declined to approve of resistance, wrote from Nuremberg that he was amazed "that Doctor Martin should so contradict himself." [13] Besides the pressure of the jurists, the following circumstances may have contributed to change Luther's attitude: First, the prospect of successful resistance as a result of the increased opposition to Rome, especially in consequence of the defection of England initiated at that time, and the prospective Protestantization of Württemberg; secondly, the Emperor's preoccupation with the hostile king of France; and, finally, the weakness and indecision of some of the Catholic estates which manifested itself at the diet of Augsburg.

As a matter of fact, Luther waxed ever more positive in his demand for armed resistance after 1531.

"We may not deviate a hair's breadth on the plea of disturbing the public peace," he wrote. "We must trust in God, who has thus far protected His Church during the most terrible wars." [14] In 1536,

[11] *Briefwechsel*, VIII, p. 344; January 15, 1531; Grisar, *Luther*, Vol. III, p. 60.
[12] Letter to a citizen of Nuremberg, March 18, 1531; Erl. ed., Vol. LIV, p. 221 (*Briefwechsel*, VIII, p. 378); Grisar, *op. cit.*, III, p. 62.
[13] See Enders in *Briefwechsel*, VIII, p. 298; Grisar, *op. cit.*, p. 59.
[14] Grisar, *Luther*, Vol. III, pp. 78 sq.

subscribing to a document which emphasized the duty to offer armed resistance for the protection of the Gospel, he said: "I, Martin Luther, will do my best by prayer and, if needs be, with the fist." [15] In his excitability and tempestuous nature he even demanded the infliction of the death penalty upon the pope and his rabble, *i. e.*, his defenders. In 1540, he gave notice that there was no other choice "but to take up arms in common against all the monks and shavelings; I too shall join in, for it is right to slay the miscreants like mad dogs." [16] In this same year he also said: "We shall not prevail against the Turks unless we slay them in time, together with the priests, and even hurl them to death." [17] Neither in this nor in similar passages is there any question of defense against force, but rather advocacy of bloody aggression. Yet, even if these ravings are outburst of impetuous anger, and not the expressions of calm deliberation, they indicate a deplorable state of mind and served upon occasion to justify the bloody crimes which resulted from the conflict between the advancing party of religious reform and the defenders of the old order.

2. THE SCHMALKALDIC LEAGUE AFTER 1531

The military League of Schmalkalden was initiated as early as February 27, 1531, by John of Saxony and Duke Ernest of Braunschweig at the instigation of the jurists. It was completed at Schmalkalden on March 29, when the remaining members affixed their seal to the document. Besides the rulers of electoral Saxony and Braunschweig-Lüneburg, there were affiliated with it Landgrave Philip of Hesse, Prince Wolfgang of Anhalt, Counts Gebhard and Albrecht of Mansfeld, and the cities of Strasburg, Ulm, Constance, Reutlingen, Memmingen, Lindau, Biberach, Isny, Lübeck, Magdeburg, and Bremen. Others joined the league later. The members bound themselves by an oath to come to the relief of any member attacked on account of the Gospel or on any other pretext.[18]

Thus a wedge was driven into the unity of the German nation at

---

[15] *Ibid.*, p. 433.

[16] *Op cit.*, Vol. VI, p. 247.

[17] *Op. cit.*, Vol. III, p. 69. Cfr. Grisar and Heege, *Luthers Kampfbilder*, n. 4 (*Lutherstudien*), pp. 138 sq., where more pertinent passages as well as Luther's cartoon: "The Pope and the Cardinals on the Gallows," may be found (p. 32); cfr. also *ibid.*, n. 31.

[18] Grisar, *Luther*, Vol. III, p. 64.

the expense of its internal strength and external development.

The Protestants were now a united political power. What Landgrave Philip and Elector John had commenced when they formed their military alliance at Gotha, in 1526, was now completed. The defense of the interests of the religious innovation passed from Luther and his theologians to the secular authorities; and the latter knew well how to pursue their selfish interests with advantage.

Luther may have been glad to remain somewhat in the background when the League was formed. The jurists and rulers were promoting his cause. If the League should prove disastrous for Germany—which actually happened—his gospel would be less exposed to criticism. Nevertheless, he had to reckon with the decline of his popularity due to the existence of the League. In no small measure he forfeited the direction of his work because of the action of the political rulers.

Schmalkalden was a small city in Hesse, situated south of Eisenach in the administrative area of Prussia. Inclosed in a pleasant valley, where the Stille flows into the Schmalkalde (a tributary of the Werra), the town presents a peaceful scene, in strong contrast with the recollections of the religious struggles in which it played a rôle. Verdant hills surround the city, the Rötberg and the Giefelsberg to the north, the Wolfsberg and the Grasberg to the south. To the east rises a hill, on which was enthroned the ancient castle of Walrab, which is now reconstructed into the stately Wilhelmsschloss. The city was encircled by a wall which has almost completely disappeared. Within its bosom the parochial church of St. George raised aloft its two spires; they are of a late Gothic design, and are still well preserved. The venerable church testifies to the pious and vigorous Catholic life that prevailed before the Protestant Reformation. The sessions of the Schmalkaldic League were held in the old-fashioned town-hall, which is still partially preserved. Luther resided in a Patrician house at the foot of the castle-hill, which still exists. Here he participated in the convention of the estates and theologians in 1537. The residence of Melanchthon, known as "Rosenapotheke," impresses the eye of present-day visitors with its antique style of architecture.

A Zwinglian element had entered this city, dominated by Lutheranism at the time the widowed sister of Philip of Hesse, Elizabeth von Sachsen-Rochlitz, took up her abode in it. Her name is associated with the change of the city to the religion of the so-called Swiss reformers. In the parish church, which was at one time richly decorated with statues, the empty pedestals bear mute evidence to the work of destruction wrought by the Zwinglian vandals. After these iconoclasts had vented their fury on the altars, statues, reliquaries and other works of sacred art, a train of wagons bearing religious objects wended its way up the hill behind the Wilhelmsschloss, where the fanatical mob consigned them to the flames.

3. THE RELIGIOUS PEACE OF NUREMBERG (1532) AND SUBSEQUENT EVENTS

While the Protestant party in Germany prudently set about to circumvent the consequences of the diet of Augsburg by procuring a temporary religious peace through intimidation, an open religious war broke out in Switzerland, in consequence of the conditions obtaining in that country. By the harsh methods under which the new religion made its appearance under Zwingli's leadership in Zurich, that city had gotten into a war with the five Catholic cantons of the Swiss Confederacy.

In the battle of Kappel, which was won by the Catholics on the eleventh of October, 1531, Zwingli was wounded and killed. This accident removed an inexorable enemy of Luther, and bettered the prospects of a more intimate union of the German Zwinglians with Lutheranism. Luther candidly expressed his satisfaction with the judgment which God had visited upon Zwingli for denying the Eucharist, just as He had once singled out Münzer for punishment. "I have been a prophet when I said that God would not tolerate the violent blasphemies of which his party was full." Thus he wrote to Link in Nuremberg.[19] Without displaying the least compassion, he consigned Zwingli to hell. Not long after Zwingli's death, on November 24, Oecolampadius died at Basle, deeply humiliated. Both men, said Luther, were to be proclaimed "damned," even though this led to "violence being offered them," because this was the best way to make people shrink from their false doctrines.[20] H. Barge, a Protestant author, justly says in his life of Karlstadt that Luther "particularly availed himself in his systematic, most experienced and malicious manner, of the forceful language he had at his command, in order

---

[19] On January 3, 1532; *Briefwechsel*, IX, p. 139.
[20] Grisar, *Luther*, Vol. IV, p. 87. *Tischreden*, Weim. ed., Vol. I, No. 1045; II, No. 2845.

to decry Zwingli as a heretic after the latter's death." [21] In a letter to Henry Bullinger, who inherited the leadership of the Zurich faction from Zwingli, and with whom he desired to be at peace, Luther declared that he had learned to esteem Zwingli as a very good man after he had made his acquaintance at Marburg, and that he mourned his death.[22]

On December 25, 1530, the Protestants at Schmalkalden protested against the election of Ferdinand as king of the Germans, which was desired by Charles V. This protest was a hostile act against the Hapsburgs. In spite of it, Ferdinand was elected at Cologne on January 5, 1531.

When the Schmalkaldians pleaded with the Emperor for the abolition of the proceedings before the "Kammergericht," they received an evasive reply, but one effect of their alliance was that the term of April 15, which the recess of the diet of Augsburg had fixed against them, was nullified. The Emperor was prevented from interfering. Even the Catholic dukes of Bavaria, instigated by their ancient hostility to the Hapsburgs, entered upon a formal alliance with the Schmalkaldians against Ferdinand at Saalfeld. Alliances with France, England, Denmark and Zapolya of Hungary were sought partly by Bavaria and partly by Philip of Hesse, and were all directed against the Emperor. The invasion of Hungary by the Turks, however, and the menace of the latter to Germany, constituted the greatest obstacle to the Emperor's plans. It was political and not dogmatic reasons that compelled Charles V to yield to the schismatics.

There were prospects of a preliminary peace. The Protestants, however, demanded that the peace should include all who in future would declare their adherence to the Augsburg Confession. Even Luther, writing to the Elector John, characterized this demand as unacceptable to the Catholic party, because it would inflict too great an injury upon them. He recommends that the opposition to Ferdinand be abandoned for the sake of avoiding war. "Who would wish to be guilty of so much bloodshed for the sake of such a cause?" [23] Finally, a treaty of peace, or, more correctly, an armistice, was signed at Nuremberg on July 23, 1532. According to its terms,

---

[21] Grisar, op. cit., IV, p. 90.
[22] May 14, 1538; Briefwechsel, XI, pp. 368 sq.
[23] Prior to May 16, 1532; Erl. ed., Vol. LIV, p. 301 (Briefwechsel, IX, p. 186).

nothing was to be done contrary to the existing religious status until the assembling of a general council. The Protestants were even assured in a secret agreement that the legal proceedings concerning the confiscation of church property would be terminated. The terms of this peace, however, were to apply only to present, not to future, adherents of the Augsburg Confession.

In the same year, 1532, Charles V proceeded to Italy, where, in February, 1533, he concluded an agreement with the Pope. Thence he repaired to Spain. It was to the great disadvantage of the Catholic cause in Germany that he did not return to the latter country until nine years later.

The state of public affairs was not essentially changed by the demise of two individuals. John, Elector of Saxony, who died in August, 1532, was succeeded in the government of his country by his son, John Frederick, who was as devoted to the cause of Lutheranism as his father had been. Pope Clement VII passed away in September, 1534, and was succeeded by Cardinal Alexander Farnese, who assumed the name of Paul III. The spirit of Catholic reform animated the latter more intensely than it had Pope Clement, and he elevated determined men to the cardinalate, such as Contarini, Pole, Sadoleto, and Caraffa. His nepotistic inclinations, however, induced him to raise two relatives to the dignity of the cardinalate, of whom one was only fourteen and the other sixteen years of age. At the very beginning of his pontificate, Paul III expressed himself in favor of convoking an ecumenical council; but political complications prevented the execution of this plan for a long time. Shortly he sent Pietro Paolo Vergerio as nuncio to Germany, in order to influence the Protestants in favor of a council. The Elector John Frederick refused to make a definite reply. It was decided to assemble the council in Mantua, in May, 1537; but the prospects of a propitious meeting were meagre because of the attitude of France and the threat of a Turkish invasion. The Protestants everywhere urged excuses for their non-participation in the council, notwithstanding that they had always clamored for one. Consequently in his circuit of the country Vergerio experienced very little coöperation, but was constrained to combat the idea of holding a German national synod instead of an ecumenical council.

On the day after Vergerio had entered Wittenberg, November 6, 1535, he invited Luther and Bugenhagen to breakfast with him in the Elector's castle.[24] He assuredly would not have invited Luther, had he been better acquainted with him, or had he examined his recently published work, "Certain Aphorisms against the Council of Constance," in which Luther indulged in the most disgraceful language about the Romish Church, "the mad, blood-thirsty, red harlot," and "the dragon's heads which peep out from the posterior of the pope-ass." The author of this offensive pamphlet availed himself of the opportunity extended by the incautious papal legate, during whose visit he delivered himself of insults to the Pope and the Catholics, and boasted of his security in the possession of his new doctrine.

In discussing the proposed council, Luther said to the papal legate: "I am willing to lose my head, if I do not defend my teachings against the world. This anger of my mouth is not my anger, but God's anger." He averred that, though he and his followers were in no need of a council, he would nevertheless attend it, in order to give testimony to the truth. He adverted to "foolish and childish matters," of which ecumenical councils treat in lieu of matters of faith. He spoke of his "priests," whom "Bishop" Bugenhagen, who was present at this interview, was ordaining according to the command of the Apostle Paul, and of a dozen other hateful things, among them that "reverend nun," his wife, who had borne him five children, of whom the eldest, Hans, was going to be a great preacher of the gospel. He evidently wished to irritate the nuncio and to confront Rome with an air of superiority.

Vergerio strangely attached great importance to Luther's readiness to attend the council, and reported it with satisfaction to Rome. In this report he also described the exterior appearance of Luther. He found him possessed of a powerful frame, with exceptionally large features. Although he was past fifty, Luther appeared to be but forty. His deportment displayed "arrogance, malevolence, and lack of consideration"; he was "a man devoid of depth, without judgment, a simpleton." He wore a heavy golden chain around his neck and several rings on his fingers. He was dressed in a doublet of dark camelot, the sleeves of which were trimmed with satin, over which he wore a coat of serge lined with fox-fur. Luther himself informs us that he had himself carefully shaved before the visit of the nuncio; it being necessary, he says, to appear youthful to the legate, so that the latter might report to his master that Luther was yet able to accomplish many things. In order to create an impression, the ex-monk solemnly rode to the castle in a coach,— "the German pope," as he said to Bugenhagen, while they were riding, "and Cardinal Pomeranus, instruments of God." Vergerio closely observed him

[24] For the following, see Grisar, *Luther*, Vol. III, pp. 424 sqq.

during the interview, especially his eyes, and writes in his report that, the longer he watched his uncanny eyes, the more he was reminded of certain persons who were regarded as possessed by the devil. He also claims to have heard from former intimate friends of Luther certain discreditable facts about the latter's youth, but refrains from mentioning their nature.

The nuncio was no model of a circumspect and reliable ecclesiastical *chargé d'affaires*. Upon his return to Italy he succeeded in obtaining a bishopric. Subsequently, in 1548, he seceded from the Catholic faith and embraced the new theology. After wandering about restlessly, agitating against the papacy, he died at Tübingen in 1565, unreconciled with the Church.

In the year in which Vergerio visited Germany in the discharge of his legatine duties, the Schmalkaldic allies received a communication from Henry VIII of England, who had dragged his kingdom into the schism. He wrote that he was not disinclined "to be admitted into the Christian league of electors and princes." It was a move which was all the more gratifying to the Schmalkaldic League, since that body had, on a former occasion, sought the friendship of this powerful monarch. But the subsequent negotiations proved fruitless, because there was no indication that the King could be induced to embrace the Lutheran dogmas.

Relative to the divorce of Henry VIII, which constituted the cause and occasion of the schism, Luther had previously proposed to the king a surprising, nay, offensive solution. In an opinion on the permissibility of divorcing Catherine of Aragon, the King's legitimate wife, which Luther delivered on September 3, 1531, he openly and candidly pronounced the marriage of the King to be indissoluble, but, in order to satisfy the King, pointed out that, with the permission of the Queen, he might "marry an additional queen, in conformity with the example of the ancients, who had many wives." [25] Owing to his narrow-minded pre-occupation with the Old Testament, Luther had gradually accustomed himself to regard bigamy as something to be permitted by way of exception also in the Christian dispensation.[26] But it is not known that he granted this exception in a single instance at any time prior to this embarrassing memorandum. Later on, however, he agreed to the bigamous marriage of Philip of Hesse, who in support of his own cause expressly referred to Luther's opinion in the case of Henry VIII.

[25] *Briefwechsel*, IX, p. 88; Grisar, *Luther*, Vol. IV, pp. 3 sqq.
[26] *Op. cit.*, Vol. III, pp. 259 sqq.

Melanchthon, on August 23, also declared in favor of the bigamous marriage of the King, saying: "The King may, with a good conscience (*tutissimum est regi*), take a second wife, while retaining the first." [27]

Blinded by passion, Henry VIII insisted upon divorcing Catherine and, in spite of the adverse decision of Rome, which refused to countenance bigamy, married Anne Boleyn as his sole queen, cut loose from the papacy, and, by means of his well-known brutal measures, compelled the English clergy to submit in all spiritual matters to his usurped ecclesiastical sovereignty.[28]

As a result of fresh advances made to the Wittenberg theologians through Robert Barnes, they were now induced to expect the King to embrace the new doctrine. Luther eagerly hugged the delusion. He wrote to Chancellor Brück that the King was "ready to accept the gospel"; that it was necessary to avail themselves of this opportunity of forming an alliance with him, since such a move would "throw the papists into confusion." Melanchthon received 500 gold pieces from Henry VIII for a work which he dedicated to him. "We have at least received fifty," Catherine von Bora said at that time with a tinge of envy.[29] The execution in the year 1535 of those noble and pious scholars, Thomas More and John Fisher, ordered by the ruthless tyrant who could not break their opposition, was sanctioned by the Wittenberg theologians. Melanchthon asserted that the use of violence against godless fanatics was a divine command.[30] Luther wrote to Melanchthon in the beginning of December, 1535: "One is apt to fly into a passion, when one realizes what traitors, thieves, murderers, yea, veritable devils the cardinals, popes, and their legates are. Would they had several kings of England to execute them." [31]

About this time, envoys of Henry VIII arrived at Wittenberg and were gratified to learn that the theologians of that town, including Luther, had abandoned their view of the validity of the former marriage of the King, which they now regarded as contrary to the natural law. In the first months of 1536, articles were drawn up, designed to effect an agreement with England in matters of faith, which had been desired by the Protestants. In the judgment of

[27] *Op. cit.*, Vol. IV, p. 5.
[28] On the attitude of Pope Clement VII, see Grisar, *op. cit.*, Vol. IV, pp. 6 sq.
[29] *Tischreden*, Weim. ed., Vol. II, n. 4957.
[30] *Corp. Ref.*, II, p. 928.
[31] *Briefwechsel*, Vol. X, p. 275: "*Utinam haberent plures reges Angliae, qui eos occiderent.*"

their Protestant discoverer, these articles reveal "a surprisingly great accommodation" even in most important questions, such as that of good works.[32] Luther describes them as "the extreme limit of what could be granted." Nevertheless, they were not accepted by the English King. The prospects of an alliance with the Schmalkaldians began to vanish. An additional reason was because the demands of Henry VIII to have a commanding influence in the affairs of the League appeared excessive to the others. The ambitious and agitated members of the League, as well as Luther himself, believed that the King intended to usurp the place of the Elector of Saxony in the leadership of the anti-papal party in Germany.

Henceforth, the Wittenberg theologians were very indignant at Henry.

Luther, in 1540, referred to him as a worthless wretch (*nebulo*).[33] To Luther's sorrow, his friend Robert Barnes was afterwards burnt at the stake because he defended the Protestant doctrine on justification. Barnes incurred the displeasure of the English tyrant also for the reason that he and Thomas Cromwell had procured a fourth wife for him in the person of Anne of Cleve; for the author of the English schism, who had divorced successively Anne Boleyn and Jane Seymour, also became tired of Anne. In the year in which Barnes was executed, Melanchthon wrote a letter to Vitus Dietrich, in which he said, respecting Henry VIII: "How very true it is that there is no sacrifice more acceptable to God than the killing of a tyrant. Would that God might inspire some courageous man with this idea!" [34]

But though the hopes of the Protestants regarding England were shattered, their position was strengthened when Philip of Hesse conquered Württemberg. Philip wrested this country from Ferdinand of Austria in 1534, by force of arms, in order to reinstate Duke Ulrich, a follower of the Reformation, who had legitimately forfeited the crown in 1519. Previous to Philip's adventure, Luther, according to his own oral report, had declared that the breach of the public peace and the spoliation of Ferdinand were "contrary to the Gospel"

---

[32] Words of G. Mentz; cfr. Grisar, *Luther*, Vol. IV, pp. 9 sqq.

[33] *Tischreden*, Weim. ed., Vol. IV, n. 5139.

[34] *Corp. Ref.*, III, p. 1076: "*Quam vere dixit ille in tragoedia, non gratiorem victimam Deo mactari posse quam tyrannum. Utinam alicui forti viro Deus hanc mentem inserat!*" On Luther and Cromwell, who was likewise executed, cfr. Grisar, *Luther*, Vol. IV, pp. 11 sq.

and "a stain upon our doctrine." [35] After the Landgrave had sub-jugated that country, and, in view of the fact that the terms of the treaty with its equivocal religious article offered the best prospects for the introduction of the new religion by Duke Ulrich, Luther expressed his delight and congratulations to the Hessian court through the preacher Justus Menius. "We rejoice," he said, "that the Land-grave has returned in safety and with the coveted peace. God is manifestly with this cause. Contrary to our common expectation, He has transformed fear into peace! He who began this work will also accomplish it. Amen." [36] Luther also informed his friends that the Landgrave, previous to his attack upon Württemberg, had visited the King of France and obtained from him a loan of 200,000 crowns in support of the war.[37]

To the best of his ability, Ulrich complied with the expectations of his friends and began to Protestantize his country.

In the year 1534, the Anabaptists obtained the upper hand at Münster by the well-known methods so characteristic of them. Their triumph proved that Luther was not wrong when he suspected that this furtive sect was capable of anything. Indeed, since the beginning of the twenties, he might have learned a lesson from the sharp criticism to which the Anabaptists subjected him. In many respects this criticism was justified. It was largely based on religious grounds. But the horrors which the capital of Westphalia was compelled to suffer, the alleged divine revelations, the cruelties and the polygamy of the Anabaptist sect, produced an outbreak of terrible fanaticism, of which the new religion and Luther's proclaimed Christian freedom were not guiltless. The sectaries of Münster now write—so Luther indignantly exclaims—that "there are two false prophets, the Pope and Luther, but of the two Luther is the worse." [38] In his preface to Urban Rhegius' work against the Anabaptists of Münster, Luther pronounced a characteristic verdict upon them: "It is perfectly evident that the devil reigns there in person, yea, one devil sits on the back of another like the toads do." [39]

When Münster, after a siege, had fallen on June 25, and the reign of terror had been ended by the execution of the ring-leader, John

[35] Tischreden, Weim. ed., IV, n. 5038.
[36] July 14, 1534; Briefwechsel, Vol. X, p. 63.
[37] Tischreden, Weim. ed., Vol. IV, n. 5038, pp. 628 and 630.
[38] Grisar, Luther, Vol. III, p. 419.
[39] Ibid.

of Leyden, and his associates, Catholicism found its position in the north somewhat strengthened.

To offset the growing popular sympathy in favor of the ancient Church, the Protestants endeavored to fortify themselves by a more intimate union of Lutheranism with the people of Upper Germany, who in the eyes of the Lutherans, were still too much inclined towards Zwinglianism. A complete understanding, especially on the question of the Eucharist, was all the more urgent, since the religious peace of Nuremberg was only temporary. The Landgrave of Hesse and Martin Bucer of Strasburg were active in trying to conclude a more intimate union with Lutheranism, without, however, wishing to abandon the Zwinglian denial of the Real Presence. Bucer endeavored to deceive the others by resorting to ambiguous formulas. Both he and Philip flattered themselves with the thought that they could succeed in inducing the people of Upper Germany and even those of Switzerland to join a league of the followers of the new gospel.

"A union between us and the Sacramentarians is being attempted with great expectations and longing," Luther wrote in August, 1535. He on his part was quite sincere in his intentions. On May 22 of the following year, he had the satisfaction of seeing the representatives of Strasburg, Augsburg, Memmingen, Ulm, Esslingen, Reutlingen, Frankfort and Constance assemble in Wittenberg. They were accompanied by two Lutheran leaders, Menius of Eisenach and Myconius of Gotha. Not one of the expected Swiss delegates appeared. All present adopted the so-called "Wittenberger Concordie," a product of Melanchthon's subtle pen.[40] The articles followed Luther in recognizing the practice of infant baptism and confession. The article on the Eucharist affirmed that the body and blood of Christ were "really and substantially" present in the Sacrament, so that even the "unworthy" verily receive the body and blood of Christ. But the interpretation which they placed upon the words showed that the Upper Germans still clung to the view that Christ is present only by that faith which even the "unworthy" may have and that He bestows on the communicant, not His flesh and blood, but merely His grace. Even Melanchthon secretly adopted this interpretation in opposition to Luther.

The issue now depended upon Luther. For the nonce he was contented with the closer union which the Upper Germans had

[40] *Op. cit.*, Vol. III, pp. 421 sq.

achieved by means of the so-called "Wittenberg Concord." By various friendly letters to the Swiss he tried "to calm down, smoothe, and further matters for the best." [41] For the time he did not wish to mention even to Bullinger of Zurich the doctrinal points in which they differed. His attitude, otherwise so abrupt, waxed strangely latitudinarian. It was similar to his conduct at the time of his negotiations with the King of England. Undoubtedly, he thought to himself—which might excuse him—that by considerate treatment the Zwinglians as a whole would gradually come over to his side, in doctrinal matters, especially since the cities of Upper Germany were in need of assistance. In this case, the wish was father to the thought. Nevertheless, even Protestant biographers have found Luther's way of ignoring the differences inherent in the Concord to be very peculiar,[42] especially in view of the fact that he had looked with suspicion upon Bucer's artful endeavors (*admonui enim ne simularet*).[43]

Distrustful of the sincerity of the Swiss, he at first distrusted the so-called Helvetian Confession, drafted in the beginning of 1536 by Bullinger, the leader of the Zurich faction, with the aid of Bucer. But in May, 1538, filled with happy expectations, he wrote to Duke Albert of Prussia: "Things have been set going with the Swiss. . . . I hope God will put an end to this scandal, not for our sake, for we have not deserved it, but for His name's sake, and in order to vex the abomination at Rome; for they are greatly affrighted and apprehensive at the new tidings." [44] Meanwhile, the Swiss "scandal" continued and disillusioned him painfully. Bullinger and Leo Judae, his associate at Zurich, persevered in their sharp opposition to Luther. Their letters contain bitter denunciations of his doctrine and character.

Leo Judae continued to write in the tone which he had adopted in 1534, when in a letter to Bucer he complained about Luther's wanton distortion of the teachings of Christ; the Apostle Paul, he said, would not have tolerated such a bishop. It was not sufficient for anyone to preach merely that Christ is our salvation. Luther was guilty of disgraceful mistakes, and ignored and execrated everybody else. "Since the Apostolic age," Leo continues, "no one has discussed the most sacred things in a manner so disgraceful, ridiculous, and irreligious as Luther." And, whilst indulging in such conduct, he (Luther) set himself up for a pope. Was not a teacher to be judged

[41] *Ibid.*, p. 422.
[42] Köstlin-Kawerau, M. *Luther*, Vol. II, p. 348.
[43] Grisar, *Luther*, Vol. III, p. 421, note 1.
[44] *Ibid.*, p. 423.

in the light of his writings? What would be left of Luther if he were to be judged by his fruits, according to the saying of Christ? Do his aspersions reflect moral grandeur? "I cannot imagine that his writings will meet with the approval of anyone whose mind is not entirely perverted." "I implore the Lord Jesus that he make Luther mild and modest. May He bestow His spirit and His love upon him, that he may discontinue his repugnant agitation; or—take him from our midst." [45]

Luther's subsequent provocative words against the Swiss and those who shared their beliefs, such as Schwenckfeld, resulted in deepening the rancorous sentiments of the Swiss. They were vexed, for instance, when he averred that Oecolampadius, a Zwinglian, was suddenly removed from this life by the devil. Bullinger discloses his mind to Bucer on the "cynical, scurrilous language" of Luther. He laments his insistence upon his own doctrines and the infallibility of his own German version of the Bible, "which, after all, was prepared with too little freedom from prejudice," etc.[46] Later on Bullinger indulged in even more violent diatribes in his "True Confession." In view of the declarations of such leaders among the Swiss theologians, it is unintelligible how, in the nineteenth century, the rulers of Prussia could urge the union of Lutheranism with the Calvinists (Zwinglians) under the name of the Reformed Evangelical Church.

4. LUTHER'S TRANSLATION OF THE BIBLE (COMPLETED IN 1534)

Luther's perseverance in working on his German translation of the Bible enabled him to publish a complete translation in 1534. It was printed by Hans Lufft at Wittenberg, and bore the title: Biblia, that is, the Entire Sacred Scriptures, Done into German by Martin Luther, Wittenberg.

The New Testament had been edited by him in September, 1522, twelve years previously, after the hasty labors begun during his sojourn at the Wartburg. It was repeatedly revised in subsequent editions. Meanwhile, the several parts of the Old Testament were edited from time to time by the translator. When the entire Bible

---

[45] Kolde, *Analecta*, p. 229; to which should be added, for purposes of consultation, the passages in *Histor. Jahrbuch*, 1919 (*Lutheranalekten*, IV), pp. 510 sqq., which have been supplemented by me from Baum's Collected Letters in the Strasburg library.

[46] Grisar, *Luther*, Vol. V, p. 409.

finally appeared, it contained Luther's marginal notes, composed in short sentences which were intended to explain the text or to render its religious meaning intelligible to the reader. These notes expressed the peculiar views of the editor. The different books were accompanied by prefaces which embody remarkable explanatory and controversial passages. The entire book was richly illustrated with wood-cuts.

In his preface to the book of Job, Luther discusses the pains it required to make a German version of the Bible. "We all," he says, "Master Philip [Melanchthon], Aurogallus, and I, labored with such care on Job that we were sometimes barely able to get through three verses in four days." . . . The reader "does not perceive what hindrances and stumbling-blocks lay in the path he now glides along as easily as down a greasy pole. To us, however, it cost much toil and sweat to remove all the hindrances and stumbling-blocks." [47]

The linguistic excellence of this German version, in contrast with former translations, which were rather clumsy because too literal, is so undisputed, even on the part of Catholic critics, that we need not print any words of appreciation of it here. The immense influence which this work exercised on the development of the German language is universally acknowledged. In his larger work on Luther, the present author has treated of these excellent features extensively, and discussed in detail the various phases of Luther's Bible and its relation to the medieval translations. [48]

The linguistic advance was achieved in a twofold manner. In the first place, Luther adopted the style of the Saxon curia, a purified form of modern High German, which had developed since the middle of the fourteenth century. He did not create this language, but made the greatest contributions toward its propagation in virtue of the popularity of his literary productions, and particularly his translation of the Bible. In the second place, he infused into the language which he had inherited, his own animated spirit, and popularized it by listening to the genuinely colloquial expressions current among the common people and introducing these into the literary language. He himself tells us that he found it of the utmost service to "look into the jaw of the man in the street," i. e., to observe closely the speech of the common people. In rejecting an inadequate expression, he was

[47] Op. cit., Vol. V, p. 497.

[48] Grisar, Luther, Vol. V, pp. 494–546. See, however, J. M. Lenhart, O. M. Cap., "Luther's Indebtedness to the Catholic Bible" in Fortnightly Review, St. Louis, May, 1930, pp. 103 ff.

apt to say: "No German speaks thus," or "The German language does not tolerate that." [49]

Besides these linguistic characteristics, the method he employed had two excellent features. He always takes pains to go back to the original text of Sacred Scripture, whereas former translators had invariably followed the Latin Vulgate. In this respect Luther followed the humanistic tendency of his age. Credit is due to Erasmus for having furnished the first great impulse to the study of the original text of Scripture by his edition of the Greek New Testament. The other excellence of Luther's version consists in the clearness he imparts by means of circumlocutions to such expressions as would otherwise be difficult of comprehension. Thus he tried to make the meaning clear to all. In doing so, however, he proceeded in an altogether too arbitrary manner, but he succeeded in making the Bible a readable and popular book.

His translation had a remarkable sale, to which the celebrity of the author and strong partisan interest naturally contributed no small share. The latest bibliographer of Luther's German Bible, Paul Pietsch, notes 34 Wittenberg impressions of the Weimar Edition alone, and 72 reprints for the rest of Germany during the decade between 1530 and 1540; and again, from 1541 to 1546, the year of Luther's death, 18 additional Wittenberg impressions and 26 reprints. It is believed, according to rather reliable investigations, that the press of Lotther at Wittenberg published no less than 100,000 complete Bibles from 1534 to 1584, to which must be added particularly the Bibles published by the press of Lufft. [50] One might almost say that Germany at this time was deluged with Bibles. What a powerful influence Luther's German Bible must have exercised in enlivening disputations about religion, is obvious; it is equally obvious that it served very much to fortify the existing prejudice that the ancient Church had withheld the Bible from the people and that it was now necessary to purify it by interpreting it in the light of Lutheran opinions.

To the end of his life, Luther devoted himself assiduously to the improvement of each subsequent edition of his German Bible. After 1539 special meetings of scholars were held at Wittenberg to assist him with their linguistic or theological knowledge in polishing his translation. In enumerating

---

[49] Grisar, *Luther*, Vol. V, p. 503. Cfr. Janssen-Pastor, *Geschichte des deutschen Volkes*, Vol. VII, 14th ed., 1904, p. 648. (English tr., Vol. XIV, pp. 401 sqq.)

[50] Grisar, *Luther*, Vol. V, p. 498.

the names of the regular or occasional members of this "sanhedrin of the best people," Mathesius [51] mentions Melanchthon, Bugenhagen, Jonas, Cruciger, Matthew Aurogallus, teacher of Hebrew at the University of Wittenberg, Bernard Ziegler, a learned Hebraist of Leipsic, and Dr. Forstemius of Tübingen. Luther's experienced amanuensis, Rörer, usually kept the minutes of these meetings. The Weimar edition of Luther's works prints what is left of the minutes of the sessions of this Bible-revision committee which met from 1539 to 1541. As a consequence of its labors, the Wittenberg Bibles published by Lufft from 1540 to 1541 show a decided improvement.

The most celebrated edition of Luther's German Bible was the so-called "Normalbibel," which appeared in 1545. It was the last to appear during his life-time. A facsimile of Luther's handwriting with parts of the Old Testament, which is reproduced in the section devoted to the "German Bible" in the new Weimar edition, enables one to see with what diligence he filed and polished the text, and how he often struggled to find the best expression for the thought.

Passing from this more exterior appreciation of his work to its intrinsic value as a translation, the so-called revised Lutheran Bible, published in 1883, has shown what a large amount of textual corrections was necessary before Luther's version satisfied the requirements of modern critical scholarship. This edition not only eliminated many errors, but also altered expressions no longer intelligible at the present time. The revised editions which have appeared since 1883 were an attempt at improving Luther's work still more.[52] Christian Josias Bunsen (d. 1860), who was the author of a Protestant "Bibelwerk," said there were "3,000 passages in Luther's Bible which call for revision." [53] Discussing the defects of scholarship which remained even after the revision of 1883, the learned Protestant philologist and Bible expert, E. Nestle, said: "A comparison with the English or Swiss work of revision shows how much farther we might and ought to have gone." [54] In 1885, the Protestant theologian and orientalist, Paul de Lagarde, vigorously criticized the Lutheran text as well as its first jejune official revision of 1883. He prints a long list of pas-

---

[51] Ibid., pp. 499 sq.

[52] A severe criticism of the official edition of 1913, by which the edition of 1892 was to be improved, in the Christliche Welt, Marburg, 1913, p. 1010.

[53] Grisar, Luther, Vol. V, p. 511.

[54] Ibid., pp. 511 sq.

sages which he holds to be manifestly mistranslations of the original, some of which are arbitrary and evidently made for theological purposes.[55]

Undoubtedly these theological variations constitute a serious defect of Luther's Bible, which diminish its value as a religious work. In the interests of his new doctrine Luther took the liberty to alter the sacred text without warrant. Döllinger's numerous exposures relative to this point met with the approval of Paul de Lagarde. Janssen has once more called attention to them in his History of the German People.[56] The Protestant Paulsen in his *Geschichte des Gelehrten Unterrichts* criticizes Luther's arbitrary alterations of the Biblical text. Notwithstanding these criticisms, the mistranslations are retained in the most recent popular editions of Luther's Bible.

Thus, in the texts which treat of justification and the significance of the law, Luther retouches the wording to suit his own doctrine. The law, according to his translation, "worketh *only* wrath"; "by the law *only* cometh the knowledge of sin." In Rom. IV, 15 and III, 20 he interpolates the word "alone."

Again, Luther's reproduction of Rom. III, 28 would have it that man is justified by faith alone. In this passage, Luther arbitrarily inserted the word "alone" and tried to justify this insertion as follows: "The text and the meaning of St. Paul demand, nay, compel this amplification." This, however, is merely a requisite of his false theory, which he imputes to the Apostle in order to square it with his own doctrinal system. The word "alone" in the Pauline text is an obtrusive recommendation of Luther's principal heresy and a subjective falsification. The context makes it quite evident, however, that, objectively speaking, the real thought of St. Paul could have been expressed by the word "alone." [57]

In Rom. III, 25 sq., Luther again fortifies his doctrine by adding the word "alone" and twice inserts the clause: "an offering of justice which availeth before God," which is not found in the original text. Luther falsely translates Rom. X, 4: "For the end of the law is Christ; he that believeth in him is righteous." The same is true of Rom. VIII, 3, where the Greek text is incompatible with the German rendition.

The illustrations above cited are all taken from St. Paul's Epistle to the Romans.

The word "pious" is persistently and designedly substituted for "just."

---

[55] *Ibid.*, p. 512.

[56] Döllinger, *Die Reformation*, Vol. III, pp. 140 sqq.; Janssen-Pastor, *op. cit.*, Vol. VII, 14 ed., pp. 654 sqq.

[57] For Luther's hectoring justification of the "alone" see *supra*.

Noe, Job, Zacharias, Elizabeth, Simeon, and Joseph, the foster-father of Christ, are all pious, but not just, as in the original text. To be pious, according to Luther, is to have faith, and, through faith, imputed justice. He does not admit real, personal justification. In like manner, Luther everywhere uses the word "congregation" instead of "church," in conformity with the tendency of his doctrine. In reproducing Bar. VI, 30, he ridicules the "priests sitting in their temples with their voluminous copes, with shaven faces and wearing tonsures." [58]

In addition there are interspersed glosses and prefaces to the several sacred books which give him a fine chance for indulging in polemics. He displays a truly marvelous dexterity in interpreting the text in favor of his new doctrine. This is particularly true of his preface to the Epistle to the Romans. [59] In his commentary on the passage which records the divine foundation of the primacy ("Thou art Peter," etc.; Matt. XVI, 18), he declares that in this passage "Peter" means "all Christians with Peter," and the creed of the congregation is the rock upon which the Church is built. The story of the anointment of Christ by Mary Magdalen elicits the following comment from him: "Thus one sees that faith alone makes the work good." [60] And so on.

After the appearance of Luther's New Testament, the Catholic ducal court of Saxony conceived the idea of publishing Luther's work without its distorted reflections on Catholic doctrine. Commissioned by Duke George, Jerome Emser undertook this task, in 1527. The conditions then prevalent in the publishing trade sanctioned such a measure. Emser did not claim that the publication was a new translation. Luther's grounds of complaint, both as a matter of fact and in law, were unfounded, although the procedure is contrary to our modern ideas. Moreover, the title merely announced that the New Testament was "restored to its original sense" in this edition.[61] Later on, after Emser's death, Augustine Alfeld published a reprint, which bore the inaccurate title: "The New Testament, translated into German by the late Emser." The Catholics, however, were determined to counteract Luther's great success by means of other tranlations. In 1534, John Dietenberger, a Mayence Dominican, published a complete translation of the Bible, in which he availed himself to a great

---

[58] Grisar, *Luther*, Vol. V, pp. 514 sq.
[59] *Op. cit.*, Vol. V, p. 526.
[60] *Op. cit.*, Vol., V, p. 518.
[61] On Emser's German New Testament, cf. Grisar, *Luther*, Vol. V, pp. 518 sqq.

extent of Luther's work. Dr. John Eck proceeded more independently in his German Bible of 1537, which, however, because of its stilted style, found but few readers.

Cochlaeus complained that Luther's work was highly regarded, even among the common people; that cobblers and old women pored over it and debated its arbitrary interpretations as if they were the word of God.[62]

The liberties which Luther took in his appraisal of entire books of the Bible were fundamentally even more reprehensible than the defects which have been censured above. It is known that he did not feel bound by the "canon" in force since the early days of the Church, which tradition and the teaching magisterium had sanctioned, and which decided what books constituted the Bible.[63]

In addition to the illustrations already given, the following examples may be adduced. The second book of the Machabees and the book of Esther were rejected, the former because it is "too much inclined to judaize," the latter on account of its "heathen naughtiness." The Epistle to the Hebrews was set aside as "a made-up epistle consisting of fragments amongst which, there is wood, hay and chaff." The Epistle of St. Jude the Apostle is ranked "below the chief books [of the Bible]." The Apocalypse he regarded as "neither apostolic nor prophetic" and said: "Let each one judge of it as he thinks fit."

He asserts that "the Epistle of St. James," which has previously been discussed, "justifies [good] works," and compared with other books of the Bible, which (he maintains) clearly proclaim the doctrine of justification by faith alone, is "but an epistle of straw," which has "nothing evangelical about it." Of this verdict, one of the most celebrated modern Protestant Bible scholars, Theodor von Zahn, says that it is "an act of injustice as incomprehensible as it is regrettable." [64] It is quite comprehensible, however, when one takes into consideration the stupendous levity with which Luther regarded his doctrine as an infallible criterion.

In rejecting the canon of the Bible, Luther destroyed the basis on which the authority of the Sacred Book had been founded. It was tragic that no Christian writer ever inflicted so much damage upon the Book of Books as the man who boasted of having favored it in so

[62] Grisar, op. cit., Vol. V, p. 529.
[63] Ibid., p. 521.
[64] Ibid., p. 523.

high a degree and represented it as the great, nay, the sole source of faith.

It is psychologically interesting to follow the motives and the general ideas which guided Luther in the course of his protracted work of translating Sacred Scripture, expressed in his own words. He intends to show the "papists" that they are not competent to translate the Bible properly, because they do not possess the "mind of Christ," and hence they ought to leave it "in peace" and undisturbed.[65]

"It is not an easy matter," he says, to find "others as sincerely devoted to the Bible as we are here at Wittenberg, who have been the first to receive the grace to reveal once more the Word of God, unadulterated and purified." "None of them knows how to translate correctly." [66] The new Bible, therefore, was to put the papists thoroughly to shame. Above all else, it was to show how mistaken they were when they reduced it to a "code" for the performance of good works, since it "condemns such works and demands faith in Christ." [67]

Hence, Luther was preëminently swayed by a polemical purpose. He wished to see the Bible read by everybody. Rich and poor alike should be enabled to judge that his doctrine was the only true doctrine. Hausrath, a Protestant biographer of Luther, writing in complete accord with the sentiments of his hero, says: "Only now could the burghers feel that they had attained to manhood in the matter of religion, and that the universal priesthood had become a reality. The head of each household now had the wellspring of all religious truth brought to his very door. . . . For a while this might lead to strange excesses, as the theology of the New Prophets showed." Still, "the advent of the German Bible was the dawn of freedom." [68]

It is easy to understand the conscious pride which filled Luther upon the completion of his work. "St. Jerome and many others have made more mistakes in translating than we." "I know that I am more learned than all the universities, those sophists by the grace of God." He invited those who censured him to "do even the twentieth part" of what he had done. "Since the Church has existed, we have never had a Bible like this one." Incidentally it is a real pleasure to him that he was able to rouse the fury (*furias concitare*) of the papists by means of such a great work.[69]

[65] Thus at the head of the edition of 1545.
[66] Grisar, *Luther*, Vol. V, pp. 526 sq.
[67] *Ibid.*, p. 528.
[68] *Luther's Leben*, I, p. 136; quoted by Grisar, *ibid.*, p. 529.
[69] *Ibid.*, p. 331.

He realized withal that he had to overcome many temptations whilst occupied with this work; thus he tells us that, whilst engaged in translating the story of Jonas, he "looked into the belly of the whale, where everything seemed given over to despair."

Besides his habitual interior struggles he was oppressed with the idea that his laborious task "would not be duly appreciated even by his own followers." [70]

He felt an interior satisfaction, however, when he recalled that his text counteracted the Jewish commentators, "who cannot know or understand what is said by Moses, the Prophets and the Psalms." [71]

The refutation of Jewish errors embodied in Luther's Bible is a satisfactory feature of his work.

Julius Köstlin declares that in his translation of the Bible, Luther "bestowed on his German people the greatest possible gift" by making of the Book of Books "an heirloom of the whole German nation." The *whole* German nation? From what has been said above it can be seen that Luther's much-lauded translation was rather a piece of subjective propaganda put forth in the interests of his own party. And as regards "his German people," it was precisely while he was engaged in this work that he applied to the German nation opprobrious epithets which place "the greatest gift" in a peculiar light. Thus the reproaches of the Prophets inspired him to use the following language: "I have begun the translation of the Prophets—a work that is quite in keeping with the gratitude I have hitherto met with from this heathenish, nay, utterly bestial nation." [72]

A word in reference to the illustrations which accompanied Luther's German Bible. The Catholics, who at that time still constituted a majority of the German nation, were aggrieved to see how their Church was ridiculed by the pictures contained in the complete Lutheran Bible of 1534, just as had been the case in the previously published New Testament. The polemical illustrations contained in the New Testament were reproduced in the complete Bible. The Babylonian harlot and the dragon once more appear crowned with the papal tiara. On the title-page of the Wittenberg edition of Luther's complete works, issued by himself in 1541, there is a picture, presumably drawn by the elder Cranach, depicting the ancient Church

[70] *Ibid.*, p. 532.
[71] *ibid.*, p. 533.
[72] *Ibid.*, p. 534.

in the act of driving men into hell; whereas the new Gospel leads them to heaven.[73] A furious looking devil in the shape of a beast, with a cardinal's hat on its head, and death in the form of a skeleton, are depicted as driving a man, clad only in a loin-cloth, into the yawning abyss of hell, where the pope, crowned with the tiara, and two other forms are burning. The obverse side of the picture glorifies the new Church. John the Baptist leads a nude penitent to the Crucified Saviour, from whose side a stream of blood gushes over a sinner who has been saved by faith. Verily, the Catholics could not regard Luther's Bible as "the greatest gift to his German nation."

When the Catholic spokesmen took into consideration Luther's principles relative to the rank and use of the Bible, they regarded themselves as justified in assuming an attitude of severe condemnation.[74] These principles contained within themselves the seeds of religious chaos. Luther held that beside, and in addition to, the words of the Bible, the "spirit" was to be the true touchstone of orthodoxy. The spirit would teach everyone to understand the sacred text. In case of doubt, the interior "feeling," which comes from above, must assume the direction of reason. Everyone stands "for himself." To the pious, according to Luther, the Word of God is perfectly clear; but he frequently emphasizes its obscurity. He holds that, owing to the absurd interpretations of many obscure passages, the Bible must almost be styled "a heretical book." Hence, in order to avoid theological anarchy, he makes the self-contradictory demand that the interpretations of the Wittenberg school, *i.e.*, his own tribunal, should always be followed. The "external Word," upon which he insists in opposition to the spirit of arbitrariness, is equivalent to his own word. Yea, penalties are to be inflicted upon those who contemn the magisterium exercised by himself.[75]

It should not be overlooked, however, that Luther's interpretation of the Bible has the undisputed merit that, in contrast with the older allegorical method of exposition, he always tries to establish the literal sense, and for this purpose lays under contribution the study of languages. Not infrequently he employs to advantage the exegetical works produced before his time, for instance, those of the celebrated

---

[73] The frontispiece of 1541 is reproduced in its original size in Grisar and Heege, *Luthers Kampfbilder*, Heft III, plate 9; cfr. the same work, pp. 19 sqq.

[74] Cf., *e. g.*, Johann Fabri, quoted in Grisar, *Luther*, Vol. V, p. 529.

[75] Grisar, *Luther*, Vol. IV, pp. 387 sqq., 420 sqq.; Vol. VI, pp. 237 sqq., 279 sqq.

Nicholas of Lyra. A well-known saying of his opponents was: *"Si Lyra non lyrasset, Lutherus non saltasset."* If Lyra (the lyre) had not played, Luther would not have danced.[76] Generally speaking, however, Luther treated the Biblical lore of the past with such supreme disregard that his neglect of the older commentators redounded to the very great disadvantage of his own work. In addition to this scientific defect of Luther's Bible, the Catholic is bound above all else to take into account the fundamental detriment to exegesis resulting from Luther's abandonment of ecclesiastical tradition. Catholics believe that the Church has been constituted by God the official interpreter of Sacred Scripture. Her voice, resounding down the ages, is sufficient guaranty that her children will not go astray in their study of the Bible. Luther repudiated her guidance, to his own detriment as well as to that of his followers, even of those who were sincere in their intentions and inclined to positive religion. He saw this fact with his own eyes and bitterly rued it. He speaks with horror of the "rubbish in Scripture."

It is easy to refute Luther's assertion that he "pulled the Bible from underneath the bench," where it lay buried, owing to its complete misunderstanding under the papacy, and because it had been denied to the laity and the clergy.[77]

Catholic exegetes are accused of having ignored the fact "that Christ forms the true content of Scripture." This accusation has been refuted by a mass of quotations from writers like Augustine and Thomas Aquinas, and also from Luther's older contemporaries, such as J. Perez of Valencia.[78] Still more striking is the assertion that the Bible was not read during the Middle Ages, nay, that its reading was prohibited by the Church.

Frederick Kropatschek, a Protestant, states in his scholarly work, *Das Schriftprinzip der lutherischen Kirche* (1904): "If everything be taken into account, it will no longer be possible to say, as the old polemics did, that the Bible was a sealed book to both theologians and laity. The more we study the Middle Ages, the more this fable tends to dissolve into thin air. . . . The Middle Ages concerned themselves with Bible translation much more than was formerly supposed."[79]

[76] Grisar, *op. cit.,* Vol. V, p. 535.
[77] *Ibid.,* pp. 536 sq.
[78] *Ibid.,* p. 541.
[79] *Ibid.,* p. 536.

Similar admissions could be cited from other Protestant scholars such as Walther Köhler, Ch. Nestle, J. Geffcken, W. L. Krafft, E. v. Dobschütz, O. Reichert, G. W. Meyer, A. Risch, etc.[80] Above all it is now agreed that the laity were never prohibited from reading the Bible, as has often been alleged. It was only when there was danger that the Bible would be abused during menacing heretical movements, that the Church authorities from time to time adopted measures forbidding the laity to read the Bible. Historical researches show that the Bible was widely circulated both in the original languages and in translations, in manuscripts and printed editions, in the age that preceded Luther. On account of the importance of the subject, a synopsis of these researches is hereby offered.

Wilhelm Walther of Rostock and Franz Falk, a scholarly clergyman of Mayence, have devoted themselves with distinction to a study of this matter. In recent times, a German-American scholar, W. Kurrelmeyer, has edited in installments *Die erste deutsche Bibel* (The First German Bible), in the Library of the Literary Society of Tübingen; these installments are supplied with critical contributions from all German translations prior to Luther.[81] The oldest complete printed German Bible appeared in 1466 and was published by Mentel of Strasburg. It was followed by thirteen other editions, some of which deviated to some extent from the first, but all appeared before the publication of Luther's Bible. The name of the editor of the Bible published by Mentel cannot be established with certainty. In consequence of the republication of this version, its text had become a kind of German Vulgate.

Dr. Falk has established the fact that no less than 156 different editions of the Latin Bible were printed in the period between 1450 and 1520.[82] In addition, there are the many extant manuscripts, which have been classified by Walther, as well as numerous prints and manuscripts of separate parts of the Bible, such as the Psalter and the Gospels and the Epistles of the ecclesiastical year.

The latter, being lessons taken from the Old and the New Testament, had been translated and collected in so-called *"plenaria"* or postils, which were to be found everywhere in the hands of the faithful. In lieu of the complete Bible, which was expensive and only partially intelligible to many, these postils supplied the people with reading material which was adapted to their needs and was explained to them during divine service. In virtue of

[80] *Ibid.*, pp. 545 sq.
[81] See Ch. Nestle in the Protestant *Enzyklopädie für Theologie*, Ergänzungsband XXIII, p. 317.
[82] Grisar, *Luther*, Vol. V, p. 536.

these "*plenaria*," all classes of the people were well grounded in the most essential and instructive portions of the Bible.

Relative to the partial and complete translations of the Bible, Sebastian Brant could truly say of the pre-Lutheran epoch: "Every country is now filled with Sacred Scripture." [83]

The extant German translations of the Bible, particularly those contained in the "*plenaria*," were by no means unknown to Luther. It may also be assumed—in fact it has been specifically demonstrated in many instances—that he made use of them more or less in his translation, as any scholar would have done when engaged in a similar work. His merit of having proceeded in an independent manner remains undiminished, even if it is to be assumed that his translation was influenced to some extent by a fixed German vocabulary expressive of Biblical words and phrases.[84]

A remark remains to be made on the practical use of the Bible during the later Middle Ages. It was an abuse that the Bible was excessively allegorized, and that it was not sufficiently used in scholastic disputations in comparison with philosophy; but it always retained its prestige in the pulpit and religious literature. Popular devotional literature furnishes a striking refutation of the claim that the Reformation rescued the Bible from oblivion, even if the statistics and facts which have been adduced above were unknown. The literature composed for the instruction and religious edification of the faithful is replete both with Biblical passages and the spirit of the Bible; at times, it is even excessive in its application of Holy Writ.

The legend of the chained Bible, which is occasionally encountered even at the present time, is little less than grotesque. In Protestant popular tracts young Luther's discovery of the Bible at Erfurt is associated with the queer notion that the copy which he happened upon while a student was fastened by a chain in the library. Copies of the Bible and other books intended for the common use of the public were frequently chained, to safeguard them from unjustifiable appropriation or removal from the room in which they were intended to be used. This very practical custom, still in vogue at present in the parlors of Italian convents, has given rise to the false notion that the Bible was kept chained in the Middle Ages.

[83] *Ibid.*, pp. 536, 540.
[84] *Ibid.*, p. 460. On "Luther's Indebtedness to the Catholic Bible" see J. M. Lenhart in the *Fortnightly Review*, St. Louis, Mo., XXXVII, 5 (May, 1930), pp. 103 ff.

5. LUTHER'S LITERARY ACTIVITY

Among the writings which Luther composed during the years in which he concluded his translation of the Bible, are many sermons and scattered prefaces written for publications of his friends and adherents. Popular religious treatises gradually become less ·frequent. One of the more noteworthy of the latter bears the title, "A Simple Method of Prayer, for a Dear Friend, Master Peter, Barber" (1535).[86] This booklet, written at the solicitation of his barber, is an appeal to all Christians who desire to lead a devout life, recommending to them particularly meditation on the "Our Father" and the Ten Commandments. Luther relates that he himself used passages from the Pater Noster and sections of the Decalogue as fuel with which to kindle a little fire within his heart. He was unfortunate in the selection of his addressee; for Barber Peter stabbed his son-in-law in the following year. Owing to Luther's intercession, the sole punishment meted out to him was exile.

A more voluminous and important treatise is that on the morals of princes and courtiers, published in 1534, under the title, "Psalm 101, with a Commentary by M. Luther." [87] In this work Luther vigorously reminds the upper classes of their duties, bewails the decline of morality in Germany, and points to intemperance as a hereditary evil. If every nation has its own devil, he says, the German devil must be a good wine-skin. At that time it was a prevalent custom at the Electoral court to indulge in riotous drinking bouts. The new Elector, John Frederick, was not the last one who might profit from Luther's admonition. In one of his Table Talks Luther expressed himself about his protector thus: "He is possessed of every virtue; but just fancy him swilling like that!" [88] Duke Henry of Braunschweig-Wolfenbüttel openly denounced the Elector as an inebriate, whereat the latter wrote a letter admitting his inebriety, "after the German custom," but said the Duke of Braunschweig was not the man to find fault, for he was an even harder drinker. Luther on one occasion refers to the appearance of the Electoral courtiers on the morning after a nightly

---

[86] Weimar ed., Vol. XXXVIII, pp. 358 sqq.; Erl. ed., Vol. XXXIII, pp. 214 sqq.

[87] Weimar ed., Vol. LI, pp. 200 sqq. and LIII, pp. 679 sqq.; Erl. ed., Vol. XXXIX, pp. 265 sqq.

[88] *Tischreden*, Weimar ed., Vol. IV, n. 4933; cfr. Grisar, *Luther*, Vol. IV, p. 203. Steinhausen (*Kulturgeschichte der Deutschen*, p. 508) calls John Frederick quite simply a drunkard.

carousal, and says that their heads appeared to have been immersed in salt brine during the night.

A work to which Luther was sincerely devoted was his exposition of the Epistle to the Galatians, which he composed in Latin in 1535. It was well known that he deemed this Pauline Epistle to be the grand citadel of his doctrine.

In 1533 he produced his controversial work, "On the Corner-Mass and the Ordination of Clerics," [89] which his friend Jonas characterized as an effective battering-ram against the papacy. The opposition which his neighbors offered to the innovations he had introduced into the divine service, was the occasion which once more induced him to attack the Mass, so dear to all good Catholics. The fiction of his nocturnal disputation with the devil, which he elaborated with great skill in this book, has become famous. The devil tries to make Luther despond because he was guilty of saying many Masses whilst still a monk, and therefore, was guilty of sacrilege. The abomination of the Mass is cleverly explained by the devil, and Luther's excuses are repudiated; he is told that he must regard himself as lost in the sight of God. He says it required his utmost efforts to retain hope for his own salvation whilst repenting of his former blindness. Some Catholic apologists have erroneously assumed that this clever bit of fiction was a confession on Luther's part that his objections to the Mass had been inspired by the devil. To the attentive reader, the objections are discernible as typical of Luther, but the disputing devil is a literary device and the overwhelming fear by which Luther pretends to have been suffocated, is pure fiction. Luther expresses the wish that all who celebrate Mass be afflicted by a similar mental agony. Such is the *punctum saliens* of the much discussed disputation.

In his treatise "On the Corner-Mass" Luther repudiated both the sacrificial character of the Mass and the Real Presence of Christ on the altar without communion. This was explained by some of his friends in the sense that, like the Sacramentarians, he denied that Christ became really present in the Eucharist by virtue of the words of institution. In the beginning of 1534 he explained this point

[89] Weimar ed., Vol. XXXVIII, pp. 183 sqq.; Erl. ed., Vol. XXXI, pp. 307 sqq. Cfr. Grisar, *Luther*, Vol. IV, pp. 518 sqq. "Corner-Mass" (*Winckelmesse*) is a contemptuous term applied to the Mass because, according to Catholic doctrine, it is equally valid whether celebrated by the priest alone in a lonely chapel or amid a concourse of faithful who unite their prayers with his and communicate with him. (Grisar, *op. cit.*, Vol. IV, pp. 519 sq.),

in a published letter,[90] in which he contended that Christ was not present in private Masses, when the priest was the sole celebrant, because there was no communion of the faithful; and that the Eucharist, because it was essentially a food, was to be distinguished from the Mass, just as God is to be differentiated from the devil. "May God"—this is his prayer—"may God bestow upon all pious Christians courage, so that, when they hear the word Mass, they may bless themselves as if they were in the presence of a Satanic abomination!" [91]

Luther's work, "On the Servile Will," which he launched against Erasmus, was answered by the latter in a vigorous and triumphant pamphlet, entitled "Hyperaspistes," published in 1526. It was an ingenious exposure of the heresies and distortions of Luther.

For a long time Luther was silent, without, however, recovering from the blow which had been administered to him. He was very much pained at the secession of the Erasmian humanists from his party, maintaining that he was justified in being angry at Erasmus because the latter, although professedly a member of the Church, minimized, nay, destroyed the essence of the Christian religion by his strictures, couched in playful and polished form. In the course of an embittered conversation, in 1532, he called Erasmus "a rogue by nature," who regarded the Blessed Trinity as ridiculous, and added: "Erasmus is as certain that there is no God, as I am certain that I see." Although that charge was a product of his hateful imagination, Luther continued to indulge in similar declarations until he finally believed them himself.

A letter from his old friend, Nicholas Amsdorf of Magdeburg, caused him to vent his pent-up wrath. On January 28, 1534, Amsdorf wrote him a letter, composed with his customary fervor, in which he said he could observe the "intervention and the miracles of God" in favor of the Gospel all around him. God, he said, produced the faith, just as He had wrought the Resurrection of Christ. George Witzel, Luther's enemy, who attacked the gospel of salvation, he said, was dependent upon Erasmus, from whom he borrowed all his weapons. Erasmus would have to be "thoroughly unmasked" by Luther "on account of his ignorance and malice." He (Amsdorf) advised Luther to perform this task in a book on the Church, since the attitude of the Erasmian party towards the Church constituted their vulnerable spot.

[90] Weimar ed., Vol. XXXVIII, p. 262; Erl. ed., Vol. XXXI, p. 377.
[91] *Briefwechsel*, Vol. X, pp. 8 sqq.; about March 11, 1534.

Luther was immensely pleased with Amsdorf's letter, but, being occupied with other matters, deferred writing the suggested treatise on the Church until 1539. However, he forthwith printed Amsdorf's letter and accompanied it by a furious attack upon Erasmus in the form of a reply to his friend at Magdeburg.[92] Resorting to the worst kind of distortions and disparagements, he tries to demonstrate that the sole purpose of Erasmus was to bring all Christian doctrine into disrepute, that he was another cynical Democritus, a second Epicurus. Melanchthon, in a letter to Erasmus, pronounced the rash publication of Luther's reply a lamentable blunder. Another friend of Erasmus, Boniface Amerbach, characterized Luther's pamphlet as "the product of a diseased brain" and asserted that Luther had been suffering from paresis (*cephalæa*) for more than a year.[93]

The calumnies which Luther had heaped upon the aged scholar of Rotterdam were too monstrous for him to leave unanswered. He gave vent to his indignation in a sarcastic Latin rejoinder: *"Purgatio adversus Epistolam non Sobriam M. Lutheri."* [94] He treats Luther as one who is drunk or mentally unbalanced. He convicts him of a long series of bare-faced lies. In his indignation, the maltreated scholar asserts that "no text is safe against his violent distortions, based upon premeditated calumny." Rather than admit the justice of Luther's malevolent charge that Erasmus was bent upon fostering infidelity, "the world will believe that Martinus has become demented through hatred, or that he suffers from some other mental disorder, or is dominated by an evil spirit."

Thereafter Luther preferred to observe silence in public; but in the company of his intimates, he expressed himself harshly about Erasmus. "This man," he said, "simply insists on believing what the pope believes"; but, "the Italians are hypocrites." "I fear," he also said, "that he [Erasmus] will die a wretched death." Not long afterwards, in 1536, Erasmus died in the city of Basle, where, due to the prevalence of the new religion, he was unable to receive the last Sacraments. He passed away, loyal to his religion and filled with sincere piety, as even the reports to Wittenberg announced, adding that his last words were: "I will bless the mercy of the Lord and His judgments." Luther did not wish to believe this, and in his Table Talks represents Erasmus's death as that of an unbelieving Epicurean. "He lived

---

[92] Grisar, *Luther*, Vol. IV, pp. 181 sq.

[93] *Ibid.*, pp. 182 sq.

[94] Amerbach had judged Luther's attack "insane"; Erasmus, on his part, addressed his biting reply to "one not sober." (Grisar, *Luther*, Vol. IV, p. 184.)

in a presumptuous security," he said, "and thus died (*securissime vixit, sicut etiam morixit*)." As late as 1544, Luther derisively says of Erasmus: "He passed away *sine crux et sine lux*"—without the Cross and without light.[95]

The great and decisive convention of the Schmalkaldic League assembled February 9, 1537, a year after the death of Erasmus.

[95] Grisar, *Luther*, Vol. IV, p. 185; *Tischreden*, Weimar ed., Vol. IV, n. 3963; 4028; 4899; 5670.

CHAPTER XV

SESSION OF THE SCHMALKALDIC LEAGUE, 1537. LITERARY BATTLES. LUTHER'S CO-WORKERS

1. THE SCHMALKALDIC ARTICLES. REPUDIATION OF THE PROPOSED GENERAL COUNCIL BY THE SCHMALKALDIANS

In view of the prevailing conditions, in particular the attitude of France, the prospects of summoning an ecumenical council, which had been the object of Vergerio's negotiations with Luther, were rather unfavorable. Nevertheless, Paul III, who was intent upon reform and the defense of Catholicism, adhered to the project and fixed the date of the council for May 23, 1537. Mantua was designated as the city where the council was to assemble. For the purpose of definitively winning over the Protestants to the idea of an ecumenical council, the Pope ordered Van der Vorst to visit Germany as his legate. The Emperor, who had intended to convoke a national council, for a while contemplated making concessions to and peaceful covenants with the estates who adhered to the new religion, in order to gain their assistance in his campaign against the Turks. But when it had been announced that the great convention of the Schmalkaldic League was to be held on February 9, 1537, Charles V sent his councilor Held to persuade the Protestants to participate in the council which they had so often demanded. Vergerio, the papal nuncio, also hastened to Schmalkalden.

Meanwhile the strength of the League had increased. The agreement was renewed for a period of ten years. Accompanied by a large retinue, the Protestant princes and the representatives of the cities entered the small town of Schmalkalden. They were accompanied by a large number of theologians—larger than any that had yet appeared at a similar assembly. It was intended that the convention should be not only extraordinarily solemn, but also decisive. Elector John Frederick of Saxony, an enthusiastic follower of Luther, would have preferred if the latter had issued a summons for a council of his own, which, in his opinion, was to be a "general and free Christian council," to which Catholic representatives were to be invited. But Luther and the theologians, as well as the jurists, persuaded him to abandon this all too daring plan. They pointed out the great discord which would probably manifest itself among the Protestants and might result in profound schisms in their own ranks. Only Bucer and a few others still adhered to the proposal of convoking a general Protestant synod.

Within a few days after assembling, the Schmalkaldic League formulated a declaration in which they decisively declined the invitation to attend the council called by Paul III. They declared that the Pope and his party did not intend to renounce their errors, that papists were not competent to pass judgment on the new religion, and that the selection of an Italian city as the seat of the council was objectionable. They contended moreover that the political situation rendered a general council impossible, and that the religious peace of Nuremberg must be preserved and extended to all members who had recently joined the League. The papal nuncio was treated with provocative disrespect by John Frederick. The delegates commissioned Melanchthon to prepare severe declarations against the papacy for adoption by the assembly and its theologians. Luther, on his part, was prepared to favor the acceptance of the papal invitation, but only under conditions to which the papacy could not agree. He desired to preserve the appearance of being conciliatory on account of the advantage which would accrue to his party from this attitude.

Luther was still at Wittenberg when, in anticipation of the approaching assembly of the League, he was compelled by an order of the Elector to draft the so-called Schmalkaldic Articles.

The Elector desired, on the one hand, a clear and definite compilation of the doctrines and practical requirements which were to be adhered to under all circumstances in opposition to the Roman Church and, on the other, a list of articles which were debatable. The summary was to be submitted to the Saxon theologians for their signature, and then proposed at Schmalkalden. At the head of the agenda, as outlined by Luther, were the sublime articles on the Divine Majesty which the partisans of the papacy did not dispute. These were followed by the articles which were rejected by the Catholics as absolutely unacceptable. The first of these was the article which set forth the Lutheran doctrine of justification by faith alone (*sola fide*). "It is not allowed either to deviate from, or to surrender this article," wrote

Luther, "even though heaven and earth should fall. Everything is founded upon this article, which we teach and by which we live in defiance of the pope, the devil, and the world."

The second article was a condemnation of the Sacrifice of the Mass, which was denounced as a "dragon's tail" that has produced much filth and vermin," namely, Purgatory, pilgrimages, confraternities, relics, indulgences, and invocation of the saints. These points are instanced without methodical order and set forth with a torrent of invectives. A third article, in similar language, demands the disestablishment of pious foundations and monasteries and the repudiation of the divine prerogatives of the papacy. The last section mentions the debatable points concerning sin, the law, penance, the Sacraments, and the marriage of priests. On these points there was to be no surrender, but it was expected that the opponents might be forced to make concessions concerning them.[1]

Luther took these articles with him when, accompanied by Melanchthon and Bugenhagen, he started out for Schmalkalden on January 31. The document was the cause of much dissension among the theologians. They quarreled particularly about the severity with which Luther expressed his belief in the real presence of Christ in the Eucharist. Ambrose Blaurer in particular declared, in opposition to Amsdorf and Osiander who defended Luther, that the conciliatory formula of the Wittenberg Concord had been violated in these articles. Melanchthon, cautiously and with reserve as was his wont, agreed with Blaurer. As other points also threatened to bring about a rupture, and Luther himself was taken ill, Melanchthon succeeded, through the mediation of the Landgrave of Hesse, in having Luther's Schmalkaldic Articles entirely withdrawn. No doubt the confused document with its exaggerations and disputable points was repugnant to the taste of this fastidious scholar, who insisted that the Augsburg Confession and the Concord of 1536 constituted an adequate profession of faith for the assembly of Schmalkalden. Melanchthon was now summoned by the estates to come forward with a declaration against the pope and the primacy of the Apostolic See. It was to be the final

---

[1] Weimar ed., Vol. L, pp. 192 sqq.; Erl. ed., Vol. XXV, 2 ed., pp. 163 sqq. Cfr. Grisar, *Luther*, Vol. III, p. 430; Vol. IV, pp. 525 sq.; Vol. VI, p. 310. Of the Sacrament of the Altar it is asserted: "We hold that bread and wine in the Last Supper are the true body and blood of Christ, and that they are communicated to and received not only by pious, but also by wicked Christians,"

breach of the German Protestants with the Church of Rome. Under pressure of the highly exasperated delegates, and during the excitement caused by the illness of Luther, Melanchthon's fickle pen imparted a very odious form to his tracts "On the Power and Primacy of the Pope" and "On the Power and Jurisdiction of the Bishops." [2] There is no longer any recognition of episcopal jurisdiction, even of the purely "human" jurisdiction which he had formerly proposed.

Thenceforth Luther's spirit asserted itself more and more in Melanchthon and produced a notable change of attitude in him toward the Catholic Church. Thus when, prior to the Schmalkadic War, he issued a new edition of Luther's "Warning to his Dear Germans" against the "papistical blood-hounds," as they are styled in this work, he accompanied it by a preface which contained unheard-of attacks upon everything Catholic.

At Schmalkalden, his writings against the pope and the bishops were subscribed to by thirty-two of the theologians and preachers there present and accepted by the convention. When, at a later date, the formulas of Concord were drawn up (in 1580) Melanchthon's above-mentioned tracts were incorporated among the "Symbolical Books" of Lutheranism. [3]

2. LUTHER'S ILLNESS AT SCHMALKALDEN. NEW POLEMICS

The illness with which Luther was seized at Schmalkalden was a violent attack of gallstone, an old trouble which had become greatly aggravated. He was no longer able to participate in the conferences of the convention. In fact, people began to fear for his life. Although he was suffering intense pains and thinking of death, he would not allow even a thought of reconciliation to arise in his soul. On the contrary, he prayed as follows: "O God, Thou knowest that I have taught Thy Word faithfully and zealously. . . . I die in hatred of the pope." [4] Once, when racked with pains, he said to a chamberlain of his Elector that his death would be a source of joy to the pope, but the latter's elation would not be of long duration; for the truth of the epitaph which he (Luther) had prepared, would remain. The tenor of this epitaph was that his death would be the death of the

[2] Grisar, *Luther*, Vol. III, pp. 438 sq.
[3] *Ibid.*, pp. 440 sq.
[4] *Tischreden*, Weimar ed., Vol. VI, n. 6974; Grisar, *Luther*, Vol. III, p. 435.

pope: *"Pestis eram vivus, moriens ero mors tua, papa."* This horrible hexameter, it is true, is not inscribed on his tomb at Wittenberg, but since about 1572, it appears upon a huge memorial tablet with his effigy which had originally been destined for Wittenberg, but was transferred to Jena.[5]

He did not want to die at Schmalkalden, but in the company of his friends at Wittenberg; for he did not wish the papal nuncio, the "legate of the devil," to enjoy the satisfaction of seeing him die in his immediate vicinity. Accordingly, on February 26, he was conveyed to a coach that was to carry him home. A multitude surrounded him as he was about to depart. He made the sign of the cross over them and said: "May the Lord fill you with His blessing and with hatred of the pope." Such was "his last will and testament," according to an expression of Mathesius in his eleventh sermon on Luther," who adds: "He [Luther] bequeathed to his friends, the preachers, *odium in papam."* [6]

On the very next day after his departure Luther experienced an improvement in his health. Having arrived at Gotha, after an exhausting journey, he made a will in writing—his so-called First Testament—in which he expressed the wish that he might live until Pentecost, in order to attack the Roman beast with even greater vigor than he had done before. In this testament he assures the princes that they need not worry over the spoliation of church property. "They do not rob like some others do; indeed, I see how, with these goods, they provide for the welfare of religion." [7] It was more of an attempted easing of his own conscience than a statement in conformity with the truth. According to the reports of his friends, he went to confession at Gotha, as was his wont, and received absolution from Bugenhagen.

He arrived safely at Wittenberg on March 14, his health having greatly improved.

When, during the ensuing period, his strength and ambition flagged, he stimulated himself by resorting to a remedy which always proved effective. He filled himself with hatred of the pope. "Then my mind is completely refreshed," he says in his Table Talks; "the

---

[5] Grisar, *Luther,* Vol. III, p. 436; Vol. V, p. 102; Vol. VI, pp. 370, 377, 389, 394, 395 sq.

[6] Mathesius, *Historien* (1566), p. 130; Köstlin-Kawerau, *M. Luther,* Vol. II, p. 389; Grisar, *Luther,* Vol. III, p. 435.

[7] Grisar, *op. cit.,* Vol. III, p. 437.

spirit is quickened and all temptations flee." [8] Certain phenomena of his inner life can hardly be judged by ordinary standards. The idea of the devil being at work in the papacy distorts all his thoughts. In the case of abnormal phenomena, among which we must reckon his imprecatory prayer, puzzling psychological problems constantly recur. He is not the victim of fixed ideas; for free-will and accountability are clearly operative in his case; but his guilt is diminished when the psychopathic condition which oppressed him since his youth and the monastic period is taken into consideration.[9] Moreover, many pages of the works and letters which he composed at Wittenberg betray this nervous condition, which was accompanied by heart disease and precordial dread.

In 1538 he published his Schmalkaldic Articles, which the convention of 1537 had suppressed, intensifying many of their polemical acerbities.[10] He represented these articles in this work as a document which had been approved by the convention, saying they were "adopted unanimously acknowledged by our party," in order that they might be "publicly submitted and introduced as our profession of faith" before a truly free council of the church. This assertion was false and it cannot be established how Luther came to make it. Can it be assumed that he had no reliable information with respect to the actual proceedings of the convention of Schmalkalden? [11]

In the same year (1538) Luther published a revision of his "Instruction of the Visitators to the Parsons," in which, besides some good exhortations, he directed the parsons to "condemn vehemently the papacy and its adherents." [12]

The larger work of the succeeding year, "On the Councils and the Churches," [13] was the execution of a proposal made by Amsdorf, who had suggested that he once and for all thoroughly repulse the Erasmians and all papists who appealed to the Church and proclaimed her right of rendering final decisions. Luther said that people constantly clamored for "the Church, the Church, the Church," in order

---

[8] *Tischreden*, Weimar ed., Vol. II, no. 2410.

[9] See the chapter: "The Darker Sides of Luther's Inner Life," Grisar, *Luther*, Vol. VI, pp. 99–186.

[10] See *supra*, n. 1.

[11] Grisar, *Luther*, Vol. III, p. 440, note 2.

[12] Weimar ed., Vol. XXVI, pp. 195 sqq.; Erl. ed., Vol. XXIII, p. 57. Cfr. Grisar, *Luther*, Vol. III, p. 438.

[13] Weimar ed., Vol. L, pp. 509 sqq.; Erl. ed., Vol. XXV, 2 ed., pp. 278 sqq. Cfr. Grisar, *Luther*, Vol. V, pp. 377 sqq.; 106 sq.

to destroy his gospel. With an impetuous diligence he read the history of ancient councils and other ecclesiastical documents in order to find material to deny the authority of the Church. The tone of this work, which is written in a self-conscious, provocative, and abusive style, constitutes a psychological problem, despite its somewhat scholarly form. "Whoever teaches differently [than we], though he be an angel from heaven," he says, "let him be anathema" (Gal. I, 8). "We desire to be the pope's masters and to trample him under foot," etc. The pope must "side with us" in the proposed council. "Emperors and kings ought to co-operate in this matter and coerce the pope into compliance." Such statements were apt to enlighten certain blind men in Germany who still good-naturedly believed that peace could be brought about by way of negotiations and religious colloquies. These so-called expectants believed that they could keep the Lutheran question in abeyance by means of a few concessions, until the ecumenical council convened.

Cardinal Albrecht of Mayence seems to have held this opinion. His immoral private life blinded his intellect and rendered his character weak. Luther was enraged at him because he had thus far declined to join the reformers. He employed the affair of a certain Anton Schönitz to vent his resentment against Albrecht in a violent pamphlet, entitled: "Against Cardinal Albrecht, Archbishop at Magdeburg," [14] which he caused to be printed against the express wish of his Elector, who did not desire to see his colleague insulted. After the book appeared, Luther had to promise the Elector not to publish anything of a personal matter without the previous censorship of the electoral curia. The incident furnished the weak Cardinal Albrecht with an opportunity of seeing how little hope there was of effecting a conciliation with the innovators. We may add that a few years later a change came over the Cardinal. A new spirit animated Mayence and its archiepiscopal court, stimulated by the activity of Giovanni Morone, the papal legate, and of Bl. Peter Faber, a companion of St. Ignatius, who came to that city in 1541. The spiritual exercises conducted by Faber influenced the worldly-minded Cardinal and induced him to become a defender of the Church and to lead a better life until his death, which occurred in 1545.[15]

[14] Weimar ed., Vol. L, pp. 395 sqq.; Erl. ed., Vol. XXXII, pp. 14 sqq. Cfr. Grisar, *Luther*, Vol. V, pp. 106 sq.

[15] Cfr. Grisar, *Luther* (German original), Vol. III, pp. 1025 sq. (omitted in the English translation by E. M. Lamond).

Duke Henry of Braunschweig-Wolfenbüttel was one of the bitterest opponents of the religious revolt. He was a personal enemy of John Frederick of Saxony and Landgrave Philip of Hesse. He was accused of many deeds of violence and led an immoral life. He was also an author and wrote a vigorous attack upon the Protestant princes and the new Church at New Year's, 1541. With impetuous haste, Luther, though afflicted with violent ear-ache, replied to him in a pamphlet entitled, "Against the Clown" (*Wider Hans Worst*).[16] The contents of this work are in accord with its contemptuous title. This uncouth lout, Luther says, is at the same time a disgraceful liar in his attacks upon the alleged evangelical heretics. In this work as well as in the one "On the Councils" Luther proposed to show where the true Church was. It is not with the papists, who lack twelve essential parts; the true and ancient Christian Church is rather on his (Luther's) side. The devil's harlot is an epithet which he applies to the papal Church, while Duke Henry, the loutish clown, is characterized as an incendiary and a dastard, who is forced to hear evil reports because of his immoral conduct.[17] Luther wrote to Melanchthon that he marveled at himself because he had observed such moderation in the composition of this book.[18]

In 1537, Luther became involved in an exciting feud with antinomianism. John Agricola of Eisleben, afterwards of Wittenberg, a former friend of Luther and one of his most renowned theologians, passionately declaimed against the law of Christian morality. He contended that the law did not effect true penance, but death and damnation. He wanted conversion and penance to be the product of love. For a considerable number of years, Luther had been wont to concede greater effectiveness to the law and the fear of punishment than he had granted in the early part of his career. Now the unsparing attacks of Agricola violently aroused him, especially since that writer quoted former statements of his own. He condemned the doctrine of Agricola as antinomianism, *i. e.*, perversion of the law.[19] On December 18, he delivered a discourse against the antinomian theses, which, however, Agricola refused to acknowledge as his own. The controversy aroused wide-spread attention. Luther's friends, among them

---

[16] Weimar ed., Vol. LI, pp. 469 sqq.; Erl. ed., Vol. XXVI, 2 ed., pp. 19 sqq.

[17] Grisar, *Luther*, Vol. IV, p. 64.

[18] April 12, 1541; see *Briefwechsel*, XIII, p. 300, on his book *Contra istum diabolum Mezentium*. Mezentius was a notorious tyrant.

[19] Grisar, *Luther*, Vol. V, pp. 15–25.

Amsdorf, bitterly complained that the pupils pretended to be wiser than their master. Luther arranged a second disputation for January 12, 1538, to justify his former position. This was followed by a third, on September 13, which proved to be an extraordinarily lengthy argument against the new "spiritual blusterers" and "conscious hypocrites." [20] Luther's work, "Against the Antinomians," published in the beginning of 1539, sealed the embittered conflict with Agricola and the numerous adherents whom the latter had attracted.[21] Meanwhile the founder of antinomianism had timidly retreated from the field of battle. Luther nevertheless printed things about him which must have hurt him keenly. In March, 1540, Agricola brought suit against Luther before the Saxon Elector, to whom he wrote that he had been trodden under foot for well-nigh three years and had slunk along at Luther's heels like a wretched cur.[22]

As a final solution, Agricola left Wittenberg about the middle of August, 1540, and betook himself to Berlin, where a position as court-preacher was offered to him by the Elector Joachim II of Brandenburg, who had been converted to the new evangel.

3. FURTHER VIOLENT MEASURES

In 1535, Joachim II succeeded his father, Joachim I, who had faithfully adhered to the ancient Church, as Elector of Brandenburg. Like his mother, Elizabeth, a friend of Luther, Joachim II had favored the new religion before his accession to the throne, but only in secret, because he had solemnly sworn to his father that he would remain true to the Catholic faith. In 1540 Joachim was persuaded by the Landgrave of Hesse to issue a ritual in his own competency as territorial bishop, in which he effected a forceful reorganization of the electorate in conformity with the new religion. The clergymen who resisted were exiled, the monasteries were suppressed, the property of the Church as well as the metallic treasures of art which adorned the churches were confiscated to the crown, whence they passed into the hands of the "silver squires" and found their way into the insatiable mint of the country.[23] The prodigality of the Elector, his buildings and mistresses, caused him immeasurable expenses. According to the

---

20 *Disputationes*, ed. Drews, Disp. I, pp. 246 sqq.; II, pp. 334 sqq.; III, pp. 419 sqq.

21 Weimar ed., Vol. L, pp. 468 sqq.; Erl. ed., Vol. XXXII, pp. 1 sqq.

22 Grisar, *Luther*, Vol. V, p. 21.

23 Janssen-Pastor, III, pp. 479 sqq.

testimony of contemporaries, the country was ruined in consequence of his misgovernment. Relative to divine service, Joachim II avoided all striking changes so carefully "that the bulk of the nation, the poor people of the countryside, did not realize what had actually happened." [24] The Elector deceptively declared that he had not introduced any new doctrine, but had merely abolished prevailing abuses. Agricola, the pliant court-preacher, faithfully assisted him. The Latin "Mass" was celebrated with churchly vestments; the host and the chalice were elevated; many feast-days were retained; meat was prohibited during the forty days of Lent; solemn processions were held as of old; and the clergy, vested in white gowns, carried the viaticum to the sick. Joachim declared that he did not wish to be bound by the ordinances of the Church of Wittenberg in these matters.

Luther, who regarded the activities of Agricola with distrust, was in the habit of characterizing him as a comedian. He approved of the new ritual only in part, and demanded that the people should comply with it only on condition that the pure gospel be preached. To Buchholzer, a preacher who felt uneasy about the retention of the clerical vestments, he wrote: "In God's name, walk about [in the procession] with a silver or golden cross and a cape or robe of velvet, silk or linen." If the Elector were not satisfied with the clergy's wearing one robe, let them put on three; if one procession did not suffice, let them hold seven, like Josue at Jericho, and let His Electoral Highness leap and dance like David before the ark of the Lord.[25] As time went on, it was but natural that these temperamental differences produced a certain opposition between Wittenberg and Berlin.

Joachim II was encouraged in his opposition to the faith of his forbears by the almost simultaneous and sudden turn in the religious situation which took place within the duchy of Saxony. Duke George, the noble, valiant and faithful defender of the ancient Church and of the Emperor, passed away on April 17, 1539, without a surviving son. His brother Henry, who succeeded him, precipitously destroyed the Catholic status of the duchy which George had sedulously nurtured since Luther commenced his public career. Luther had always hoped for the death of Duke George. The judgment of God, so he said in 1522, would inevitably overtake him.[26] After the Duke had

[24] J. G. Droysen, quoted *ibid.*, p. 481.

[25] December 4, 1539; *Briefwechsel*, XII, p. 317; Janssen-Pastor, *l. c.*, p. 482; Grisar, *Luther*, Vol. V, p. 313.

[26] Grisar, *op. cit.*, Vol. IV, p. 190.

died a Christian death, Luther predicted that his race would perish.[27]

Like Joachim II, the new duke had favored Lutheranism before he succeeded to the throne. As the arbitrary ruler of the Church in his duchy, he commenced his reign by ruthless measures against the Catholics. Luther came temporarily from Wittenberg in order to aid him by his sermons and counsel. Melanchthon, Jonas, and Cruciger associated themselves with him for the purpose. In July, 1539, scarcely four months after the demise of his predecessor, Duke Henry, following the example of the Elector of Saxony, decreed a so-called evangelical visitation, as the most practical method of Protestantizing his people. The decree was executed by Luther's preachers.

The Catholic clergy were forcibly removed and replaced by apostate priests and monks, nay, sometimes even by ordinary laborers, who, though devoid of all education, pushed themselves to the fore by their fluency of speech and a hastily acquired stock of Biblical quotations.

Luther was not pleased with the conditions which speedily developed at court and among the nobility and the people. His letters reveal a gloomy picture. At the court of the aged and feeble prince he sees nothing but "arrogance and the desire of amassing wealth," coupled with an "inordinate repugnance to promoting the cause of God." [28] In his depressed mood he believes that the scandals of the court are "ten times worse" than the scandal caused by the bigamous union of the Landgrave of Hesse, styles the courtiers and nobles "the harpies of the land," and says that they will end by "eating themselves up by their own avarice." Despite their continuous appropriation of the property of the Church, he charges them with allowing the preachers to starve. He advises a pastor, who was to have been chosen visitator, as follows: "Even should you get nothing for the visitation, still you must hold it as well as you can, comfort souls to the best of your power, and, in any case, expel the poisonous papists." [29] Thus, Luther's idea of advancing the kingdom of God is bound up with the harshest and most unfair methods and he extols the introduction of the new religion into the duchy of Saxony as a wonderful work of God for the salvation of souls.

The religious apostasy made progress also in the North German jurisdiction of Albrecht of Mayence, namely, in the archbishopric of Magdeburg and the bishopric of Halberstadt. In 1541, Justus Jonas introduced the new religion into his native city of Halle.

27 *Tischreden*, Weimar ed., Vol. IV, n. 4623; Grisar, *l. c.*

28 Grisar, *op. cit.*, Vol. IV, p. 194.

29 *Ibid.*, p. 195.

As early as 1533, Protestantism made great gains in the duchy of Jülich-Cleve, in Anhalt-Köthen, and in Mecklenburg. In March, 1534, Anhalt was completely Protestantized, on which occasion Luther sent congratulations and best wishes to the ruler of that city. In July of the same year, the city and district of Augsburg adopted the new religion. In 1539, the archbishopric of Riga in Livonia was brought under Protestant control.

In 1534, dukes Barnim and Philip of Pomerania forced their subjects to embrace the new evangel, despite the resistance offered by the nobility and the prelates. Bugenhagen, who was a Pomeranian, aided the rulers by his unflinching energy and talent for organization. In order to strengthen the new religion, Duke Philip married a sister of the Saxon Elector. During the marriage ceremony, which Luther solemnized according to his new rite, the wedding ring happened to fall to the floor. For a moment Luther was nonplussed, but then exclaimed: "Do you hear, devil, this wedding does not concern you; you will labor in vain." [30]

Bugenhagen was actively engaged in the promotion of Lutheranism, not only in Pomerania, but also in Braunschweig, Hamburg, and Lübeck. From 1537 to 1539 he labored in the service of King Christian III, who introduced the new religion with extremely violent measures in Denmark.

On February 4, 1538, Bugenhagen joyfully reported to Luther from Copenhagen that "the Mass was now prohibited throughout the entire country;" that the mendicant friars had been exiled as "sedition-mongers" and "blasphemers" because they refused to accept the offers of the king; that all the canons had been ordered to attend the Lutheran communion on festivals, and that every effort would be put forth to subject the four thousand parishes to the new evangel.[31] The tyrannical ruler caused all the bishops within his territory to be incarcerated. According to an account of the superintendent of Zealand, who had come to Denmark from Wittenberg in the company of Bugenhagen, some of the monks were hanged.

The King was solemnly crowned by Bugenhagen on August 12, 1537. "Everything proceeds favorably," Luther wrote to Bucer in Denmark. "God is working through Pomeranus. He crowned the king and queen like a true bishop." [32]

In few countries were the external ritualistic forms so little disturbed as

[30] Köstlin-Kawerau, M. Luther, Vol. II, pp. 290 sq.
[31] Grisar, Luther, Vol. III, p. 413.
[32] Ibid.

in Denmark under the calculating influence of Bugenhagen. Even at the present time, the number of Catholic practices, commencing with the celebration of high Mass to the ringing of the angelus bells, is amazingly great in Denmark, Norway, and the duchies formerly united to the Danish crown. The Protestant ministers, when celebrating "Mass," still frequently vest themselves in a chasuble made of red silken velvet, which is worn over an alb of white linen. They also perform the elevation of bread and wine after the so-called consecration, which is pronounced in the middle of the altar.

In Sweden also Catholic ritualistic solemnities were retained for a long time. In his career of royal hierarch Gustavus Wasa, who had Protestantized that country as early as 1527, continued to rule in disregard of all the liberties of the people. He maintained friendly relations with Luther, from whom he procured a tutor for his son Eric in the person of George Normann, a native of Pomerania, who came to Sweden fully empowered to supervise the bishops and the clergy. The impetuous spokesmen of the new religion in Denmark spread rumors to the effect that King Gustavus was not sufficiently in earnest about the new gospel. Gustavus pleaded with Luther to protect him from such reports. In 1539, Luther wrote a testimonial certifying that "his piety was marvelously extolled above that of other princes," that he was imbued by God with a loftier spirit not only for the cause of religion, but also for the cultivation of the sciences. He exhorted the King to establish schools throughout his kingdom, particularly in connection with the cathedral churches; for this was the principal obligation of a pious prince.[33] He had in mind schools that were founded upon his gospel and labored efficaciously to promote the same—such as he himself advocated for Germany.

4. BELLIGERENT AND PACIFIC MOVEMENTS IN THE EMPIRE

In 1537, a more intimate union of the Catholic princes against the Schmalkaldic League, which was threatening war, became a necessity. After many efforts on his part, the imperial ambassador, Held, succeeded in March, 1538, in drafting a plan for a "defensive league" at Spires. It was adopted at Nuremberg on the tenth of June. Emperor Charles and King Ferdinand headed the League, whose other members were: Bavaria, Duke George of Saxony, Dukes Henry and Eric of Braunschweig, and the Elector Albrecht of Mayence (for

[33] *Briefwechsel*, XII, p. 132; April 18, 1539.

Magdeburg and Halberstadt). Owing to the fact that other Catholic princes kept aloof, this so-called Holy League did not attain to the importance which might have been expected.

The Schmalkaldic League soon afterwards sustained a disadvantage, due to the armistice signed at Nizza (June 17, 1538) between the Emperor and France, in consequence of which the League lost all hope of obtaining the aid of France, which it had sought. Emperor Charles, on his part, needed all his forces against the Turks. This confirmed him in his project of friendly negotiations with the Protestants. But the Schmalkaldic League prepared for war. Landgrave Philip labored unceasingly to bring it about.

Luther effectually supported the political programme of the Schmalkaldians in a memorandum which decisively advocated armed resistance, though he regretted the war and would have preferred to see Germany invaded by "a pestilence" rather than ravaged by bloody strife. In conjunction with Jonas, Bucer, and Melanchthon, at the end of January, 1539, he drew up a formal opinion, wherein he indicated to his Elector that the imperial constitution as well as the natural law permitted princes to engage in aggressive war in defense of the menaced gospel and the ecclesiastical possessions which it had acquired. In the event that the Emperor would have recourse to arms, he said, his status would have to be regarded as that of a mercenary in the service of the pope, or as that of a highway robber, for there was no difference between a common assassin and the Emperor, especially since he tried to force his subjects to commit blasphemy and idolatry.[34]

In February, 1539, the leaders of the Schmalkaldic League, whilst in a similar frame of mind, convoked an assembly which was to meet in Frankfort on the Main.[35] It was attended by delegates of the Emperor and of King Ferdinand. At this convention, Saxony and Hesse declared themselves in favor of aggressive war, "in order to get the better of the enemy." However, they were confronted with opposition in the assembly. It was asserted that the programme adopted by the Catholic League at Nuremberg expressly declared that peace must be preserved. Although France promised to aid the Protestants, the war, which was expected to break out at any moment, was avoided for the present. The so-called peace of Frankfort was brought about,

[34] Köstlin-Kawerau, M. Luther, Vol. II, pp. 401 sq.
[35] Janssen-Pastor, Gesch. d. deutschen Volkes, Vol. III, pp. 460 sqq.

chiefly because it appeared that there was no leader competent to conduct the war, Philip of Hesse being severely ill. As frequently in the past, so now, Philip was stricken with an attack of syphilis, which he had contracted by his dissolute life. He left Frankfort on April 17, and hastened to Giessen for medical treatment.

The Frankfort peace provided an arrangement which redounded to the advantage of the new religion. The peace was to endure fifteen months, with temporary suspension of all lawsuits pending in the "Kammergericht" (the supreme court of judicature). At the same time it obliged the signers to participate in a religious conference soon to be held for the sake of effecting a "Christian and laudable union." These proposals were combated by the Catholics. Conrad Braun, a jurist of the imperial supreme court of Spires, maintained in his writings that the reference to a religious conference was a violation of the rights of the proposed Church council. He held that the use of force against sedition-mongers and despoilers of the Church was perfectly proper.[36] These views were favorably received by many ecclesiastical authorities. But where was there any prospect of the successful application of violent measures under the then prevailing circumstances? The strength of the Schmalkaldic League was increased by the very fact that it gained time through the constant extension of the tolerance which was granted to it.

The ecumenical council convoked by Paul III could not take place at Mantua, as planned. It was at first deferred and then summoned to convene at Vicenza, on May 1, 1538. On account of untoward circumstances, it had again to be postponed, until it was finally opened at Trent, November, 1542, at the urging of the Emperor. On July 6, 1543, it had to be adjourned because the war between the Emperor and France prevented many bishops from attending.

An unlucky star also governed the contemplated religious conference. The Emperor ordered it to be held at Hagenau, in June, 1540, but it miscarried, because most of the Protestant theologians departed in consequence of a dissension that had arisen among them relative to certain preliminary questions. The conference was resumed at Worms in the fall. Its deliberations were presided over by the imperial chancellor Granvella. Each side had appointed eleven delegates as spokesmen, among the Catholics so appointed being Eck, Coch-

---

[36] G. Kawerau, *Reformation und Gegenreformation*, p. 135; cfr. Janssen-Pastor, *op. cit.,* III, p. 447.

laeus, and John Gropper, whilst the Protestants selected Melanchthon, Bucer, and Calvin. The Augsburg Confession was presented by Melanchthon as one of the bases for discussion. It was not the original text, however, but the so-called *Confessio Variata,* which had been altered and published by Melanchthon in 1540. The alterations were important. In treating the doctrine of the Eucharist, Melanchthon had met the wishes of the Swiss theologians. In respect of justification, he had attenuated the Lutheran position, eliminated the doctrine of strict imputation and assumed a certain righteousness in man which was imputed to him by God. As regards good works and the observance of the law, "actual changes, or at least attenuations of a dogmatic nature" had likewise been made." [37] To all these changes Luther raised no objections, whereas Dr. Eck during the conference at once charged his opponent, Melanchthon, with arbitrarily changing the basic document; he did not, however, terminate the negotiations, which were soon after transferred by the Emperor to Ratisbon, where the diet was then in session.

Eck was convinced that the conference was bound to prove futile because the question at issue was loyalty to the Catholic Church or positive rejection of her teaching authority. For this reason, he also found fault with the attenuation of Catholic dogmas, especially that of justification, attempted by Gropper. Gropper and Julius Pflugk, being the most moderate representatives of the older religion, differed from the other Catholic theologians in some respects. Gropper participated with Bucer in drawing up certain compromise articles which were proposed for discussion. The whole movement was finally frustrated by the justified objection of Rome to the proposed formula on justification, in which human co-operation and merit were omitted; and, on the other hand, by Luther's declaration that the articles of compromise were "impossible proposals" which neither party could accept.[38]

Although an agreement was reached as to some other non-essential points, the plans for reunion were regarded as shattered on May 22. Cardinal Gasparo Contarini had vainly tried to help matters by his personal participation at the conference as papal legate. Under the influence of the Emperor and of his own fond expectations, he went rather far in accepting the Lutheran idea of justification, at least in

[37] The phrase in quotes is Theodore Kolde's. Cfr. Grisar, *Luther,* Vol. III, pp. 440 sq.
[38] *Briefwechsel,* XIII, p. 341; cfr., pp. 267 sq.

certain expressions. After the close of the conference he expounded his views in a much discussed "Letter on Justification" (*Epistola de Iustificatione*). Despite the many attacks directed against this letter, Pope Paul III continued favorably disposed towards the Cardinal.[39]

At the close of the diet of Ratisbon, during which the opposition between the two parties became constantly more acute, the Nuremberg peace pact of 1532, but also the strict decrees of Augsburg were renewed, subject, however, to a declaration (which was not accepted by the Catholic estates) that the ecclesiastical property usurped by the Protestants be protected and that the application of the Augsburg decree be restricted to religious matters. All this was to be in force up to the assembly of the proposed ecumenical council or a new diet.

The Catholic cause unexpectedly profited by the weakening of the League. Philip of Hesse, its mainstay, began to vacillate in consequence of an event that was creditable neither to himself nor to the Protestant party. The consequences of the bigamous marriage which he contracted (to be discussed later) affected the political affairs of the Empire. When the matter became known publicly, he was threatened with severe penalties under the laws of the Empire. In order to evade them, he resolved, in 1541, to make terms with the Emperor. His abandonment of the military League of Schmalkalden was an irretrievable loss to that organization, which now began to decline.

5. LITERARY DEFENDERS OF THE CATHOLIC CAUSE AFTER 1530

The literary defense of the Catholic cause proceeded with unabated vigor, in spite of the great difficulties which the Catholic writers encountered.

It was not encouraging for authors who wrote in defense of the Church or of the outraged rights of Catholics, to realize that they were exposed to the vulgar invectives to which Luther and his disciples resorted in their replies, or that the products of their industry could be published only amid the greatest difficulties and at the cost of severe sacrifices, because there was no adequate Catholic press. The bishops continued to withhold their support. Papal subsidies were shared only by a few, who succeeded in presenting their petitions to Rome through powerful intercessors. Many talented apologists were

---

[39] The *Epistola*, newly edited, with a critical introduction, in *Corpus Catholicorum*, Vol. VII (1923) by F. Hünermann (*G. Contarini, Gegenreformatorische Schriften*).

driven from the monasteries or ecclesiastical positions in the course of the religious upheaval and, deprived of material support, endeavored in vain to wield their pen in the service of the faith. Had there been a number of periodicals at the disposal of talented Catholic writers, as is the case to-day; had there been available an organized Catholic daily press as a means of reaching the masses, the position of the Church would have been quite different.

The necessity of moral reform, among Protestants as well as Catholics, was greater, however, than the need of scientific or popular instruction; for the new freedom promoted moral decadence in a very high degree. Catholic writers complained that their efforts were largely offset by the rejection of the precepts of the Church and by the unheard-of compulsion exercised by the courts and magistrates of many cities, and against which no remedy could be found. As a result, some ecclesiastics, who might have been able to wield a mighty influence in the literary sphere, dedicated themselves to preaching and practical action. Others were deterred from literary work by the inconsistency and fatuousness of the claims made by the Protestants, who asserted one thing to-day and denied it to-morrow and demanded recognition in one place for what they rejected in another.

Among the books which exercised a powerful influence before and after 1530 were the earlier and later literary productions of Eck, Cochlaeus, and Faber.

Dr. John Eck, of the University of Ingolstadt, was called "the Achilles of the Catholic party" by Cardinal Pole.[40] His practically arranged "Manual against the Lutherans" (*Enchiridion*) was in general use among Catholics and, up to 1600, went through some fifty editions. In addition to his sermons on the Sacraments, his principal achievement consisted in his commentaries on the Gospels for Sundays and feast-days. Intended for the clergy, they evidenced their author's intimate acquaintance with the errors of the day. No less than seventeen editions of the Latin version of these sermons, which comprised several volumes, appeared up to the year 1579. In 1530, Eck began to reissue at Augsburg his writings against Luther, the first installment being entitled *Prima Pars Operum contra Ludderum*.[41] They were followed by a long series of new works, among which were treatises on Purgatory and the Mass, dissertations against Zwinglian-

[40] Janssen-Pastor, *op. cit.*, Vol. VII, p. 593.
[41] Wiedmann, *Johann Eck*, Ratisbon, 1865, p. 586.

ism and against the errors of the Jews, memoranda composed for princes and religious conferences, and commentaries on various books of the Bible. Eck displayed incredible energy up to the time of his death, in 1543. This humble priest never coveted ecclesiastical dignities. When offered honorary canonries, as was frequently the case, he invariably declined them, saying: "I desire to remain a schoolmaster as long as I live." [42] Courageously he bore the slanders which were heaped upon him by the Lutheran party as well as the derision to which he was subjected.

He felt more keenly the studied silence with which his enemies met his arguments. In his Apology of 1542, he addresses his opponent Bucer thus: "Listen, you apostate; does not Eck quote the words of Sacred Scripture and the Fathers? Why do you not reply to his writings on the primacy of Peter, on penance, the Mass, Purgatory, or to his many homilies and other writings? . . . Do you believe you were right," he asks, "when you said at the beginning of the controversy that Eck would be unable to advance any other authorities than his Scotus, Ockham, Thomas, etc.?" [43] As a matter of fact, Eck's scholarly use of Sacred Scripture and the Church Fathers constituted one of the principal merits of his controversial method. Consistency and fortitude were characteristic of the activity of this man, who also made a striking impression by his athletic appearance. "At the religious conference in Ratisbon, in 1541, the superficiality of the friends of the Interim gave way to the lucidity of his principles and his solidity." [44] His vivacious temperament and blunt honesty, coupled with a fine sense of humor, doubtless inspired many a harsh passage in his writings which it would have been better to omit. But it was a boisterous and turbulent arena to which he was summoned by his vocation. [45]

John Cochlaeus in his literary activity revealed not so much a profound theologian as an ever ready and eloquent controversialist. Hardly a year passed but that this man, who was small of stature, participated in the controversies of the day, which he conducted with great versatility. Descriptions of the age in which he lived, exhortations, admonitions, and at times violent personal attacks fill the books of this active controversialist after 1530 as well as before that time.

[42] Janssen-Pastor, op. cit., Vol. VII, p. 592.
[43] From Eck's Apologia; cfr. Wiedemann, op. cit., p. 275.
[44] Thus Janssen-Pastor, VII, p. 587.
[45] On certain blemishes in his private life cf. Janssen-Pastor, VII, p. 592, n. 4.

When Eck died, Cochlaeus took over and vigorously prosecuted the work of the latter. The high-minded Duke George of Saxony, in whose service he labored, supported him in every possible way. When, in 1539, George was succeeded by his brother Henry, who favored Lutheranism, Cochlaeus saw his labors suddenly interrupted; his publisher, Nicholas Wolrab, of Dresden, was thrown into prison; books in defense of the Church by Witzel and Nausea, which Wolrab had in press at the time, were cast into the water. Only with difficulty Cochlaeus succeeded in inducing a relative of his to open a print-shop for Catholic books in Mayence. The printer, Francis Behan, succeeded in establishing the foremost printing establishment for Catholic works in Germany, which flourished at Mayence together with that of Cologne, the second most important center for Catholic publications.

"For twenty years," Cochlaeus wrote in 1540, "there was nothing more disadvantageous for us Catholic authors, in contrast with the heretics, than the great unreliability of our publishers. . . . The publishers were almost all Lutherans, and we were able to obtain their services only at a great outlay of money."

He instances the sad experiences of Eck, Nausea, Mensing, and others, with whom he had attended the religious conference at Worms.[46] His own material condition was improved by a canonicate at Breslau. In 1548 and 1549 he lived at Mayence. He died at Breslau in 1552, exhausted by his labors. The works which he wrote after the diet of Augsburg (1530) embrace an excellent treatise on the saints, various publications on the question of holding an ecumenical council, an effective and thorough reply to Bullinger, "On the Authority of the Canonical Books and the Church," which is ranked among the best of his books, and his pointed "Philippica" against Philip Melanchthon, in which he attacks, among other things, the "serpentine artifice and hypocrisy" of that innovator.[47] Cochlaeus deserves special credit for his Latin "History of the Acts and Writings of Luther" (*Commentaria*, etc.), which first appeared at Mayence in 1549, and was frequently reprinted. It embraces the entire controversial period and depicts the course of the great religious upheaval as his keen eye observed it. The story is copiously supported by

---

[46] Janssen-Pastor, *l. c.*, p. 566.

[47] *Ibid*. The treatise in Cochlaeus' works on the veneration of the saints (1534) is actually the product of Arnoldus Vesaliensis.

citations from his own works and those of the unfortunate author of the schism. The work proved to be a mine of information for later Catholic writers.

John Faber, formerly vicar-general of Constance, became bishop of Vienna in 1530, through the influence of Ferdinand, and as such continued his very successful activity against Lutheranism by means of the spoken and written word, especially by advising the princes. In 1535 he wrote in defense of the Mass and the priesthood against Luther. In the following year he wrote on faith and good works. There is extant an instructive memorandum intended for the religious conferences, addressed by him to the Catholic leaders. He was esteemed by his fellow-Catholics for his learning and wisdom, and for the purity of his morals—which fact did not prevent Justus Jonas, in a pamphlet composed at the instigation of Luther, to characterize Faber as a "patron of harlots," because he combated the marriage of priests. He could afford to ignore all such insults. He died at Vienna in 1541.[48]

Faber was succeeded in the episcopal see of Vienna by his friend Frederick Grau, called Nausea, another energetic and gifted apologist who opposed the heretical deluge. Grau was a man of excellent culture and thoroughly trained in the sciences of language and jurisprudence, no less than in theology. Originally employed as secretary by the papal legate Campeggio, he afterwards functioned as a preacher and writer in Mayence. His sermons are noted for their correct interpretation of Sacred Scripture. Owing in part to his lack of means, he was unable to publish his excellent catechism before 1543. In his work on the council, he favored the granting of communion under both forms, thinking that the Protestants could be won over by this concession. He likewise urged the pope to abolish the law of sacerdotal celibacy for the sake of removing scandal. He participated in the Council of Trent, and died in that city in 1552.[49]

Of the large number of other defenders of the Catholic Church and her doctrines we will mention only a few of the more prominent. A man of very striking characteristics was George Witzel (Wicel), a priest who travelled much and was extremely active. He died at Mayence in 1573. Influenced by the writings of Erasmus, he embraced Lutheranism and married, but after having acquired a more intimate

[48] Janssen-Pastor, op. cit., VII, pp. 580 sqq.
[49] Ibid., pp. 582 sqq.

knowledge of the true aims of Luther and seeing the moral decline which followed the new religion, he returned to the Catholic Church and at once, in 1532, published an excellent treatise on good works, followed by a book on justification, another on the Church, and an apologia of himself. During his varied career he composed nearly a hundred works, all characterized by combativeness and learning. No one scourged the conditions within the bosom of the Lutheran Church so effectively as Wicel; few experienced such adversities on this account as he, so that—as he himself laments—"I am scarcely safe anywhere, even in my own home, and I cannot travel without exposing myself to the greatest danger." [50] From 1533 to 1538 he was pastor of the few Catholics remaining in the town of Eisleben. During this period, he was compelled, as he himself says, "to live in the midst of wolves." As protégé of Duke George of Saxony, he lived in better circumstances for a short time at Dresden. At Fulda, where he stayed with Abbot John, life was made intolerable for him by persecutions. In Mayence he was assailed by the Lutherans because he defended the imperial interim of 1548, which was repugnant to them. This conciliatory interim, which was designed to end the schism and hence made undue concessions to the Protestants, was in harmony with Wicel's ideal to win over the opposition by means of conciliatory measures. He wished to stand above the disputants of both parties. Without abandoning Catholic dogma, as he understood it, he wished to prepare the way for a reconciliation, which, however, proved ineffectual and was, in part, impossible. In this respect his Erasmian training was a hindrance to him. He even censured the theologians at Trent because they refused to adopt his peculiar methods for the re-establishment of peace.

The lively discussions which this obstinate man had to carry on with his fellow-Catholics were evidence of the fact that the latter carefully weighed the idea of religious peace. If the idea itself was regarded as impracticable, this was not due to a blind refusal of conciliation. Wicel himself was forced to realize the extent of the injury from which the Church was likely to suffer in consequence of such ill-advised concessions, when, imbued with the best of intentions, he enthusiastically participated in the new ecclesiastical régime introduced by Joachim II of Brandenburg, which in the end Protestantized that country.

[50] *Ibid.*, p. 570.

Another Catholic spokesman who deserves to be mentioned is the Augustinian eremite, John Hoffmeister. He began to unfold a splendid literary activity, commencing with 1538, when he wrote his "Dialogues" and a refutation of the Schmalkaldic Articles. He continued his efforts even after he had been made vicar-general of his Order for all Germany. He, too, was animated by the delusive hope of conciliating the Protestants.

The Franciscans furnished many renowned and learned defenders of the ancient faith, e. g., Augustine von Alfeld (died about 1533), Nicholas Herborn (died 1535), Conrad Kling (died 1556), and the excellent pulpit orator John Wild of Mayence (died 1554).[51] Caspar Schatzgeyer, a Minorite, was the model of them all in gentleness and the noble style of his popular writings. Henry Helmesius, John Heller, John of Deventer, Francis Polygranus were other Franciscans who defended the Catholic cause.

The most celebrated Dominican authors were: Michael Vehe (died 1539), who produced one of the first German hymnals; Bartholomew Kleindienst (died 1560), who, among other literary compositions, addressed a "Right Catholic Admonition" to "his dear Germans," in imitation of the title of one of Luther's books; John Dietenberger (died 1537), the author of a number of small popular pamphlets, a refutation of the Augsburg Confession, and an excellent catechism; and John Mensing, who actively opposed Protestantism until his death (about 1541), unhindered by the high offices which he held, among which was that of auxiliary bishop of Halberstadt.[52] The University of Frankfort on the Oder honored the memory of his temporary professorship there. Conrad Wimpina, a theologian of that university, did not long continue his labors in refutation of the Augsburg Confession which he had commenced in Augsburg, but died in 1531, and left behind him, among other works, a brief but excellent history of the religious sects in the *Anacephalaeosis Sectarum*.

As in former times, so also now, prominent men outside of Germany opposed the prevalent heresy. A splendid figure was the learned Stanislaus Hosius, leader of the Polish episcopate. He became bishop of Ermland in 1551, and later on a cardinal. To the select circle of his friends belonged Frederick Staphylus, who had studied at Witten-

---

[51] On Wild see Janssen-Pastor, *op. cit.*, Vol. VII, pp. 546–550.
[52] On Mensing see Grisar, *Luther*, Vol. I, p. 79; Vol. III, p. 195; Vol. IV, pp. 121, 160, 303, 385; Vol. VI, pp. 276, 391, 409 sq., 482 sq.

berg as a Protestant, became a convert to Catholicism in 1552, and composed an "Epitome of the Doctrine of Luther" which became famous. Italy and other countries, especially the Netherlands and France, likewise produced eminent antagonists of Lutheranism before as well as after 1530. Ambrosius Catharinus, a native of Siena, continued his literary activity for ten years in France. On account of his criticism of Cardinal Cajetan, he was out of harmony with his Italian confrères. In Italy, not only courageous members of the monastic Orders, such as the Franciscan Giovanni Delfino, but also men who had been elevated to the cardinalate, like Jacopo Sadoleto, Marino Grimani, and Gasparo Contarini, contributed by their writings to the defense of the Catholic religion.

6. LUTHER'S FELLOW-COMBATANTS

After 1530, the friends of Luther, particularly at Wittenberg, made every effort to promote his cause.

Philip Melanchthon, while devoting his energies mainly to his humanistic studies, at the same time actively intervened in the theological controversies up to the time of his death. Because of the success of his labors in behalf of the new creed, it can truthfully be said that he "created Evangelical theology" and "established the Protestant ecclesiastical system." [53] But it is equally true that in course of time he changed his teaching in many points and deviated widely from Luther. His *Confessio Variata* shows a different complexion from the original Augsburg Confession. Commencing with the edition of 1535, his *Loci Communes,* or "Outlines," differ considerably from the earlier editions. As early as 1532, his Commentary on St. Paul's Epistle to the Romans contained a different theology. "He was no longer the interpreter of Luther's ideas," says Frederick Loofs, one of the most respected Protestant historians of dogma.[54] How different is the attitude of the Catholic apologists with their uniformly consistent doctrine! Even though liberty of action prevails among them, and they differ amongst each other in making unessential concessions, they occupy firm common ground in all dogmatic questions.

Melanchthon at first disapproved of Luther's denial of free-will

[53] Thus Gustav Krüger; *see* Grisar, *Luther,* Vol. III. pp. 349 sq.
[54] Grisar, *ibid.*

and abandoned the doctrine of unconditional predestination. Subsequently, he also opposed Luther's exaggerated estimate of the doctrine of justification by faith alone and his low valuation of good works. He gave a more tolerable form to his master's views on penance and fear as a motive of contrition. In later years he even applied the epithet "blasphemous" to the principal thesis of Luther's chief work on the "Enslaved Will." Relative to the doctrine of the Lord's Supper, a deep chasm separated Melanchthon from Luther, who was always more inclined to favor Zwinglianism.[55] Luther was aware of these differences of opinion in matters of doctrine, but nevertheless adhered to Melanchthon; for he could and would not dispense with his talents and reputation. Melanchthon on his part carefully avoided whatever might have led to an open rupture.

No matter how far he was prepared to go in his attempts at reconciliation, Melanchthon never denied his Protestant sympathies. Because of his fundamental deviations from Lutheranism, however, he was violently assailed by his Wittenburg colleagues. Thus Conrad Cordatus, Luther's table companion, passionately attacked him in 1536. Luther found an excuse for Melanchthon, but, displeased with his philosophical ideas, said: "I shall have to chop off the head of philosophy, and may God help me do it; for so it must be."[56] Jacob Schenk, an eloquent and aggressive Lutheran pastor, in 1537, accused Melanchthon of making treasonable concessions to the Catholics. The Elector was drawn into the controversy and privately consulted Luther with reference to it. Luther again expressed his regard for Melanchthon and deprecated his "being driven from the University" of Wittenberg.[57] But events soon conspired to induce Melanchthon, under pressure of his adversaries and broken down by his silent conflict with Luther, seriously to contemplate abandoning Wittenberg.[58] He remained, however, for he was unable to form any firm resolutions. "Let us cover our wounds," he afterwards wrote to Bucer, "and exhort others to do the same."[59] The Catholic spokesmen increasingly revealed his inconstancy and weakness of character, which was the

[55] On Melanchthon's doctrinal deviations from Luther see Grisar, *Luther*, Vol. III, pp. 346 sqq.; Vol. V, pp. 252 sqq.

[56] Grisar, *op. cit.*, Vol. III, p. 371.

[57] *Ibid.*

[58] *Ibid.*, p. 370.

[59] *Ibid.*, p. 377.

cause of his suffering. Mercilessly they censured his pliancy, which approached perfidy. Cochlaeus warned the humanist Andrew Cricius, bishop of Plozk, against the connection which Melanchthon endeavored to form with him. His admonition was based on the opinion which he had formed of Melanchthon from personal observation at Augsburg, in 1530. "Take care lest he cheat you with his deceitful cunning, for, like the Sirens, he gains a hearing by sweet and honeyed words. . . . He seduces [men's hearts] with dishonest words." [60]

Luther on one occasion aptly styled his friend "the Erasmian intermediary." [61]

Melanchthon was so deeply immersed in his humanistic views, which he shared with the much admired Erasmus, that his theology, which he·had studied only *en passant*, was affected by his rationalistic and immature philosophy. Although far removed from the Catholic truth, he nevertheless contended that he fundamentally agreed with the religious position of Erasmus.[62] His concepts of faith, its foundation and postulates, were rather shallow. It was deplorable that this philologian, who lacked profound theological learning, was able to wield so much influence in the sphere of theology. "When barely eighteen years of age," says John Faber, bishop of Vienna, "he began to teach the simple and by his soft speeches has disturbed the whole Church beyond measure." [63] The Catholic apologists soon discovered the shallowness of his theology and philosophy. He delights in speaking of the "celestial academy," where men sit in the *schola* of the apostles, prophets, etc. He bedecks revelation in a vesture of classicism. But, not content with style, he alters the content of religion for the sake of sophistry or expediency or to promote his irenic endeavors. In brief, he is dominated by a desire to reduce all things to a humanistic level.

It was his supreme desire to pursue his humanistic studies in peace and tranquillity. The princes, as "theocrats," he held, should establish such a state for himself and the faithful. He placed all religious authority in their hands. In this he was aided by his ideas of classical antiquity. He was of the opinion that the growing corruption could be overcome only by the civil authority in religious matters.[64]

[60] Grisar, *op. cit.*, Vol. V, p. 267.
[61] *Op. cit.*, Vol. III, pp. 343 sqq.
[62] *Op. cit.*, Vol. V, p. 268.
[63] *Ibid.*, p. 267.
[64] *Op. cit.*, Vol. V, p. 584; Vol. VI, p. 673.

His ability to describe the decadence of the age approached that of the convert Wicel.[65]

Did Melanchthon counsel his mother to remain a Catholic? A report which made its first appearance in 1605, has him say to her: "The new religion seems more acceptable, but the old one is safer" (*Haec plausibilior, illa securior*). According to this account he did not desire to see his mother disturbed in her faith—an attitude quite conformable with his character. One may say with the author of the article "Melanchthon" in the Protestant "Encyclopädie für Theologie": "The story is at least not improbable, even if it cannot be demonstrated as true." [66]

An entirely different type was the ex-priest John Bugenhagen, a Pomeranian, pastor of Wittenberg, and Luther's right bower in the propagation of Protestantism in northern Germany. Köstlin characterizes him as a man "endowed with great and sturdy natural powers of mind and body." [67] Indefatigable self-sacrifice and tireless industry were characteristics of this robust and stern man. While not a great theologian, he was gifted with an unusual talent for organizing, as his ecclesiastical ordinances show. In the preface to Bugenhagen's published Commentary on the Psalms, Luther says: "I venture to assert that Pomeranus is the first person on earth to give an explanation of the book of Psalms." This eulogy, however, appears "strange" to Albrecht, the Protestant editor of the preface, who observes: "Luther had no clear perception of the defects of Bugenhagen's exegetical method." [68] Luther freely unbosomed himself to Bugenhagen and acknowledged that he often derived great consolation from a single word that came out of his mouth. When his friend labored in distant parts, Luther felt his absence keenly. He classified Bugenhagen with those who were able to offer "strong limbs" to the temptations of the devil; of such, he said, "there must be some *in ecclesia* who are well able to bear the brunt of the devil's blows." [69] He rejoiced that his associate heartily despised the ring of the Catholic apologist. One of Bugenhagen's statements against the apologists of the ancient Church ran as follows: "Dear Lord Jesus Christ, arise with Thy holy

[65] *Op. cit.*, Vol. V, pp. 178 sq. On Melanchthon's demand for a council composed of followers of the new religion, *ibid.*, Vol. V, pp. 169 sqq.

[66] Grisar, *Luther*, Vol. V, pp. 270 sqq.

[67] Grisar, *op. cit.*, Vol. III, pp. 404 sqq.

[68] *Ibid.*

[69] *Tischreden*, Weimar ed., Vol. II, n. 1307.

angels and thrust down into the abyss of hell the diabolical murder and blasphemy of Antichrist!"[70] Luther's opponents in his own camp were likewise an abomination to Bugenhagen, and once when Luther complained of Karlstadt, Grickel, and Jeckel (*i.e.*, Agricola and Schenk), Bugenhagen interrupted him and proposed this radical remedy: "Doctor, we should do what is commanded in Deuteronomy (XIII, 5 sqq.), where Moses says they should be put to death." And Luther acquiesced.[71] Pomeranus was blunt and superstitious. When, on one occasion, the devil crawled into his churn and spoilt the butter, he proceeded to insult his satanic majesty by easing himself in the churn. Luther praised this act as most effectual.[72]

Nicholas von Amsdorf, superintendent of Magdeburg, proved to be a second Luther. Because of his fidelity to the new evangel, based upon a certain mystic disposition, he impressed many favorably. After Luther's death he published a book entitled, "That the Proposition 'Good Works' are harmful to Salvation is a Sound Christian One."[73] Luther styled him "a born theologian."

Other less famous friends of Luther were: John Brenz, co-founder of Protestantism in Swabia; George Burkhardt, surnamed Spalatin, promoter of Lutheranism at the court of the Elector Frederick, and, after the latter's demise, Lutheran pastor at Altenburg; Nicholas Hausmann, pastor at Zwickau; Wenceslaus Link of Nuremberg; John Lang of Erfurt, etc. Because of their activity in distant parts of the country, Luther often revealed his inmost soul to them in his epistolary correspondence. Of Brenz he says: "Amongst all the theologians of our day there is not one who knows how to interpret and handle Holy Scripture like Brenz."[74]

The second of the above-mentioned associates of Luther, Spalatin, was actively engaged in historical research. In practice he was a model of intolerance, particularly in the Protestantizing of Meissen. Nevertheless, when, on one occasion, he visited his native Catholic city of Spalt, he delivered himself of this advice: "Stick to your own form of divine service."[75] He presented the congregation of Spalt with a picture of Our Lady, which had. once belonged

---

[70] Grisar, *Luther*, Vol. III, p. 412.
[71] *Ibid.*, p. 409.
[72] *Tischreden*, Weimar ed., Vol. III, n. 3491; Grisar, *op. cit.*, Vol. III, p. 230,
[73] Grisar, *op. cit.*, Vol. VI, p. 409.
[74] *Op. cit.*, Vol. III, p. 405.
[75] *Op. cit.*, Vol. III, p. 285.

to the castle-church at Wittenberg; this image is venerated at Spalt even at the present day. In the same city he founded a yearly Mass for his deceased parents. In his later days Spalatin was much disquieted by melancholy and temptations to despair. Luther endeavored to comfort him; but he counseled him in vain "to find consolation even against his own conscience." [76]

Of the more intimate friends of Luther, Justus Jonas remained longest with him at Wittenberg. [77] He was a lover and master of sociability, and, when Luther was depressed by melancholy, willingly complied with Kate's summons to the "Black Monastery" to entertain him with his agreeable conversation. He was an able humanist and versed in jurisprudence. His Latin translations of Luther's works were highly praised. His original productions were less numerous, but, being a courageous fighter, he earned the respect of his friends for his various publications on the religious question. He calumniously attacked Catholic apologists, such as Faber and Wicel. Besides Melanchthon, Bugenhagen, and Cruciger, Jonas was one of the most circumspect participants in the transactions and legal opinions that issued from Wittenberg. Luther, who was wont to eulogize the talents of his friends, said that Jonas had all the gifts of a good orator, "save that he cleared his throat too often." [78] As provost of the castle-church of Wittenberg Jonas had an income, though it was never adequate for his needs. He was dean of the theological faculty from 1523 to 1533, and took part in all the important actions of Lutheranism, such as the Marburg Conference, the diet of Augsburg, the visitations in electoral Saxony after 1528, and the introduction of Protestantism into the duchy of Saxony. In 1541 he founded and subsequently directed the affairs of the Lutheran Church in the city of Halle, which up to that time had been the residence of Cardinal Albrecht of Mayence. [79] When qualms of conscience and theological doubts assailed Jonas, Luther had to be at hand to encourage him. On one occasion he sent Jonas the consoling words with which he was wont to find comfort in similar circumstances. [80] On another occasion, Jonas expressed the opinion, approved by Luther, that since a

---

[76] *Op. cit.*, Vol. III, p. 285; Vol. V, p. 330.

[77] Grisar, *Luther*, Vol. III, pp. 413 sqq.

[78] *Tischreden*, Weimar ed., Vol. II, n. 2580.

[79] Cfr. Grisar, *Luther*, Vol. V, pp. 165 sq.

[80] *Tischreden*, Weimar ed., Vol. IV, n. 4852; Grisar, *op. cit.*, Vol. III, pp. 414 sq.

man could not comprehend the articles, it was sufficent to begin with a mere assent.[81] "Yes," said Luther, "if a man could but believe it." [82] When Jonas railed at the infidelity of the country people around Wittenberg, Luther admitted that he knew only one peasant in all the villages who seriously instructed his household in the Word of God and the Catechism. "The others," he said, "are all going to the devil." [83] In consequence of "spiritual temptations" (G. Kawerau) which he suffered after the Schmalkaldic Wars, Jonas developed a severe mental disorder similar to the *morbus melancholicus* of Spalatin. It is said that his death (1555) was happier than his life. [84]

It is remarkable with what frequency the contemporary documents mention this disease as occurring within the Protestant fold, especially in the later years of life. Melancholia may almost be considered as the chief malady of the age of the Reformation. [85] Nicholas Paulus has latterly again called attention to this peculiar phenomenon, which had been previously noted by others. He supports his contention with a mass of documentary evidence. [86] Among other things he mentions that Jerome Baumgärtner of Nuremberg, Luke Osiander, and Zachary Rivander speak of healthy people everywhere suffering from fear, lack of consolation, and mental strain; that the number of suicides increased in so frightful a manner as to cause one's hair to stand on end; and that they believed it was a sign forecasting the approach of doomsday. Jerome Weller, whom Luther endeavored to console in various ways, Nicholas Hausmann, his intimate intellectual associate, Simon Musaeus, who wrote two treatises against the "melancholy devil," Nicholas Selnecker, the editor of Luther's Table Talks, Wolfgang Capito, the celebrated spokesman of the new religion at Strasburg, and Joachim Camerarius, an intimate friend of Melanchthon, who in a letter to Luther expresses his despair because of the moral decadence of the age, were all affected by this disease of chronic religious melancholy, not to speak of a number of less famous preachers, scholars, and authors who professed the new religion.

[81] *Tischreden*, Weimar ed., Vol. V, n. 5562.
[82] *Tischreden*, Vol. IV, n. 4864.
[83] *Ibid.*, II, n, 2622b; Grisar, *op. cit.*, Vol. III, p. 415.
[84] *Ibid.*, p. 416.
[85] Concerning the following, see Grisar, *Luther*, Vol. III, p. 416; Vol. IV, pp. 218 sqq.
[86] Cfr. Grisar, *op. cit.*, Vol. IV, p. 225, n. 3.

When the preacher Nicholas Beyer narrated in the presence of Luther how the devil had tempted him to stab himself, Luther consoled him by confessing that he had been assailed by similar temptations, though we have no evidence that he was ever seriously tempted to commit suicide. Mathesius, Luther's pupil and eulogist, "could not bear the sight of a knife in the last year of his life because it enticed him to commit suicide" (G. Loesche). The Nuremberg preacher George Besler, a victim of melancholy induced by the religious conditions of the time, committed suicide with a "hog-spear" during Luther's lifetime.

Antonius Musa, pastor of Rochlitz, confided to Luther that he was depressed in his mind because he could not believe what he preached to others. Thereupon Luther replied as follows, according to Mathesius: "Praise and thanks be to God that this also happens to others. I fancied it was true only in my case." Mathesius adds: "Musa never forgot this consolation all his life." He says that Musa himself told him this story.[87] The same eulogist of Luther writes: "There are many who lead a languishing existence and despair; there is no longer any joy or courage among men." A peculiar kind of literature became popular at that time, consisting of consolatory exhortations for those afflicted with melancholy. A Hamburg preacher, J. Magdeburgius, wrote: "The need of consolation was never felt more keenly than at present." Amsdorf lamented that many who were afflicted by melancholia returned to Catholicism, because "they were at their wit's end" on account of the doctrinal dissensions of Protestantism.

One of those thus tormented was Luther's table companion, John Schlaginhaufen. His suffering was increased by a profound sense of guilt. The interviews with Luther, which he reports in writing, are a vivid reflection of the prevalent malady of that age. Schlaginhaufen was disinclined to believe Luther when the latter maintained that Satan alone could cause such dread melancholia, but Luther insisted. "The devil," he said, "feels his kingdom is coming to an end, hence the fuss he makes." The troubled man, however, grew more gloomy, because he could "not distinguish between the law and the Gospel." Luther consoled him by saying that he himself and the Apostle Paul

[87] Grisar, *op. cit.*, Vol. V, p. 364.

had "never been able to get that far," namely, to make a proper distinction between the law and the Gospel. Finally, Luther resorted to his authority and said: "I have God's authority and commission to speak to you and to comfort you." [88]

[88] Grisar, *op. cit.*, Vol. IV, pp. 226 sq.; *Tischreden*, Weimar ed., Vol. II, n. 1263, 1289, 1492, 1557.

CHAPTER XVI

PERSONAL AND DOMESTIC AFFAIRS

1. ENGAGING CHARACTERISTICS

In reviewing the life of Luther in the former Black Monastery of Wittenberg, our attention is first attracted to his relations with Catherine. Although there were weighty objections to their marriage from the Catholic point of view, and although it was severely censured by the jurists who upheld the canon law of the Church, it nevertheless presented a favorable exterior appearance. It had to be admitted that peace, harmony, and mutual good will governed the union of the ex-monk and the former nun. So far as known, neither ever violated the pretended marriage. Luther expressed himself in words of gratitude and appreciation for the aid and comfort which he derived from his wife, even though, on occasion, he scourged her willfulness in partly serious and partly facetious language.

Luther's children were compelled to learn and practice their religion. As they grew up, they, on the whole, caused no dishonor to the family. They were not endowed with any special talents, nor did they distinguish themselves in their positions in life.

The home life of the family was subject to considerable unrest, caused by the fact that relatives and students occupied the former monastic cells and ate at Luther's table. In addition, quite a few strangers visited Wittenberg, who wished to see and converse with Luther. Moreover, the agitation caused by Luther's controversies, which so visibly vibrates in his correspondence, quite naturally affected his domestic life, as his Table Talks frequently testify.

On the other hand Luther's family life displayed many attractive traits. Thus, when his daughter Magdalen, a sweet and pious child, died at the age of thirteen, Luther was seized with a sorrow so profound as to move even the modern reader to tears.[1] Thanks to his letters, his admirers are likewise enabled to participate in the happy hours he spent in his family circle. Luther is frequently pictured as

---

[1] Cf. Köstlin-Kawerau, M. *Luther*, Vol. II, p. 596.

a happy father sitting with his family under the Christmas tree. But the Christmas tree was not introduced till several centuries after his death. Luther's family life at Wittenberg is usually celebrated by Protestant biographers as the model and archetype of that of an evangelical pastor. But we must not forget—to mention only one point—that the Reformer's home, being the center of a tremendous religious conflict, cannot have been so devout and tranquil as we are asked to believe.

Luther desired every father of a family to interpret the Bible to his family and to address them on religious matters in accordance with a prescribed plan. He himself set the example. When, in 1532, sickness prevented him from preaching in church, he preached to his household in the Black Monastery. This custom gave rise to his "*Hauspostille*," *i. e.*, book of instructions for home use. It was intended as a guide for others and undoubtedly did much good. It was first edited in 1544 by Vitus Dietrich.[2] Of larger scope and wider influence was the "*Kirchenpostille*," a collection delivered in public. Of these, he published the sermons for the winter semester in 1540. The sermons for the summer semester were brought into shape and published by Cruciger in 1545.[3] A very large number of Luther's sermons had been circulating in separate editions or in smaller compilations since their delivery.

Luther's sermons are invariably distinguished by great freshness and practicality. They display a forcefulness of diction and a diversity of thought, the like of which is scarcely met with elsewhere. He possessed sufficient talent to become a second Berthold of Regensburg. It must be admitted, however, that the addresses are often monotonous on account of frequent repetitions and show lack of preparation and reliance upon the author's innate gift of speech. Sometimes his auditors were bored by his noisome and tedious attacks upon the ancient Church and her doctrines. Despite these defects, however, Luther's sermons were so diligently copied that a large number of copies, made by various individuals, are still extant. The new Weimar edition of Luther's works reproduces them all, thereby occasionally bestowing unmerited honor on addresses which were delivered without due preparation and order.

[2] Weimar ed., Vol. LII; Erl. ed., Vols. I–VI.

[3] Cf. Weimar ed., Vol. VII, p. 463; 10, I, 1; 17, II, 21; 22. Erl. ed., Vol. VII, 2 ed., p. 134; Vol. VIII, pp. 11, 173; Vol. IX, p. 1; Vol. X, 2 ed., p. 133; Vol. XI, p. 191; Vol. XII, p. 1.

In their originality some of his better sermons, and also some of the inferior ones, are reminiscent of Luther's maxim: "Ascend the pulpit, open your mouth, and then stop." [4] Luther frequently addressed similar maxims to his preachers.

Despite his facility in the use of words, the voluminousness of his sermons is a source of amazement. He was anxious to produce moral effects no less than to confirm his new doctrine and to eradicate popery. Relative to morality, he felt a profound obligation to counteract the decline of ethical standards, which was a concomitant of the new freedom proclaimed by his gospel. His very desire to preserve the good repute of his religious innovation impelled him to issue frequent warnings and reproofs. Moreover, as he had abolished the holy Sacrifice of the Mass, the office of preaching was advanced to the most prominent place in his church. Everything was made dependent upon the "Word," which was supposed to be experienced interiorly and to persist without the aid of the Catholic means of grace and the weight of ecclesiastical authority.

Luther intended to introduce the interdict when to his sorrow he saw how weak was the influence exercised by his Wittenberg pulpit and how scandals grew apace. He always had felt the need of some kind of ecclesiastical discipline, though at the same time he never gave up the idea of a "church apart of true believers," who having expressly obligated themselves to observe religion and morality, should take their stand alongside the partly heathen masses of the national Church.[5] The plan proved impracticable. As the Protestant theologian Drews says, Luther himself "was uncertain and wavered in the details of his plan. He had but little bent to sketch out organizations even in his head; to this he did not feel himself called." [6] This was also the reason why his proposal to introduce the ban, which he made in 1538, and again in a sermon at Wittenberg on February 23, 1539, came to naught. He was compelled to lament: "They refuse to hear of excommunication." [7] Which utterance recalls the words of the Elector: "If only people could be found who would let themselves be excommunicated!" And yet there was question only of the so-called minor excommunication, namely, exclusion from

---

[4] Thus Kroker (*Tischreden*, Weimar ed., Vol. VI, p. 643) translates the saying (*ibid.*, Vol. IV, n. 5171a): "*Ascendat suggestum, aperiat os et desinat*" (cf. *ibid.*, n. 5171b.)

[5] Cfr. Grisar, *Luther*, Vol. V, pp. 133 sqq.

[6] Grisar, *op. cit.*, Vol. V, p. 140.

[7] *Ibid.*, p. 186,

divine worship, or at least from the Lord's Supper, and prohibition to act as sponsor at baptism. It was Luther's intention that not only the ecclesiastical authorities, but the entire congregation, should inflict the ban, just as was the rule in Hesse, under the "Regulations for Church Discipline" drawn up for that country.

Luther, to be sure, was not unwilling to exercise severity. Thus he writes to Antony Lauterbach at Pirna: "I am pleased with Hesse's example of the use of excommunication. If you can establish the same thing, well and good. But the centaurs and harpies of the court will look at it askance. May the Lord be our help! Everywhere license and lawlessness continue to spread among the people, but it is the fault of the civil authorities." [8]

In a sermon of February 23, 1539, wherein he vigorously developed the idea of the lesser excommunication, he maintained the duty of the entire congregation to co-operate in the enforcement of the ban. After the public denunciation of an obdurate member, the congregation was to lift its voice in prayer against him, assist in the formal expulsion, and participate in the readmission of the excommunicate to public worship.[9] When he saw that his zeal was not appreciated, Luther threatened public offenders all the more violently with harsh treatment after death: "Let them go to the devil, and if they die, let them be buried on the rubbish-heap like dogs." Whoever obstinately remains away from the Lord's Supper lives "in a self-inflicted ban" and is to be delivered to the civil authority.[10]

The civil government was obliged by law to lend its aid to support ecclesiastical discipline. Luther favored this procedure; for "facts have shown"—thus he wrote to Spalatin in 1527—"that men despise the evangel and insist on being compelled by the law and the sword." [11] In 1529 he demanded that even those who had no religion yet should "be driven to attend the sermon" in order that they may know what is right or wrong.[12] According to his Small Catechism, the masses must be "held and driven to the faith." Particularly should they be held to attend catechetical instruction, as he advised Margrave George of Brandenburg. At Wittenberg those who persistently neglected to

---

[8] On April 2, 1543; *Briefwechsel*, Vol. XV, p. 131; cfr. Grisar, *Luther*, Vol. V, p. 188.
[9] *Ibid.*
[10] Grisar, V, p. 189, where more passages are given. *Tischreden*, Weimar ed., Vol. IV, n. 5174; Vol. V, n. 5438.
[11] Grisar, *Luther*, Vol. VI, p. 262.
[12] *Ibid.* pp. 743 sq., where the following passages may be found.

attend the sermons were threatened with "banishment and the law." The court ordained that there be "universal attendance at church." In 1557 we hear of a fine imposed upon violators; in case of poverty they were "to be punished by being fastened to the church or a prison by means of an iron collar." The oppressive policy of the State Church of Saxony resulted from the force of circumstances and the endeavor to achieve some kind of union among Protestants. The State transferred its rule to the spiritual sphere, which usurpation, even at its inception, provoked loud protests from Luther and many preachers. Nevertheless, the process of evolution could not be arrested.

History is obliged to chronicle many instances where Luther displayed great courage for the sake of preserving religious discipline and ecclesiastical customs. A case in point is that of Hans von Metzsch, a haughty captain and governor of Wittenberg, who led a dissolute life. In 1531 Luther notified this powerful man that he was excluded from ecclesiastical communion and forbade him—though not publicly—to receive the Lord's Supper. When Metzsch married his mistress in accordance with the prescribed regulations, a reconciliation was effected. Nevertheless, in 1538, Luther again censured the governor, this time with increased vigor, because of his affronts against public worship and the preachers. He pronounced invalid the absolution which the deacon Fröschel had granted to him, and, in a statement served upon him by two deacons, demanded that Metzsch reform and become reconciled with the Church and with those whom he had offended. At the same time he apprised him that he would incur excommunication if he refused to conform with these demands. Metzsch was also threatened with major excommunication on the part of the prince in case he continued recusant. The subsequent course of events is doubtful; it appears, however, that some kind of peace was again patched up.[13] In the following year, Luther inveighed from the pulpit against a citizen of Wittenberg who had approached the Lord's Supper though he had committed a murder and was unreconciled with the Church. He insisted that this man render strict satisfaction before being readmitted to church.

Mention has been made on a previous page of the courage which Luther displayed at the time of the pestilence. Unmindful of the danger of contagion, he remained at his post, although many proved

[13] Köstlin-Kawerau, M. *Luther*, Vol. II, pp. 438 sq.

themselves deserters. He resolutely endeavored to be of service to the afflicted and to encourage his clerical assistants in persevering by the power of his example. As early as 1527, during those critical days when Wittenberg and its environs were ravaged by the epidemic, he composed a treatise: "Whether One Should Flee from Death," which contained beautiful and encouraging thoughts calculated to comfort the afflicted.[14]

Courageously and lovingly he used his influence on many occasions to secure redress for those who were the victims of injustice.[15] Because of the esteem in which he was held, and his willingness to minister to others, his aid and intercession with the Elector were frequently invoked. His petitions, as a rule, were effective. His protestations against oppression, even though they assumed most vigorous forms, were usually heeded at court. On one occasion he called himself the supporter of the poor and defender of their rights. At times it happened that, in his short-sightedness, he permitted himself to become interested in cases where justice was on the side of the other party. Frequently he displayed undue credulity and anger. A case in point—it was on the occasion when he assumed the honorary titles quoted above—is furnished by his advocacy of the cause of Hans von Schönitz of Halle, who had been legally executed by the Elector Albrecht of Mayence for serious crimes which he had committed. The brother of the executed man together with one Louis Rabe succeeded in convincing Luther that the Archbishop, whom Luther cordially hated, was guilty of murder. In 1535, and again in 1536, Luther published two letters against Albrecht concerning this case. In 1538 he composed a treatise on the alleged Schönitz scandal, in which he forcibly vented his indignation.[16]

A merchant from Kölln on the Spree, Hans Kohlhase, who had failed to obtain a favorable verdict in a lawsuit, became enraged and declared a private feud against the entire commonwealth of Electoral Saxony. It was a procedure incomprehensible to our age, which finds its explanation only in the then prevalent conditions. With the aid of a mercenary mob from Brandenburg, Kohlhase began to "rob,

---

[14] Weimar ed., Vol. XXIII, pp. 333 sqq.; Erl. ed., Vol. XXII, pp. 317 sqq.; Köstlin-Kawerau, M. *Luther*, Vol. II, pp. 171 sqq.

[15] Köstlin-Kawerau, *op. cit.*, p. 420.

[16] Grisar, *Luther*, Vol. V, pp. 106 sq.; Köstlin-Kawerau, *op. cit.*, Vol. II, pp. 419, 422; see also the note in the third German ed. of Grisar's *Luther*, Vol. III, pp. 1009 sqq. (this note is not contained in Lamond's English translation).

burn, capture, and hold to ransom," according to his own formal announcement. Conflagrations, attributed to his revengeful spirit, broke out in Wittenberg and its environs. The Elector was disposed to effect an amicable settlement and Kohlhase sought Luther's advice. He received a trenchant reply, in which Luther vigorously espoused the cause of law and order and demanded that vengeance be left to God. At the same time he addressed ardent religious exhortations to the offender. Kohlhase, however, being dissatisfied with the offers of the Elector, continued his depredations. Luther prophesied in his Table Talks that Kohlhase would be drowned in his own blood. He was executed at Berlin, March 22, 1540, being broken on the wheel on account of excesses committed in Brandenburg. Fable has seized upon the story of this gruesome adventurer and his relation to Luther. Popular biographers of Luther still love to relate how Kohlhase, in disguise, knocked at Luther's door one dark night and, being admitted by the latter, explained his quarrel in the presence of Melanchthon, Cruciger, and others, became reconciled with God and his fellowmen, and promised to abstain from violence in future.[17]

To some extent this legend (originating with a chronicler who gives no authority for his statements) is reminiscent of the conciliatory attitude which Luther assumed toward his enemy Karlstadt when the latter, plunged in direst need after the Peasants' War, approached Luther in 1525 and asked him to intercede for him with the Elector, so that he might be permitted to return to the country. Luther, having obtained Karlstadt's promise that he would change his doctrines, magnanimously procured for him the permission he craved.[18]

Luther was frequently generous towards the poor, even beyond his humble means. His simple way of life made it possible for him to practice benevolence. He lived frugally and was satisfied with but little of this world's goods. This fact was generally known and, in view of his meager income, the court and the city gladly helped him along with gifts of money and food. Poor students were the chief beneficiaries of his solicitude; for he was very much concerned that the support of the students of the University of Wittenberg should be assured. His amiable disposition and sociability strongly attracted

[17] Grisar, *Luther* (Engl. tr.), Vol. V, pp. 117 sqq.; *Tischreden*, Weimar ed., Vol. IV, n. 4088, 4315, 4536.

[18] Köstlin-Kawerau, M. *Luther*, Vol. I, pp. 718 sq.

the students, who were charmed by his fame no less than by his robust physique and characteristically flashing eyes.

Luther's lectures, which began in the early hours of the morning, were carefully prepared and embodied practical directions for the usually large audiences which attended them. His graphic interpretations of the Bible and his meditations, which at times bordered on the mystical, were interspersed with frequent sallies (not always phrased in choice language) against Catholic dogmas, the papists, and the enemies in his own camp, the so-called *Schwärmer* (fanatics). When they disagreed with him, he did not spare even the most highly esteemed Fathers of the Church. With a self-consciousness that made a profound impression on the short-sighted young men to whom he lectured, he exalted his own opinions above those of others. Proofs of this are amply supplied by his Commentary on St. Paul's Epistle to the Galatians and his exposition of Genesis, which he commenced in 1535, but which was published by someone else, and not very accurately.[19]

There is extant also a collection of proverbs made by Luther, which did not, however, appear in print until 1900.[20] It reflects his efforts to preserve and increase the treasury of German proverbial sayings of which he was wont to avail himself so liberally. Besides these, we have the theological disputations held before the faculty under his direction and amid constant interruptions on his part. These disputations (1535–1545) were edited in a stately volume by Dr. Paul Drews in 1896. They show many traces of Luther's passionate nature and are characterized by rude diction and an attempt to go to extremes in expression as well as content.

2. RELIGIOUS POETRY AND CHURCH HYMNS

A new sphere was opened to Luther's successful endeavors in the field of hymnology. In the days of his youth he had become familiar with the hymns of the Catholic Church and learned to appreciate the value of congregational singing. He realized that poetry and songs within and without the church are apt means for conveying religious thoughts to the hearts of the people. Quite naturally he made use of this means in the furtherance of his gospel. By his successful

[19] Weimar ed., Vols. XLII–XLIV.
[20] Weimar ed., Vol. LI, pp. 645 sqq.

poetical compositions he created a preëminent and efficacious position
for the religious hymn within the Protestant cult. It supplemented
the sermon and the defective liturgy within the church and aroused
the minds of the faithful with a religious and also a militant fervor
outside the church walls.

The thirty-fifth volume of the Weimar edition of Luther's works
contains all the hymns composed by him, as collected by Lucke.[21]
The series commences with "Ein neues Lied wir heben an" (composed
in 1523) and, "Nu freut euch, liebe Christen gemein." In the following year Luther was most prolific in the production of church
hymns. His "Enchiridion geistlicher Gesänge," published in that
year, consisted of twenty-five hymns, of which fifteen were his own
work. Somewhat later in the same year, Luther and John Walther,
a cantor stationed at the court of Torgau, published a "Geistliches
Gesangbüchlein" in Wittenberg. This hymn-book, as revised in 1529,
contained several new hymns, notably the celebrated "Ein' feste Burg
ist unser Gott" (A mighty fortress is our God) [22] and also, "Verleih
uns Frieden gnädiglich" and "Herr Gott, dich loben wir." Other
hymns of Luther originated in the period from 1535 to 1546. The
battle-hymn, "Erhalt uns, Herr, bei deinem Wort, Und steur des
Papsts und Türken Mord" (Preserve us, O Lord, in Thy Word, and
check the atrocities of Pope and Turk), was written in 1537.

Luther did not set any of his hymns to music. The melodies were
partly supplied by Walther and many of them are adaptations of earlier melodies or chorals familiar to the people from Catholic days.

The singing of anthems or secular songs (chorals) by the younger
members of Luther's household was a favorite means of recreation
after meals. Luther gives expression to his delight thereat in a poem,
"To Lady Music," which prefaced an edition of one of the above-
mentioned hymnals. The conclusion of the poem ardently eulogizes
the nightingale because of her praise of God: "She sings and flits in
praise of Him, And naught her ardent soul can dim; Thus, too, my
lyre would sound His praise, And thank Him through the endless
days." In another preface Luther develops an excellent discourse on
the educational value of spiritual hymns. In his opinion they should
assist the young "in getting rid of amorous and carnal songs." All
should be convinced that "not all the arts are overthrown by the

---

[21] Cf. also Erl. ed., Vol. LVI, pp. 291 sqq.

[22] Grisar, *Lutherstudien*, n. 2: "Luthers Trutzlied." Cf. Lucke, Weimar ed., Vol. LIII.

gospel, . . . but I would like to see all the arts, especially music, serve Him who has bestowed and created them."

Ratzeberger, the physician, tells of another motive of Luther's predilection for the art of music. Luther, he says, "discovered that he was relieved of great depression by music during his temptations and melancholy spells." [23] In matter of fact, the soothing strains of the church hymns often helped to assuage the storms that agitated his soul. In a letter to the composer Senfl, who was in the service of Duke William of Bavaria, and whose motets he esteemed very highly, he acknowledged that music had often "refreshed his spirit and relieved him of great troubles." [24] He requested Senfl to set to music the text of the Psalm, "In peace I will sleep and rest" (Ps. IV, 9); for this verse afforded him consolation for his approaching death. He was as weary of the world as it was of him. The letter to Senfl incidentally embodied an attempt on Luther's part to regain the favor of the Bavarian court. Luther, who was desirous of obtaining a foothold in Bavaria, evidently attached great importance to the friendship and activity of this highly esteemed composer.

3. THE TABLE TALKS

Luther's Table Talks are of great importance as sources for his personality and work. These original effusions from his communicative lips are a profound revelation of his inmost being and often cast a bright light on the events of his age and life.

Formerly the utilization of the Table Talks was a difficult matter, as there were only inadequate editions extant, such as the old German compilation of John Aurifaber, the Latin *Colloquia* of H. Bindseil, originally collected by Antony Lauterbach, and other collections. There was wanting a critical compilation going back to the oldest textual tradition, as embodied in the transcript of Luther's utterances made by various individuals. This task has now been performed by a painstaking Protestant investigator, Ernst Kroker. In six large volumes he has collected 7,075 speeches or addresses, reproduced in the most exact possible order and in accordance with the sequence of the recorders and the time.[25] In this manner, the value of the Table Talks as historical sources is very much enhanced.

[23] Grisar, *Luther*, Vol. II, p. 171.
[24] *Ibid.*
[25] *Tischreden*, Weimar ed., Vols. I–VI (1912–1921).

The students who had found lodging in the cells of the former Black Monastery were wont to assemble daily about Luther's table, where the places of honor, next to Luther and his Kate, were occupied by invited guests from afar, or by friends who lived in the city of Wittenberg. The students listened attentively to the conversations, in most of which Luther acted as spokesman. Many instructive matters were discussed here, many notable thoughts uttered for the benefit of the education of his auditors, designed to be imparted later on to their friends and acquaintances. The students soon grew accustomed to take down in shorthand, either in Latin or in German, as much of the conversation as they could. Luther observed this, but did not protest; on the contrary, he frequently asked them to write down this or that utterance. Kate once jestingly remarked that the copyists should be obliged to pay for this privilege, just as they were obliged to pay for their lectures at the university.[26]

Nevertheless, the conversation was quite unconstrained. Luther often uttered remarkable opinions on Biblical passages, on theological or philosophical doctrines, on individuals of both camps, the Protestant as well as the Catholic, or on his own experiences, on natural phenomena, on matters pertaining to the present or the future. The conversation became especially animated when strangers participated therein. Before all else, however, the audience liked to listen to Luther himself, the honored and admired oracle of his younger disciples. Cordatus, one of the copyists, repeatedly expressed his displeasure, when the loquacious Kate or the talkative Jonas did not allow Luther sufficient opportunity for speaking.

The first direct copies were made by the students in their rooms. They were somewhat polished and either jealously preserved or circulated for the instruction of others. There were collectors who compiled reports which were derived from diverse sources and originated at various times. Anton Lauterbach's collection, made with great diligence, is the largest. In it the talks are grouped according to the topics discussed and the various points of view expressed. Besides Lauterbach's printed work, many such collections have come down to us, whereas none of the original papers written at table have been preserved. The general fidelity of the old copies is vouched for not only by the character and the purpose of the authors, but also by the observation that, where the same discourse is reported by various parties, there is

[26] Cf. the exposition in Grisar, *Luther*, Vol. III, pp. 217–241, for which, however, Kroker's edition was not yet available.

usually substantial agreement, despite grammatical or other formal variations. Misunderstandings of one or the other copyist, omissions, even in important matters, mistakes owing to inadvertence in the course of reproduction, are, of course, not excluded. This circumstance must be taken into consideration when the Table Talks are quoted.[27]

Kroker in his edition supplies the parallel passages and furnishes pertinent emendations. Hence, these literary remains of Luther's table must be regarded, in general, as an adequate historical source concerning his character and life. Kroker rightly rejects, for example, the objections of Otto Scheel to important passages which differ from the latter's theories.[28]

Of course, it must not be overlooked that the Table Talks are ephemeral—"children of the moment." While they correctly and vividly reproduce the ideas of the speaker, minus the cool reflection which prevails in the writing of letters and still more of books, they contain frequent exaggerations and betray a lack of moderation. The lightning-like flashes which they emit are not always true. The momentary exaggerations of the speaker at times beget contradictions which conflict with other talks or literary utterances. Frequently humorous statements were received as serious declarations. Humor and satire of a very pungent kind play a great part in these talks.

The recording of the Table Talks commenced with the year 1531, or possibly 1529. They are continued, with interruptions, in longer or more abbreviated and detached communications of the students up to the last meal taken by Luther.

In point of time the transcripts of Vitus Dietrich and those embodied in the collection of Dietrich and Rörer are the first.[29] These are followed by three groups of copyists and collectors. The older group consists of John Schlaginhaufen (for years 1531 and 1532), Cordatus (after 1531), Lauterbach, Weller and Corvinus. The middle group, who compiled the *Tischreden* from 1536 to 1539, consists of some of the above-mentioned writers. Among these Lauterbach is especially noted for his diaries, which cover the years 1538 and 1539. The later group, from 1540 to 1546, is composed of John Mathesius, who supplies an excellent source of information, Caspar Heydenreich, Jerome Besold, Magister Plato, John Stoltz, and John Aurifaber.[30] In

---

[27] See Kroker's introduction to Vol. I of his edition.

[28] *Tischreden*, Weimar ed., Vol. V, pp. XIV sqq.

[29] *Ibid.*, Vol. I, p. XVI. Cfr. Kroker in the *Lutherstudien*, edited by the collaborators of the Weimar edition (1917), pp. 178 sqq.

[30] Cfr. *Tischreden*, Weimar ed., Vol. I, p. XI and the introductions to the various parts in the following volumes.—The transcripts of Besold are to be published in the Weimar ed. by J. Haussleiter. Cf. his treatise in the *Archiv für Reformationsgeschichte*, Vols. XIX sqq.

addition to this, each one of these groups embraces various smaller manuscripts, such as those of Pastor Khumer and George Rörer.

The most ample information is furnished by Anton Lauterbach, who has arranged his notes in topical order.[31] The most exact reporter, however, is George Rörer, the versatile secretary of the committee which revised Luther's translation of the Bible.

In the course of the present work we have cited many a typical passage from the Table Talks. These, and the multifarious discourses themselves, display extraordinary versatility and profound feeling. Even though we are compelled to criticize these Talks severely, it must be acknowledged that Luther's utterances are permeated by many sound, stimulating, and pious thoughts.[32] Thus there are beautiful expressions on the attributes of God, particularly His love and mercy, on the duties of the faithful and their obligations in everyday life, on the cure of souls, on preaching and education, on charity, on the vices of the age, on the virtues and vices of great men, past and present, and so on. It was as much the purpose of the Table Talks to benefit the hearers spiritually as to cheer them up and to amuse them. If we take up at random numbers 5553 to 5577, in which Mathesius, availing himself of Heydenreich's notes, supplies his readers with detailed information, we may well marvel at the abundance of profound and practical ideas. In discoursing on the blindness of the Jews and the night of God's wrath against them, for example, Luther becomes so deeply moved that he folds his hands in prayer and exclaims: "O heavenly Father, let us remain in the light of the sun, and permit us not to become recreant to Thy Word!"[33] It is not to be wondered at that Protestants have published many anthologies of interesting and instructive passages taken from Luther's Table Talks. Their good features, with which alone most Protestants are familiar, have contributed to a general overestimation of the Table Talks.

Voluminous collections of the Table Talks were published at an early period. That by Aurifaber appeared in 1566 at Eisleben and went through several editions. It was reprinted by K. Förstemann and H. Bindseil in 1844 [34] and found its way into the Erlangen edition

---

[31] These notes form the essential, nay, almost literal content of Bindseil's *Colloquia.*

[32] Cfr. Grisar, *Luther,* Vol. IV, pp. 262 sqq.

[33] *Ibid.,* III, 225 sqq.

[34] *M. Luthers Tischreden oder Colloquia.* (Based on Aurifaber's text, but collated with the redactions of Stangwald and Selnecker.)

of Luther's collected works as late as 1854 sqq.[35] This version is defective, not only because of frequent arbitrary rearrangements of the subject-matter and changes in the style of the original text (which changes were made for the sake of fluency or clearness), but also on account of an attempt at rendering certain utterances less objectionable and at toning down extremely blunt expressions.

The learned historian J. G. Walch (died in 1775), in common with other Protestant scholars, regretted the publication of the Table Talks. He says that passages in Luther's colloquies "were revealed which should have remained unpublished" and surmises that his indiscretions were the result of "a perversion of the human will."

On the other hand, many friends of Luther were edified by the Table Talks. Among the original copyists, for instance, Cordatus places them at the head of Luther's writings and regards them as "more precious than the oracles of Apollo." Mathesius recalls with gratitude the "many precious things" he heard at Luther's table, and certifies that the ex-monk never uttered "an improper word."[36] In his more recent and popular edition of Luther's Table Talks, Förstemann declares them to be the most important part of Luther's spiritual legacy because in them "the stream of his genius flows clearest." According to Bindseil and Müllensiefen, in their introduction to the *Colloquia*, Luther's Table Talks display "the noblest flower of his nation," and the repulsive and uncouth passages, while, of course, not entirely excusable, contribute to the "complete characterization of the great man," since they show the "furrows and faults that formed a part of his personality."[37]

The "furrows and faults" revealed in the Table Talks are, as a matter of fact, so prominent that they overshadow the better features and the eulogies which we have quoted are well-nigh beyond understanding. Among these glaring defects are innumerable unjust accusations, polemical exaggerations, and crying distortions of the Catholic faith. This applies above all to Luther's immoderate and blunt expressions, not to say the vulgar obscenities with which he assails the pope, the monastic orders, the Mass, etc. The earlier champions of the Catholic cause are to be pardoned for having again and

---

[35] Vols. LVII–LXII.

[36] Cfr. Grisar, *Luther*, Vol. III, pp. 224 sq.

[37] The cited passages are given more completely in Grisar, *op. cit.*, Vol. III, pp. 223, 228, 221, 228 sq., 222.

again adverted to the sad phenomenon of this filth in their characterization of Luther. The Table Talks were known to the Catholics of a later period mostly through the selections thus made from them by the earlier controversialists. Hence, the opinion formerly entertained by many Catholics that the Table Talks were mainly a collection of obscenities. This opinion is as much an exaggeration as the Protestant eulogies mentioned above. To convince oneself that the colloquies abound in vulgar and obscene passages, side by side with excellent features, one need but read a few pages of them at random or peruse the excerpts which the author of the present book felt it necessary for the sake of historical truth to reproduce in his larger work on Luther.[38]

Suffice it to remark here that the sphere of the ventral functions constitutes the most fertile soil of his amplifications and comparisons. The students around his table frequently indicate improper remarks in their manuscripts by signs, such as I or X, where their pen hesitates to express the dirty word. As noticed before, Luther employs such expressions with predilection in his references to the pope and Catholicism. The hatred which inspires his shameless utterances makes them all the more repulsive. In the entire scope of German letters there is nothing that may be compared with these excrescences of Luther's eloquence, least of all among the representatives of religion or the heralds of the religious reformation, to whom, of course, he wishes to belong, though it is quite true that his century was distinguished for its coarseness.[39] Caspar Schatzgeyer, one of the mildest among the Catholic apologists, in rebuking Luther's coarseness and vulgarity, says that he befouls the face and garments of his foes with such a mass of vituperative filth (*conviciorum stercora*) that they are forced to save themselves by flight from the intolerable stench and dirt. "Never," he says, "in any literary struggle has a larger array of weapons of that sort been seen." [40]

Luther used these weapons also against some of those who professed the new faith. Thus he censures the nobility who refused to provide an income for the Protestant ministers. They exasperate us unto evacuation, he says, and continues: "Then *adorabunt nostra stercora . . .* we are as ready to part as *ein reiffer dreck und ein weit*

[38] Grisar, *Luther*, Vol. III, pp. 228 sqq.
[39] *Ibid.*, pp. 236 sq.
[40] *Ibid.*, p. 237.

Arssloch." [41] Naturally the devil who inspires him and others with doubts and fears, receives his share of abuse. The manner in which he teaches his hearers to despise Satan is too revolting to be quoted. A hint is supplied by the previously mentioned butter-vat of Bugenhagen. On the other hand, it should be noted, if this be necessary, that it is not his object to arouse sensuality. His language is coarse, not lascivious; it arouses disgust, not the evil passions of man's lower nature.

In that age and in the succeeding century the unhappy aftereffects of this coarseness led to a certain corruption of the German language, due to the fact that it came from the mouth of a man who was so highly admired as Luther, and that his Table Talks were read in every home. The dregs of vulgarity which had been stirred up by Luther were for a long time a sad dowry of the so-called "Grobian Age" and the polemical literature against Catholics.

[41] *Ibid.*, p. 233.

CHAPTER XVII

PERSONAL AND DOMESTIC AFFAIRS (Continued)

I. DURATION AND WANING OF TEMPTATIONS

Luther's vigorous, nay, coarse language was not infrequently intended by him to drown the interior scruples about his conduct and teaching.

He called his phobias "temptations" (*Anfechtungen*). From 1527 to 1528, a particularly stormy period in his life, they attained to an extraordinary intensity. After a brief calm, during his sojourn in the castle of Coburg, the gloomy spells returned. He tells us that at that time affliction and sadness of spirit seized him to such an extent as to produce a contraction of the heart.[1] Thereupon the struggle gradually abated. Of his serious illness during the diet of Schmalkalden, 1537, he says: "I would have died in Christ, without any temptations and very composedly." Recollecting this same affliction in 1540, he said to his friends: "At the close of life, all temptations cease; for then the Holy Spirit abides with the faithful believer, forcibly restrains the devil, and pours perfect rest and certainty into the heart."

He ascribed the acquisition of his strong faith to the terrible storms he had experienced. Heretics, on the other hand—so he assures us—were devoid of strong faith, even if they died for it; they possessed only obstinacy, inspired by the devil.

For two weeks he experienced a "spiritual malady," as he styles it in 1537, during which he practically lived without food and sleep. He consoled himself, however, by having recourse to the Apostle Paul, who was also "unable to comprehend" what was proper. When such "spiritual temptations present themselves," he says, "and when I add: 'cursed be the day on which I was born,' then there is trouble."

Again, in 1537, when exhausted in consequence of overwork and indisposition, he protests that he was willing to die; for now he was

---

[1] Cfr. Grisar, *Luther*, Vol. V, pp. 346 sqq., for the passages quoted in the text.

"exceedingly happy and peaceful of heart." [2] Nevertheless, the fears of the spiritual struggles at once rearose in his mind—a mental state in which man regards God as his enemy and feels himself as if pierced by a lance. Then "one does not know whether God is the devil or the devil God." [3]

On October 7, 1538, he again says that he is in the throes of a mortal agony. In this same year he complains that the devil "accused him severely before God." But soon after he declares that while he is assailed by doubts and stumbles at times, this is often the case with Christians; "even though I stumble, yet I am resolved to stand by what I have taught." Only fanatics, he thinks, never stumble, "they stand firm."

In order to overcome his phobias, Luther makes use of the most diverse remedies, some of which have already been referred to in this book. "Quickly inveigh against the papists," was his slogan, especially during temptations concerning the doctrine of justification. He excites in himself a "bold anger" or some other distracting emotion. According to his own confession, he also sought a remedy in sexual enjoyment with his Kate and in jovial intercourse with his friends. "A strong drink of beer," according to his directions, is apt to be of benefit when melancholy thoughts afflict one. Of course, devotional and theological helps are also to be applied. "When I seize the Bible, I have triumphed." Only the correct text did not always suggest itself to him or excitement rendered it lame when it was found. The thought: "Thou shalt become a great man through temptation" was invoked, but often proved inoperative. [4]

The defects of his concept of faith strongly re-acted upon his scruples and temptations. According to that doctrine, life powerfully inspired by faith lacked sufficient support. Faith meant the acceptance of revelation, but more frequently and aggressively, a confident trust in God. The acceptance of revelation was made difficult for him, nay, logically impossible by the arbitrary way in which he impugned the books of the Bible, which form the basis of revelation. [5] In his interpretation of those parts of the Bible which he acknowledged as authentic, Luther opened wide the gates of a subjectivism diametri-

[2] *Tischreden*, Weimar ed., Vol. IV, n. 4777.
[3] Grisar, *Luther*, Vol. V, p. 352.
[4] *Ibid.*, p. 355.
[5] *Op. cit.*, Vol. IV, pp. 387 sqq.

cally opposed to faith.[6] In dealing with faith as fiduciary confidence in the mercy of God he was exposed to the oppressive experience that, notwithstanding his boldness, this faith was unstable in its presuppositions. It depended on vacillating emotions. The appropriation of the merits of Christ, the cloak of His justice, was a very difficult and mostly unattainable matter for a conscience weighed down by guilt. Moreover, he himself had declared that man was not free to do good, but God alone could infuse a feeling of the possession of the merits of Christ into the heart. But who could vouch for the operation of God? Owing to his theory of predestination, Luther and his followers did not even know whether they were destined for eternal punishment by the mysterious will of the Most High, despite their acquired feeling of certitude. How, then, were doubts and disquietude to be cured? One realizes that the temptations suffered by Luther must have found a fertile soil in his doctrinal system.[7]

He confesses, in 1543, that he did not feel quite sure that his was a steadfast, fiduciary faith, but that it still lagged behind that of ordinary believers. "I cannot believe it," he said in 1540, "and yet I teach others. . . . I know it is true, but I am unable to believe it. . . . Oh, if only a man could believe it!" [8] By means of these words, he naturally does not intend to deny his faith, but to describe the freshness of that religious fervor which distinguishes a true Christian and which he, in the days of his youth, had observed everywhere among Catholics. Not a day does he waste, he writes in 1542; "but the devil is an evil spirit . . . as I do not fail to realize day by day; for a man waxes cold, and the more so, the longer he lives."

Even in his last sermon at Eisleben, he speaks of "the sin which still persists in us, and which compels us not to believe. We, the best of Christians, also do the same. . . . In view of the weakness of faith, we feel trepidation and anxiety."

Toward the close of his life, Luther's temptations became fewer. At least the discussion of them becomes constantly rarer in his writings and conversations. It seems that he had succeeded, to a certain degree, in lulling them to sleep. The application of the antidotes which have been enumerated above, may not have been ineffectual.

---

[6] *Op. cit.*, Vol. V, pp. 356 sqq.

[7] *Tischreden*, Weimar ed., Vol. IV, n. 5462; Grisar, *Luther*, Vol. V, p. 361.

[8] *Tischreden, ibid.*, n. 4864; Grisar, *op. cit.*, V, 360 sq. The following passages, *ibid.*, pp. 361 and 368.

The gymnastics of which he had made use to stifle his conscience produced an unenviable result: lassitude and indifference appeared simultaneously. "Towards the close of life," he says, "such temptations cease, whilst other maladies remain."

The other maladies which continued to afflict him, were his morbid states, which at all times had co-operated with his temptations and had at least contributed to strengthen them. His permanent heart trouble, as is known, often resulted in precordial distress; and his overwrought nerves exacted their tribute in the form of mental suffering. Thus, in connection with other bodily infirmities, an intolerable psychological condition developed, namely, a tormenting sense of fear, which restlessly sought and found an object in the unrest of his conscience. As a result, his "temptations" often assumed an intensity akin to that of the death agony, a phenomenon which would hardly be capable of explanation without the presence of bodily infirmities.[9] Inversely, the poor man's physical condition was undoubtedly affected by his struggles of conscience. On the other hand, he assures us that there were frequent periods of temptation which he sustained in a state of perfectly good health.

Without any doubt, the phobias originated not merely in disease, as has been maintained; but disease and spiritual attacks combined to assail his soul, and his conscience had to bear the brunt of the attack.[10]

Indeed, his violent apostasy from the Catholic Church, then universally acknowledged, could not have taken place without a lengthy and profound agitation of conscience. It cannot be repeated too often that Luther's terrific assault upon the papacy was inevitably accompanied by a life of interior storm and stress, which could scarcely be allayed, especially in a man who had enjoyed the interior peace of the Church for so long a time. It is of such struggles of conscience as the real objects of his temptations that the unfortunate man speaks when he tremblingly asks himself the questions: Are you alone gifted with understanding? Has mankind been in error until your advent? Did the Almighty really abandon His Church and acquiesce in her being immersed in error? Even his consciousness of great success and the eulogies of his adherents were bound to prove ineffectual in view of such terrible thoughts.

[9] *Ibid.*, V, p. 333.
[10] Grisar, *Luther*, Vol. V, pp. 321 sqq.

If he was less frequently assailed by storms of conscience in his advanced years, this is due in part to the exhaustion which finally overpowered him and which produced a certain apathy. Other dismal features of his mental life associated themselves with this condition, which, in its totality, constituted a truly abnormal state of soul.

2. ABNORMAL PSYCHOLOGICAL TRAITS

The first of the abnormal traits of Luther's psychology was his fear of the devil.

Numerous facts and utterances hitherto quoted attest how consciously and persistently he moved in the imaginary sphere of the power of darkness.

Fearfully he ever beholds this power about him. As he progresses in age, the whole world becomes more and more the "kingdom of the devil," as he styles it in 1544. The devil governs it and devastates it by his tools, "the Turk, the Jew, the pope"; but, he maintains, "he shall be under Christ to all eternity." [11]

Before Luther's time popular belief in the devil had assumed an exaggerated form. It had become firmly established, especially among the mining folk, from whom Luther descended, in consequence of the uncanny labors which they performed within the bowels of the earth. Even learned men were infected by this superstition. Had the sober doctrine of Holy Writ and the Church been adhered to, the faithful would have been preserved from many aberrations in this sphere. Luther magnified and coarsened the maniacal ideas which his parental home and the tendency of his age had implanted in his mind. He confirmed this belief among the Germans, whereas, had he wished to be a true reformer of ecclesiastical life, he would have found a very useful field for his activity in correcting them and the other moral diseases of his age. Up to his time, however, no one had delineated the devil and his works with so much detail, no one had addressed the people on the subject with such a weight of personality and such urgent and apparently religious instructions as Luther.

In his Large Catechism, where he speaks of the damage wrought by the devil, he tells how Satan "breaks many a man's neck, drives others out of their mind or drowns them in the water"; how he "stirs up strife and brings

[11] *Ibid.*, V, 275.

murder, sedition, and war; also causes hail and tempests, destroying the corn and the cattle, and poisoning the air," etc.[12] In a similar vein he writes in his Home-Postil and in his Church-Postil, where he attributes to Satan every evil with which mankind is afflicted. His own experiences are frequently reflected in his excited ebullitions, especially when he touches upon the demoniac fury with which his faith had been assailed. In connection with the latter he asserts that the devil is more at home in Holy Scripture than all the universities and scholars. "Whosoever attempts to dispute with him," he says, "will assuredly be pitched on the ash heap." He is convinced that madness is in every case due to the devil, who always employs mad men as his instruments. How many people, he says, has the devil seized bodily, especially when they had caused him trouble in virtue of a pact! According to his own confession, Luther often was frightened by demons. There are less of them at large now because they have entered into his enemies, the heretics, Anabaptists, and fanatics. Luther has the faculty of furnishing a fertile account of the various species of devils, their habitations, and the forms which they assume.

He is most prolix, however, in his statements and reflections on the demons' attitude toward himself. It is he whom the evil powers have selected to make war upon, because of his great mission. This mania throws him into a state of misery and mental darkness and he imagines "nightly encounters" in which he is compelled to contend with the enemy of the Gospel; hence, all the supposed obstacles to the rapid propagation of his religion among the papists; hence, all those remarkable phantoms which hold his mind in their powerful spell.

When, towards the end of his life, in 1546, he was compelled to journey to Eisleben, he writes that an assembly of devils congregated in that town in order to prevent the establishment of peace which he contemplated.[13] Indeed, he believed that he actually saw the devil, even more plainly than at the time he sojourned in the castle of Coburg.[14] Thus, one evening, as he stood praying at the window of his domicile, he saw the devil perched on a nearby street fountain, jeering at him, thus insinuating that he was his sworn enemy. He hastened to his friend, Michael Coelius, the court preacher of Mansfeld, who lived in the house, and amid tears apprised him of what he had seen. Coelius narrates the incident in his funeral oration on Luther. His physician, Ratzeberger, adds that Luther informed Coelius

12 *Ibid.*, p. 278. The following citations *ibid.*, pp. 279, 281, 284.
13 *Ibid.*, p. 297.
14 *Op. cit.*, Vol. VI, p. 130.

and Jonas that the devil had showed him his posterior and told him
that he would achieve nothing in Eisleben.

The whole affair, naturally, was purely a hallucination. It is
reminiscent of the hallucinations which Luther had at other times, for
example, at the Wartburg and the Coburg, as a result of his excited
mental condition.

Once, at Wittenberg, he descried the devil in the garden beneath
his window in the shape of a huge wild boar, which disappeared when
he boldly jeered at it.[15] On the other hand, the disputation with the
devil on the Mass, as was shown above, was but a fiction of his pen.
It may be questioned whether the frequent nightly attacks launched
by Satan always occurred without hallucinations. According to his
own statement, a vulgar "*Leck mich . . .*" often banished them. He
seriously states in his Home-Postil: "The devil is always about us in
disguise, as I myself have witnessed, taking, *e. g.*, the form of a hog, of
a burning wisp of straw, and such like." [16]

Luther was also much annoyed by witches, whom he calls "harlots of the devil." "I wanted to burn them myself," he says, "according to the usage of the law, where the priests commenced to stone the
guilty ones." [17] On another occasion he declares against the female
corrupters of milk, that "the method of Doctor Pommer is the best"—
a reminiscence of the latter's treatment of the butter-vat. Luther's
declarations against witches, as contained in his Table Talks, became
universally known and together with his writings, which are replete
with demoniac thoughts, fatefully contributed to the bloody persecution of witches.[18]

Luther was very much inclined to assume that persons subject to
violent attacks of hysteria were possessed by the devil. However, he
did not wish to resort to the customary ecclesiastical exorcism with
its commands addressed to the devil, but restricted himself to prayer.
"God knows the time when the devil must depart." The success of
prayer, however, usually appeared rather dubious.

In January, 1546, he experienced a peculiar encounter with the supposed
devil in the sacristy of the parish church of Wittenberg. In the presence of

---

[15] *Ibid.*, pp. 131 sq.

[16] *Ibid.*, VI, 132.

[17] *Tischreden*, Weimar ed., Vol. IV, n. 3979.

[18] N. Paulus, *Hexenwahn und Hexenprozess, vornehmlich im 16. Jahrhundert* (1910),
pp. 488 sqq.

several doctors, ecclesiastics, and students, the devil was to be driven out of a girl of eighteen, a native of Ossitz, near Meissen, by the prayers of Luther and his attendants. It is evident from the accounts of two participants that the girl was in a highly hysterical condition. These two witnesses are Frederick Staphylus, a future convert to Catholicism, and Sebastian Fröschel, Luther's deacon. When, after the recitation of a somewhat lengthy prayer, Luther noticed no sign of the devil's departure, he applied his foot to the patient to signify his disdain for the devil. The poor creature whom he had thus insulted, followed him with threatening looks and gestures. The door could not be opened, as it had been bolted, and the key mislaid. Since the window, which was bolted with iron bars, did not permit of escape, Luther, the devil's greatest and best-hated foe on earth, says Staphylus, "ran about hither and thither, seized with fright," constantly pursued by the infuriated girl, and writhed and deported himself like a person in despair. Finally the sacristan passed in a hatchet, with which Staphylus burst open the door, and thus liberated Luther from his desperate plight. The pious Fröschel says that afterwards reports came to Wittenberg to the effect that the evil spirit no longer tormented the girl, as formerly.[19]

Luther's expectation of the end of the world is another dark trait which pervades his life and assumes a more vivid hue in his later years. He makes various estimates as to when the end may be expected.[20] On one occasion he says it will come in fifty years. Then again he predicts that the catastrophe will have happened by 1548. "We shall yet experience the fulfillment of the Scriptures." The idea circulated widely. His eccentric pupil and friend, Michael Stiefel, despite Luther's opposition, anticipated the date by assigning the year 1533, the eighteenth of October, at exactly eight o'clock in the morning, as the date of the world's end. At this hour he assembled his trembling parishioners in church, and, as nothing happened, was severely censured by Luther.

The end of the world was frequently predicted by other, even by great, men. In Luther's case, however, the expectation is accompanied by unusual agitation and morbid symptoms. It springs from the idea of his vocation and success. He revealed Antichrist in the papacy, and this revelation, according to the Bible, was to be followed immediately by the advent of the Great Judge. This theory he sets forth in detail and with the greatest seriousness in his tract against Catharinus,

[19] Grisar, *Luther*, Vol. VI, pp. 137 sq.
[20] *Op. cit.*, Vol. V, pp. 242, 248.

appealing to the celebrated passage of St. Paul's Epistle to the Thessalonians and the misunderstood prophecy of Daniel.

There is something visionary about his proclamations concerning the end of the world, and for this reason they deserve closer consideration.[21]

Many signs in nature, human society, and the empire of Satan, he held, announced the end of the world, as did also the ever increasing brutalization of the masses and the upper classes. In his fantastic interpretation of the monk-calf, he adduces the horrors of the papacy in corroboration of his prophecy. In old age he says of himself: "Let the Lord call me hence, I have committed, seen, and suffered sufficient of evil." At that time he was able to find even a certain consolation in reflecting on the end of the world, and to speak of the "dear Judgment Day," which was to liberate him from the difficulties which surrounded his work, and from the struggles within his own soul. The great successes which he finally experiences, appear to him to signify the last flaring up of the light. "The light is approaching extinction; it still makes a mighty effort, but thereafter it will be extinguished in a twinkle." Oppressive dreams of the impending judgment visit him. He overcomes the impression by hoping vigorously and longing for his departure from this vale of tears. Thus a mixture of dread and consolation, of fear and satisfaction is prevalent in his expectation of the end of the world.

So sure is he in his calculations that, in view of the brevity of time still allotted, he does not concern himself particularly about the discipline of the Church in the future, e. g., about the institution and order of public worship.[22]

The spiritual exhaustion which overwhelmed him towards the end of his life had a share in this indifference. It also belongs to the dark side of his spiritual life. Luther exclaims in his apathy: "Let everything collapse, stand, perish, as it may. Let matters take their course as they are, since, after all, matters will not change. . . . Germany has had its day and will never again be what it once was." Thus he writes in 1542.[23] He is "tired of this life," he writes in the same year;

[21] For proofs of the following *ibid.*, pp. 242 sqq. Gf. the passages cited by Kroker, *Tischreden*, Weimar ed., index to Vol. VI, *s. v.* "Tag, jüngster."

[22] Cfr. Köstlin-Kawerau, *M. Luther*, Vol. II, p. 522.

[23] In a letter to the preacher Probst at Bremen, on March 26, 1542. *Briefwechsel*, XIV, p. 218; Grisar, *Luther*, Vol. V, p. 226; the following passages, *ibid.*, pp. 230 sq., 246 sqq.

"all thoughts concerning plans and rendering aid begone from me! All is vanity." And again in 1543: "We will let things take their course as they may." He regards his words: "Let happen what may" as inspired by Christ, who will seize the reins Himself. The ailments, too, which he suffered, contributed to this despondency. He was afflicted alternately by oppression of the heart and by violent and whirling sensations in the head, accompanied by a ringing in the ears, and by sufferings caused by gallstone and other maladies.

"Distemper, melancholy, and severe afflictions," says Ratzeberger, oppressed him. This physician believes that the mental sufferings which Luther sustained contributed to his death.[24] Luther is profoundly grieved at his inability "to proceed effectively" against the papists, "so great is the immensity of the papistic monster." [25] He sees the advent of the Tridentine Council and he execrates and curses it.[26] With avidity he gives credence to the fable that the Emperor and the Pope had despatched ambassadors to the Grand Turk with gifts and an offer of peace, ready to prostrate themselves before the infidel ruler in long Turkish garments. He says that this is "a token of the coming of the end of all things." [27] Indeed, in the disturbed state of his mind he believed the most incredible things. He felt that he was repeatedly saved from the danger of being poisoned by the papists, who pursued him with deadly intent. He preached in poisoned pulpits without injury to himself. Witches endeavored in vain to destroy him and his family. Hired incendiaries convulsed the districts which adhered to him; but the devil raved in vain.

Dissatisfaction with Wittenberg finally induced him to abandon that city forever. Although he had bidden adieu to his Wittenberg hearers on a former occasion, and although he wanted to depart from the ungrateful city in the beginning of 1544, he did not carry out his plan until the end of July, 1545. After careful preparation [28] he betakes himself to Zeitz, whence he addresses a letter to his wife, declaring that he will never come back and requesting her to return to the estate of her family at Zulsdorf and to restore the Black Monastery to the Elector. He says he is resolved to beg for his bread in his old age. From Zeitz he repairs to Merseburg, where, on August 2, he con-

24 Grisar, op. cit.
25 Ibid., IV, 344.
26 Ibid.
27 Ibid.
28 Ibid., pp. 341 sqq.

fers upon the canon of the cathedral chapter, George von Anhalt, a so-called ordination as bishop of the diocese that had been abolished by Duke August of Saxony. From Merseburg he proceeds to Leipsic, where he preaches on the twelfth of August. He was prevailed upon to return to Wittenberg only after most strenuous efforts put forth by Melanchthon and Bugenhagen, who had been appointed emissaries of the city, the University, and the Elector.

After his return he felt better for a while. Owing to the devotion shown him by his followers, his mental depression yielded to a lively spirit of enterprise. It was a sudden transition, such as not infrequently occurred in his interior life, an idiosyncrasy of psychopathic sufferers.[29] The enemies were made to sense the old Luther in the new polemical literature which he produced. But melancholia once more returned, though apparently not accompanied by his former temptations.

Because of his suspicion of the teaching of others, association with him is described as intolerable, since he always suspected deviations from his own doctrinal position and would brook no differences of opinion. Melanchthon, who held different opinions on various points, e. g., on the Eucharist, complained bitterly and wrote afterwards that he was forced to put up with "an ignominious servility" in his association with Luther. He compares himself with the unfortunate Prometheus chained to the rock and describes Luther as the demagogue Cleon and the impetuous Hercules.[30] Forced to linger, as it were, in the cave of Cyclops, and not feeling secure against the secret wrath of Luther, he also desired to leave Wittenberg and announced his readiness "to slink away"—such is his expression.[31]

One particularly prominent trait in the spiritual life of Luther is his extraordinary capacity for self-delusion. The inward necessity of continually justifying anew to the world, and no less to himself, his pretended calling, the overwhelming ambition of belittling his antagonists and augmenting the number of his own followers and,

---

[29] John Joseph Mangan, in *Life, Character, and Influence of Desiderius Erasmus of Rotterdam* (1927), at pp. 87–88 of volume two, makes the following observations on Luther, which confirm Father Grisar's position. He says: "As our study of Erasmus has led us to decide definitely that he was a neurasthenic, so our study of Luther has convinced us that he was a psychopath, if not always, then most assuredly at intervals."—The author advances a number of proofs in substantiation of his assertion, which appear very interesting, as some of them are based upon medical observations. (Tr.)

[30] Grisar, *Luther*, Vol. V, pp. 252 sqq.

[31] *Ibid.*, VI, 347.

finally, his inevitable and constant perplexities, resulted in most curious expressions of self-delusion, which sometimes contradicted the views he entertained at other times.

Thus the moral corruption developing under the new evangel on occasion would appear terrible to him only because the gospel which he preached was pure and holy, and light intensifies the shadows. As there is no light in the papacy, he contends, its horrible evils and vices are not so noticeable. He ascribes the corruption of his followers to the devil, who would discredit the evangel, but on other occasions admits that it was caused by his *sola fides* doctrine which implied the inefficacy of good works.[32]

A few examples will show how arbitrarily his mental processes contravened the ordinary laws of experience and the rules of logic, in order to conform with the idea of his vocation, which dominated him with morbid force.

God continuously performs miracles in confirmation of his doctrine. In response to the prayers of the Lutherans, He destroys the enemies of His teaching. "By my prayers I have brought about the death of Duke George of Saxony; by means of our prayers we intend to encompass also the death of others." With the greatest apparent naïveté he finds his doctrines confirmed by the ancient doctors of the Church, such as St. Augustine, whereas in matter of fact they state the exact contrary. He cannot comprehend why the whole world does not agree with him and says that malice alone prevents the papists from accepting what is so evidently right; or, rather, they accept it in secret, as the pope and the Roman curia do, but they do not wish to honor him and the truth. The most horrible infidelity is rampant under the papacy. The papists do not heed "that God incessantly attacks them with many wounds, plagues, and signs." Has He not confirmed the Lutheran religion by the sudden death of Zwingli?

I am in duty bound to proclaim to the world what I "feel inwardly through the spirit of God." Indeed, I permit myself to be guided by God "as the wind and the waves propel the ship." Opposition and the din of battle are but the seal of divine approbation on my work. In the Peasants' War he boldly asserted that God commanded him to proclaim that the peasants were to be slain like dogs. In a spirit of defiance he afterwards vouches, with regard to his whole doctrinal system, that he will abide "by the first mandate of the vocation received from on high," by the "firstfruits of the received spirit," even "if God or Christ should announce the contrary" (!) He may not yield, since, in his own imagination, his victory over the papacy is already assured. "This majesty has fallen," "it has been destroyed" by the "spirit of the mouth of the Lord." "The Church will be without a pope,"

---

[32] Cfr. Grisar, *Luther*, Vol. IV, pp. 210 sqq.; Vol. VI, pp. 331 sq.

since he will fall just as the Turk. "Even now he is singing Eli, Eli," because he has been struck. Soon men will say, *Expiravit*—"he has breathed his last." "My adversaries will have neither the Word nor the Cross." They all avoid the Cross.

"Here I, a poor monk, and a poor nun must come to the rescue. We two comprehend the article of the Cross and raise it up; for this reason the Word and the Cross are sufficient; they give us assurance."

Thus the series of illusions outlined above is concluded with the remarkable tableau showing how Luther and his Kate raise up the the Cross in the sight of the world—they who had bound themselves by a solemn vow before the altar of God to embrace His Cross in a life of voluntary chastity, poverty, and obedience. How different the reality! To what extent the Cross disappears in Luther's conception of the married state and sexual life will be seen in a subsequent section.

3. FROM FREEDOM TO VIOLENT INTOLERANCE

The reversion of his early attitude on religious liberty and spiritual independence also belongs to the remarkable features of Luther's later life. This contradiction must be emphasized because rationalist Protestants of the present time like to quote Luther's earlier utterances, which seem to imply the destruction of all positive Christian belief.[33]

It is well known that Luther by no means intended to substitute rationalism for revealed Christianity. Nevertheless, in the first years of his polemics he advanced to such an extent in his antagonism to Catholic doctrine as apparently to antagonize all dogma. Relative to practice, he at that time permitted the obligation and dignity of the law to recede in an unwarranted manner. It is known that the liberty of opinion which emerged in consequence, and the loose morals of his adherents, as disclosed especially by the visitations of 1527–1528, led him to employ greater caution. The law and the fear of divine chastisement were inculcated by him more strictly, and belief in the revealed doctrines which he regarded as certain was emphasized with great severity. The controversy with Zwingli caused Luther to draw up a formal series of articles of faith. The Augsburg Confession fur-

[33] *Tischreden*, Weimar ed., Vol. V, n. 5515,

nished a certain basis, which was afterwards expanded and sanctioned by the publication of the so-called Schmalkaldic Articles. The controversy aroused by the Antinomianism of Agricola once more restored the law to its legitimate position and set new limits to liberty of teaching. Present-day Protestant theologians speak of a restriction of teaching and doctrinal torpidity on the part of the aging Luther. Many would prefer to progress along the path which he blazed in his early career as a reformer, holding that a healthy evolution can only take place where there is complete freedom, and lamenting that Luther's promising spring was succeeded by no summer.[34]

It is not true, however, that Luther's declarations in favor of liberty ceased altogether in his later years. His principle of the untrammeled formation of a personal religious conviction on the part of each individual in accordance with his private interpretation of the Bible, was never abandoned. After he had rejected the teaching authority of the Church, instituted by God for the preservation of dogma, there was really nothing left for him to do but to uphold an unlimited subjectivism. He contradicts himself, therefore, when he demands unconditional adherence to an objective sum of truths. All the more so, as he boldly sets up his own personal opinions in place of the venerable authority of the Church. True, he tried to conceal this substitution as much as possible. He assures his adherents that they must follow Christ, not him, but at the same time proceeds, in part unconsciously, on the assumption that his mandates must be obeyed. But, it may be asked, where is the necessary guarantee of truth if his judgment, hence the view of one person, is to be depended upon as to what constitutes the teaching of Christ, and what part of the ancient teaching and revelation is to be retained in the prescribed articles of the new evangel?

The reversions to a more positive attitude, occasionally noticed in Luther, were, therefore, fundamentally only a more brutal emphasis of the Wittenberg doctrine, which was his own. For him the change was a necessity; and even though it appears as grossly inconsistent, it nevertheless redounded to the future benefit of Protestantism by assisting it in carrying on during the coming centuries, until the scepticism of a new era and the advent of the so-called historical method and the modern spirit of independence shook Lutheranism with destructive force.

[34] Grisar, *op. cit.*, Vol. VI, pp. 237 sqq.

In his tribunal at Wittenberg Luther strove to protect *his truth* by all means. He hurled the most violent invectives not only at the papists, but also at the "heretics" in his own camp, who dared to deviate from his theological teaching. He assails not only the Zwinglians, but also Karlstadt, Bucer, Capito, Grickel (Agricola) and Jeckel (Jacob Schenck) among many others.

"They are knaves," thus he inveighs against them. "They would readily assail and surprise us, just as if we were blind and ignorant of their methods." [35] "By God's grace I am more learned than all the sophists and theologians of the schools." But "they have a high opinion of themselves, which, indeed, is the cause and well-spring of all heresies, for, as St. Augustine says, 'Ambition is the mother of all heresies.' " "It all comes from obstinacy and conceit and the ideas of natural reason, which puffs itself up."

Whilst in this frame of mind, it appears to have been impossible for Luther to realize that he actually condemned himself by these declarations uttered at various times.

The heretics—he says on another occasion—cannot be sure of their cause. First of all, they ought "to be certain of their mission." "One ought to be certain of it before God, whilst by all means one ought to be able to say before the people: 'If anyone knows better, let him say so; I will gladly yield to God's Word when I am better instructed.' "

He asks them: Where are your miracles? With a boldness that is truly extraordinary he demands miraculous signs from the sectaries. He himself needs none in attestation of his teaching; for his mission is an ordinary one, whereas their pretended mission is extraordinary. Were he to petition God, he says, God would endow him with "the gift of raising the dead, or of performing other miracles." However, he does not ask God for these gifts, since "the rich gift of interpreting the Scriptures is sufficient" for him.

In his reaction against the doctrinal liberty which he himself inaugurated Luther goes so far as to advocate compulsory measures against those who differ with him. In 1525 he had enunciated the principle: "The [secular] authorities are not to hinder anyone from teaching and believing what he pleases." [36] In 1530—originally induced thereto by the agitation of the Anabaptists—he demands the exercise of force and bloody repression on the part of his Elector and the other Protestant rulers. Not only are those Anabaptists who rebel against the authority of the State to be dealt with harshly, but also those who

---

[35] *Tischreden*, Weimar ed., Vol. III, n. 2896b. The other passages cited in small print will be found *apnd* Grisar, *op. cit.*, Vol. VI, pp. 279 sqq.

[36] This and the following quotations *ibid.*, VI, pp. 248 sqq.

are not in rebellion. "These also are not to be tolerated, but are to be treated as public blasphemers." To deviate from his teaching is equivalent to "public blasphemy" and deserving of death. "The authorities shall hand over knaves of that ilk to their proper master, to wit, Master Hans" (*i. e.*, the hangman). The Sacramentarians and the papists, too, being blasphemers, must not be tolerated.

At the end of October, 1531, Melanchthon, who was known for his humane disposition, developed in detail the reasons for employing the sword against the Anabaptists. These reasons apply to all who "reject the office of public preaching and teach that men can become holy in some other manner, without sermons and ecclesiastical worship." Luther subscribed his name to these reasons, saying, "It pleases me." In his sermons on St. Matthew, which were delivered about this time, he says: "It is not allowed to everyone to excogitate his own ideas, formulate his own doctrine, permit himself to be called Master and dominate or censure anyone else"; "it is one of the greatest and most injurious vices on earth, whence all factious spirits originate."

Thus sectaries, especially Anabaptists, were executed in Electoral Saxony, the rulers appealing to the Wittenberg theologians and jurists in justification of their procedure.[37] Luther never revoked his intolerant views; on the contrary, he constantly intensified them as he approached the end of his life.[38]

Certain formidable barriers which had been erected by him and Melanchthon at the faculty of Wittenberg, were intended to safeguard this supreme tribunal and citadel of pure orthodoxy against the incursions of "heretical" opinions. The statutes of the theological faculty, which were probably drawn up in 1533, invested that body with the right of deciding all matters of faith. The proper observance of this provision was guaranteed by the fact that Luther presided over the faculty uninterruptedly from 1535 until his death.[39] Moreover, after 1535, there was prescribed, at the instigation of the Elector, an "Ordination Oath," preceded by a theological examination, for all preachers and pastors sent out by the University. In the certificate of ordination of Heinrich Bock (dated May 17, 1540, and signed by Luther, Bugenhagen, Jonas, and Melanchthon) it is set forth that

[37] *Ibid.*, pp. 254 sq.

[38] *Ibid.*, pp. 256 sqq. Cfr. N. Paulus, *Protestantismus und Toleranz im 16. Jahrhundert* (1911), Ch. I.

[39] Grisar, *Luther*, Vol. VI, pp. 262 sq.

Bock had undertaken to "preach to the people steadfastly and faith-fully the pure doctrine of the gospel which our Church confesses." It is also stated that he adheres to the "consensus" of the "Catholic Church of Christ." [40] "Catholicity" here is understood in a sense which does not ordinarily attach to the word. "Ordination" merely consisted in the declaration that the candidates were authorized to serve as ministers.

Naturally many opponents within his own camp reproached Luther with lack of liberty in the exercise of the ministry. They charged, and not without justification, that the Wittenbergers proposed "to breathe new life into despotism, to seat themselves in the chair, and to exercise jurisdiction just as the pope had done heretofore." [41] Luther was dubbed "the Pope of Wittenberg" (*Papa Albiacus*), an epithet which became increasingly popular when his talented and scholarly opponent, Sebastian Franck, whose writings enjoyed a wide circulation, developed Luther's subjectivism to its logical conclusions and combated the Lutheran ecclesiastical system, demanding unre-stricted liberty. This intrepid challenger was everywhere pursued by verdicts and demands for execution on the part of Luther and Me-lanchthon.[42] Simon Lemnius (Lemchen), a Protestant humanist of Wittenberg, was another public opponent of Luther's theological despotism. Banished from Wittenberg in 1538, he avenged himself by the publication of a caustic "Apology," the complete text of which became known to historians but recently. In it he unmercifully castigates the spiritual tyranny exercised by Luther. "He sits like a dictator at Wittenberg and rules"; thus the "Apology," "and what he says must be taken as law." [43] However, it must be noted that Lemnius, because of other attacks upon the conduct of Luther's cir-cle, did not bequeathe to posterity the reputation of a respectable controversialist, his attacks being very frivolous in diction and con-tent and also untrue. He composed a revolting poem in which he depicts Luther as suffering from dysentery. Luther retorted with a "Merd-Song" of his own, in which he paid his respects to Lemnius in language that was no less vulgar than his opponent's.[44]

In spite of such attacks Luther maintained his tribunal at Witten-

[40] *Ibid.*, p. 265.
[41] *Ibid.*, p. 315.
[42] *Ibid.*, pp. 266 sqq.
[43] *Ibid.*, p. 288.
[44] *Tischreden*, Weimar ed., Vol. IV, n. 4032. Cfr. Grisar, *Luther*, Vol. VI, p. 288.

berg. "Whosoever shall despise the Wittenberg School," he declared, "is a heretic and an evil man; for in this school God has revealed His Word." [45] And he adhered to this solemn pronouncement. In 1542 he went so far as to demand that the leading citizens of Meissen, who had embraced his doctrine, should "signify their approval of everything which has hitherto been done by us and shall be done in the future." [46]

Luther's intolerance also animated his co-workers, especially Melanchthon.[47] A. Hänel in the *Zeitschrift für Rechtsgeschichte* passes the following judgment upon the latter: As far as Protestantism is concerned, "liberty of belief" was "denied at every point." In fervent words Melanchthon sanctioned the execution of the "heretic" Michael Servetus by Calvin in 1554 as "a pious and memorable example for all posterity." [48] It has been previously noted that he wished God would send a "bold assassin" to "despatch" the heretical King Henry VIII of England.[49] Martin Bucer, to mention but one more of Luther's associates, asserted that the civil authority "was obliged to abolish false doctrine and perverse public worship," and that all the bishops and the clergy must obey it as the sole existing authority.[50]

The new religion was, as a matter of course, capable of enforcing such demands only by availing itself of its intimate connection with the secular authority. By surrendering the religious discipline to the civil government, the Protestant Church became a compulsory State institution, a nursery of despotic encroachments upon the spiritual domain. Luther himself says of it: "Satan is still Satan; under the papacy he pushed the Church into the world sphere and now, in our day, he seeks to bring the State system into the Church." [51]

The Church, whose invisibility and purely spiritual power Luther had hitherto so forcibly emphasized, in his hands became a visible institution, which asserted its visibility all too strongly, and became accustomed to marshal all temporal forces and to insure its preservation with the aid of the secular arm. The tragic fate of Luther's theory

[45] *Tischreden, ibid.*, n. 5126; Grisar, *op. cit.*, Vol. V, p. 170.
[46] Grisar, *ibid.*, VI, p. 279.
[47] *Ibid.*, p. 265.
[48] Grisar, *op. cit.*, VI, pp. 266 sqq.
[49] Grisar, *op. cit.*, VI, pp. 269 sqq.
[50] *Ibid.*, Vol. IV, p. 12. Respecting Melanchthon, Bucer, etc., see the proofs in Paulus, *Toleranz.*
[51] Grisar, *op. cit.*, Vol. VI, p. 320.

of the Church has led many a Protestant scholar to assert, quite truly, that there is no room for a church in Luther's system. It is even doubted whether he intended to found a church in any true sense of the word.[52] Protestants have frankly exposed the inherent contradiction between his pronouncements on religious authority and the duty of secular rulers and his persistent assertion of individual liberty and the claims of his gospel.[53]

Luther's retreat from the position which he had originally assumed merely contributed to a clearer disclosure of the contradictions inherent in the principal ideas of his system. The intrinsic contradictions are especially manifest in the sphere of morality. For this reason, we will devote a special chapter to the ethical aspects of Luther's doctrine and practice.

[52] *Ibid.*, p. 307, quoting Martin Rade.
[53] *Ibid.*, pp. 321 sq. Cfr. Th. Pauls, *Luthers Auffassung von Staat und Volk*, Bonn, 1925, a book which unjustifiably credits Luther with too much systematization.

CHAPTER XVIII

LUTHER ON MORALITY AND MATRIMONY. THE BIGAMY OF PHILIP OF HESSE

1. LUTHER'S ETHICAL TEACHING IN GENERAL

The ethical system of Luther was vitally influenced by his conception of the gospel, which in his opinion was essentially only forgiveness of sin, a cloak covering guilt, the quieting of an "affrighted conscience." To gain a sense of confidence was the starting-point of the new doctrine. Luther's supreme gain was to acquire certainty of salvation through an active faith in the appropriation of the merits of Christ. This thought is the guiding star also of his ethics.

Protestants say that Luther erected ethics upon its genuine foundation, which had been ignored up to his time. This claim, however, is disproved by certain leading declarations of his, which raise the question how a true ethical system could originate under such conditions. Luther taught that man is not a free agent, but a mute "pillar of salt," either controlled by the grace of God which is operative within him, or subject to the domination of the devil, without any activity on his part. His reason in religious matters resembles a lunatic." In consequence of an ineradicable original guilt, sin persists in man's inordinate concupiscence; even the just man, i. e., he who is regarded as just by God, remains a sinner. Sin is merely covered up by fiduciary faith in the blood of Christ. The "golden cloak of grace" due to the merits of the Redeemer does everything. Good works are devoid of supernatural merit and have no significance for Heaven. Every man is predestined for Heaven or hell by a hidden decree of God.[1]

It is fair to ask: What moral inducement is there in Luther's hypothesis to combat the perversity of human nature? Is there any moral responsibility? Can there be any such thing as Christian morality? At a time when the renown of Luther was not so great as it is since the last decades of the nineteenth century, the Protestant theologian K. F. Stäudlin openly declared that "no genuine Christian ethic could

[1] Cfr. Grisar, *Luther*, Vol. V, pp. 3 sqq.

exist" on the basis of Luther's principles.[2] Many other Protestant authors share this view. As a matter of fact, Luther's work "On the Enslaved Will" marks the death of ethics.

He inculcates humility because sin is in man and man is completely dependent upon God, without any capacity or volition on his part. But this sort of humility is no basis for a system of ethics.

Luther errs in his fundamental presupposition that the assurance of possessing salvation, contained in fiduciary faith, will move man to observe true morality, and particularly to perform acts inspired by love, which alone are pleasing to God. Lack of morality demonstrates that one has not the right kind of faith, which, in his system, takes the place of Christian perfection and virtue.

Practical Christianity is relegated to the background in Luther's system, for the only obligatory works of divine worship are faith, praise, and thanksgiving. The others are to be "directed towards our neighbor"; yet there are no good works except such as have been commanded by God. Indeed, without faith the good works which man performs amount to sin, just as the virtues of the pagans were *splendida vitia*.[3] "Faith" causes the Church and the world to be two entirely different empires, so completely separated that the exterior office of a Christian, *e. g.*, of a ruler, has nothing to do with his Christian belief. To strive for perfection as Catholics do, is folly. There are no evangelical counsels, and even the most pious believers are sinners. Saints must be "good, hearty sinners"—an expression which recalls to mind his declaration: "Sin boldly, but believe more boldly."

But in spite of these intellectual aberrations, the sermons and writings of Luther contain a rich treasure of ethical doctrines. He so urgently and eloquently exhorts men to the practice of virtue that his voice is scarcely distinguishable from that of the ancient Church. Many illustrations of this have been furnished in the foregoing chapter. Thus, in point of morality Luther actually pursued a far better course than his theological opinions would lead one to expect. His lack of consistency proved a decided advantage. In his ethical teaching, as in other respects, he did not carry his avowed principles to their logical conclusions. He desired to be helpful to others in his own way as a spiritual director and to demonstrate that the new Gospel was morally sound and profitable.

---

[2] *Geschichte der Moral*, Göttingen, 1806, p. 209.
[3] Cfr. Grisar, *Luther*, Vol. V, pp. 47 sqq.

Luther never attempted to formulate a system of ethics, and his theoretical principles would have rendered the attempt futile. But Protestantism has reason to congratulate itself that its founder, even without a system, scattered so many seeds of Christian morality in his emphatic and popular way, though it should not be overlooked that he derived his supply from the heritage of the ancient Church, upon which he drew freely.

Protestant writers have lamented the fact that Luther bequeathed to his followers no systematic introduction to the devout life so that even to the present day Protestantism lacks any definite rule of piety. Julius Kaftan laments that Luther slighted the doctrine of piety and that of "redemption from the world," in the narrower sense. The salvation "bestowed by Christ is not merely justification and forgiveness of sins," but rather the "everlasting possession" to be reached by a Christlike life. Justification is but the road to this possession. The Church has other "vital interests." [4]

In his writings no less than in his life Luther neglected the true methods of self-reform. Catholic authors, on the other hand, such as St. Bernard and Gerson, from whom Luther derived enlightenment at a former period of his life, showed that true piety is based on self-denial. In Luther's opinion self-denial is of far less importance than the ready surrender of the "fretful" so-called traditional prejudices of renunciation and restraint in worldly affairs. The ill-considered expression: "What matters it if we commit a fresh sin?", since there is forgiveness in faith, supplies us with a profound insight into his mentality.

Retirement, examination of conscience, and solitude, were to be shunned, according to his view. Quietude, he says, "calls forth the worst of thoughts." [5] In his directions for praying, one misses the salt of sorrow and contrition; they lack the fragrance of true humility and are far removed from that charity which resigns itself to God and submits with equanimity to the divine will, especially with reference to one's vocation in life. To render his prayers fervent, he must spice them with curses against the "papists." There is anger and passion in his practical attitude; megalomania, jealousy and irritation in his appeal to violence; there are, finally, examples of untruthfulness and dishonesty in his polemics, so that Erasmus is constrained to exclaim: "You pretend to be a teacher of the Gospel!" [6]

[4] *Op. cit.*, Vol. V, pp. 89 sqq.
[5] *Ibid.*, p. 93.
[6] *Ibid.*, pp. 112 sqq.

His teaching on "self-improvement and the reformation of the Church," considered in the light of Luther's conduct, furnishes numerous other and no less damaging objections to his ethical doctrine.[7] Suffice it to say that reform, to be effective, should have commenced with a sincere improvement of morals, enforced by the example of his own life. Instead, he commenced with arbitrary changes of doctrine. It was necessary at that time to counteract the subjectivism and scepticism produced by the Renaissance. Luther, on the contrary, encouraged this evil. He favored the divergent tendencies of the nations and took no account of the new tasks imposed on the Church by the discovery of new countries. Allowing the masses to read the Bible was no compensation for the want of truly great objects of reform.

The Bible in consequence of the use that was made of it rather became the means of theological and social confusion. It seemed, as Luther himself declared, as if everyone was desirous "of boring a hole wherever his snout happened to be." [8] In his pessimism, with which he infected the world, he descries how even in the first centuries "the devil had broken into Holy Scripture and caused such a disturbance as to give rise to many heresies." [9]

As a reformer, he did not direct the unfavorable currents of his age into better channels, but to a certain extent permitted himself to be carried off by them. Thus, in the beginning of his career, he adopted the pseudo-mysticism which pervaded his age. From contemporary humanism, he not only adopted disrespect for authority and the spirit of rebellion, which he augmented, but also promoted the excessive use of authority on the part of ambitious princes at the expense of their subjects. Finally, in his writings and addresses on marriage and sexual questions, he cultivated the crude naturalism of the Renaissance with an abandon that was astounding, particularly in his fight upon sacerdotal celibacy and monasticism. At times, says the Protestant philosopher Frederick Paulsen, this naturalism causes Luther to speak "as if abstention from the works of the flesh spelled rebellion against the will and command of God."

[7] *Ibid.*, pp. 84 sqq.
[8] *Ibid.*, p. 129.
[9] *Ibid.*, p. 130.

2. MATRIMONY AND SACERDOTAL CELIBACY

We shall not revert here to the examples which have been previously adduced to show how Luther availed himself of the lure of the married state in order to gain adherents among priests and religious. Nor shall we refer to his afore-mentioned writings on his favorite theme of matrimony, such as his treatises "On the Matrimonial Life," "On Things Matrimonial," and his interpretation of the seventh chapter of the First Epistle to the Corinthians. We will consider only a few of the general principles and viewpoints prominent in these works.

Luther's doctrine on matrimony cannot be treated as a complete system because of the author's numerous contradictions and vacillations. It is manifest from many ardent expressions that Luther regarded Christian matrimony as an exalted state of life. His own marriage, which had been contracted in defiance of the Church laws, afforded him frequent opportunities of eulogizing matrimony as an institution ordained by God. He waxes enthusiastic in emphasizing its chief purpose, namely, the procreation of children for the welfare of State and Church, even though at the same time he continually exaggerates the danger of incontinence as its most urgent motive. In a hundred passages he describes how married life operates as a stimulus to good works, how it protects the faith of husband and wife, awakens love, and fosters discipline and domesticity. He delineates family life in such captivating terms that the single life appears quite unattractive. The moral features which he delights in mentioning in the course of these descriptions have led Protestant writers to say that Luther's views on matrimony spell the very apex of morality. Why disregard the sensual and dangerous aspects of his teaching and example?

It was fatal to Luther's teaching on matrimony that it was the product of a twofold struggle—that against the state of virginity and that against the authority of the Church.

The sexual and sensual admixture of his doctrine derives from his antagonism to the state of virginity. His hostility to the sacerdotal and monastic states leads him to degrade celibacy beyond all measure. [10] In order to assail the Catholic position more effectively he as-

[10] Cfr. Grisar, *Luther*, Vol. III, pp. 241 sqq., and the excellent work of S. Baranowski, *Luthers Lehre von der Ehe* (1913), pp. 34 sqq.

serts, as the starting-point of his own doctrine, that the sexual instinct in man operates as an irresistible law of nature and tolerates no restriction in the form of vows, which can result in unchastity. In his invectives against the vow of chastity human dignity and decency are set aside. The means of grace offered by the Church for the successful conquest of the sexual instinct and for leading a higher life, are ignored. Nature, in his opinion, compels practically all men to embrace the matrimonial state. It is a "miracle" if anyone is able to live continently.[11] For the rest, he goes much farther than the Catholic Church by declaring the sexual instinct sinful in itself. He refuses to acknowledge that the involuntary movements of the sexual instinct are no sin, and that it is virtuous to resist them for the sake of God or to keep a deliberate vow.

His position was influenced not only by his antagonism to sacerdotal celibacy and the religious vow of chastity, but likewise by his fight on the authority of the Church. Her venerable and salutary traditions for the protection of the matrimonial state and family life, which she ever esteemed most highly, counted for nothing in his eyes. He rejects without investigation the teaching of the Church on matrimonial impediments and divorce. An artificial Biblical or a merely natural argument is sufficient for him to open a wide road to what he calls Christian liberty. The efforts made at the present time to abolish marriage as a social institution were unconsciously inaugurated by Luther when he denied the time-honored authority of the Church in matrimonial matters.

In his system, which did not recognize matrimony as a sacrament, the Church, which regulates and administers the sacraments, was replaced by the secular authority. His original endeavor to regulate matrimonial matters with the aid of his preachers and pastors, was defeated by a multiplicity of problems and controversial cases. The State usurped authority in this sphere and Luther favored this tendency. He could not consistently have done otherwise after he had declared matrimony to be a purely secular affair. But in doing so he nevertheless created a contradiction which cannot be spanned; for, on the one hand, he praises the matrimonial state as "most holy," and on the other, he divorces it from the Church, to whom holy things are subject.[12]

11 Cfr. Grisar, Luther, Vol. III, pp. 246 sqq.
12 Baranowski, op. cit., p. 177.

In vain one seeks to find in Luther a true concordance between the service of the world and the service of God in matrimony. There is discord and antithesis everywhere. At times he extols sexual intercourse in matrimony as a lofty divine service; then again he characterizes it as religiously indifferent, nay, even as stained with sin. He exhorts parents to be one in their prayers and in the Christian education of their offspring, yet asserts the validity of marriage between Christians and pagans, because this does not affect the faith. He arbitrarily relaxes the ties of matrimony, and at the same time unduly contracts the duties of the domestic sphere; for the subjection of the wife to the authority of the husband, and that of the children to the will of the parents, as advocated by him, appears to exceed the bounds of what is lawful to personal conduct and individual self-determination.[13] His attitude on the latter subject provoked the celebrated, lengthy and violent controversy on the validity of marriage contracted without parental consent, which consent he designated as necessary for a valid union of the children.

Even more subversive were his principles concerning divorce.[14]

As early as 1520 Luther refused to assert the indissolubility of the marriage tie. As time went on, the complaint raised against him became ever more justified, that (to quote his own words) "he arbitrarily trifled with the dissolution and the confirmation of matrimony." [15] Though he regards divorce as a serious matter, injurious to the Christian polity and the State, he finds that adultery is an immediate ground for divorce, with liberty to remarry. After breaking with the Biblical doctrine and with tradition in this critical matter, he subsequently proposed a second ground for divorce, namely, willful desertion. He did this in order to come to the aid of those unfortunates who had been forced to adopt celibacy. Other grounds for divorce recognized by him are persistent irascibility and violent incompatibility of temper. If either one of the parties concerned cannot restrain himself, he says, "let him (or her) woo another in the name of God." [16] This was the extent to which the idea of the ir-

---

[13] *Ibid.*, p. 209. Similarly an examination of Luther's utterances on vocation would show how confused were his views of marriage and celibacy, and also of the secular and the spiritual vocation. On "vocation" in the Middle Ages and Luther's idea of it see N. Paulus in *Histor. Jahrbuch*, Vol. 32, pp. 725 sqq., and Vol. 45, pp. 308 sqq.

[14] Grisar, *Luther*, Vol. IV, pp. 3–79; Baranowski, *Luthers Lehre von der Ehe*, pp. 115 sqq.

[15] *Briefwechsel* VIII, p. 398.

[16] Baranowski, *op. cit.*, p. 124.

resistibility of the sexual urge had led him. As a matter of course, Luther permits divorce (*divortium*) where the life of one conjugal partner is jeopardized by the other; but the passage in question does not clearly indicate whether or not he means a complete dissolution of the matrimonial bond. It frequently appears that he is little concerned with the important distinction between a complete dissolution of the marriage bond and a mere separation from bed and board. He extends the so-called Pauline Privilege to Christian couples and to cases where one party urges the other to "unchristian conduct," to "theft, adultery or any unrighteousness towards God." But, as regards these matters, he also repudiates the civil authority, which ought to devise remedial measures. He holds that physical impotence not only dissolves matrimony where it previously existed, but also when subsequently contracted, even in the case of marriages blessed with offspring.

There are two other grounds for divorce which he admits. In the case of obstinate refusal to render the *debitum,* the injured party may enter upon a new marriage. "If you are unwilling," to quote the easily misconstruable and insidious assertion of Luther, "then another shall; if the wife is unwilling, then the maid shall come." At all events, Luther holds that, in case of refusal, the secular authorities ought to intervene. Finally, he also regarded serious illness, especially leprosy, as an adequate ground for divorce, at least in the internal forum of conscience, thereby proposing a principle which, according to a recent Protestant critic, " is apt by its consequences to shake the institution of matrimony to its very foundations." [17] If this be true of this one ground, what must be said of the collective effect of all the grounds that have been mentioned?

In the practical application of these ideas Luther mingled the strangest contradictions. He requires the verdict of the civil authorities for the validation of divorce, yet regards marriage as already dissolved and to be treated as dissolved in secret. He grants the right of remarriage to one party and at the same time denies it to the other. In the forum of conscience he concedes grounds for divorce which he refuses to defend in public, and so forth.[18]

In his narrow purview he discovers ecclesiastical domination and pretensions, if not avarice, in the traditional diriment impediments

[17] *Theol. Studien und Kritiken,* 1881, p. 445.
[18] Baranowski, *op. cit.,* p. 131.

upheld by the Church. He particularly rejects the dilatory impediments.[19] "Freedom," he says, "may not be abolished by the superstition and stupidity of others." [20] Suffice it to mention that, on the basis of the Old Testament, he regards only the second degree of consanguinity and the first degree of affinity as impediments arising from relationship, and that on other occasions he indirectly exempts even the first degree of affinity. The precedent of an Old Testament patriarch counts for more with him than "100,000 popes." [21]

The precedent of the patriarchs also confused his views of the unity of marriage. While he would not tolerate the introduction of bigamy, he nevertheless, as indicated elsewhere, allowed a certain scope to it.[22] As early as 1520 he gave expression to this sentimental inclination of his, preferring bigamy to divorce in case of necessity.[23] In 1524 he expressed himself more decisively toward Chancellor Brück: "I admit that I am unable to prohibit a man from marrying several wives; it does not contradict Holy Writ." But scandal and sound ethics, he adds, establish objections to the practice.[24] He repeats these statements frequently. In the subsequent account of the bigamous marriage of Landgrave Philip of Hesse, the consequences of Luther's and Melanchthon's attitude will be seen. This one case clearly reveals the fact that the so-called reformers "lacked a comprehensive insight into the true ethical nature of matrimony." [25]

How different in this respect are the Middle Ages, particularly the time which preceded Luther, with its numerous popular treatises on matrimony as a sacrament—writings which abounded in attractive profundity and solid theological content. In the tender delineations of domestic life found in these "marriage booklets" justice is accorded the human side of the marital relationship and protection is afforded the sublimity and purity of this institution by the faithful reproduction of the precepts of the Church.[26]

The Protestant claim that the esteem of womanhood originated with Luther is entirely unfounded. The dignity of woman, her social

[19] Weimar ed., Vol. X, ii, p. 287.

[20] Ibid., VI, p. 558.

[21] Ibid., XVI, p. 405.

[22] Grisar, Luther, Vol. IV, pp. 13 sqq.; Baranowski, op. cit., p. 162 sqq.; Rockwell, Die Doppelehe Philipps von Hessen (1904), pp. 247 sqq.

[23] Weimar ed., Vol. VI, p. 559.

[24] Briefwechsel, IV, pp. 282 sq.; January 27, 1524.

[25] This pertinent observation is by Baranowski, op. cit., p. 168.

[26] Grisar, Luther, Vol. IV, pp. 135 sqq.

mission, the esteem and veneration which her position demands, could not be more thoroughly effective than in a society firmly founded on a religion which appreciated and extolled virginity equally with motherhood, and honored the supreme type of motherhood in Mary, Virgin and Mother, the protectress of Christendom.[27]

It is impossible to follow the utterances of Luther on marriage and sexual matters without ever and anon being repelled by the vulgarity of his language and his sensuality. [28]

For example, here is a sentence which surely does not honor womanhood: "The word and work of God is quite clear, *viz.*, that women were made to be either wives or prostitutes." [29] We add a few others: "Had we opportunity, time, and occasion," he says in his bombastic manner, "we should all commit adultery"; he thus intends to indicate the power of concupiscence, and then continues: "We are so mad, when once our passions are aroused, that we forget everything." [30] Marriage ought to be contracted by "a boy not later than the age of twenty, and a girl when she is from fifteen to eighteen years of age. Then they are still healthy and sound, and they can leave it to God to see that their children are provided for." [31] "Even though one may have the gift to be able to live chastely without a wife, yet he ought to marry in defiance of the pope, who insists so much on celibacy." [32]—"Were all those living under the papacy kneaded together, not one would be found who had remained chaste up to his fortieth year." [33]—"I am satisfied that the saints stick in the mud just like we do." [34]

Certain indecorous German utterances of Luther are reproduced in Latin in the present writer's more exhaustive work.[35] In a letter of December 6, 1525, Luther speaks of his marriage and that of Spalatin in a manner that is not fit for reproduction. The older editors (Aurifaber, De Wette, Walch) omitted the passage in question.[36]

It is a notorious fact that the undignified vulgarity of Luther's language, spiced with sexual allusions, attains its height in the objurgations which he metes out to the papacy and the Roman Church.[37] Thus the pope is com-

[27] *Ibid.*, pp. 131 sqq.
[28] *Op. cit.*, Vol. III, pp. 264 sqq.
[29] *Ibid.*, p. 243.
[30] *Ibid.*, p. 245.
[31] *Ibid.*, p. 246.
[32] *Tischreden*, Weimar ed., II, n. 2129b; cf. a; see also Grisar, *Luther*, Vol. III, p. 246.
[33] *Ibid.*, p. 251.
[34] *Ibid.*
[35] *Luther*, Vol. III, pp. 251 sq., n. 3.
[36] *Ibid.*, p. 269, n. 2.
[37] *Ibid.*, pp. 265 sqq.

pared with the detestable pagan god, Priapus. In giving vent to such utterances, Luther, as his excuses demonstrate, was quite conscious that he had transcended even the freedom which his coarse age was wont to grant. In 1541 he writes against the loyal Catholics: [38] "You are the runaway apostate, strumpet Church as the prophets term it"; "you whoremongers preach in your own brothels and devil's churches"; "your conduct is such as if the bride of a beloved bridegroom were to allow every man to abuse her at his will." Unable to satiate himself with this image, he continues: "This whore, once a pure virgin and beloved bride, is now an apostate, a vagrant, a whore, a house-whore," etc. "You old whores bear in your turn young whores, and so increase and multiply the pope's Church, which is the devil's own." "You reduce many true virgins of Christ, who have been regenerated by baptism, to arch-harlots." [39]

3 · THE BIGAMY OF PHILIP OF HESSE

On December 9, 1539, Martin Bucer visited Luther in Wittenberg and presented him with a request by the Landgrave Philip of Hesse for an opinion sanctioning his intended bigamous marriage with Margaret von der Sale.[40]

Luther and Melanchthon were alarmed at the disclosure made by Bucer in accordance with his written directions. The argument which the Landgrave advanced in his petition was that, in consequence of the immoral life he had hitherto led, he was constrained by his conscience to take unto himself another wife, in addition to the one he already had, as a substitute for the "debauched women" with whom he had hitherto consorted. It was his desire that the new marriage, as well as the formal opinion of Luther and Melanchthon permitting the same, be "publicly proclaimed to the world" by gradual stages, so that his second wife "be not regarded as a dishonorable person." What alarmed the two leaders of Protestantism most was Philip's threat that, in the event of their non-acquiescence, he would appeal to the Emperor; in other words, that he, in complete contradiction to the attitude which he had hitherto observed, would endeavor by means of concessions to obtain the favor of the most hated and most powerful opponent of Lutheranism, in order to procure from him toleration of his step, notwithstanding the severe imperial laws which pro-

---

[38] Grisar, *Luther*, Vol. VI, p. 331.

[39] *Ibid.*, p. 332; cfr. III, pp. 270 sqq.

[40] For proofs pertaining to this section let it suffice to refer in general to my lengthy exposition in *Luther*, Vol. IV, pp. 13-79. In a few cases only are references given here.

hibited it. Plainly, Philip contemplated a fatal betrayal of the Protestant cause.

Luther and Melanchthon had previously expressed themselves in favor of the permissibility of bigamy in particular cases.[41] They believed that there was justification for it in the Old Testament, citing the cases in which polygamy was permitted by God in exceptional instances. In certain cases, Luther, too, as he himself says, had counseled the contraction of bigamous marriage, when, for instance, husbands complained of severe and incurable disease of their wives or of their refusal to render the *debitum*. Philip of Hesse was acquainted with these public pronouncements as well as with Luther's proffer of bigamy to Henry VIII of England. Martin Bucer cited all these facts with persuasive eloquence.

On the other hand the Wittenberg theologians were well aware that polygamy had been abolished by the divine Founder of the Church in the New Testament. Even though they were prepared to tolerate exceptions in extraordinary cases, they yet held that polygamy ought not to be reintroduced generally. Thus Melanchthon asserted that the words of Christ, "they two shall be one flesh" should be observed as a "universal Christian law." [42]

Philip's demand for permission to contract a bigamous marriage appeared to open the gates to polygamy. Hence, the embarrassment which seized both Wittenberg reformers at the unheard-of proposition of the Landgrave.

Philip, who had just partly recovered from a severe venereal attack, had cast his eyes upon Margaret, the seventeen-year-old daughter of the lady in waiting of his sister, the Duchess Elizabeth of Sachsen-Rochlitz. He obtained a promise from Margaret's ambitious mother that his desire would be gratified, but only on condition that Margaret would become his wife and true landgravine, not merely a despised concubine. This unsavory plan, coupled with the aforesaid condition, was furthered by the Protestant pastor of Melsungen, John Lening, an apostatized Carthusian monk, who was reputed to be leading an immoral life himself. The afore-mentioned sister of the landgrave, however, violently opposed the bigamous marriage as soon as she became aware of it, not indeed for any ethical

---

[41] Grisar, *Luther,* Vol. III, pp. 259 sqq.

[42] Cf. Rockwell, *Die Doppelehe Philipps von Hessen,* p. 194; Camerarius in *Corp. Ref.,* III, pp. 1077 sq.; Grisar, *Luther,* Vol. IV, pp. 62 sq.

motive (her own moral conduct as a widow was blameworthy), but because she regarded her brother's marriage to the daughter of her governess as a disgrace to the reigning family. Philip's declaration that, after a dissolute life, he was constrained to ease his conscience by means of a new, duly contracted marriage, was but a pretext which served as a cloak to cover his unrestrained sensuality. He despatched the complaisant physician Sailer, also a Protestant, to win over for his plan the theologian Bucer, whom he had selected to conduct the negotiations at Wittenberg. Sailer writes that Bucer was "highly amazed" when he communicated to him the invitation to visit Philip regarding this affair, but that he finally consented to come and act as mediator, to avert the defection of the Landgrave from the Protestant cause. Bucer undertook the mission and received written instructions from the prince, of which the text is still extant. The authentic text of the reply made by Luther and Melanchthon is preserved in the government archives at Marburg.[43]

On December 10, the day after the arrival of Bucer, they delivered to him the fatal document which had been composed with remarkable haste by the skilled pen of Melanchthon. It styles itself a "testimonial," and states that the contemplated marriage is not contrary to the law of God and may be entered upon by the Landgrave because of a "necessity of conscience." [44] The deponents demand that the new marriage, as well as the "testimonial," should remain secret, in order to avoid scandal and to prevent polygamy from becoming general. They might have foreseen that this desire was destined to remain unfulfilled in view of the declared intention of the autocratic Landgrave to divulge the entire matter.

The document is not devoid of sound, moral exhortations, but, on the other hand, the alleged divine "dispensation" to contract a bigamous marriage is treated as a sort of initiation of the petitioner into a "retired state" with the intimation that the marriage with Margaret would entail "no particular scandal," since the people would regard her as a concubine, and concubines were not uncommon in many courts. At the very beginning of the document, the Landgrave is invited to continue to act as loyal protector of the new religion and to hold himself aloof from the imperial party. The conclusion contains an angry remark of Luther charging the Emperor with

---

[43] Printed in Luther's *Briefwechsel*, Vol. XII, pp. 326 sqq. An excerpt in Grisar, *Luther*, Vol. IV, pp. 19 sq.

[44] The document declares that, in a very special case, "a husband" might "take another wife with the advice of his pastor."

being utterly devoid of faith and aiming only at mutiny in Germany; pious Christians, Luther contended, are forbidden to associate with him.

It is evident that the acquiescence of the two Wittenberg reformers was dictated by their desire to retain Philip in his rôle of protector of their party.

The other protector of the Protestant cause was the Elector John Frederick of Saxony. Bucer, gratified with his success, at once repaired to his court in order to communicate Philip's plan and the Wittenberg "testimonial" to John Frederick and to put him in a favorable mood by various political promises. Due to his powers of persuasion, Bucer succeeded in obtaining the promise of the Elector "to give his fraternal aid at all times" to Philip in this matter.[45]

On December 23, Philip was in possession of the "testimony" of the two theologians and the favorable reply of the Elector. He caused the theological opinion to be subscribed by his own Hessian theologians, in order that it might carry greater weight. It was signed by Lening, Melander, Corvinus, and three other Protestant ministers. The solemn nuptials were celebrated on March 4 in the chapel of the castle of Rotenburg on the Fulda, in the presence of Bucer, Eberhard von der Thann, who represented the Elector of Saxony, and various other witnesses. Melanchthon also, after a heated argument with the participants, graced the occasion with his presence. Thus, with the aid of the theologians, Philip had taken a step which was fraught with serious consequences.

The new princess was sent to the castle of Wilhelmshöhe, because the Landgrave was still intent upon secrecy. But the impossibility of concealing the marriage soon became manifest. Too many knew the secret. Thus, when Philip sent a barrel of wine to Luther, as a mark of his gratitude, and also remembered Catherine with a gift, the mayor of Lohra openly discussed the destination of the wine in the presence of all the peasants and declared he "knew for certain the prince had taken a second wife." The courts and the aristocracy were informed of the marriage principally through the sister of the Landgrave, Elizabeth von Rochlitz, who was greatly agitated over and vehemently protested against it. Amid tears she proclaimed that Luther and Bucer were consummate villains. The ducal court of Saxony also was apprehensive and indignant. The Elector now began to fear that the Emperor would interfere, on account of the general scan-

---

[45] Grisar, *op. cit.*, IV, pp. 23 sq.

dal, especially since the news had reached King Ferdinand and Rome. It was recalled that, as recently as 1532, the code of laws known as "Carolina" had prescribed "capital punishment" for bigamists.

Due to the universal indignation, the Landgrave, awaking from his dream, began to speak of a reconciliation with the Emperor, nay, even with the Pope. Bucer and his apprehensive Hessian theologians, who were joined by Schnepf, Osiander, and Brenz, urged Philip to extricate himself from his embarrassing situation by publicly passing off Margaret von der Sale as his concubine, and not as his wife, and to have a new and suitable contract drawn up instead of the matrimonial certificate inscribed at Rotenburg; thus, they thought, he might be able to silence the hostile court of Dresden and other opponents. The Landgrave declined, saying that God never permitted lying and that he expected a change of public opinion from the publication of the "testimony" of the Wittenbergers.

This dreadful threat and the whole embarrassing situation promptly became known at Wittenberg, and on June 10, 1540, Jonas wrote to George von Anhalt that Melanchthon was "very much perplexed and Doctor Martin full of thought." [46] Luther's predicament increased when his own elector became very apprehensive and indicated to him through Chancellor Brück that he had gone too far, as universal bigamy might result from his conduct. Luther hit upon a way of extricating himself from this dilemma by suggesting that his "testimony" to Philip of Hesse be represented as a secret advice given in the confessional and consequently subject to the seal of confession. He wrote to his ruler that, even if the Landgrave would publish the document, he would not be ashamed of his Biblical standpoint nor of his advice in an extreme case of conscience, "even should it come before the world." [47] Nevertheless, the danger of publication continued to be a source of terror to him. It does not redound to his credit that he assured the elector that he was not aware at the time he drafted his "testimony" for Philip of Hesse that the noble lady of Eschwege was also at the disposal of the petitioner as a concubine and that he did not expect a new princess, but had hoped that the Landgrave would only "keep an honorable maiden secretly in clandestine marriage to satisfy the great necessity of his conscience, even though it had an illegitimate appearance before the eyes of the world," since

[46] *Ibid.*, p. 36.
[47] *Ibid.*, p. 37.

he (Luther) had given the same advice to various pastors and bishops relative to their housekeepers.

There could be no question here of the seal of confession, though Luther cites the words "confession" and "advice given in confession" as often as three times in this letter. In matter of fact neither the Landgrave nor anyone at Wittenberg thought of confession. What Philip desired was not absolution, but something quite different. And where was there an auricular confession in the ecclesiastical sense which would have entailed the seal? Where was the Landgrave's willingness to perform any action demanded by the secrecy of the confessional, in lieu of the publicity desired by him? Only a natural obligation of secrecy might arise, just as in the case of any delicate and confidential transaction; but this obligation was annulled by the conduct of Philip, who did not care that the sordid reasons for his "necessity of conscience" became even more widely known than they already were.

In this dilemma Luther, on June 27, recommended to the Hessian courtier Eberhard von der Thann that, if hard pressed, the Landgrave should deny the whole affair and declare to the Emperor that he had merely taken a concubine.[48] About the middle of July Luther wrote in a similar vein to another Hessian councillor, who has been identified as the Chancellor John Feige, asking him to state that the Landgrave had contracted no secret union and assuring him that he had answered inquirers by stating that "the Landgrave's other marriage is all nonsense." This, continues Luther, he was justified in doing, on the theory of the secrecy of confession. At the same time he warned the Chancellor that he would strongly resent it if Philip would undertake to make public his (Luther's) "testimonial," and that he (Luther) would know how to "extricate" himself from the quandary. He admitted the impossibility of defending the bigamous marriage "before the world *iure nunc regente*." [49]

Luther's agitation at this time is reflected in his familiar discourses, especially the Table Talks.[50] "I am not pleased with what has happened," he laments; "would that I could alter it!" "Would that it might not become more aggravated!" Since this trial has been imposed upon us by God, "we must put up with the devil and his filth." etc. "The papists may deride us;

[48] *Ibid.*, p. 40.
[49] *Ibid.*, p. 41 sq.
[50] *Ibid.*, p. 43 sqq.

they, however, merit still less pardon on account of their infidelity." In his perplexity he consoles himself with the impending decline of popery. In his habitual manner, he devises acrimonious witticisms: "What do the papists intend to make of this incident? They kill men, whereas we labor in behalf of life, and take several wives."

Luther's chief source of worry is the fear that the Landgrave might come to an understanding with the Emperor and desert the party of the reformers. In mentioning this danger, he exclaims: "He is a strange man"; "he was born under a star; he is bent upon having his own way." It is noteworthy that both Luther and Melanchthon repeatedly suggest the prevalence of hereditary madness in the family of the Hessian ruler. On one occasion Luther said: "This is a fatal curse in his family." Melanchthon said that "this [the bigamous marriage] is the beginning of his [Philip's] insanity."

The haughty Landgrave had undoubtedly at first believed that he would have the whole Protestant world behind him in his bigamous adventure, and that, protected by public opinion, he could afford to ignore the supreme court and the Emperor. The disappointment which he experienced and his subsequent clashes with Luther were all the more apt to impel him to seek a reconciliation with the Emperor.

The fear lest Philip should desert their party and the disgrace resulting from the Landgrave's bigamous marriage affected Melanchthon to such an extent that he became seriously ill in Weimar on his journey to the religious conference to be held at Hagenau. Luther hastened to his bedside, and as a result of his strong exhortations, Melanchthon speedily recovered. In Luther's eyes this was a benevolent dispensation of Providence, which he describes in his correspondence as a "manifest miracle of God." The fanciful embellishment which he gave to the incident when narrating it, has left its traces in his friend Ratzeberger's account.[51] Melanchthon now advanced the excuse that he and Luther had been "deceived" by Philip when they formulated their "advice." That it was a disgraceful matter he concedes. In publishing Melanchthon's letters, Camerarius printed that of September 1, 1540, addressed to him by Melanchthon, only with omissions and additions. The genuine text was not made public until 1904.[52]

Philip of Hesse's bigamy led to an official conference of theo-

---

[51] *Ibid.*, p. 48.

[52] Melanchthon says therein among other matters: "Either love gained the upper hand [in the case of the Landgrave] or [it was] a beginning and prelude to the insanity, which exists in the family."

logians and councillors from Hesse and the electorate of Saxony, which commenced on July 15, 1540, at Eisenach. Luther, too, put in an appearance. He vigorously opposed the intention of the Landgrave not to permit the new marriage to be represented as a form of concubinage and consequently to publish the "testimony" of the Wittenbergers and the fact of his marriage at Rotenburg. In the event that his opinion were to see the light, he (Luther) was prepared to admit that he had "played the part of a fool," to confess his disgrace and beseech God to restore his good name. His idea was either to retract, or to publish the lie that Philip's second wife was a mere concubine. According to the minutes, he declared on the first day of the Eisenach conference: "What harm could it do if a man told a good, lusty lie in a worthy cause and for the sake of the Christian Church?" [53] On July 17 he said: "To lie in case of necessity, or for convenience, or in excuse, would not offend God, who was ready to take such lies on Himself."

Philip, indignant at Luther's attitude, addressed to him a letter in which Luther's threat of retracting the advice and of saying that he had "acted foolishly" was denounced as "a bit of folly." "Nothing more dreadful has ever come to my ears," he writes, "than that it should have occurred to a brave man to retract what he had granted by a written dispensation to a troubled conscience. . . . If you can answer for it to God, why do you fear and shrink from the world?" [54] He finally asks Luther to proceed vigorously against the vices rampant in his own circle and to invoke the ban (which he himself had caused to be introduced) "against adultery, usury, and drunkenness," which are no longer regarded as sins. Sarcastically he adds of his new wife: "I confess that I love her . . . that I should have taken her because she pleased me is only natural, for I see that you holy men also take those that please you."

Luther was unable to appease the wrath of Philip in his reply of July 24, in which he permitted himself to pen the following provocative words: "When it comes to writing, I shall be quite competent to wriggle out of it and to leave Your Grace in the lurch." [55] To which the prince replied that it was a matter of indifference to him whether

[53] Grisar, *Luther*, Vol. IV, p. 51; excerpted from Philip's *Briefwechsel*, ed. by Lenz, pp. 373, 375.

[54] Grisar, *op. cit.*, Vol. IV, pp. 55 sq.

[55] It is significant that in this same letter he threatens to take the Emperor to task because "he raves against the truth of God."

Luther extricated or implicated himself by means of his pen; let him but reflect that the marriages of the Wittenberg preachers were not recognized by the law of the empire, because they had been monks and priests; he, however, looked upon Margaret as his "wife according to God's word and your advice; such is God's will; the world may regard my wife, your wife, and the other preachers' wives as it pleases." [56]

In the same letter he makes grave charges against the Elector John Frederick of Saxony, in order, if possible, to bring him around. He accuses him of having committed an atrocious crime (sodomy) under his (Philip's) roof at Cassel and again at the time of the first diet of Spires. He mentions this matter also in a letter to Bucer (dated January 3, 1541), [57] in which he expresses the belief that he ought to speak in definite terms of this crime because at that time Justus Menius, the "superintendent" of the Elector, boasted of the virtues of his master and threatened to attack the bigamous marriage of the Landgrave in print. Many an ugly rumor was current about the immoral conduct of the Saxon Elector, who was addicted to excessive drinking. Both the Landgrave and the Elector, says the Protestant biographer of Luther, Adolf Hausrath, "did their best to make mockery of the claim of the Evangelicals that their gospel would revive the morality of the German nation." [58]

Bucer wrote from Marburg to Landgrave Philip, in 1539, of the effect which these and other examples of persons in high station was sure to have on the masses: "The people are lapsing into barbarism, and the lascivious state of affairs goes on increasing." And, in a letter written in the same year, Luther applies the expression "a horrible Sodom" to the conditions then existing in Wittenberg and in the Electorate of Saxony.[59]

This side-light on contemporary conditions is indispensable to understand the history of the bigamous marriage of the Landgrave of Hesse.

In a vigorous pamphlet against Philip of Hesse and Luther, written in November, 1540, Duke Henry of Brunswick, an active opponent of Luther and the new theology, proclaimed that the Landgrave had incurred

[56] Op. cit., p. 59.
[57] Op. cit., pp. 202 sqq.
[58] Op. cit., p. 203. Hausrath, Luthers Leben, Vol. II, p. 391.
[59] Grisar, op. cit., IV, pp. 201, 208.

the severe penalty prescribed by the imperial laws, as a result of his bigamous marriage authorized by the biblical experts of Wittenberg. Luther replied to him acrimoniously and abusively in his pamphlet entitled "Wider Hans Worst." For this reason, a reply which the Duke of Brunswick published in May, 1541, characterized Luther as "that most insidious arch-heretic, that impious arch-miscreant and hopeless knave." [60]

About the same time John Lening—that physical and spiritual monster, as Luther and Melanchthon call him—who had been the first to promote the bigamous marriage of Philip, undertook a serious defense of the Landgrave's conduct which was agitating all Germany. He did this in a book entitled "Dialogue of Huldericus Neobulus," which Philip caused to be printed at Marburg. The "dialogue" but vaguely refrains from advocating the universal practice of bigamy. The Wittenbergers believed that Lening aimed at legalizing polygamy. Luther prepared a refutation, which, however, was not published because of the intervention of his elector, who did not wish to add fuel to the fire. Later on he (Luther) himself deemed it better "not to strengthen the clamor" by additional writings and "to have the filth stirred up under the noses of the whole world." [61]

It was not to be marveled at that the obstinate Landgrave, who had never possessed any profound Protestant convictions, having been left in the lurch by Luther, finally resolved to abandon his protectorate over the new theology, and appealed to the Emperor, to whom he made liberal offers which were unfavorable to the Protestant party, but by means of which he expected to arrive at a settlement and to escape the penalty which he had incurred.

The politicians of the imperial court found Philip's offers acceptable. He was permitted to retain Margaret von der Sale, though she was not to be regarded as his wife. All his other mistakes were pardoned. In return, he promised to support the recruiting of soldiers by the imperial forces and to remain neutral in the Emperor's impending campaign against Jülich. As a result of his change of attitude, the Schmalkaldians were forced to sever their connections with the King of France and to forego the assistance of Denmark and Sweden. As a consequence of this move and of Philip's resignation of his command, the power of the Schmalkaldic League was paralyzed.[62] It was the

---

[60] *Ibid.*, pp. 61, 63 sqq.

[61] *Ibid.*, pp. 64 sqq., 67.

[62] G. Kawerau, *Geschichte der Reformation und Gegenreformation*, p. 146; Grisar, *Luther*, Vol. IV, pp. 76 sq.

severest blow which could be inflicted upon the political position of the religious innovators. The way was prepared for the triumph of Charles V over the leaders of the Protestants in the Schmalkaldic War, which was waged soon after Luther's demise (1547). It is not impossible that the wily Hessian Landgrave, when he allied himself with the Emperor, perceived the confused and desperate condition of the Protestant cause and that his change of front was inspired also by a tactical reason. It was legally confirmed by the Treaty of Ratisbon, June 13, 1541.

Luther was bitterly requited for his unfortunate decision of December 10, 1539, wherein he permitted himself to be governed "by political ideas and political manipulations," instead of acting under the inspiration of "the unvarnished truth and an incorruptible conscience," as the Protestant historian Julius Böhmer expresses it. The same historian declares that in this entire affair Luther showed himself to be "weak, nay, flabby in his moral judgments." [63]

Another Protestant, the historian Paul Tschackert, characterizes the Hessian affair as "a dirty story," which is and must remain "a shameful blot on the German Reformation and on the life of our reformers." Theodore Kolde, in a work which is otherwise decidedly favorable to Luther, holds that "the attitude which the reformers took up [towards this affair] at a later date, is even more offensive than Luther's advice itself. He refers to the lie which Luther recommended and which he was prepared to tell, according to his own public declaration. "With devilish logic," says Adolf Hausrath, the Protestant biographer of Luther, "one false step induced them [the Protestant ecclesiastical leaders] to take another which was even worse." [64]

To mitigate these abundant condemnations, an attempt has been made by Protestant writers to hold the Catholic Church and the ideas of the Middle Ages at least partly responsible for Luther's attitude. These writers cite the reformer's opinion in the case of Philip of Hesse as an advice given as a secret matter of conscience, under the seal of confession. The "egg-shells of a previous period of Church history" are said to have clung to the Wittenberg doctor in his "testimonial" to the Landgrave and the ensuing negotiations. It is sufficient to note

[63] *Ibid.*, p. 71.
[64] The quoted and other passages of Protestant historians, *ibid.*, pp. 72, 78 sq.

that these ideas are an invention of Martin Luther, for the "secret of confession" which he claimed, never existed in the Catholic Middle Ages.[65]

Certain established facts, which are generally overlooked in the Protestant condemnation of this affair, are more important than the refutation of the "egg-shell" theory. In the first place, there is a close connection between the "testimonial" of December 10, 1539, and Luther's fundamental attitude towards the Bible. It was only because he disregarded ecclesiastical tradition in the interpretation of Holy Scripture and had accustomed himself to introduce his own ideas into the sacred text, that he was able to discover that the New Testament permitted bigamy in exceptional cases. His attitude towards the authority of the Church must also be taken into consideration. Only because he substituted the subjective opinion of an individual, *i.e.*, his own, for the teaching and governing authority of the Church, which he had repudiated, was he able to propose his own erroneous opinion as a moral guide. Finally, Luther arrived at his lamentable accommodation because Lutheranism was compelled to seek the aid of the secular rulers to insure the permanency of the new Evangel.[66] Hence, it is obvious that the incident casts a shadow upon the entire interior structure of Lutheranism, and that it cannot be regarded simply as an accidental disfiguration.

4. "THE BOLD, LUSTY LIE"

This subject demands a special note. It was part of Luther's theological system. Strange as this statement may sound, yet his attitude towards lying is based upon principles which he formally defended.[67] He taught, and endeavored to demonstrate on diverse occasions, that lying is permitted as a matter of expediency or of necessity, provided that it redounds to the advantage of the new Evangel or to the real benefit of others. He excludes only the lie that works an injury. He proposed this theology of lying as early as 1524. Points of contact with the past were not entirely wanting, notwithstanding the contrary teaching of St. Augustine on the unlawfulness of lying

---

[65] *Ibid.*, pp. 72 sq.

[66] Spontaneously the attention is here directed to the entirely different attitude of the Catholic Church towards Henry VIII's attacks upon the sanctity of matrimony and his introduction of the schism.

[67] For the following cf. Grisar, *Luther*, Vol. IV, pp. 80–178.

in every form. But never before was the lawfulness of lying brought into a system.

By degrees, Luther reduces the lie of convenience or necessity to a virtue. "Lying is a virtue," he says, "if it is indulged in for the purpose of preventing the fury of the devil, or made to serve the honor, the life, and the welfare of one's fellowmen." He likewise regarded it as permissible if intended to secure a personal advantage pleasing to God or, in general, to promote His glory.[68] In confirmation of his attitude he repeatedly appeals to misconstrued examples from the Old Testament.

In the long war which he waged upon the Catholic Church, and which he believed to be for the glory of God, he so habituated himself to the application of his fundamental principle, viz., that everything was permissible in the warfare against Antichrist, as to feel no reluctance in resorting to notorious falsehoods. Indeed, it is probable that, owing to his peculiar practice of auto-suggestion, he finally believed his unfair and offensive inventions, in consequence of his frequent repetition of them, especially since they offered him an apparent composure in his qualms of conscience. The author has collected a veritable arsenal of untrue assertions made by Luther, especially against the "papists," in his larger work on Luther, in which he has also offered a psychological explanation of the strange phenomenon of Luther's mendacity and tried to give an insight into the infectious results of his lying.[69]

[68] Ibid., pp. 108 sqq., 116 sqq., 131 sqq.
[69] Ibid., Vol. IV, pp. 80 sqq.

Chapter XIX

THE ECCLESIASTICAL SCHISM ANTERIOR TO LUTHER'S DEATH

1. THE EVE OF THE RELIGIOUS WAR. THE COUNCIL

In the early forties of the sixteenth century Germany was in a strained condition, politically and religiously, and no signs of an early turn for the better were visible. The Turks, more menacing than ever before, continued their assaults upon the eastern frontiers of the Empire. In 1541 they gained a foothold in Hungary, whence they threatened destruction against Germany. In the west, the King of France was entering upon his fourth war against Charles V, which dragged on from 1542 to 1544.

To fill the measure of domestic misery caused by the religious schism, the Bundestag of Schmalkalden, in March, 1540, declared against the toleration of Catholic worship. The fruitlessness of the religious conference of Worms and of the diet of Ratisbon (up to May 22, 1541) convinced the Catholic spokesmen, John Eck, Julius von Pflug, and John Gropper, as well as all other intelligent observers, that the hope of religious reunion was vain.

The diet of Ratisbon closed with the armistice of the so-called Interim. Two later diets, that of Spires (1542), and that of Nuremberg (1543) endeavored to unite the nation against the Turkish peril. But the Protestants, because of their extravagant religious demands, obstinately refused to come to the assistance of the Emperor, as they were in duty bound to do. The victory of Charles V over the Duke of Cleve, notwithstanding the support which the latter received from France and from the Elector of Saxony, proved to be an advantage for the Catholic cause. In July, 1542, however, that cause was injured by the violent and victorious irruption of the Schmalkaldian forces into the duchy of Brunswick, which resulted in the imprisonment of Henry of Brunswick, the Catholic Duke "Heinz," whom Luther pursued with implacable hatred (October 20, 1545).

Halle, the see city of Cardinal Albrecht of Mayence, which had so long defended itself against Lutheranism, was Protestantized by Justus Jonas through the efforts of Luther, and Albrecht was compelled to establish his residence at Mayence and Aschaffenburg. He transferred his celebrated collection of relics to these and other cities. The antinomian, Agricola, who, to escape the wrath of Luther had taken refuge with the Elector of Brandenburg, supported the measures which that prince employed to promote the Reformation. The religious upheaval continued unimpeded in the duchy of Saxony. The bishop of Meissen, John von Maltitz, complained as early as 1540 to Bishop John Faber, of Vienna, that the Catholic press of his diocese had been reduced to silence, and the prescriptions of the Lutheran "inspectors" were enforced, whilst the bishop was unable to bestir himself. "I fear," he wrote, "that the wrath of God will be visited upon the Pope, the Emperor, and King Ferdinand, because they permit the decline and suppression of the Catholic faith." The deeds of violence, he continued, were too potent; divine services could no longer be conducted at Meissen and the sermons in the local church were preached by a Lutheran minister who had been forced upon the people.[1]

It was a lamentable accommodation by which, in 1543, the new religion was permitted to invade the bishoprics of Münster and Osnabrück. The venerable see of Cologne, the "German Rome," was assailed by the innovators with every prospect of success under the administration of the weak-kneed and uneducated elector, Herman von Wied.

In his reports to Rome, the far-seeing papal legate, Morone, uttered bitter complaints—and not without reason—concerning the attitude of the great majority of German ecclesiastical princes. He charged that many flourishing parts of the German Church had been lost in virtue of their dilatoriness and worldly-mindedness and predicted that the ruin would assume unlimited proportions if the bishops did not arouse themselves and offer resolute resistance.

In consequence of the deficiency of the German resistance, the Emperor also lapsed into a complaisance which displeased the more zealous Catholics. Notwithstanding his loyalty to the Church, he succumbed to the influence of the subversive movement which had been going on for many years. His advisers, even Granvella, were not competent

[1] L. Cardauns, according to Vatican manuscripts in the sixth volume of the *Nuntiaturberichte* (1910), pp. 233 and 237 sq.

to cope with the difficulties of the situation. At the diet of Spires, in February, 1544, the empire made undue concessions to the innovators, although the position of the Emperor had been fortified by the return of Landgrave Philip of Hesse to his former allegiance. In the recess of June the tenth, the religious controversy was adjourned by leaving the adherents of the new theology in substantial possession of their usurped ecclesiastical rights and properties. It was resolved that a "free Christian council of the German nation" should shortly attempt a settlement. The very term, "a free council," was bound to excite the apprehension that the papal authority would be eliminated. If the council were restricted to the German nation and conducted as a mixed spiritual-temporal assembly, composed of Catholics and Protestants, as was to be feared, it was bound to give rise to the greatest anxiety. In either event, the expectations connected with a legitimate general council of Christendom, as planned by the Church authorities, could not be realized.

On November 9 of the same year Pope Paul III convoked the ecumenical council which had so often been deferred because of the belligerency of the times. It was to meet at Trent on the fifteenth of March, 1545.

The Bull of convocation proclaims that it was intended to put an end to the religious schism, to effect the reform of the whole of Christendom, and to achieve unity in the defense of the Cross against the Crescent. On the twelfth of December of the same year, the council was opened by a splendid address by Cardinal Del Monte, the future Julius III. Attended by only thirty-four voting members, the council faced the prospect of being compelled soon to transfer the seat of its deliberations elsewhere. In March, 1547, the state of public affairs forced it to continue its deliberations at Bologna. The opening of the Tridentine Council took place at almost the same time when the congress of the Schmalkaldic League, assembled at Frankfort on the Main, issued its protest against the ecumenical council, which had so often been demanded by the Protestants themselves.

On August 24, 1544, the Pope had addressed grave remonstrances to the Emperor because of the latter's attitude toward the religious schism in Germany.

In a Brief transmitted to Cardinal Morone, which was communicated also to King Ferdinand and the Catholic estates of the empire, he wrote that he was deeply grieved to see that the recess of the diet of Spires excluded from the deliberations of religious affairs the Pope, who from the foundation of the Church had been invested with supreme authority in all such matters. The Emperor had reason to fear the penalties set forth in Holy Writ against those who infringed upon the rights of God and His representatives. The Emperor is not the directive head of the Church, but only its protector. The increasing complaisance of Charles had made the reclamation of the separated brethren all the more difficult. He must withdraw the concessions which (in a spirit of undue clemency) had been made to the enemies of the Church, otherwise, the Pope could no longer be content with mere admonitions.[2]

Owing to his Christian convictions, Charles was not prepared to satisfy the opponents of the papacy by allowing matters to develop into a rupture with Paul III. In defense of himself, he caused an oral reply to be made to some of the charges contained in the papal Brief. "After calm deliberation he could not but perceive that the complaints which were preferred by the Pope with so much determination were not without justification."[3]

In 1556, Charles V, under the pressure of his office, which weighed heavily upon him, transferred his crown to Philip II, and retired to the Spanish monastery of San Yuste, where he spent the remainder of his life.

In opposition to the Catholic estates, and still more in view of the approaching council, the Protestants endeavored to unite their forces and organize more effectively. A result of this endeavor was the so-called "Wittenberg Reformation," which on the fourteenth of January, 1545, Luther and the theologians associated with him at Wittenberg presented to the Elector of Saxony in response to the latter's request for an official demonstration. Melanchthon had drafted the document in such a cautious and apparently mild form that Chancellor Brück wrote that there is "no trace of Doctor Martinus' boisterousness" in it. This "Wittenberg Reformation" treats successively of doctrine, the sacraments, the office of preaching, the episcopal government, etc. It pretends that the bishops ought to be retained— provided they embrace the new theology! This was a well-known and favorite dream of Melanchthon's. He does not speak of forcing new bishops into office. Notwithstanding the fact that the authors of the document appeared to be moderate in their language, the pronounce-

---

[2] The text is most accurately reproduced in Ehses, *Concil. Trident.*, Vol. IV, pp. 364 sqq.; cfr. Pastor, *Geschichte der Päpste*, Vol. V (1909), pp. 504 sq.

[3] Thus Pastor, *l. c.*, p. 507.

ment characterizes the papacy as "idolatry." Whatever might savor of concession is rejected. Only a few external forms of the old Catholic worship are tolerated, mainly as a means of deceiving those who were accustomed to them.[4]

2. "CONSECRATION" OF THE BISHOP OF NAUMBURG AND DEDICATION OF THE CHURCH AT TORGAU

The manner in which Luther at that time intended to proceed with the installation of bishops for his churches, was exemplified in the celebrated case of the "consecration" of Nicholas Amsdorf as "Evangelical bishop" of Naumburg.[5]

The legitimate bishop of this city, Philip, palsgrave of the Rhine and duke of Bavaria, had died in 1541, after exposing his people entirely too much to the infiltrations of Protestanism. The selection of a successor precipitated a crisis, owing to the arbitrary and violent measures taken by the elector, John Frederick of Saxony, who was resolved upon obtaining possession of this ancient and wealthy bishopric. The see of Naumburg was directly subject to the imperial government and enjoyed the personal protection of the emperor. The elector's powers were limited to certain privileges of arbitration. After Bishop Philip's death a Lutheran preacher, Nicholas Medler, in compliance with the elector's instructions, began to function as "superintendent of Naumburg" and to deliver sermons in the cathedral. Soon after the admirable and scholarly provost, Julius von Pflug, was legitimately elected by the chapter. The elector forcibly prevented Pflug from entering upon his new office. He prosecuted the conquest of the city and the territory with such vehemence that his procedure seemed rash even to the Wittenberg theologians. Luther wrote to the elector: "What cannot be carried off openly, may be won by waiting." Pflug, however, was not recognized as bishop by the Wittenbergers, who at first intended to erect only a Lutheran consistory in the city of Naumburg, but changed their mind and favored the appointment of a new bishop by the elector. Up to this time, no steps had been taken anywhere in Germany towards the direct installation of a Protestant bishop. Melanchthon in particular hesitated to go to such lengths, as his "Wittenberg Reformation" evinced.

---

[4] On the "Wittenberg Reformation," see Grisar, *Luther*, Vol. V, pp. 385 sqq.; Vol. III, pp. 448 sq.

[5] For the following see Grisar, *op. cit.*, Vol. V, pp. 192 sqq.

The curious procedure at Naumburg remains practically an isolated case.

Luther and his friends wanted to force the issue by the election of Prince George of Anhalt, canon of Magdeburg and Merseburg, who shared the Wittenberg views. The elector, however, feared that, owing to his position, this prince might not prove an easy tool in his sovereign's hands. Not until 1545 did Prince George attain to the "episcopal dignity," when Luther "consecrated" him bishop of Merseburg, which see had been occupied in 1541 by August, the brother of Duke Maurice of Saxony, and had since then been governed by George as spiritual administrator. The "consecration" of Prince George of Anhalt, besides that of Amsdorf at Naumburg, was the only act of the kind which Luther performed.[6]

In lieu of George von Anhalt, the Saxon elector destined Nicholas von Amsdorf for the see of Naumburg. Amsdorf at the time was actively engaged in preaching Luther's doctrine at Magdeburg. Luther thoroughly approved of the appointment and eulogized Amsdorf in a letter to the elector as "learned and proficient in Holy Scripture, more so than the whole crowd of papists; also a man of good morals and upright life." Melanchthon was not so favorably disposed towards this hot-blooded theologian, nor did he approve of his conduct, but charged him with having had adulterous relations with the wife of his deacon at Magdeburg.

In order to give the proceedings connected with the "consecration" at Naumburg a semblance of legitimacy, the Protestant councillors of that city and of Zeitz, and the Protestant members of the gentry, were asked to vote for Amsdorf. Many of them had sworn everlasting fidelity to the Catholic Chapter under the former bishop. Luther solved their scruples by advising them that no oath taken by the sheep to the wolves could be of any account, and that "no duty could be binding which ran counter to God's commandment to do away with idolatrous doctrine."[7]

On January 20, 1542, Luther himself "consecrated" the new Protestant "bishop" in the sacred precincts of the cathedral of Naumburg. This magnificent structure, one of the most beautiful medieval cathedrals of Germany, a noble type of the later Romanesque and Gothic style, was begun as early as 1045 under Bishop Cadalus, and through

[6] *Ibid.*, pp. 193 sq.

[7] Köstlin-Kawerau, *Martin Luther*, Vol. II, pp. 554 sq.

the mouths of its numerous and wonderful statues of saints and pious princes seemed to utter a loud protest against the unheard-of proceedings within its walls. Many guests of high rank assembled in the choir between the magnificent rood-loft, with its richly ornamented passages, and the altar. The elector had arrived two days previously, accompanied by an escort of 200 mounted knights, all clothed in black. At his side were his brother, John Ernest, and Duke Ernest of Brunswick. The councillors and knights of Zeitz and Naumburg acted as electors and witnesses. In response to an address by Nicholas Medler, they signified their choice in the name of the congregation, to which the people assented by saying "Amen." Luther deemed it very important to emphasize on this occasion his old idea of the importance of the congregation in contrast with the arbitrary action of the elector. The entire ceremony was to proceed in accordance with the example of the earliest centuries of the Church, in which the bishop, as it were, married the congregation of the faithful who had elevated him. The accompanying ancient rites, however, were omitted; above all the transfer of legitimate ecclesiastical jurisdiction to the new "bishop." In place of the neighboring bishops who, in conformity with the practice of antiquity, were wont to participate, three superintendents and an apostate abbot were invited to perform the rite of the laying on of hands. Melanchthon, in his usual weakness, had also complied with the summons to be present.

Luther preached to the superintendents of the Church on the text of St. Paul, where he teaches that "the Holy Ghost hath placed you bishops to rule the church of God." After the sermon Amsdorf knelt before the altar, surrounded by the four assistants, and the "Veni Creator" was sung. Luther reminded the future bishop concerning his episcopal duties, and on the latter giving a satisfactory answer, in common with the four others, he laid his hands on his head; after this Luther alone offered a prayer for him. This was followed by the "Te Deum," sung in German. The "consecration" took place in a manner similar to the ordination of preachers, namely, by imposition of hands and prayer.

Shortly after the ceremony Luther wrote to a friend that it was "a daring act" on the part of the "Heresiarch Luther," which "will arouse much hatred, animosity, and indignation against us"; and that he was hard at work "in hammering out a book on the subject." [8] This

[8] Grisar, *Luther*, Vol. V, p. 195.

book was to justify the "consecration" at Naumburg and to present the procedure as a model. It was composed at the request of the elector and appeared in 1542, under the title *Exempel, einen rechten christlichen Bischof zu weihen* (Example How to Consecrate a Genuine Christian Bishop). In many respects it is opposed to the cautious and mild "Wittenberg Reformation," which knows naught of such an "example of how one might wish to reform bishoprics and organize bishoprics in a Christian manner." Luther states in this book that the new bishop was ordained "without any chrism, without even any butter, lard, fat, grease, incense, charcoal, or any such-like holy things." He dismisses his opponents with insolent remarks, even resorting to language borrowed from the category of human evacuations, and adduces in the following form a list of Catholic apologists: "Doctor Sow (Eck), Witling, Blockhead, Dr. Dirtyspoon (Cochlaeus), Lick-dish, Urinal, Heinz, Mainz, etc. Extensive repetitions, moreover, are characteristic of the book. Luther had evidently overwritten himself. His disgust with life, due to bad health, the forerunner of his fatal sickness, spoiled his work.

In his later correspondence with the new "bishop," Luther refers to Amsdorf's bitter complaint that practically nothing was being done by the elector to establish order in the ecclesiastical régime of Naumburg. Luther bewailed with him that the government "so often take rash steps, and then, when we are down in the mire, snore idly and leave us in the lurch." [9] "All Germany," he says, "presents a terrible scene of demoralization and decadence."

"It is Christ's business to see to this," he writes on another occasion, "since He Himself by His Word has called forth so much evil and such great hatred on the part of the devil." In a pseudo-mystical strain he consoles himself and Amsdorf by reflecting that it would be safest to allow oneself to be "carried along" by the guidance of God, who has created the bishop and disposed everything that has happened. "The blinder we are, the more God acts through us." We can only look forward hopefully to the end of the world.

Amsdorf, the whilom Catholic priest, found little pleasure in his episcopal status. He and his preachers received but a meager sustenance. Soon after Luther's death he was deposed as a result of the decisive victory of the imperial forces over the Schmalkaldic League.

[9] *Ibid.,* p. 197.

He had to retire to Magdeburg, where he did his best to develop that city into a strong citadel of ultra-Lutheranism. In Magdeburg he also wrote his notorious book: "That Good Works are Injurious to Salvation." [10]

Due to the change of events that followed the battle of Mühlberg, in which the Protestant forces were defeated, the venerable cathedral of Naumburg once more decked itself out in festive garments to welcome its legitimate bishop, Julius von Pflug. But the bishopric had been Protestantized, and Catholics were permitted to celebrate divine service only in the cathedral at Naumburg and the collegiate church of Zeitz. A painting in the cathedral, though unfortunately much damaged, preserves the features of the noble Bishop Pflug, who, after a life replete with hardships and disappointments, died in 1564 and was interred in Zeitz. He was particularly saddened by his experiences with the Augsburg Interim of 1548, in the drafting of which he had participated. Pflug's expectation of obtaining papal consent to sacerdotal marriages and the lay-chalice, for the sake of reconciling the non-Catholics, proved futile. Other remedial measures were necessary. It pained him to see how many members of his clergy lived in concubinage in this era of mental and moral confusion—a fact that explains the propositions which he himself and others submitted for the sake of obtaining far-reaching concessions from the Holy See.

After having been so successful in seizing the bishopric of Naumburg, the elector of Saxony sought to obtain control of that of Meissen also. Luther and Amsdorf assisted him in this undertaking. In consequence, a feud (known as the "Wurzer Fehde," after the town of Wurzer) arose between him and the youthful Duke Maurice of Saxony, an adherent of the new religion.[11] In order to terminate the controversy, both parties agreed to divide the spoils. The elector appropriated that part of the bishopric which lay about Wurzen, which he forthwith Protestantized, whilst the remaining part, including Meissen, fell to Duke Maurice, who also exercised violence in religious matters. Both in Meissen and in Wurzen treasures of Catholic art were removed from the churches and dissipated with that brutal barbarity which was employed against so many churches abounding

[10] *Ibid.*, p. 198.

[11] On the "Wurzer Fehde" and Luther's attitude toward the same see Grisar's *op. cit.*, Vol. V, pp. 200 sqq.

in rare and noble works of art.[12] In his feud with the elector, Luther denounced Maurice of Saxony as "a mad blood-hound." For various reasons, this prince developed such a degree of antipathy to Protestantism, that he abandoned the Schmalkaldic League and commenced to gravitate toward the Emperor. As a result, the elector and Luther became all the more intimately allied.

When, in 1544, John Frederick of Saxony had completed the castle-church at Torgau on the Elbe, the first newly erected Protestant church in Saxony, he invited Luther to officiate at its dedication. The ceremony, which Luther performed as if he were a bishop, paralleled the pseudo-consecration of the Protestant bishop of Naumburg. The ancient church ritual was set aside for the "service of the Word." The intimate participation of the congregation in the act, which was supposed to take place in the name of the people, was once more clearly expressed. Luther's sermon, which replaced the rite of consecration, was published by Caspar Creutziger (Cruciger).[13] In it he develops, among others, his doctrine that every Christian believer is a priest. He so strongly emphasized the unity of his act with the congregation that here, too, one is constrained to think of opposition against the elector. In this address he incidentally ascribes to the Christian congregation the right of transferring the celebration of Sunday to some other day of the week, if circumstances demand it. He boldly stated, without fear of contradiction, that man is the master of the Sunday, not Sunday the master of man.[14] Another novelty was the singing of a fugue, composed by John Walther, which contained the words: *"Vive Luthere, vive Melanchthon, vivite nostrae lumina terrae* (Long live Luther, long live Melanchthon, long live the lights of our earth), with an ostentatious amplification of their merits.[15]

3. ATTACKS UPON THE ARCHBISHOPRIC OF COLOGNE AND THE DUCHY OF BRUNSWICK

In 1543 Luther joyfully boasted to Duke Albrecht of Prussia that the archbishopric of Cologne had embraced his Evangel in earnest,

[12] For illustrations see Grisar, *op. cit.*, Vol. V, pp. 203 sqq.; II, 352 sq.; Vol. IV, p. 196; Vol. VI, 277 sq.

[13] Erlangen ed., Vol. II, pp. 218 sq.; Köstlin-Kawerau, M. *Luther*, Vol. III, pp. 573 sq.

[14] Erl. ed., Vol. II, p. 223.

[15] Text, *ibid.*, p. 219.

despite the strenuous opposition of the canons of the cathedral, and that matters were progressing famously in the duchy of Brunswick.[16]

Herman von Wied, archbishop and elector of Cologne, was a worldly-minded man, uninstructed in ecclesiastical matters, of whom Charles V once said to Philip of Hesse: "Why does he start novelties? He knows no Latin, and, in his whole life, has only said three Masses, two of which I attended myself. He does not even understand the Confiteor. To reform does not mean to bring in another belief or another religion." [17]

After 1539 Bishop Herman was persuaded by the preacher Peter Medmann, and still more by Martin Bucer, to effect a change in religion in the archdiocese of Cologne. The powerful resistance which he encountered in his cathedral chapter as well as in the city council led Luther to speak of "seven devils, who sit in the highest temple, whom God will overthrow, who breaks down the cedars of Lebanon." [18] In the courageous defense of the Catholic cause at Cologne, three men distinguished themselves: John Gropper, a member of the secular clergy, a true guiding spirit of the archbishopric in its hour of danger; Eberhard Billick, the learned and indefatigable provincial of the Carmelites, and Peter Canisius, a member of the newly-founded Society of Jesus.

The situation became critical when Melanchthon, in 1543, settled at Bonn and, in conjunction with Bucer, devoted his energies to promoting the plans of the misguided archbishop. Melanchthon wrote a pamphlet against Billick, in which he accuses the Rhinelanders of "idolatry." In order to draw the people away from the Church, he, aided by Bucer, published the so-called "Cologne Reformation," whereby he gained over many Catholics. The Catholic leaders on their part addressed urgent representations against Herman von Wied to the Holy See, and also endeavored to procure the intervention of the Emperor. Herman von Wied, however, issued a summons for a provincial diet to be held at Bonn on January 6, 1546, for the purpose of definitely introducing a new form of religion, which, to the great chagrin of Luther, but conformably with the designs of Bucer and Melanchthon, was a compound of Lutheranism and Zwinglianism.

---

[16] Grisar, *Luther*, Vol. V, p. 166.
[17] *Ibid.*, V, p. 166.
[18] *Ibid.*, p. 233.

The youthful Canisius at that time rendered excellent services to the Church of Cologne, a prelude of his future activity as "Apostle of Germany." He sojourned at Cologne with several brethren of his Order, for the sake of study. When Emperor Charles visited Cologne, in August, 1545, Canisius, then a deacon, eloquent of speech, well informed, and courageous, appeared before that monarch at the urgent importunities of Gropper, and warmly requested him to protect the religion of his Rhenish subjects. The ensuing exhortations and admonitions of the Emperor had no influence upon the archbishop. Before the assembly of the dreaded diet of Bonn, Canisius, already highly esteemed by the citizens of Cologne, was asked to make a hurried trip to the Netherlands, to plead with the Emperor for assistance. He succeeded in obtaining an order which inhibited the archbishop from making any decision in religious questions prior to the next diet. Because of the persistent danger, Canisius, in February, 1546, undertook another journey, and visited the Emperor at Nymwegen, the birthplace of Canisius. In the name of Cologne, he requested the removal from the city of certain clamorous adherents of Archbishop Wied, and an imperial letter to the magistrates, encouraging them in their opposition to the religious innovation.[19] The efforts of the Catholic leaders of Cologne resulted in the deposition and excommunication of the Archbishop on April 16, 1546. After this Herman von Wied disappears from history. He was succeeded by a zealous Catholic, Adolf von Schaumburg. Cologne was saved to the faith and continued to be a citadel of the Catholic religion and the heart of the Catholic Rhineland. In the same year, 1546, the year of Luther's death, Canisius, who was afterwards canonized by the Church, was ordained to the priesthood and published a Latin edition of the works of St. Cyril of Alexandria and a revised text of the writings of Pope St. Leo the Great, in order to demonstrate the traditional teaching of the Church.

In Northern Germany, Duke Henry of Brunswick-Wolfenbüttel was the militant leader of the Catholic league against the Schmalkaldians. This position made him highly obnoxious to Luther and his friends, but their hatred was augmented by his defense of the Catholic cause in writing. His forceful attacks upon the bigamous mar-

---

[19] The visits of P. Canisius to the Emperor are mentioned by O. Braunsberger, *Petrus Canisius*, 2nd and 3rd ed., 1921, p. 32. Relative to the last journey, Braunsberger remarks, without indicating his source: "first revealed through the latest researches."

riage of Philip of Hesse provoked Luther to write his pamphlet "Wider Hans Worst," which was directed against Duke Henry. Luther followed this up with a bitter incitement against the "bloodhound and incendiary Heinz," as he styled the militant Duke.

For the rest, his criticism of the private life of Duke Henry was not unfounded. Not only his controversial methods, but also his moral character were quite objectionable. But the charge of arson in the territories of the new religion, which Luther made against him, was the product of a morbid imagination.[20] It is rumored, he says, that "Heinz" has dispatched "many hundreds of incendiaries against the Evangelical estates." He maintained in all seriousness "that the Pope is said to have given 80,000 ducats towards it." History is ignorant of any such transaction. Certain alleged confessions extorted on the rack have no significance.

In 1542, when Duke Henry attempted to enforce the ban which the Imperial Supreme Court had declared against the city of Goslar, the war which the Elector of Saxony and the Landgrave of Hesse had long prepared against him, finally broke out. Luther was aware at that time of prophecies which foretold the end of the "son of perdition,"—a "warning example, instituted by God, for the tyrants of our time." [21] The two allied Protestant princes took possession of the Duke's territory and committed many atrocities. They introduced Protestantism there with the aid of Luther and especially Bugenhagen. Due to Henry's determination to regain his principality, a new war broke out in 1545, which ended in even more striking success for his enemies, who took the Duke captive.

When, in deference to the Emperor, Philip of Hesse and others favored the release of Duke Henry, Luther published an open letter to Philip and the elector,[22] in which he characterizes the idea of setting free that "mischievous, wild tool of the Roman idol," as an open attack not merely on the Evangel, but even on the manifest will of God, as clearly displayed in the recent war, which had been waged "by His angels." In this remarkable document Luther rose to the pinnacle of his morbidly mystical conception of life: God Himself has kindled this conflagration against his adversaries, God, who calls Himself a consuming fire. His friends, as well as he, had

---

[20] Grisar, *Luther*, Vol. IV, pp. 293 sq.

[21] *Op. cit.*, Vol. V, p. 236.

[22] Erl. ed., Vol. XXVI, ii, pp. 251 sqq.; De Wette, *Briefe*, VI, pp. 385 sqq. Cfr. Grisar, *Luther*, Vol. V, pp. 394 sq.

always prayed and clamored for peace, but "the pope and the papists would gladly see us all dead, body and soul, whereas we for our part would have them all to be body and soul happy, together with us." [23] Luther represents this document as his own exclusive and personal affair. "Nevertheless," says Köstlin-Kawerau, "it is not to be doubted" that Luther "performed a task that had been ordered with the intention of influencing the Landgrave." [24] Chancellor Brück had inspired him with the ideas set forth in that document, for it was extremely important to the elector to prevent the release of Duke Henry.

The last armed champion of the Catholic cause in Northern Germany succumbed with Henry of Brunswick. Not until the Schmalkaldic War of 1547, after Luther's death, did a favorable change come, at least temporarily.

[23] *Ibid.*, p. 395.
[24] Köstlin-Kawerau, *Martin Luther*, Vol. II, p. 612.

CHAPTER XX

LUTHER'S FINAL STRUGGLES AND DEATH

1. THE MILITANT SPIRIT OF LUTHER IN WORD AND PICTURE

During the first half of the forties, the thought of death frequently engaged the mind of Luther. His apprehension was most strongly expressed on November 10, 1545, when he celebrated his sixty-first birthday in the circle of his friends, Melanchthon, Bugenhagen, Cruciger, Major, Paul Eber, and some others, who surrounded him at the festive board. He said then that he would not live to see Easter and spoke sorrowfully of the future apostasy of certain brethren, which would inflict a blow upon the Gospel greater than any of which the papists were capable, who, for the most part, were rude, ignorant Epicureans. He spoke of his impending death in a similar vein, though less definitely, in his declining years.

And yet these years furnish an exemplification of the incessant activity of this man, who was afflicted with melancholia. His literary productions, some of which have already been noted above, must be considered first.

With his impetuous pen he commenced a vigorous onslaught on the Jews and the Jewish religion. In the first years of his public career he had spoken of them in a different tone. At that time, as we have seen above, he harbored the seductive idea that they might be converted to the new Evangel. His treatise of 1523 was inspired by this visionary idea.[1] The acceptance of his Gospel on the part of the Jews was to be a divine seal of approval. But his expectations came to naught. As a result, indignation at their infidelity, their blasphemies against Christianity, and their oppression of non-Jews in Germany, took hold of him. With the sanction of Luther, John Frederick expelled the Jews from electoral Saxony in 1536, whilst King Ferdinand granted them an asylum in his territories.

Luther first proceeded against the infidelity and proselytizing zeal

[1] Grisar, *Luther*, Vol. V, pp. 411 sq.

of the Jews in his "Epistle against the Sabbatarians," published in 1538. The Jews had succeeded in introducing the observance of the Sabbath and other rites in some localities, even among Christians. Then, commencing with 1542, he launched a violent attack, intended to annihilate the hostile Jewry. In the year mentioned he published his tract "On the Jews and their Lies." [2] Immediately afterwards he completed his tract, "On Shem Hamphoras and the Generation of Christ"—a work which exhibits greater forcefulness, but overflows with attacks and is saturated with vulgarities.[3] Shem Hamphoras (or "peculiar name"), according to Luther, was a cabbalistic formula of the Jews, supposed to be endowed with great power, by means of which Jesus was alleged to have wrought His miracles. In 1543 followed another literary attack upon the Jews, which bore the title: "On the Last Words of David." [4] An ardent zeal for outraged Christianity is reflected in these productions, which bear evidence of an agitated frame of mind. Luther's zeal for truth and justice, however, does not improve matters because that work abounds in extravagant appeals to inflict violence upon a race struck with religious blindness and weighed down by injustice.

Once more he raised his voice against that persecuted race in his last sermon at Eisleben, on February 14, 1546: [5] "You rulers," he said, "ought not to tolerate, but to expel them." By indirection it was a summons to rise against the Jews, who were favored in the neighboring country of Mansfeld, but had become notorious by their fraudulent and usurious practices.

Usury was an evil which Luther also attacked in other vigorous pamphlets. Having written two sermons against it as early as 1519 and 1520, and having condemned it anew in his tract, "On Commerce and Usury," written in 1524,[6] he once more returned to this favorite topic in 1540, when he wrote his "Appeal to Pastors to Preach against Usury." [7] Although he manifested an exaggerated zeal against the abuses connected with money loans, he revealed no

[2] Weimar ed., Vol. LIII, pp. 412 sqq.; Erl. ed., Vol. XXXII, pp. 99 sqq.; cfr. Grisar, op. cit., Vol. V, pp. 402 sqq.

[3] Weimar ed., Vol. LIII, pp. 573 sqq.; Erl. ed., Vol. XXXII, pp. 275 sqq.; cfr. Grisar, op. cit., Vol. V, pp. 404–407.

[4] Erl. ed., Vol. XXXVII, pp. 1 sqq.

[5] Grisar, op. cit., Vol. VI, p. 374.

[6] Grisar, op. cit., Vol. VI, pp. 86 sqq.

[7] Weimar ed., Vol. LI, pp. 331 sqq.; Erl. ed., Vol. XXIII, pp. 282 sqq.; Köstlin-Kawerau, Martin Luther, Vol. II, p. 432; Grisar, l. c.

insight into the commercial and trade relations whose development had then practically begun, and which appeared to justify a fair rate of interest on loaned capital. He condemns interest-taking outright,[8] and makes but one exception, by granting that the aged and widows and orphans might, if necessary, exact interest on loans in order to secure a livelihood.

An "Exhortation to Prayer against the Turks," which he wrote in 1541, is superior in tone and contents to Luther's previous pamphlets against the Turks.[9] The elector had urged the people to pray against the Saracen menace, which constantly grew more threatening. It is the will of God, Luther declares, that Christians should beseech the Lord for aid in a penitential spirit and sincere faith. The Turk and the pope are on the decline and Judgment Day will soon console the faithful. We have here a repetition of the thoughts on which he delighted to dwell in view of his approaching death. His "Computation of the Years of the Word" (*Supputatio Annorum Mundi*), which is in line with this tendency of his mind, appeared in the same year and was re-edited with alterations in 1545.[10] His dreams of Antichrist and the end of the world form the subject-matter of his work on "The Twelfth Chapter of Daniel," which was published at the same time.[11]

This series was followed by a preface to Ezechiel, as well as two works, not devoid of merit, which were intended to combat the Koran, and his booklet, "Consolation for Wives who have not Fared well in Bearing Children," a practical work designed to meet the spiritual wants of the nation. In 1543 began the publication of his lectures on Genesis, based upon notes made by his hearers under the editorship of Vitus Dietrich. Luther himself at this time, was engaged in the interpretation of the Messianic prophecies of Isaias, a work which was published only after his death.

His "Brief Profession of Faith in the Blessed Sacrament" (1544) [12] was the fruit of the deeply felt need of once more settling accounts with those who opposed his teaching of Christ's real presence in the Eucharist. "I, who am about to die," he says, "wish to take with me before the judgment seat of my Lord this testimony, that, in com-

---

[8] Thus Köstlin, *l. c.*

[9] Weimar ed., Vol. LI, pp. 585 sqq.; Erl. ed., Vol. XXXII, pp. 74 sqq.; Köstlin-Kawerau, *Martin Luther*, Vol. II, p. 563. Cfr. Grisar, *op. cit.*, Vol. V, pp. 167, 417 sqq.

[10] Weimar ed., Vol. LIII, pp. 151 sqq.

[11] Erlangen ed., Vol. XLI, pp. 294 sqq.

[12] *Ibid.*, Vol. XXII, pp. 396 sqq.

pliance with God's command in Tit. III, 10, I have earnestly condemned and avoided the fanatics and adversaries of the Sacrament,
Karlstadt, Zwingli, Oecolampadius, Stenkefeld (*i. e.*, Schwenckfeld),
and their disciples at Zurich, or wherever they may be." He answers
their objections with the question, whether, by the same token, they
are not compelled to deny belief in the humanity and divinity of
Christ. "We must," he says, "either believe everything, wholly and
entirely, or nothing." For God is omnipotent. The adversaries, with
their "infernal hearts and lying mouths" are not even deserving of
prayer.

This angry tract was occasioned by the new movement of the Swiss
reformers against belief in the Real Presence and by the above-
mentioned so-called "Reformation of Cologne," composed by Melanchthon and Bucer, which, to the chagrin of Luther, spoke in
Bucer's sense of a purely spiritual communion with the body and blood
of Christ in the Last Supper.[13] Melanchthon, who had collaborated in
the "Reformation of Cologne," was worried about himself and his
fate. It was said at Wittenberg that Luther was about to propose a
formula to which all would be compelled to subscribe. When this
formula ("Brief Creed") appeared, there was rejoicing because it
contained no reference to Melanchthon and Bucer. Luther had suppressed his chagrin and did not care to cast suspicion upon these men
in public. All the more ruthlessly, however, did this tract sever his
relations with the Swiss innovators, which, notwithstanding the theological controversies, had gradually become more tolerable.

The Swiss reformers soon issued energetic counter-declarations.
Bullinger, above all, entered the lists against Luther with his "True
Creed" of the Zurich theologians,[14] in which he states that the abusive
language of the Wittenbergers would not be reciprocated by him. He
severely censured the violent and indecent effusions of an aged and
otherwise highly respected man, and especially the autocratic manner
of his decisions. The theological reasons which Bullinger advances for
the Eucharistic beliefs of Zwingli's disciples are not very impressive.

Whilst Melanchthon was still engaged in the composition of his
cautious "Wittenberg Reformation," which was intended to be a
programme in opposition to the Council of Trent, which was then
commencing, Luther summoned all his available strength to deliver

---

[13] Köstlin-Kawerau, *Martin Luther*, Vol. II, p. 581.
[14] Cfr. Grisar, *Luther*, Vol. IV, pp. 325 sq.; Vol. V, p. 409.

a new blow against the papacy, for his hatred was not yet quenched. This fresh outburst was contained in a work, the first part of which bore the title, "Against the Papacy at Rome founded by the Devil" (1545).[15] He attacks the papacy along the entire line and frequently in a furious fashion, because it refused to succumb to his assaults, nay, even dared to gain new vigor at the Council. Luther held that the papacy originated in hell and was sustained by infernal powers. This is drastically illustrated by a picture on the title page of this pamphlet,[16] which represents the pope seated on his throne in the widely distended and terrible jaws of hell, and borne upward by ropes drawn by devils. Whilst adoring the prince of hell, who flees before him, he is crowned with a tiara which tapers into a point composed of human excrements.

We may be permitted to omit quotations from this horrible pamphlet, which contains repetitions of former ideas, but clothed in forms which seem to force an irrevocable decision concerning the mental state of its author, which, as is known, frequently obtruded itself upon the reader of his former writings.[17]

Luther arrived at the unfortunate resolution of publishing this pamphlet with illustrations.

He had already increased the number of his previously published polemical illustrations by some which were calculated to arouse the brutal passions of the masses.[18] One pamphlet depicted the pope as Satan.[19] A frightful, savage and nude giant, with an immense tail, wears the triple crown and is adorned with the ears of an ass. In his right hand he holds the trunk of a tree resembling a club; in his left, which is extended in a threatening manner, he holds a large, broken key. Amid fire and smoke, this "pope-ass" expectorates worms and filth, like the dragon in the Apocalypse (c. XVI). The wings of a bat, serrated after the manner of flames, can be seen on his back. Beneath him, the fires of hell burst forth. A devil wearing a cardinal's hat and seated at the right on a papal Bull, devours a bishop, and allows his excrements to drop upon the papal seal.

[15] Erl. ed., Vol. XXVI, ii, pp. 131 sqq.
[16] Grisar and Heege, *Luthers Kampfbilder*, n. 4 (*Lutherstudien*, V), p. 20.
[17] Passages from this pamphlet quoted in Grisar, *Luther*, Vol. V, pp. 381 sqq., 421 sqq.; Vol. III, p. 151.
[18] Cf. Grisar und Heege, *Luthers Kampfbilder*, n. 2 and 3.
[19] *Ibid.*, n. 4, plate 2, with text, pp. 67 sqq.

One series of controversial illustrations furnished by Luther is entitled, "Illustrations of the Papacy." It was published in 1545 and was intended to illustrate, as it were, his "Papacy founded by Satan." It contains the following caricatures:[20] "The Pope-Ass of Rome, a monster found in the Tiber in 1496"; the ascent of the pope from hell; the mockery of the ban by two rogues with exposed backs and emitting blasts of wind against the pope. Again, there are illustrations deriding the papal government by the most crude defilement of the papal arms, depicting a wretch discharging his faeces into them whilst two others are getting ready to follow his example. Another illustration depicts the great keys on the papal arms as master-keys in the hands of thieves. The fifth illustration shows the manner in which the papacy rewards the emperors—the fictitious decapitation of Conradine by the hand of a pope. Sixth, there is "the reward of the most Satanic pope and his cardinals," represented by the death of the pope on the gallows in the company of two cardinals and a priest. The seventh and eighth cartoons, which appear on one page, represent the pope riding a sow and offering to the world steaming human excrements with his blessing, which was designed to be an insult to the proposed Council; the other illustration (intended to be a mockery of the pope's biblical exegesis) depicts him in the capacity of an ass performing on the bag-pipe. The last and ninth cartoon is designed to suggest that the pope was born of a nude she-devil, a scene vulgar beyond all description.

A wood-cut, which depicts Pope Alexander III placing his foot on the neck of Emperor Barbarossa, as well as the pope-ass above described, do not belong to this series. The two repulsive illustrations of the origin of Antichrist, i. e., the papacy, and the origin of the monastic life, were free supplements, for which Luther seems to be partially responsible. The entire collection has become extremely rare, owing probably to the outraged sensibilities of those who were offended by them. In recent times, these cartoons have been resubmitted to the public in the interests of history, but not by partisans of Luther.[21]

Luther's active participation in the "Illustrations of the Papacy" has been placed beyond question by recent research. He even as-

[20] *Kampfbilder*, n. 4.
[21] *Ibid.*, plate 3 and text, pp. 92 sqq.

sisted the "artist" with his crayon, besides contributing the ideas and the crude verses that accompanied the cartoons.[22] His name is attached to the illustrations of the series, as well as to the cartoon of the pope-devil. The drawings themselves were without exception the product of his confidant, Lucas Cranach, an artist who had previously achieved fame by his fine religious paintings.

Hence, it is historically untenable if Protestant authors hold Cranach solely responsible for the disgraceful cartoons of the papacy and ascribe only the text to Luther. These illustrations are his spiritual property in the fullest sense of the word, and Luther himself described them as his last will and testament to the German nation.[23]

He expressed the wish that these cartoons might enter every home and workshop, and thus bear effective witness against the papacy.

Luther did not even shrink from designing a cartoon which represented the death of the pope on the gallows, clearly intended to provoke deeds of violence.[24] This cartoon deserves special mention because of its sanguinary and inciting character. The pope is distinguishable as the then reigning pontiff, Paul III. His tongue has been pulled out of his throat, and an executioner is engaged in nailing it to the gallows, as had already been done to three others who had been hanged thereon, namely, Cardinal Albrecht of Mayence, Cardinal Otto Truchsess of Augsburg(?), and the priest Cochlaeus(?). Four devils convey the souls of the executed felons to hell. Despite his exhortations to the contrary, there are numerous passages in the writings of Luther which incite, or are apt to incite, to sanguinary deeds of violence against the clergy and the monks.[25] Of course, it cannot be inferred from such expressions of passionate rage that Luther was actually prepared to indorse the assassination of ecclesiastical dignitaries, or personally to take a hand in them. It is quite patent, however, that bloody results were apt to follow the dissemination of cartoons such as those described, especially the last brutal gallows scene, in conjunction with Luther's sanguinary cries for violence.

[22] *Ibid.*, pp. 73 sqq., 86, p. 89, p. 91 and the testimony of Christoph Walther, Aurifaber, and Amsdorf. Luther had some proficiency in drawing; cf. *Kampfbilder*, n. 3, pp. 59 sqq.

[23] *Kampfbilder*, n. 4, p. 86.

[24] *Ibid.*, plate 1 in actual size, and text, p. 26.

[25] *Ibid.*, pp. 137–139, where twelve passages are quoted. Cf. the cartoon published by Luther in 1538, which picture Paul III as Judas. (*Kampfbilder*, n. 4, p. 4.)

2. IN THE MIDST OF RUINS

Many contemporary writings contain doleful lamentations, not only on the part of Protestants, but also on that of Catholics, concerning the decay of the internal life of the Church brought about by the Protestant Reformation. Thus when, in 1549, John Cochlaeus printed the preface to his great work, "On the Work and Writings of Luther," he deplored the wounds of the Church in melancholy terms.[26] He was grieved, above all, by the unhappy lot of the souls that had been severed from the Church, the fountain of salvation. "The bond of charity and concord which unites Christian people," he says, "has been loosened, discipline undermined, reverence for God destroyed, wholesome fear extinguished, and obedience cast aside. In lieu of these prevail sinfulness and a freedom that is alien to God." This courageous defender of the Church died at Breslau in the year 1552.

John Wild, who died two years later, was a distinguished cathedral preacher of Mayence and a Franciscan Observantine. He paints an impressive picture of the moral decadence which had set in and proved so detrimental to Catholic religious life.[27] "Alas," he exclaims, "all fear of God is driven out of the hearts of men by dint of sermons lacking all sense of modesty and urging faith alone. . . . The other, namely, good works, has been trodden in the mire. The result is that we are now for the most part Christians merely in name, but so far as works are concerned, more depraved and wicked than even Jews or Turks. The cause of the very grievous sufferings of the Church," he says, is "that her children have been and are so lamentably led astray that they refuse any longer to acknowledge their own mother."

With depressed feelings Wild views his German fatherland torn by factions and become a byword to its neighbors. "Everybody wants a bit of us." People say: "Ha, these are the haughty Germans who . . . have a finger in every war; now they are going to set to on each other."

Duke William of Bavaria, another opponent of the Reformation, presented the diet of Ratisbon (1541) with a memorial in which he bitterly complained of the "great injury and corruption" into

---

[26] *Commentaria de Actis*, etc., part I, Cfr. Grisar, *Luther*, Vol. IV, pp. 365 sq.

[27] Cf. N. Paulus, *Johann Wild* (*Dritte Vereinsschrift der Görresgesellschaft*, 1893), p. 15; Grisar, *Luther*, Vol. IV, pp. 366 sq.

which his fellow-Catholics were being led by the Protestantizers. "Contrary to the commandment of God, in defiance of law and Christian usages . . . churches and monasteries are seized by force . . . religious foundations and property are torn from them mercilessly." And yet "the Catholics have no dearer wish than order and justice."[28] Once more the religious and judicial grievances of the Catholics were prominently brought forward at the diet of Worms (1545). It was maintained that the opponents of the faith were suppressing everything; yet they complained about being suppressed themselves. "What the Protestants call proclaiming the Word of God, is for the most part, as they themselves complain, mere slander and abuse of the pope." "Nothing constant any more," says the Cologne Doctor Carl von der Plassen, "discipline, loyalty, and respectability have vanished." He is pained to observe the evil reaction of the religious innovation on the lives of Catholics. "What misery results from want of clergy and schools even in the lands which have remained Catholic!"

Besides the alarming increase in the number of violations of sacerdotal celibacy, already mentioned above, the decrease in the reception of the sacraments and attendance at divine worship in the Catholic parts of Germany was especially lamentable. Thus Peter Canisius complains in his letters about Ingolstadt that communions in that Catholic city had practically ceased. He writes in 1550 that, although two bells are rung to summon the people to Mass, which is said in a church located in the center of the city, "still, we cannot induce two persons to attend Mass, even if we would pay them for coming." The law of fasting had become practically obsolete in the academy known as the Georgianum.[29] In Austria the state of Catholicism was scarcely less disheartening. Esteem for the clergy had profoundly declined. Almost in no wise did the shepherds measure up to the tasks of their vocation. Monastic discipline had deserted most of the cloisters. Ignorance and barbarity prevailed among the masses. The University of Vienna had deteriorated very appreciably. In the course of twenty years this institution, which had formerly yielded such abundant fruits for the Church, scarcely produced one student a year for the priesthood.[30]

Luther always tried hard to propagate his doctrines in Austria.

---

[28] For these and the following two passages see Grisar, *op. cit.*, Vol. IV, pp. 367 sq.
[29] Braunsberger, *Canisius*, 2nd and 3rd ed., 1921, pp. 44–47.
[30] *Ibid.*, pp. 51 sq.

Among others, he endeavored to attract the Moravian Brethren to his cause. Notwithstanding important variations of doctrine, he treated the senior of the Brethren, who came to Wittenberg in 1540 and again in 1542, with great distinction. He exhorted the Brethren in writing to persevere with him to the end in unity of doctrine and spirit, since he expected soon to depart this life.[31] Wittenberg did not adopt any part of the ecclesiastical discipline which the Moravian Brethren maintained. Nor was there ever any spiritual connection between them. Later on, in 1772, the congregation of Moravian Brethren (Herrnhuter) in Saxony resulted from a rapprochement between Lutheranism and the Brethren.

In Transylvania, also, efforts were made, towards the end of Luther's life, to effect a closer union with Wittenberg and an increased separation from Rome. In 1542, the preacher William Farel despatched a letter from Metz requesting a union of the followers of the new religion with the Schmalkaldic League. About this time overtures were begun in Vienna for the sake of obtaining Luther's advice and direction. They were, however, devoid of notable results. Italy was preserved from religious subversion by the watchfulness of the Inquisition. For the rest, the weakness of the new religion was too little known abroad.

The extent to which authority, spiritual as well as temporal, was shaken in consequence of Luther's rebellion against the ancient faith, became clearly manifest in Germany. Preachers who were highly esteemed by Luther were treated with contempt and derision by their own followers. Wenceslaus Link, once the honored successor of Staupitz as vicar of the Augustinians, was derisively hailed in Nuremberg as "Pfaff" by the magistrates whilst carrying on his Protestant activities in that town. Luther consoled him by writing: "The civil authorities have ever been, and always will be, enemies of the Church." "Our respected domestic opponents," he continues, "are dangerous to us, according to the prophecy: 'After the revelation of Antichrist, there will come men who say, there is no God!' "[32] "Each will desire to be his own rabbi," he says on another occasion, "whence the greatest devastation will ensue."[33]

Under Link as vicar-general, the Augustinian congregation began

[31] Köstlin-Kawerau, *Martin Luther*, Vol. II, p. 579.
[32] Grisar, *Luther*, Vol. V, p. 325.
[33] *Tischreden*, Weimar ed., Vol. III, n. 3900.

to decline. The three succeeding vicars witnessed its complete ruin. The Saxon province of the Order also fell a victim to the religious innovation. Its own members promoted subversion and confusion.[34] Melanchthon, and still more Bucer, continued to cherish the fervent hope that, during the prevalence of this state of confusion, "our princes and estates will bring about a council or some kind of harmony in doctrine and worship, lest everybody proceed on his own responsibility" (Melanchthon). That a council would only be productive of greater disunion, Luther perceived more clearly than the others. The reason was because there was no sanction, and this was the permanent cause of the ruination.

"In God's kingdom, in which He rules through the Gospel," Luther taught as a fundamental truth of his theology, "there is no going to law, nor have we anything to do with law, but everything is summed up in forgiveness, remission and bestowing, and there is no anger or punishment, nothing but benevolence and service of our neighbor." [35] As a consequence, doctrines and ethical precepts were invalidated, as there was no authority to enforce them. Luther's system is altogether devoid of an authoritative foundation, such as the Catholic Church possesses in her constitution; everything is "opinion and advice," as he himself avers.[36] He is neither able nor does he desire to lay down precepts. Since, however, he cannot afford to do without some force that binds men, he appeals to civil authority, to the State, which must be Lutheran, and to which he even ascribes the right of deciding doctrinal controversies, provided only that the decision is "in conformity with Scripture." In this manner—as the Protestant theologian, Christopher Ernest Luthardt, is compelled to acknowledge in his *Ethik Luthers*—Luther arrived at propositions which are "at variance with his fundamental views," and at suppositions concerning the secular authority "which he decisively denies where he lays down principles." [37]

Nor did Luther have an authoritative argument by which he might have convinced those of his opponents who denounced the Blessed Trinity, as happened first in Protestant Nuremberg, if the civil government did not proceed against them. He and Melanchthon refused

[34] Cfr. Kolde, *Die deutsche Augustinerkongregation*, Gotha, 1879, last chapter.
[35] Grisar, *op. cit.*, Vol. V, p. 565.
[36] *Ibid.*, p. 566.
[37] *Ibid.*, p. 567.

to reply to Campanus, who denied the Trinity, lest they advertise his opinions.

Antinomianism, for which Luther had persecuted Agricola, continued its course beneath the ruins, being promoted by the eloquent and active Jacob Schenck, who was for a time court-preacher at Weimar. In a sermon which he delivered at Eisenach in 1540, Luther discovered a confirmation of his suspicion that Schenk's "opposition to the law" furnished the common people with an occasion of moral laxity. Schenk was called to the electoral court of Joachim of Brandenburg, as assistant to the antinomian Agricola, and it is claimed that he starved himself to death in a spell of melancholia.[38] When Agricola again visited Wittenberg, in company with his wife and daughter, in 1545, the old differences manifested themselves anew; despite the fact that he brought with him a letter of recommendation from his elector. Luther refused to see the "arrogant and impious fellow," as he had branded him on a former occasion, though he received his wife and daughter. After Luther's death, Agricola, bowing to the situation that existed at the Brandenburg court, posed as a defender of genuine Lutheranism against the "Philippists," i.e., the adherents of Melanchthon. The solemn religious services which he conducted in honor of the Reformation in the court-chapel at Berlin, in 1563, were a sort of triumphal assertion of what pretended to be orthodox Lutheranism. "Thus the man whom Luther had proscribed, contributed to the triumph of rigorous Lutheranism."[39] Agricola died during an epidemic in 1566.

Another characteristic feature of the spreading theological ruin was Agricola's impassioned opposition to Melanchthon's revision of the Augsburg Confession, the so-called *Confessio Variata* of 1540. Melanchthon, as is well known, underwent a process of theological development which took him farther and farther away from Luther. He interpreted essential portions of the Augsburg Confession, which he himself had composed in 1530, so that Agricola spoke of the "Variata" as a "falsified" Confession and availed himself of Melanchthon's arbitrary changes as an argument in his indictment of "Philippism." Melanchthon, on his part, stated at the religious conference of Augsburg that the only changes he had made were certain modifications

[38] Köstlin-Kawerau, *Martin Luther*, Vol. II, p. 467.
[39] Kawerau in the *Realenzyklopädie für Theologie*, etc., Vol. I, 3rd ed., p. 253.

of language with a view to greater clearness of doctrine.[40] The doctrines of justification, good works, and penance, however, had actually been altered in accordance with the ideas which Melanchthon had proposed in 1535 in his *Loci Theologici,* and which approximated the Catholic teaching. The propositions on the Last Supper reveal concessions to the Swiss reformers, who denied the real presence of Christ in the Eucharist. "That there was question of actual changes, ought never to have been denied," writes Theodore Kolde, a Protestant authority on Luther.[41] Luther himself never publicly rejected the "Confessio Variata." He did not wish to provoke an open breach with his learned and indispensable ally. But after his death Melanchthon experienced the ill-will of the theologians of the New Gospel. How bitterly he felt it may be gathered from the fact that, shortly before his demise (April 19, 1560), he wrote with his own hand that among the reasons why he did not fear death so much was this: "You will be delivered from all trouble and the fury of the theologians." [42]

A compliant attitude towards dogma, similar to that of Luther towards Melanchthon's "Confessio Variata," is discovered in the position taken by both these men toward the Articles of Agreement elaborated by the English Protestants in 1536, proposing a union between Anglicanism and Lutheranism. At that time it was a question of winning over an important country.[43] After the attempt had failed, the German reformers were rewarded by hostility on the part of the new Anglican Church toward Lutheranism. Luther himself declared that he was glad to be rid of the "blasphemer" (Henry VIII).[44] He was very much depressed, however, when the King (in 1540) executed Luther's friend Barnes, who had played the rôle of mediator for years between Wittenberg and Henry VIII. Barnes was put to death as a heretic because he promulgated Luther's doctrine of justification.

A strong rival of Luther's ecclesiastical polity appeared during the declining years of his life in Calvinism, which deviated widely from the Wittenberg school. John Calvin, who had established his politico-religious rule at Geneva, in 1541, began by opposing Luther's assertion of the real presence of Christ in the Eucharist. The Genevan

[40] Grisar, *Luther, l. c.*

[41] *Symbolische Bücher,* ed. by H. T. Müller, 10th ed., Introduction, p. XXV.

[42] Cfr. Grisar, *op. cit.,* Vol. V, p. 265.

[43] G. Mentz; cfr. Grisar, *op. cit.,* Vol. V, p. 260.

[44] Köstlin-Kawerau, *Martin Luther,* Vol. II, p. 400.

innovator flatly denied this doctrine and described the intentionally vague formulas of Melanchthon and Bucer as "mere vaporing," intended to deceive their opponents. Also with regard to predestination, Calvin discarded the hypocrisies of the Lutheran position by asserting that it is not free will which governs men's efforts to save their souls, but the irresistible providence of God in a deterministic sense. Calvin was a most pronounced and consistent champion of unconditional predestination. From the practical standpoint, it was important that he rejected Luther's fundamental principle of the separation of the spiritual and temporal kingdoms and in its place set up a theocracy at Geneva, where his theology permeated every fibre of public life and he himself governed with a reckless absolutism. Subsequently, this type of political religion was adopted to a greater or less degree by the Calvinistic churches in other countries. Notwithstanding the differences between their respective doctrines, however, Luther and Calvin mutually eulogized each other. Calvin was treated with consideration by Luther and, in his turn, acknowledged the influence which Luther had exercised upon him. Had Luther lived longer, the two reformers would no doubt have become embroiled in violent altercations.[45]

In view of Zwinglianism and Calvinism, Protestants often speak of a complete and free evolution of Protestantism. It would be more proper to speak of a multiplication of ruins, which the spirit of innovation wrought within the domain of dogma.

Continuing the discussion of German Lutheranism—when we turn from the sphere of dogma to that of practical affairs, we discover that the greatest damage during Luther's declining years was done to ecclesiastical property. Luther was fully aware of the fact that the confiscation of the temporal possessions of the Church would constitute a powerful stimulus for the civil governments to open their territories to the new ecclesiastical régime. With sentiments of self-satisfaction he refers his elector to the "considerable wealth, which increases daily." [46] Whatever the territorial ruler did not appropriate, was confiscated by the magistrates of the different municipalities. These seized pre-eminently the minor benefices which, as a rule, depended either upon them or upon prominent families. The emolu-

[45] On the relations between Calvin and Luther see Grisar, *Luther*, Vol. V, pp. 399 sqq.
[46] *Ibid.*, Vol. III, p. 35.

ments, so Luther and the rulers frequently asserted, were intended for the maintenance of schools, preachers, and parishes. Still, there are numerous complaints made by Luther and his followers that such was not the case, or that the "harpies" among the nobility interfered, in order to enrich themselves. Who, in surveying that age, can calculate the immense sums derived from the confiscation of bishoprics, clerical benefices, and monasteries, which were forever alienated from the spiritual or educational purposes for which they had been given, including the foundations of Christian charity which dispensed help with a lavish hand? Even if the former use of these properties was not always in conformity with the pious intentions of their founders; even if the revenues from these ancient endowments were allowed to accumulate excessively, when contrasted with the possessions of the bourgeoisie, a fact which gave rise to many complaints and altercations—yet the spoliation, perpetrated by ineffable acts of violence, was assuredly not the proper solution of the existing problem. It merely caused ruin and destruction.[47]

As these ruins accumulated, the theologians of Wittenberg gave up the idea of regulative intervention. When, in 1544, the magistrate of a certain city requested Luther to advise him, according to Sacred Scripture, on the question of the confiscation of ecclesiastical property, he replied: "This matter does not concern us theologians. Such things must be decided by the lawyers." It was a formal evasion of questions which the theologians themselves had raised.[48] They saw with their own eyes and acknowledged the curse which always follows the spoliation of the Church. Thus Paul Eber, Luther's Wittenberg friend, speaks of the penury which was visited upon the devotees of the Lutheran Church in consequence of the spoliation, and predicts that the future will reveal even more clearly how the confiscated Church property will react upon its beneficiaries, who "so greatly warmed and fattened themselves by means of these spiritual possessions." [49]

A particularly sad chapter in the history of the dissipation of the property of the Church is furnished by the destruction of numerous works of ecclesiastical art that adorned the churches. In Lutheran Germany this destruction was not as great as in the Zwinglian parts

[47] On the fate of the Church property, cfr. Grisar, *Luther, passim* (see index).

[48] Grisar, *op. cit.*, Vol. V, pp. 206 sq.

[49] *Ibid.*, Vol. IV, pp. 59 sqq.

of Switzerland and of southern and western Germany, where a veritable mania developed against images, altars, and other objects of sacred art. Thus the city of Nuremberg, for instance, owed the preservation of many precious art treasures to the indulgent attitude of the populace and its civic spirit. Still, Lutheran communities also became the scene of much destruction. There is extant a catalogue of Blasius Kneusel, which lists the objects of ecclesiastical art destroyed at Meissen. He enumerates fifty-one objects of great value which had been robbed by spoliators—amongst them a golden cross "of the weight of 1,300 gulden, heavy with precious stones," a diamond cross worth 16,000 gulden, several golden crosses adorned with precious stones and pearls, a gold plate appraised at a thousand gulden, a large bust of St. Benno, made of precious metals, weighing more than 36 pounds, which had been purchased with the charitable gifts of the members of the parish of Meissen. From time to time, even now, treasures of religious art are discovered in hiding places which were purloined at that time. In its avarice, this barbaric age did not hesitate to consign to the melting-pot the most precious monstrances, chalices, and patens, excusing itself on the strength of the commonplace Lutheran charge of "idolatry." Luther's hostility to pictorial representations became fatal to art, even though he moderated his expressions on this subject as time went on. His unchanging attitude was that the religious images would gradually disappear if his doctrine prevailed. The creation of a religious image or statue was no longer counted as a good work.[50] The decline of artistic development in Germany, which had justified the highest expectations at the close of the Middle Ages, was brought on by Luther's work.

Moreover, a perceptible retrogression in the care of the poor resulted from the destruction of ecclesiastical revenues. The practice of Christian charity sustained a severe blow. The assertion that good works were of no value was bound to weaken the spirit of charity, so splendidly manifested towards the close of the Middle Ages by the foundation of hospitals and other charitable institutions under ecclesiastical auspices. Luther intended to substitute for them the so-called community poor-boxes and a more intensive care of the poor on the part of the civil authorities. But these boxes were success-

---

[50] On Meissen, op. cit., Vol. V, pp. 203, 169; on destructive activities in Erfurt, ibid., pp. 213 sqq.; on Luther's attitude toward the veneration of images in general, cfr. ibid., pp. 207 sqq.

fully operated only in a few places. Luther's failure at Leisnig and elsewhere produced a deterrent effect. Luther, moreover, wished to see begging completely prohibited. His movement was directed against the mendicant Orders of the Catholic Church, but it produced no far-reaching social results.[51]

Complaints that the moral sense, which in the last analysis must sustain all charitable endeavors, was becoming extinguished, were multiplied by Luther and his partisans. Under the papacy, he says, people had been eager to make sacrifices for the poor, but now they had grown cold.[52] In his opinion the society of true Christians, planned by him, was bound to cultivate the spirit of sacrifice in the era of the new Gospel; but, he says, "would that we had nations and individuals who sincerely desired to be Christians!" In one of his sermons he exclaims: "Woe unto you peasants, burghers, and members of the nobility, who appropriate all things unto yourselves, who scrape and hoard, and yet desire to be good evangelicals!" It was a proof that he was "unsophisticated," as a modern sociologist mildly puts it, that Luther ascribed to the "faith" which he preached the sole power of overcoming the obstacles to charity by means of the community poor-box.[53]

Adolph Harnack concedes that, "where Lutheranism was in the ascendant, social care of the poor was soon reduced to a worse plight than ever before." [54] The lack of resourcefulness of the Protestant system of poor-relief continued for a long time.

Protestant authors, by way of contrast, have referred to the excellent systems of poor-relief that flourished in the cities of South Germany at the time of the religious schism. But these institutions were a heritage of the fifteenth century, that is, of the Catholic Middle Ages. They owed as little to Lutheranism as the excellent institutions and arrangements for the poor which existed in the Catholic Netherlands, such as, for instance, at Ypres, in 1525. It was Catholic idealism, humanism, and the rising civic spirit of the municipalities as they attained to independence, which created those praiseworthy institutions. Protestantism, on the other hand, even after Bugenhagen had improved the parish treasuries in virtue of his superior genius for organization, as a rule attained only to inadequate governmental regulations of the system of poor-relief with a tinge of religious influence. These

[51] *Op. cit.*, Vol. VI, pp. 50 sqq.
[52] *Ibid.*, pp. 54 sq.
[53] Feuchtwanger, quoted *ibid.*, pp. 56 sq.
[54] *Reden und Aufsätze*, Vol. II (1904), p. 52.

"poor-chests" were occasionally described by envious parties as "clerical and usury funds," which does not, however, prove that in certain localities, such as Hesse and Straṣburg, they did not really benefit the poor, especially when administered by men of truly Christian charity.

William Liese, the most recent Catholic writer on the history of charity, correctly observes that "in practice the olden Catholic ideals and motives continued to operate," but "it can scarcely be affirmed" that there was a Protestant impetus in the interest of poor-relief, or a growth of charity in early Protestantism, whilst, on the other hand, "new principles are wont to make their influence felt most clearly in the beginning," and in the history of Christianity it was "precisely the primitive age" that "produced the noblest fruits of charity." [55]

Relative to the schools, also, the aging Luther failed to see about him that revival for which he had appealed in various writings; on the contrary, here, too, he observed increasing dissolution and decline. "Now that it is a question of founding true schools," he laments, "every purse is closed with iron chains, and no one is able to give." This deplorable state of affairs made him beg of God a happy death, so that he might not live to witness Germany's punishment.[56] Even more frequent and persistent are the complaints of Melanchthon, who was a professional educator, on the failure of his endeavors in this sphere. In consequence of the decadence of Christian schools, he once wrote, we shall yet become pagans.[57] In Catholic districts a similar deplorable retrogression of the school system ensued in consequence of the religious controversies. At first, indeed, Protestantism was able to retrieve itself in virtue of the support given it by those princes who were intent upon procuring recruits for their bureaucratic system and favored the general education of the people.[58] That Luther is the founder of the "Volksschule" is as unfounded a claim as that he is to be regarded as the author of poor-relief and a promoter of charity on a grand scale. These claims are but the extreme expressions

[55] Geschichte der Caritas, Vol. I (1922), pp. 255 sq. Liese reports the findings of Feuchtwanger, Püschel, Otto Winckelmann (1922), and others, and concludes: "If we review the recent vivid discussion of the subject, we find substantial agreement on the following points: (1) The Reformation has not promoted, but rather injured charity; (2) it has given a powerful impetus to governmental poor-relief, as is revealed by the multitude of municipal ordinances passed from 1520 to 1530."

[56] Grisar, Luther, Vol. VI, p. 53. On the decline of schools, ibid., pp. 22 sqq., and Janssen-Pastor, Vol. VII, 14th ed. (1904), pp. 5 sqq., 81 sqq.

[57] Grisar, ibid.

[58] Grisar, op. cit., Vol. VI, p. 435.

of a Luther cult which has no basis in history. His claims as a champion of culture are equally baseless. Beginning with the Peasants' War he spoke and wrote rabidly against the peasants and the mob and continued to do this to the end of his life. He had adopted the maxim: "It does not do to pipe too much to the mob, or it will too readily lose its head." [59] In his speeches he frequently works himself into a veritable rage against the mob, calling it "Master Omnes," the "many-headed monster," etc. As a Protestant author, Feuchtwanger, says, Luther is not far removed from the politico-social ideas of Machiavelli, who counsels rulers to keep a tight rein on the masses.[60] Gradually he began to claim absolute authority. "If compulsion and the law of the strong arm still ruled," he says, "as in the past, so that if a man dared to grumble, he got a box on the ear—things would fare better; otherwise it is all of no use." [61] "Christ does not wish to abolish serfdom," he says in another passage on the oppressed condition of the peasants, whose lot was constantly growing worse. "What cares He how the lords or princes rule [in temporal matters]?" In his sermons on the first book of Moses, he actually represents serfdom as a relatively desirable state. "If society is to endure, . . . it will be necessary to re-establish it." [62] Possibly these declarations were but the outbursts of a transient mood; yet they betray sufficiently the sentiments which he harbored toward the lower classes.

One truly interested in the advancement of civilization should be intent upon the preservation of ancient popular usages, especially those whose cultural worth resides in the maintenance of the spiritual and particularly the religious life. In many respects Luther proved himself an enemy of the popular customs of the Middle Ages, because he suspected hidden idolatry in those quite indifferent customs of which the people had become fond and which were rooted in primitive ages. He passionately declaimed not only against the abuses which were connected with them; but, although he was himself descended from the common people, he blindly combated popular usages which were characteristic and educational.

A proof of this, among others, is contained in the memorandum which he presented to the Elector of Saxony during the diet of Augsburg, in 1530. This memorandum was connected with his object of

[59] *Op. cit.*, Vol. V, p. 577, n. 1.
[60] *Op. cit.*, Vol. VI, p. 57.
[61] *Op. cit.*, Vol. VI, p. 74.
[62] *Ibid.*

promoting a scheme which he had devised for the purification of the Church.[63] The lengthy list of "abuses" was intended, according to his own words, to make known "the great, nay, atrocious injuries which were inflicted upon souls and consciences."

It impresses one as strange that he includes the custom of St. John's fire, which has remained popular even to the present day. The people build a bonfire in mid-summer, on June 24. It was taken over from paganism, but divested of its heathen accompaniments. Similarly he condemns the use of St. John's wine, which was taken on December 27, the feast of the Apostle John. He does not spare either the innocent celebration of St. Martin's eve, with its old custom of children bearing lights, or the ancient German funeral banquets, which were primarily arranged for the benefit of mourners who had come from afar.

Luther condemned the very popular semi-dramatic plays, inherited from the devout and childlike Middle Ages. They were presented on the high feast-days of the Church with a view to elevate the minds of the faithful, and required only a little refurbishing here and there to be entirely acceptable. Such were the cherished Christmas plays enacted at the manger of the Christ Child; the Palm Sunday procession with the figure of Christ riding on an ass; the solemn processional veneration of the Holy Cross during the last days of Holy Week; the customary touching celebration of the Resurrection, symbolized by the elevation of the Cross above the tomb; the dramatic representation of the Ascension by means of a statue rising on high; and the coming of the Holy Ghost by means of an ornamented dove. These were all extremely ancient popular usages, which had taken deep root and imparted ardor to the religious life of the people. It goes without saying that a general war of extermination was declared on all specifically Catholic customs.

How profoundly the religious life of the people was affected by these changes may be seen from the fact that the above-mentioned memorial proposed to abolish all confraternities with their religious demonstrations, which were so frequently inspiring, all pilgrimages and processions, the customary blessing of the fields by devout processions with the Cross, and the elevating public solemnities in commemoration of the departed on All Souls'. Furthermore the use of bells, candles, candlesticks, banners and the vestments worn at divine service.

It was also proposed to discontinue the custom of carrying biers into church. The offering of the pence during divine services was to be proscribed. The veiling of images during the season of Lent, as well as the hanging up of the so-called black cloth that covered the altar during Lent,

<hr>

[63] *Briefwechsel,* Vol. VII, pp. 256 sqq. (March, 1530.)

were to be discontinued. All these practices were dear to the people. Fasting, the recitation of the Divine Office, the solemn rites of consecration, the ceremony of the washing of the feet on Maundy Thursday, the use of Holy Water, and the celebration of the Roman Jubilee were to be inhibited.

Further study of Luther's writings shows that an endless number of other deep-seated religious customs, which reflected the active participation of the people in the life of the Church, were condemned to extinction.

Divine worship and the religious life of the people necessarily languished after the forcible abolition of these popular customs. The radical innovations of Lutheranism, so foreign to human feeling, produced ruins where formerly the seeds of civilization had been strewn in abundance, even though they were frequently in need of better care in order to blossom forth vigorously. The aging Luther did not sense this very noticeable decline of cultural life, but imagined that he had taught the people to worship God in the spirit, whilst even among his own followers complaints were rife that he failed to do adequate justice to human nature, which, in the final analysis, is a composite of body and soul.

On the other hand, he admitted the existence of other and, in some respects, even greater ruins. They are touched upon here only in passing, since most of them have been treated of in a previous part of this work.

He saw domestic life undermined as a consequence of his arbitrary loosening of the conjugal tie. His parsons importuned him on this point with endless letters. Poignantly and frequently he sensed the decline of the liberty of the Church resulting from the intervention of civil authority. The position of his jurists, who partly endeavored to observe the old canon law and partly favored the religious innovations, became impossible. Ecclesiastical regulations and consistories but too frequently proved inadequate aids, until they assumed the character of administrative governmental measures. Luther witnessed a certain decline in the power of the Schmalkaldic League after the Landgrave of Hesse had drawn closer to the Emperor. He heard the coming uproar of the religious war and trembled for its issue, knowing scarcely any consolation but the day of judgment. The empire itself, its unity and power, and especially the authority of the Emperor, were weakened to their very foundation. That his work was one of the causes of the unhappy condition of the empire was a thought which he had to bear to his grave.

The ruins which Luther saw round about him, did not, however, prevent him from asserting his claims. He did not live to see the decisive defeat of the Schmalkaldians at Mühlberg.

3. AT DEATH'S DOOR

The last will and testament which Luther made during his severe illness in 1537 at Gotha upon his return from the Schmalkaldian conference, boldly declared that he had done right in "storming" the papacy "with the aid of God's Word." [64] A second and final testament, dated January 6, 1542, the original of which is preserved in the Archives of the Augsburg Confession at Budapest, refers with equal solemnity to his claim that "the Father of all mercies has entrusted to him the Gospel of His beloved Son." He styles himself "God's notary and witness in His Gospel." [65]

This testament, as well as the first, lacks the necessary legal formalities. His controversy with the lawyers, who refused to regard his marriage as valid and his five children as his legitimate heirs, induced him to disregard the notarial form and accounts for the fact that he styles himself a notary of God, whereby he sought to justify himself, and also for the high-sounding words he used in that document: "Let it be admitted that I am the kind of person which I truly am, namely, public, one who is known in heaven and on earth, as well as in hell, and who possesses sufficient reputation and authority to be trusted and believed in preference to any notary." At the same time he styles himself a "condemned, poor, undeserving, miserable sinner."

He testifies in this document that his "dear and faithful house-wife, Catherine," "ever treated him with love, appreciation, and affection as an upright and faithful consort." He demands that his children should "look into her hands," not she into theirs. He bequeathes to her his estate at Zulsdorf and a house he had purchased from Bruno Bauer; also his "goblets and jewels, such as rings, chains, and show coins, of gold and silver," valued at about 1,000 gulden. These bequests, however, were subject to the obligation of liquidating his debts, which amounted to approximately 450 gulden. Ready cash,

---

[64] Text *ibid.*, Vol. XI, pp. 209 sq., of February 28, 1537. Cfr. Grisar, *Luther*, Vol. III, pp. 436 sq.

[65] Text in *Briefwechsel*, Vol. XIV, pp. 149 sq.

he says, he had none, owing to the expense of keeping their house in repair and maintaining the household. The monastery in which he resided automatically reverted to the Elector, whom he requests "graciously to guard and administer" his legacy to Catherine. The authenticity of his signature is confirmed at the bottom of the document by Melanchthon, Cruciger, and Bugenhagen. An imperial decree required that a testament which was not drawn up by a notary, should bear signatures of seven witnesses, together with their seals. But the elector supplied these deficiencies and officially confirmed Luther's last will and testament on April 11, 1546.

At the age of sixty, Luther wrote to his elector, on March 30, 1544, that he was "old and cold and ungainly, weak and sickly." He feared that evil times were coming, but the consolation of the "dear Word of God," and of prayer, would ever remain to his territorial lord. "The devil, the Turk, the Pope and his followers, cannot enjoy" these two unspeakable treasures.[66] This, in a certain sense, was his farewell letter to his protector.

The sufferings of which Luther complained were constriction of the chest and heart, a result of hardening of the arteries, and renewed "phobias," in addition to the extraordinary nervousness which accompanied him throughout life; finally, dizzy spells and pains from gall-stone.

Notwithstanding his afflictions, he continued to take part in literary controversies almost until his last breath.

Immediately after the publication of his treatise "Wider das Papsttum zu Rom vom Teufel gestiftet," he issued a description of the attitude of Popes Hadrian IV and Alexander III towards the Emperor Frederick Barbarossa.[67] It was translated from the Latin history of the popes by Robert Barnes—a thoroughly unreliable and hostile book, which Luther furnished with a preface and annotations. This pamphlet was intended to incite the temporal rulers of his time against the papacy, which was charged with contempt for, and abuse of, princes. The prefaces to the various sections of the second volume of his collected German writings, and the still more important prefaces to those of the first volume of his Latin works in the Wittenberg edition, date from 1545. In the general preface to the latter volume he essays a historical presentation of the origin and develop-

[66] Grisar, *Luther*, Vol. VI, p. 341.
[67] Erl. ed., Vol. XXXII, pp. 358 sqq.

ment of his agitated life.[68] This narrative is a strongly colored and
deliberate recasting of his early career. "The picture of his youth
is made to tally more and more with the convictions of his later
years." [69] It may be well to make a résumé of this artificial account
in its main outlines, since Protestant biographers accept it as the
truth. According to this fiction, Luther was a blameless, penitent
monk, who was swept into the controversy with the Church only
by his unavoidable opposition to the abuses connected with the sale
of indulgences. At first he was unaware of the stupendous theological
abyss which separated him from the teaching of the Church and quite
unconscious of his ardent desire to obtain recognition for the dogmatic system which he had excogitated for the sake of quieting his
neurotic fears. Until he got into the controversy with Tetzel, Luther
was a simple monk who had died to the world and was given to heroic
mortifications, seeking nothing else but a merciful God. But he was
unable to discover this merciful God in the monastery and, as a result of gruelling experiences, became convinced that God was not
in the papacy. While he was engaged in public controversy about indulgences, in 1518, he was suddenly enlightened on the truth that man
is justified by faith alone.

No further word is necessary on the perverted form in which he
desired to hand down to posterity the development of his theoretical
ideas by means of the preface to his collected Latin works. The whole
incident is characteristic of the controversial spirit that moved him
to the last. The fiction thus concocted was intended to be a blow to
the Catholic Church and a vindication of his agitated life.

In 1545 he issued a pamphlet against the theologians of Louvain
University, who had taken a stand against him at the outset of his
career. In a certain sense, this pamphlet was a return to the beginning of his religious innovation. The Louvain theologians had published thirty-two articles against him in the previous year. He replied in seventy-six antitheses, "Against the Louvain Theologasters,"
of which his Protestant biographer Köstlin says that they are "abusive
and derisive rather than convincing." [70] It had been his intention to
expand this pamphlet into a treatise entitled, "Against the Asses in

[68] *Opp. Lat. Var.*, I, pp. 15 sqq.

[69] Thus Hausrath; see Grisar, *Luther*, Vol. VI, p. 191. For the following cf. ch. XXXVII
of the same volume: "Umdichtung des jungen Luther durch den alternden."

[70] *Opp. Lat. Var.*, IV, pp. 486 sqq.; German in the Erl. ed. of his works, Vol. LXV, pp.
169 sqq. Cfr. Köstlin-Kawerau, *Martin Luther*, Vol. II, p. 609.

Paris and Louvain," but death snatched the pen from his hand before he was able to complete it.[71] As a definite determination of his doctrinal position, the two last-mentioned productions, inspired by an unbroken opposition to the ancient religion, are significant, in so far as they categorically repeat his three principal dogmas, the articles of the "standing and falling Church," as he termed them; *i. e.*, that of justification and grace, that of the law, and that of sin continuously inherent in man. To study theology without these articles he said, as his opponents in those learned seats of harlotry did, was like trying to teach an ass to play the lyre. Among his past publications was his reply to a "mendacious pamphlet" [72] describing his alleged frightful death; also various hymns and prefaces.

Archbishop Albrecht of Mayence, who did not embrace Lutheranism, figures in Luther's letters as the "pestilence of all Germany" down to the very end of his correspondence. Albrecht departed this life on September 24, 1545, at peace with the Church. During the years 1542 and 1543, as mentioned above, this ecclesiastical prince had associated intimately with Morone and Blessed Peter Faber, whom he kept near him. He issued commendable regulations for the protection and prosperity of the Church during his declining years.[73] As late as 1542, Luther had ridiculed the cardinal-elector because of the latter's collection of relics and distributed among the masses a fabricated list of these. This list mentions "a piece of the left horn of Moses, three flames from the burning bush on Mt. Sinai, two wings and one egg of the Holy Ghost," etc. The pamphlet was characterized by lawyers as a public libel (*libellus famosus*) against a prince of the empire, which was punishable at law. Luther wrote to Jonas that even if his pamphlet were a libel in the legal acceptation of the term, which was impossible, he nevertheless claimed the right to write thus "against the cardinal, the pope, the devil and all their crew." If he lived long enough, he hoped to tread yet another measure with the bride of Mayence, despite asses and jurists.[74] The reforms which the

[71] G. Buchwald, *Luthers letzte Streitschrift* (Leipzig, 1893). In the fragment published by Buchwald, Luther declares that the theologians of Louvain and Paris were doomed to hell (*absque dubio peribunt*) and that the same fate would overtake the respective rulers, unless they opposed them.

[72] Erl. ed., Vol. XXXII, pp. 426 sqq.

[73] Cfr. L. Cardauns, *Zur Geschichte der Kirchl. Unions- und Reformbestrebungen*, 1910, pp. 210–276.

[74] Grisar, *Luther*, Vol. IV, p. 293.

cardinal, in his zeal for religion, endeavored to introduce, had excited the wrath of Luther, who, after the dignitary's death, unhesitatingly consigned him to hell.

Luther's rudeness enabled him to gain the victory in his contest with the lawyers of the imperial consistory in the matter of the validity of "clandestine marriages" contracted without parental consent. In January, 1544, he delivered a sermon which contained brutal attacks against the jurists who opposed his attitude in this matter. Never before in his life, not even in his controversy with the pope, he says, had he been so much agitated as in these contentious days.[75] In this connection, he was also agitated by an affair of his own house. Caspar Beier, a student, endeavored to dissolve a clandestine marriage which he had contracted, in order to take another wife. Only with the special aid of the elector, Luther succeeded in having all such marriages declared invalid until the consent of the parents had been obtained, or until a decree had been delivered by the consistory which pronounced parental resistance as groundless. The "divine precept" of preaching the fourth commandment of the Decalogue, which, he said, had been entrusted to him, finally won the day and he triumphantly conducted Beier to his new bride. No one was able to resist the all-powerful dictator. Catherine Bora had assisted Beier, who was a relative of hers, in winning the intervention of Luther on his behalf. Cruciger on this occasion called her "the domestic torch" (*fax domestica*).[76]

4. LUTHER'S DEATH

Despite his weakened condition, Luther, at the beginning of October, 1545, undertook a journey to Mansfeld. Count Albert of Mansfeld, a protagonist of Lutheranism, had solicited his aid in the adjustment of some lawsuits in which he was involved with his brother Gebhard and his nephew on account of certain revenues from mines and various legal claims. This first journey to Mansfeld was followed by a second, on Christmas. Luther requested Melanchthon to accompany him, which the latter did grumblingly, as he disliked to listen to the quarrels of contentious people. When Melanchthon took sick, Luther returned with him to Wittenberg. The litiga-

[75] *Op. cit.*, VI, 358 sq.
[76] *Ibid.*, p. 359.

tion at Mansfeld induced him to set out, in January, 1546, for his native city of Eisleben, which was also to be the city of his death. Undoubtedly, these frequent journeys were inspired, at least in part, by that unrest which so often leads men to change their habitation at the approach of death, and also by that discontent with Wittenberg which had driven him to visit Zeitz, Merseburg, and Leipsic but a short time previously.

On the twenty-third of January, in spite of the rigors of the winter, Luther once more left Wittenberg, accompanied by his sons, their tutor and his amanuensis, John Aurifaber, the future editor of the Table Talks. At Halle he was compelled to spend three days with Jonas on account of floating ice in the Saale river. The devil, he wrote, dwells in the water, but he was resolved not to get drowned to give the pope and his myrmidons cause for delight.[77] In a sermon delivered in Halle he poured forth his anger against popery and demanded the expulsion of the "lousy monks" who still remained in that locality. "You ought to drive the imbecile, sorry creatures out of town!" On January 28, he and his escort, which now included Jonas, resumed their journey across the swollen Saale. Whilst riding in his carriage in the vicinity of Eisleben, the bitter wind caused him to experience difficulty in breathing, vertigo, and great debility. "The devil always plays me this trick," so he consoled himself, "when I have something great on hand." Arrived at his destination, he jocosely wrote to Catherine that the Jews who lived at Rissdorf had raised the cold wind against him and attempted to turn his brain to ice.

The litigant counts and their counselors were already present in Eisleben. They assigned the house of the town-clerk, which still stands, to Luther, Jonas, and Aurifaber, and liberally provided for their sustenance. Luther extols the Naumburg beer, says that his three sons had gone on to Jena; two of them returned to the narrow quarters at Eisleben, but spent a great deal of their time in Mansfeld, which lay close by. Luther's friend, Coelius, who was court-preacher in Mansfeld, was also in the house. Luther entertained his friends every evening in a room on the ground-floor beneath the quarters which he occupied; he enjoyed his meals, drank heartily, and exhibited a jovial disposition. When Catherine again expressed fears about his health, he replied in a jocose vein, giving her an account

[77] *Ibid.*, p. 372.

of all that her anxious thoughts had brought upon him: the fire that broke out just in front of his door, had almost burnt him up; the plaster that fell down from the ceiling of his room had nearly killed him. "I fear, if you don't put your fears to rest, the earth will finally open and swallow us up." [78]

While he sojourned at Eisleben, Luther preached four sermons, which severely taxed his strength. In one of them he attacked the Jews, contending that, if they did not become Christians, the rulers were obliged to expel them. He upbraided the Jews of Mansfeld not only for hating the Christians, but also for cheating them and practicing usury—which charge was not without justification. In assailing the Jews he was well aware that the Countess of Mansfeld was regarded as their protectress. Twice Luther partook of the Lord's Supper while at Eisleben, after having "absolution" administered to him, as is reported. On the occasion of his second communion, he ordained two priests, in conformity with what he alleged was apostolic practice.

He was annoyed to find that the negotiations designed to effect a reconciliation between the counts proceeded in an extremely tedious manner. He blamed the devil for the stubborn resistance that was offered to the proposals of mediation put forth by the experts and by himself. All the devils, he said, had convened at Eisleben to cast mockery upon his efforts in this sorry affair. He writes that he was prepared to rush in upon the disputants like a "hobgoblin" and "to grease the wagon with his anger." In the excess of his excitement he experienced the above-mentioned hallucination of the devil seated on a fountain—a scene which, as Coelius writes, caused him to shed tears because of the malicious indecency which Satan exhibited towards his person. In the end a satisfactory settlement was reached. On February 14 he wrote to his "dear and amiable wife": "God has shown great favor here; for the rulers have practically settled all their differences with the aid of their councilors." He announced at the same time: "We expect to return home this week, if it so please God."

On February 16, sickness and death were the topics of a very lively discussion during supper, according to the notations of Aurifaber. During these discourses, Luther said: "When I shall arrive at home

[78] *Ibid.*, pp. 373 sq.

in Wittenberg, I shall lay me in a coffin and offer the maggots an obese doctor to feed on." [79] As yet, he did not anticipate that death would overtake him at Eisleben.

Worry over the religious situation to some extent diverted Luther's thoughts from the fate which confronted him. He learned how strictly the Emperor insisted upon submission to the Council which had already begun; how fruitless were the proceedings of the religious conference at Ratisbon; how, after the failure of all attempts at reunion, the empire was preparing for the oft-threatened war against the Schmalkaldians. Other disquieting reports were brought by Prince Wolfgang von Anhalt and Count Henry von Schwarzburg, two friends of Luther, who had come to Eisleben to act as arbitrators for the counts of Mansfeld. "The Emperor is unalterably opposed to us," sighed Luther; "he reveals now what he has hitherto concealed." His solicitude for his elector inspired him to utter these words: "God save our gracious Lord; he is due for a struggle!" On one occasion he absented himself from his fellow-boarders, as they were at supper, exhorting them to "pray for the realization of the designs of God, that it may go well with the affairs of the Church; the Council of Trent displays a great deal of indignation."

At the same time, his spirit was wrapped in gloom because of the violent opposition that developed on the part of the Swiss and other Sacramentarians to his doctrine of the Last Supper. These renewed attacks had been called forth by his recently published "Brief Confession." His displeasure with them was undoubtedly heightened because of the further fact that he reread those of his works in which he had vented his anger during the controversy on the Eucharist, and which were included in the volume of his German works just then in course of publication. Hence, in his sermons at Eisleben, he paid his respects to the Sacramentarians and in forceful words warned his hearers against the arbitrary interpretation of Sacred Scripture by "that prostitute, human reason." His last notes, written on Feb. 16, 1546, appear to be a reference to the misuse of the Bible by the Sacramentarians. "No one," he says, "has sufficiently tasted the Sacred Scriptures who has not governed churches with the prophets for a hundred years." He claims, moreover, that one must have been a shepherd or a farmer for five years in order to understand the Bucolics and Georgics of Vergil; and, in order to appreciate Cicero's let-

---

[79] *Tischreden*, Weimar ed., Vol. VI, n. 6975.

ters, it was necessary for one to have spent twenty-five years in the service of an important state.[80] Shortly before he had inscribed in the postil of a friend the following words, based upon John VIII, 51, which sound like a presentiment of death: "If any man keep my word, he shall not see death forever." In this connection he also wrote: "Blessed in the Word is he who believes and goes to sleep and dies over it." [81] This was a favorite thought with him. Frequently during these days he also quoted the text: "God so loved the world," etc., which he undertook to explain in a lengthy address to his friends.

The first indication that his heart trouble was growing worse was noticed on the 17th of February, when he grew restless and said, among other things: "Here at Eisleben I was baptized. What if I were to remain here?" In the evening he was seized with oppression on the chest, a pain he had experienced in former ailments. He felt relieved when rubbed with hot cloths and went down for supper with his companions, with whom he ate and drank copiously in his usual jovial mood, recounting anecdotes and participating in the serious discussions which were carried on. Among other things the mutual recognition of friends in Heaven was debated. In Heaven, he said, we shall recognize each other in virtue of the illuminating spirit of God, who caused Adam immediately to recognize Eve as flesh of his flesh, whom He had built from a rib taken from his own body whilst he was asleep. He also discussed his own death and the devil. He said he had lived to be sixty-three years of age in order that he might witness all the malice, faithlessness, and misery which was caused by the devil in the world. The human race is like sheep being led to slaughter.[82] Shortly afterwards he repaired to his room. It was still early in the evening; he recited his prayers at the open window, as was his custom, and then retired for the night.

While at prayer, a new severe attack of heart oppression came on. His friends again hurried to his aid, tried to give him relief by rubbing him with hot cloths. He got an hour's sleep on a sofa in his room, after Count Albrecht, who had been summoned, and his relatives offered him various remedies. He refused to have the doctors called, as he did not think there was any danger. Having told his friends, who in the meantime had come to see him, to retire, he

[80] *Briefwechsel*, Vol. XVII, p. 60.
[81] Köstlin-Kawerau, *Martin Luther*, Vol. II, p. 620.
[82] Grisar, *Luther*, Vol. IV, pp. 376 sq.

withdrew to his chamber. Jonas and a servant, Rudfeld by name, had a couch in the same room, which was small and lacking in ventilation. The couch which Luther occupied may still be found in the self-same crowded room. He slept in his bed only from ten or eleven o'clock until about one in the morning, when he got up and awakened Jonas, saying to him: "Oh, my God, how ill I feel!" Aided by Jonas and the servant he dragged himself into the sitting-room, saying he would probably die at Eisleben after all, and repeating the prayer: "Into thy hands I commend my spirit!" As he lay outstretched on the couch, the constriction of his heart became unbearable.

The inmates of the house, the counts and the princes, who appeared at intervals to express their solicitude and sympathy, were kept informed of the condition of the patient. Two physicians, one a doctor and the other a master of medicine, were hurriedly summoned. Before they appeared, however, the malady had completely overcome the patient. They found him lying on the couch unconscious and with no perceptible pulse. After a brief interval, however, Luther recovered consciousness, and, bathed in the cold sweat of death, was heard to exclaim: "My God, I am so ill and anxious; I am going." He also recited some prayers, in which he expressed his thanks to God for having revealed to him His Son Jesus Christ, in whom he believed, whilst the hateful pope had blasphemed Him.[83] Thrice he repeated the familiar verse: "God so loved the world," etc. In vain Count Albrecht and his relatives offered strengthening or refreshing draughts to the patient. As he again lay practically unconscious, Jonas and Coelius, in order to obtain a confession from him in the presence of the attendants, shouted into his ear the question whether he remained steadfast in the faith in Christ and His doctrine which he had preached; to which they caught the reply: "Yes." That was his last word. He did not recall his life's partner at Wittenberg, nor did he mention his children. It seems the stroke had stupefied him and blotted out the memory of those dear to him.

About three o'clock in the morning Luther drew a deep breath and departed this life to return his soul into the hands of the eternal Judge. It was a frosty morning (February 18, 1546), and the earth was still veiled in darkness.

During this last crisis, or soon after, John Landau, an apothecary

[83] *Ibid.*, p. 378.

of Eisleben, was sent for with the request to attempt to restore animation by the application of a clyster. Landau was a convert to the Catholic Church and a nephew of the famous controversialist Wicel. He came at once, but, after examining Luther, who had already departed this life, declared: "He is dead; of what use can an injection be?" The physicians, however, insisted upon a try with the instrument, so that the patient might again come to himself if there still was life in him. When the apothecary inserted the nozzle he noticed some flatulency given off into the ball of the syringe. The two physicians disputed together as to the cause of death. The doctor said it was a fit of apoplexy, for the mouth was drawn down and the whole of the right side discolored. The master, on the other hand, maintained that so holy a man could not have been stricken down by the hand of God and that it was rather the result of a suffocating catarrh and that death was due to choking. Neither knew anything of Luther's chronic disease affecting the arteries of the heart.[84] The true cause of his death was neither apoplexy nor catarrh.

After Luther's death, all the distinguished guests assembled in his chamber. Jonas, who sat at the head of the bed, wrung his hands and wept aloud. He assured the others that Luther had been more cheerful on the previous evening than for many a day. "Oh, God Almighty, God Almighty!" he exclaimed. The apothecary was bidden to administer a thorough rubbing to the nose, mouth, forehead, and left side of the corpse with a costly scented fluid which the counts had brought. The guests still expected to see signs of life and remarked that on several former occasions Luther had lain for a long time motionless and was thought to be dead, for instance, at Schmalkalden, in 1537, when he was tormented with gall-stone. The apothecary soon ascertained that rigor mortis had set in. Jonas then suggested that a detailed report be at once dispatched by courier to the Elector of Saxony. About four o'clock in the morning, he composed a comprehensive account of the event, assisted by Coelius and Aurifaber.

[84] Cf. the opinion of Dr. Guido Jochner in the Innsbruck *Zeitschrift für kathol. Theologie*, Vol. 45 (1921), pp. 486 sqq., and also that of Dr. Tscharnak in Janssen-Pastor, Vol. III (18 ed.), p. 601. Of material importance is Jonas's letter in Kawerau's edition of his correspondence, Vol. II, pp. 182 sq., where he says Luther suffered from heart disease in the year before his death. In *Ioh. Manlii Libellus Medicus* (Bâsle, 1563), pp. 24 sq., it is stated that καρδιακή i.e., heart disease, was the cause of Luther's death. Manlius also says: *"Paulo ante mortem mihi scripsit, se eo morbo rursum tentatum esse."* Melanchthon wrote to V. Theodorus (*Corp. Ref.*, VI, p. 68): *"Non apoplexia, non asthmate extinctus est."* But the real cause of Luther's death he did not know either.

In the meantime the corpse, still lying on the couch, was re-arranged so as to enable the expected visitors to obtain a better view of it. After sunrise Luther's friends sent for a painter to draw the features of the departed. The picture, which represents Luther lying on the couch, was unsatisfactory and a second picture, based in part on the first, was made the following day. The painter of the second picture was Lucas Fortenagel of Halle; when he went to work, Luther already lay in his coffin. This portrait is preserved in the university library of Leipsic, which also preserves a less perfect representation depicting Luther's head as resting on a pillow. It is probable that this latter picture is the one drawn immediately after his demise.

If a Catholic opponent of Luther, familiar with his life and deeds, a man noble-minded and sympathetic of heart, had entered that room in the morning after the reformer's death, what would have been his thoughts? Above all else he would have implored God to be merciful to the soul of the departed man, thus complying with the teaching of Him who commands men to love even their worst enemies. Then, there would have flashed before his mind's eye the monstrous and embittered attacks launched by Luther upon that sacred institution, the indestructible Church established by Jesus Christ at the price of His blood and founded upon Peter and his successors. In spirit, he would have beheld the deep wounds inflicted upon that Church by this man, so remarkably endowed with eloquence, will-power, and energy. How many thousands of souls redeemed by Christ, he would have said to himself, have been torn from the Saviour's living body by this man, without any fault of their own, and frequently without their knowledge, bequeathing their misfortune to posterity. But yielding to mercy, he would also have recalled the fateful enthusiasm of the dead reformer for his own cause, and that profound and serious self-delusion which domineered his ardent temperament with ever increasing force since the inception of his contest with Rome. Did not Luther, thus the spectator might have soliloquized, eventually find himself in a state of true mental obsession, though, of course, of his own volition and which, at least in its inception, had been caused by himself? Was it an obsession which allowed him to see naught else but his supposed vocation as the promulgator of a new and true Gospel, directed against Antichrist and the demoniac forces, just as he imagined the imminent dissolution of the world and the advent of the

Great Judge? Did this delusion, in the evening of his life, incapacitate him for receiving even one ray of light?

If our hypothetical friend, thus absorbed in reflection at the bier of Luther, had been granted an insight into the mental evolution of the deceased, *i. e.*, into his psychological condition since he left the parental roof, his frightening experiences at entering the monastery, as well as the state of despondency and the constant struggles caused by his disease, he would have felt all the more inclined to pronounce a charitable judgment on the dead reformer. Was Luther a great man? he might have asked himself, as he left the chamber of death impressed by these reflections. There could be no other answer than this: If he is to be called great, his greatness is negative. As our observer later in life recalled the stirring scene in Luther's death chamber, he might have entertained the hope that the misguided reformer would be saved. Janssen, the great Catholic historian who penetrated so deeply into the inwardness of the Reformation period, used to recommend to converts who sought his guidance to pray for the repose of Luther's soul.[85] God alone searches the hearts and reins of men. Human understanding is too limited.

The account we have given of the circumstances of Luther's demise is based, first, on the report made the same day by Jonas to the Elector; secondly, on letters written by other eye-witnesses either on the day of Luther's death or immediately afterwards; thirdly, on the account of the Catholic apothecary Landau, on the funeral orations, and especially on the "Historia" of Luther's death composed at Wittenberg by Jonas, Coelius, and Aurifaber and apparently published about the middle of March.[86] While it cannot be denied that the letter of Jonas and the "Historia" contain palpable exaggerations concerning the pious aphorisms and prayers of Luther—expressions of devotion of which he was hardly capable in consequence of his

[85] Cited by Pastor toward the close of his biography of Janssen.

[86] The "Historia" in Walch's edition of Luther's Works, Vol. XXI, pp. 280 sqq. Landau's account first appeared in Cochlaeus, *Ex Compendio Actorum M. Lutheri* (Moguntiae, 1548; cf. Grisar, *Luther*, Vol. VI, p. 379, n. 2). All the accounts of Luther's death were more recently collected by Jak. Strieder, *Bericht über Luthers letzte Lebensstunden* (1912; cfr. the same writer's article, *Luthers letzte Stunden*, in the *Histor. Vierteljahsschrift*, 1912, No. 3), and Christoph Schubart, *Die Berichte*, etc., (1917), which contains a more detailed account based on all the letters. The best exposition according to the sources is supplied by N. Paulus, *Luthers Lebensende* (1898), whose conclusions have not been affected by the less important sources which have since come to light.

repeated lapses into unconsciousness,[87] there is, however, no adequate warrant for impugning the substantial credibility of this and other accounts, as has been done in recent times. In view of certain accounts that originated in foreign countries and were written for polemical purposes, it has been asserted that Luther was found dead in bed at daybreak, and that, accordingly, all the occurrences reported of the night of his death are fictions invented for the purpose of concealing the disagreeable facts in the case. But such a colossal deception was an impossibility because of the large number and the rank of those who knew the facts at first hand, including several women. The calm and detailed account which Landau, the Catholic apothecary, published in 1548, absolutely forbids the acceptance of the above-noted arbitrary theory of deception. Moreover, a falsification of facts, such as is here supposed, would most assuredly have assumed a different form. It would not have failed to mention that Luther spoke affectionately of his Catherine, and to describe a touching scene in which the dying father bade farewell to his children.

The fable of Luther's alleged suicide, which some writers (notably P. Majunke) have exploited in recent years, is based on an apocryphal letter, attributed to an alleged servant of Luther, whose name is not mentioned. It was circulated about twenty years after Luther's death among his opponents, particularly in foreign countries. The story of the unknown servant was mentioned for the first time in a book which the Italian Oratorian, Thomas Bozius, published at Rome in 1591. The Franciscan, Henry Sedulius, was the first to print the text of the letter in a book published at Antwerp in 1606. In this letter, the servant is quoted as stating that he discovered "our Master Martin suspended from his bed, wretchedly strangulated." [88]

The fable belongs to a category of inventions, quite common at the time, devised for the purpose of imputing a disgraceful death to an opponent, especially if he happened to be an ecclesiastic. Many prominent men were made to die in despair and impenitent, or to terminate their lives by suicide.[89] Luther himself was notorious for this

[87] In the *Lutherkalender* for 1911, p. 93, A. Spaeth concedes that the first letter of Jonas and the "Historia," may have been inspired by a desire to represent Luther's death in as favorable and edifying a manner as possible.

[88] In the *Allg. Deutsche Biographie*, Vol. LII (1900), pp. 156 sq., we read that the fable of Luther's suicide is no longer defended by any serious Catholic, nay, that Catholics have been among its foremost opponents.

[89] Cf. Grisar, *Luther*, II, 303 sq.

form of fabrication, and readily placed credence in reports of this kind.

Strange, too, are the amplifications made by certain authors regarding the legends of Luther's decease. It is claimed that he had "his nun" with him on the fatal night of his death; yea, that Catherine Bora strangled him during a quarrel. Others allege that the devil either carried him off alive or murdered him.

The above-noted accounts of Luther's death are not surprising in view of the mass of false statements made about the reformer in succeeding ages by short-sighted and uncritical Catholic authors, who were horrified at the way in which he ravished the Church. Thus it was alleged that he inwardly abandoned all his doctrines in his old age; that he contemplated a return to the papacy, without, however, being converted; that he said to Catherine on one occasion, as she admired the starry firmament, that heaven was not for them. It was asserted that he had three children apart from those born of his marriage; that he indulged in "orgies" with escaped nuns; that he began his fight upon the Church in order that he might be able to marry while yet a monk; that at a later date he advised people in writing to pray for many wives and few children; that he was the author of the saying: "Who loves not woman, wine, and song, remains a fool his whole life long." [90]

Rumors were circulated especially about his inebriety and habitual excesses at table, which have already been mentioned, in connection with which certain misconstrued jokes were reproduced. It is claimed that he indulged excessively in eating and drinking on the eve of his death. He was described as extremely corpulent, a characteristic supposed to be verified by his own previously adduced phrase of the "obese doctor." He was rather stoutish, as the portraits of his corpse reveal; but this was only after he had reached middle age. Such exaggerations as that contained in the celebrated verse of Gothe's "Faust" are to be rejected.

His inveterate opposition to the pope, which he reaffirmed shortly before his death at Eisleben, was embellished by a very questionable flourish of his friend Ratzeberger, who was not even in Eisleben at the time. He informs us that Luther, as he partook of his last meal,

---

[90] These slanders are incidentally repudiated in our text; see also our larger work, *Luther*, Vol. III, pp. 280 sqq.; Vol. V, p. 372. On the charge of inebriety, cfr. Vol. III, pp. 294 sqq.

wrote the following celebrated verse on the wall with a piece of chalk: *"Pestis eram vivus, moriens ero mors tua, papa"* (In life, O Pope, I was thy plague, in dying I shall be thy death). The silence of other sources, particularly that of the panegyrics, where Luther's previous use of this verse is mentioned, renders Ratzeberger's account rather incredible.[91] The so-called death-mask of Luther, preserved at Halle, is also the product of an erroneous Protestant tradition. According to the investigations of Frederick Loofs, professor of theology at Halle, it originated in the eighteenth century.[92] There was a natural desire to have authentic memorials of the famous man. Likewise most of the objects exhibited at the present time as having supposedly been left behind by the deceased, are insufficiently attested.

Catholic controversialists distorted his obsequies.[93] They alleged that when the funeral procession arrived at Wittenberg, the coffin was found empty. According to others, the hearse had to be abandoned on the road to Wittenberg because of the horrible stench emanating from the corpse. A number of rooks circling in the air about the corpse at Halle were later made out to have been devils, "who came to attend the burial of their prophet." Persons who were possessed by the devil remained unmolested at that time, since all the devils were taking part in the funeral, and so forth. These tales merely prove how greatly the Catholics had been horrified at Luther's conduct.

Having waded through the legends occasioned by the death of Luther, we must now attend to his obsequies. The body was enclosed in a tin coffin at Eisleben. After Jonas and Coelius had delivered memorial addresses there, the remains were conveyed to Halle, on February 20, thence to Wittenberg, on the morning of February 22. At the Elster Gate—the scene of the famous burning of the Bull of Excommunication—the coffin was received by the university, the town-council, and the burghers, and escorted to the Schlosskirche, where, by order of the Elector, Luther's mortal remains were to find their last resting-place. On Feb. 22, they were interred in front of the pulpit, where they still rest at the present day.[94] It is worthy of note that the

[91] Grisar, *op. cit.*, Vol. V, p. 102; Vol. VI, pp. 377–394.

[92] Loofs in *Religiöse Kunst* (1918), No. 1, pp, 2–15.

[93] Grisar, *op. cit.*, Vol. VI, pp. 394 sqq.

[94] An investigation made February 14, 1892, revealed the presence of Luther's remains in the Schlosskirche at Wittenberg. Hence, they were not removed, as was charged, after the entry of the victorious imperial troops in the Schmalkaldic War.

day of Luther's interment was the Feast of the Chair of St. Peter, or, as formerly known in the Catholic Church, the Feast of the Institution of the Papal Primacy.

When the procession that escorted the corpse arrived at the castle-church, Bugenhagen delivered a funeral oration. This was followed by a eulogy pronounced by Melanchthon. All the addresses delivered on this occasion, including those of Jonas and Coelius, previously referred to, have been preserved in print.[95] In the mind of Bugenhagen, Luther was "without doubt the angel of which the Apocalypse speaks in Chapter XIV: 'And I saw an angel flying through the midst of heaven, who had an eternal gospel to preach!' " God the Father, according to Bugenhagen, "revealed" the *evangelium aeternum,* the great mystery, through Luther, "the divinely appointed reformer of the Church." Melanchthon, in his funeral oration, similarly extolled the deceased as one of a long line of divine tools starting in Old Testament times, as a man taught by God and exercised in severe spiritual combats of a friendly nature, not at all passionate or quarrelsome, and only inclined to be violent when such medicine was required by the ailments of the age. He said Luther was endowed with all the gifts of God enumerated by the Apostle Paul in his Epistle to the Philippians (IV, 8), where he says: "Whatsoever things are true, whatsoever modest, whatsoever just, whatsoever lovely, whatsoever of good fame." Now, he concluded, he has gone to join the company of the prophets in Heaven.

No more impressive contrast to these eulogies can be conceived than the hymns of praise chanted by the Church on this very day in honor of Blessed Peter, and of his successor in the Apostolic See: *"Tu es Petrus"*—thou art Peter, the holder of the see, against whom the gates of hell shall not prevail.

In a bulletin in which he announced the death of Luther to the students of Wittenberg University, Melanchthon said: "Alas, the chariot of Israel and the driver thereof have departed (4 Kings, II, 12), who has ruled the Church in this old age of the world. Human wisdom has not discovered the doctrine of the remission of sins and fiduciary trust in the Son of God, but God has revealed it through this man."

In Coelius' address at Eisleben, Luther was represented as appearing a "true Elias and Jeremias," a "John the Baptist or an apostle before

---

[95] Cf. Grisar, *Luther,* Vol. VI, pp. 387 sqq., where excerpts are given.

the great day of the Lord." Jonas in his sermon prophesied that now all papists and monks would "turn to dust and perish," as Luther himself had frequently predicted as a consequence of his death; thus the death of the prophet would exercise a peculiar influence on the godless and impenitent; yea, within two years the deluded papists would be overtaken by a "dreadful punishment."

In harmony with these effusions medals were struck bearing Luther's celebrated verse, *"Moriens ero mors tua, papa."* Epitaphs appeared both in verse and in prose, particularly at Wittenberg, replete with the most exaggerated praise. A noteworthy leaflet of this character, appearing anonymously, was probably the product of Paul Eber.[96] The shop of Cranach flooded Protestant Germany with portraits of Luther, which were of questionable worth. The defiant, coarse-grained nature of the man is strongly emphasized in these representations, which, though they by no means completely corresponded with each other, form the basis of the typical portrait of Luther which came into use later on. A cloud of spoken and written encomiums, uttered in the style of funeral sermons, overcast the memory of Luther, fascinated the impressionable masses and prevented thousands from obtaining a true insight into the facts of the case and the real character of the man.

5. AFTER LUTHER'S DEATH

The glorification of Luther by his biographers deserves a special treatment on account of its after-effects.

Among the earliest biographies, or rather the attempts at such, which were destined to establish the fame of Luther, mention must be made of the biographical sketch which Melanchthon published at the beginning of the second volume of Luther's Latin works, which appeared in 1546. The writer either closed his eyes to the defects of Luther's character, or excused them. In his admiration of Luther's greatness, he completely forgot the pique which he suffered at his hands.

John Mathesius, an enthusiastic disciple of Luther, but of no pronounced talent, while pastor of Joachimstal in Bohemia, delivered a

---

[96] O. Clemen, *Gedichte auf Luthers Tod*, in the *Jahrbuch der Luthergesellschaft* (1919), pp. 59 sqq.; the same, *Flugschriften aus den ersten Jahren der Reformation*, Leipsic, 1907; cfr. *Zeitschrift für katholische Theologie* (1922), pp. 137 sqq.

series of sermons on Luther which were crammed with historical and unhistorical assertions—"pious panegyrics," as they are properly styled by the Protestant historian William Maurenbrecher. In his eagerness to edify his hearers, Mathesius disregarded the facts. His sermons appeared in print at Nuremberg, in 1566, twenty years after Luther's death, under the title, "Historien von des ehrwirden in Gott seligen thewren Manns Gottes Doctoris M. Lutheri Anfang, Lehr, Leben und Sterben." Due to their popular style, they have enjoyed a wide circulation up to the present time.

In the same year, John Aurifaber, one of the witnesses of Luther's death, published at Eisleben his "Colloquia oder Tischreden" of Luther, to which we have already adverted. The preface, addressed to the "imperial cities of Strasburg, Augsburg, Ulm, Nuremberg," etc., eulogizes Luther as "the venerable and highly enlightened Moses of the Germans." The contents of this work, partly entertaining and partly instructive, display a popular and rather blunt style and wielded an incredibly powerful influence on the masses and thereby confirmed the domination of Luther over many minds. Others, notably Stangwald (1571) and Selnecker (1577), were inspired by Aurifaber's success to issue similar publications.[97]

Cyriacus Spangenberg, a fanatical admirer of Luther, composed a book entitled, "Theander Lutherus," which was divided into sermons. The principal title is followed by a high-sounding, lengthy subtitle, which enables one to infer the tendency and worth of the whole work. In this subtitle Luther is called "the esteemed man of God," "a prophet," "an apostle," and "an evangelist," "the third Elias," "the second Paul," and "the true John," "a most excellent theologian," "the angel of the Apocalypse," etc. These sermons, delivered at Mansfeld in 1562, first appeared separately, but were afterwards published in a collective edition (1589). They did not, however, attain to the popularity of Mathesius' "Historien."[98]

Flacius Illyricus, a professor at the University of Wittenberg, and Nicholas Amsdorf, were two of the most enthusiastic champions of Luther, who achieved eminence not by writing biographies of their hero, but by eulogizing and battling for him. Thus Flacius, in his book on "The Marks of the True Religion" (Magdeburg, 1549), treated of the mark of sanctity, which he discovered not only in the

---

[97] On these and other biographers of Luther see Grisar, *op. cit.*, Vol. VI, pp. 388 sqq.
[98] *Ibid.*, p. 391.

doctrines of his deified master, but also in his extraordinarily pious life, abounding in examples of Christian virtue. Amsdorf, likewise, describes Luther as a saint, the equal of St. Paul. He maintains that Luther was "raised by a special grace and given to the German nation." He strongly stresses his German nationality. By laying emphasis on Luther's patriotism, efforts were put forth at a very early date to persuade the "German nation" of its obligation to honor its great leader. German nationality, German customs, and German patriotism were made to serve as effective levers to raise the figure of Luther to a high pedestal.

However, the authors just mentioned, like many later eulogists of Luther, cannot avoid painful references to the serious schisms and counter-currents of the time. Many theologians and preachers differ in their teaching from the so-called orthodox or Gnesio-Lutherans, without ceasing to extol Luther. Amsdorf complains about these "pretenders to wisdom," Flacius Illyricus fulminates against them as "apostates." Many were persecuted by the inflamed theologians of the new religion. Mathesius is alarmed at seeing "all sorts of impure and poisoned water" penetrating the "pipes of Wittenberg," through which the waters of life are dispensed.

What Luther had frequently foretold came to pass after his death. The profound theological controversies that agitated the schools and churches soon entailed the intervention of the civil governments. The names used to describe the controversies (such as Osiandric, Majorite, Adiaphoristic, and Synergistic disputes) are reminiscent of movements that were as replete with theological contrasts as with passions and hatred.[99] How the Gnesio-Lutherans, and particularly Flacius and his followers, were singled out for attack, may be seen from a cannon in the fortress of Coburg, cast at that time, in which the favorite court-preacher is portrayed in the act of seizing an adherent of Flacius by the throat and strangling him. In electoral Saxony, the classic land of the Lutheran Reformation, Cryptocalvinism, so-called, gained the ascendancy under the Elector August, who became ruler in 1553. The representatives of this movement published a *Corpus Doctrinae Philippicum,* extracted from the writings of Melanchthon, which deviated from the teaching of Luther. Although protected by the civil authorities, Melanchthon and the "Philippists,"

[99] *Ibid.,* pp. 408 sqq.

as his followers were called, suffered much from the persecution of the Lutheran theologians.

More tranquil times dawned only after "orthodox" Lutheranism had established its rule. The extravagant praises of Luther resounded everywhere during this period; but soon the Age of Enlightenment came and effected a considerable decline of Luther's influence among scholars and the educated laity. The contradictory nature of his doctrines and their defects were more widely recognized and conclusions drawn from his premises which, while they were not illogical, would have been very unwelcome to Luther himself. Some even dared to criticize publicly the character and private life of the founder of Protestantism. Finally, the rise of the historico-critical method threatened to impair the esteem harbored for his doctrines and person. About the time of the centenary celebration of Luther's birth (1883), however, a reaction favorable to his reputation set in among influential Protestants in Germany. This was due to various circumstances, not the least of which was aggravated opposition to a newly ascendant Catholicism. In conformity with modern ideas, Luther was now hailed as a champion of liberty and civilization, a guide to a new spiritual future, as well as the representative of the national ideals and customs of Germany.[100] In the World War he was to be the hero of unadulterated and triumphant German tradition and inspiration; but the defeat of the Central Powers disappointed the audacious hopes of Lutheranism.[101]

In the meantime, especially since the revolution, the religion of Luther has, in many respects, assumed the rôle of a so-called "German religion" without dogmas. The Protestant churches, honoring his name as a symbol of their title, are actively engaged in securing their future under a new form, the former system of national churches having ceased to exist. Some laudably endeavor to preserve for Protestantism the positive Christian elements which Luther retained. In general, however, the religious Luther is relegated to the background. Though his admirers ought to consider him primarily as a religious

[100] Probably only a few individuals, however, regarded criticism as prohibited to such a degree as the author of a prominent jubilee book for 1917, who wrote: "After four hundred years, we do not feel justified in criticizing the shade of this great and singular man." But he admits that he "likes the Luther of the diet of Worms better than the Luther of the year 1545."

[101] Cf. H. Grisar, Der deutsche Luther im Weltkrieg und in der Gegenwart, Augsburg, 1924.

innovator, they abandon, with striking unanimity, the religious phase, and, instead, celebrate Luther as a champion of modern culture. This became evident in 1917, at the time of the fourth centenary of the Reformation, and during the celebrations commemorative of that event in the ensuing years, such as that at Worms.[102] A closer inspection of the voluminous scientific and popular literature of this period, and of the flood of published addresses delivered at the larger festival assemblies, elicit amazement at the thoroughness with which the historic Luther has been obliterated. His teaching is discarded as unimportant, and the highest aims of his life are tacitly treated as antiquated and obsolete. Public attention is directed to the excellence of his German style, the literary skill shown in his translation of the Bible, the popular appeal of his hymns, and, naturally, his alleged genuine "Germanism." [103] His undaunted courage was eulogized and his boast re-echoed throughout Germany: "No one, please God, shall awe me so long as I live." [104] Just as though the moral value of the ends pursued, as well as the morality of the means employed, are not a necessary element in evaluating courage and perseverance! This very defiance which would assail heaven, the very quality of "superman," induced many admirers to refer to Luther as a great historical phenomenon. Most of them, however, base their admiration upon something quite different. Luther's courage has begun to gain that unrestrained spiritual liberty which they desire to enjoy. Luther destroyed for his adherents the authority of the old Church. It is this destructive phase of his activity which makes him so important to our modern age. The freedom of the intellect which he won by his struggles, we are told, must be extended. Men must advance beyond the beginnings which he inaugurated, and strive for a more natural Christianity. In the attainment of this end Luther must be our guide. That is the slogan of the great majority of Protestant scholars.[105] Luther's responsibility for such a fate, which is tantamount

[102] Grisar, *Lutherstudien*, n. 1: "*Luther zu Worms und die jüngsten drei Jahrhundertfeste der Reformation*," Freiburg, 1921.

[103] Grisar, *Die Literatur des Lutherjubiläums 1917, ein Bild des heutigen Protestantismus*, in the *Zeitschrift für kathol. Theologie*, Vol. XLII (1918), pp. 591–628 and 785–814.

[104] Cf. Grisar, *Luther*, Vol. VI, pp. 396 sqq., where other similar passages are reproduced.

[105] According to Friedrich Loofs, *Wer war Jesus?* (Halle, 1916, p. 216), "all learned [Protestant] theologians of Germany—even those who do not express themselves openly—are agreed that the ancient orthodox theology of the two natures in Christ cannot be maintained in its traditional form." Belief in the divinity of Christ is relinquished. "All systematic theologians are seeking new ways in Christology." (Cf. p. 180).

to a disavowal of his life's work, cannot be denied. And yet, with the aid of Lutheran propositions, *i. e.*, a selection of his doctrines on the religion of Christ, reproduced in his own forceful language, it is possible to deliver a scathing indictment against the ever-increasing ranks of his admirers.

BIBLIOGRAPHY

Analecta Lutherana. Letters and documents pertaining to the history of Luther. Containing at the same time a supplement to his hitherto collected correspondence. Edited by Th. Kolde. Gotha, 1883.

Analecta Lutherana et Malanchthoniana; cf. Mathesius, *Aufzeichnungen.*

Archiv für Reformationsgeschichte. Texte und Untersuchungen. Edited by W. Friedensburg. Berlin (afterwards Leipsic), 1903–1904 sqq.

BALAN P. *Monumenta Reformationis Lutheranae ex Tabulariis S. Sedis Secretis.* 1521–1525. Ratisbonae, 1884.

BARANOWSKI S. *Luthers Lehre von der Ehe.* Münster, 1913.

BARGE H. *Andreas Bodenstein von Karlstadt.* 2 vols., Leipsic, 1905.

BELOW G. v. *Die Ursachen der Reformation.* (Histor. Bibliothek., Vol. 38), 3rd ed., Berlin, 1917. (Cfr. *Theol. Revue,* 1919, p. 49.)

—— *Die Bedeutung der Reformation in der politischen Entwicklung.* Leipsic, 1918. (Cfr. *Theol. Revue,* 1919, p. 112.)

BERGER A. E. *Martin Luther in kulturgeschichtlicher Darstellung.* (Collection "Geisteshelden.") 3 Parts. Berlin, 1895–1921.

BEZOLD F. v. *Geschichte der deutschen Reformation.* Berlin, 1890.

BICHLER FR. *Luther in Vergangenheit und Gegenwart.* Ratisbon, 1918. (Cfr. *Theol. Revue,* 1921, p. 59; *Hist.-polit. Blätter,* 163 [1919], p. 66.)

BIEREYE JOH. *Die Erfurter Lutherstätten.* With 13 Plates. Erfurt, 1917.

BÖHMER H. *Luther im Lichte der neueren Forschung.* (Aus Natur und Geisteswelt, No. 113.) Leipsic, 1906; 5th ed., 1918.

—— *Luthers Romfahrt.* Leipsic, 1914.

—— *Der junge Luther.* Gotha, 1925. 393 pages with 39 Portraits.

BRANDENBURG E. *Luthers Anschauung von Staat und Gesellschaft.* Schriften des Vereins für Reformationsgeschichte, No. 70, Halle, 1901.

BRAUN W. *Die Bedeutung der Concupiscenz in Luthers Leben und Lehre.* Berlin, 1908.

—— *Biographisches und theologisches Verständnis der Entwicklung Luthers.* Berlin, 1917.

BRIEFWECHSEL; see CORRESPONDENCE.

BRIEGER TH. *Aleander und Luther. Die vervollständigten Aleander-Depeschen nebst Untersuchungen über den Wormser Reichstag.* Part I. Gotha, 1884.

—— *Die Reformation.* Berlin, 1914.

—— *Martin Luther und wir. Das reformatorische Christentum Luthers.* 2nd ed., Gotha, 1918.

BUCHWALD GEORG. *Dr. M. Luther.* 3rd, revised ed. Leipsig, 1917.

BURKHARDT C. A. *Geschichte der sächsischen Kirchen- und Schulvisitationen von 1524 bis 1545.* Leipsic, 1879.

CALVIN JOHN. *Opera quae Supersunt Omnia.* Edited by G. Baum, E. Cunitz, E. Reuss. 59 vols. (29–87 in *Corpus Reformatorum.*) Brunsvigae, 1863–1900.

COCHLAEUS JOHN. *Commentaria de Actis et Scriptis M. Lutheri. . . . ab a. 1517 usque ad a. 1536 conscripta.* Moguntiae, 1549.

COHRS FERD. *Phil. Melanchthon. (Schriften des Vereins für Reformationsgeschichte,* No. 55.) Halle, 1897.

(COLLOQUIA, ed. Bindseil), BINDSEIL H. E., *D. Martini Lutheri Colloquia, Meditationes, Consolationes, Iudicia, Sententiae, Narrationes, Responsa, Facetiae e Codice ms. Bibliothecae Orphanotrophei Halensis cum perpetua collatione editionis Rebenstockianae Edita et Prolegomenis Indicibusque Instructa.* 3 vols. Lemgoviae et Detmoldae, 1863–1866.

(*Commentarius in Epist. ad Galat.*) M. *Lutheri Commentarius in Epistolam ad Galatas.* Ed. I. A. IRMISCHER, 3 vols. Erlangae, 1843 sq.

(CORDATUS, *Tagebuch*) WRAMPELMEYER H., *Tagebuch über Dr. Martin Luther, geführt von Dr. Konrad Cordatus,* 1537. First edited in Halle, 1885.

Corpus Catholicorum. Works of Catholic Authors in the Age of the Reformation; founded by J. GREVING. Vol. I (containing plan of the undertaking). Münster, 1919; Vol. II to VII (containing Contarini's Documents of the Counter-Reformation, edited by FRIED. HÜNERMANN), Münster 1919 to 1923.

Corpus Reformatorum. Ed. BRETSCHNEIDER et BINDSEIL. Halis Saxoniae, 1834 sqq. Vols. I–XXVII: *Melanchthonis Opera;* Vols. XXIX–LXXXVII: *Calvini Opera;* Vols. LXXXVIII–XCVI: *Zwingli Opera. Supplementa Melanchthoniana.* 1 vol.: The Dogmatic Writings, edited by O. CLEMEN. Leipsic, 1909.

(*Correspondence.*) M. *Luther's Briefe, Sendschreiben und Bedenken vollständig gesammelt von M. de Wette.* Sect. I–V. Berlin, 1825–1828; Sect., VI, ed. by J. K. SEIDEMANN, Berlin, 1856.

(*Correspondence.*) *Dr. Martin Luthers Briefwechsel. Bearbeitet und mit Erläuterungen versehen von L. Enders.* Vols. I–XI. Frankfort on the Main, thereafter Stuttgart, 1884–1907; Vols. XII–XVI: revised by G. KAWERAU, Leipsic, 1910–1915; Vol. XVII, revised by G. KAWERAU and P. FLEMMING, *ibid.,* 1920; Vol. XVIII, revised by P. FLEMMING and O. ALBRECHT *ibid.,* 1923.

(*Correspondence.*) *Luthers Briefwechsel, mit vielen unbekannten Briefen und unter Berücksichtigung der De Wetteschen Ausgabe,* ed. by C. A. BURKHARDT. Leipsic, 1866.

——Briefwechsel des Beatus Rhenanus, gesammelt und herausgegeben von A. *Horawitz und K. Hartfelder.* Leipsic, 1886,

—— *Briefwechsel der Brüder Ambrosius und Thomas Blaurer*, 1509–1548, ed. by TR. SCHIES. Vol. I. Freiburg i. B., 1908.

—— *Briefwechsel des Justus Jonas, gesammelt und bearbeitet von G. Kawerau.* 2 vols. Halle, 1884.

—— *Briefwechsel Landgrafs Philipps des Grossmütigen von Hessen mit Bucer*, ed. by M. LENZ. (*Publikationen aus dem Kgl. Preuss. Staatsarchiv.*) 3 vols. Leipsic, 1880–1891.

—— *Akten und Briefe zur Kirchenpolitik Herzog Georgs von Sachsen*, ed. by F. GESS. Vol. I–II, Leipsic, 1905–1917.

—— *Erasmi Opus Epistolarum*, ed. P. S. ALLEN. Vol. IV: 1519–1521. London (Oxford), 1922.

CREUTZBERG, H. A. *Karl von Miltitz. Sein Leben und seine geschichtliche Bedeutung.* (*Studien und Dartellungen aus dem Gebiete der Geschichte*, edited under the auspices of the Goerres-Gesellschaft, Vol. VI, no. 1). Freiburg i. Br., 1907.

CRISTIANI, L. *Du Luthéranisme au Protestantisme. Thèse de Clermont.* Paris, 1911.

DENIFLE, H. (O. P.) *Luther und Luthertum in der ersten Entwicklung, quellenmässig dargestellt.* Vol. I, 1st ed., Mayence, 1904; 2nd ed., Part I, *ibid.*, 1904; Part II, supplemented and edited by A. W. WEISS, O. P., *ibid.*, 1906.

—— *Quellenbelege zu Bd. I, 2te Aufl., Abt. 1–2: Die abendländische Schriftauslegung bis Luther über Justitia Dei (Rom. 1, 17) und Justificatio. Beitrag zur Geschichte der Exegese, der Literatur und des Dogmas im Mittelalter. Ibid.*, 1905. Vol. II of the main work, edited by A. M. WEISS, O. P., *ibid.*, 1909.

—— *Luther in rationalistischer und christlicher Beleuchtung. Prinzipielle Auseinandersetzung mit A. Harnack und R. Seeberg.* Mayence, 1904.

—— Works provoked by Denifle; cf. Wolf, *Quellenkunde*, Vol. II, Sect. 1, p. 230, note 4.

Deutsch-evangelische Blätter. Zeitschrift für den gesamten Bereich des deutschen Protestantismus. Halle, 1891 sqq.

DILTHEY W. *Glaubenslehre der Reformatoren.* (*Preussische Jahrbücher*, Vol. 75).

—— *Gesammelte Schriften.* Vols. 1, 2, 4. Leipsic, 1914 sqq.

(*Disputations.*) DREWS P., *Disputationen Dr. Martin Luthers, in den Jahren 1535–1545 an der Universität Wittenberg gehalten. Zum ersten Mal hg. Göttingen*, 1895.

(*Disputations.*) STANGE C., *Die ältesten ethischen Disputationen Dr. Martin Luthers.* (*Quellenschriften zur Geschichte des Protestantismus*, Vol. I). Leipsic, 1904.

DÖLLINGER J. v. *Luther. Eine Skizze.* Freiburg i. Br., 1890. (Also in Wetzer and Welte's *Kirchenlexikon*, 1st and 2nd ed., article, "Luther.")

—— *Die Reformation, ihre innere Entwicklung und ihre Wirkungen im Umfange des lutherischen Bekenntnisses.* 3 vols. Ratisbon, 1846–1848 (Vol. I, 2nd ed., 1851).

DOUMERGUE E. *Jean Calvin.* Vol. I–V. Lausanne, 1899–1917.

ECK IOH. *Opera contra Ludderum* Pars I–V. Ingolstadii, 1530–1535.

—— *Epistola de Ratione Studiorum suorum 1538,* ed. I. METZLER in *Corpus Cath.,* no. 2; cfr. *Theol. Revue,* 1922, p. 147.

—— *Pfarrbuch U. L. Frau in Ingolstadt,* ed. by J. GREVING. Leipsic, 1908.

ECKART R. *Luther und die Reformation in Urteilen bedeutender Männer.* 2nd ed. Halle, 1917.

EHSES St. *Geschichte der Packschen Händel. Ein Beitrag zur Geschichte der deutschen Reformation.* Freiburg i. Br., 1881.

ELLINGER G. *Philipp Melanchthon. Ein Lebensbild.* Berlin, 1902.

ERASMUS D. *Opera Omnia Emendatiora et Auctiora.* Ed. CLERICUS. 10 vols. Lugd. Batavorum, 1702–1706.

Erläuterungen und Ergänzungen zu Janssens Geschichte des deutschen Volkes, ed. by L. v. PASTOR. Freiburg i. Br., 1898–1925.

EVERS G. *Martin Luther. Lebens- und Charakterbild, von ihm selbst gezeichnet in seinen eigenen Schriften und Korrespondenzen.* 6 vols. Mayence, 1883–1891.

FALK F. *Die Bibel am Ausgang des Mittelalters.* Mayence, 1905.

—— *Die Ehe am Ausgang des Mittelalters. (Erläuterungen und Ergänzungen zu Janssens Geschichte des deutschen Volkes,* Vol. VI, no. 4). Freiburg i. Br., 1908.

Flugschriften aus den ersten Jahren der Reformation, ed. by O. CLEMEN. Leipsic and New York, 1907 sqq.

Flugschriften aus der Reformationszeit in Faksimiledrucken, ed. by O. CLEMEN. No. 1–4. Leipsic, 1921. See *Zeitschrift für kath. Theologie,* Vol. 46 (1922), pp. 137–140.

FÖRSTEMANN C. E. *Neues Urkundenbuch zur Geschichte der evangelischen Kirchenreform.* 1 vol. only. Hamburg, 1842.

FRIEDENSBURG A. *Geschichte der Universität Wittenberg.* Halle, 1917.

GÖLLER E. *Der Ausbruch der Reformation und dis spätmittelalterliche Ablasspraxis.* Freiburg i. Br., 1917.

GOTTSCHICK J. *Luthers Lehre.* Tübingen, 1914.

GRISAR H. (S. J.) *Luther.* Vol I: *Luthers Werden. Grundlegung der Spaltung bis 1530.* 3rd ed. with supplementary notes, Freiburg i. Br., 1924. Vol II: *Auf der Höhe des Lebens,* 3rd ed., with supplementary notes, *ibid.,* 1924. Vol. III: *Am Ende der Bahn. Rückblicke.* 3rd ed., with supplementary notes, *ibid.,* 1925.—(The *Nachträge* to the 3rd ed. of this work can be had separately.)

—— *Luther.* Authorized translation from the German by E. M. Lamond, edited by LUIGI CAPPADELTA. London and St. Louis, 1913–1917. 6 vols.

—— *Luther-Studien. Luthers Kampfbilder. In Verbindung mit Franz Heege*
S. J. *hg. Heft 1: Passional Christi und Antichristi. Eröffnung des Bilder-*
kampfes. Heft 2: Der Bilderkampf in der deutschen Bibel. Heft 3: Der
Bilderkampf in den Schriften von 1523 bis 1545. Heft 4: Die "Abbildung
des Papsttums" und andere Kampfbilder in Flugblättern 1538–1545.—
Luther zu Worms und die jüngsten drei Jahrhundertfeste der Reformation.
—Luthers Trutzlied "Ein' feste Burg" in Vergangenheit und Gegenwart.
Freiburg i. Br., 1921 sqq.

—— *Der deutsche Luther im Weltkrieg und in der Gegenwarst.* Augsburg,
1924.

—— Articles on Luther and Melanchthon in relation to education, in the
Lexikon der Pädagogik by Roloff. Freiburg i. Br., 1921.

—— *Luther-Analekten, I–VII. (Historisches Jahrbuch der Görres-Gesell-*
schaft, Vol. XXXIX–XLII. Munich, 1919–1922.

—— *Prinzipienfragen moderner Lutherforschung. (Sonderabdruck aus den*
Stimmen aus Maria-Laach, Bd. 83, Heft 10). Freiburg i. Br., 1912.

—— *W. Köhler über Luther und die Lüge. (Sonderabdruck aus dem His-*
torischen Jahrbuch der Görres-Gesellschaft, Bd. 23, Heft 1). Munich,
1913.

—— *Literatur des Lutherjubiläums von 1917, ein Bild des heutigen Pro-*
testanismus. (Sonderabdruck aus der Zeitschrift für katholische Theologie,
Bd. 42 [1918], S. 391, 628, 785–814.) Innsbruck, 1918.

—— *Einige Bemerkungen zur protestantischen Kritik meines Lutherwerkes.*
(*Theol. Revue,* 1919, pp. 1 sqq.)

GRÜTZMACHER R. H.; see *Reformationsschriften.*

HALLER JOH. *Die Ursachen der Reformation.* Tübingen, 1917.

HANSEN H. *Stimuli et Clavi, Spiesse und Nägel (zur Reformationsfeier* 1917).
Altona, 1917. (Cfr. Grisar, *Literatur des Lutherjubiläums,* pp. 596–598).

HARNACK A. *Lehrbuch der Dogmengeschichte.* Vol. III: *Die Entwicklung*
des kirchlichen Dogmas. II and III, 4th revised ed., Tübingen 1910.

—— *Luther und die Grundlegung der Reformation.* Berlin, 1917.

—— *Die Reformation. (Internationale Monatschrift für Wissenschaft* usw.,
1917, Heft 11, pp. 1281–1364.) Reprinted in *Reden und Aufsätze,* Vol.
VI, Giessen, 1923, pp. 71–136.

HARTFELDER K. *Phil. Melanchthon als Praeceptor Germaniae. (Mon. Germ.*
Paedagogica, tom. VII.) Berlin, 1889.

HAUCK A. *Die Reformation in ihren Wirkungen auf das Leben.* Leipsic,
1918. Cfr. *Hist.-politische Blätter,* Vol. 163 (1919), pp. 34–42.

HAUSRATH A. *Luthers Leben.* 2 vols. Berlin, 1904. (2nd and 3rd imprint
with supplementary notes by H. v. Schubert.)

HEEGE F. See GRISAR, *Lutherstudien.*

HERMELINK H. *Reformation und Gegenreformation* in *Handbuch der*
Kirchengeschichte by G. Krüger, Vol. III.) Tübingen, 1911.

HOLL K. *Gesammelte Aufsätze zur Kirchengeschichte.* Vol. I: *Luther.* 2nd and 3rd ed., Tübingen, 1923.

HUMBERTCLAUDE H. *Erasme et Luther.* Fribourg i. Sw., 1909.

HUNZINGER A. W. *Luther-Studien.* Heft 1–2. Leipzig, 1905. Cfr. Wolf, *Quellenkunde,* Vol. II, Sect. 1, p. 236.

HUTTEN ULR. *Opera.* 5 vols., ed. E. BÖCKING. Lipsiae, 1859–1862.

IMBART DE LA TOUR P. *Les Origines de la Réforme.* 3 Vols. Paris, 1905–1914.

(JANSSEN-PASTOR.) JANSSEN J., *Geschichte des deutschen Volkes seit dem Ausgang des Mittelalters.* 19th and 20th ed. by L. VON PASTOR. Vol. I: *Die allgemeinen Zustände des deutschen Volkes beim Ausgang des Mittelalters,* Freiburg i. Br., 1913; Vol. II: *Vom Beginn der politisch-kirchlichen Revolution bis zum Ausgang der sozialen Revolution von 1525, ibid.,* 1915; Vol. III: *Bis zum sogenannten Augsburger Religionsfrieden von 1555, ibid.,* 1917. Cf. also *Erläuterungen und Ergänzungen.*

—— *An meine Kritiker. Nebst Ergänzungen und Erläuterungen zu den drei ersten Bänden meiner Geschichte des deutschen Volkes.* Freiburg i. Br., 1882.

—— *Ein zweites Wort an meine Kritiker. Nebst Ergänzungen und Erläuterungen zu den drei ersten Bänden meiner Geschichte des deutschen Volkes.* Freiburg i. Br., 1883.

JORDAN Herm. *Luthers Staatsauffassung.* Munich, 1917.

KALKOFF P. *Forschungen zu Luthers römischem Prozess.* (*Bibliothek des Kgl. Preuss. Histor. Instituts in Rom,* Vol. II), Rome, 1905.

—— *Luther und die Entscheidungsjahre der Reformation. Von den Ablassthesen bis zum Wormser Edikt.* Leipsic, 1917.

—— *Der Wormser Reichstag von 1521.* Munich and Berlin, 1922.

—— *Das Wormser Edikt.* Munich, 1917.

—— *Erasmus, Luther und Friedrich der Weise.* Leipsic, 1920.

—— *Ulrich von Hutten und die Reformation.* Leipsic, 1920.

—— *Zu Luthers römischem Prozess.* Gotha, 1912 (with a list of Kalkoffs previous writings, pp. v ff.)—Cfr. G. KRÜGER, *Kalkoffs Studien zur Frühgeschichte der Reformation* in *Theol. Studien und Kritiken,* 1918, pp. 144 sqq.

KAMPSCHULTE F. W. *Johannes Calvin, seine Kirche und sein Staat in Genf.* 2 vols. Leipsic, 1869 and 1899.

—— *Die Universität Erfurt und ihr Verhältniss zum Humanismus und zur Reformation.* 2 vols. Treves, 1858 and 1860.

KAULFUSS-DIESCH Karl. *Das Buch der Reformation, geschrieben von Mitlebenden.* Leipsic, 1917.

KASER KURT. *Reformation und Gegenreformation* (in *Weltgeschichte,* ed. by Ludo M. HARTMANN, Vol. VI, Sect. 1.) Stuttgart, 1922.

KAWERAU GUST. *Reformation und Gegenreformation.* 3rd ed., Freiburg, 1907 (in MÖLLERS *Lehrbuch der Kirchengeschichte,* Vol. III.)

—— *Die Versuche, Melanchthon zur katholischen Kirche zurückzuführen.* (*Schriften des Vereins für Reformationsgeschichte,* Heft 73.) Leipsic, 1903.

—— *Luthers Schriften nach der Reihenfolge der Jahre verzeichnet.* (*Zweite Publikation des Vereins für Reformationsgeschichte.*) Leipsic, 1917.

—— *Glossen zu Grisars "Luther"* (*Schriften des Vereins für Reformationsgechichte,* Heft 105.) *Leipsic,* 1911. Cfr. GRISAR, *Luther,* (Engl. tr.), Vol. VI. and *Stimmen aus Maria-Laach,* 1913, Heft 1, pp. 9 sqq.

——*Luthers Randglosses zum Marienpsalter des Markus von Weida* (*Theol. Studien und Kritiken,* 1917. pp. 81 ff.)

KIEFL F. X. *Katholische Weltanschauung und modernes Denken.* 2nd and 3rd ed., Ratisbon, 1922.

Kirchenordnungen, Die evangelischen des 16. Jahrhunderts, ed. by E. SEHLING. I: *Die Ordnungen für die ernestinischen und albertinischen Gebiete,* Leipsic, 1902; II: *Die vier geistlichen Gebiete* usw., *ibid.,* 1904; III: *Die Mark Brandenburg* usw., *ibid.,* 1909.

KIRN P. *Friedrich der Weise und die Kirche. Seine Kirchenpolitik vor und nach Luthers Auftreten im Jahre* 1517. Leipsic, 1926.

KLINGNER ERICH. *Luther und der deutsche Volksaberglaube.* Berlin, 1912.

KÖHLER WALTER. *Katholizismus und Reformation. Kritisches Referat über die wissenschaftlichen Leistungen der neueren katholischen Theologie auf dem Gebiete der Reformationsgeschichte.* Giessen, 1905.

—— *Luther und die Kirchengeschichte.* Vol. I, Sect. 1. Erlangen, 1900.

—— *Luther und die deutsche Reformation.* Leipsic, 1916.

—— *Luther der deutsche Reformator.* 2nd ed., Contance, 1917.

—— *Luther und die Lüge.* Leipsic, 1912. (*Schriften des Vereins für Reformationsgeschichte.*)

—— *Dokumente zum Ablaszstreit von* 1517. Tübingen, 1902.

—— *Zwingli und Luther. Ihr Streit über das Abendmahl.* Vol. I. Leipsic, 1924.

KÖSTLIN JUL. *Luthers Leben.* 9th ed., Leipsic, 1891.

—— *Luthers Theologie in ihrer geschichtlichen Entwicklung und in ihrem Zusammenhang dargestellt.* 2 vols., 2nd ed. completely recast. Stuttgart, 1901.

(KÖSTLIN-KAWERAU). KÖSTLIN J., *Martin Luther. Sein Leben und seine Schriften.* 2 vols., 5th revised ed., continued by G. KAWERAU. Berlin, 1903.

KOLDE TH. Cfr. *Analecta Lutherana.*

—— *Die deutsche Augustinerkongregation und Johann v. Staupitz. Ein Beitrag zur Ordens- und Reformationsgeschichte nach meistens ungedruckten Quellen.* Gotha, 1879.

—— *Martin Luther. Eine Biographie.* 2 vols. Gotha, 1884–1893.

KROKER ERNST. *Katharina von Bora.* 2nd ed., Leipsic, 1925.

KURRELMEYER W. *Die erste deutsche Bibel.* Vols. I–X. Tübingen, 1903–1915.

LAUCHERT FRIEDR., *Die italienischen literarischen Gegner Luthers.* (*Erläuterungen und Ergänzungen zu Janssens Geschichte*, Vol. VIII.) Freiburg i. Br., 1912.

(LAUTERBACH's *Tagebuch*). SEIDEMANN J. K., A. *Lauterbachs Tagebuch auf das Jahr 1538. Die Hauptquelle der Tischreden Luthers.* Dresden, 1872.

LEWIN REINH. *Luthers Stellung zu den Juden.* Berlin, 1911.

LOESCHE G. Cfr. Mathesius, *Aufzeichnungen, Historien.*

LOOFS F. *Leitfaden zum Studium der Dogmengeschichte.* 4th, completely recast ed., Halle a. d. S., 1906.

LÖSCHER V. E. *Vollständige Reformationsacta und Documenta.* 3 vols. Leipsic, 1720–1729.

LUTHARDT C. E. *Die Ethik Luthers in ihren Grundzügen.* 2nd revised ed., Leipsic, 1875.

LUTHER MARTIN. (1) collected editions of his writings, see *Werke, Opera Lat. Var., Opera Lat. Exeg., Commentarius in Epist. ad Galatas, Römerbriefkommentar.* (2) Correspondence, see *Correspondence, Analecta.* (3) Table Talk, see *Tischreden* ed. by Aurifaber and Förstemann; also *Werke*, Weimar ed., Erl. ed., Vols. LVII–LXII; *Werke*, Halle ed., Vol. XXII; *Colloquia, Cordatus, Lauterbach, Mathesius, Schlaginhaufen.* (4) Various writings, see *Analecta, Disputations.*

LUTHER-GESELLSCHAFT (Wittenberg): *Jahrbuch*, 1919 sqq.; *Flugschriften*, 1919 sqq.; *Mitteilungen* (now *Luther*). *Vietrteljahrsschrift.*

Luther-Studien von den Mitarbeitern der Weimarer Lutherausgabe. Weimar, 1917.

MATHESIUS J., *Aufzeichnungen*: Loesche G., *Analecta Lutherana et Melanchthoniana. Tischreden Luthers und Aussprüche Melanchthons hauptsächlich nach den Aufzeichnungen des Johannes Mathesius, aus der Nürnberger Handschrift im Germanischen Museum mit Benützung von Seidemanns Vorarbeiten hg. und erläutert.* Gotha, 1892.

MATHESIUS J. *Historien von des ehrwirdigen in Gott seligen thewren Manns Gottes Doctoris Martini Luthers Anfang, Lehr, Leben und Sterben.* Nuremberg, 1566; ed. by G. LOESCHE in the *Bibliothek deutscher Schriftsteller aus Böhmen*, Vol. IX, Prague, 1898; 2nd ed., 1906. (Our quotations are from the Nuremberg edition.)

MATHESIUS J. *Tischreden*: KROKER E., *Luthers Tischreden in der Mathesischen Sammlung. Aus einer Handschrift der Leipziger Stadtbibliothek.* Leipsic, 1903.

MAURENBRECHER W. *Studien und Skizzen zur Geschichte der Reformationszeit*, Leipsic, 1874.

—— *Geschichte der katholischen Reformation*, Vol. I, Nördlingen, 1880.

MELANCHTHON, see MATHESIUS; also *Vita Lutheri.*

MELANCHTHON, *Opera Omnia*. Ed. BRETSCHNEIDER. (*Corpus Reformatorum*, vols. I to XXVIII.) Halis Saxoniae, 1834–1863.

—— *Supplementa Melanchthoniana. Werke Philipp Melanchthons, die im Corpus Reformatorum vermisst werden*. Ed. by the Verein für Reformationsgeschichte, Leipzig.

MENTZ GEORG. *Deutsche Geschichte im Zeitalter der Reformation, 1493–1648*. Tübingen, 1913.

MÖHLER J. A. *Symbolik oder Darstellung der dogmatischen Gegensätze der Katholiken und Protestanten nach ihren öffentlichen Bekenntnisschriften*. 1st ed., Ratisbon, 1832. 10th ed., with supplementary notes by J. M. RAICH. Mayence, 1889.

MÖLLER W. *Lehrbuch der Kirchengeschichte*. Vol. III: *Reformation und Gegenreformation*, by G. KAWERAU, 3rd revised and enlarged ed., Tübingen, 1907.

MÜLLER ALFONS VIKT. *Luthers theologische Quellen*. Giessen, 1912. Cfr. M. Grabmann in the *Katholik*, Vol. XCIII, pp. 151 sqq.

—— *Luther und Tauler*. Bonn, 1918.

—— *Luthers Werden bis zum Turmerlebnis*. Gotha, 1920. See *Theol. Revue*, 1920, pp. 297 sq.

MÜLLER H. T., *Die symbolischen Bücher der evangelisch-lutherischen Kirche, deutsch und lateinisch. Mit einer neuen historischen Einleitung von Th. Kolde*. 10th ed., Gütersloh, 1907.

MÜLLER KARL. *Luther und Karlstadt. Stücke aus ihrem gegenseitigen Verhältnis untersucht*. Tübingen, 1909.

—— *Kirche, Gemeinde und Obrigkeit nach Luther*. Tübingen, 1910.

—— *Kirchengeschichte*. Vols. I and II. Tübingen, 1902–1919.

—— *Luthers Äusserungen über das Recht des bewaffneten Widerstandes gegen den Kaiser*. Munich, 1915.

MÜLLER NIK. *Die Wittenberger Bewegung von 1521 bis 1522*. 2nd ed., Leipsic, 1911.

MÜNZER TH. *Hochverursachte Schutzrede und Antwort wider das geistlose sanftlebende Fleisch zu Wittenberg*, ed. by ENDERS, *Neudrucke deutscher Literaturwerke*, No. 118, Halle, 1893.

MURNER THOMAS, O. S. FR. *Von dem Lutherischen Narren*, ed. by P. MERKER (see *Theol. Lit.-Zeitung*, 1919, 224).—*Die Mühle*, ed. by the Elsäss. Verein (*Murners Schriften*, Vol. IV) 1923.—*Ausgewählte Dichtungen*, ed. by GEORG SCHUMANN, Ratisbon, 1915.

MYCONIUS FRIEDR. *Reformationsgeschichte*, ed. by O. CLEMEN. (*Voigtländers Quellenbücher*, Heft 68), 1915.

NEUBAUER TH. *Luthers Frühzeit*. (*Jahrbücher der Akademie zu Erfurt*, Vol. XLIII), 1917.

Nuntiaturberichte aus Deutschland nebst ergänzenden Aktenstücken. Part I: 1533–1559, ed. by the Kgl. Preuss. Institut in Rom and the Kgl. Preuss.

Archivverwaltung; Vol. V: *Nuntiaturen Morones und Poggios; Legationen Farneses und Cervinis* 1539–1540, ed. by L. CARDAUNS; Vol. VI: *Gesandtschaft Campeggios; Nuntiaturen Morones und Poggios 1540–1541*, ed. by L. CARDAUNS. Berlin, 1909.

Opera Latina Exegetica.—M. *Lutheri Exegetica Opera Latina.* Cura C. Elsperger. 28 vols. Erlangae, 1829 sqq.—Printed separately: *D. M. Lutheri Commentarius in Epistolam ad Galatas*, ed. I. A. IRMISCHER. 3 vols. Erlangae, 1843 sq.

Opera Latina Varia.—M. *Lutheri Opera Latina Varii Argumenti ad Reformationis Historiam Imprimis Pertinentia.* Cura H. SCHMIDT. Vols. I–VII. Francofurti, 1865 sqq. (Forms part of the Erlangen ed. of Luther's *Werke.*)

OERGEL G. *Vom jungen Luther. Beiträge zur Lutherforschung.* Erfurt, 1899.

PASTOR L. v. *Geschichte der Päpste seit dem Ausgang des Mittelalters. Mit Benutzung des Päpstlichen Geheimarchivs und vieler anderer Archive bearbeitet.* Vols. I and III, 8th and 9th revised ed.; Vol. III, 5th to 7th ed.; Vol. IV, 8th to 9th ed.; Vol. V, 8th to 9th ed.

PAULS THEODOR, *Luthers Auffassung von Staat und Volk. (Bonner Staatswissenschaftliche Untersuchungen*, Heft 12). Bonn and Leipsic, 1925.

PAULSEN F. *Geschichte des gelehrten Unterrichtes auf den deutschen Schulen und Universitäten vom Ausgang des Mittelalters bis zur Gegenwart. Mit besonderer Rücksicht auf den klassischen Unterricht.* Leipsic, 1885, 2 vols.; 2nd ed., 1896–1897; 3rd ed., Berlin, 1921.

PAULUS N. *Die deutschen Dominikaner im Kampfe gegen Luther, 1518–1563. (Erläuterungen und Ergänzungen zu Janssens Geschichte des deutschen Volkes*, Vol. IV, Heft 1 and 2.) Freiburg i. Br., 1903.

—— *Hexenwahn und Hexenprozess vornehmlich im 16. Jahrhundert.* Freiburg i. Br., 1910.

—— *Luther und die Gewissensfreiheit (Glaube und Wissen*, Heft 4), Munich, 1905.

—— *Luthers Lebensende. Eine kritische Untersuchung. (Erläuterungen und Ergänzungen zu Janssens Geschichte des deutschen Volkes*, Vol. I, Heft 1.) Freiburg i. Br., 1898.

—— *Kaspar Schatzgeyer, ein Vorkämpfer der katholischen Kirche gegen Luther in Süddeutschland. (Strassburger Theologische Studien*, Vol. III, Heft 1.) Freiburg i. Br., 1898.

—— *Johann Tetzel, der Ablassprediger.* Mayence, 1899.

—— *Bartholomäus Arnoldi von Usingen. (Strassburger Theologische Studien*, Vol. I, Heft 3.) Freiburg i. Br., 1893.

—— *Zu Luthers Romreise* (in the *Histor. Jahrbuch*, 1901, Vol. XXVI, pp. 79 sqq. and in the *Hist.-polit. Blätter*, 1912, I, pp. 126 sqq.) Cfr. Grisar, *Luther-Analekten*, I.

—— *Protestantismus und Toleranz im 16. Jahrhundert.* Freiburg i. Br., 1911.

—— *Geschichte des Ablasses im Mittelalter.* 3 vols. Paderborn, 1922–1923.

PFLUGK-HARTTUNG J. v. *Im Morgenrot der Reformation.* Hersfeld, 1912 (*Sammlung von Abhandlungen verschiedener Verfasser und von Abbildungen.*)

PREUSS HANS, *Unser Luther. Jubiläumsgabe.* Leipsic, 1917.

—— *Luthers Frömmigkeit,* Leipsic, 1917. (Cfr. *Zeitschrift für Kath. Theologie,* Vol. XLIII [1919], pp. 150–155.)

—— *Lutherbildnisse.* 2nd ed., Leipsic, 1922.

Quellen und Forschungen aus dem Gebiet der Geschichte in Verbindung mit ihrem historischen Institut zu Rom. hg. von der Görres-Gesellschaft. Paderborn, 1892 sqq.

—— *aus den italienischen Archiven und Bibliotheken,* hg. vom Kgl. Preuss. *Histor. Institut in Rom.* Rome, 1897 sqq.

OLDECOP JOH. ed. by K. Euling. (*Bibliothek des literarischen Vereins von Stuttgart,* Vol. CXC), Tübingen, 1891.

RADE. *Martin Luther in Worten aus seinen Werken.* Berlin, 1917.

—— *Luther und die Communio Sanctorum.* Berlin, 1917. (Cfr. *Stimmen der Zeit,* Vol. XCV, 1918), pp. 501 sq.)

—— *Das königliche Priestertum der Gläubigen.* Tübingen, 1918.

—— *Luthers Rechtfertigungsglaube.* Tübingen, 1917.

RATZEBERGER M. *Handschriftliche Geschichte über Luther und seine Zeit,* ed. by Ch. G. NEUDECKER. Jena, 1850.

RAYNALDI *Annales Ecclesiastici. Accedunt Notae Chronologicae etc., auctore* I. D. MANSI. Tom. 12–14. Lucae, 1755.

Reformationsgeschichtliche Studien und Texte, ed. by J. GREVING. Münster i. W., 1908 sqq.

Reformationsschriften, ed. by R. G. GRÜTZMACHER. Leipzig, 1917, sqq.

Reichstagsakten, Deutsche. First Series, Vol II: *Deutsche Reichstagsakten unter Karl V.,* ed. by ADOLF WREDE. Gotha, 1896.

RIFFEL K., *Christliche Kirchengeschichte der neuesten Zeit, von dem Anfange der grossen Glaubens- und Kirchenspaltung des 16. Jahrhunderts.* 3 vols. Mayence, 1842–1846.

RISCH ADOLF. *Luthers Bibelverdeutschung (Schriften des Vereins für Reformationsgeschichte,* No. 135). Leipsic, 1922.

RITSCHL A. *Rechtfertigung und Versöhnung.* 3 vols. 2nd ed. Bonn, 1882–1883.

RITSCHL O. *Dogmengeschichte des Protestantismus.* Vols. I and II. Leipsic, 1908 sq.

—— *Luthers religiöses Vermächtnis.* Bonn 1918. (See *Theol. Revue,* 1919, p. 111.)

ROCKWELL W. W. *Die Doppelehe des Landgrafen Philipp von Hessen.* Marburg, 1904.

Römerbriefkommentar. FICKER J., *Luthers Vorlesung über den Römerbrief 1515–16. 1 Teil: Glossen; 2 Teil: Scholien (Anfänge reformatorischer Bibelauslegung, hg. von. J. Ficker).* Leipsic, 1908.

ROST H. *Der Protestantismus nach protestantischen Zeugnissen.* Paderborn, 1920.

SCHÄFER E. *Luther und die Juden.* Gütersloh, 1917.

—— *Luther als Kirchenhistoriker.* Gütersloh, 1897.

SCHEEL O. *Luthers Stellung zur Heiligen Schrift. (Sammlung gemeinverständlicher Vorträge und Schriften aus dem Gebiete der Theologie, No. 29).* Tübingen, 1902.

—— *Martin Luther. Vom Katholizismus zur Reformation.* Vol. I, 3rd ed. Tübingen, 1921; Vol. II, 1917. See *Theol. Revue,* 1920, pp. 207 sqq; *Zeitschrift für kath. Theologie,* Vol. XLIV (1920), pp. 586–593; *Stimmen der Zeit,* Vol. CIII (1922), p. 382.

—— *Dokumente zu Luthers Entwicklung.* Tübingen, 1911.

SCHLAGINHAUFEN. *Tischreden Luthers aus den Jahren 1531 und 1532 nach den Aufzeichnungen von Johann Schlaginhaufen aus einer Münchener Handschrift hg. von.* W. PREGER. Leipsic, 1888.

SCHRECKENBACH P., and NEUBERT F. *Martin Luther. Mit 384 Abbildungen besonders aus alten Quellen* (text by Schreckenbach). 3rd ed., Leipsic, 1921.

Schriften des Vereins für Reformationsgeschichte. Halle, 1883 sqq. No. 100: *Jubiläumsschrift,* Leipsic, 1910. (With contributions by Friedensburg, Scheel, Bauer, Hermann, Benrat, and Kawerau).

SCHUBART CHR. *Die Berichte über Luthers Tod und Begräbnis.* Weimar, 1917.

SCHUBERT HANS v. *Luther und seine lieben Deutschen.* Stuttgart, 1917.

—— *Luthers Frühentwicklung. (Schriften des Vereins für Reformationsgeschichte, No.* 124).

SECKENDORF V. L. DE. *Commentarius Historicus et Apologeticus de Lutheranismo sive de Reformatione Religionis ductu D. Martini Lutheri . . . recepta et stabilita.* Lipsiae, 1694.

SEEBERG REINH. *Die Lehre Luthers. (Lehrbuch der Dogmengeschichte,* Vol. IV, Part I, 2nd and 3rd ed. Leipsic, 1917; Part II, 2nd and 3rd ed., 1920. See *Theol. Revue,* 1919, pp. 241–247 and 1921, pp. 386 sqq.)

—— *Luthers Anschauung von dem Geschlechtsleben und der Ehe und ihre geschichtliche Stellung (Jahrbuch der Luthergesellschaft,* Vol. VII, pp. 77–122).

SEHLING E. *Geschichte der protestantischen Kirchenverfassung.* 2nd ed. Berlin, 1914.

SPAHN M. *Johann Cochläus. Ein Lebensbild aus der Zeit der Kirchenspaltung.* Berlin, 1898.

SPANGENBERG CYRIACUS. *Theander Lutherus*, 1589. (See Kawerau in the *Real-Enzyklopädie für prot. Theologie*, 3rd ed., Vol. XVIII, p. 567; DÖLLINGER, *Die Reformation*, Vol. II, pp. 270 sqq.)

STÄHELIN R. *Huldreich Zwingli*, 2 vols. Bâsle, 1895–1897.

STANGE CARL. *Luther und das sittliche Ideal*. Gütersloh, 1919. (See *Theol. Revue*, 1921, p. 99.)

—— *Zur Einführung in die Gedanken Luthers*. Gütersloh, 1921.

STROHL H. *L'Évolution Religieuse de Luther jusqu'à 1515*. Strasbourg, 1922.

—— *L' Épanouissement de la Pensée Religieuse de Luther de 1515 à 1520*. Strasbourg, 1924.

Studien zur Reformationsgeschichte, G. Kawerau dargebracht. Leipsic, 1917.

Tischreden oder Colloquia M. Luthers, ed. by AURIFABER, 2 vols. Eisleben, 1564–1565. Edited by FÖRSTEMANN.

—— *Nach Aurifabers erster Ausgabe, mit sorgfältiger Vergleichung sowohl der Stangwaldschen als der Selneccerschen Redaktion*. 4 Vols. (Vol. IV, ed. with the co-operation of H. E. Bindseil.) Leipsic, 1844–1848.

TROELTSCH E. *Protestantisches Christentum*. (*Kultur der Gegenwart*, Vol. I, Heft 4), 2nd ed., 1909.

—— *Soziallehren der christlichen Kirchen*. (*Gesammelte Schriften*, Vol. I), 1911.

—— *Die Bedeutung des Protestantismus für die Entstehung der modernen Welt*. (*Histor. Bibliothek*, No. 24. 3rd ed., 1924, Munich.) (See WOLF, *Quellenkunde*, Vol. I, p. 46.)

ULENBERG C. *Historia de Vita . . . Lutheri, Melanchthonis, Matth. Flacii Illyrici, G. Maioris et Andr. Osiandri*. 2 vols. Coloniae, 1622.

Vita Lutheri. In *Vitae Quatuor Reformatorum* by Melanchthon, Berolini, 1841. Also in *Corp. Reform.*, Vol. VI, pp. 155 sqq., and previously as preface to Vol. II of the Wittenberg edition of Luthers Latin writings.

WALTHER W. *Für Luther, Wider Rom. Handbuch der Apologetik Luthers und der Reformation den römischen Anklagen gegenüber*. Halle a. S., 1906.

—— *Luthers deutsche Bibel*. Berlin, 1917.

—— *Die deutsche Bibelübersetzung des Mittelalters*. Braunschweig, 1889–1892. See WOLF, *Quellenkunde*, Vol. I, p. 186.

—— *Das Erbe der Reformation*. Vol. I–IV. Leipsic, 1909–1917.

—— *Luthers Charakter*. 2nd ed., Leipsic, 1917.

—— *Luther und die Juden*. Leipsic, 1921.

—— *Deutschlands Schwert durch Luther geweiht*. 2nd ed., Leipsic, 1919.

WARD F. G. *Darstellung der Ansichten Luthers vom Staat*. Halle, 1898.

WEISS A. M. (O. P.), *Lutherpsychologie als Schlüssel zur Lutherlegende. Denifles Untersuchungen kritisch nachgeprüft*. 2nd ed., Mayence, 1906.

—— *Luther und Luthertum*. Vol. II; see DENIFLE.

WORKS, Erl. ed., M. *Luthers sämtliche Werke.* 67 vols., ed. by J. G. Ploch-mann and J. A. Irmischer. Erlangen, 1826–1868. Vols. I–XX und XXIV–XXVI, 2nd ed. by L. Enders, Frankfort a. M., 1862 sqq.—The Erl. ed. comprises the *Opp. Lat. Exeg.,* the *Comment. in Epist. ad Galat.,* die *Opp. Lat. Var.* and *Briefwechsel,* ed. by L. Enders (cf. these four titles above).

—— Weimar ed., *Dr. Martin Luthers Werke. Kritische Gesamtausgabe.* Wei-mar, 1883 sqq. Under the editorship of J. Knaake, G. Kawerau, P. Pietsch, N. Müller, K. Drescher, and W. Walther.

—— (Weimar ed.) *Tischreden* in 6 vols. 1912–1921; ed. by ERNST KROKER.

—— Altenburg ed., 1661–1664. 10 vols. (German); reimpression, Leipsic, 1729–1740. 22 vols.

—— Eisleben ed. (Supplement to the Wittenberg und Jena editions) by J. AURIFABER. 2 vols. 1564–1565.

—— Halle ed., by J. G. Walch. 24 vols. 1740–1753 (German). New ed. under the auspices of the German Lutheran Synod of Missouri, Ohio, and other States. St. Louis, Mo. 22 vols. 1880–1904. Vol. 23 (Index vol.), 1910.

—— Jena ed., 8 vols. German and 4 vols. Latin. 1555–1558.

—— Wittenberg ed., A. 12 vols. German (1539–1559) and 7 vols. Latin (1545–1558).

—— *Luthers Werke in Auswahl.* Ed. by OTTO CLEMEN and ALB. LIETZ-MANN. Vols. I to IV. Bonn 1913 sq.

—— *Luthers ausgewählte Werke.* Ed. by H. H. BORCHERDT. 6 vols. Munich, 1913–1923.

—— *Martin Luther. Auswahl,* by NEUBAUER, in *Denkmäler der älteren deutschen Literatur,* Vol. III, Heft 2 and 3. 3rd ed., 1903–1907.

—— *Ausgewählte Schriften Luthers.* Ed. by ARNOLD BERGER. 3 vols. Leipsic, 1917.

—— *Auswahl,* ed. by BUCHWALD, KAWERAU, KÖSTLIN, RADE, etc., (Known as "Braunschweiger Ausgabe"). 8 vols. 3rd ed. Braunschweig and later Berlin, 1905 sqq. Also 2 supplementary vols.

WERNLE PAUL. *Der evangelische Glaube nach den Hauptschriften der Re-formation.* Vol. I: *Luther.* Tübingen, 1912. (Vol. II: *Zwingli;* Vol. III: *Calvin*).

WIEDEMANN TH. *Johann Eck, Professor der Theologie an der Universität Ingolstadt.* Ratisbon, 1865.

WOLF GUSTAV. *Quellenkunde der deutschen Reformationsgeschichte.* Vol. I: *Vorreformation und allgemeine Reformationsgeschichte,* Gotha, 1915; Vol. II, Part 1: *Kirchliche Reformationsgeschichte,* 1916; Vol. II, Part 2: *Kirchliche Reformationsgeschichte, Fortsetzung,* 1922.

ZICKENDRAHT K. *Der Streit zwischen Erasmus und Luther über die Willens-freiheit.* Leipsic, 1909.

Zwingli H. *Opera*. 5 vols., ed. by Emil Egli und Georg Finsler, since 1910 by Finsler and Walter Köhler. 1905–1925. (*Corpus Reformatorum*, Vols. LXXXVIII sqq.)

INDEX

Abnormal psychological traits, 490 ff.
Abuses, Ecclesiastical, 80 f., 90 ff., 560 f.
Accolti, Pietro, 153
"Acta Augustana," 105
Address to the German nobility, 158 f., 169 f., 171
Adrian VI, 238
Æsop, Fables of, 394 f.
Age, The new, 122 ff.
Agricola, John, 128, 270, 330, 387, 445 ff., 529, 553
Albrecht, Grand Master of the Teutonic Order, 317
Albrecht of Brandenburg, 90 f., 95, 137, 240 f.
Albrecht of Mayence, 242, 293, 309 f., 382, 444, 529, 566
Aleander, 175 f., 180 f., 183, 184, 189, 191
Alexander VI, 54, 81, 83
Alfeld, Augustine von, 142, 149, 369, 425, 460
"Altarists," 127 f.
Altenburg, 226 ff.
Amerbach, Vitus, 370; Boniface, 436
Amsdorf, Nicholas, 75, 189 f., 193, 274 f., 290, 371, 435 f., 440, 465, 533 ff., 582
Anabaptists, 213, 254 ff., 319 f., 332, 341, 417 f., 501
Anglicanism, 554
Ann, St., 23, 38
Annates, 125
Antichrist, 113, 132, 148, 159, 171, 194, 196, 197 f., 209 f., 247, 280, 298, 376, 401, 527, 544
Anticlericalism, 125
Antinomianism, 445 f., 499, 553
Apobolymaeus, see Findling
Apocrypha of the Lutheran Bible, 264
"Apologia Confessionis Augustanae," 378
Appearance, Personal, of Luther, 216 f., 413 f.
Architecture, 134
Aristotle, 23 sqq., 50, 77, 79, 117

Arnoldi, Barth., of Usingen, 20, 22, 24, 28, 37, 49, 178, 306, 310, 370, 377; Francis, 396 f.
Art, 54, 135
"Assertio Omnium Articulorum," 172
Augsburg Confession, 375 ff., 453, 553 f.
Augsburg, Diet of, 374 ff.
Augustine, St., 51, 77 f., 107, 303, 430, 497, 526
Augustinian Order, 39 f., 45 f., 52 ff., 177 f., 208, 370, 551 f.
Aurifaber, 217, 277, 358, 479, 482, 568, 581
Aurogallus, Matthew, 421, 423
Austria, 550 f.
Authority, Luther on secular, 244 f.

Babylonish Captivity of the Church, Luther on the, 158, 162 ff., 170
Baccalaureate, Biblical, 48
Bachelor's degree, 21
Bader, Augustine, 320
Ban, Year of the, 141 ff., Sermon on, 152
Baptism, 257 f., 267, 335; see also Anabaptists
Barber Peter, 433
Barnes, Robt., 415 f., 564
Bartholomew, Master; see Arnoldi
Bebel, August, 259
Beier, Leonard, 96
Benefices, Ecclesiastical, 124, 125
Bernhardi, B., 74
Bezold, Fr. von, 285
Bible, Before Luther, 132 f.; Luther and the, 25, 44, 50, 58, 85 f.; Luther's translation of, 211 f., 381 f., 420 ff.; His criticism of, 263 ff.; Post-Reformation Catholic translations, 362, 431; The so-called revised Lutheran, 423; Catholics and the, 430 f.
Bibliography, 586 ff.
Biel, Gabriel, 46, 48, 79, 84 f.
Bigamy of Philip of Hesse, 515 ff.

Billican, Theo., 370
Bishops, 129 sq., 454; Apostate, 318
Blaurer, Ambrose, 276, 321, 440
Bodenstein, Andrew, of Karlstadt; see Karlstadt
Böhm, Hans, 139
Böhmer, Julius, 525
Boleyn, Anne, 415
Bonaventure, St., 59
Bora, Catherine von, 233, 241, 271, 293 ff., 340, 354, 357, 415, 480, 498, 518, 563 f., 567, 568, 576, 577
Borna, Luther's "heroic" letter from, 215 f.
Brant, Sebastian, 135
Braun, John, 16, 19, 32
Brenz, John, 97, 465, 519
Brethren of the Common Life, 12 sq.
Breviary, 62
Brunswick, Attacks upon the duchy of, 537 ff.
Bucer, Martin, 97, 183, 252, 275, 320, 349, 379, 390, 418, 419, 420, 449, 453, 456, 503, 515 ff., 523, 538, 545, 552, 555
Bugenhagen, John, 224, 231, 274 f., 294, 319, 352, 355, 371, 405, 412 f., 423, 440, 449, 464 f., 558, 579
Bull "Exurge Domine," 154 ff., 164 ff., 325
Bullinger, Henry, 411, 419, 420, 545
"Bundschuh," 139, 186
Bunsen, Chr. J., 423
Burial, 578
Burkhardt, John, see Spalatin

Cajetan, Cardinal, 101 ff., 111, 137, 141, 153 f., 362, 364, 371, 461
Calvin, John, 303, 453, 503, 554 f.
Calvinism, 554 ff.
Camerarius, Joachim, 272, 296 f., 467
Campeggio, Cardinal Lorenzo, 239 f., 272, 377, 396, 458
Canisius, St. Peter, 539, 550
Canon law, Luther burns the book of, 173 f.
Capito, Wolfgang, 252, 270
Caraccioli, 175, 180
Cartoons, 340 f., 365, 546 ff.
Catechisms, Luther's, 334 f.
Catharinus, Ambrose, 164, 182, 196, 362, 364, 371

Catholic apologetics against Luther, 359 ff., 454 ff.
Celibacy, Sacerdotal, 127, 151, 159, 177, 200 f., 392, 509 ff.
Censorship, 192 f.
Chalice for the laity, 339 f.
Character sketch, 574 f.
Characteristics, Engaging, 470 ff.
Charity, 125
Charles V, 123, 139, 141, 162, 175, 180 f., 184, 187, 190 ff., 323 ff., 373 ff., 411, 412, 438, 451, 528 ff., 538 f.
Chastity, 31, 230
Chemnitz, Martin, 250
Chieregati, 238 f.
Children, 358 f., 470 f.
Christian II, of Denmark, 372 f.
Christian III, of Denmark, 449
Church, Doctrinal authority of, 79 f.; Abuses in, 80 f.; Wealth of the, 125; Luther's ideal of, 246 f.; And the Bible, 430 f.
Clement VII, 239 f., 298, 323 ff., 379, 412
Clerical proletariat, 128
Clerical state, Tract against, 232 f.
Clichtovaeus, J., 364, 371
Cloaca, 108 f.
Coburg, Luther at the Castle of, 380 ff.
Cochlaeus, John, 42, 55, 183, 187, 189, 222, 223, 261, 360 f., 366, 377, 378, 396, 397, 398, 405, 426, 456 f., 549
Coelius, Michael, 491 f., 568, 569, 579
Cognac, Holy League of, 323
Cologne, Attacks upon the archbishopric of, 537 ff.
Commandments, 146, 304
Concord of Wittenberg, 418 f., 440
Concubinage, 126 f.
Concupiscence, 73
Confession, 68, 150, 196 f., 218 f.; Seal of, 520, 526
"Confessio Variata," 553 f.
"Confutatio" of the Augsburg Confession, 377
Congregational church, 246 f.
Congregational singing, 8
Conscience, Freedom of, 188
"Consecration" of the Bishop of Naumburg, 532 ff.
Constance, Council of, 115, 116, 154, 165, 413
Contarini, Gasparo, Cardinal, 453 f., 461

Cordatus, Conrad, 108, 277, 462, 483
Corpus Catholicorum, 360
Corruption within the Church, 130
Cotta, Kuntz, 15 sq.
Councils, 443 f.
"Courtesans," 125
Cranach, Lucas, 365, 428, 548
Crotus Rubeanus, 26, 29, 43, 116, 136, 153
Cruciger, 349, 423
Cryptocalvinism, 582
Culture, Luther as a champion of, 560
Cusa, Cardinal Nicholas of, 126 f.
Customs, Popular, 560 ff.

Daniel, 196, 198
Death, 567 ff.
Death-mask, 578
Decadence, Moral, a result of the Protestant Reformation, 549
"De Captivitate Babylonica," 162, 170
Defenders of the Catholic cause, Literary, 454 ff.
De Lagarde, Paul, 423 f.
Denifle, H. (O. P.), 72, 107 f.
Denmark, Protestantism in, 449 f.
"De Planctu Ecclesiae," 135
"De Ruina Ecclesiae," 135
"De Servo Arbitrio," 298 ff.
"De Squaloribus Curiae, 135
Despondency, 35
Dessau, League of, 285 f., 316
"Deus absconditus," 302 f.
Devil, 42, 182, 196, 200, 202, 203, 204, 215, 251, 283, 288, 289, 291, 294, 300, 305, 311, 345, 354, 355, 357, 363 f., 369, 382 ff., 420, 429, 434, 443, 485, 487, 490 ff., 503, 508, 546, 564, 568, 569, 578
Devotio moderna, 12
Dietenberger, John, 363, 368, 425, 460
Dionysius the (Pseudo-) Areopagite, 60
Discipline, Ecclesiastical, 472 ff.
Discovery in the Tower, The, 105 ff.
Divorce, 511 f.
Doctorate in theology, 56 f., 86
"Doctor plenus," 358
Doctrinal system, 73 f.
Döllinger, 424
Dominicans, 100, 322, 367 f.
Drunkard, Luther not a, 357 f., 364, 577
Dungersheim, Jerome, 30 f., 118, 370

Dürer, Albrecht, 195

Eberbach, Peter and Henry, 29, 136
Eberlin, John, 369
Eck, Dr. John, 96, 111 ff., 120 f., 126, 135, 149, 153, 156, 164 f., 166, 175, 360, 365 f., 375, 377, 378, 426, 455 f.
Eck, John von, 184 f.
Edict of Worms, 190 ff., 216, 239, 240, 326 f., 347, 377, 379
Education, 394
Eilenburg, 228
"Ein' feste Burg," 355
Eisenach, 15 sqq.
Eisleben, 1 sqq.
Elevation, 254
Elizabeth, St., 16, 198
Elizabeth von Sachsen-Rochlitz, 409 f., 516, 518
Ellenbog, Nicholas, 370
Emser, Jerome, 30, 116, 119, 149, 176, 360 f., 425
Eobanus Hessus, 29, 136, 306
Epistolae Obscurorum Virorum, 29, 136
Epitaphs, 580
Erasmus, 136 ff., 175, 223, 268 ff., 284, 299, 354, 358, 360, 363, 364, 422, 435 ff., 463
Erfurt, 19 sqq., 51, 182, 195, 305 ff.
Ernest of Braunschweig, 408
Ethics, 505 ff.
Eucharist, 150 f., 249 ff., 341 ff.
Excommunication, 100, 155 f., 174, 219, 472 f.

Faber, John, 273, 360, 366 f., 377, 458
Faber, John (Augustanus), 367
Faber, Peter, 444
Fabri, John, 368
Faith, 145, 166 ff., 206, 267, 425, 487 f., 506
Falk, F., 370, 431
Family life, 470 f.
Fanaticism, Epistle against, 252
Fear, Morbid, 49, 59, 62, 63, 489
Feldkirch, Barth., 200
Ferdinand, Archduke of Austria, Brother of Charles V, 238, 316, 325, 346, 374, 411, 416, 519, 529
Fichte, 170
Findling, John, 362, 370
Fisher, John, 371, 415

Flacius Illyricus, 581 f.
Florentina of Oberweimar, 234
Force as a means of Protestant propaganda, 225 f.
Forerunners of the Reformation, Alleged, 82 ff.
Forstemius, Dr., 423
Francis I (King of France), 237, 323
Franciscans, 322, 369 f.
Franck, Seb., 502
Frankfort, Peace of, 452
"Fraternal Union of Knighthood," 197
Frederick "the Wise," of Saxony, 91, 96, 97, 101 f., 103, 104, 119, 120, 141, 143, 155, 180, 214 f., 216, 238, 241 f.
Free Christianity, 265 ff.
Free-will, see Will
Fugger, 91, 375

Galatians, Lectures on the Epistle to the, 75, 119, 143, 434
Geiler von Kaysersberg, 81, 128, 135
George of Anhalt, 535
George of Saxony, Duke, 81, 97, 115, 193, 215, 238, 287 ff., 309, 315 f., 338, 396 ff., 447
German Bible, Luther's, 420 ff.
"Germanism," Luther's, 583 f.
Ghosts, 202 ff.
Glapion, John, 183
Glorification of Luther by his biographers, 580 ff.
Goethe, 169, 170
Grace, 73 f., 78, 86
Grace, Frederick, 458
Gravamina, 126, 181
Groote, Gerard, 12, 60
Gropper, John, 453
Günther, Franz, 77
Gustavus Wasa, 372

Haller, Joh., 159
Harnack, Adolph von, 170, 264, 558
Hauspostille, 471
Hausrath, Adolph, 525
Hebrews, Epistle to the, 426
Henry of Braunschweig-Wolffenbüttel, 445, 523 f., 528, 539 f.
Henry of Saxony, 447 f.
Henry VIII, "Defender of the Catholic Faith," 260; Attacked by Luther, 260 f., 287, 337, 371; Divorce of, 414 ff., 503, 554

Heretics, Protestant proceedings against, 332 f.
Hilten, John, 18
Hochstraten, Jacob, 119, 169, 360, 368
Hoffmann, Melchior, 319 f., 359
Hoffmeister, John, 460
Holy League, 451
Hosius, Stanislaus, 460
Hubmaier, Balthasar, 280, 339
Humanism, The new, 136 ff.
Humility, 506
Hus, John, 83, 154, 191, 229
Hussite heresy, 138
Hutten, Ulrich von, 137, 161
Hymnbook, First Lutheran, 250 f.
Hymns, 250 f., 477 f.

Ickelsamer, Val., 254 f.
Iconoclasm, 212, 321, 351, 556 f.
Illness, 441 ff
Images, Sacred, 212, 218, 557
Impediments, Matrimonial, 513
"In caena Domini," Bull, 211
Indulgences, 54, 77, 81, 82, 89 ff., 111, 115
Insanity, 99 f., 364, 396, 436
Inspiration, 264
Interdict, 472
Interest, 262
Interference of secular authorities in church affairs, 129
Intolerance, 333, 498 ff.

James, Epistle of St., 170, 426
Janssen, Joh., 132, 424
Jews, 261 f., 542 f., 569
Joachim II, of Brandenburg, 446 f., 459
Job, 421
John Frederick, Duke of Saxony, 182, 309, 390, 412, 438 f., 518, 523
John of Saxony, 143, 244, 311 ff., 347, 349, 408, 409, 412
John of Wesel, 81 f.
Jonas, Justus, 117, 136, 224, 273 f., 295, 311, 349, 387, 388, 405, 406, 423, 448, 466 f., 519, 529, 566, 568, 572 ff., 580
Julius II, 54, 55, 81
Jurisprudence, Roman supplants German system, 138 f.
Justification, 58, 74, 78, 86, 105 ff., 414, 453 f.
Justitia Dei, 105 f.

Kaftan, Julius, 507
Kant, 170
Karlstadt, Andrew, 57, 75, 112 ff., 120, 165, 200 f., 209, 212 f., 217, 219, 252 ff., 278 f., 342, 358 f., 476
Kattenbusch, 301, 303, 305
Kauxdorf, Andrew, 228
Keys, Treatise on the, 392
Kirchenpostille, 471
Kling, Conrad, 310, 370, 460
Köhler, Walter, 332, 431
Kohlhase, Hans, 475 f.
Kolde, Theo., 290, 316, 525, 554
Köllin, Conrad, 368
Köstlin-Kawerau, 274, 303, 345, 428, 541
Kroker, Ernst, 479, 481
Kronberg, Hartmuth von, 223
Kropatschek, Fr., 430
Kurrelmeyer, W., 431

"Ladies' Peace" of Cambrai, 323
Landau, John, 572 f., 575 f.
Lang, John, 29, 51, 66, 75, 77, 120, 136, 305, 307, 308, 465
Lang, Matthew, Cardinal Archbishop of Salzburg, 120, 178
Language, Uncouth, 259 f.
Last will and testament, 442, 563 f.
Latomus, see Massoon
Law, Study of, 27 f.
Lectures, 477
Legends, 188 f., 205, 385 f., 576 ff.
Leipsic, Disputation of 1519, 111
Leisnig, Attempt to establish a model congregation at, 247 f., 558
Lemnius, Simon, 502
Lening, John, 524
Leo Judae, 419 f.
Leo X, 90, 95, 98, 104, 111, 121, 129, 141, 153 ff., 180, 192, 238
Liberty of a Christian, Luther on, 144, 165 ff.; As a Lutheran shibboleth, 224 f., 267
Licentiate in theology, 57
Lichtenberg, 229 f.
Lies, 388, 526 ff.
Lightning, 37 f., 41
Link, Wenceslaus, 75, 114, 161, 182, 226, 275, 321, 389, 406 f., 465, 551
Livonia, 251, 319, 449
"Loci Communes" of Melanchthon, 118, 206 f., 272, 461, 554

Love affair, Early, 29 f.
Lupinus, Peter, 75
Luther, Derivation and forms of name, 3 f.
Luther, Hans, 1 ff., 41, 47 f., 386 f.
Lutheranism, Spread of, 221 ff.; The new State Church, 311 ff.
Lyra, Nicholas of, 430

Magdeburg, 11 sqq.
"Magnificat," Interpretation of, 210 f.
Majunke, P., 576
Mansfeld (city), 4 sqq.
Mansfeld, Count Albrecht von, 234
Mantuanus, 136
Marburg, Luther and Zwingli meet at, 349 ff.; The 15 articles of, 350 f.
Marriage, Luther's, 289 ff.
Marriages, Clandestine, 337, 567
"Martyrs," The first two Lutheran, 275, 338 f.
Mary, Bl. Virgin, 26, 210 f.
Mass, Luther's first, 46 ff.; Laxness in saying, 62; Attacks upon, 207 ff., 220, 221 f., 242 f., 393, 434, 440; The Lutheran substitute for, 248 f., 332, 447, 450; Denial of its sacrificial character, 249 f.; Suppression of, 314
Masson, James, 197, 370
Master's degree, 23, 27, 46, 219
Mathesius, John, 13, 26, 42, 50, 203, 277, 357, 423, 468, 580 f., 582
Matrimony, Sermon on, 120; Luther and, 258 ff., 335 ff., 509 ff.
Maximilian I, Emperor, 101, 104, 123
Mayr, John; see Eck
Mazzolini, Sylvester; see Prierias
Melancholia, 34, 37, 49, 201, 290, 382, 467 ff., 486, 495
Melanchthon, Philip, 40, 117 f., 194, 205 ff., 209, 213 f., 218, 221, 235, 270 ff., 292, 296 f., 311, 315, 330, 348, 349, 353, 375 ff., 387 f., 405, 406, 415, 421, 423, 436, 440 f., 451 ff., 461 ff., 496, 501, 515 f., 518, 519, 521, 524, 531, 533, 538, 545, 552, 553 f., 555, 567, 579, 582 f.
Melchiorites, 319 f.
Mendacity, 363, 526 ff.
Menius, Justus, 349, 417, 418
Mensing, John, 368, 460
Merd-song, 502

Metzsch, Hans von, 474
Miltitz, Karl von, 103 f., 118, 141, 165, 166
Moller, Henry, 275
Monasteries, Auxiliaries from the, 229 ff.
Monastery, Luther's entry into, 34 f., 37 ff.; First years in, 44 ff., 64
Monk-Calf of Freiberg, 234 f., 494
Monstrosities, 235 f.
Monument at Worms, 83
Morality, 505 ff.
Moravian Brethren, 551
Morbus melancholicus, 467
More, Sir Thomas, 260 f., 371, 415
Morone, Cardinal, 529 ff.
Mosellanus, see Schade
Münster, Anabaptist regime at, 417 f.
Münzer, Thomas, 186, 213, 219, 254, 255 ff., 278 ff.
Murner, Thomas, 164, 169, 207, 360 f., 370
Musa, Antonius, 468
Music, 26, 63, 251, 478 f.
Mutianus, Conrad, 136, 273
Mutianus, Rufus, 29
Myconius, 349
Mysticism, 58 ff., 68, 76, 169, 292

Nathin, John, 42, 48, 52, 65, 178, 310
Nationalism, 123
Nausea, see Grau, Frederick
Nervousness, 35, 40 ff.
Nestle, E., 423
Nobility, Address to the German, 158, 169, 171
Nominalism, 24, 84 ff.
Novitiate, 44 ff.
Nuns, Fugitive, 233 f., 271 f., 288, 292, 297, 577
Nuremberg, Religious peace of, 410 ff.

"Oblation," 162
Obsequies, 578 ff.
Ockham, William of, 24, 26, 84 f., 305
Oecolampadius, 120 f., 276, 321, 343, 349, 420
Oldecop, John, 38, 43, 53, 97
"On the Corner-Mass," 434 f.
"Onus Ecclesiæ," 135
Operationes in Psalmos, 106, 119
Ordination, Luther's, 46
"Ordination Oath," 501 f.

"Orthodox" Lutheranism, 582 f.
Osiander, Andrew, 321, 322, 440, 467, 519
Outlawry, Sentence of, 190

"Papa Albiacus," 502
Papacy, Luther on the, 142 f., 298 f., 546
Parentage, 2 sqq.
"Passion of Martinus," 193
Patronage, 128
Paul, St., 71 ff.
Paul III, 412, 438, 530 f., 548
"Pauline privilege," 512
Paulsen, F., 268, 424, 508
Paulus, Nicholas, 333, 467
Peace, Exhortation to, 281 f.
Peasants' War, 278 ff.
"Pecca forfiter," 205 ff.
Pelargus, Ambrose, 368 f.
Pelayo Alvarez, 135
Pelican, Conrad, 275
Penance, 63 f., 68
Penitents, Instructions for, 176
Perez, J., 430
Pestilence, 45
Peter Lombard, 50
Peter, Primacy of, 111 ff.
Pflug, Julius von, 536
Philip II, Landgrave of Hesse, 315 f., 328, 347, 348, 349, 377, 378, 379, 390, 409, 411, 414, 416 f., 418, 451, 454, 513, 515 ff., 530, 540
"Philippists," 553 f., 582 f.
Pictures, Polemical, 340 f., 546 ff.; In Luther's German Bible, 428 f.
Pirkheimer, Charitas, 322; Willibald, 121, 145, 165, 195, 223, 363, 364
Pirstinger, Berthold, 135
Plague, 355 f., 474 f.
Plays, Popular, 561
Plenaria, 431 f.
Polentz, Georg von, 317 f.
Pollich, Martin, 75 f.
Polygamy, 516
Poor-relief, 557 f.
Pope-Ass of Rome, 235 f., 546 f.
Pope, Luther's hatred of the, 442 f.
Portraits, 580
Postillæ, 25, 431 f.
Poverty, Voluntary, 67
Prayers, 198 f., 390 f., 507
Prayer-book, 237

Preaching, 132
Predestination, 69 f., 78, 270, 301 ff., 488
Prierias, Sylvester, 100 f., 105, 147, 148 f., 371
Priesthood, Luther's ordination to, 46
Primacy of the pope, 111
Princes, Ecclesiastical regime of territorial, 123 ff.
Printing press, 133, 192, 361
Private judgment, 170
Probst, Jacob, 275
Proles, Andrew, 46, 62
Propaganda, Lutheran methods of, 221 ff.
"Prophet of the Germans," 395
Protestants, Origin of name, 347
Protest of 1529, 346 ff.
Proverbs, 477
"Proviso of the Gospel," 387 ff.
Prussia, 317 f.
Psalms, Lectures on, 58, 66, 106, 172
Purgatory, Treatise on, 191 f.

Queiss, Eberhard von, 318

Rationalism as the result of Luther's work, 583 ff.
Ratzeberger, 13, 63, 202, 405, 479, 491, 495
Rauch, Peter, 368
Real Presence, Doctrine of, 252, 276, 342 ff., 390, 418, 434, 440, 544 f.
Reform, Need of, 80 ff., 124, 455
Reformation, Why it made such rapid progress, 319
Reissenbusch, Wolfgang, 230
Relics, 566
Renaissance, 122 ff.
Resistance to authority, 406 ff.
"Resolutions," 97 ff., 113 f.
Responsio to the theologians of Cologne and Louvain, 149
Reuchlin, 83
Rhadinus, Thomas, 272
"Ritter Görg," 194 ff.
Romans, Interpretation of the Epistle to the, 71 ff., 124 f., 131
Rome, Journey to, 52 ff.
Rörer, George, 109, 481, 482
Rural vicar, 61

Sacramentarians, 343, 349, 354, 355, 418, 434, 501, 570

Sacrament, Blessed, Sermon on, 150; Under both forms, 117 f., 339 f.; Profession of faith in, 544 f.
Sacraments, 163, 267
Saints, Invocation of, 393
Savonarola, 83
Saxony, State Church of, 328 ff.
Schade, Peter, 115, 270, 277
Schalbe, Caspar, 136; Henry, 15; Ursula, 15
Schatzgeyer, Caspar, 363, 364 f., 369 f., 460, 484
Schaumburg, Sylvester, 161
Scheel, O., 36, 301
Schenk, Jacob, 462, 553
Scheurl, Christopher, 75, 77
Schiele, F. M., 394
Schism, The ecclesiastical, 528 ff.
Schlaginhaufen, John, 108 f., 203, 468 f.
Schleinitz, John von, 150
Schmalkalden, League of, 403 ff., 438
Schmalkaldic Articles, 438, 525
Schnepf, Erhard, 97
Scholasticism, 64 f., 77, 85
School discipline, 5 sq.
Schools, 393 f., 559 f.
Schultz, Jerome, 95
Schurf, Jerome, 75, 184, 275, 294, 337
Schwabach, Articles of, 351
Schwarzburg, Count Johann Heinrich, 228 f.
Schwenckfeld, Caspar, 276 f., 420
Scultetus; see Schultz
Secularization, 123 f., 312, 555 ff.
Self-delusion, 496 f.
Self-righteousness, 67, 80, 222
Senfl, 479
"Sententiarius," 48, 50
Sermon, in Lutheran worship, 249
Sermons, 433, 471 f.
Servetus, M., 503
Servitia, 125
"Shem Hamphoras," 543
Sickingen, Franz von, 137, 161, 196 f.
Sigismund, King of Poland, 318
Sin, 206, 293, 304 f., 392
"So help me God, Amen," 185
Sola fide, 108, 301, 393, 424
Soldiers, 311
Soliman, Sultan, 325
Spalatin, George, 29, 103, 114, 117, 131, 136, 148, 149, 151, 182, 194, 206, 243, 312 f., 331, 355, 387, 465 f.
Spengler, Lazarus, 165, 321, 389, 405, 406

Spenlein, George, 67 f., 206
Speratus, Paul, 372
Spires, Diet of, 346 ff.; Defensive League of, 450 f.
"Squire George," 194 ff., 216
Stahl, F. J., 160
Staphylus, Frederick, 460 f., 493
Staupitz, John, 44, 49, 51 ff., 55, 56, 57, 61, 62 f., 65, 68 f., 75, 81, 87, 92, 94, 98, 120, 131, 161, 171, 178, 199
Stiefel, Michael, 493
Student years, Luther's, 19 sqq., 48 f.
Studies, Luther's, 48 ff.
Sturm, Jacob, 349
Subjectivism, 266 f.
Suicide, Luther's alleged, 576 f.
"Summissaries," 128
Superstitions, 10 sq.
"Supputatio Annorum Mundi," 544
Sweden, Protestantism in, 450
Sword, Appeal to the, 148
Sylvius, Peter, 363
Syphilis, 290

Table Talks, 109, 470, 479 ff., 581
Tauler, John, 59, 60, 99, 169
Teacher, Luther's First experience as, 48
Temptations, 31, 62, 70, 87, 199, 291, 352 ff., 384 ff., 428, 486 ff.
Terminism, 24
"Tessaradekas," 119, 143
Testament, 442
Tetzel, John, 91 ff., 104, 149
Teutonic Knights, 231 f., 317 ff.
"Theander Lutherus," 581
"Theologia deutsch," 59, 60
Thomas à Kempis, 133
Thomas, Aquinas, St., 24, 64, 430
Thunderbolt at Stotternheim, 37 f., 41, 99
Tischreden, see Table Talks
Torgau, Treaty of, 286; League of, 316
Translations of the Bible, see Bible
Transubstantiation, 254 ff.
Trebonius, John, 17 sq., 28, 32
Trent, Council of, 452, 495, 530, 545
Trial, The Roman, 153 ff.
Trithemius, 135
Trutvetter, Jodocus, 20, 22, 24, 28
Tschackert, Paul, 525
"Turkish bell," 9
Turks, 9, 18, 325 f., 348, 352, 528, 544
Twelve Articles, 280

Ulrich of Augsburg, Fable attributed to, 177
Ulrich of Württemberg, 416 f.
Usingen, see Arnoldi
Usury, 262, 543
Utraquists, 116, 247

Vehe, Michael John, 369, 460
Vergerio, P. P., 412 f., 414, 438
Vio, Cajetan de; see Cajetan
Violence, 225 f., 403 f.
Virginity, 509 f.
Vischer, Herman, 133
Visitation of the Lutheran churches in Saxony, 329 f.
Vituperation, 484 f.
Volta, Gabriel della, 95
Vows, Luther's solemn, 45; Praise of monastic, 80; Tract against, 200 ff., 510

Walch, J. G., 483
Waldus, Peter, 83
Walther, John, 250 f., 321; Wm., 348, 431
Wappler, P., 332 f.
War, 404 f.
Wartburg, 16 f., 189 ff., 193 ff.
Wessel Gansfort, 81 f.
"Why the Books of the Pope have been Burnt by Dr. M. Luther," 174 f.
Wicel, George, 41, 223 f., 370, 435, 458 f.
Wiclif, John, 83, 154, 229
"Wider die Bulle des Endchrists," 172
Wied, Herman von, 538
Wild, John, 370, 460, 549
Will, Freedom of, 268 ff., 298 ff., 435, 506
William of Anhalt-Zerbst, 14
Wimpfeling, Jacob, 133, 135, 223
Wimpina, Conrad, 95, 370, 378, 460
Witches, 492
"Wittenberger Concordie," 418 f., 440
"Wittenberg Reformation," The so-called, 531 f., 535, 545
Wives, Luther's three, 292
Womanhood, Dignity of, 513 f.
Works, Good, 143 ff., 313
Worms, Luther monument at, 83; Diet of, 180 ff., 550
"Wurzer Fehde," 536 f.

Youth, Luther's, 1 sqq.

Zasius, 223, 284
Zell, Matthew, 320
Ziegler, Bernard, 423
Zwickau, Prophets of, 213 f., 219 f., 252

Zwilling, Gabriel, 208 f., 212, 225 f., 373
Zwingli and Zwinglianism, 252, 253 ff., 320 ff., 341 ff., 348 ff., 378, 379, 409 f., 418, 555

CARMELITE M...
       B...
  B...